Introducing

PHILOSOPHY
a text with readings
third edition

Introducing
PHILOSOPHY
a text with readings
third edition

ROBERT C. SOLOMON
University of Texas at Austin

UNDER THE GENERAL EDITORSHIP OF ROBERT J. FOGELIN
Dartmouth College

HARCOURT BRACE JOVANOVICH, PUBLISHERS

San Diego   New York   Chicago   Atlanta   Washington, D.C.
London   Sydney   Toronto

For
Vita P. Solomon,
who brought me into life
and taught me it was art.

Cover art:
Helen Frankenthaler, "Essence Mulberry,"
woodcut printed and published by Tyler Graphics Ltd.
© copyright Helen Frankenthaler/Tyler Graphics Ltd. 1977.

ISBN: 0-15-541560-3

Library of Congress Catalog Card Number: 84-81498

Printed in the United States of America

Preface

Introducing Philosophy: A Text with Readings presupposes no background in the subject and no special abilities. Intended primarily as a textbook for a one- or two-semester introductory course, the book provides not so much a course in itself as the materials for a course from which instructors and students can focus on a variety of problems and perspectives. The point of this text is to present students with alternatives on every issue and let them arrive at their own individual conclusions. These conclusions should be based on arguments in class and with friends or classmates, as well as on the discussions in the book. The assumption here is that the purpose of philosophy is to encourage everyone to think for himself or herself and that no single source of arguments or information can take the place of personal dialogues and discussions. A textbook is ultimately a sourcebook; everything in it is to be taken as a cause for further argument, not as a final statement of results. This text does not attempt to sway students toward any particular philosophical positions but rather presents basic philosophical problems and powerful philosophical arguments to enable students to think for themselves. That is what philosophy is about — thinking for oneself on basic issues.

This book derives from twenty years of teaching in very different schools in various states and cities. It is based on the belief that philosophy is a genuinely exciting subject, accessible not only to specialists and a few gifted undergraduate majors but to everyone. Everyone is a philosopher, whether enrolled in a philosophy course or not. Most of us are concerned with the same basic problems and use the same essential arguments. The difference is that someone who has studied philosophy has the advantage of having encountered stronger and more varied arguments than might have been available otherwise. In this book, the views of the major philosophers of the past twenty-five hundred years are used to give students these various arguments. This has the advantage of offering introductory students the opportunity of having direct contact with substantial readings from significant works in the history of philosophy, but without the unreasonable demand that they confront these often difficult works in full and without commentary or editing, as they would in the originals or in most anthologies. This book is not, however, a historical introduction as such but rather an introduction to the **problems** of philosophy and the various ways in which they have been answered. The history of philosophy thus serves to illuminate these problems and replies, not the other way around.

Although the language of philosophy is often specialized and sometimes difficult, this book is as free of jargon and special terminology as is possible. Where necessary, the most important and widely used philosophical terms are carefully introduced within the text and also summarized in glossaries at the end of each chapter. At the end of the book there are biographies of the philosophers discussed in the text. Although the book deals principally with their ideas rather than with their lives, it is nevertheless valuable to have the student learn their place in history.

The responses to the first two editions of *Introducing Philosophy* have been both gratifying and helpful in this third revision for a new generation of students. In this edition, some of the longer readings have been cut down, some new ones have been added, and more explanatory material has been added throughout the book. For example, the discussion of Kant's philosophy has been made more substantial, and new original material from Kant's writings has been added. The religion chapter has been bolstered by a more extensive discussion of the problem of evil, by more material on the meaning of religious language, and by the addition of sections on Buddhism, Hinduism, and Islam. The original two ethics chapters in the first edition have been consolidated but also enlarged by the addition of readings and material on metaethics, including classic readings from Moore and Ayer. The "Mind-Body" chapter has been brought up to date with a discussion of "functionalism," as well as with an expanded discussion of "the identity theory." The epistemology chapters have been strengthened by a more extensive discussion of the pragmatists, including some original readings, and by sections on hermeneutics and relativism. The logic section has once again been redone and expanded, with additional help in symbolization and a more extensive discussion of the informal fallacies. The format of the book has also been changed considerably in order to make the readings more pronounced and to make life easier for both student and instructor.

FOR THE INSTRUCTOR: HOW TO USE THIS BOOK

Introducing Philosophy is written for a complete course, and the chapters build on one another in a logical sequence. But the book is also flexible, and each chapter has been written as an independent unit so that it is possible to use the text in a variety of ways and for a variety of courses. Within each chapter, too, various sections can be selected for shorter discussions. For example, some instructors may want to use only the first sections of Chapter 6 ("Religion") or only a few key sections from Chapters 7 ("Self-identity") and 9 ("Freedom").

A full course might include the Introduction and all eleven chapters, but this may be a heavy load for an average one-term course. At the other extreme, a short course (for example, a summer term or a class that meets only once a week, a quarter system, or a class that prefers to treat a few central issues in more detail) might use only half the chapters. The following outlines are suggestions for a variety of uses of the book adapted to different lengths and kinds of classes:

> Maximum course (one very full term):
> Introduction, Chapters 1–11.
> Minimum course (summer, part-time, quarter):
> Introduction, Chapters 1, 3, 6, 9, and either 7 or 8; possibly 10.
> Two-term course:
> First term: Introduction, Chapters 1–6;
> Second term: Introduction, Chapters 7–11.
> Average course (14–16 week term; chapters in parentheses are optional):
> Introduction, Chapters 1, (2), 3, (4), 6, 7, 8, 9, (10), (11).
> Ethics and Religion course:
> Introduction, Chapters 6, 7, 9, 10, (11).
> Metaphysics and Epistemology course:
> Introduction, Chapters 1, 2, 3, 4, (5), (6), (7), 8, 9.

Chapters 4–5 are the most difficult and thus may be the first dropped by some classes. Other classes may prefer to begin with either Chapter 6 ("Religion") or Chapter 10 ("Ethics") and reorder the sequence of chapters. Chapter 2 (which discusses Spinoza's and Leibniz's metaphysics) also may be skipped for many shorter courses. The basic course, therefore, tailored to the average one-term, 14–16 week class, meeting three times a week, would be

Introduction, Chapters 1, 3, 6, 7, 8, 9, 10.

The remaining chapters can be added as time and interest permit.

FOR THE STUDENT: *DOING* PHILOSOPHY

Your attempt to develop your own thoughts — to "do" philosophy as well as to read what others have done — is central to any study of philosophy. Philosophy, more than any other "field," is not so much a "subject" as it is a way of thinking, one that can be fully appreciated only by joining in. While reading each section, therefore, do not hesitate to put the book down at any time and do your own thinking and writing. When reading about metaphysics, for example, think about how you would develop your own view of reality and how you would answer the questions raised by the first philosophers of ancient Greece. When confronted by an argument, consider how you might argue for — or against — the same position. And when facing a problem, always be certain that you make the attempt to answer it in your own terms as well as read through the answers offered by earlier thinkers. In philosophy, unlike physics or biology, your own answer may be just as legitimate as those given by the philosophers of the past. That is what makes philosophy so difficult to learn at first, but it is also what makes it so personally valuable and enjoyable.

ACKNOWLEDGMENTS

This book and its revisions have been made possible through the encouragement and help of many people, most importantly the several thousand introductory students I have had the pleasure of meeting and teaching over the past decade. More immediately, I want to thank Susan Zaleski, for her very special insights and criticism of the manuscript in its early stages; Robert Fogelin, Yale University, John McDermott, Texas A & M, and George Cronk, Bergen Community College, for their encouragement and helpful suggestions; and Terry Boswell, Lisa Erlich, David Blumenfeld, Paul Woodruff, Harry O'Hara of University of Texas at Austin, Stephanie Lewis of Kidder-Peabody, and Barbara Barratt for their time and good advice. Robin Dumas gave me considerable help with the index. Revisions for the Second Edition were suggested by Paul Woodruff, Billy Joe Lucas, and Cheshire Calhoun. I have benefited in the Third Edition from advice from Peter Hutcheson, Richard Palmer, Norman Thomas, Greta Reed, Edward Johnson, Paul Woodruff, Don Branson, Hoke Robinson, Robert Fogelin, Meredith Michaels, Bruce Paternoster, and Maxine Morphis. I owe a special debt of gratitude to Bruce Ballard, both for his editorial suggestions and for his extensive help with the revised manuscript. Bill Pullin originally convinced me to write this book for HBJ. Bill McLane encouraged me to undertake both revisions and was extremely encouraging all the way through. Marlane Agriesti has been an essential source of advice and encouragement during the preparation of this edition, and John Holland, Sid Zimmerman, Laurel Miller, Gail Majdalany, Anne Boynton, Christine Pearson, Dorothea von Elbe, and Robert Watrous have helped me put the various manuscripts through production. My thanks to all of them, but mainly, my thanks to my own teachers — Robert Hanson, Doris Yokum, Elizabeth Flower, James Ross, C. G. Hempel — who provided me with the models and the material for an ideal introductory philosophy course, and to many of the students who still continue to make the teaching of philosophy one of the more satisfying professions in a not easily satisfying world.

Robert C. Solomon

Contents

PREFACE   v

Introduction: Philosophy   1

Socrates   1
What Is Philosophy?   10
A Modern Approach to Philosophy   13
A Brief Introduction to Logic   18
    Deductive Arguments   19
    Inductive Arguments   26
    Argument by Analogy   29
    Argument by Counter-Examples   31
    Reductio ad Absurdum   32
    The Worst Kinds of Fallacies   33

Part One   Knowing the World, and Beyond   43

1 Reality: Ancient Views   45

"The Way the World Really Is": The Pre-Socratics   45
Two Kinds of Metaphysics: Plato and Aristotle   53
Two Important Assumptions   74
Summary and Conclusion   76

2 Reality: Two Modern Views   80

Benedictus de Spinoza   82
Gottfried Wilhelm von Leibniz   91
Summary and Conclusion   103

3 Knowledge   105

The Rationalist's Confidence: Descartes   109
Concerning Human Understanding: John Locke   120
The Empiricist Theory of Knowledge   125
Common Sense Undone: Bishop Berkeley   133
The Congenial Skeptic: David Hume   141
Summary and Conclusion   156

4 Truth   160

What Is Truth?   162
Theories of Truth   165
     The Coherence Theory   166
     The Pragmatic Theory   168
     The Semantic Theory   174
Kant's Revolution   178
The Battle in Europe after Kant: Relativism and Absolutism   186
Hermeneutics: The New Quest for Understanding   189
Relativism Reconsidered   193
Summary and Conclusion   201

5 Necessity   205

Analytic Truths   207
The Truths of Arithmetic and Geometry   210
     The Empiricist Argument   211
     The Rationalist Response   220
The Truths of Metaphysics   230
Summary and Conclusion   232

6 Religion   237

The Traditional Conception of God   237
Can We Know That God Exists?   240
     The Ontological Argument   241
     The Cosmological Argument   249
     The Teleological Argument   252
What Is Religious Belief?   257
Knowledge and Faith   264
     The Problem of Evil   270
     Faith and Irrationality   284

Other Gods (Islam, Buddhism, Hinduism)   293
Doubt   302
Is Religion Nonsense?   307
The Attack on Religion: Marx, Nietzsche, and Freud   312
Summary and Conclusion   317

Part Two   Knowing Oneself, and Acting   321

7 Self-identity   323

The Enduring Self and Self-consciousness: From Descartes to Kant   324
Facts and Fantasies: Existentialism and Beyond   341
One Self? Any Self? The Eastern Alternative   349
The Individual and the Community   353
Summary and Conclusion   363

8 Mind and Body   365

What Is Consciousness?   365
"Incorrigibility" as the Mark of the Mental   369
The Problem of Dualism   372
The Rejection of Dualism   377
    Radical Behaviorism   377
    Logical Behaviorism   378
The Identity Theory   386
Changing Our Minds: Alternative Conceptions   396
Functionalism: The Mind and the Computer   407
Summary and Conclusion   416

9 Freedom   419

Determinism   420
Are We Cogs in the Universe? "Hard Determinism"   422
Is Determinism True? Determinism Versus Indeterminism   424
The Role of Consciousness   427
"Soft Determinism"   429
Compulsion   437
A Champion of Determinism   442
Demanding to Be Free: Libertarianism   448
Existentialism   453
Freedom and Perversity   457
Summary and Conclusion   459

10 Ethics   462

Morality   464
Is Morality Relative?   466
Egoism and Altruism   471
Morality as Virtue: Aristotle   477
Morality and Sentiment: Hume and Rousseau   490
Morality and Reason: Kant   497
Utilitarianism   512
The Creation of Morality: Nietzsche and Existentialism   523
Ethics Unnaturalized: Metaethics and Its Consequences   535
Summary and Conclusion   549

11 Politics   553

The Problem of Justice   555
The Legitimacy of the State   571
   Five Theories of Legitimacy   573
   The Social Contract   575
Individual Rights and Freedom   587
A Different Sense of Freedom: Marx   594
The Absolute State: Fascism   604
The Alternative to Government: Anarchism   609
Summary and Conclusion   613

BRIEF BIOGRAPHIES   617
BIBLIOGRAPHY   629
INDEX OF GLOSSARY TERMS   635
SUBJECT INDEX   638

Reading Selections by Chapter

INTRODUCTION

Aristophanes, *Clouds*   2
Plato, *Apology*   2–4
Plato, *Crito*   4–8
Plato, *Phaedo*   8–9
Plato, *Republic*   9–10
Plato, *Apology*   13
Descartes, *Discourse on Method*   17

1.

Plato, *Republic*   55–59
Plato, *Meno*   60–66
Aristotle, *Metaphysics*   73

2.

Spinoza, *Ethics*   82–91
Leibniz, *Monadology*   92–102

3.

Russell, *The Problems of Philosophy*   106–108
Descartes, *Meditation I*   110–11, 112–14
Descartes, *Meditation II*   114–18
Descartes, *Meditation VI*   119–20
Locke, *Essay Concerning Human Understanding*   121–23
Leibniz, *New Essays on the Human Understanding*   123–24
Locke, *Essay*   125–33
Berkeley, *Principles of Human Knowledge*   134–41
Hume, *Enquiry Concerning Human Understanding*   142
Hume, *Treatise of Human Nature*   142–44, 146–56

4.

Blanshard, *The Nature of Thought*   167
*Pierce, "How to Make Our Ideas Clear"   169–72
James, *Pragmatism*   172–74
Tarski, "Semantic Theory of Truth"   175–76
*Kant, *Prolegomena*   182–83
Husserl, "Philosophy as a Rigorous Science"   188–89
*MacIntyre on Gadamer's *Truth and Method*   191–92
*Swoyer, "Relative Truth"   194–201

5.

Aristotle, *Metaphysics*   209
Ayer, *Language, Truth and Logic*   212
Mill, *A System of Logic*   213–17
Hempel, "On the Nature of Mathematical Truth"   218–20
Kant, *Critique of Pure Reason*   222–24
Kant, *Prolegomena*   224–25
Husserl, *Ideas*   226–27
*Husserl, "Phenomenology"   228–30

6.

Anselm, *Proslogion*   241–43
Descartes, *Meditation IV*   243–45
Kant, *Critique of Pure Reason*   247–48
Aquinas, "Five Ways"   249–51
Einstein, "Religion and Science"   252–53
*Hawking, "God and the Universe"   253–54
Aquinas, "Five Ways"   254
Hume, *Dialogues*   255
Wisdom, "Gods"   256–57
Flew, Hare, Mitchell, *Symposium*   257–64
Kant, *Critique of Practical Reason*   265–66
James, *The Will to Believe*   267–69
*Pascal, *Pensées*   269
*Augustine, from *Confessions*   271–74
*Bayle, "The Problem of Evil"   276–79
Dostoevsky, *Brothers Karamazov*   281–84
Kierkegaard, *Concluding Unscientific Postscript*   287–88
Kierkegaard, *Philosophical Fragments*   288–89
Tillich, *Dynamics of Faith*   290–92
*Smith, *Religions of Man*   293–302
Dostoevsky, *Brothers Karamazov*   303–307
Ayer, *Language, Truth and Logic*   307–11

*indicates selections new to this edition

Marx, *Early Writings*   312–13
Nietzsche, *Beyond Good and Evil*   313–14
Nietzsche, *The Antichrist*   314–15
Nietzsche, *Joyful Wisdom*   315–16
Freud, *Future of an Illusion*   316–17

7.

Descartes, *Meditation VI*   325–26
Locke, *Essay*   326–29
Hume, *Treatise*   331–32, 333–34
Kant, *Prolegomena*   336–37
*Michaels, "Personal Identity"   338–41
Sartre, *Existentialism as a Humanism*   343–45
Sartre, *Being and Nothingness*   346
Sartre, *No Exit*   347–49
Hesse, *Steppenwolf*   350
Buddha, *Teachings*   351–52
Nietzsche, *Joyful Wisdom*   354–56
Kierkegaard, *Concluding Unscientific Postscript*   357–58
Heidegger, *Being and Time*   358
Reisman, *Individualism Reconsidered*   359
Hegel, *Phenomenology of Spirit*   360
Hegel, *Reason in History*   360–61
Kierkegaard, *Concluding Unscientific Postscript*   361–62
Marx, *Early Writings*   362

8.

Descartes, *Meditation VI*   366–68
Freud, *Introductory Lectures*   370–71
Descartes, "Passions of the Soul"   374–75
Ryle, *Concept of Mind*   378–84
*Smart, "Sensations and Brain Processes"   386–90
Shaffer, *Philosophy of Mind*   391–96
Aristotle, *De Anima*   397
Strawson, "Persons"   397–400
James, "Does Consciousness Exist?"   402–407
*Fodor, "The Mind-Body Problem"   408–16

9.

Holbach, *System of Nature*   423–24
Mill, *A System of Logic*   430–34
Hume, *Enquiry Concerning Human Understanding*   435–36
Aristotle, *Ethics*   437–38

*indicates selections new to this edition

Hospers, "What Means This Freedom?"   439–41
Skinner, "Freedom and the Control of Men"   443–45
Skinner, *Walden II*   445–46
Burgess, *A Clockwork Orange*   447
Campbell, *In Defense of Free Will*   449–53
Sartre, *Being and Nothingness*   454–56
Dostoevsky, *Notes from Underground*   457–59

10.

Augustine, *On Freedom*   464–65
Stace, *Concept of Morals*   468–71
Plato, *The Republic*   472–73
Butler, *Five Sermons*   474–76
Aristotle, *Ethics*   477–90
Hume, *Inquiry Concerning the Principles of Morals*   491–94
Rousseau, *Emile*   494–97
Kant, *Fundamental Principles of the Metaphysics of Morals*   498–510
Bentham, *Principles of Morals and Legislation*   513–16
Mill, *Utilitarianism*   517–23
Nietzsche, *Joyful Wisdom*   527
Nietzsche, *Beyond Good and Evil*   527–30
Sartre, *Existentialism as a Humanism*   531–34
*Moore, *Principia Ethica*   537–40
*Ayer, *Language, Truth and Logic*   540–44
*MacIntyre, *After Virtue*   544–49

11.

Plato, *Republic*   557–59
Aristotle, *Ethics*   559–62
Mill, *Utilitarianism*   563–67
Hume, *Inquiry Concerning the Principles of Morals*   567–68
Rawls, "Justice as Fairness"   568–71
Hobbes, *Leviathan*   576–80
Rousseau, *The Social Contract*   582–86
Jefferson *et al.*, *The Declaration of Independence*   587
Locke, *Second Treatise on Government*   589
Mill, *On Liberty*   591–94
Marx, *Early Writings*   595–96
Marx and Engels, *Communist Manifesto*   597–604
Mussolini, "The Doctrine of Fascism"   605–606
Machiavelli, *The Prince*   607–609
Tucker, *Instead of a Book*   610–13

*indicates selections new to this edition

Introducing

PHILOSOPHY
a text with readings
third edition

Introduction: Philosophy

The unexamined life is not worth living.

Socrates

SOCRATES

He was not the first philosopher, but he was, and is still, the ideal of philosophers. Once assured by the oracle at Delphi that he was the wisest man in Athens, Socrates (470–399 B.C.) borrowed his view of life from the inscription at Delphi, "Know Thyself." Mixing humility with arrogance, he boasted that his superiority lay in his awareness of his own ignorance, and he spent the rest of his life making fools of the self-proclaimed "wise men" of Athens.

In the opinion of Socrates and other critics of the time, the government of Athens was corrupt and notoriously bumbling, in marked contrast to the "Golden Age" of Pericles a few years before. Philosophical arguments had become all cleverness and demagoguery, rhetorical tricks to win arguments and legal cases; political ambition replaced justice and the search for the good life. Socrates believed that the people of Athens held their principles glibly, like banners at a football game, but rarely lived up to them and even more rarely examined them. Against this, he developed a technique of asking seemingly innocent questions, trapping his audience in their own confusions and hypocrisies, exploding the pretentions of his times. And against their easy certainties, he taught that "the unexamined life is not worth living." He referred to himself as a "gadfly" (an obnoxious insect with a painful bite), keeping his fellow citizens from ever becoming as smug and self-righteous as they would like to have been. Accordingly, he made many enemies and was satirized by Aristophanes in his play the *Clouds*.

from *The Clouds,* by Aristophanes

STUDENT OF SOCRATES: Socrates asked Chaerephon how many of its own feet a flea could jump—one had bitten Chaerephon's brow and then jumped to Socrates' head.

STREPSIADES: And how did he measure the jump?

STUDENT: Most ingeniously. He melted wax, caught the flea, dipped its feet, and the hardened wax made Persian slippers.

Unfastening these, he found their size.

STREPSIADES: Royal Zeus! What an acute intellect!

STUDENT: But yesterday a high thought was lost through a lizard.

STREPSIADES: How so? Tell me.

STUDENT: As he gaped up at the moon, investigating her paths and turnings, from off the roof a lizard befouled him.[1]

In the play, Aristophanes made Socrates and his students look utterly ridiculous, and the Athenian public enjoyed Aristophanes' sarcasm as a mild form of vengeance for Socrates' constant criticisms. Aristophanes' "clouds" refer to that confusion which we mean when we talk of someone "having his head in the clouds." Aristophanes probably expressed the general public opinion when he described Socrates as "shiftless" and merely a master at verbal trickery.

Socrates' students, however, virtually worshipped him. They described him as "the bravest, most wise and most upright man of our times" and perceived him as a martyr for the truth in a corrupted society. The price of his criticism was not merely the satire of the playwrights. Because he had been such a continual nuisance, the government arranged to have Socrates brought to trial for "corrupting the youth of Athens" and being an "atheist." And for these trumped up "crimes," Socrates was condemned to death. But at his trial, he once again became a "gadfly" to those who condemned him.

from *The Apology,* by Plato

There are many other reasons for my not being angry with you for convicting me, gentlemen of the jury, and what happened was not unexpected. I am much more surprised at the number of votes cast on each side, for I did not think the decision would be by so few votes but by a great many. As it is, a switch of only thirty votes would have acquitted me. I think myself that I have been cleared on Meletus' charges, and it is clear to all that, if Anytus and Lycon had not joined him in accusing me, he would have been fined a thousand drachmas for not receiving a fifth of the votes.

He assesses the penalty at death. So be it. What counter-assessment should I propose to you, gentlemen of the jury? Clearly it should be a pen-

[1] Aristophanes, *Clouds,* in *The Complete Plays of Aristophanes,* trans. Moses Hadas (New York: Bantam, 1962).

alty I deserve, and what do I deserve to suffer or to pay because I have deliberately not led a quiet life but have neglected what occupies most people: wealth, household affairs, the position of general or public orator or the other offices, the political clubs and factions that exist in the city? I thought myself too honest to survive if I occupied myself with those things. I did not follow that path that would have made me of no use either to you or to myself, but I went to each of you privately and conferred upon him what I say is the greatest benefit, by persuading him not to care for any of his belongings before caring that he himself should be as good and as wise as possible, not to care for the city's possessions more than for the city itself, and to care for other things in the same way. What do I deserve for being such a man? Some good, gentlemen of the jury, if I must truly make an assessment according to my deserts, and something suitable.

Socrates here suggests that the state should give him a pension rather than a punishment, for being a public benefactor and urging his students to be virtuous.

It is for the sake of a short time, gentlemen of the jury, that you will acquire the reputation and the guilt, in the eyes of those who want to denigrate the city, of having killed Socrates, a wise man, for they will say that I am wise even if I am not. If you had waited but a little while, this would have happened of its own accord. You see my age, that I am already advanced in years and close to death. I am saying this not to all of you but to those who condemned me to death, and to these same jurors I say: Perhaps you think that I was convicted for lack of such words as might have convinced you, if I thought I should say or do all I could to avoid my sentence. Far from it. I was convicted because I lacked not words but boldness and shamelessness and the willingness to say to you what you would most gladly have heard from me, lamentations and tears and my saying and doing many things that I say are unworthy of me but that you are accustomed to hear from others. I did not think then that the danger I ran should make me do anything mean, nor do I now regret the nature of my defence. I would much rather die after this kind of defence than live after making the other kind. Neither I nor any other man should, on trial or in war, contrive to avoid death at any cost. Indeed it is often obvious in battle that one could escape death by throwing away one's weapons and by turning to supplicate one's pursuers, and there are many ways to avoid death in every kind of danger if one will venture to do or say anything to avoid it. It is not difficult to avoid death, gentlemen of the jury, it is much more difficult to avoid wickedness, for it runs faster than death. Slow and elderly as I am, I have been caught by the slower pursuer, whereas my accusers, being clever and sharp, have been caught by the quicker, wickedness. I leave you now, condemned to death by you, but they are condemned by truth to wickedness and injustice. So I maintain my assessment, and they maintain theirs. This perhaps had to happen, and I think it is as it should be.

Now I want to prophesy to those who convicted me, for I am at the point when men prophesy most, when they are about to die. I say gentlemen, to those who voted to kill me, that vengeance will come upon you immediately after my death, a vengeance much harder to bear than that which you took in killing me. You did this in the belief that you would avoid giving an account of your life, but I maintain that quite the opposite will happen to you. There will be more people to test you, whom I now held back, but you did not notice it. They will be more difficult to deal with as they will be younger and you will resent them more. You are wrong if you believe that by killing people you will prevent anyone from reproaching you for not living in the right way. To escape such tests is neither possible nor good, but it is best and easiest not to discredit others but to prepare oneself to be as good as possible. With this prophecy to you who convicted me, I part from you.[2]

In prison, he was given the opportunity to escape. He refused it. He had always taught that "the really important thing is not to live, but to live well." And to "live well" meant, along with the more enjoyable things in life, to live according to your principles. When his friend Crito tried to persuade him otherwise, Socrates responded

from *Crito,*
by Plato

SOCRATES. My good Crito, why should we care so much for what the majority think? The most reasonable people, to whom one should pay more attention, will believe that things were done as they were done.

CRITO. You see, Socrates, that one must also pay attention to the opinion of the majority. Your present situation makes clear that the majority can inflict not the least but pretty well the greatest evils if one is slandered among them.

SOCRATES. Would that the majority could inflict the greatest evils, for they would then be capable of the greatest good, and that would be fine, but now they cannot do either. They cannot make a man either wise or foolish, but they inflict things haphazardly.

CRITO. That may be so. But tell me this, Socrates, are you anticipating that I and your other friends would have trouble with the informers if you escape from here, as having stolen you away, and that we should be compelled to lose all our property or pay heavy fines and suffer other punishment besides? If you have any such fear, forget it. We would be justified in running this risk to save you, and worse, if necessary. Do follow my advice, and do not act differently.

SOCRATES. I do have these things in mind, Crito, and also many others.

CRITO. Have no such fear. It is not much money that some people require to save you and get you out of here.

. . . . . .

Besides, Socrates, I do not think that what you are doing is right, to give up your life when you can save it, and to hasten your fate as your

[2]Plato, *Apology,* in *The Trial and Death of Socrates,* 2nd ed., trans. G. M. A. Grube (Indianapolis, Ind.: Hackett, 1974).

enemies would hasten it, and indeed have hastened it in their wish to destroy you.

· · · · ·

SOCRATES. My dear Crito, your eagerness is worth much if it should have some right aim; if not, then the greater your keenness the more difficult it is to deal with. We must therefore examine whether we should act in this way or not, as not only now but at all times I am the kind of man who listens only to the argument that on reflection seems best to me. I cannot, now that this fate has come upon me, discard the arguments I used; they seem to me much the same. I value and respect the same principles as before, and if we have no better arguments to bring up at this moment, be sure that I shall not agree with you, not even if the power of the majority were to frighten us with more bogeys, as if we were children, with threats of incarcerations and executions and confiscation of property. How should we examine this matter most reasonably? Would it be by taking up first your argument about the opinions of men, whether it is sound in every case that one should pay attention to some opinions, but not to others? Or was that well-spoken before the necessity to die came upon me, but now it is clear that this was said in vain for the sake of argument, that it was in truth play and nonsense? I am eager to examine together with you, Crito, whether this argument will appear in any way different to me in my present circumstances, or whether it remains the same, whether we are to abandon it or believe it. It was said on every occasion that one should greatly value some opinions, but not others. Does that seem to you a sound statement?

· · · · ·

Examine the following statement in turn as to whether it stays the same or not, that the most important thing is not life, but the good life.

CRITO. It stays the same.

SOCRATES. And that the good life, the beautiful life, and the just life are the same; does that still hold, or not?

CRITO. It does hold.

SOCRATES. As we have agreed so far, we must examine next whether it is right for me to try to get out of here when the Athenians have not acquitted me. If it is seen to be right, we will try to do so; if it is not, we will abandon the idea. As for those questions you raise about money, reputation, the upbringing of children, Crito, those considerations in truth belong to those people who easily put men to death and would bring them to life again if they could, without thinking; I mean the majority of men. For us, however, since our argument leads to this, the only valid consideration, as we were saying just now, is whether we should be acting rightly in giving money and gratitude to those who will lead me out of here, and ourselves helping with the escape, or whether in truth we shall do wrong in doing all this. If it appears that we shall be acting unjustly, then we have no need at all to take into account whether we shall have to die, if we stay here and keep quiet, or suffer in another way, rather than do wrong.

CRITO. I think you put that beautifully, Socrates, but see what we should do.

SOCRATES. Let us examine the question together, my dear friend, and if you can make any objection while I am speaking, make it and I will listen to you, but if you have no objection to make, my dear Crito, then stop now from saying the same thing so often, that I must leave here against the will of the Athenians. I think it important to persuade you before I act, and not to act against your wishes. . . .

SOCRATES. Then . . . I ask you: when one has come to an agreement that is just with someone, should one fulfill it or cheat on it?

CRITO. One should fulfill it.

SOCRATES. See what follows from this: If we leave here without the city's permission, are we injuring people whom we should least injure? And are we sticking to a just agreement, or not?

CRITO. I cannot answer your question, Socrates, I do not know.

SOCRATES. Look at it this way. If, as we were planning to run away from here, or whatever one should call it, the laws and the state came and confronted us and asked: "Tell me, Socrates, what are you intending to do? Do you not by this action you are attempting intend to destroy us, the laws, and indeed the whole city, as far as you are concerned? Or do you think it possible for a city not to be destroyed if the verdicts of its courts have no force but are nullified and set at naught by private individuals?" What shall we answer to this and other such arguments? For many things could be said, especially by an orator on behalf of this law we are destroying, which orders that the judgments of the courts shall be carried out. Shall we say in answer, "The city wronged me, and its decision was not right." Shall we say that, or what?

CRITO. Yes, by Zeus, Socrates, that is our answer.

SOCRATES. Then what if the laws said, "Was that the agreement between us, Socrates, or was it to respect the judgments that the city came to?" And if we wondered at their words, they would perhaps add: "Socrates, do not wonder at what we say but answer, since you are accustomed to proceed by question and answer. Come now, what accusation do you bring against us and the city, that you should try to destroy us? Did we not, first, bring you to birth, and was it not through us that your father married your mother and begat you? Tell us, do you find anything to criticize in those of us who are concerned with marriage?" And I would say that I do not criticize them. "Or in those of us concerned with the nurture of babies and the education that you too received? Were those assigned to that subject not right to instruct your father to educate you in the arts and in physical culture?" And I would say that they were right. "Very well," they would continue, "and after you were born and nurtured and educated, could you, in the first place, deny that you are our offspring and servant, both you and your forefathers? If that is so, do you think that we are on an equal footing as regards the right, and that whatever we do to you it is right for you to do to us? You were not on an equal footing with your father as regards the right, nor with your master if you had one, so as to retaliate for anything they did to you, to revile them if they reviled you, to beat them if they beat you, and so with many other things. Do you think you have this right to retaliation against your country and its laws? That if we undertake to destroy you and think it right to do so, you can undertake to destroy us, as far as you can, in return? And will you say that you are right to do so, you who truly care for virtue? Is your wisdom such as not to realize that your country is to be honoured more than your mother, your father and all your ancestors, that it is more to be revered and more sacred, and that it counts for more among the gods and sensible men, that you must worship it, yield to it and placate its anger more than your father's? You must either persuade it or obey its orders, and endure in silence whatever it instructs you to endure, whether blows or bonds, and if it leads you into war to be wounded or killed, you must obey. To do so is right, and one must not give way or retreat or leave one's post, but both in war and in courts and everywhere else, one must obey the commands of one's city and country, or persuade it as to the nature of justice. It is impious to bring violence to bear against your mother or father, it is much more so to use it against your country."

What shall we say in reply, Crito, that the laws speak the truth, or not?

CRITO. I think they do.

SOCRATES. "Reflect now, Socrates," the laws might say "that if what we say is true, you are not treating us rightly by planning to do what you are planning.

. . . . .

"So decisively did you choose us and agree to be a citizen under us. Also, you have had children in this city, thus showing that it was congenial to you. Then at your trial you could have assessed your penalty at exile if you wished, and you are now attempting to do against the city's wishes what you could then have done with her consent. Then you prided yourself that you did not resent death, but you chose, as you said, death in preference to exile. Now, however, those words do not make you ashamed, and you pay no heed to us, the laws, as you plan to destroy us, and you act like the meanest type of slave by trying to run away, contrary to your undertakings and your agreement to live as a citizen under us. First then, answer us on this very point, whether we speak the truth when we say that you agreed, not only in words but by your deeds, to live in accordance with us." What are we to say to that, Crito? Must we not agree?

CRITO. We must, Socrates.

SOCRATES. "Surely," they might say, "you are breaking the undertakings and agreements that you made with us without compulsion or deceit, and under no pressure of time for deliberation. You have had seventy years during which you could have gone away if you did not like us, and if you thought our agreements unjust. You did not choose to go to Sparta or to Crete, which you are always saying are well governed, nor to any other city, Greek or foreign. You have been away from Athens less than the lame or the blind or other handicapped people. It is clear that the city has been outstandingly more congenial to you than to other Athenians, and so have we, the laws, for what city can please if its laws do not? Will you then not now stick to our agreements? You will, Socrates, if we can persuade you, and not make yourself a laughingstock by leaving the city.

"Be persuaded by us who have brought you up, Socrates. Do not value either your children or your life or anything else more than goodness, in order that you may have all this as your defence before the rulers there. If you do this deed, you will not think it better or more just or more pious, nor will any one of your friends, nor will it be better for you when you arrive yonder. As it is, you depart, if you depart, after being wronged not by us, the laws, but by men; but if you depart after shamefully returning wrong for wrong and injury for injury, after breaking your agreement and contract with us, after injuring those you should injure least — yourself, your friends, your country and us — we shall be angry with you while you are still alive, and our brothers, the laws of the underworld, will not receive [you] kindly, knowing that you tried to destroy us as far as you could. Do not let Crito persuade you, rather than we, to do what he says."

·   ·   ·   ·   ·

CRITO. I have nothing to say, Socrates.

SOCRATES. Let it be then, Crito, and let us act in this way, since this is the way the god is leading us.[3]

Socrates believed that the good of his "soul" was far more important than the transient pleasures of life. Accordingly, he preferred to die for his ideas than live as a hypocrite. An idea worth living for may be an idea worth dying for as well.

And while he was saying this, he was holding the cup, and then drained it calmly and easily. Most of us had been able to hold back our tears reasonably well up till then, but when we saw him drinking it and after he drank it, we could hold them back no longer; my own tears came in floods against my will. So I covered my face. I was weeping for myself — not for him, but for my misfortune in being deprived of such a comrade. Even before me, Crito was unable to restrain his tears and got up. Apollodorus had not ceased from weeping before, and at this moment his noisy tears and anger made everybody present break down, except Socrates, "What is this," he said, "you strange fellows. It is mainly for this reason that I sent the

[3]Plato, *Crito*, in *The Trial and Death of Socrates*, 2nd ed., trans. G. M. A. Grube (Indianapolis, Ind.: Hackett, 1974).

women away, to avoid such unseemliness, for I am told one should die in good omened silence. So keep quiet and control yourselves."

. . . . .

Such was the end of our comrade, Echecrates, a man who, we would say, was of all those we have known the best, and· also the wisest and the most upright.[4]

Is there anything that you believe so passionately that you would die for it? Is there anything that you·believe so passionately that it really makes your life worth living? For most people, now as always, life is rather a matter of "getting by." One of the more popular phrases of self-praise these days is "I'm a survivor." But, ironically, a person who is not willing to die for anything (for example, his or her own freedom) is thereby more vulnerable to threats and corruption. To be willing to die — as Socrates was — is to have a considerable advantage over someone for whom "life is everything."

If you look closely at your life, not only at your proclaimed ideals and principles but your desires and ambitions as well, do the facts of your life add up to its best intentions? Or are you too just drifting with the times, dissatisfied with ultimately meaningless jobs and mindless joyless entertainments, concerned with the price of gasoline and some stupidity of the government, the petty competitions of school and society, the hassles of chores and assignments, car troubles and occasional social embarrassments, interrupted only by all too rare and too quickly passing pleasures and distractions? What we learn from Socrates is how to rise above all of this. Not that we should give up worldly pleasures — good food and fun, sex, sports, and entertainment — and put our heads in the "clouds"; but we should see them in perspective, and examine for ourselves that jungle of confused reactions and conditioned responses that we have unthinkingly inherited from our parents and borrowed from our peers. The point is not to give up what we have learned or to turn against our "culture." Rather, the lesson to be learned from Socrates is that thinking about our lives and clarifying our ideals can turn it from a dreary series of tasks and distractions into a self-conscious adventure, one even worth dying for and certainly worth living for. It is a special kind of abstract thinking, rising above petty concerns and transforming our existence into a bold experiment in living. This special kind of thinking is called — philosophy.

SOCRATES. Do you agree, or not, that when we say that a man has a passion for something, we shall say that he desires that whole kind of thing, not just one part of it and not the other?

GLAUCON. Yes, the whole of it.

SOCRATES. The lover of wisdom, we shall say, has a passion for wisdom, not for this kind of wisdom and not that, but for every kind of wisdom?

GLAUCON. True.

[4]Plato, *Phaedo*, in *The Trial and Death of Socrates*, 2nd ed., trans. G. M. A. Grube (Indianapolis, Ind.: Hackett, 1974).

SOCRATES. As for one who is choosy about what he learns, especially if he is young and cannot yet give a reasoned account of what is useful and what is not, we shall not call him a lover of learning or a philosopher, just as we shall not say that a man who is difficult about his food is hungry or has an appetite for food. We shall not call him a lover of food but a bad feeder.

GLAUCON. And we should be right.

SOCRATES. But we shall rightly call a philosopher the man who is easily willing to learn every kind of knowledge, gladly turns to learning things, and is unsatiable in this respect. Is that not so?[5]

WHAT IS PHILOSOPHY?

Philosophy is not like any other academic subject; rather it is a critical approach to all subjects. Philosophy is a style of life, a life of ideas or the life of reason, which a person like Socrates lives all his life, which many of us live only a few hours a week. It is thinking, about everything and anything. But mainly, it is living thoughtfully. Aristotle, the student of Plato, who was the student of Socrates, called this "contemplative" or philosophical life the ideal life for man. He did not mean, however, that one should sit and think all of the time without doing anything. Aristotle, like the other Greek philosophers, was not one to abstain from pleasures of all kinds or from political and social involvement for the sake of isolated thinking. Philosophy need not, as commonly believed, put our heads in the clouds, out of touch with everyday reality. Quite to the contrary, philosophy takes our heads out of the clouds, enlarging our view of ourselves and our knowledge of the world, allowing us to break out of prejudices and harmful habits that we have held since we were too young or too naive to know better. Philosophy puts our lives and our beliefs in perspective, by enabling us to see afresh the ways in which we view the world, to see what we assume, what we infer, and what we know for certain. It allows us to see the consequences of our views and sometimes their hopeless inconsistencies. It allows us to see the justification (or lack of it) for our most treasured beliefs, and to separate what we will continue to believe with confidence from what we should consider doubtful or reject. Philosophy gives us the intellectual strength to defend what we do and what we believe to others and to ourselves. It forces us to be clear about the limits as well as the warrants for our acts and beliefs. And, consequently, it gives us the intellectual strength to understand, tolerate, and even sympathize with views very different from our own.

Philosophy is first and foremost a discipline that teaches you how to hold and defend beliefs that, perhaps, you have always held, but without having to articulate and argue them. For example, suppose you have been brought up in a deeply

[5]Plato, *The Republic*, Bk. V, trans. G. M. A. Grube (Indianapolis, Ind.: Hackett, 1974).

religious home; you have been taught respect for God and Church, but you have never had to learn to justify or argue for your beliefs. You know that, although there are people who would disagree with you, your belief is a righteous and necessary one, but you have never had to explain this to anyone, nor have you ever tried to explain it to yourself. But now you enter college and immediately you are confronted by fellow students, some of whom you consider close friends and admire in many ways, who are vocally antireligious. Your first reactions may be almost physical; you feel weak, flushed, and anxious. You refuse to listen, and if you respond at all, it is with a tinge of hysteria. You may get into fights as well as arguments. You feel as if some foundation of your life, one of its main supports, is slipping away. But slowly you gain some confidence; you begin to listen. You give yourself enough distance so that you will consider arguments about religion in just the same way you would consider arguments about some scientific or political dispute. You ask yourself *why* they don't believe. Are their arguments persuasive, their reasons *good* reasons? You begin asking yourself how you came to believe in your religion in the first place, and you may well come up with the answer (many freshmen do) that you were "conditioned" by your parents and by society in general. Consequently, you may, perhaps for a time, perhaps for a lifetime, question or reject the ideas you had once "naturally" accepted. Or you may reaffirm your faith with new commitment, determined that, whatever the source, your beliefs are right. But after further consideration and argument, perhaps with some new religious experience, you now see both sides of the arguments. For the first time, you can weigh their merits and demerits against each other without defensively holding onto one and attacking the other. You may remain a believer; you may become an atheist or an agnostic (a person who admits not knowing whether there is a God or not). Or you may adopt a position in which you give all religions (and nonreligion) equal weight, continuing to believe but not insisting that your belief is the only correct one or that you are necessarily a superior person because of it. But whatever you decide, your position will no longer be naive and unthinking. You know the arguments, both for and against. You know how to defend yourself. And, most importantly, you have confidence that your position is secure, that you have considered its objections, and that you have mastered its strengths. So it is with all philosophical problems and positions. Philosophy does not pull us away from our lives; it clarifies them. It secures them on intellectual ground in place of the fragile supports provided by inherited prejudices, fragments of parental advice, and mindless slogans borrowed from television commercials and televised demagogues.

"Philosophy" sounds like a new and mysterious discipline, unlike anything you have ever encountered. But the basic ideas of philosophy are familiar to all of us, even if we have not yet formally confronted the problems. In this sense, we are all philosophers already. Watch yourself in a crisis, or listen to yourself in an argument with a friend. Notice how quickly abstract concepts like "freedom," "mankind," "self-identity," "nature" and "natural," "relative," "reality," "illusion," and "truth" enter our thoughts and our conversations. Notice how certain basic philosophical principles—whether conservative or radical, selfish or idealistic, confident or skeptical, pedestrian or heroic — enter into our arguments and our thinking as well as our actions. We all have some opinions about God, about morality and its principles, about the nature of man and the nature of the universe. But because we haven't questioned them, they are merely the **assumptions** of our thinking. We believe many things without having thought about them, merely assuming them, sometimes without evidence or good reasons. What the study of philosophy does for us is to make our ideas explicit, to give us the means of defending our presuppositions, and to make alternative suppositions available to us as well. Where once we merely assumed a point of view, passively and for lack of alternatives, we now can argue for it with confidence, knowing that our acceptance is active and critical, systematic rather than merely a collection of borrowed beliefs (who knows from where). To be **critical** means to examine carefully and cautiously, willing, if necessary, to change one's own beliefs. It does not need to be nasty or destructive. There is "constructive criticism" as well. And to "argue" does not mean "to have a fight"; an **argument** may simply be the justification of our beliefs.

So what is philosophy? Literally, from the Greek *(philein, sophia)*, it is "the love of wisdom."[6] It is an attitude of critical and systematic thoughtfulness rather than a particular subject matter. This makes matters very difficult for the beginner, who would like a definition of philosophy of the same kind received when he or she began biology, as "the study of living organisms." But the nature of philosophy is itself among the most bitter disputes in philosophy. Many philosophers say that it is a science, in fact, the "Queen of the Sciences," the womb in which physics, chemistry, mathematics, astronomy, biology, and psychology began their development before being born into their own distinguished worlds and separate university departments. And insofar as one says that philosophy is the road to reality and that the goal of philosophy is truth, that would seem to make it the ultimate science as well. But it has also been argued, as far back as Socrates, that the main business of philosophy is a matter of definitions — finding clear meanings for such important ideas as truth, justice, wisdom, knowledge, and happiness. Accordingly, many philosophers have taken advantage of the sophisticated tools of modern logic and linguistics in their attempt to find such definitions. Other philosophers, however, would insist that philosophy is rather closer to morality and religion, its purpose to give meaning to our lives and lead us down "the right path" to "the good life." Still others insist that philosophy is an art, the art of criticism and argumentation as well as the art of conceptual system building. There are philosophers who place strong emphasis upon proof and argument; there are others who place their trust in intuition and insight. There are philosophers who reduce all philosophizing to the study of experience; there are philosophers who take it as a matter of principle not to trust experience. There are philosophers who insist on being practical, in fact, who insist that there are no other considerations but practicality; and then there are philosophers who

---

[6]The word was invented by Pythagoras (whom we shall meet in the next chapter). When he was asked if he was already a wise man, he answered "No, I am not wise, but I am a *lover* of wisdom."

insist on the purity of the life of ideas, divorced from any practical considerations. But philosophy cannot, without distortion, be reduced to any one of these preferences. All enter into that constantly redefined critical and creative life of ideas that Socrates was willing to die for. In fact, Socrates himself insisted that it is the seeking of wisdom that is the essence of philosophy and that anyone who is sure that he or she has wisdom already is undoubtedly wrong — Socrates included. In the *Apology*, for example, he makes this famous disclaimer:

from *The Apology*, by Plato

The effect of these investigations of mine, gentlemen, has been to arouse against me a great deal of hostility, and hostility of a particularly bitter and persistent kind, which has resulted in various malicious suggestions, including the description of me as a professor of wisdom. This is due to the fact that whenever I succeed in disproving another person's claim to wisdom in a given subject, the bystanders assume that I know everything about that subject myself. But the truth of the matter, gentlemen, is pretty certainly this: that real wisdom is the property of God, and this oracle is his way of telling us that human wisdom has little or no value. It seems to me that he is not referring literally to Socrates, but has merely taken my name as an example, as if he would say to us 'The wisest of you men is he who has realized, like Socrates, that in respect of wisdom he is really worthless.'

That is why I still go about seeking and searching in obedience to the divine command, if I think that anyone is wise, whether citizen or stranger; and when I think that any person is not wise, I try to help the cause of God by proving that he is not. This occupation has kept me too busy to do much either in politics or in my own affairs; in fact, my service to God has reduced me to extreme poverty.[7]

A MODERN APPROACH TO PHILOSOPHY

The approach to philosophy in this book is essentially a modern approach. This means not only that it is the approach (or set of approaches) that has dominated the last three hundred years of philosophy but also that it has an identifiable character that distinguishes it from most previous philosophies and makes it extremely close to our own ideas. Historically, modern philosophy has its origins in the rise of science and technology. (As we shall see, philosophy and science both emerged in ancient Greece.) We should understand science, however, not just as a particular discipline or subject matter, but rather as a state of mind, a way of looking at the world. It considers the world to be understandable and every event in the world to be explainable. It sees the universe as *rational*—operating

[7]Plato, *The Last Days of Socrates*, trans. Hugh Tredennick (Harmondsworth, Middlesex: Penguin, 1954).

according to universal laws. And it sees the human mind as rational too — in the sense that it can grasp and formulate these laws for itself. Though science is essentially a team effort, requiring the labor and thinking of thousands of men and women, the great breakthroughs in science have often been the insights of one man or woman alone. The most famous modern example of this individual genius is the British philosopher-scientist Isaac Newton. In the eyes of his contemporaries and followers, he single-mindedly mastered the laws of the universe, while sitting (so the story goes) under an apple tree. So too is the ideal of modern philosophy. It is, in a phrase, *thinking for yourself*. That is, philosophy is thinking for yourself about basic questions — about life, knowledge, religion, and what to do with yourself. It is *using* the rationality built into your brain to comprehend the rationality (or lack of it) in the world around you.

Accordingly, the central demand of modern philosophy is *the autonomy of the individual person*. This means that each of us must be credited with the ability to ascertain what is true and what is right, through our own thinking and experience, without just depending upon outside authority: parents, teachers, popes, kings, or a majority of peers. Whether you believe in God or not must be decided by you, by appeal to your own reason and arguments that you can formulate and examine by yourself. Whether you accept a scientific theory, a doctor's diagnosis, a newspaper's version of the news, or the legitimacy of a new law are also matters to be decided by you on the basis of evidence, principles that you can accept, and arguments that you acknowledge as valid. This stress on individual autonomy stands at the very foundation of contemporary Western thought. We might say that it is our most basic assumption. (Accordingly, we shall have to examine it as well; but the obvious place to begin is to assume that we are — each of us — capable of carrying out the reflection and criticism that philosophy demands of us.)

Historically, the position of individual autonomy can be found in Socrates, most famously, who went against the popular opinions of his day and, consequently, sacrificed his life for the "Laws" and principles he believed to be right. It also appears in many medieval philosophers, some of whom also faced grave danger in their partial rejection or questioning of the "authority" of the Church. The stress on individual autonomy comes to dominate Western thinking in that intellectually brilliant period of history called "the Enlightenment," sometimes called "the Age of Reason." It began in the late seventeenth century and continued through the French Revolution (1789). It appeared in different countries with varying speed and intensity, but ultimately it influenced the thinking of Europe, from England and France to Spain and Russia, and it became the ideology of young America, which used Enlightenment doctrines in the formulation of a "Declaration of Independence," a war for its own autonomy, and a new government established solely on Enlightenment principles. And those principles were, whatever the variations from one country or party to another, the autonomy of the individual and each person's right to choose and to speak his[8] own religious,

---

[8]Not, at that point in history, *hers* as well. The concept of a woman's autonomy and right to choose is a late nineteenth-century idea that has only recently become accepted.

political, moral, and philosophical beliefs, to "pursue happiness" in his own way, and to lead the life that he, as a reasonable person, sees as right. And if these principles have often been abused, creating confusion and sometimes anarchy, encouraging ruthlessness in politics and strife in a mixed society, they are principles that we are capable of challenging only with great difficulty and a sense of imminent danger. Once we deny the individual the right or the ability to decide such matters for himself or herself, who shall decide? We no longer agree on any single unambiguous set of instructions from the Scriptures. We no longer trust everyone in power. We are rightfully suspicious of those who attack the individual, because we always wonder what else they have in mind. Whatever the abuses, and whatever political, social, or economic systems might be required to support it, philosophical autonomy is our starting point.

The metaphor of enlightenment is common to many cultures. The comparison of clear thinking with illumination is to be found in ancient, Christian, and Eastern thought as well as in comic book symbolism and modern philosophy. The most important employer of that metaphor, for our purposes, is a French philosopher of the seventeenth century, René Descartes. Descartes was one of the founders of the Enlightenment, and he is generally recognized as the father of modern philosophy. Like Socrates two thousand years before, Descartes believed that each of us was capable of ascertaining what beliefs were true and what actions were right. But where Socrates searched through dialogue and discussion, Descartes searched for the truth in the solitude of his own thinking. With considerable risk to his safety, he challenged the authority of the French government and the Catholic Church. He insisted that he would accept as true only those ideas that were demonstrably true to him. Against the obscure teachings of the Church and the often opaque commands of his government, Descartes insisted upon "clear and distinct ideas" and arguments based upon "the light of reason." The modern philosophy of individual autonomy begins with Descartes. As a matter of fact, his results were quite conservative. He retained much of his medieval teachings; he continued to believe in God and the Church; and he made it his first "moral maxim" to "obey the laws and customs of my country." His challenge to authority was rather his method, which signified one of the greatest revolutions in Western thought. From Descartes on, the ultimate authority was to be found in our own thinking and experience, nowhere else.

None of this is meant to deny authority as such. We still make appeals to authority, but authorities are never to be taken as absolutes. For example, none of us would particularly like to go out and establish on our own the figures of the 1980 census of the U.S. population. But it is up to us whether or not to accept the official "authoritative" figures, to question, if necessary, the integrity or motivation of the authorities, and to appeal, if necessary, to alternative sources of information.

For anyone beginning to study philosophy today, Descartes is an essential figure. His method is both easy to follow and very much in accord with our own independent temperaments. Descartes proceeded by means of logical arguments, giving us a long monologue of presentations and proofs of his philosophical doubts and beliefs. Like Socrates before him, Descartes used his philosophy to cut through the clouds of prejudice and unreliable opinions. He was concerned with their truth, no matter how many people already believed them, and no matter how few. Descartes's arguments were his tools for finding this truth and distinguishing it from falsehood and mere opinion.

Philosophy has always been concerned with truth and our knowledge of reality. Not coincidentally, Descartes's new philosophy developed in the age of Galileo and the rise of modern science. In ancient Greece, the origins of philosophy and the birth of Greek science were one and the same. The truth, however, is not always what most people believe at any given time. (Most people once believed that the earth was flat, for example.) But, at the same time that they simply refuse to accept "common sense," philosophers try not to say things that common sense finds absurd. For example, a philosopher who denied that anyone existed besides himself would clearly be absurd. So too, the philosopher who argued that he knew that nobody ever knows anything is caught in an obvious absurdity. Accordingly, two of the most important challenges in the philosopher's search for truth are (1) skepticism and (2) paradox. In **skepticism,** the philosopher finds himself or herself unable to justify what every sane person knows to be the case; for example, that we are not merely dreaming all of the time. In a **paradox,** an absurd conclusion seems to result from perfectly acceptable ways of thinking. For example, there is the familiar paradox of Epimenides the Cretan, who claimed that "all Cretans are liars." (That sounds reasonable enough.) But . . . if what he said was true, then he was lying and what he said, accordingly, was false. But how can the same statement be both true and false? What Epimenides said was true only if it was false at the same time. That is a paradox. And whenever a philosophical argument ends in paradox, we can be sure that something has gone wrong.

Skepticism begins with *doubt*. The philosopher considers the possibility that something that everyone believes is possibly mistaken. Some doubt is a healthy sign of intellectual autonomy, but excessive doubting becomes skepticism, which is no longer healthy. It has its obvious dangers: If you doubt whether you are ever awake or not, you might well do things that wouldn't have serious consequences in a dream but would be fatal in real life (jumping out of a plane, for example). Philosophers who have doubts about the most ordinary and seemingly unquestionable beliefs are called *skeptics*. But however challenging skeptics may be as philosophers, in practice their skepticism is impossible. Accordingly, one of the main drives in philosophy has been to refute the skeptic and return philosophy to common sense (to prove, for example, that we are *not* dreaming all of the time). Opposed to skepticism is an ancient philosophical ideal, the ideal of **certainty,** the ability to prove beyond a doubt that what we believe is true. Socrates and Descartes, in their very different ways, tried to provide precisely this certainty in our most important beliefs, and thus refute the skeptics of their own times.

For Descartes, certainty is the **criterion,** that is, the test, according to which our beliefs are to be evaluated. But do we ever find such certainty? It seems that we do, at least in one discipline Descartes suggests — in mathematics. Who can doubt that two plus two equals four? or that the interior angles of a triangle total

180°? Using mathematics as his ideal, Descartes (and many generations of philosophers following him) attempted to apply a similar method in philosophy. First, he must find, as in Euclidean geometry, a small set of "first principles" or **axioms** that are obvious or **self-evident.** They may be assumed without proof or are so fundamental that they seem not to allow any proof. These will serve as **premises** or starting points for the *arguments* that will take us from the self-evident axioms to other principles that may not be self-evident at all. But if they can be **deduced** from other principles that are already certain, like the theorems of geometry, then they share the certainty of the principles from which they have been derived. (We will discuss "deduction" on page 19.)

Descartes was a scientist and a mathematician as well as a philosopher. With that in mind, we can understand his *Discourse on Method.* Descartes set out four basic rules that would define philosophy for many years:

from *Discourse on Method,* by Descartes

The first of these was to accept nothing as true which I did not clearly recognise to be so; that is to say, carefully to avoid precipitation and prejudice in judgments, and to accept in them nothing more than what was presented to my mind so clearly and distinctly that I could have no occasion to doubt it.

The second was to divide up each of the difficulties which I examined into as many parts as possible, and as seemed requisite in order that it might be resolved in the best manner possible.

The third was to carry on my reflectons in due order, commencing with objects that were the most simple and easy to understand, in order to rise little by little, or by degrees, to knowledge of the most complex, assuming an order, even if a fictitious one, among those which do not follow a natural sequence relatively to one another.

The last was in all cases to make enumerations so complete and reviews so general that I should be certain of having omitted nothing.[9]

One might say that the essence of these rules is to be cautious and to think for oneself. The premises, upon which all else depends, must be utterly beyond doubt, "perfectly certain," otherwise all else is futile. The test or criterion of such a premise is that it be "a clear and distinct idea," self-evident, and "springing from the light of reason alone."

We shall see much more of Descartes in the following chapters. In Chapter 3, we shall see that Descartes's technique for assuring the certainty of his premises will be what he called the method of doubt (or *methodological doubt*). In order to make sure that he does not accept any principle too quickly ("too precipitously") before being convinced of its "perfect certainty," he resolves to doubt every belief until he can prove it true beyond question, and to show that the very

[9]René Descartes, *Discourse on Method,* in *The Philosophical Works of Descartes,* trans. Elizabeth S. Haldane and G. R. T. Ross (Cambridge: Cambridge University Press, 1911).

act of doubting this belief leads to an intolerable paradox. The point of this kind of argument is not to become a skeptic, but, quite the contrary, to find those premises that even the skeptic cannot doubt. And from those premises, Descartes and many generations of philosophers following him will attempt to prove that we do indeed know what we think we know. Like Socrates, Descartes begins by questioning what no one else but a philosopher would doubt and ends up changing the way we think about ourselves and our knowledge for several centuries.

A BRIEF INTRODUCTION TO LOGIC

Descartes's strategy, and the main technique of philosophers in general, is to present arguments for what they believe. In Plato's *Crito*, Socrates and Crito offer arguments for their views, and Socrates wins because his arguments are better. An argument is a verbal attempt to get other people to accept a belief or opinion by providing reasons why they should accept it. We usually think of an argument as a confrontation between two people. When they try to convince each other, they usually resort to a certain verbal means and it is with these means that a philosopher is concerned. Of course, there are other ways of getting people to agree with you — tricks, bribes, brainwashing, and threats of physical force. But arguments are the most durable and trustworthy as well as the most respectable way of getting others to agree. Freedom of speech is the cornerstone of democracy (and the bane of totalitarianism) just because of our faith in the ability of arguments to determine the best among competing opinions.

You don't have to be arguing with anyone in particular in order to construct an argument. Editorials in newspapers, for example, argue for a position, but not necessarily against anyone. But whether your argument is a letter to a magazine, in which you are trying to convince the entire American population of your views, or a personal letter, in which you are trying to convince a friend not to do something foolhardy, the main point of argument is *persuasion*. A scientist describing an experiment tries to persuade other scientists of the truth of his or her theory. A politician tries to persuade his or her constituency of the need for higher taxes. A philosopher tries to persuade us of a certain view of life, a certain view of reality, a certain view of ourselves. In each case, these people try to give as many reasons as possible why other people should accept their view of things, in short, they use arguments to persuade others.

Argument involves at least two components: **logic** and **rhetoric.** Logic concerns those reasons that should hold for anyone, anywhere, without appealing to personal feelings, sympathies, or prejudices. Rhetoric, on the other hand, does involve such personal appeals. Personal charm may be part of rhetoric, in a writer as well as in a public speaker. Jokes may be part of rhetoric. Personal pleas are effective rhetorical tools; so is trying to be sympathetic to readers, or playing off their fears. None of these personal tactics are part of logic, however. Logic is impersonal, and for this reason logic may be less flamboyant and personally exciting, but it has the advantage of being applicable to everyone. A logical argument goes beyond rhetorical appeal. But it is important to understand that logic and rhetoric virtually always function together. Although it is possible to be persuasive through pure rhetoric without being at all logical, such efforts often disappear as soon as readers have had a chance to think again about how they have been persuaded. One can also be logical without attention to rhetoric, but such arguments will be dry and unattractive, even if they do convince anyone who would take the time to read them. However, logic and rhetoric in combination can be very persuasive and are rarely separable in any great work of philosophy. In all of the readings in this book, you will notice the combination of impersonal logic and personal appeal, all aimed at getting us to agree with the author's point of view.

There are good arguments and there are bad arguments. Just as the success of a logically inadequate argument may depend upon the passing mood of a reader or the fact that he or she has not yet heard the other side, so a good argument must survive passing moods, reflection, and criticism. This requires good logic as well as effective rhetoric, and so it is important to master the basic rules of argument, as well as to be aware of the all too common pitfalls that lie in wait for those who ignore the rules. Knowing these rules and warnings will not only help you avoid what are called **fallacies** — that is, mistakes in logic — but it will also allow you to effectively criticize other people's arguments as well. Have you ever heard someone say, "Well, there's something wrong with that argument, but I'm not sure what it is"? Knowing a little logic will let you see very clearly what is wrong with an argument.

Standard logic textbooks emphasize two primary forms of logical argument:

(1) **Deductive arguments** reason from one statement to another by means of accepted logical rules, such that anyone who accepts the premises *must* accept the conclusion.

(2) **Inductive arguments** infer one statement from another, but it is possible for the conclusion to be false even if all of the premises are true. The most familiar example of an inductive argument is a **generalization** from a set of particular observations to a general statement called a **hypothesis.**

Deductive Arguments

A deductive argument is valid when it correctly conforms to the rules of deduction. Some examples of the most familiar rules are:

1) It had to be either Phyllis or Fred. (It was Phyllis *or* it was Fred.)
   It wasn't Phyllis.
   Therefore, it had to be Fred.
2) Both Tom and Jerry went to the circus last night. (Tom went to the circus last night *and* Jerry went to the circus last night.)
   Therefore, Tom went to the circus last night.

3) *If* Carol did that all by herself, *then* she's courageous.
    Carol did it all by herself.
    Therefore, Carol is courageous.

It is important to emphasize that whether or not an argument is valid depends only on the form of the argument. A valid argument — one in the correct form — can still have a conclusion that is false. Consider:

4) If Carol did that all by herself, then elephants can fly.
    Carol did it all by herself.
    Therefore, elephants can fly.

Notice that example 4 is identical in form to example 3. The conclusion is patently false, but the argument is still valid.

Logicians would state the form of each of the preceding arguments in symbols, and it is sometimes convenient, when testing the validity of an argument, to translate it into such symbols to see whether or not it fits a correct form of deduction. In symbolic form, the arguments look like this (the 'p' and 'q' letters are called "propositional variables," because they can be replaced by any propositions):

1') Either p or q.
     Not p.
     Therefore q.
2') p and q.
     Therefore, p.
3') and 4') If p then q.
     p.
     Therefore q.

But what good is a deductive argument if its conclusion can be false? The answer is that if the initial statements are true, then the truth of the conclusion is guaranteed. The initial statements are called **premises,** and if the premises are true, then the conclusion must be true if the argument form is valid. It is important to remember that a deductive argument cannot prove its own premises. To be effective, you must be sure of the premises before beginning the deductive argument. Thus the following argument, although it is valid, is an appallingly bad argument.

5) If someone argues for socialized medicine, then he or she must be a communist.
    Communists want to kill people. (If someone is a communist, then he or she wants to kill people.)
    Therefore, if someone is for socialized medicine, he or she wants to kill people.

This argument has the valid form:

5') If p then q.
     If q then r.
     Therefore, if p then r.

But although the argument is valid, its premises are not true, and therefore they provide no guarantee that the conclusion is true. A valid argument guarantees the truth of the conclusion only if the premises are true. Therefore, in using or evaluating any deductive argument, you must always ask yourself two things:

a) Are the premises true?
b) Is the argument valid?

If the answer to both of these is "yes," then the argument is said to be **sound.**

   An argument in an essay may not appear exactly in the form provided by the rules of deduction. This does not mean that the argument is invalid. In example 5, the second premise, "communists want to kill people," must be restated in "If . . . then . . ." form. In fact, straightforward copying of the rules of deduction in an essay makes boring reading, so arguments usually must be restated in order to fit these forms exactly. When you are writing an argument, it is necessary to pay attention both to the validity of the argument and to stating it in an interesting way. Sometimes it is permissible to leave out one of the premises, if it is so obvious to every reader that actually stating it would seem absurd. For example,

6) Kathy decided that no women should go to the meeting. Therefore, Kathy decided not to go to the meeting.

The missing premise, of course, is

Kathy is a woman.

But it would be unnecessary in most contexts to say this. When using deductive arguments effectively, rhetorical considerations are important too.

   One of the best-known forms of deductive reasoning is called the **syllogism.** Sometimes the term "syllogism" is applied to all deductive arguments, but traditionally it refers to one kind in particular: deductive arguments, usually with two premises and a conclusion, that depend on the words "all," "some," and "none." (These words are called **quantifiers.**) The best-known example is

7) All men are mortal.
   Socrates is a man.
   Therefore, Socrates is mortal.

The first statement, "All men are mortal," is called the *major premise;* the second statement, "Socrates is a man," is called the *minor premise.* The final statement, following from the other two, is the *conclusion* and is generally preceded by the word "therefore." In this example, the words "men" and "man" are called the *middle term,* the word "mortal" is called the *predicate,* and the name "Socrates" is called the *subject.* The middle term serves to link the subject and the predicate, both of which are joined in the conclusion. The form of this syllogism is

7′) All A's are B's.
   C is an A.
   Therefore, C is a B.

Any nouns can be substituted for the 'A', 'B', and 'C' in this deductive form. For example,

> 8) All cows are pigeons.
> George Washington is a cow.
> Therefore, George Washington is a pigeon.

In the two examples above, the letters no longer stand for propositions but for subjects and predicates. 'C' stands for the subjects "Socrates" and "George Washington." 'A' and 'B' stand for the predicates "is a man," "is a cow," "is mortal," and "is a pigeon." In quantificational logic, however, a far more useful set of symbols has been developed using the following notation:

Small letters 'a,' 'b,' 'r,' 's' are names of individual subjects ("Socrates," "George Washington").

Capital letters 'F,' 'G,' 'H,' etc. are the names of predicates ("is a man," "is red," "has an I.Q. of less than 40").

The combination of a capital letter and a small letter expresses a simple statement (or proposition) such as:

> Fs = Socrates is fat.
> or Ga = Albert is green.

We can represent more complex statements by a variety of combinatory techniques, such as

> Fs and Ga = Socrates is fat and Albert is green.
> or Hsa = Socrates hits Albert. (where H = "hits" is
> a "two place relational predicate")

The small letters "x," "y," and "z" are given a special role as individual *variables;* that is, they do not stand for particular subject names but, like pronouns, leave open the place for a name:

> Fx = something is fat.
> Hxy = something hits someone.

The quantificational symbols for all and none are

> "(x)" is read "for all x's"

and

> "($\exists$x)" is read "There is at least one x."

So

> "(x)Fx" is read "Everything is fat."
> "($\exists$x)Gx" is read "Someone is green."
> "(x) ($\exists$y) Hxy" is read "Everyone hit someone."
> "(x) (If Fx then Gx)" is read "Everyone who is fat is green."

For the connective "if . . . then . . . " logicians often use the symbol for material implication — "⊃."
We can rewrite example 5'):

> (x) (Sx ⊃ Cx) ("If anyone argues for socialized medicine, then he is a communist.")
> (x) (Cx ⊃ Kx) ("If anyone is a communist, then he or she. . . . ")
> (x) (Sx ⊃ Kx) ("If anyone argues for . . . , then he or she. . . . ")

and 7'):

> (x) (Mx ⊃ Nx)
> Ms
> Ns

Argument 8 is of the same form:

> 8') (x) (Cx ⊃ Px)
> Cg
> Pg

Argument 8 is valid, although its conclusion is false. The reason, of course, is that the premises are false. Again, a valid argument does not guarantee a true conclusion unless the premises are true. So always be certain that you have adequately defended the premises before beginning your deduction.

Valid arguments sometimes proceed from negative premises as well as positive assertions. For example,

> 9) No women have ever been astronauts.
> Eleanor Roosevelt was a woman.
> Therefore, Eleanor Roosevelt was not an astronaut.

The form is

> 9') No A's are B's.
> C is an A.
> Therefore, C is not a B.
> or (x)(Ax ⊃ not Bx)
> Ac
> Not Bc

Another common argument is

> 10) Some elephants weigh more than two thousand pounds.
> Elephants are animals.
> Therefore, some animals weigh more than two thousand pounds.

The form, with a little rephrasing, is

10′) Some A's are B's. (Some elephants are more than two thousand pounds in weight.)
All A's are C's. (All elephants are animals. The "all" is implicit.)
Therefore, some C's are B's. (Some animals are more than two thousand pounds in weight.)
or ($\exists$x)(Ax and Bx)
(x)(Ax $\supset$ Cx)
($\exists$x)(Cx and Bx)

Not all deductive arguments are syllogisms in this traditional sense. For example, the following is a valid deductive argument, but not a syllogism:

11) Jones is an idiot, and he (Jones) is also the luckiest man alive.
Therefore, Jones is an idiot.

The form of this argument is

11′) p and q.
Therefore, p.

In the discussion that follows, therefore, we will talk about deductive arguments in general and not worry whether they are properly to be called "syllogisms" or not.

SOME BASIC RULES OF DEDUCTIVE INFERENCE

1. Modus Ponens
p $\supset$ q
p
$\therefore$ q

2. Modus Tollens
p $\supset$ q
not q
$\therefore$ not p

3. Hypothetical Syllogism
p $\supset$ q
q $\supset$ r
$\therefore$ p $\supset$ r

4. Disjunctive Syllogism
p or q
not p
$\therefore$ q

5. Constructive Dilemma
(p $\supset$ q) and (r $\supset$ s)
p or r
$\therefore$ q or s

6. Absorption
p $\supset$ q
$\therefore$ p $\supset$ (p and q)

7. Simplification
p and q
$\therefore$ p

8. Conjunction
p
q
$\therefore$ p and q

9. Addition
p
$\therefore$ p or q

It is impossible in this introduction to list all of the correct forms of deduction. We will, however, describe some of the most dangerous *fallacies*, mistakes in deductive form. The following example is one, for it looks dangerously like example 10,:

12) Some elephants are domesticated.
    Some camels are domesticated.
    Therefore, some elephants are camels.

This form,

12') Some A's are B's.
    Some C's are B's.
    Therefore, some A's are C's.
  or (∃x)(Ax and Bx)
    (∃x)(Cx and Bx)
    (∃x)(Ax and Cx)

is *invalid* (not valid), and is thus a fallacy. This fallacy often appears in political arguments, for example,

13) We all know that some influential Republicans have been corrupt.
    And we all know that at least some communists are corrupt.
    Therefore, we know that at least some Republicans are communists.

When stated so simply, the fallacy is obvious. But when this argument is spread through a long-winded speech, such fallacies are often accepted as valid arguments. Using the logician's symbolic forms to analyze a complex speech or essay will often make clear the validity or invalidity of an argument.

Another common fallacy closely resembles the deductive form in example 3):

14) If this antidote doesn't work, then the patient will die.
    The patient died.
    Therefore, the antidote doesn't work.

This looks valid at first glance, but it is not. The patient may have fallen out of a window, proving nothing about the antidote. The form of this argument is

14') If p then q.
    q.
    Therefore, p.

The correct deductive form of example 3 was

If p then q.
p.
Therefore, q.

Be particularly careful of the difference between these two.

"If . . . then . . ." statements are often used in another pair of arguments, one valid, one invalid. The valid one is

15) If this antidote doesn't work, then the patient will die.
The patient didn't die.
Therefore, the antidote worked.

The form is

15′) If p then q.
Not q.
Therefore, not p.

This is valid, although one might insist on adding an explicit qualification to the first premise. The qualification is, "for nothing else whatever can save him," since one might argue that something else, perhaps a miracle, might save the patient rather than the antidote. Notice that this qualification doesn't save the invalid argument in example 14, however, nor does it save the invalid argument in the following example:

16) If this antidote doesn't work, then the patient will die.
The antidote works.
Therefore, the patient won't die.

Again, the patient might very well die of other causes, despite the antidote. The form,

16′) If p then q.
Not p.
Therefore, not q.

is invalid.

Most valid and invalid deductive argument forms are a matter of common sense. What makes fallacies so common is not ignorance of logic so often as sloppy thinking or writing, or talking faster than you can organize your thoughts in valid form. Most important, therefore, be careful in thinking and writing. And yet, even the greatest philosophers commit fallacies, and you will see some of them.

Inductive Arguments

In deduction, the conclusion never states more than the premises. (It is often said that the conclusion is already "contained in" the premises.) In an inductive argument, the conclusion *always* states more than the premises. It is, therefore, a less certain form of argument, but that does not mean that it is any less important. Many of the premises in deductive arguments will come from inductive ones, and most of our knowledge and almost all of science depend upon induction. Induction takes various forms and defies rigid characterization. One general form of an inductive argument is

Every A we have observed is a B.
Therefore, every A is a B.

The argument, in other words, is from an observed set of things to an entire class of things, for example, from

17) Every crow we have observed in the past 20 years is black.

to

All crows are black.

But induction, unlike deduction, does not guarantee the truth of the conclusion, even if we know that the observations are all correct. So the conclusion of example 17 should properly read

It is probable that all crows are black.

The form of the inductive argument should be further corrected:

Every A we have seen is a B.
Therefore, we can suppose that every A is probably a B, at least until we find an A that isn't a B.

This tentative conclusion is called a **hypothesis.** A hypothesis is an educated guess on the basis of the evidence collected so far. It is always possible, when we are using induction, that a new piece of evidence will turn up that will refute the hypothesis. This new piece of evidence is called a **counter-example.** Inductive arguments must always be ready for such counter-examples; it must be admitted that no inductive argument guarantees certainty. This is always the possibility that a counter-example will be found, or that a better hypothesis will be formulated. This is not to say, however, that we should not accept such arguments. Human beings have observed millions of rabbits, and never has a rabbit weighed more than two thousand pounds. This does not mean that it is impossible to find a two-thousand-pound rabbit, but neither does it mean that we should therefore hesitate to believe that no rabbits weigh over two thousand pounds. Induction is never certain, but, on the basis of the evidence, we can nevertheless agree on the best hypothesis. It is worth noting, however, that some philosophers, following David Hume (see Chapter 3), have claimed that induction is without rational justification, no matter how undeniably useful it may be.

There are good (sound) and bad (unsound) inductive arguments. The most familiar reason for an unsound inductive argument is generalization on the basis of too few examples. For instance, the following is clearly unsound:

18) Every American president from the state of Pennsylvania has been a Democrat.
Therefore, we can suppose that every American president from the state of Pennsylvania will be a Democrat.

There has only been one president from Pennsylvania, and the intricacies of politics are clearly such that it is probably just as likely that the next president from Pennsylvania will be a Republican as a Democrat. Similarly,

19) The driver of every Italian bus we rode had a beard.
Therefore, all Italian bus drivers have beards.

is unsound. Although the sampling involves more than one example, this is still
not sufficient to make a sound inductive generalization. How many examples are
required? It varies with the case. If a chemist, conducting an experiment, adds
chemical g to chemical h and gets chemical j, that in itself will probably warrant
a hypothesis that

$$g + h \rightarrow j,$$

although this hypothesis, like all hypotheses, will have to be tested by further
experiments and observations. (Deductions, on the contrary, do not have to be
tested, assuming the truth of their premises.) A chemist can usually assume that
one set of pure chemicals will react like any other set of the same chemicals. But
when the hypothesis is about people, generalizations should be made with
extreme caution, especially when writing about such a sensitive subject as
"national character." For example, "Italians are . . . ," "Russians tend to be . . . ,"
"Americans are too . . ." require extreme care. But caution does not mean that it
is impossible to write about such subjects. It has often been done brilliantly, and
you might even agree that a person who refuses to see the general differences
between different peoples and societies is even more foolish than someone who
generalizes too quickly and carelessly. But all generalizations (even this one) must
be made with care for the context and the subject matter.

A different kind of inductive unsoundness comes from generalizing to a
hypothesis that goes too far beyond what the evidence will support. For example,

20) Every graduate we know of Delmonico High School is an excellent
athlete.
Therefore, we can suppose that the physical education teachers there
must be very good.

The problem here is not too small a sampling; in fact, we might even look at
every graduate of Delmonico High School. The problem is that this kind of evidence isn't sufficient to prove anything about the teachers. The students might
come from athletic homes. Or the food in the student cafeteria might be loaded
with extra vitamins and protein. Or the students may enjoy playing sports outside
of school, even though their gym classes are badly taught. It is important to be
sure that the hypothesis you defend is supported by the right kind of evidence.
In this case, we need evidence about the physical education teachers, not just
about the students.

Not every inductive argument proceeds from evidence to a generalization. For
example, detectives use inductive arguments in moving from the evidence to the
indictment of a particular individual. (What Sherlock Holmes refers to as his
"powers of deduction" is in fact his remarkable ability with induction.) It is
worth noting that not every philosopher thinks that induction is so important for
knowledge. For example, the contemporary British philosopher Karl Popper

believes that the logic of science (and police investigations) proceeds not by way of induction but by way of the *disconfirmation* of proposed hypotheses with counter-examples. In other words, knowledge preceeds from hypothesis to hypothesis, not from evidence to hypothesis by way of induction. But whatever one thinks of the justifiability of induction and its importance, it is essential not to think of induction as occurring in a vacuum. Inductive reasoning always goes on against a background of other hypotheses, theories, and scientific viewpoints as well as an abundance of other evidence that is taken for granted, built into the hypothesis itself or, perhaps, ignored as irrelevant, undependable, or unimportant. Because of its formality, deduction can deal with isolated arguments. But induction, even when subjected to the formal rigors of probability theory, can never be so understood out of context. Background conditions and the state of knowledge at the moment are always in some sense presupposed. Because of this informal (if not chaotic) complexity, induction is just as much a matter of insight as logic.

A very different kind of problem arises for induction when the hypothesis is *self-confirming*. A self-confirming hypothesis creates its own confirmation or, alternatively, blocks all possible counter-examples from the start. Two familiar examples: a policeman (in uniform) tries to evaluate the driving patterns of the cars that pass him, making sure that they all drive at the legal speed. Of course they do! But the same sort of self-confirmation often goes on in subtle ways, in science, for example, where the equipment itself is designed to present precisely the evidence it is supposed to be looking for. The other example is the paranoid, who advances the hypothesis that "they're all out to get me." And, given that way of looking at the world, indeed they are. Not only does the paranoid systematically interpret other people's behavior in a hostile way, he also behaves in such a way that people really do become wary of him, if not hostile to him. But again, this extreme case has thousands of more everyday instance; a person who feels friendless may easily work on a mild version of the paranoid hypothesis and confirm his own thesis. A person who entertains the hypothesis that "all people are basically selfish" will have little trouble finding what he or she is looking for, and, within that investigation, some selfish motive can always be found (for example, "in order not to feel guilty") for even the most generous and unselfish behavior. (We might note that there are also *self-defeating* hypotheses; the policeman may hypothesize that everyone breaks the law and goes out (in uniform) to catch them, thereby undermining his own hypothesis.)

Argument by Analogy

A form of inductive argument that is sometimes objected to unfairly is **argument by analogy**. An argument by analogy defends the similarity between some aspect of two things on the basis of their similarity in other respects. For example, a politician defends the need for more efficient government and fewer unnecessary jobs on the basis of an argument by analogy between government and business.

A government is like a business, the politician argues. It has a certain product to turn out, namely, services to the people, and receives a certain income from the sale of that product, namely, taxes. It employs a certain number of people, whose job it is to turn out that product and who are paid with that income. Their business is to produce the product as cheaply but as well as possible, to keep the cost down, and make a profit in order to be able to offer new and better services. Thus, the politician argues, the more efficiently it is run and the fewer unnecessary employees it must support, the better a government will be.

Such an argument is valuable in getting people to see similarities and in clarifying complex and confusing issues. The danger, and the reason why many logicians reject arguments by analogy altogether, is that no two things are similar in every respect. (Otherwise, they would be the same.) And just because two things are similar in certain respects, it doesn't follow that they will be similar in others. But this objection is too strong. If two things are similar in several respects, it is at least plausible to suggest that they will be similar in others. For example, running the government is like running a business. Both involve managing an organization. Both require skill in handling money. The success of both depends on the quality of the products and services they produce. Therefore, the way to handle the city transportation problem is to ask which plan will give the most service for the least money.

Arguments by analogy may employ both deductive and inductive arguments; insofar as *A* (government) is like *B* (a business), deductions appropriate in discussing *A* will be appropriate in discussing *B* as well. And if *A* and *B* are similar in so many ways, then it is inductively plausible that they will be similar in other ways too. So arguments by analogy are at least a valuable form of reasoning, if not always a reliable form of proof. It is important, however, to pay careful attention to each particular analogy, to make sure that the two things compared are significantly similar and, most importantly, that the aspect that is argued about is significantly similar in both cases. Arguments by analogy are extremely valuable, but they must always be used with care.

The three kinds of arguments discussed above, deductive, inductive, and argument by analogy, are attempts to defend a view or an opinion. But part of almost every argument is an attack on alternative views and opinions. In general, you can attack someone else's position by asking the following questions:

a) What is he or she arguing? Is the position clear?
b) What are the arguments? Are they deductive? inductive? or by analogy?
    If deductive:
        What are the premises and are they all true?
        Are the deductive arguments valid?
    If the answer to either of these questions is "no," you have a good counter-argument to show that your adversary has not given us a reason for accepting his or her view.
    If inductive:
        Is there enough evidence to support the hypothesis?

Does the evidence support the hypothesis?

Is the hypothesis sufficiently clear?

Is this the best hypothesis to explain the evidence?

If the answer to any of these is "no," you have a good counter-argument to show that your adversary has not defended his or her general claim.

If argument by analogy:

Are the things compared similar?

Are the things similar in the particular respect in question?

If the answer to either of these is "no," you have a good argument to show that your opponent's analogy is not a good one.

c) Does the conclusion mean what your opponent says it means?

Argument by Counter-Examples

Whenever anyone makes a general claim, it is possible to attack with an example that seems to go against the claim. This is a *counter-example*. We already mentioned counter-examples with respect to inductive generalizations; a counter-example that refutes an hypothesis, such as "here is an *a* that is not *b*," will always give trouble to someone who argues that "all *a*'s are *b*'s." For example, if a bigot says, "All people from Poland are naturally unintelligent," the single counter-example of Copernicus, a Pole, is sufficient to undermine that claim. Counter-examples may also work in the face of deductively defended claims, however. Consider a common philosophical argument (which we shall discuss in Chapter 9):

22) All events in nature are determined by physical forces. (Gravity, chemistry, electromagnetic forces, and so on.)
All human actions are events in nature.
Therefore, all human actions are determined by physical forces.

This syllogism is a valid argument, of the form,

22') All A's are B's.
All C's are A's.
Therefore, all C's are B's.

One way to attack this valid argument, even if you don't see any reasons to reject the premises as such, is to use the method of counter-examples: "Look. I decided to come to this college of my own free will. I thought about it for a few days, and I remember the exact moment when I made my decision, while eating pizza at Harry's restaurant. Now I made that decision. It wasn't caused in me by physical forces. Therefore, I reject your conclusion."

What has happened here is this: On the one hand, if we accept the premises as true and the argument as valid, it would seem that we have to accept the conclusion. But what the counter-example does in this case is force the person who has argued the syllogism to clarify what is meant by "determined by phys-ical forces" in both the premise and the conclusion. Does this mean only that there must be *some* forces present? If so, the argument is not nearly so interesting as we thought, for everyone will admit that when a person makes a decision there is an electrical charge or a chemical change in the brain. Does it mean rather that there are *only* physical causes present, in which case "free will" is indeed excluded? But what then of the counter-example (your college decision)? The bur-den of proof is on the person who argued the syllogism; he or she is forced to explain how it seems that you made a decision of your own free will when in fact there is no such thing as free will. You can see how this philosophical argu-ment could become very complicated, but we only want to make a simple point. A single, well-placed counter-example can open up a whole new discussion, even when it might seem as if the matter had already been settled.

A general comment is necessary here. It might seem to you as if arguments are conclusive, one way or the other. In fact, this is almost never the case. An argument can be convincing and persuasive, but there is always room for further argument if someone is stubborn or persistent enough. A good counter-example can always be explained away, and even a large number of counter-examples might be explained away. What ultimately sinks a bad hypothesis or general claim is the weight of the extra explanations it needs. For example, someone argues that there are Martians currently living on the earth. You point out that no one has ever seen a Martian. Your opponent explains this away by suggesting that the Martians are invisible to the human eye. You argue that the atmosphere of the earth would not support Martian life. Your opponent argues that they are a different form of life, different from any that we can understand. You ask your opponent what these Martians do, and how we might come to test his or her view. He or she says that the Martians don't want us to know that they are here, so that they are careful not to do anything that would let us discover their presence. At this point, you will probably walk away in disgust. You have not silenced your opponent. In fact, he or she might go on inventing new ways out of your argu-ments forever. But, at a certain point, your opponent's explanations will have become so complicated and based on so much dubious knowledge that you and everyone else will be completely justified in ignoring him or her. The point of argument, remember, is to persuade. Absolute proof is impossible. But this means too that persuading some people is also impossible. There are limits to argu-ment — at least, practical limits.

Reductio ad Absurdum

One last argument deserves mention. It is usually called by its Latin name, **reductio ad absurdum,** and is a form of deductive argument. It consists of taking your opponent's view and showing that it has intolerable or contradictory consequences. For example, someone argues that one can never know whether minds exist other than one's own. You counter by pointing out that the very act of arguing this (with you) contradicts his point. He replies, no doubt, that he can't *know* that you exist. You show that he cannot even know that *he* exists. What you have done is reduce your opponent's view to absurdity, showing that it leads to consequences that no one could accept, in this case, the idea that if one has exclusive self-knowledge, then he cannot have self-knowledge at all. A reductio ad absurdum argument, like a good counter-example, is often an excellent way of forcing other people to clarify their positions and explain a lot more carefully exactly what they mean to argue.

The Worst Kinds of Fallacies

There are fallacies, more general than those we discussed previously under deductive arguments (page 25). No brief survey of logic would be adequate without them. Whatever kind of arguments you employ, be careful that you *never* use the following:

MERE ASSERTION   The fact that you accept a position is not sufficient for anyone else to believe it. Stating your view is not an argument for it, and unless you are just answering a public opinion survey, every opinion always deserves a supporting argument. There are statements, of course, that everyone would accept at face value, and you need not argue those. But that does not mean that they cannot be argued, and even the most obvious facts of common sense must be argued for when challenged, and this is what much of philosophy is about.

BEGGING THE QUESTION   Another fallacy is something that looks like an argument but simply accepts as a premise what is supposed to be argued for as a conclusion. For example, suppose you are arguing that one ought to be a Christian and your reason is that the Bible tells you so. This may, in fact, be conclusive for you, but if you are trying to convince someone who doesn't believe in Christ, he or she will probably not believe what the Bible says either. As an argument for becoming a Christian, therefore, referring to the Bible begs the question. Question begging often consists of a reworded conclusion, as in "this book will improve your grades because it will help you to do better in your courses."

VICIOUS CIRCLE   Begging the question is similar to another error, which is often called arguing in a "vicious circle." Consider a more elaborate version of the above fallacy. A person claims to know God exists because she has had a religious vision. Asked how she knows that the vision was religious rather than just the effect of something she ate, she replies that such an elaborate and powerful experience could not have been caused by anyone or anything but God. Asked how she knows this, she replies that God Himself told her—in the vision. Or, "he must be guilty because of the look on his face." "How do you know that he looks guilty rather than frightened or sad?" "Because he's the one who did it, that's why!" If you argue A because of B, and B because of C, but then C because of A, you have argued in a vicious circle. It is vicious because, as in begging the question, you have assumed just what you want to prove. But the following is worth remembering. Ultimately, all positions may come full circle, depending upon certain beliefs that can be defended only if you accept the rest of a great many beliefs. Debates between religious people and atheists are often like this, or arguments between businessmen and Marxists, where many hours of argument show quite clearly that each person accepts a large system of beliefs all of which depend on the others. Some logicians call this a "virtuous circle," but this does not mean that there are no vicious circles. A virtuous circle is the development of an entire world-view, and it requires a great deal of thinking and organizing. Vicious circles, like begging the question, are usually shortcuts to nowhere that result from careless thinking.

IRRELEVANCIES   You have seen people who argue a point by arguing everything else, throwing up charts of statistics and complaining about the state of the universe and telling jokes; everything but getting to the point. This may be a technique of wearing out your opponent; it is not a way of persuading him or her to agree with you. No matter how brilliant an argument may be, it is no good to you unless it is relevant to the point you want to defend.

AD HOMINEM ARGUMENTS   The most distasteful kind of irrelevancy is an attack on your opponent personally instead of arguing against his or her position. It may well be that the person you are arguing against is a liar, a sloppy dresser, bald and ugly, too young to vote or too old to work, but the only question is whether what he or she says is to be accepted. Harping on the appearance, reputation, manners, intelligence, friends, or possessions of your opponent may sometimes give your readers insight into why he or she holds a certain position, but it does not prove or disprove the position itself. As insight into an opponent's motives, personal considerations may, in small doses, be appropriate. But more than a very small dose is usually offensive, and it will usually weigh more against you than against your opponent. Whenever possible, avoid this kind of argument completely. It usually indicates that you don't have any good arguments yourself.

UNCLEAR OR SHIFTING CONCLUSIONS   One of the most frustrating arguments to read is an argument that has a vague conclusion or that shifts conclusions with every paragraph. If something is worth defending at all, it is worth stating clearly and sticking with it. If you argue that drug users should be punished, but aren't clear whether you mean people who traffic heroin or people who take aspirin, you are not worth listening to. If you say that you mean illegal drug offenders, then don't argue that drugs are bad for your body, since this is equally true for both legal and illegal drugs. If you say that you mean amphetamine users, then don't switch to talking about the illegality of drugs when someone explains to you the several medical uses of amphetamines. Know what you are arguing, or your arguments will have no point.

CHANGING MEANINGS   It is easy to miss a fallacy when the words seem to form a valid argument. For example, consider this:

People are free as long as they can think for themselves.
Prisoners in jail are free to think for themselves.
Therefore, prisoners in jail are free.

This paradoxical conclusion is due to the ambiguity of "free," first used to refer to a kind of mental freedom, second to physical freedom. An interesting example is the argument made by the famous British philosopher John Stuart Mill that "whatever people desire, that is what is desirable." But notice that he is playing with an ambiguity between something being able to be desired, which something obviously is if it is in fact desired, and "desirable," which means "should be desired." Not everything that is in fact desired should be desired (for example, alcohol by alcoholics), so the argument is invalid. Be careful that the key terms in your argument keep the same meaning throughout.

DISTRACTION   Another familiar form of fallacy is the "red herring," the some-times long-winded pursuit of an argument leading nowhere — except away from the point at issue. For example, in the middle of an argument about the relation between the mind and the brain, a neurologist may well enjoy telling you, in impressive detail, any number of odd facts about neurology, about brain opera-tions he has performed, about silly theories that neurology-ignorant philosophers have defended in the past. But if these do not bear on the issue at hand, they are only pleasant ways of spending the afternoon, not steps to settling a difference of opinion. Distraction is a fallacy that is especially advantageous when the time for argument is limited. (For this reason, it is particularly prevalent in the classroom.)

PSEUDO-QUESTIONS   Sometimes fallacious reasoning begins with the very ques-tion being asked. For example, some philosophers have argued that asking such questions as "how is the mind related to the body?" or "could God create a moun-tain so heavy that even He could not move it?" are pseudo-questions, that is, they look like real questions — even profound questions — but are ultimately unan-swerable because they are based on some hidden piece of nonsense. (In these two cases, it has been suggested that there is no legitimate distinction between mind and body, and therefore any question about how they are "related" is pointless; the second question presumes that God is "omnipotent" in the sense that he can do the logically impossible, which is absurd. We will see more of these issues in Chapters 6 and 8.) Pseudo-questions, like distractions, lead us down a lengthy path going nowhere, except that, with pseudo-questions, we start from nowhere too.

DUBIOUS AUTHORITY   We mentioned earlier that modern philosophy is based on the assumption that we have a right — and sometimes a duty — to question author-ity. And yet, most of our knowledge and opinions are based on appeals to author-ities — whether scientists or the Bible or people who are known to be particularly wise. It would be extremely foolish, if not fatal, not to so appeal to authorities, especially in a world that has grown so technologically and socially complicated. We ask an economist what will happen if interest rates fall. We ask Miss Manners which fork to use for the salad. The fallacy of dubious authority arises when we ask the *wrong* person, when we appeal to an expert who is not in fact an expert in the area of concern. For example, when physicians are asked questions about nuclear policy, or physicists are asked questions about high school education, their expertise in one field does not necessarily transfer to the other. Appealing to opinions in books and newspapers depends on the authority of the authors and the publications in question. What is in print is not necessarily authoritative.

SLIPPERY SLOPE   Metaphors often pervade arguments. One of the more common metaphors is the "slippery slope," the greased incline which, once trod, inevitably carries us to the bottom. (In politics, it is sometimes called "the domino theory.") For example, it is argued that any interference with free speech whatsoever, even forbidding someone to scream "fire" in a crowded auditorium, will sooner or later lead to the eradication of free speech of every kind, including informed, responsible political discussion. But is it the case that, by attacking an extreme instance, we thereby endanger an entire institution? Sometimes, this may be so. But more often than not, the slippery slope metaphor leads us to think that there is such inevitability when in fact there is no such thing.

ATTACKING A STRAW MAN   Real opponents with real arguments and objections are sometimes difficult to refute, and so the easy way out is to attack an unreal opponent with easily refutable arguments and objections. This unreal fellow is called "a straw man," and it provides us with the extra advantage of not fighting back. For example, a writer of religion viciously attacks those who have suggested that Jesus never existed, when in fact his opponents have only questioned a particular interpretation of His divinity. A writer discussing the mind-body problem lampoons those who believe that there is *NO* possible connection between the mind and the body—a position that has been argued by virtually no one.

PITY (AND OTHER EMOTIONAL APPEALS)
   Some forms of fallacy appeal to the better parts of us, even as they challenge our fragile logical abilities. The appeal to pity has always been such an argument. Photographs of suffering people may well be an incentive to social action, but the connection between our pity—which is an undeniable virtue—and the social action in question is not yet an argument. The appeal to pity—and all appeals to emotion—have a perfectly legitimate place in philosophical argument, but such appeals are not yet themselves arguments for any particular position. An orator may make us angry, but what we are to do about the problem must be the product of further argument.

APPEAL TO FORCE   Physical might never makes philosophical right. Sometimes a person can be intimidated, but he or she is not thus refuted. Sometimes one has to back up a philosophical conviction with force, but it is never the force that justifies the conviction.

INAPPROPRIATE ARGUMENTS   The last fallacy we will mention has to do with choice of methods. To insist on deductive arguments when there are powerful inductive arguments against you is a fallacy too, not a fallacious argument, perhaps, but a mistake in logic all the same. For example, if you are arguing deductively that there cannot be any torture going on in a certain country, since Mr. Q rules the country and Mr. Q is a good man (where the implicit premise is that "Good men don't allow torture in their country"), you had better be willing to give up the argument when dozens of trustworthy eyewitnesses publicly describe the tortures they have seen or experienced. To continue with your deduction in the face of such information is foolish. This may not tell you where your argument has gone wrong: Perhaps Mr. Q is not such a good man. Perhaps he has been overpowered. Perhaps good men can't prevent torture if they aren't told about it. But in any case, the argument must now be given up.

The same may be true the other way around. There are certain abstract questions that seem to be answerable only by deduction. When arguing about religious questions, for example, looking for evidence upon which to build an inductive argument may be foolish. What is at stake are your basic concepts of religion and their implications. Evidence, in the sense of looking around for pertinent facts, may be irrelevant. Very abstract questions often require deductive arguments only.

To be caught in one of these fallacies is almost always embarrassing and damaging to your overall argument. If you have a case to make, then make it in the most powerfully persuasive way. An intelligent combination of deductive and inductive arguments, coupled with analogies and proper criticisms of alternative positions, is the most effective persuasion available. If you think your opinions are important, then they deserve nothing less than the best supporting arguments you can put together.

As you proceed with your course, you will have the opportunity to use many of these logical forms, not only on the great philosophers of the past but on your own thinking as well. You will find that philosophical criticism is a powerful tool in the arguments you have with your friends and the debates you carry on, whatever the topic. Most importantly, philosophy is a valuable aid to getting together your own thoughts about things, about the problems of philosophy that you will encounter in this book, and about "life in general." For that is what philosophy is ultimately about.

GLOSSARY

abstract: a general consideration, independent of particular concerns or objects. For example, a philosopher may attempt to ascertain the nature of justice without particular reference to any concrete practical case.

ad hominem argument: an argument against the person instead of the position; for example, attacking a philosopher's living habits instead of asking whether or not his theories are true.

argument: process of reasoning from one claim to another. An argument may, but need not be, directed against an explicit alternative. A philosophical argument does not require an opponent or a disagreement.

assertion: a statement or declaration, taking a position. *Mere* assertion, when presented as an argument, is a fallacy; arguments not only consist of assertions but reasons for them as well.

assumption: a principle taken for granted, without argument or proof.

autonomy: intellectual independence and freedom from authority; the presumed ability to determine the acceptability of one's own beliefs and actions.

axiom: a principle that is generally accepted from the beginning and so may be used without further debate as a starting point of argument.

begging the question: to put forth as the solution to a problem merely a restatement of the problem itself. For example, "Why do oysters give me indigestion? Because they upset my stomach."

Cartesianism: concerning Descartes. In particular, concerning his philosophical method. (Descartes's followers are generally called "Cartesians" and their method "Cartesianism.") The Cartesian method is essentially a deductive method, as in geometry, starting with self-evident axioms and deducing the rest.

certainty: beyond doubt. But it is important to insist that certainty in the philosophical sense is more than the common psychological use of certain ("feeling certain"). One can feel certain and yet be wrong or foolish. One can be certain, in this philosophical sense, only if one can prove that the matter is beyond doubt, that no reasons for doubt could be raised.

coherence: logical connection. A statement by a witness in a courtroom coheres with other testimony and evidence when it fits in and follows from that other testimony and evidence. To say that a philosophy must be coherent is to say that its various principles must fit together in an orderly and logically agreeable fashion.

consistent: fitting together in an orderly logical way. Two principles are consistent if they do not contradict each other. A philosophy is consistent if none of its principles contradict each other.

contradiction: logical relation of two principles in which the truth of one requires the falsity of the other. A witness's statement in court contradicts other testimony if both statements cannot be true.

counter-example: an example that contradicts a generalization, such as "all elephants have tusks." A counter-example would be an elephant without tusks.

criterion: the test or standard according to which a judgment or an evaluation can be made. For example, a test for a substance being an acid is that it turns litmus paper red.

critical: thinking carefully; not necessarily nasty.

declarative sentence: a sentence in which one takes a position, states a fact, asserts a proposition.

deduction (deductive argument): a process of reasoning from one principle to another by means of accepted rules of inference. In a deductive argument, a conclusion follows necessarily from the premises, and so if you are certain of the premises, you can be certain of the conclusion, too.

dialectic: argument through dialogue, disagreement, and successive revisions, out of which comes agreement.

doubt: lack of certainty; lack of reasons to believe and perhaps having reasons not to believe. It is important to distinguish doubt in this philosophical sense from doubt in the ordinary psychological sense. Mere personal uncertainty or distrust is not sufficient; there must be a demonstrable reason for doubt, that is, reasons for not accepting the beliefs in question.

Enlightenment: an important cultural and philosophical movement in the eighteenth century in Europe defined by a new confidence in human reason and individual autonomy. Some of the major figures of this movement were René Descartes, the metaphysician Baron Henri d'Holbach, the political philosopher Jean-Jacques Rousseau, and the political reformer-writer Voltaire in France. In Great Britain, Enlightenment philosophers were John Locke and David Hume; in Germany Immanuel Kant.

fallacy: an error in reasoning, an unsound or invalid argument.

first principles: those axioms and assumptions from which a philosophy begins. These must be solid and indisputable principles; they need not be those principles that one happens to first believe.

formal logic: a branch of logic that is concerned with the principles of reasoning as such, in which it is the relationships between symbols that are studied and not their interpretation.

generalization: usually, a proposition about all of a group or set of things on the basis of a limited acquaintance with some of its members. In logic, however, a generalization may be universal ("all x's are y's") or existential ("there are some x's that are y's").

hypothesis: a provisional conclusion, which is accepted as most probable in the light of the known facts.

implication: one statement logically follows from another. Statements imply one another. We infer one from the other.

incoherent: not fitting together in an orderly or logically agreeable fashion. Using fancy jargon that has no precise meaning may be a source of incoherence. So is a mere list of random beliefs, without any order or logic to hold them together. (They may even contradict each other as well.) An incoherent philosophy may be insightful and true in parts, but because it never coheres into a single system, it may well appear to be nonsense, or simply a jumble of words and phrases. In other cases, an incoherent philosophy may be one that makes no sense, whose terms are utter gibberish or whose principles are mere ramblings without intelligible connection or interpretation. (Opposite of coherent.)

inconsistent: not compatible; contradictory. One might also say that a person's actions are inconsistent with his or her principles. People as well as other principles can be inconsistent with a principle.

inductive argument: a process of reasoning in which the characteristics of an entire class or set of things is inferred on the basis of an acquaintance with some of its members. In an inductive argument, although the conclusion is supported by the premises, it does not follow necessarily from the premises and its truth is not guaranteed by them.

inference: reasoning from one set of principles to another, as in an argument. Deductive inference is but a single kind of inference.

invalid: not correctly following agreed-upon rules of inference in an argument. Always applied to arguments, not to statements. (Opposite of valid.)

logic: the study of the rules of valid inference and "rational argument." In general, a sense of order.

method: (sometimes, **methodology**) approach and strategy for resolving philosophical problems. For example, the appeal to experience, the appeal to divine revelation, the insistence upon mathematical logic, confidence in reason or trust in authority: all of these are aspects of philosophical methodology.

method of doubt: (or **methodological doubt**) Descartes's technique for discovering those principles of which we can be "perfectly certain"; namely, doubt everything, until you discover those principles that cannot be doubted.

paradox: a self-contradictory conclusion drawn from seemingly acceptable premises. For example, suppose you try to help all and only those people who do not help themselves. That sounds reasonable enough. But then, do you help yourself? If you do help everyone, then you would also help yourself. But if you don't help yourself, then you aren't helping all who don't help themselves. This is a paradox.

predicate: that which is asserted or denied of a thing, which refers to a property of things. Some familiar predicates would be "is red," "is an animal."

premise: the principle or one of those principles upon which an argument is based. The starting point of an argument.

presupposition: a principle that is assumed as a precondition for whatever else one believes, which itself may remain unexamined and uncriticized throughout the argument. For example, a lawyer presupposes that the court aims at justice and has some idea what is just. It is the philosopher, not the lawyer, who challenges those claims.

proof: in a deductive argument, a proof is a sequence of steps, each according to an acceptable rule of inference, to the conclusion to be proved.

proposition: an assertion that is either true or false.

reason: the ability to think abstractly, to form arguments and make inferences. Sometimes referred to as a "faculty" of the human mind (a leftover from eighteenth-century psychology). More specialized meanings will be discussed in later chapters.

reasons: explanations, justifications, evidence, or some other basis for accepting a proposition.

reductio ad absurdum: a form of argument in which one refutes a statement by showing that it leads to self-contradiction or an otherwise intolerable conclusion.

reflection: to think about something, to "put it in perspective." We often do this with our beliefs and our emotions. For example, "This morning I was furious at you, but after reflecting on it at lunch, I decided that it was nothing to be angry about." One might say that philosophy is reflection about life and knowledge in general.

rhetoric: the persuasive use of language to convince other people to accept your beliefs.

rule of inference: a generally accepted principle according to which one may infer one statement from another. (We have not yet said anything about the nature of these "generally acceptable" rules; for now, we have simply presupposed that some such rules are acceptable to everyone; for example, "if *either* A is true *or* B is true, but we know that B is false, then we can conclude that A is true.")

self-contradictory: a contradiction within one and the same statement or set of statements. What I say may contradict what you say; but what I say might also contradict something else that I said, in which case I am being self-contradictory. Moreover, in a few strange cases, my own statement may be self-contradictory; for example, "I do not exist."

self-evident: obvious without proof or argument; for Descartes, a "clear and distinct idea," one about which there could be no doubt and it is obvious that there could be no doubt.

skepticism: the philosophical belief that knowledge is not possible, that doubt will not be overcome by any valid arguments. A philosopher who holds this belief is called a skeptic. Again, skepticism is not mere personal doubt; it requires systematic doubt with reasons for that doubt.

sound: an argument whose premises are true and that is valid.

syllogism: a kind of deductive reasoning; the best-known examples are those arguments of the form,

> All P's are Q's. (Major premise)
> S is a P. (Minor premise)
> _____
> *Therefore*, S is a Q. (Conclusion)

The major premise is a general claim, the minor premise is a specific statement.

system: an orderly formulation of principles (together with reasons, implications, evidence, methods, and presuppositions) that is comprehensive, consistent, and coherent and in which the various principles are interconnected as tightly as possible by logical implications.

trivial: obvious and not worth saying.

unsound: an argument whose premises are false or that is invalid.

valid: an argument that correctly follows agreed-upon rules of inference. Always applies to arguments, not statements.

vicious circle: use of two propositions or arguments to support one another with no other support. For example, "He must be guilty because he's got such a guilty look on his face. . . . Well I can tell it's a guilty look because he's the one who is guilty."

PART ONE

Knowing the World, and Beyond

1

Reality: Ancient Views

It must be that what can be spoken and thought is:
for it is possible for it to be,
and it is not possible for what is nothing to be.

Parmenides

"THE WAY THE WORLD REALLY IS":
THE PRE-SOCRATICS

The beginning of philosophy, and a major step in the intellectual development of the Western world, was a seemingly odd claim made by the Greek philosopher Thales on the coast of Turkey sometime around 580 B.C. He suggested that the source of everything was water. The earth floats upon water, and it and all things on it are made of water. Aristotle later called his theory "childish." But it is one of the remarkable claims of the ancient world, not because it is so implausible (as his own students pointed out to him) but because it was the first recorded attempt to describe "the way the world really is," beyond all appearances and day-to-day opinions. Accordingly, Thales' theory marks the beginning of Western science as well as philosophy. He was the first thinker to break with common sense and religion and offer a general theory about the ultimate nature of reality. In place of mythological accounts of nature and human behavior in terms of divine agencies (gods, goddesses, and spirits), the Greeks provided explanations in terms of laws and abstract generalizations. Knowledge became and end in itself, one of the noblest pursuits of humanity.

Thales was the first of a group of philosophers—or rather, the first of several groups of philosophers, scattered around the various Greek islands and the coasts of Asia Minor who lived in the sixth and fifth centuries B.C., just before the time of Socrates. Accordingly, they are called **Pre-Socratics.** Their opinions varied greatly. Between them, they developed a wide range of systematic views of the universe and the ultimate nature of reality. Unlike Socrates and most later philosophers, they were not very concerned with questions of method. They went straight to the heart of the question, to the nature of the universe itself. And some of them, as we shall see, came strikingly close to our modern scientific conceptions.

We are all aware that the way the world really is may not correspond to our everyday views of the world, the way it seems to be. For example, we casually talk of "sunrises" and "sunsets," and surely it does seem as if the sun goes "up" and "down," while we and our earth stay in place. It took several thousand years for people in general to recognize that, despite appearances, our earth actually moves around the sun. We now accept that without question, even if there is little in our everyday experience to support it. Similarly, consider the chair on which you are sitting: Does it seem to you that it is composed mostly of empty space and tiny electrically charged colorless particles whirling about at fantastic speeds? Of course not, but modern science has taught you that "solid" objects are indeed made up of just such spaces and particles. The world is not as it seems. And the beginnings of both philosophy and science were the first attempts of men and women to see beyond their "common sense" views of things and try to find the reality behind them.

What is the way the world really is? How would you answer that question? Very likely you will appeal to the authority of modern science, and that is probably a reasonable beginning. But you know that the "science" of one generation is seen as the superstitions of another. (Once people believed that the earth was flat.) And you have probably, at least once in your school career, caught one of the "authorities" — perhaps a teacher, perhaps even a noted scientist — in a mistake. Can we simply accept what scientists tell us without question, any more than Descartes could accept the teachings of his teachers without question? Have you ever examined the evidence for the theory that the earth goes around the sun? If not, why should you believe it? Or, to take a very different example, scientists are generally agreed that some version of Darwin's theory of evolution is true. Does that mean that you have to believe it? There are many people who do not, because it seems to contradict the story of creation in the Bible. And so you have to decide which to believe. Even within science there are always disagreements and debates. There are different theories to answer the same questions, and you have to decide. Which are you to believe?

Your view of reality is influenced by modern science but it is also influenced by 2500 years of Western philosophy, even if you've never studied it before. We can say, with some confidence, that we know much more about the world than the ancient Greek philosophers. But we must not be too confident. Not only are there still many scientific problems unsolved, there are and always will be conflicting views of how we are to see our world in more general terms. How much faith should we have in religion? How much should we see the world as a world of people and how much as a world of physical objects? How much should we accept "common sense" (which changes all the time) and how much should we indulge in scientific and philosophical speculation (which changes all the time also)?

THE FIRST PHILOSOPHERS   The first Greek philosophers did not have the advantage of either our scientific sophistication or a long history of philosophical thinking to give them support. Thus, Thales' answer, that ultimate reality is water, should not surprise us nearly so much as the fact that he attempted such a theory at all. Indeed, we should be impressed by the fact that he even asked the question, "What is the world really like?" because, as far as we know, no one had attempted to ask such a question before him. Of course, there were lots of opinions about reality; all of the ancient religions had them. But Thales' approach was different. He was not willing to accept the opinions and mythologies that had been handed down for generations. He insisted, instead, on observing the world for himself, on thinking out his own answer, and on discussing it with his friends and neighbors, many of whom, no doubt, thought that he was slightly peculiar. (It is also said, however, that his cosmic speculations helped him to make a fortune in the olive oil business. No doubt his neighbors respected that.)

The idea that everything was water did not satisfy Thales' friends and students. They appreciated his attempt to find the "One Reality," but they thought that it must be something else. Thales' first student, named Anaximander, argued against his teacher that some things, for example, the dry, dusty cliffs of Asia Minor, could not possibly be made of water, which was naturally wet and never dry. Anaximander was the first recorded student to talk back to his teacher (which in philosophy, unlike most other subjects, is considered a virtue rather than a discourtesy). Thales had made the first gigantic step, rejecting the "obvious" answers of common sense and trying to find out "the way the world really is." But notice that Thales' answer to that question still appeals to a common-sense ingredient, water, which is so familiar to us. And Thales' defense of his thesis also depended on some very common-sensical claims: for example, the idea that if you dig deep enough into the earth, you will eventually hit water.

Once Thales had made the break with common sense and said that the way the world really is need not be at all like the way it seems to us, it was no longer necessary to suppose that reality was anything like our experiences. Anaximander, consequently, argued that ultimate reality could not be composed of any of the then known elements—earth, air, fire, or water—since these were each so different from the others. They might be mixed together, as when earth and water are mixed to make mud or clay, but it made no sense to suppose that any of them might really be made up of any of the others. So Anaximander suggested that the ultimate nature of reality was something else—let us simply call it "primordial stuff"—that is not like anything we could ever experience. The word Anaximander actually used was *apeiron*, which is sometimes translated as "indefinite" or "unlimited." *Apeiron*, or primordial "stuff," was a chaotic mixture of elements, which separated out to yield the variety of things in the world. This notion of "stuff" was a second major step in philosophy and science. Today, we feel comfortable with the idea that things are made of "stuff" (atoms and molecules) that we never experience in everyday life. But in the ancient world, this suggestion must have seemed extremely exciting.

Anaximander's student, Anaximenes, thought his teacher's notion of "stuff" was too mysterious, but he also rejected Thales' theory and replaced it with the idea that air is the basic "stuff." Just as our soul, which is air, integrates us, so breath and air surround the whole cosmos. Air makes up the other elements and the various things of the world by becoming thicker and thinner. (Think of steam condensing to form water, and then ice.) Anaximenes thus introduced the idea that changes in the quantity of basic elements can produce changes in quality as well—a key principle of modern science.

HERACLITUS Heraclitus, another philosopher of the same period, defended the idea that fire was the fundamental "stuff" of the universe, arguing that the heat of living organisms and the constant changing of the things of this world could best be explained as manifestations of this fascinating element. "This world that is the same for all, neither any god nor any man shaped it, but it ever was and is and shall be ever-living Fire that kindles by measures and goes out by measures." (Think of a flame, constantly active, consuming itself and always changing.) Heraclitus' view of the importance of change brought him to the view of reality itself as flux, thereby placing him in opposition to the established notion that reality is unchanging. (The famous example, "You can't step twice into the same river," is often attributed to him because of his belief in reality as flux.) But the fact that we refer to the river at all shows that, although the matter (the water) may change continually, the *form* of the river remains more or less constant. So too, Heraclitus argues, our ever-changing reality has an underlying form—or logos— which remains the same. Heraclitus' view of reality was to have a profound effect on the philosophers of the nineteenth and twentieth centuries.

MONISM AND MATERIALISM The attempt to reduce all of the varied things in the world to one kind of thing is called **monism.** It is the search for ultimate reality, which might be very different from the appearance of everyday life, that has motivated philosophy and science for twenty-five hundred years. So the debate began: Was the world really made of water, or air, or fire, or perhaps some other kind of "stuff" that we could never experience? Today, the debate continues: Is everything made up of matter, or energy, or matter-energy? Are there basic particles that cannot be reduced to anything else? Scientists once thought that atoms were such particles; then they discovered electrons, protons, and neutrons that made up atoms. And since then, they have discovered dozens of other particles, and today they are debating a mysterious particle called a quark, which physicists now think may provide the ultimate answer to Thales' ancient question. But notice that all of these views are strictly physical. That is, they are concerned about basic questions of what we now call physics and chemistry, concerned about the material "stuff" of which all things are composed. This was true of Thales; and it is still true of modern "quark" theorists. Accordingly, the philosophies of all of these thinkers can be called **materialism,** the view that reality is ultimately composed of some kind of material "stuff." (In this context, "materialism" does not mean concern about the material things in life — money, cars, jewelry, or getting a new garbage disposal every year.)

DEMOCRITUS, ATOMS, AND PLURALISM   Not all materialists thought that there was only one ultimate component of reality. A number of philosophers appeared in the ancient world who believed in **pluralism,** that is, that more than one basic "stuff" made up the universe. The best known of the pluralists was Democritus, who suggested that the universe was made up of tiny bits of "stuff" that he called *atoms*. These combined together to form the many different things and qualities of the world. (The soul, he suggested, consists of smooth, round, unusually mobile atoms, disposed throughout the body.) Other pluralists stressed the idea that these different bits of "stuff" were very different in kind as well, so that the bits of stuff that composed water, for example, would be very different from the bits of "stuff" that composed fire. You can appreciate how modern these are, given our current ideas in chemistry and physics. These ancient Greek issues and answers have not become obsolete; they have changed and become more refined. Some have been more in favor at one time and others at other times. But they are still very much with us.

IMMATERIAL "STUFF"   If you think like a physical scientist, the idea that the universe is made up of some kind of material "stuff" sounds very plausible. In fact, you might wonder, what else could it be made of? Consider this; there are some things in the universe that could not plausibly be made of material "stuff." For example, what about your thoughts and feelings? Are they simply bits of matter, or are they composed of some entirely different kind of "stuff," perhaps some kind of mental or spiritual "stuff"? Heraclitus, who had argued that everything was made of fire, was already groping for some such conception of **immaterial** "stuff," something not material, but rather spiritual or nonphysical. ("Immaterial," in a philosophical context, does not mean "unimportant.") Accordingly, he introduced his idea that underlying all of the things and changes in the universe is the *logos*, which might be called a logic. Thought had a role in the universe as well as material "stuff," and Heraclitus tried to argue that "thought is Being," in other words, that everything is composed of thought as well as matter. People had (and still have) a very difficult time trying to understand what he meant by this, but it is at least clear what he was trying to do. Heraclitus was concerned to recognize something that had previously been neglected, namely, thought, which was not just another kind of material "stuff."

PYTHAGORAS   Another Pre-Socratic philosopher, Pythagoras, also attempted to defend a view of the world that did not depend upon the usual kinds of material "stuff." He taught that numbers were the real nature of things, and he taught his students to worship the mathematical order of the universe. He was particularly inspired by new Greek discoveries in music and harmony, and he saw the universe itself as a grand *harmony*. (The term, "the music of the spheres," was part of his teachings.) Unlike the other Pre-Socratic philosophers we have met, Pythagoras was much more of a religious figure. He was a mystic and the leader of a powerful underground cult that believed in reincarnation and the **immortality** of the soul. In accordance with this religion, he gave the mind and the soul a much more prominent place in his view of the world than other Pre-Socratic philosophers. But despite the sometimes mysterious views of Pythagoras and his cult, he is still recognized as one of the most important thinkers of the ancient world. Together with Heraclitus, he was one of the first to defend a view of reality that depended more on logic and thought than purely material "stuff." (The "Pythagorean theorem," that you learned in high school, is named after him.)

These ancient attempts to find out the way the world really is should not be thought of as clumsy attempts to find out the things that modern scientists now know. All the theories of "stuff" were indeed the precursors of modern physics and chemistry. But you can already see that these philosophers were also concerned with what we would call the mental and the spiritual aspects of the world. Even the most materialistic among them, for example, Thales, did not believe that the basic matter of the universe was cold and lifeless "stuff." All of these philosophers believed that the universe itself, as well as everything in it, was alive in at least some limited way. That is, they all believed in **animism,** the doctrine that everything, volcanoes and stones as well as elephants and flowers, are living things. Furthermore, animism has not disappeared because of the advances of science, though in certain periods (like our own) it has been treated less favorably than in others. But even in the nineteenth century, when physics and chemistry were making some of their most spectacular advances, animism was an extremely popular doctrine, even among scientists. And there are still a great many people today who accept a modified version of it. So don't think that the problems discussed by these ancient philosophers have been solved by science or simply gone away. The place of mind and spirit in a world of matter and energy is still among our basic problems. The ancient search for the way the world really is is still very much with us.

There were a great many philosophers in the Pre-Socratic period, but it is not our purpose to provide a history of them. We just want to get some idea of the questions and answers that have defined philosophy since ancient times. But before we can understand the truly magnificent breakthrough that comes with Socrates, Plato, and Aristotle, it is necessary to see how these earlier theories ran into troubles that they could not solve. First, what had been presupposed by everyone we have discussed is the idea that reality, whatever it is, must be eternal and unchanging. For Thales, water was the eternal and unchanging element, although the forms it took might be very different and change constantly. For Democritus, atoms were unchanging and indestructible, although the things they combined to compose might change and be destroyed. For Pythagoras, numbers, unlike the particular things in the world, were eternal and unchanging. Only

Heraclitus seemed to have some reservations about this presupposition; because he believed that the ultimate nature of reality was fire, he appreciated the importance of change, as in the flickering of a flame. But even he insisted that the *logos*, or logic, that underlay the constant changes in the world was itself eternal and unchanging. And we shall see that this presupposition, that reality cannot change, however much things seem to change, will remain one of the most important beliefs in Western culture. (In Christianity, for example, the eternal and unchanging nature of God and the human soul are built upon the same philosophical foundation.)

PARMENIDES AND ZENO   But this insistence on the eternal and unchanging nature of ultimate reality raises a serious problem. The philosopher who brought it out most clearly was the Pre-Socratic Parmenides. He was an accomplished mathematician who thought far more of the eternal certainties of arithmetic than he did of the transient things of everyday experience. He too was a monist and believed in a single reality, "the One." Because he shared the assumption that reality must be eternal and unchanging, he came to an astonishing conclusion: This world, the world of our experience, cannot be real! Our world is constantly changing: Objects are created and destroyed; organisms live and die; people grow old, change their appearance, and move from place to place. And so this world, with all its changes, could not be the real world, nor could we ever know the real world, since we are as inconstant and changing as the other things of our experience. We are, at best, living in a kind of illusion, not in reality at all!

Since Thales, the main achievement of philosophy had been to break away from common sense and ordinary experience in order to find out the way the world really is. But now we can see how far away from common sense and ordinary experience this breaking away can lead us. In Parmenides' philosophy, if the results of his logic are incompatible with common sense and ordinary experience, so much the worse for common sense and ordinary experience. The followers of Parmenides, particularly the mathematician Zeno, carried these bizarre conclusions even further. Zeno argued, by means of a series of famous paradoxes, that all motion and change was nothing but an illusion.

The following generation of philosophers, who called themselves **sophists** (who have ever since given "sophistry" a bad name because of their rhetorical debating tricks), went even further. They argued that there was no reality, and even if there were, we couldn't know anything about it anyway. (So argued the sophist Gorgias.) And the teaching of Protagoras, another sophist, is still well known today; he said, "Man is the measure of all things," which means that there is no reality except for what we take to be reality. We shall later see that the sophists, despite their bad reputation, anticipated many of the most important philosophical concerns of the twentieth century. In particular, they stressed the *practical* questions rather than abstract questions, and thus anticipated our own American *pragmatists*. And, in suggesting that truth is *relative* to people, they anticipated the much disputed question of *relativism,* the idea that truth might be different at different times for different people. Wandering around the countryside, giving lessons in debating and rhetoric, the sophists used the accomplishments of the earlier philosophers to ridicule philosophy and make fools of practically everyone. That is, until they met Socrates, whose arguments against them changed the course of philosophy and Western thought in general.

The second difficulty ancient theories ran into was this: All of the Pre-Socratic philosophers, including Heraclitus and Pythagoras, gave primary emphasis to material things and the relations between them; they gave only secondary and passing attention to immaterial objects, thoughts, and numbers, for example. They were groping for a way of dealing with them, but their attempts were never satisfactory. Pythagoras did not view numbers as immaterial objects but only as aspects of material objects. It would remain for Socrates and his student Plato, in the fourth century B.C., to finally give the immaterial aspects of reality their full recognition.

These various theories about the way the world really is have a proper name. They are called **metaphysical doctrines,** and the attempt to develop such doctrines, in which we have been taking part for these past pages, is called **metaphysics.** The business of metaphysics is to ask and attempt to answer the most basic questions about the universe, its composition and the "stuff" of which it is composed, the role of man and mind, and the nature of the immaterial aspects of the universe as well as its physical nature. But now that we are about to discuss metaphysics in its maturity, with Plato and Aristotle, let us also give "stuff" its proper name. It is called (first by Aristotle) *substance.* Accordingly, metaphysics, the study of "the way the world really is," begins with the answers to a series of questions about substance and how it is manifested in particular things (such as people and trees).

1. How many substances are there? (Monism versus pluralism.)
2. What are they? (Water, air, fire, numbers, something unknown, minds, spirit, atoms?)
3. How are individual things composed? (And how do we tell them apart, identify them, reidentify them?)
4. How do different things and (if there is more than one) different substances interact?
5. How did substance come into being? (Created by God? Or has it always been there?)
6. Are substances "in" space and time? Are space and time substances? (If not, what are they?)

The first four questions are usually referred to as **ontology,** the study of being as such. The last questions are referred to as **cosmology,** the study of the universe. (For the Pre-Socratics, these were the same.) Cosmological questions are necessarily shared between philosophers, physicists, and astronomers, and it is impossible for us to give them more than a cursory review within a strictly philosophical book. Ontology, on the other hand, is still considered by many philosophers to be the heart of metaphysics. It is with ontology, therefore, that this chapter will be primarily concerned.

(Ontology and cosmology are not all there is to metaphysics. A further set of problems must be singled out because it is of particular personal importance to us. [The division follows that of the great German metaphysician Immanuel Kant, whom we shall meet in later chapters.] Kant summarized this second set of problems with the abbreviation "God, Freedom, and Immortality," problems that "the human mind will never give up." The existence of God is both an ontological problem [God has been identified as the "substance of the universe"] and a cosmological problem [God as creator; God as eternal]. But the existence and nature of God quite obviously deserve separate study, however intricately bound up they may be with other ontological and cosmological problems. [We shall provide this separate study in Chapter 6.] The problem of the existence of the human soul is often tied to religious questions, particularly in the Christian tradition [which is the context Kant intended]. But it is more than this: We shall see how Plato used the concept of an immortal soul to explain our ability to know eternal truths. In a more secular and transient context, there is the metaphysical problem of the relationship between mind and body [Chapter 8]. Finally, the question of metaphysical freedom [the only one of these questions not deeply considered by any of the Greek philosophers] needs to be examined in detail before we can move on to any more "practical" questions involving human action [Chapter 9].)

TWO KINDS OF METAPHYSICS:
PLATO AND ARISTOTLE

The term "metaphysics" is relatively new (from about 70 B.C. or so), but it is generally agreed that the first great systematic metaphysicians were Plato (428–348 B.C.) and Aristotle (384–322 B.C.). Plato had been a student of Socrates and his most faithful recorder. (Almost all that we have of Socrates' teachings comes to us through Plato.) Yet Socrates was a moralist, not a metaphysician, and most of the metaphysical doctrines that Plato discusses using Socrates as his mouthpiece are probably Plato's own. Aristotle never tried to be a faithful disciple of Plato, and he became his teacher's harshest and most famous critic. It has been said of each of them that the history of philosophy is nothing more than a series of footnotes to their brilliant dialogues and treatises of twenty-four hundred years ago.

Metaphysics is what Aristotle called "first philosophy," the investigation of "Being as Being," or ultimate reality. What does it mean for something to exist?

What is it for something to change? What makes one thing like another? Sometimes these questions, or at least the answers to these questions, are presupposed in our everyday thinking, whether we actually think about them or not. For example, we "naturally" believe that a tree continues to exist when we aren't looking at it. But why do we believe this? Even when such questions are the creations of philosophers, they outline views of the world that nonphilosophers share with them. The problem is, as we shall see, that people disagree violently about these issues, even from one generation to the next (for example, from Plato to Aristotle). And what seems to be clear and obvious to one philosopher will seem obscure, merely metaphorical, or downright paradoxical to another. But as we watch the warring history of metaphysics, we too should be humbled by it, for it cannot be that all of those geniuses got it wrong while we now have it right. We too, whether explicitly or not, have metaphysical views, and we too may have to be ready to give them up as we think more about them and face further arguments.

With Plato and Aristotle, metaphysics becomes a cautious consuming enterprise, producing monumental systems of many volumes that require a lifetime of study to master. All we can do here is to present a thumbnail sketch, with some brief selections, of Plato's metaphysics and a very brief introduction to Aristotle's philosophy, which seems, at first glance, to be primarily a refutation of Plato. But like so many philosophers who seem to be attacking each other from completely opposed viewpoints, Plato and Aristotle have much in common. Both attempted to resolve the problems they inherited from the Pre-Socratics: to find the ultimate substance of the universe, to understand what was eternal and unchanging, to understand change, and to show that the universe as a whole was intelligible to human understanding. Plato, following Parmenides and the other Pre-Socratics who trusted their reason more than common sense, gave reason a grander position in human life and in the universe in general than it had ever received before. Aristotle, although he too defended reason, insisted that philosophy return to common sense and have a respect for ordinary opinion, which many of the Greek philosophers seemed to have lost. But whatever their differences, it is the shared grandeur of their enterprise that should impress us most about Plato and Aristotle. Between them, they established what we today call "philosophy." And between them, they also laid the intellectual foundations for Christian theology. Saint Augustine, for example, was very much a Platonist, and Saint Thomas Aquinas was thoroughly indebted to Aristotle.

Plato

The most important single feature of Plato's philosophy is his theory of **Forms.** (The Greek word is *Eidos.*) Plato's Forms are sometimes referred to as **Ideas,** but Plato does not mean "ideas" in a person's mind, but rather *ideal forms* or perfect examples — the perfect circle or perfect beauty. To avoid confusion, we shall not use the word "Ideas," but only "Forms."

Forms are the ultimate reality. Things change, people grow old and die, but Forms are eternal and unchanging. Thus Plato could agree with Heraclitus that the world of our experience is constantly changing; but he could also agree with Parmenides, who insisted that the real world, the eternal and unchanging world, was not the same as the world of our experience. According to Plato, it was a *world of Forms*, a world of eternal truths. There were, in other words, two worlds: (1) the world in which we live, a world of constant change or a *world of becoming*, and (2) a world of ideas, an unchanging world, the real world or the *world of being*. Our only access to this latter world, the real world, was through our reason, our capacity for intellectual thought. Plato's "two-worlds" view was to have a direct and obvious influence on Christian theology. It would also affect philosophers, mathematicians, mystics, poets, and romantics of all kinds until the present day. But in his own time it had a more immediate importance; it allowed him to reconcile Heraclitus and Parmenides, to resolve the problems of the Pre-Socratics, and to finally give ideas their proper place in human thought.

For Plato, it is the world of Forms, the world of being, that is real. But this is not to say (as Parmenides had argued) that the world we live in, the world of becoming, is unreal. It is, however, less than real, not an illusion, but without those qualities of eternity and necessity that were the marks of true reality. This might seem like a verbal trick; it is not. The idea of a hierarchy of realities was already familiar in religions that antedated Plato's philosophy by centuries. And we still use such notions in our own thinking, comparing, for example, the world of film and novels to "the real world," or the dreary humdrum of working-day life to "really living." But the best illustration of Plato's two-worlds view is his own, which he offers us in a parable called the "Myth of the Cave."

It is a parable about bringing people from the less real to the really real. Indeed, one of the most striking features of Plato's philosophy (and much of Greek philosophy in general) is its emphasis on the *love* of wisdom, the irresistibility of reality; and what is too easily lost in translation is the almost sexual imagery Plato uses to describe our passion for the truth. The "Myth of the Cave" not only illustrates two kinds of knowledge, two kinds of worlds; it is also a parable about human timidity, the difficulties we have in facing the truth, and our resistance to the dazzling light of truth itself.

from *The Republic*, by Plato

SOCRATES. Imagine men to be living in an underground cave-like dwelling place, which has a way up to the light along its whole width, but the entrance is a long way up. The men have been there from childhood, with their neck and legs in fetters, so that they remain in the same place and can only see ahead of them, as their bonds prevent them turning their heads. Light is provided by a fire burning some way behind them and on a higher ground, there is a path across the cave and along this a low wall has been built, like the screen at a puppet show in front of the performers who show their puppets above it.

GLAUCON. I see it.

SOCRATES. See then also men carrying along that wall, so that they overtop it, all kinds of artifacts, statues of men, reproductions of other animals in stone or wood fashioned in all sorts of ways, and, as is likely, some of the carriers are talking while others are silent.

GLAUCON. This is a strange picture, and strange prisoners.

SOCRATES. They are like us, I said. Do you think, in the first place, that such men could see anything of themselves and each other except the shadows which the fire casts upon the wall of the cave in front of them?

GLAUCON. How could they, if they have to keep their heads still throughout life?

SOCRATES. And is not the same true of the objects carried along the wall?

GLAUCON. Quite.

SOCRATES. If they could converse with one another, do you not think that they would consider these shadows to be the real things?

GLAUCON. Necessarily.

SOCRATES. What if their prison had an echo which reached them from in front of them? Whenever one of the carriers passing behind the wall spoke, would they not think that it was the shadow passing in front of them which was talking? Do you agree?

GLAUCON. By Zeus, I do.

SOCRATES. Altogether then, I said, such men would believe the truth to be nothing else than the shadows of the artifacts?

GLAUCON. They must believe that.

SOCRATES. Consider then what deliverance from their bonds and the curing of their ignorance would be if something like this naturally happened to them. Whenever one of them was freed, had to stand up suddenly, turn his head, walk, and look up toward the light, doing all that would give him pain, the flash of the fire would make it impossible for him to see the objects of which he had earlier seen the shadows. What do you think he would say if he was told that what he saw was foolishness, that he was now somewhat closer to reality and turned to things that existed more fully, that he saw more correctly? If one then pointed to each of the objects passing by, asked him what each was, and forced him to answer, do you not think he would be at a loss and believe that the things which he saw earlier were truer than the things now pointed out to him?

GLAUCON. Much truer.

SOCRATES. If one then compelled him to look at the fire itself, his eyes would hurt, he would turn round and flee toward those things which he could see, and think that they were in fact clearer than those now shown to him.

GLAUCON. Quite so.

SOCRATES. And if one were to drag him thence by force up the rough and steep path, and did not let him go before he was dragged into the sunlight, would he not be in physical pain and angry as he was dragged along? When he came into the light, with the sunlight filling his eyes, he would not be able to see a single one of the things which are now said to be true.

GLAUCON. Not at once, certainly.

SOCRATES. I think he would need time to get adjusted before he could see things in the world above; at first he would see shadows most easily, then reflections of men and other things in water, then the things themselves. After this he would see objects in the sky and the sky itself more easily at night, the light of the stars and the moon more easily than the sun and the light of the sun during the day.

GLAUCON. Of course.

SOCRATES. Then, at last, he would be able to see the sun, not images of it in water or in some alien place, but the sun itself in its own place, and be able to contemplate it.

GLAUCON. That must be so.

SOCRATES. After this he would reflect that it is the sun which provides the seasons and the years, which governs everything in the visible world, and is also in some way the cause of those other things which he used to see.

GLAUCON. Clearly that would be the next stage.

SOCRATES. What then? As he reminds himself of his first dwelling place, of the wisdom there and of his fellow prisoners, would he not reckon himself happy for the change, and pity them?

GLAUCON. Surely.

SOCRATES. And if the men below had praise and honours from each other, and prizes for the man who saw most clearly the shadows that passed before them, and who could best remember which usually came earlier and which later, and which came together and thus could most ably prophesy the future, do you think our man would desire those rewards and envy those who were honoured and held power among the prisoners, or would he feel, as Homer put it, that he certainly wished to be "serf to another man without possessions upon the earth"[1] and go through any suffering, rather than share their opinions and live as they do?

GLAUCON. Quite so, I think he would rather suffer anything.

SOCRATES. Reflect on this too. If this man went down into the cave again and sat down in the same seat, would his eyes not be filled with darkness, coming suddenly out of the sunlight?

GLAUCON. They certainly would.

---

[1] *Odyssey* 11, 489–90, where Achilles says to Odysseus, on the latter's visit to the underworld, that he would rather be a servant to a poor man on earth than king among the dead [transl. note].

SOCRATES. And if he had to contend again with those who had remained prisoners in recognizing those shadows while his sight was affected and his eyes had not settled down — and the time for this adjustment would not be short — would he not be ridiculed? Would it not be said that he had returned from his upward journey with his eyesight spoiled, and that it was not worthwhile even to attempt to travel upward? As for the man who tried to free them and lead them upward, if they could somehow lay their hands on him and kill him, they would do so.

GLAUCON. They certainly would.

SOCRATES. This whole image, my dear Glaucon, must be related to what we said before. The realm of the visible should be compared to the prison dwelling, and the fire inside it to the power of the sun. If you interpret the upward journey and the contemplation of things above as the upward journey of the soul to the intelligible realm, you will grasp what I surmise since you were keen to hear it. Whether it is true or not only the god knows, but this is how I see it, namely that in the intelligible world the Form of the Good is the last to be seen, and with difficulty; when seen it must be reckoned to be for all the cause of all that is right and beautiful, to have produced in the visible world both the light and the fount of light, while in the intelligible world it is itself that which produces and controls truth and intelligence, and he who is to act intelligently in public or in private must see it.

GLAUCON. I share your thought as far as I am able.

SOCRATES. Come then, share with me this thought also: do not be surprised that those who have reached this point are unwilling to occupy themselves with human affairs, and that their souls are always pressing upward to spend their time there, for this is natural if things are as our parable indicates.

GLAUCON. That is very likely.

SOCRATES. Further, do you think it at all surprising that anyone coming to the evils of human life from the contemplation of the divine behaves awkwardly and appears very ridiculous while his eyes are still dazzled and before he is sufficiently adjusted to the darkness around him, if he is compelled to contend in court or some other place about the shadows of justice or the objects of which they are shadows, and to carry through the contest about these in the way these things are understood by those who have never seen Justice itself?

GLAUCON. That is not surprising at all.

SOCRATES. Anyone with intelligence would remember that the eyes may be confused in two ways and from two causes, coming from light into darkness as well as from darkness into light. Realizing that the same applies to the soul, whenever he sees a soul disturbed and unable to see something, he will not laugh mindlessly but will consider whether it has come from a brighter life and is dimmed because unadjusted, or has come from greater ignorance into greater light and is filled with a brighter dazzlement. The former he would declare happy in its life and experience, the latter he would pity, and if he should wish to laugh at it, his laughter would be less ridiculous than if he laughed at a soul that has come from the light above.

GLAUCON. What you say is very reasonable.

SOCRATES. We must then, if these things are true, think something like this about them, namely that education is not what some declare it to be; they say that knowledge is not present in the soul and that they put it in, like putting sight into blind eyes.

GLAUCON. They surely say that.

SOCRATES. Our present argument shows that the capacity to learn and the organ with which to do so are present in every person's soul. It is as if it were not possible to turn the eye from darkness to light without turning the whole body; so one must turn one's whole soul from the world of becoming until it can endure to contemplate reality, and the brightest of realities, which we say is the Good.

GLAUCON. Yes.

SOCRATES. Education then is the art of doing this very thing, this turning around, the knowledge of how the soul can most easily and most effectively be turned around; it is not the art of putting the capacity of sight into the soul; the soul possesses that already but it is not turned the right way or looking where it should. This is what education has to deal with.

GLAUCON. That seems likely.[2]

Our world is like a set of shadows of the real world; that does not make it an illusion, but it does make it a mere imitation of the bright originals. Notice, too, the savior-like role of the philosopher that Plato is setting up here. (His famous argument that philosophers should be kings, and kings philosophers, is included here too.) Like Pythagoras, Plato believed that knowledge of pure Forms, knowledge of the world of "Being," is a person's only hope for salvation and the "good life."

Socrates had taught his students, Plato among them, that the truth, if we can know it at all, must be in us. Plato (using his teacher as his literary spokesman) gives this revelation a new twist. It begins with a puzzle. How is it possible to learn anything? If we don't already know it, how will we recognize it when we find it? And if we already do know it, it makes no sense to say that we "learn it." Now this puzzle sounds like nonsense if we think only of examples such as "What is the beer consumption rate in Omaha, Nebraska?" To answer such questions, obviously we can't simply "look into ourselves"; we have to go out into the world and get information. But Plato insists that he is after much bigger game than "information"; he wants Knowledge (with a capital K), knowledge of reality, to which we have access only through thinking. That world, unlike the world of change and "information" in which we live, is characterized by the fact that everything in it is eternal and necessary. In this eternal world, reality is not dis-

[2]Plato, *The Republic*, Bk. VII, trans. G. M. A. Grube (Indianapolis, Ind.: Hackett, 1974).

coverable merely through observation and experience. For example, consider the simple truth, $2 + 2 = 4$; it never changes, no experience is necessary to know it; it is one of those eternal truths that deserves its place in Plato's world of Being. But then how do we know it? How can it already be "in us"?

The second principle of Plato's metaphysics, our bridge between the two worlds, is the immortality and immateriality of the human soul. Our souls contain knowledge of the world of Being that is already in us at birth. Such knowledge and ideas are called **innate.** Experience only triggers them off and allows us to "remember" them. Here is the extravagant answer to Plato's puzzle, "How is it possible to learn a truth about the world of Being?" The answer is: We already "know" it; it's just a matter of recalling it. Consider his famous illustration of this second doctrine in his dialogue, *Meno:*

from *Meno,*
by Plato

MENO. How will you look for it, Socrates, when you do not know at all what
it is? How will you aim to search for something you do not know at
all? If you should meet with it, how will you know that this is the thing
that you did not know?

SOCRATES. I know what you want to say, Meno. Do you realize what a debater's argument you are bringing up, that a man cannot search either for
what he knows or for what he does not know? He cannot search for
what he knows — since he knows it, there is no need to search — nor for
what he does not know, for he does not know what to look for.

MENO. Does that argument not seem sound to you, Socrates?

SOCRATES. Not to me.

MENO. Can you tell me why?

SOCRATES. I can. I have heard wise men and women talk about divine matters . . .

MENO. What did they say?

SOCRATES. What was, I thought, both true and beautiful.

MENO. What was it, and who were they?

SOCRATES. The speakers were among the priests and priestesses whose care
it is to be able to give an account of their practices. Pindar too says it,
and many others of the divine among our poets. What they say is this;
see whether you think they speak the truth: They say that the human
soul is immortal; at times it comes to an end, which they call dying, at
times it is reborn, but it is never destroyed, and one must therefore live
one's life as piously as possible:
    Persephone will return to the sun above in the ninth year the souls
    of those from whom she will exact punishment for old miseries, and
    from these come noble kings, mighty in strength and greatest in wis-
    dom, and for the rest of time men will call them sacred heroes.
As the soul is immortal, has been born often and has seen all things
here and in the underworld, there is nothing which it has not learned;
so it is in no way surprising that it can recollect the things it knew

before, both about virtue and other things. As the whole of nature is akin, and the soul has learned everything, nothing prevents a man, after recalling one thing only — a process men call learning — discovering everything else for himself, if he is brave and does not tire of the search, for searching and learning are, as a whole, recollection. We must, therefore, not believe that debater's argument, for it would make us idle, and fainthearted men like to hear it, whereas my argument makes them energetic and keen on the search. I trust that this is true, and I want to inquire along with you into the nature of virtue.

MENO. Yes, Socrates, but how do you mean that we do not learn, but that what we call learning is recollection? Can you teach me that this is so?

SOCRATES. As I said just now, Meno, you are a rascal. You now ask me if I can teach you, when I say there is no teaching but recollection, in order to show me up at once as contradicting myself.

MENO. No, by Zeus, Socrates, that was not my intention when I spoke, but just a habit. If you can somehow show me that things are as you say, please do so.

So far, Socrates has only asserted that we have innate ideas, knowledge that we are born with but may not recognize. What he must do now is demonstrate that this is so. He asks Meno to call over a nearby slave, a young boy.

MENO. Certainly. You there, come forward. [to a slave boy]

SOCRATES. Is he a Greek? Does he speak Greek?

MENO. Very much so. He was born in my household.

SOCRATES. Pay attention then whether you think he is recollecting or learning from me.

MENO. I will pay attention.

SOCRATES. Tell me now, boy, you know that a square figure is like this?

SLAVE BOY. I do.

Socrates draws a square ABCD. The sides are of course equal, and the lines joining the middle points of these sides, which also go through the center of the square, namely EF and GH. He then assumes the sides to be two feet.

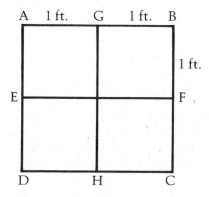

SOCRATES. A square then is a figure in which all these four sides are equal?

SLAVE BOY. Yes indeed.

SOCRATES. And it also has these lines through the middle equal?

SLAVE BOY. Yes.

SOCRATES. And such a figure could be larger or smaller?

SLAVE BOY. Certainly.

SOCRATES. If then this side were two feet, and this other side two feet, how many feet would the whole be? Consider it this way: if it were two feet this way, and only one foot that way, the figure would be once two feet?

SLAVE BOY. Yes.

SOCRATES. But if it is two feet also that way, it would surely be twice two feet?

SLAVE BOY. Yes.

SOCRATES. How many feet is twice two feet? Work it out and tell me.

SLAVE BOY. Four, Socrates.

SOCRATES. Now let us have another figure twice the size of this one, with the four sides equal like this one.

SLAVE BOY. Yes.

SOCRATES. How many feet will that be?

SLAVE BOY. Eight.

SOCRATES. Come now, try to tell me how long each side of this will be. The side of this is two feet. What about each side of the one which is its double?

SLAVE BOY. Obviously, Socrates, it will be twice the length.

SOCRATES. You see, Meno, that I am not teaching the boy anything, but all I do is question him. And now he thinks he knows the length of the line on which an eight-foot figure is based. Do you agree?

MENO. I do.

SOCRATES. And does he know?

MENO. Certainly not.

The boy is mistaken, of course. The side of a square whose area is 8 has to be $\sqrt{8}$, the square root of 8. But what Socrates (Plato) is defending here is his entire philosophical method, in which he shows people how mistaken they are in order to open up their minds to the truth. Socrates shows the boy just how wrong he is and leads him to see the correct answer. The important point in the demonstration is that Socrates does not tell the boy the answer, but rather draws it out of him. The problem itself is quite easy. The side of a square double the area of the first must be the diagonal of the first square ($\sqrt{8}$), and Socrates gets the slave boy to recognize this by simply drawing three more squares, such that the four diagonals together make up the new square in question.

SOCRATES. Look then how he will come out of his perplexity while searching along with me. I shall do nothing more than ask questions and not

teach him. Watch whether you find me teaching and explaining things
to him instead of asking for his opinion.

SOCRATES. You tell me, is this not a four-foot figure? You understand?

SLAVE BOY. I do.

SOCRATES. We add to it this figure which is equal to it?

SLAVE BOY. Yes.

SOCRATES. And we add this third figure equal to each of them?

SLAVE BOY. Yes.

SOCRATES. Could we then fill in the space in the corner?

SLAVE BOY. Certainly.

*Socrates now builds up his sixteen-foot square by joining two four-foot
squares, then a third, like this.*

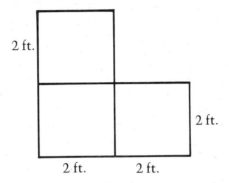

*Filling "the space in the corner will give another four-foot square, which
completes the sixteen-foot square containing four four-foot squares."*

SOCRATES. So we have these four equal figures?

SLAVE BOY. Yes.

SOCRATES. Well then, how many times is the whole figure larger than this
one?[3]

SLAVE BOY. Four times.

SOCRATES. But we should have had one that was twice as large, or do you
not remember?

SLAVE BOY. I certainly do.

SOCRATES. Does not this line from one corner to the other cut each of these
figures in two?

SLAVE BOY. Yes.

[3]"This one" is any one of the inside squares of four feet [transl. note].

Socrates now draws the diagonals of the four inside squares, namely FH, HE, EG and GF, which together form the square GFHEG. We should note that Socrates here introduces a new element, which is not the result of a question but of his own knowledge, though the answer to the problem follows from questions. The new square contains four halves of a four foot square and is therefore eight feet.

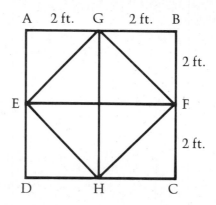

SOCRATES. So these are four equal lines which enclose this figure?

SLAVE BOY. They are.

SOCRATES. Consider now: how large is the figure?

SLAVE BOY. I do not understand.

SOCRATES. Each of these lines cuts off half of each of the four figures inside it, does it not?

SLAVE BOY. Yes.

SOCRATES. How many of this size are there in this figure?

SLAVE BOY. Four.

SOCRATES. How many in this?

SLAVE BOY. Two.

SOCRATES. What is the relation of four to two?

SLAVE BOY. Double.

SOCRATES. How many feet in this?

SLAVE BOY. Eight.

SOCRATES. Based on what line?

SLAVE BOY. This one.

SOCRATES. That is, on the line that stretches from corner to corner of the four-foot figure?

SLAVE BOY. Yes.

SOCRATES. Clever men call this the diagonal, so that if diagonal is its name, you say that the double figure would be that based on the diagonal?

SLAVE BOY. Most certainly, Socrates.

Now, Socrates draws his own conclusions:

> SOCRATES. What do you think, Meno? Has he, in his answers, expressed any opinion that was not his own?
>
> MENO. No, they were all his own.
>
> SOCRATES. And yet, as we said, he did not know a short time ago?
>
> MENO. That is true.
>
> SOCRATES. So these opinions were in him, were they not?
>
> MENO. Yes.
>
> SOCRATES. So the man who does not know has within himself true opinions about the things that he does not know?
>
> MENO. So it appears.
>
> SOCRATES. These opinions have now just been stirred up like a dream, but if he were repeatedly asked these same questions in various ways, you know that in the end his knowledge about these things would be as accurate as anyone's.
>
> MENO. It is likely.
>
> SOCRATES. And he will know it without having been taught but only questioned, and find the knowledge within himself?
>
> MENO. Yes.
>
> SOCRATES. And is not finding knowledge within oneself recollection?
>
> MENO. Certainly.
>
> SOCRATES. Must he not either have at some time acquired the knowledge he now possesses, or else have always possessed it?
>
> MENO. Yes.
>
> SOCRATES. If he always had it, he would always have known. If he acquired it, he cannot have done so in his present life. Or has someone taught him geometry? For he will perform in the same way about all geometry, and all other knowledge. Has someone taught him everything? You should know, especially as he has been born and brought up in your house.
>
> MENO. But I know that no one has taught him.
>
> SOCRATES. Yet he has these opinions, or doesn't he?
>
> MENO. That seems indisputable, Socrates.
>
> SOCRATES. If he has not acquired them in his present life, is it not clear that he had them and had learned them at some other time?
>
> MENO. It seems so.
>
> SOCRATES. Then that was the time when he was not a human being?
>
> MENO. Yes.
>
> SOCRATES. If then, during the time he exists and is not a human being he will have true opinions which, when stirred by questioning, become knowledge, will not his soul have learned during all time? For it is clear that during all time he exists either as a man or not.
>
> MENO. So it seems.

SOCRATES. Then if the truth about reality is always in our soul, the soul would be immortal so that you should always confidently try to seek out and recollect what you do not know at present — that is, what you do not recollect?

MENO. Somehow, Socrates, I think that what you say is right.

SOCRATES. I think so too, Meno.[4]

The doctrine of the immortality of the soul was not original with Plato, of course. The ancient Egyptians had believed in it many centuries before the first Greek philosophers, and Pythagoras had taught it to his students. But Plato's doctrine had more than religious significance; it was his answer to the skeptics and our bridge to the eternal world of Being. Of course, as a student of Socrates, he also appreciated the advantages of believing in an afterlife. Socrates could face death so calmly, he told his students, just because he believed in life after death. But for Plato it signified something more; it provided us with knowledge in this life as well as continued existence in another.

Plato's doctrines of the world of Being and the immortality of the soul introduce a clearly immaterialist conception of reality, as opposed to all of the more or less materialist conceptions we have encountered so far (the world as "stuff"). Even Pythagoras' numbers and Heraclitus' *logos* had their materialistic foundations, for neither philosopher was willing to grant these things independent existence, independent, that is, of the material things of this world. The things of Plato's world of Being can exist apart from them.

What is in this "other world," this world of Being? We have already met one of its inhabitants: the simple truth, $2 + 2 = 4$. Its inhabitants are Forms. Consider the following familiar example: You are asked by your geometry teacher to prove that the internal angles of a triangle total 180°. Simple enough. You remember how: You extend the base of the triangle, draw a line parallel to the base through the apex, and then proceed with your proof. But now, how do you know that you have not only shown that the internal angles of *this* triangle total 180°? As a matter of fact, it is pretty obvious that what you have drawn isn't even a triangle; the sides sag, one of the angles is broken, and the lines are fat (after all, a real line has no width at all). But yet you claim to have proved something about all triangles. Well, it is clear that you needn't do the proof even twice, much less an infinite number of times, to make your claim. How come? Because, you will answer, what you have been working with is not this particular poorly drawn triangle in your notebook but an ideal triangle, the form of all and any triangles. And there it is — Plato's Form of a triangle. It is not identical to any particular triangle. (How could it be, for it would have to be acute, isosceles, right, and nonright all at the same time!) It is their ideal Form, which each particular triangle approximates, that has its own existence in the world of Being. Plato says that every triangle that we can draw participates in the ideal Form and that it is

---

[4]Plato, *Meno*, trans. G. M. A. Grube (Indianapolis, Ind.: Hackett, 1976).

only through reason, not through observation of particular triangles, that we come into contact with these ideal Forms.

Plato's Forms are what different things of the same kind have in common and what make them things of the same kind. For example, two horses have in common the Form horse, and you recognize a horse, Plato would say, because of its Form. Suppose that you've never seen a horse before. Is it possible for you to know what a horse is? The answer is, "of course." It is enough that you have learned what a horse is (from pictures or descriptions) even if you've never seen one. But how is such learning possible? According to Plato, it is possible because we know a **definition** and thus recognize the Form of a horse, like the ideal Form of a triangle, and with it we are able to know what a horse is, even if we have never seen one, and we recognize horses when we do see them. In Plato's terms, we can recognize all horses, no matter what their age, shape, color, or peculiarities, just because they "participate" in the Form horse. And for Plato, the Form horse has even more reality than particular, flesh-and-blood horses.

The concept of Form allows Plato to explain what it is that one comes to understand when one learns that two or more things are of the same kind. But for Plato the notion of Form serves another purpose as well. In addition to what we know about things from experience, we also know some things independent of experience, and we know these things with certainty (the same certainty Descartes sought in our introduction). For example, we know that every horse is an animal. We know this not simply because every horse that we have seen has turned out to be an animal, but because we know, apart from any particular experiences with horses, that the very Form horse includes the Form animal. (In our times, we would say that the meaning of the English word "horse" already includes the concept of "being an animal"; accordingly, philosophers refer to this kind of truth as **conceptual truth**. But this term was not available to Plato.)

To know a Platonic Form is not just to "see" something. It is to fall in love with it; in fact, it is to fall madly in love. And so Socrates, in nearly all of Plato's dialogues, repeats the claim that a philosopher is a kind of lover. Indeed, he says that to know the Forms is to want to reproduce, to propagate, to teach everyone else to see them and to love them too. The Myth of the Cave, and the metaphor of the Sun and shadows, has two sides. The first is that the changing world of our everyday experience is only a shadow, an imitation of reality. But the second side is that the world of our everyday experience is also an image of the divine and ultimate reality, and so in the things of everyday life we get at least a glimpse of perfection.

Among the Forms are those ideals of human perfection, which it is up to us not only to recognize but to try to realize here in the world of Becoming: Wisdom, Justice, Beauty, and Goodness. It is to these ideals of perfection that each of us aspires, and it is the definition of these ideals that is the task of every philosopher. His or her job (and Socrates' main task in all of Plato's dialogues) is to sort out our common confusions about such vital matters. The business of the philosopher, in short, is to make us recognize eternal Forms and make it possible to achieve that heroic wisdom to which Plato's teacher, Socrates, had devoted his life.

I hope that you can appreciate, even from this brief sketch, the power of the metaphysical doctrines Plato has developed. You may also be aware of some of their difficulties. Most importantly, the gap between our world and the real world makes us exceedingly uncomfortable; none of us likes to think of ourselves living merely in the shadows. (And Plato himself warns, "wouldn't the prisoners who had never been released . . . laugh at him and even . . . kill" the philosopher who thus instructs them?) The connection between the world of Being and our own world of Becoming is not at all clear. Plato does say that the things of this latter world "participate" in the Forms of the former, but one thing that we shall have to learn right away in philosophy (and in every other discipline) is that words that pretend to be explanations are often only cosmetic cover-ups. It looks as if we have a theory when in fact we have only a word. This is particularly true of Plato's word "participates" (*methexis*), and he himself raises serious doubts about it in his later dialogues. But the real attack comes, as it should come in philosophy, from his own students, and in particular, from one, perhaps the greatest of them all, Aristotle.

Aristotle

Aristotle claimed that he did not understand Plato's concept of "participation." (When a philosopher claims "not to understand" something, it means that he is pushing for a better account of it, that he is not at all satisfied so far. Aristotle probably understood Plato as well as anybody ever has.) Aristotle's objection was, essentially, that Plato had failed to explain the relationship between the Forms and particular things, and that the word "participation" was no more than "a mere empty phrase and a poetic metaphor."[5] Furthermore, Plato's emphasis on the Forms made it impossible to appreciate the full reality of particular things, and the eternal permanence of the Forms made them useless for understanding how particular things could change. Indeed, the question "How do things change?" becomes the central theme of Aristotle's philosophy.

Aristotle also wanted to determine the nature of reality. But Plato had argued that reality was something other than the world of our experience. Aristotle, a practical man of the earth, a great biologist, physicist, and worldly tutor to Alexander the Great, would have none of this. This world, our world, is reality. He agreed with Plato that knowledge must be universal and concerned with what things have in common, but he rejected Plato's idea that these common universal ingredients — the Forms of things — could be separated from particular things. But this meant that Aristotle also rejected Plato's separation of the human soul from the body, and Aristotle, unlike Plato, saw human beings entirely as creatures of nature, "rational animals" — but still animals. Metaphysics, for Aristotle, was not the study of another world, recollected in our eternal souls; metaphysics was simply the study of nature *(physis)*, and, as importantly, the study of ourselves.

[5]Aristotle, *Metaphysics*, trans. W. D. Ross (Oxford: Oxford University Press, 1924).

Accordingly, he brought metaphysics back home. But it must not be thought that he made it any simpler. The beginning student of Aristotle — as well as the trained scholar — will attest to the fact that he is among the most difficult authors in philosophy.

The doctrines of Aristotle's metaphysics sound as simple as they could be. This world, the world of our experience, is reality; there is no other world. The ultimate things of reality, which he calls substances, are individual things — men, horses, trees, and butterflies. Change is real and reality changes (thus rejecting the chief presupposition of most who came before him). The soul is not immortal, and Forms have no existence apart from the things that are instances of them. But don't think that Aristotle thereby rejected the 250 years of Greek philosophy preceding him. Aristotle, despite the common-sense quality of his metaphysics, knew better. He was not simply returning philosophy to "common sense." Quite the contrary, he was still answering the problems of Plato and his ancestors and making use of their answers as well.

We can divide Aristotle's metaphysics into an ontology and a cosmology. For beginning philosophers, the latter is far more interesting, the former extremely difficult. Aristotle's ontology is based upon the all-important notion of substance, his technical term for the Pre-Socratic conceptions of the ultimate "stuff" of the universe. He says, "The question that was asked long ago, is asked now, and always is a matter of difficulty, 'What is Being?' is now the question, 'What is Substance?'"[6] "Substance," in other words, is "that which is," or reality. (It does not mean "physical material," as in "there's a gooey substance stuck to the bottom of my shoe.")

For Aristotle, the primary substances are individual things; secondary substances (less real than individuals) are what he called the species and the genus to which a thing belongs. To return to our equestrian example, this particular horse, for Aristotle, is the primary substance. The species, "horse," and the even broader genus, "animal," are less real than the horse itself. Aristotle, like Plato, has a hierarchy of reality. But he turns Plato's hierarchy upside down. Plato holds that the more abstract things are the more real; Aristotle argues that the more concrete things, individuals, are the more real. For Aristotle, as in common sense, the more tangible things are considered to be the most real things.

What is a substance? Aristotle spends many pages giving a number of definitions, enough to keep the philosophers of the Middle Ages busy for a thousand years sorting them out. For our purposes, it will be enough to mention three different descriptions of substance, each of which is important for Aristotle and for later philosophy. The first characterization of substance is presented in terms of grammar. Aristotle says, "a substance is that which is neither predicable of a subject nor present in a subject; for instance, the individual man or horse."[7] More simply, a substance is the thing referred to by a noun, which is the subject of a

---

[6]Aristotle, *Metaphysics*, trans. Hugh Tredennick (Cambridge, Mass.: Harvard University Press, 1933).
[7]Aristotle, *Categories*, trans. J. L. Ackrill (Oxford: Oxford University Press, 1963).

sentence; for example, "the man is . . ." or "Socrates is . . ." or "the horse is. . . ." (This characterization would have been less confusing in Greek.) A more ontological way of saying this, but unfortunately very confusing too, is to say that a substance is independent of anything else. (We shall see how important this becomes in the modern metaphysics of Spinoza and Leibniz.) Other things might depend upon a substance, but a substance does not depend upon them. This is an awkward way of saying, perhaps, that the color of a horse could not exist without the horse; indeed, nothing could be true of a horse if it did not exist.

A second way of characterizing substance is to say that substance is what underlies all of the properties and changes in something. In this sense, you can say that you are the same person (that is, the same substance) that you were ten years ago, despite the fact that you are, quite obviously, very different in a great many ways. (Aristotle says, "Substance, while remaining the same, is capable of admitting contrary properties.") Combining these two characterizations, we can say that a substance is whatever is most basic to reality, like the Pre-Socratic philosophers' notion of "stuff." It is the concrete individual thing, which remains constant despite the fact that it changes and has different properties at different times. You are the same person before and after you've gotten a haircut, tried on a new suit of clothes, or had your appendix removed.

The third characterization of substance requires the introduction of another new term, which became a central concern of philosophers before this century. A substance can be defined in terms of what is *essential*. An **essence** (or an **essential property**) is that aspect of an individual that identifies it as a particular individual. For example, it is part of the essence of being Socrates that he is a human being, that he lived in the fourth century B.C., and that he was wise. Anything that does not have these properties could not possibly be Socrates. There are other properties that Socrates has, of course, for example, the fact that he had a wart on his nose. But this is not an essential property. (Aristotle calls it an *accident* or an *accidental property*.) Socrates still would have been Socrates without it. But Socrates could not have been a centipede, for it is part of his essence to be human.

In working out the notion of essence, Aristotle also evolves his theory of change. The essence of a thing cannot change (or it would no longer be the same thing), and it is of little metaphysical importance if accidents change. So what does change? It is here that Aristotle introduces a distinction that is familiar to us now, but that was difficult to make out in his day. It is the distinction between *form* and *matter*. (Notice that "form" is written with a small *f* here, although Aristotle uses the same word as Plato, *eidos*. His word for matter is *hylē*.) Form and matter, he says, can be distinguished everywhere in nature, but the best examples can be found in human craftsmanship. One can take a lump of clay, for example, and make it into a bowl of any number of shapes. Or one can take a piece of silver and make it into a fork, a spoon, a bracelet, or a couple of rings. The clay or the silver is the matter; the shape and the function define the form. But Aristotle also says that the matter itself can be analyzed in terms of form and matter. The matter of the clay and the silver would be the basic elements—earth, air, fire, and water. The form would be the shape and proportion these elements assume to make clay or silver. Indeed, Aristotle even holds that the basic elements themselves can be analyzed in terms of more primitive matter—hotness, coldness, dryness, and wetness—which combine to give the form of the elements. It is the form of things that we can know and explain, according to Aristotle, never the matter. But it is the matter of things that stays the same when things change; it is the form that changes. Thus, by changing their form, tadpoles turn into frogs, and seeds into fruits and flowers, while the matter stays (more or less) the same. In a sense, the essence of a frog is already present in the tadpole and of a fruit in its seed.

You may already anticipate certain troubles that will plague later philosophers. How much can we change a person, for example, and still have him or her be the same? provide a haircut? a college education? a ten-year jail sentence? a sex change operation? But before we worry about such problems, let us appreciate the importance of this notion of essence in Aristotle's philosophy. With it, he can do everything that Plato wanted to do with his special notion of Forms, but without invoking anything other-worldly. According to Aristotle, we can know that Socrates is a man, for instance, just because the essence of Socrates includes the property of being a man. We can know that a horse is an animal because the essence of being a horse includes the property of being an animal. In Plato, a conceptual truth of this kind was a truth about eternal Forms; for Aristotle, it is the form that changes, and a conceptual truth is rather a statement about essences.

In Chapter 2, we shall see why the two concepts of substance and essence are so important to later philosophy. But for now, let us turn to a much more exciting aspect of Aristotle's philosophy, his cosmology. It has inspired literally thousands of great thinkers, notably Saint Thomas Aquinas, who used Aristotle's metaphysics to build one of the great theological systems of Christianity.

To understand Aristotle's cosmology, we have to begin with a notion that is extremely foreign to people today; it is that the universe as a whole, and all things in it, have a purpose, a goal. The Greek word for "purpose" or "goal" is *telos*, and Aristotle's view is called **teleology.** Teleology can be directly contrasted with our modern scientific view of reality, which is primarily a *causal* view. Teleology explains something by looking for its purpose, goal, or end; causal explanations seek to understand *how* something came about, not *why* it came about. If you were asked why a frog has a heart, for example, the teleological answer would be "in order to keep it alive, by pumping the blood through its body." The causal answer, on the other hand, would be an explanation of the genetics, the evolutionary process, the development of the frog. If you were asked why a plant turns its leaves towards the sunlight, the teleological answer would be "in order to face the sun." The causal explanation, instead, would refer you to the fact that the cells grow faster on one side of the stem and that certain light-sensitive chemicals do such-and-such, and so on. In modern science, a causal answer is always preferable, and if a teleological answer is allowed at all it is always with the qualification that either there is an underlying causal explanation, or we do not yet have (but someday will have) an adequate causal explanation. In Aristotle's metaphysics, on the other hand, one does not have an explanation at all unless one knows what purpose a thing or an event serves. "Nature does nothing in vain" is the motto of the teleologist.[8]

Aristotle believed that every substance, every individual thing whether human, animal, vegetable, or mineral, had its own internal principles, certain tendencies that were part of its essence. This was, for example, the basis of his famous theory of falling objects, which was not refuted for two thousand years (by Galileo and others). Every object has its "place," and if that object is moved, it will return to its rightful place on its own power. That means that any object of sufficient size, whose place is on (or under) the ground, will fall toward the earth immediately if it is lifted into the air. And larger objects, which are not slowed down by the air's resistance, will fall faster than smaller ones. Indeed, this seemed so inherently reasonable to Aristotle and everyone around him that it never occurred to them to test it under experimental conditions. But gravitation, which Newton would not discover for another two millennia, is essentially a causal concept. Aristotle's explanation was a teleological one, which the Greeks found far more convincing. Moreover, even if they had had the equipment for a test, which they did not, the Greeks still might not have believed the answer, for they trusted their reasoning far more than they trusted experience.

A reader who begins Aristotle may be initially confused by his use of the word "cause" *(aition)* to include not only what we have been calling causal explanation but teleological accounts as well. In fact, Aristotle lists four different kinds of **cause,** all of which together explain why a thing is as it is at any given time. The first of these is the matter that makes it up, the **material cause,** the silver in the spoon or the flesh and blood that make up our bodies. The second is the principle or law by which it is made, the **formal cause,** the architect's blueprint or the craftsman's model. The third is what we would call "the cause," which Aristotle calls the **efficient cause,** the person or event that actually makes something happen, by doing something — pushing a button, working at a project, calling the person in charge. Fourth, there is the purpose of the thing, its **final cause,** its **telos.** Now notice that Aristotle's four causes are better suited for explaining human activities than giving what we would call scientific explanations about things that happen in nature. But this is indeed Aristotle's paradigm, and he even says in *Physics,*[9] "If purpose is present in art, it must also be present in nature." It is the final cause that provides us with the most important explanation.

We can understand this without any difficulty when we are explaining human activities. We want to know, first of all, what purpose a person has in

[8]Aristotle rejected a theory of natural selection argued by Empedocles 2300 years before Darwin because it was not a teleological theory.
[9]Aristotle, *Physics*, trans. W. D. Ross (Oxford: Oxford University Press, 1936).

doing something. But when it comes to nature, we do not generally ask about purpose, but are more likely to ask about (efficient) causes. We might ask of an animal, what purpose is served by a long neck, or certain features in its feet, or some kind of fur, but we are less likely to ask that of a plant and would find such a question unintelligible with reference to rocks, clouds, and stars. Aristotle and his fellow Greeks would not find this unintelligible at all. Indeed, he believed (and thousands of scientists followed him until the seventeenth century) that everything that existed had to be accounted for in terms of its inner purposes and the overall purpose it served in nature. ·Thus a magnet literally "attracts" little pieces of metal, and the stars really do have a purpose in their heavenly wanderings. And not only do all the things and creatures of the universe have their purposes, but the universe itself has its purpose too. Indeed, it is this ultimate purpose of the universe that gives all the particular things their significance. Indeed, for Aristotle, the idea that the universe as a whole might *not* have a purpose would have been absurd. And one of his most famous arguments is aimed at showing why there must be an ultimate purpose, a "first (Final) cause," or what he calls, "the prime mover."

> Moreover, it is obvious that there is some first principle, and that the causes of things are not infinitely many either in a direct sequence or in kind. For the material generation of one thing from another cannot go on in an infinite progression (e.g. flesh from earth, earth from air, air from fire, and so on without a stop); nor can the source of motion (e.g. man be moved by air, air by the sun, the sun by Strife, with no limit to the series). In the same way neither can the Final Cause [that is, purposes] recede to infinity — walking having health for its object, and health happiness, and happiness something else: one thing always being done for the sake of another. And it is just the same with the Formal Cause [that is, the essence]. For in the case of all intermediate terms of a series which are contained between a first and last term, the prior term is necessarily the cause of those which follow it; because if we had to say which of the three is the cause, we should say "the first." At any rate it is not the last term, because what comes at the end is not the cause of anything. Neither, again, is the intermediate term, which is only the cause of one (and it makes no difference whether there is one intermediate term or several, nor whether they are infinite or limited in number). But of series which are infinite in this way, and in general of the infinite, all the parts are equally intermediate, down to the present moment. Thus if there is no first term, there is no cause at all.[10]

The argument, simply stated, is that teleological explanations cannot go on forever, or what philosophers sometimes call an **infinite regress.** For Aristotle, if x exists for the purpose of y and y exists for the purpose of z, there must

[10]Aristotle, *Metaphysics*, trans. Hugh Tredennick (Cambridge, Mass.: Harvard University Press, 1933).

be some ultimate purpose that will explain them all. A similar argument can be made with regard to efficient causes, that if *p* makes *q* happen and *r* makes *p* happen and so on, there must be an end to the "and so on," and so too with the material cause and the formal cause. But the most exciting aspect of this infinite regress argument is the idea that the universe itself must have a purpose, a Final cause, a "prime mover" that Aristotle characterizes as "pure thought, thinking about itself." It is an obscure but intriguing idea, which was taken up by Christian theology as an apt characterization of the Christian God (see Chapter 6). But Aristotle's prime mover has few of the characteristics of the Judeo-Christian-Islamic God; he (it) did not create the universe and has no special concern for man. The prime mover is more of a metaphysical necessity than a proper object of worship. But it is not too far-fetched to say that Aristotle, like most of the Greeks, viewed the universe as something like a cosmic organism, with an ultimate purpose, whose ultimate goal was thinking itself.

We can appreciate how this cosmology would become a source of inspiration for a great many philosophers, poets, and religious people. In more recent centuries, for example, it was used as a welcome alternative to the "nuts and bolts" materialism of modern Newtonian science (as we shall see in Leibniz). Tied to the technical details of Aristotle's ontology is an extremely imaginative cosmology; the picture of a purposeful universe, developing according to its own goals and principles. It is a fascinating picture and still an attractive alternative to the lifeless picture of the physical universe that is so central to our modern scientific outlook.

TWO IMPORTANT ASSUMPTIONS

We have just reviewed the two greatest metaphysical theories in the history of human thought. With Plato, humanity first began to appreciate the extent to which its world was structured by abstract Forms. With Aristotle, people began to realize the significance of language in structuring that world. But despite their intimate connections, Plato and Aristotle offer us very different **paradigms** (that is, ideal examples) of the nature of metaphysics. In Plato there is the leap into the realm of pure Forms, the thrill of esoteric argument, and the elegance of the proofs against common sense. In Aristotle, there is always the anchor of common sense and everyday experience, the cautious and piecemeal analysis of the concepts we use every day in talking about our world, in Aristotle's view, the only world. In an important sense, the history of philosophy is the interplay of these two paradigms. And philosophy is still very much involved in a debate between the two.

Before we skip two millennia to modern times, it is important that we make explicit two assumptions or presuppositions that have been generally accepted until very recently. These were assumed by the Pre-Socratics from the very start of their venture; they were accepted by Plato and Aristotle and would be presupposed by most medieval and modern philosophers as well. Those assumptions are:

1) The world is intelligible. Every attempt to understand the world presupposes that the world can be understood, and understood by us. Another way of stating this is to say that all metaphysics assumes that our thought is adequate to understanding the world, or at least, to understanding the limits of our understanding (as, for example, in our attempts to understand God). It is this faith in thought as a guide to reality that Heraclitus was groping for with his *logos*, a first crude approximation of the doctrine that "thought" is a dependable guide to "Being." Plato assumed that thought could discover the world of Being. Aristotle, who didn't accept Plato's two-worlds view, nevertheless accepted Plato's confidence that an examination of the language we speak will allow us to discover truths about reality. So too, metaphysicians from Thales to Alfred North Whitehead in our own century have made the same assumption: Language and thought are more or less accurate vehicles for representing and recognizing reality, and that reality is thereby intelligible to us.

It is only very recently that this assumption has been seriously questioned. Without this assumption an embarrassing doubt arises. Why should we suppose that what we describe as the way the world really is is anything more than an autobiographical account of the only way that we can describe it? Perhaps our view of the world is determined by the structures and limitations of the language we learned from our parents and peers? Moreover, how can we even know that reality has any "structure" at all, apart from those structures that we impose upon it with our language? For example, could it not be that the distinctions Aristotle applies to reality are nothing other than a reflection of the structure of the Greek language? And could not the necessary truths we discover about reality be nothing other than the conceptual truths that are built right into the meanings of our words? Here the skeptic is armed with a particularly powerful set of arguments. If we give up the assumption that our language mirrors reality, then we must face the skeptic and we can never be assured of having a grasp of "the way the world really is" at all. For this reason, most philosophers have always felt compelled to hold on to this important assumption. Descartes, for example, though he tried to doubt everything, never for a second doubted the trustworthiness of his own language. But today, such leading scientist-philosophers as Albert Einstein have insisted that the intelligibility of the universe is itself a problem, a problem surmounted only by faith.

2) It is usually assumed that all statements about reality in metaphysics are **necessary truths.** Several times we have mentioned the fact that metaphysical claims are not simply statements about "the way the world really is" but actually claims about "the way the world *must* be." Every statement in metaphysics, in other words, must be taken as if the reality it described had to be that way, according to some rational principle or reason. This is what Descartes

required of his "first principles." He demanded that they be "perfectly certain," and he insisted throughout his philosophy that the only truths really worth the honorific title of "knowledge" were those that could be known beyond all possible doubt. In Plato, we saw that necessary truth was the earmark of reality, eternal and unchanging. And in Aristotle, although the matter becomes more subtle, it is clear that he considered all of his principles — even his principles of natural science — as matters of necessity. This emphasis on necessity is of tremendous importance. We shall devote two later chapters to it (Chapters 4 and 5).

SUMMARY AND CONCLUSION

Metaphysics is the study of ultimate reality, the attempt to find out the way the world really is. The first recognized metaphysical theory in Western philosophy is Thales' suggestion that everything is ultimately made of water. After Thales, a number of schools of metaphysics suggested alternative theories, all of them depending on the speculative powers of human reason and diverging in various and important ways from "common sense." But these thinkers were not only the first significant Western philosophers; they were also the first theoretical scientists, anticipating in many ways some of the most sophisticated theories of contemporary physics, astronomy, and chemistry.

The first turning point in Western metaphysics came with Socrates, although Socrates himself was more interested in moral issues than in metaphysics as such. Socrates' student, Plato, and his student in turn, Aristotle, became the first great systematic metaphysicians, and philosophy ever since has been deeply indebted to them. Plato introduced an elaborate theory in which ultimate reality consisted of Forms, in contrast with the particular and changing things of everyday life. To support this "two-worlds" theory of Forms versus individual things, he offered a theory of learning, a "theory of recollection," in which he argued that the human soul is immortal and that each of us already knows, in some sense, what we appear to learn in our lives. Aristotle argues instead that only individual things deserve the ultimate claim to reality, for these individual things are the primary substances. Since Aristotle, metaphysicians have typically used the term "substance" as the name of the basic entities that compose reality.

GLOSSARY

animism: the view that things (or, at the extreme, all things) are alive. It may also be the view that the universe as a whole is one gigantic organism.

Becoming: (In Plato) the "world of Becoming" is the changing world of our daily experience, in which things and people come into being and pass away.

Being: (In Plato) the "world of Being" is the realm of eternal Forms, in which nothing ever changes. It is, for him, reality, and, in general, Being is used by philosophers to refer to whatever they consider ultimately real (substance, God).

cause: that which brings something about. Philosophers usually add, "as a matter of necessity." In Aristotle, "cause" means something like "reason," and he distinguishes four different kinds of "causes" of a change: (1) the *formal* cause, the principle or essential idea according to which a change comes about (think of a blueprint for a building, or the plans for a project); (2) the *material* cause, the matter that undergoes the change (think of the raw materials for building a house — lumber, bricks, cement); (3) the *efficient* cause, that which initiates the change (the construction workers and their tools); (4) the *final* cause, or the purpose of the change (to build a place where Socrates and his family can live, for example).

conceptual truth: a statement that is true and that we can see to be true by virtue of the meanings of the words (or we should say, the "concepts") that compose it. For example, "a horse is an animal" is a conceptual truth because anyone who speaks English and knows the meanings of the words "horse" and "animal" knows that such a statement must be true. (We shall discuss such statements in greater detail in Chapters 4 and 5.) In Plato, a conceptual truth is a truth about Forms. In Aristotle, a conceptual truth is a matter of describing the essence of a thing. (See *Form*, *essence*.).

cosmology: the study of the universe in its entirety (from the Greek word for "universe" — "*cosmos*").

essence: the necessary or defining characteristics or properties of a thing. "That which makes a thing what it is," in other words, those features which one must list in a definition or uniquely identifying description. (For example, the fact that Socrates is a man is part of his essence, the fact that he never smoked on Saturdays is not.)

Form: (In Plato) an independently existing entity in the world of Being, which determines the nature of the particular things of this world. In Aristotle, forms have no independent existence.

Idea: In Plato, a Form.

immaterialism: the metaphysical view that accepts the existence of nonspatial, nonsensory entities such as numbers, minds and ideas. The weak version asserts merely that there are such entities. The strong version asserts that there are *only* such entities (that is, there are no physical objects).

immortality: the idea that the soul survives death (and, in some belief systems, precedes birth).

infinite regress: a sequence going back endlessly. For example, "A is caused by B, and B by C, and C by D . . . and so on to infinity." Aristotle believed such a regress to be an intellectual absurdity.

innate ideas: knowledge that is "programmed" into us from birth and need not be learned. Experience may be necessary to "trigger off" such ideas, but they are already "in" all of us. In Plato, the theory of innate ideas is part of a general theory of the immortality of the soul.

materialism: the metaphysical view that only physical matter and its properties exist. Such intangible entities as numbers, minds, and ideas are really properties of physical bodies. To talk about energy, for example, is, in a way, to talk about physical potential; to talk about minds is, as a kind of shorthand, to talk about behavior; to talk about ideas is, in a misleading way, to talk about the various structures and interrelationships between objects. Numbers have no existence of their own but only represent sets of sets of objects (the set of all sets of eight things is the number eight, for example). Materialism has always been a powerful world view in modern scientific culture. It was also the most common view among the Pre-Socratic philosophers.

metaphysics: most simply, the study of the most basic (or "first") principles. Traditionally, the study of ultimate reality, or "Being as such." Popularly, any kind of very abstract or obscure thinking. Most philosophers today would define metaphysics as the study of the most general concepts of science and human life, for example, "reality," "existence," "freedom," "God," "soul," "action," "mind." In general, we can divide metaphysics into: ontology, cosmology, and an ill-defined set of problems concerning God and the immortality of the human soul. (See *ontology, cosmology,* and Chapters 7–10.)

monism: the metaphysical view that there is ultimately only one substance, that all reality is one. Less strictly, it may be applied to philosophers who believe in only one kind of substance.

necessary truth: a statement which could not possibly be false under any conceivable circumstances; for instance, "2 + 2 = 4." (See Chapters 4 and 5.)

ontology: the study of being. That is, that part of metaphysics that asks such questions as "What is there?" "What is it for something to exist?" "What is an individual thing?" "How do things interact?" Traditionally, these questions were formulated as questions about substance (see page 52). Today, much of ontology is part of logic and linguistics and is the study of the concepts we use to discuss such matters. Sometimes ontology is used as a synonym for metaphysics, but usually the latter is the broader discipline.

paradigm: an ideal example. Philosophers often talk about "a paradigm such-and-such" or "a paradigm case of. . . ." For example, "a paradigm case of willpower is my getting up early on Sunday morning."

participation: Plato's obscure and unexplained relationship between the things of this world and the Forms of which they are manifestations. He tells us that individual things "participate" in their Forms.

pluralism: the metaphysical view that there are many distinct substances in the universe, and, perhaps, many different kinds of substances as well.

prime mover: in Aristotle's the "cause-of-itself," the first cause, which (Who) initiates all changes but is not itself (Himself) effected by anything prior. Aristotle believes there must be a prime mover if we are to avoid an infinite regress, which he considers an absurdity. Aristotle also refers to the prime mover as "God," and medieval philosophers (for example, St. Thomas Aquinas) have developed these views into Christian theology.

property: properties are generally distinguished from the substances in which they "inhere" by pointing to the fact that a property cannot exist without being a property of something; for example, there can be any number of red things but no redness that exists independently. (Many philosophers have challenged this idea, but this problem, which is called the "problem of universals," will not be discussed in this introductory course.)

reason: in our introduction, we defined "reason" as simply "the ability to think abstractly." In metaphysics, however, it often has a more controversial meaning, namely, that human ability to go beyond experience to determine, through thought alone, what reality is really like.

sophists: ancient Greek philosophers and teachers who believed that no reality exists except for what we take to be reality.

substance: the essential reality of a thing or things that underlies the various properties and changes of properties. Its most common definitions: "that which is independent and can exist by itself," and "the essence of a thing which does not and cannot change." In traditional metaphysics, substance is the same as "ultimate reality," and the study of substance is that branch of metaphysics that studies reality, namely, ontology. (See *essence, ontology*.)

teleology (teleological): the belief that all phenomena have a purpose, end, or goal (from the Greek *telos*, meaning "purpose"). Aristotle's metaphysics is a teleology, which means that he believes that the universe itself — and consequently everything in it — operates for purposes and can be explained according to goals.

2

Reality: Two Modern Views

The greatest good is the knowledge of the union which the mind has with the whole of nature.

Benedictus de Spinoza

The best way to learn modern metaphysics is to study the works of the great philosophers. We can also study the problems of ontology and cosmology as separate subjects, but then what is lost is the most striking aspect of metaphysics — the sense of system that ties these separate problems together and distinguishes the great metaphysicians from lesser philosophical technicians. It is within the scope of such all-encompassing systems or world views that these problems are unified into a matter of deep intellectual and cultural concern. Accordingly, an excellent way to get a sense of modern metaphysics is to study the works of two of the most systematic and brilliant philosophers following Descartes. The first is a Jewish philosopher, excommunicated for his heresies, who lived his life in poverty on the outskirts of Amsterdam. He is Benedictus[1] de Spinoza (1632–1677). The second is his slightly younger contemporary, Gottfried Wilhelm von Leibniz (1646–1716), Germany's first great modern philosopher. Together, they present us with the best possible lesson in modern metaphysics.

Modern metaphysics begins with Descartes, his insistence upon perfect certainty and mathematical deduction as the legitimate methodology. But methodology aside, metaphysics is a continuous enterprise from the Greeks through medieval philosophy, with Descartes its direct heir. We should not be surprised, for example, to find that the central concept of Descartes's metaphysics is *substance*, and that his definition of it (and the term itself) comes straight from Aristotle: "a thing existing in such a manner that it has need of no other thing in

---

[1]Born Baruch: he changed his name after he was excommunicated from the Jewish faith.

order to exist." Both Spinoza and Leibniz follow Descartes in taking substance as their central concept, and they follow him also in their method. (The three philosophers are usually grouped together as a single school of thought often called *Rationalism.*)

At first glance, the problems of modern metaphysics appear to be the same that faced the Pre-Socratics: How many substances are there? What are they? How are individuals distinguished? How do different things (or substances) interact? How does substance come into being? Is there a beginning to the universe? But two momentous changes in the intervening centuries forced modern philosophers to deal with problems that had barely even occurred to Greek philosophers.

The long and powerful hold of Christianity had given immaterialism (including the immortality of the human soul and the existence of a spiritual God) a status it had only rarely enjoyed in materialistic Greece. Accordingly, few philosophers held to the ancient view that only material "stuff" existed, that is, the view we call materialism. It was now obligatory for any philosopher to account for those mysterious immaterial entities, minds. And, of course, God. Descartes's metaphysics, for example, began by acknowledging two kinds of "created substances," one physical, one mental. And then there was one (and only one) "uncreated substance" — God. Other philosophers, Leibniz for one, went so far as to argue that there were only immaterial substances. Such a position is now called **idealism.** In modern philosophy, materialism ("it's all matter, never mind") and idealism ("it's all in the mind, no matter") have been fighting it out for three centuries. Idealism typically carries with it a religious conviction, for the concept of mind and the concept of spirit are never far apart. (In German, for example, they are the same word, *Geist.*) Materialism, on the other hand, usually draws its power from the remarkable advancements in the sciences, and here we find our second momentous change.

With the rise of modern science, it became the generally accepted view that the universe was a giant machine, perhaps set up by God, but in any case a well-coordinated and predictable mechanism. Isaac Newton's discovery of the causal laws of motion and gravity only brought to a climax a scientific world-view that had been in the making for centuries. And though ancient animism was still alive and belief in God and spirituality was still virtually universal, the modern mechanical view of reality was an absolutely unavoidable consideration for any metaphysician.

Both Spinoza and Leibniz fully appreciated this modern scientific view, although they interpreted it very differently. They were both religious men. (Spinoza, ironically, was branded an atheist and his philosophy banned from most of Europe.) They both accepted Descartes's "rationalist," deductive method and both developed their thinking along the lines of a geometrical system. They both began by considering the concept of substance. Yet Spinoza emerged as a monist, Leibniz as a pluralist. In viewing their impressive systems of thought, it is important to keep in mind the long history we have quickly reviewed, the powerful influences of Christianity and science and, most importantly, the various metaphysical problems to which we were introduced in the preceding chapter.

BENEDICTUS DE SPINOZA

Spinoza's *Ethics* is one of the few modern works that is accepted as an unqualified classic by virtually everyone in philosophy. It is the author's only major work. Spinoza was an avid political reformer, particularly on the issue of religious toleration, and even in liberal Amsterdam, that made him a dangerous person to know. The following work, which, as you will see, is much more than a study in "ethics," was his most forceful contribution to the issue of tolerance. Spinoza introduced a shockingly radical re-interpretation of God and his relation to the universe. He also gave an equally shocking theory of our roles in the universe. So while you are attempting to comprehend these difficult statements and proofs about "substance," keep your mind open for the dramatic changes in the way Spinoza teaches us to look at our world.

As in geometry, Spinoza begins with a set of definitions:

from *Ethics,*
by Spinoza

DEFINITIONS

I. By that which is *self-caused,* I mean that of which the essence involves existence, or that of which the nature is only conceivable as existent.

II. A thing is called *finite after its kind,* when it can be limited by another thing of the same nature; for instance, a body is called finite because we always conceive another greater body. So, also, a thought is limited by another thought, but a body is not limited by thought, nor a thought by body.

III. By *substance,* I mean that which is in itself, and is conceived through itself: in other words, that of which a conception can be formed independently of any other conception.

IV. By *attribute,* I mean that which the intellect perceives as constituting the essence of substance.

V. By *mode,* I mean the modifications of substance, or that which exists in, and is conceived through, something other than itself.

VI. By *God,* I mean a being absolutely infinite — that is, a substance consisting in infinite attributes, in which each expresses eternal and infinite essentiality.

VII. That thing is called free, which exists solely by the necessity of its own nature, and of which the action is determined by itself alone. On the other hand, that thing is necessary, or rather constrained, which is determined by something external to itself to a fixed and definite method of existence or action.

VIII. By *eternity,* I mean existence itself, in so far as it is conceived necessarily to follow solely from the definition of that which is eternal.[2]

---

[2]Benedictus de Spinoza, *Ethics,* in *The Rationalists,* trans. R. H. M. Elwes (New York: Doubleday, 1960). All subsequent quotations from Spinoza are from this edition of *Ethics.*

These definitions sound much more forbidding than they really are. Notice first how many of these terms and definitions are familiar to us from Aristotle: for example, the definition of substance as the basic "stuff" that has various properties but is dependent only on itself and can be thought of without thinking of anything else. **Attributes** and **modes,** on the other hand, are properties: attributes consist of essential characteristics of a substance; modes are modifications of attributes. (For example, having a body is an attribute of substance; being blond and blue-eyed are merely modes.) The **cause-of-itself** is like Aristotle's prime mover, but with some very important differences. Spinoza's "mover" turns out to be identical to the universe, and Spinoza's "God" is much more than "thought thinking itself," as in Aristotle. But the basic starting point of the entire system, as summarized in these definitions and axioms, is the Aristotelian notion of substance. Like the ancient metaphysicians, Spinoza insists that whatever really exists, exists eternally (Def. VIII). But that also means—there can be no Creation and no Creator!

As in geometry, the definitions are followed by a set of *axioms*, that is, principles that are so obvious that they need no defense. In plane geometry, such an axiom would be "the shortest distance between two points is a straight line." Spinoza's axioms may not seem quite so obvious at first glance, partly because of the unfamiliarity of his metaphysical terminology.

AXIOMS

I. Everything which exists, exists either in itself or in something else.

II. That which cannot be conceived through anything else must be conceived through itself.

III. From a given definite cause an effect necessarily follows; and, on the other hand, if no definite cause be granted, it is impossible that an effect can follow.

IV. The knowledge of an effect depends on and involves the knowledge of a cause.

V. Things which have nothing in common cannot be understood, the one by means of the other; the conception of one does not involve the conception of the other.

VI. A true idea must correspond with its ideate or object.

VII. If a thing can be conceived as non-existing, its essence does not involve existence.

You can see that the axioms follow approximately the same sequence as the definitions, and the axioms in most cases are based on the definitions, although they do not strictly follow from them. For example, Axiom 1, like Definition 1, concerns the idea that everything has an explanation. Definition 1, although stated in terms of "cause" ("self-caused"), concerns that which must exist if it can just be thought of. Axiom 1 says that everything must either be explainable through itself (that is, "self-caused") or through something else. Similarly, Definition 2 uses a technical term ("finite after its kind") to talk about things that can be explained only by reference to something greater, while Axiom 2 says that anything that cannot be so explained must be explained simply in terms of itself ("self-caused" again). Axioms 3 and 4 outline the basic principles of cause and effect; that is, that a cause makes its effect happen necessarily, and without the cause, there would be no effect, and that the knowledge of the effect depends on knowing the cause. (These principles have had a long and important history in both metaphysics and theories of science and knowledge. They will play a key role in Spinoza's theory of determinism [the idea that everything happens necessarily because of its causes] and in "deterministic" theories generally. These will be discussed in Chapter 9 in detail.) Axioms 5–7 return to the central theme of explanation begun in Axioms 1 and 2; Axiom 5 insists that one thing can be explained in terms of another only if they have "something in common." Thus you explain one physical event in terms of another physical event (since they have in common certain physical properties). Axiom 6 repeats the important assumption we made explicit at the end of Chapter 1, namely, that our ideas are capable of grasping reality. (This axiom also states a seemingly innocent theory of truth, often called "the correspondence theory of truth," which says that "a true idea corresponds with some actual fact [*ideate* or *object*] in the world." This is discussed in Chapter 4.) Axiom 7 returns to the idea of "essence involving existence," in other words, that which is self-caused, or substance or God. Axiom 7 is stated negatively, however, and says that if we can think of something as not existing (for example, we can imagine what it would be like to live in a world without freeways, or without stars, or even without other people) then "its essence does not involve existence." That is, existing is not one of its essential characteristics and it is not "self-caused."

The general theme of the axioms, therefore, is that everything has an explanation for its existence, either by reference to something else or because it is "self-caused" or self-explanatory, that is, its "essence involves its existence" or it is entirely "in itself and conceived through itself." This last phrase is from the definition of "substance" (Definition 3), so you can see how, even in his axioms and definitions, Spinoza is setting up his main thesis, that there can only be one substance.

Starting with these definitions and axioms, which he takes to be unobjectionable, Spinoza begins the "proofs" of his "propositions," which follow like the theorems of Euclidean geometry from the definitions of terms like "line," "point," and "parallel." Again, these look forbidding, but their philosophical relevance should be clear.

PROPOSITIONS

PROP. I. *Substance is by nature prior to its modifications.*
Proof. — This is clear from Deff. iii. and v.
PROP. II. *Two substances, whose attributes are different, have nothing in common.*

Proof.—Also evident from Def. iii. For each must exist in itself, and be conceived through itself; in other words, the conception of one does not imply the conception of the other.

PROP. III. *Things which have nothing in common cannot be one the cause of the other.*

Proof.—If they have nothing in common, it follows that one cannot be apprehended by means of the other (Ax. v.), and, therefore, one cannot be the cause of the other (Ax. iv.). *Q.E.D.* [Latin, *quod erat demonstrandum*, a phrase used in traditional logic meaning "thus it is proven."]

PROP. IV. *Two or more distinct things are distinguished one from the other either by the difference of the attributes of the substances, or by the difference of their modifications.*

Proof.—Everything which exists, exists either in itself or in something else (Ax. i.),—that is (by Deff. iii. and v.), nothing is granted in addition to the understanding, except substance and its modifications. Nothing is, therefore, given besides the understanding, by which several things may be distinguished one from the other, except the substances, or, in other words (see Ax. iv.), their attributes and modifications. *Q.E.D.*

PROP. V. *There cannot exist in the universe two or more substances having the same nature or attribute.*

Proof.—If several distinct substances be granted, they must be distinguished one from the other, either by the difference of their attributes, or by the difference of their modifications (Prop. iv.). If only by the difference of their attributes, it will be granted that there cannot be more than one with an identical attribute. If by the difference of their modifications—as substance is naturally prior to its modifications (Prop. i.),—it follows that setting the modifications aside, and considering substance in itself, that is truly, (Deff. iii. and vi.), there cannot be conceived one substance different from another,—that is (by Prop. iv.), there cannot be granted several substances, but one substance only. *Q.E.D.*

PROP. VI. *One substance cannot be produced by another substance.*

Proof.—It is impossible that there should be in the universe two substances with an identical attribute, *i.e.* which have anything common to them both (Prop. ii.), and, therefore (Prop. iii.), one cannot be the cause of another, neither can one be produced by the other. *Q.E.D.*

Corollary.—Hence it follows that a substance cannot be produced by anything external to itself. For in the universe nothing is granted, save substances and their modifications (as appears from Ax. i. and Deff. iii. and v.). Now (by the last Prop.) substance cannot be produced by another substance, therefore it cannot be produced by anything external to itself. *Q.E.D.* This is shown still more readily by the absurdity of the contradictory. For, if substance be produced by an external cause, the knowledge of it would depend on the knowledge of its cause (Ax. iv.), and (by Def. iii.) it would itself not be substance.

So far, the main point is quite simple: if there is more than one substance, they could have no possible relation to each other. Therefore, by a kind of *reductio ad adsurdum* argument, there can only be one substance. In the propositions that follow (and especially the note to Prop. VIII), this is demonstrated again:

PROP. VII. *Existence belongs to the nature of substance.*

Proof.—Substance cannot be produced by anything external (Corollary, Prop. vi.), it must, therefore, be its own cause—that is, its essence necessarily involves existence, or existence belongs to its nature.

PROP. VIII. *Every substance is necessarily infinite.*

Proof.—There can only be one substance with an identical attribute, and existence follows from its nature (Prop. vii.); its nature, therefore, involves existence, either as finite or infinite. It does not exist as finite, for (by Def. ii.) it would then be limited by something else of the same kind, which would also necessarily exist (Prop. vii.); and there would be two substances with an identical attribute, which is absurd (Prop. v.). It therefore exists as infinite. *Q.E.D.*

Note.—No doubt it will be difficult for those who think about things loosely, and have not been accustomed to know them by their primary causes, to comprehend the demonstration of Prop. vii.: for such persons make no distinction between the modifications of substances and the substances themselves, and are ignorant of the manner in which things are produced; hence they attribute to substances the beginning which they observe in natural objects. Those who are ignorant of true causes, make complete confusion—think that trees might talk just as well as men—that men might be formed from stones as well as from seed; and imagine that any form might be changed into any other. So, also, those who confuse the two natures, divine and human, readily attribute human passions to the deity, especially so long as they do not know how passions originate in the mind. But, if people would consider the nature of substance, they would have no doubt about the truth of Prop. vii. In fact, this proposition would be a universal axiom, and accounted a truism. For, by substance, would be understood that which is in itself, and is conceived through itself—that is, something of which the conception requires not the conception of anything else; whereas modifications exist in something external to themselves, and a conception of them is formed by means of a conception of the thing in which they exist. Therefore, we may have true ideas of non-existent modifications; for, although they may have no *actual* existence apart from the conceiving intellect, yet their essence is so involved in something external to themselves that they may through it be conceived. Whereas the only truth substances can have, external to the intellect, must consist in their existence, because they are conceived through themselves. Therefore, for a person to say that he has a clear and distinct—that is, a true—idea of a substance, but that he is not sure whether such substance exists, would be the same as if he said that he had a true idea, but was not sure whether or not it was false (a little consideration will make this plain); or if anyone affirmed that substance is created, it would be the same as saying that a false idea was true—in short, the height of absurdity. It must, then, necessarily be admitted that the existence of substance as its essence is an eternal truth. And we can hence conclude by another process of reasoning—that there is but one such substance.

This last phrase summarizes the key doctrine of the entire *Ethics,* that there can be but one substance. The argument in this note, which insists that the essence of substance includes its existence, was a very popular argument throughout the Middle Ages. It means, quite simply, that if you can even imagine something whose essence includes existence, then you know that thing necessarily exists. In a further digression (but it is the digressions that often contain the most philosophy), Spinoza adopts Aristotle's insistence (see p. 72) that everything (or every event) must have its cause:

> There is necessarily for each individual existent thing a cause why it should exist.
> This cause of existence must either be contained in the nature and definition of the thing defined, or must be postulated apart from such definition.

It is such an assertion that gives Aristotle the basis for his "prime mover" argument. But Spinoza, unlike Aristotle, has no qualms about the idea of an "infinite regress"; and so, in his view, the universe extends back in time forever, has always existed, and at no time ever came into existence.

What then follows is the working-out of the notion that there is one substance:

> PROP. IX. *The more reality or being a thing has, the greater the number of its attributes* (Def. iv.).
> PROP. X. *Each particular attribute of the one substance must be conceived through itself.*
> *Proof.* — An attribute is that which the intellect perceives of substance, as constituting its essence (Def. iv.), and, therefore, must be conceived through itself (Def. iii.). *Q.E.D.*

Spinoza goes on to explain that, although we might think of different attributes separately (for example, think of minds and bodies as totally different from each other), we must not conclude that they are different substances. They are rather separate properties of one and the same substance. He then concludes that:

> Consequently it is abundantly clear, that an absolutely infinite being must necessarily be defined as consisting in infinite attributes, each of which expresses a certain eternal and infinite essence.
> If anyone now ask, by what sign shall he be able to distinguish different substances, let him read the following propositions, which show that there is but one substance in the universe, and that it is absolutely infinite, wherefore such a sign would be sought for in vain.

Now this looks complicated, but we can appreciate its straightforward significance by looking at it through our earlier questions in ontology and cosmology (p. 52): first, how many substances does Spinoza say that there are (and must be)? Only one — he is a monist, like the earliest Pre-Socratics. Descartes, Spinoza's immediate predecessor, had argued that there are three kinds of substance: bodies, minds, and God. Spinoza, however, argues that the very definition of substance makes it necessary that there be only one substance, and that bodies and minds are attributes of this one substance, not substances themselves. So the answer to our second ontological question, "what kind of substances?" is "one infinite substance," the full nature of which we cannot know. But at least we know two of its properties, namely body and mind. Now notice that this gets around a problem that will plague Descartes (see Chapter 8): How can different substances, which by definition are independent, interact with one another (our fourth question)? If mind and body are separate substances, then how can they come together to form a person? For Spinoza, since there is only one substance, this problem does not arise. With regard to our third question, "how do we distinguish different things (attributes, bodies, and minds)?" Spinoza's answer is fantastic; there is ultimately only one body, namely the physical universe, and one mind, namely all of the thinking in the universe (which in turn are different attributes of the one substance). This means that distinctions between our bodies ("my" body and "your" body) and between our bodies and the rest of the physical universe are ultimately unwarranted, a humanistic pretention that has no basis in reality. But even more surprising is the idea that there is but a single mind, and that our individual minds are somehow only "part of it" (that is, particular modes) but not individual minds at all! Your pride in your "individuality," therefore, has no foundation in reality. You are only a part of that one cosmic substance, the universe.

But the universe is also God. Here is where the innocent-looking obscurity of Spinoza's system becomes the heresy that was banned throughout Europe. By Proposition X, Spinoza has proved that God, substance, and the cause-of-itself are all identical. In the next few propositions, he proves that God necessarily exists (we shall see similar proofs in Chapter 6). Then, Proposition XIV: *"Besides God, no substance can be granted or conceived."* This means that God and the universe are one and the same. This position, called *pantheism* (literally, "everything is God"), was considered sacrilege, even in liberal Amsterdam. It means, against all traditional Judeo-Christian teachings, that God has no existence independent of the universe and that He therefore cannot be its Creator. Look again at the explanation to Definition VIII and then at Proposition XV and those that follow:

PROP. XV. *Whatsoever is, is in God, and without God nothing can be, or be conceived.*

PROP. XVI. *From the necessity of the divine nature must follow an infinite number of things in infinite ways—that is, all things which can fall within the sphere of infinite intellect.*

PROP. XVII. *God acts solely by the laws of his own nature, and is not constrained by anyone.*

PROP. XVIII. *God is the indwelling and not the transient cause of all things.*

PROP. XIX. *God, and all the attributes of God, are eternal.*

PROP. XX. *The existence of God and his essence are one and the same.*

PROP. XXI. *All things which follow from the absolute nature of any attribute of God must always exist and be infinite, or, in other words, are eternal and infinite through the said attribute.*

PROP. XXII. *Whatever follows from any attribute of God, in so far as it is modified by a modification, which exists necessarily and as infinite, through the said attribute, must also exist necessarily and as infinite.*

PROP. XXIII. *Every mode which exists both necessarily and as infinite must necessarily follow either from the absolute nature of some attribute of God, or from an attribute modified by a modification which exists necessarily and as infinite.*

PROP. XXIV. *The essence of things produced by God does not involve existence.*

PROP. XXV. *God is the efficient cause not only of the existence of things, but also of their essence.*

Yes, Spinoza believes in God. But God is nothing other than the universe. He has few of the characteristics traditionally attributed to Him and worshipped in Him. For example, Spinoza goes on to argue, on the basis of what he has said already, that God has no will, that He doesn't do anything, and ultimately, He doesn't care about anything either, including humanity. Here is a scientific world view that is so unrelenting that even Newton himself would be shocked by it. This does not mean that Spinoza is a materialist; quite to the contrary, the importance of his constant insistence upon "the infinite attributes of God," of which we are capable of knowing only two (could you imagine what some of the others might be like?) is to say that God has not only physical existence but (at least) mental existence as well. But where the scientific outlook becomes most dramatic is in Spinoza's defense of the doctrine we shall call **determinism,** the thesis that every event in the universe necessarily occurs as the result of its cause. The ultimate cause is God, which is to say, the universe itself. Once again, the terms come from Aristotle, but it is therefore important to insist that Spinoza does not believe — with either Aristotle or Christendom — that the universe has any purpose whatsoever. Nor does he believe that the universe or God has any beginning or end, thus answering our two sets of cosmological questions with a single necessary truth, once again, derived directly from the definition of substance.

The ultimate meaning of Spinoza's arguments for determinism is that no action, whether of man or God, is ever free. Everything in the universe, according to Spinoza, is exactly as it must be; the universe couldn't be any other way. Nothing is so pointless as struggling against a universe in which everything, including our own natures and actions, is already determined.

PROP. XXVI. *A thing which is conditioned to act in a particular manner has necessarily been thus conditioned by God; and that which has not been conditioned by God cannot condition itself to act.*

PROP. XXVII. *A thing, which has been conditioned by God to act in a particular way, cannot render itself unconditioned.*

PROP. XXVIII. *Every individual thing, or everything which is finite and has a conditioned existence, cannot exist or be conditioned to act, unless it be conditioned for existence and action by a cause other than itself, which also is finite and has a conditioned existence; and likewise this cause cannot in its turn exist or be conditioned to act, unless it be conditioned for existence and action by another cause, which also is finite and has a conditioned existence, and so on to infinity.*

PROP. XXIX. *Nothing in the universe is contingent, but all things are conditioned to exist and operate in a particular manner by the necessity of the divine nature.*[3]

PROP. XXX. *Intellect, in function finite, or in function infinite, must comprehend the attributes of God and the modifications of God, and nothing else.*

PROP. XXXI. *The intellect in function, whether finite or infinite, as will, desire, love, &c., should be referred to passive nature and not to active nature.*

PROP. XXXII. *Will cannot be called a free cause, but only a necessary cause.*

PROP. XXXIII. *Things could not have been brought into being by God in any manner or in any order different from that which has in fact obtained.* [God is determined too.]

PROP. XXXIV. *God's power is identical with his essence.*

PROP. XXXV. *Whatsoever we conceive to be in the power of God, necessarily exists.*

PROP. XXXVI. *There is no cause from whose nature some effect does not follow.*

Part II of the *Ethics* discusses "the Nature and Origin of the Mind." It begins with a further set of definitions and axioms, most importantly, the definition of body as "extended thing," that is, extended in space (which Spinoza got directly from Descartes and the medieval philosophers) and idea, "the mental conception which is formed by the mind as a thinking thing." Mind, unlike body, is defined as **unextended** (that is, it has no spatial dimensions). It is in this part that Spinoza argues those surprising doctrines that we have already summarized: Mind and body are each one of an infinite number of attributes of God, not substance themselves (as they were for Descartes), and that our individual minds are really indistinguishable modifications of the one Great Mind of the One Substance. And Spinoza joins with all of his metaphysical colleagues in insisting that "the order and connection of ideas is the same as the order and connection of things" (Prop. VII). Here again is Spinoza's affirmation of his confidence in thought to grasp reality. (Remember Heraclitus, "thought is Being.")

The upshot of Part II, and the subject that dominates the *Ethics* for the remaining three Parts, is Spinoza's determinism.

---

[3]We are all determined by the nature of God or the universe. But then, here is a problem: are we not then compelled to struggle, and can't help but doing so? If so, what is the point of Spinoza's urging us not to. This Spinoza never answers.

> PROP. XLVIII. *In the mind there is no absolute or free will; but the mind is determined to wish this or that by a cause, which has been determined by another cause, and this last by another cause, and so on to infinity.*

Spinoza has none of Aristotle's fears of an "infinite regress," and if he believes in a "cause-of-itself," that is not the same as a "first cause," for there is no such thing. We shall talk more about this "free will and determinism" problem in Chapter 9, but it is worth noting, as a way of summing up, Spinoza's drastic answer to the problem. As an unyielding determinist, he rejects every attempt to save some space for freedom of human action. But he assures us that we can, with heroic effort (Prop. XLVII), understand the nature of this determinism, and accept it gracefully. The folly is in the fighting, he tells us. The remainder of the *Ethics* is given over to the attempt to draw out the logical consequences of this stoic conclusion. Part III is a long argument against emotions and what we would call "emotional involvement" as the needless cause of suffering and vice. Against them, Spinoza argues the virtues of human reason, which penetrates the useless involvements of the emotions and allows us to understand the causes of our actions and feelings. And to understand an emotion, Spinoza believes, is to change and eliminate it. For example, to understand why one is angry, according to Spinoza, is sufficient to let us get rid of our anger. To realize that we are unable to change, according to Spinoza, is the only freedom we can really be said to have.

What you have just seen is modern metaphysics at its most brilliant. The geometrical method, however, is no longer fashionable, and much of Spinoza's language is, to us, antiquated and unnatural. But the intricacies of his system, the way he ties so many different ideas together, the answers he gave to ancient philosophical problems, and the boldness with which he sets out a new vision of the universe, have made Spinoza's philosophy widely appreciated despite his difficult style. What you are about to read, though, is no less astonishing, no less brilliant, and its author no less remarkable a genius. The work from which these excerpts come is a very short work (of about 90 paragraphs) written by Leibniz, who begins with much the same concepts and definitions as Spinoza, but ends up with a wholly different metaphysical system. (Leibniz and Spinoza met several times and discussed these issues. But Leibniz found Spinoza's opinions too shocking and acquaintanceship with him too dangerous.)

GOTTFRIED WILHELM VON LEIBNIZ

Leibniz begins with the same technical notion of substance, but from it he weaves an entirely different but equally fantastic picture of the universe. Where Spinoza's universe was mechanical and wholly dependent upon causes, Leibniz's universe is very much alive, and everything happens for a purpose (as in Aristotle's ancient teleology). The guiding principle of Leibniz's philosophy is called "The

Principle of Sufficient Reason," which says, simply, that there must be a reason for everything. Even God, on this account, cannot act capriciously, but must have a reason for whatever He has created. We shall see that this principle is among the most important guidelines to Leibniz's philosophy. From it, he develops a radical alternative to Isaac Newton's physics and a spectacularly optimistic view that, because God acts according to this principle, this world that He created must be "the best of all possible worlds."

Where Spinoza argues that there can be at most one substance, Leibniz argues that there are many. He calls them **monads.** Every monad is different from every other, and God (who is something of a supermonad and the only "uncreated monad") has created them all. The work presented here, accordingly, is called the *Monadology* ("the study of monads"), written in 1714. It is a very condensed summary of Leibniz's metaphysics:

> 1. The Monad, of which we will speak here, is nothing else than a simple substance, which goes to make up composites; by simple, we mean without parts.
> 2. There must be simple substances because there are composites; for a composite is nothing else than a collection or *aggregatum* of simple substances.[4]

A simple substance is one that cannot be divided. The argument is curious: any "composite" is obviously divisible. That means that every composite must be "composed" of some simple substances that make it up. (There is a hidden infinite regress argument here: if there weren't ultimately simple substances, then we could go on dividing things forever.) But if the simple substances were extended in space, then they too would be further divisible, for anything that has length, for example, no matter how small, can be cut in two (at least in theory). Therefore, Leibniz concludes, these basic simple substances or monads must be immaterial and have no extension. They can have neither parts, nor extension, nor divisibility:

> 3. Now, where there are no constituent parts there is possible neither extension, nor form, nor divisibility. These Monads are the true Atoms of nature, and, in fact, the Elements of things.

Here, in Leibniz's first three propositions, are the answers to our first two ontological questions: "How many substances are there?" Many. This answer makes Leibniz a pluralist. "What kind of substances are they?" Simple and immaterial substances, which makes Leibniz an *immaterialist*. (Don't be misled by the term "atoms": we are used to thinking of atoms as the smallest material substances,

---

[4]Gottfried W. von Leibniz, *Monadology*, in *The Rationalists*, trans. George Montgomery (New York: Doubleday, 1960). All subsequent quotations from Leibniz are from this edition of *Monadology*.

but Leibniz's atoms are *im*material.) And now, in three more propositions, Leibniz answers our first cosmological question: "Are these substances eternal, or do they come into being at some time? How do they come into being? And are they destructible?":

> 4. Their dissolution, therefore, is not to be feared and there is no way conceivable by which a simple substance can perish through natural means.
> 5. For the same reason there is no way conceivable by which a simple substance might, through natural means, come into existence, since it cannot be formed by composition.
> 6. We may say then, that the existence of Monads can begin or end only all at once, that is to say, the Monad can begin only through creation and end only through annihilation. Composites, however, begin or end gradually.

Spinoza had argued that the one substance could neither be created nor destroyed; it had neither beginning nor end. Leibniz's substances, or "monads," can be created or destroyed, but not by any "natural" means. They can be created or destroyed only "all at once." Anticipating later propositions, we can guess that Leibniz will have God (who is something of a supermonad) create them. But notice that compounds of monads, for example, "material objects," can be created and destroyed "naturally."

Now our third question, "How do we distinguish different substances or monads?":

> 8. Still Monads must have some qualities, otherwise they would not even be existences. And if simple substances did not differ at all in their qualities, there would be no means of perceiving any change in things. Whatever is in a composite can come into it only through its simple elements and the Monads, if they were without qualities, since they do not differ at all in quantity, would be indistinguishable one from another. For instance, if we imagine *a plenum* or completely filled space, where each part receives only the equivalent of its own previous motion, one state of things would not be distinguishable from another.
> 9. Each Monad, indeed, must be different from every other. For there are never in nature two beings which are exactly alike, and in which it is not possible to find a difference either internal or based on an intrinsic property.

Only God could actually know everything about every monad in order to compare and contrast them. But even God can distinguish different monads only because they in fact have differences between them. This leads Leibniz to suggest one of his most controversial principles, the so-called "Principle of the Identity of Indiscernibles": no two monads can have the same properties (Prop. 9). Why is this? According to the "Principle of Sufficient Reason" (Prop. 32) nothing can be without good reason. Even God, therefore, would have no good reason for duplicating any monad. If two monads were identical, Leibniz argues, God could have no reason for putting one in one place and the other in another place, or for creating them both in the first place. Therefore, no two monads could be exactly alike. A strange kind of argument, but very much at the heart of Leibniz's philosophy, as we shall see later.

How does a monad, which is by definition "simple," alter or combine with other monads to form the changing and familiar universe of our experience? (Here you should be reminded of the similar problems that faced the ancient Pre-Socratics and Plato.) Here is our fourth question, and the most difficult Leibniz has to answer: "How do substances interact?" By definition, monads cannot literally "interact." And so Leibniz's answer is extremely speculative and imaginative:

> 7. There is also no way of explaining how a Monad can be altered or changed in its inner being by any other created thing, since there is no possibility of transposition within it, nor can we conceive of any internal movement which can be produced, directed, increased or diminished there within the substance, such as can take place in the case of composites where a change can occur among the parts. The Monads have no windows through which anything may come in or go out.

The problem is that different substances, by definition, are independent and cannot, therefore, have anything to do with one another. Descartes, as we shall see in Chapter 8, had a terrible time getting together his two substances of mind and body. Spinoza, as a monist, solved the problem in the simplest possible way; since there is only one substance, no question of "interaction" is applicable. But Leibniz is a pluralist; there are many substances. They cannot interact as such. They cannot even perceive each other in the usual sense. They "have no windows," in his peculiar but now famous expression; "nothing can come in or go out." And unlike the ancient (and modern) materialist atomists, Leibniz cannot have his monads simply combine and recombine to form new compounds in any usual sense. They cannot, in Leibniz's words, "be altered or changed in [their] inner being by any other created thing." So, how do monads change? They must have all changes already created (by God) within themselves.

Remember the animism that was so prevalent in the ancient Greek philosophers. For them, the phenomenon of life was the model for metaphysics. The idea of Newtonian mechanics would have been incomprehensible to them. Leibniz, we may now say, was vehemently anti-Newton. He was, we may also say, one of the outstanding modern animists. A monad is as different as can be from a Newtonian material atom; a monad is alive, and its changes come from within, never from without. (Except, that is, for its initial creation.) Think of a monad as a living being, "programmed" (to use a modern word) with all of the information and experiences it needs to develop in a certain way, like an acorn developing into an oak tree. Thus the changes in the monad are all internal, programmed by God at the creation. Now keep in mind that a monad is immaterial, and so its "growth" cannot be thought of as a development in the physical world. The growth too, therefore, must be internal, and the apparent interaction between monads must really be changes in the perceptions of the monads themselves.

10. I assume it as admitted that every created being, and consequently the created Monad, is subject to change, and indeed that this change is continuous in each.

11. It follows from what has just been said, that the natural changes of the Monad come from an internal principle, because an external cause can have no influence upon its inner being.

12. Now besides this principle of change there must also be in the Monad a manifoldness which changes. This manifoldness constitutes, so to speak, the specific nature and the variety of the simple substances.

13. This manifoldness must involve a multiplicity in the unity or in that which is simple. For since every natural change takes place by degrees, there must be something which changes and something which remains unchanged, and consequently there must be in the simple substance a plurality of conditions and relations, even though it has no parts.

14. The passing condition which involves and represents a multiplicity in the unity, or in the simple substance, is nothing else than what is called Perception. This should be carefully distinguished from Consciousness.

Leibniz argues here that what we call interactions between things are really changes in perceptions; for example, what we are really talking about when we describe a squirrel climbing a tree is our perception of a squirrel climbing a tree. This makes Leibniz an idealist, for he is claiming that the sense in which material things exist in space is that we experience *(perceive)* them as existing. What is ultimately real, therefore, is perception, and it is perception that changes, within each monad, to create the appearance of a moving and changing material world. Notice that Leibniz carefully distinguishes "Perception" from what he calls "Consciousness." Perception is experience, in general, and is present, in some degree, in every monad. Consciousness, on the other hand, is a very special kind of experience, reflective and articulate, and is to be found only in a few monads. (It is worth noting that, with this distinction, Leibniz precociously introduces the concept of "the unconscious" into German philosophy two hundred years before Freud.)

15. The action of the internal principle which brings about the change or the passing from one perception to another may be called Appetition. It is true that the desire is not always able to attain to the whole of the perception which it strives for, but it always attains a portion of it and reaches new perceptions.

16. We, ourselves, experience a multiplicity in a simple substance, when we find that the most trifling thought of which we are conscious involves a variety in the object. Therefore all those who acknowledge that the soul is a simple substance ought to grant this multiplicity in the Monad. . . .

17. It must be confessed, however, that Perception, and that which depends upon it, are inexplicable by mechanical causes, that is to say, by

figures and motions. Supposing that there were a machine whose structure produced thought, sensation, and perception, we could conceive of it as increased in size with the same proportions until one was able to enter into its interior, as he would into a mill. Now, on going into it he would find only pieces working upon one another, but never would he find anything to explain Perception.

Here is the attack on Newton's more materialist view of the universe. Such a view, Leibniz complains, cannot account for experience (perception), in other words, the immaterial aspects of the universe.

It is accordingly in the simple substance, and not in the composite nor in a machine that the Perception is to be sought. Furthermore, there is nothing besides perceptions and their changes to be found in the simple substance. And it is in these alone that all the internal activities of the simple substance can consist.

18. All simple substances or created Monads may be called Entelechies, because they have in themselves a certain perfection. There is in them a sufficiency which makes them the source of their internal activities, and renders them, so to speak, incorporeal Automations. [In other words, every monad is alive, to a certain extent.]

19. If we wish to designate as soul everything which has perceptions and desires in the general sense that I have just explained, all simple substances or created Monads could be called souls. But since feeling is something more than a mere perception I think that the general name of Monad or Entelechy should suffice for simple substances which have only perception, while we may reserve the term Soul for those whose perception is more distinct and is accompanied by memory. [Again, Leibniz insists that "Perception" is most primitive and is common to all monads.]

20. We experience in ourselves a state where we remember nothing and where we have no distinct perception, as in periods of fainting, or when we are overcome by a profound, dreamless sleep. In such a state the soul does not sensibly differ at all from a simple Monad. As this state, however, is not permanent and the soul can recover from it, the soul is something more.

21. Nevertheless it does not follow at all that the simple substance is in such a state without perception. This is so because of the reasons given above; for it cannot perish, nor on the other hand would it exist without some affection and the affection is nothing else than its perception. When, however, there are a great number of weak perceptions where nothing stands out distinctively, we are stunned; as when one turns around and around in the same direction, a dizziness comes on, which makes him swoon and makes him able to distinguish nothing. Among animals, death can occasion this state for quite a period. [!]

22. Every present state of a simple substance is a natural consequence of its preceding state, in such a way that its present is pregnant with its future. [Here is Leibniz's version of the thesis that one cause necessarily follows another.]

23. Therefore, since on awakening after a period of unconsciousness we become conscious of our perceptions, we must, without having been con-

scious of them, have had perceptions immediately before; for one perception can come in a natural way only from another perception, just as a motion can come in a natural way only from a motion.

24. It is evident from this that if we were to have nothing distinctive, or so to speak prominent, and of a higher flavor in our perceptions, we should be in a continual state of stupor. This is the condition of Monads which are wholly bare.

25. We see that nature has given to animals heightened perceptions, having provided them with organs which collect numerous rays of light or numerous waves of air and thus make them more effective in their combination. Something similar to this takes place in the case of smell, in that of taste and of touch, and perhaps in many other senses which are unknown to us.

.   .   .   .   .

29. It is the knowledge of eternal and necessary truths that distinguishes us from mere animals and gives us reason and the sciences, thus raising us to a knowledge of ourselves and of God. This is what is called in us the Rational Soul or the Mind.

30. It is also through the knowledge of necessary truths and through abstractions from them that we come to perform Reflective Acts, which cause us to think of what is called the I, and to decide that this or that is within us. It is thus, that in thinking upon ourselves we think of *being*, of *substance*, of the *simple* and *composite*, of a *material* thing and of *God* himself, conceiving that what is limited in us is in him without limits. These Reflective Acts furnish the principal objects of our reasonings.

The answer to our fourth question is, "Monads don't interact." Each is locked into itself, and contains within itself its own view of the universe as a whole.

56. Now this interconnection, relationship, or this adaptation of all things to each particular one, and of each one to all the rest, brings it about that every simple substance has relations which express all the others and that it is consequently a perpetual living mirror of the universe.

57. And as the same city regarded from different sides appears entirely different, and is, as it were multiplied respectively, so, because of the infinite number of simple substances, there are a similar infinite number of universes which are, nevertheless, only the aspects of a single one as seen from the special point of view of each monad.

But, of course, the perspective of any one monad is extremely one-sided and confused.

60. Besides, in what has just been said can be seen the *a priori* reasons why things cannot be otherwise than they are. It is because God, in ordering the whole, has had regard to every part and in particular to each monad; and since the monad is by its very nature *representative*, nothing can limit it to represent merely a part of things. It is nevertheless true that this representation is, as regards the details of the whole universe, only a confused

representation, and is distinct only as regards a small part of them, that is to say, as regards those things which are nearest or greatest in relation to each monad. If the representation were distinct as to the details of the entire universe, each monad would be a Deity. It is not in the object represented that the monads are limited, but in the modifications of their knowledge of the object. In a confused way they reach out to infinity or to the whole, but are limited and differentiated in the degree of their distinct perceptions.

Now Leibniz has an alternative to Newton: bodies (composite monads) only seem to interact; in fact, it all happens within each monad, programmed and created by God in "pre-established harmony."

61. In this respect composites are like simple substances, for all space is filled up; therefore, all matter is connected. And in a plenum or filled space every movement has an effect upon bodies in proportion to this distance, so that not only is every body affected by those which are in contact with it and responds in some way to whatever happens to them, but also by means of them the body responds to those bodies adjoining them, and their inter-communication reaches to any distance whatsoever. Consequently every body responds to all that happens in the universe, so that he who saw all could read in each one what is happening everywhere, and even what has happened and what will happen.

62. Thus although each created monad represents the whole universe, it represents more distinctly the body which specially pertains to it and of which it constitutes the entelechy. And as this body expresses all the universe through the interconnection of all matter in the plenum, the soul also represents the whole universe in representing this body, which belongs to it in a particular way.

Every monad develops as a reflection of the development of all the other monads in the universe as well. If, for example, we are watching a squirrel climb around a tree, Leibniz's view is that the reality of the squirrel climbing around the tree is actually our perception of this. But you can see that this alone is not sufficient; we might simply dream or hallucinate this view, and it would then not be "real" at all. The difference between the dream and the reality is the changes in the other monads, for instance, the monads that constitute the squirrel, and any other observers of the same scene, including God. Reality is composed of the totality of all monads, each perceiving from its own perspective (although God, Leibniz insists, perceives from all perspectives at once). The "pre-established harmony" guarantees that all of these views from all of these perspectives are in agreement, so that our view of the squirrel, for example, is matched by the squirrel's view of us.

This view of the pre-established harmony between monads allows Leibniz to give a surprising answer to our fourth question, "How do different substances interact?" By definition, substances cannot interact as such. But they can seem to interact if their perceptions are coordinated. Thus, the collision of two billiard balls is in fact a harmony of perceptions about the collision of two billiard balls. Two people fighting is in fact a harmony of perceptions by each of the two people (and anyone else who is watching) about those two people fighting. This answer may seem to be extreme, but given Leibniz's conception of the universe as composed of a great number of immaterial substances, it is an answer that is necessary for his philosophy to be consistent. It is an answer that is also necessary, however, to enable him to reject Newton's cosmology, which he and many of his contemporaries found even more extreme and difficult to understand than Leibniz's own strange view of interaction.

The last of our initial set of questions about substance and our second cosmological question is, "Are space and time themselves substances?" According to Leibniz, the answer to this question is an emphatic "no!" It is on this question that Leibniz makes his sharpest break with Newton's physics. Are monads "in" space? Leibniz would have said "no." But he also seems to give the surprising answer that not only are monads not "in" space (since they are immaterial) but they are, strictly speaking, not "in" time either. The monad does not change in time, but rather, time is in the monad. That is, time is a relation between experiences of the monad. It is not something independent. These views of space and time are intimately tied to Leibniz's analysis of the only seeming "interaction" between monads. Both are rejections of Newton's theory, and an attempt to offer an alternative.

To our way of thinking, Leibniz's views seem bizarre, compared to the almost common-sense character of Newton's theory. Newton had argued that the universe was the motion of (material) atoms in empty space, acting against each other according to the laws of motion, force, and gravity that he had so elegantly formulated. But Newton's theories, which seem almost quaintly obvious to us now, contained what most people of his and Leibniz's time — including Newton himself — considered to be manifest absurdities. One, relating to our fourth ontological question, was the idea of **action-at-a-distance,** the idea that one object could affect another although the two were not even in contact. (For example, the idea that the moon and the earth have gravitational attraction for each other.) Thus Leibniz's conception of windowless monads, each seeming to interact with others but in fact only developing within itself, would have seemed to his contemporaries no more absurd than Newton's view of causality. Leibniz didn't need causality, he had his "pre-established harmony." Newton, meanwhile, had a great deal of trouble reconciling his mechanistic theories with the traditional ideas of God and Creation, which he continued to hold for the rest of his life.

The most famous disagreement between Leibniz and Newton concerns the nature of space and time, a topic that is still being debated because of the impact of Einstein's theory of relativity at the beginning of this century. Newton's mechanical theory seemed to presuppose the existence of some permanent container, namely space, in which the material atoms of his theory could mutually attract and bounce against each other. This container, which could exist independently of its contents is called **absolute space.** In itself, this sounds entirely reasonable; we talk about things "moving in space" and "taking up space." But then, can we also talk about the entire universe being "in" space, the way a basketball can be said to be "in" the basket? This idea has some absurd consequences that led Leibniz and many of his contemporaries to reject it. The idea that space could exist apart from all things in it, perhaps even entirely empty (or what many philosophers called the **void**), would mean that it makes sense to talk about movement or location in space even when there isn't anything in space, not even points and rulers with which to measure distances or dimensions. Bertrand Russell, one of Leibniz's most famous followers, pointed out the absurdity of this idea by asking, "if space is absolute, then wouldn't it make sense to suggest that the universe might have doubled in size last night?" But what would it mean to say that the universe has gotten larger? An elephant or a planet or even a galaxy can get larger, but only in comparison to some measuring stick and a frame of reference. It is only by such comparisons that such "size" talk makes sense. But to say that the universe doubles in size is to say that our measuring stick, and we ourselves, double in size also. So all comparisons remain the same. Similarly, what would it mean to say that the universe in its entirety moved one foot to the left? All of the one-foot measurements are in the universe. There is no way to talk about the universe itself moving. On the basis of such considerations, Leibniz rejected Newton's idea of absolute space as absurd. In its place, he insisted that space is relative, that is, relative to measurements and things that are measured. There is no absolute space; there is only space relative to the various positions of the monads, that is, to observers.

The same is true of time. Newton believed in **absolute time** also, time as existing apart from anything happening "in" it. But the same consequences follow this initially reasonable idea. If time is absolute, it seems to make sense to ask, "when did the universe begin?" (In fact, astronomers are again asking this question.) But what could this "when" refer to? It can't refer to any measurement in the universe (clocks, the age of rocks or stars) for it is the universe itself that is being measured. And, there aren't any measures of time outside of the universe. Consequently, Leibniz rejected absolute time along with absolute space. Both are relative to the monads and have no possible existence of their own. This means, among other things, that there could be no void or empty space, nor could there be any sense of time in which literally nothing happened. Space and time, according to Leibniz, are relative to our own perceptions.

Now I said many pages ago that such cosmological issues were never the domain of philosophy alone, and you are well aware that current physics and astronomy are still very much involved with these questions. And both alternatives, from Newton and from Leibniz, are still very much alive. Scientists do indeed still talk about the beginning of the universe, and with awesome sophistication; and of course they also talk in strictly relativistic terms, like Leibniz, but now à la Einstein. To delve into these issues any further, therefore, we should have to leave eighteenth-century metaphysics and move into twentieth-century physics. What is often relevant to these philosophical debates are the new and sometimes strange experimental findings that are always emerging from the sciences. Recently, for example, experiments with the speed of light have brought about startling changes in our views of space and time. One consequence of this changed view is the idea that we cannot talk intelligibly about two events happening "at the same time" if they are a sufficiently great distance apart, say several billion light years. The discovery of radiation from outer space and the expansion of galaxies has raised old issues about creation in a new way: whether the universe was created all at once and then started to expand and change (the "big-bang theory") or whether there is continuous creation going on even now (the "steady-state theory"). Because of recent theories in science, philosophers are now willing to say things that would have seemed like utter nonsense to both Newton and Leibniz — for example, that "space is curved."

These are not issues to be settled by scientists alone, however; it is philosophical theories that give structure and meaning to the scientific experiments. But neither can philosophers simply cut themselves off from science and pretend that they can solve these problems "just in their heads." At the outer reaches of science, you will find philosophy, just as, at the beginnings of philosophy, you will find the unanswered problems of science.

In an earlier chapter, we stressed the importance of a basic assumption of all metaphysics, that the universe is intelligible. In Leibniz's philosophy, this assumption is presented as one of the basic presuppositions of all thinking; he calls it,

> 32. . . . *the Principle of Sufficient Reason,* in virtue of which we believe that no fact can be real and no statement true unless it has a sufficient reason why it should be thus and not otherwise. Most frequently, however, these reasons cannot be known to us.

They can, however, be known to God, who knows everything. It is on the basis of this principle, for example, that Leibniz defends the claim he made in Prop. 9, that two monads can never be identical ("the identity of indiscernibles"). The reasoning is this: Since God is the supremely rational Being (monad), He must have a reason for all that He does. But Leibniz also argues (Prop. 58) that God must have created the universe "with the greatest possible variety together with the greatest order that may be." Here is the reason why God would not have created any two monads alike. But the Principle of Sufficient Reason has a further implication; it also serves as a principle of divine ethics. Among the various possible worlds (that is, among the infinitely many ways in which the world might have been), God chooses the most perfect, that is, "the best of all possible worlds." Here is the doctrine of cosmic optimism that Voltaire so brilliantly lampooned in his novel, *Candide*. But Leibniz took this concept of "the best of all possible worlds" very seriously. In the next century, it was to provide a foundation for much of the optimism of the Enlightenment. And in Leibniz's own metaphysics, it provides the concluding propositions of *Monadology*, a joyous optimism that creates as close to a "happy ending" as one can expect to find in a serious philosophical treatise.

85. Whence it is easy to conclude that the totality of all spirits must compose the city of God, that is to say, the most perfect state that is possible under the most perfect monarch.

. . . . .

90. Finally, under this perfect government, there will be no good action unrewarded and no evil action unpunished; everything must turn out for the well-being of the good; that is to say, of those who are not disaffected in this great state, who, after having done their duty, trust in Providence and who love and imitate, as is meet, the Author of all Good, delighting in the contemplation of his perfections according to the nature of that genuine, pure love which finds pleasure in the happiness of those who are loved. It is for this reason that wise and virtuous persons work in behalf of everything which seems conformable to presumptive or antecedent will of God, and are, nevertheless, content with what God actually brings to pass through his secret, consequent and determining will, recognizing that if we were able to understand sufficiently well the order of the universe, we should find that it surpasses all the desires of the wisest of us, and that it is impossible to render it better than it is, not only for all in general, but also for each one of us in particular, provided that we have the proper attachment for the author of all, not only as the Architect and the efficient cause of our being [our Creator] but also as our Lord and the Final Cause [purpose of our existence] who ought to be the whole goal of our will, and who alone can make us happy.

This theological "happy ending" is not an afterthought for Leibniz; it is the heart of his philosophy. Like his older contemporary Spinoza, his involvement in metaphysics is ultimately a very personal concern for religion and for his own view of himself and his place in the world. From this perspective, it is revealing to see the vast differences between the two philosophers. Spinoza's view of humanity is extremely anti-individualistic, and each individual is wholly submerged in the concept of the one substance. In Leibniz, however, his pluralism reinforces the view that each individual is a world in himself or herself, and his idealism places an emphasis on mind and thought that is in sharp contrast with Spinoza's balance between thought and body (although many critics have charged Spinoza with emphasizing body to an alarming degree). Spinoza's determinism and his view that ultimately we can do nothing but understand is surely a gloomy view compared to Leibniz's happy confidence that this is the "best of all possible worlds." And, of course, Spinoza's heretical view of God as the one substance (sometimes called *pantheism*) is very different from Leibniz's more traditional and pious view.

Of equal importance, however, are the more technical issues that are raised by Leibniz and Spinoza, for these have preoccupied scientists and metaphysicians alike for over two centuries. The nature of ultimate reality ("substance") and the nature of space and time are still unresolved questions. These questions are still the subject of some of the most current investigations in science and philosophy. And many of the current answers are modeled after those of Spinoza and Leibniz. In addition to the content of their theories, the methods of Spinoza and Leibniz also continue to dominate much of modern philosophy. Leibniz's logic, for example is considered by many modern logicians, Bertrand Russell for one, to be one of the most important advances in modern thinking.

Our concern in this chapter has been to study the best modern examples of a metaphysical system. For this purpose, Spinoza's *Ethics* and Leibniz's *Monadology* serve excellently. But now that we have investigated these two systems and come to appreciate their admirable intelligence as well as some of their obscurities, it is necessary to end on a note of doubt. We have seen two of the most brilliant minds in the history of philosophy begin with the same basic concept, "substance," and use similar methods of deduction to arrive at wholly different views of reality. How could they disagree so radically? And, thinking of ourselves, how are we to decide which of them to agree with? How can we defend one system against the other? Since the systems flatly contradict each other on several points (for example, whether there is only one or whether there are many substances), we cannot logically agree with both of them. Thus the question arises, how can one prove a metaphysical theory? How can we know the way the world really is? Or, more skeptically, can we know the way the world really is?

SUMMARY AND CONCLUSION

In this chapter we have summarized the thought of two of the greatest metaphysical thinkers of modern times. Both begin from the concept of "substance" and attempt to use deduction as a method for proving the ultimate nature of reality. Their answers, however, are extremely different. Spinoza argues that there can only be one substance; Leibniz argues that there are many. For Spinoza, God is identical to the universe, to the one substance; for Leibniz, God is distinct from all other substances, which He created. For Spinoza, mind and body are but two of an infinite number of attributes of God, the only two that we can know; for Leibniz, all substances are ultimately immaterial. But beneath these technical concerns is a struggle by both philosophers to answer the most important problems of human existence: the nature of God and proper religion, the place of man and woman in the universe, and the role and foundations of science.

GLOSSARY

absolute (space and time): the view that space and time exist independently of objects and events "in" them, a view defended by Newton. In general, absolute, as used in philosophy, means independent and nonrelative, unqualified and all-inclusive.

action-at-a-distance: the idea that one object can have a causal effect on another from a distance, as in Newton's laws of gravitational attraction. Leibniz's rejection of this idea as "absurd" led him to develop a noncausal interpretation of the same phenomena.

animism: (see Glossary, Ch. 1)

attribute: in Spinoza, an essential property of God; for example, having a physical nature, having thoughts. In general, an attribute is a property (as in Aristotle).

best of all possible worlds: Leibniz's view that God demands a perfect universe and makes it "the best possible," all things considered.

cause-of-itself *(causa sui):* that which explains its own existence, often said of God. It also follows from the usual definitions of substance.

determinism: the view that every event in the universe is dependent upon other events, which are its causes. On this view, all human actions and decisions, even those which we would normally describe as "free" and "undetermined," are totally dependent on prior events that cause them. (This problem will be examined in Ch. 9.)

extended: having spatial dimensions. Philosophers (for example, Descartes, Leibniz, and Spinoza) often define bodies as "extended," minds and ideas as "unextended."

idealism: the metaphysical view that only minds and their ideas exist.

Identity of Indiscernibles: a principle of Leibniz's philosophy according to which no two things can possibly have all of the same properties, or be absolutely identical in all respects.

modes: in Spinoza, inessential properties or modifications of attributes.

monad: in Leibniz, the simple immaterial substances that are the ultimate constituents of all reality. God, the one uncreated monad, created all of the others as self-enclosed ("windowless"), predetermined entities.

Principle of Sufficient Reason: in Leibniz, the insistence that all events must have a justification and that ultimately all events must be justified by God's reasons. The principle is sometimes invoked to assert that everything must have some explanation, whether or not God is involved. (For example, scientists use such a principle in their work, as we shall see in the following chapter.)

pre-established harmony: the belief that the order of the universe is pre-arranged by God. In Leibniz, this view allows him an alternative to Newton's theory of causal relationships.

unextended: not having spatial dimensions. Philosophers (for example, Descartes, Leibniz, and Spinoza) often define mind and ideas as unextended.

void: empty space.

3

Knowledge

The Chinese philosopher awakened with a start, for he had been dreaming that he was a butterfly. And for the rest of his days, he did not know whether he was a Chinese philosopher dreaming that he was a butterfly, or a butterfly who was now dreaming that he was a Chinese philosopher.

Chuang-Tzu

After an evening of heated but fruitless metaphysical debate with a number of his friends, the British physician John Locke turned to them and asked, "Shouldn't we first determine whether we are capable of answering such questions?" They agreed. Perhaps you are thinking much the same thing. These great metaphysical systems are surely monuments to human intelligence. But do they achieve what they are intended to? Do they tell us "the way the world really is?" Since each of the contending systems claims that it does, how can it be that they disagree? Which is right? And how can we decide?

In 1690 Locke took philosophy around a sharp turn, one that had been suggested by Descartes a half century before. But Descartes had broached the question "What can we know?" only as a preface to his metaphysics. Locke, on the other hand, decided to put questions about reality on the shelf until he could develop an adequate theory of human knowledge. Accordingly, his great book is not primarily an inquiry into substance or reality or God or truth (although all of these enter in); it is *An Essay Concerning Human Understanding.* From metaphysics, the study of ultimate reality, we now turn to **epistemology,** the study of human knowledge — how we get it, what it is, whether we have it, or why we don't.

Even before Plato, Parmenides had seen that between knowledge and reality are the appearances of reality, which might be very different from the reality itself. Plato's "Parable of the Cave" is a graphic illustration of this distinction. Descartes, although he distrusted his senses and wasn't certain that they gave accurate representations of reality, at least could be certain of the appearances themselves — he could not be mistaken about them. And here is the problem that has defined modern epistemology, the seeming abyss between reality and mere appearance. Perhaps we know the appearances of things, but how can we know that we know the reality "behind" them?

Let us return for a moment to the central idea of traditional metaphysics, that of substance. Substance is that which underlies all of the various properties of a thing (or things); and it is the properties, never the substance itself, that are experienced by us. Now, presumably, there can be no properties unless they are properties of something. That seems to be a platitude. But yet, we cannot experience the nature of the substance itself. And here begins the embarrassment of metaphysics.

The problem was stated succinctly by the best-known British philosopher of this century, Bertrand Russell, in a little volume called *The Problems of Philosophy*. He says:

from *The Problems of Philosophy*, by Bertrand Russell

In daily life, we assume as certain many things which, on a closer scrutiny, are found to be so full of apparent contradictions that only a great amount of thought enables us to know what it is that we really may believe. In the search for certainty, it is natural to begin with our present experiences, and in some sense, no doubt, knowledge is to be derived from them. But any statement as to what it is that our immediate experiences make us know is very likely to be wrong. It seems to me that I am now sitting in a chair, at a table of a certain shape, on which I see sheets of paper with writing or print. By turning my head I see out of the window buildings and clouds and the sun. I believe that the sun is about ninety-three million miles from the earth; that it is a hot globe many times bigger than the earth; that, owing to the earth's rotation, it rises every morning, and will continue to do so for an indefinite time in the future. I believe that, if any other normal person comes into my room, he will see the same chairs and tables and books and papers as I see, and that the table which I see is the same as the table which I feel pressing against my arm. All this seems to be so evident as to be hardly worth stating, except in answer to a man who doubts whether I know anything. Yet all this may be reasonably doubted, and all of it requires much careful discussion before we can be sure that we have stated it in a form that is wholly true.

To make our difficulties plain, let us concentrate attention on the table. To the eye it is oblong, brown and shiny, to the touch it is smooth and cool and hard; when I tap it, it gives out a wooden sound. Any one else who sees and feels and hears the table will agree with this description, so that it might seem as if no difficulty would arise; but as soon as we try to be more precise our troubles begin. Although I believe that the table is 'really' of the same colour all over, the parts that reflect the light look much brighter than the other parts, and some parts look white because of reflected light. I know that, if I move, the parts that reflect the light will be different, so that the apparent distribution of colours on the table will change. It follows that if several people are looking at the table at the same moment, no two of them will see exactly the same distribution of colours, because no two can see it from exactly the same point of view, and any change in the point of view makes some change in the way the light is reflected.

For most practical purposes these differences are unimportant, but to the painter they are all-important: the painter has to unlearn the habit of thinking that things seem to have the colour which common sense says they 'really' have, and to learn the habit of seeing things as they appear. Here we have already the beginning of one of the distinctions that cause most trouble in philosophy — the distinction between 'appearance' and 'reality', between what things seem to be and what they are. The painter wants to know what things seem to be, the practical man and the philosopher want to know what they are; but the philosopher's wish to know this is stronger than the practical man's, and is more troubled by knowledge as to the difficulties of answering the question.

To return to the table. It is evident from what we have found, that there is no colour which preeminently appears to be *the* colour of the table, or even of any one particular part of the table — it appears to be of different colours from different points of view, and there is no reason for regarding some of these as more really its colour than others. And we know that even from a given point of view the colour will seem different by artificial light, or to a colour-blind man, or to a man wearing blue spectacles, while in the dark there will be no colour at all, though to touch and hearing the table will be unchanged. This colour is not something which is inherent in the table, but something depending upon the table and the spectator and the way the light falls on the table. When, in ordinary life, we speak of *the* colour of the table, we only mean the sort of colour which it will seem to have to a normal spectator from an ordinary point of view under usual conditions of light. But the other colours which appear under other conditions have just as good a right to be considered real; and therefore, to avoid favouritism, we are compelled to deny that, in itself, the table has any one particular colour.

The same thing applies to the texture. With the naked eye one can see the grain, but otherwise the table looks smooth and even. If we looked at it through a microscope, we should see roughnesses and hills and valleys, and all sorts of differences that are imperceptible to the naked eye. Which of these is the 'real' table? We are naturally tempted to say that what we see through the microscope is more real, but that in turn would be changed by a still more powerful microscope. If, then, we cannot trust what we see with the naked eye, why should we trust what we see through a microscope? Thus, again, the confidence in our sense with which we began deserts us.

The *shape* of the table is no better. We are all in the habit of judging as to the 'real' shapes of things, and we do this so unreflectingly that we come to think we actually see the real shapes. But, in fact, as we all have to learn if we try to draw, a given thing looks different in shape from every different point of view. If our table is 'really' rectangular, it will look, from almost all points of view, as if it had two acute angles and two obtuse angles. If opposite sides are parallel, they will look as if they converged to a point away from the spectator; if they are of equal length, they will look as if the nearer side were longer. All these things are not commonly noticed in looking at a table, because experience has taught us to construct the 'real' shape from the apparent shape, and the 'real' shape is what interests us as practical men. But the 'real' shape is not what we see; it is something inferred from what we see. And what we see is constantly changing in shape as we move about the room; so that here again the senses seem not to give us the truth about the table itself, but only about the appearance of the table.

Similar difficulties arise when we consider the sense of touch. It is true that the table always gives us a sensation of hardness, and we feel that it resists pressure. But the sensation we obtain depends upon how hard we press the table and also upon what part of the body we press with; thus the various sensations due to various pressures or various parts of the body cannot be supposed to reveal *directly* any definite property of the table, but at most to be *signs* of some property which perhaps *causes* all the sensations, but is not actually apparent in any of them. And the same applies still more obviously to the sounds which can be elicited by rapping the table.

Thus it becomes evident that the real table, if there is one, is not the same as what we immediately experience by sight or touch or hearing. The real table, if there is one, is not *immediately* known to us at all, but must be an inference from what is immediately known. Hence, two very difficult questions at once arise; namely, (1) Is there a real table at all? (2) If so, what sort of object can it be?[1]

In these few pages, Russell succeeds in summarizing the problems that have dominated British philosophy since Locke's original epistemological studies. But why say "British philosophy"? Why should this problem have been more serious there than on the continent of Europe, where most of the great metaphysicians were working? Why should it have had more impact on Locke and his followers than on Descartes, Spinoza, Leibniz, and their latter-day followers? Because of a single profound difference, which has always created a general gap in understanding between British-American philosophy and European philosophy. Descartes, Spinoza, and Leibniz retained their faith in human reason's ability to give us knowledge of reality, despite the fact that reality was beyond our every possible experience. Because of their confidence in the powers of reason, they are usually called **rationalists**. And because it happens that all three were Europeans (Descartes was French; Spinoza, Dutch; and Leibniz, German), they are often called *continental rationalists*. The movement developed by John Locke, on the other hand, is generally called **empiricism,** because of its insistence upon the data of experience (or *empirical* data) as the source of all knowledge. (A **datum** [plural, *data*] is a bit of "given" information; modern empiricist philosophers sometimes talk of **sense-data,** that is, the information immediately given by

[1]Bertrand Russell, *The Problems of Philosophy* (Oxford: Oxford University Press, 1912).

the senses.) Also included in this group of empiricists are Bishop George Berkeley[2] and David Hume, whom we shall also meet in this chapter. And because they were all from Great Britain, they are often called *British empiricists*. (Berkeley was Irish; Hume, Scottish; Bertrand Russell is generally considered a more contemporary member of this same movement.)

So, how are we to know reality? by retaining traditional confidence in our own powers of abstract reason? or by appeal to experience, which carries with it the threat that we may never know reality beyond our experience at all? In the pages that follow, you will see one of the most vigorous and long-lasting dialogues in modern philosophy, not only between the rationalists and the empiricists but (as we saw in the juxtaposition of Spinoza and Leibniz in Chapter 2) between the various rationalists and empiricists as well. Among the issues in dispute are not only the emphasis and faith in reason versus experience but also the nature of reason and the nature of experience. What is an idea that can be known to be true by reason alone — a "truth of reason"? How can we infer from the nature of our private experience what the world "outside" is like? How do we even know that there *is* an "external" world? How is it possible to have "abstract" ideas, that is, ideas that are not simply based on the concrete particulars of experience, such as *this* dog, *this* table, *that* star over there to the left of the Big Dipper? How do we get the idea, for example, of "dog" in general, not this dog or that dog or big dog or little dog or Chihuahua or German Shepherd but just "dog," which includes all of them? Most of these disputes, you will notice, are ancient, and were already debated by the Pre-Socratics, Plato, and Aristotle. The question of *substance* comes up again and again; what is a substance? how do we know of substances? And, a more specific set of questions: What aspects of a thing are *in it*? what aspects of a thing are rather *in us*, that is, in the way we perceive it, in the mental apparatus that we use in our knowledge? But beneath the welter of questions and debates, there is a singular shared concern. All of the rationalists and empiricists are men of science who appreciate the advances of modern physics and its kindred disciplines, who think of knowledge as one of the highest human attributes, and who want to understand that knowledge and its foundations as a way of justifying their faith in science. At the bottom of all of these disputes, in other words, is that basic admiration and concern for knowledge as such, and the question "how is this knowledge possible?" is itself an extension of that same admiration and concern.

THE RATIONALIST'S CONFIDENCE: DESCARTES

Let's return to the philosopher who began the modern emphasis on methodology, René Descartes. We have already mentioned his "method of doubt," but the goal of this method is not to defend the doubts but, quite to the contrary, to move from doubt to knowledge and certainty. Descartes's doubt is intended only to

[2]Bishop Berkeley traveled to America; Berkeley, California is named after him.

separate what is doubtful from what is not. He never doubted, nor did his follow-ers, that he would be able to find beliefs that were beyond doubt and use them to prove all sorts of other beliefs about reality. These beliefs would be "clear and distinct" and "perfectly certain." (Spinoza refers to such ideas as "adequate ideas"; Leibniz calls them "truths of reason.") Once Descartes had found even one such belief, he could use it as a premise from which he could deduce all of his other beliefs about reality. And none of this depends upon the data of experience; it is entirely a process of reason, of examining the clarity of his beliefs and the logical connections between them.

Once again, it is important to remind ourselves that these problems and their sometimes radical complications and solutions do not appear in a vacuum. Des-cartes lived in the time of Galileo, and Galileo's new science is always in the background of Descartes's method of doubt. In undermining the traditional sci-ence of Aristotle and the Middle Ages, Galileo had raised the doubt that what we think that we see we might not really see at all. Colors, for example, seemed to be more in the minds of men and women than in the objects themselves. But if we could be mistaken about something so seemingly certain as the color of objects, Descartes reasons, could we not be mistaken about much else besides? Indeed, could we not be mistaken in our perceptions *in general?* It is for this reason that Descartes appeals to reason rather than to experience (although, as we shall see, he dangerously calls reason into question as well). We might also add that, although he was a devout Catholic, Descartes could not help but be affected by Martin Luther's challenge to church authority, the century before. Thus the insistence of resolving these doubts for oneself, instead of appealing to established authority, was very much a part of the radical temperament of the time.

In six famous "meditations," Descartes begins with the resolve to doubt every-thing that he believes, that is, until he can find a first premise that is beyond doubt, from which he can then argue for the truth of other beliefs, which he can then use as premises to prove more beliefs, and so on. In the first meditation, he states his method of doubt and begins to eliminate all of those beliefs about which he could possibly be mistaken. He doubts his senses; could they not mislead him, as they do in an optical illusion or a hallucination? He examines his belief in God; could it be that his Jesuit teachers had been fooling him? He even doubts the existence of the world; is it not conceivable that he is merely dreaming? Here is the first of the meditations.

from *Meditation I,* by Descartes

Of the Things Which May Be Brought Within the Sphere of the Doubtful

It is now some years since I detected how many were the false beliefs that I had from my earliest youth admitted as true, and how doubtful was everything I had since constructed on this basis; and from that time I was convinced that I must once for all seriously undertake to rid myself of all the opinions which I had formerly accepted, and commence to build anew from the foundation, if I wanted to establish any firm and permanent structure in the sciences.

In order to "build anew" his system of beliefs and eliminate false beliefs, Descartes resolves to doubt everything that he believes. But this does not mean that he has to list every belief he has; that might take forever. Instead, it is necessary only for him to examine those "first principles" upon which all of his other beliefs are based.

> Now for this object it is not necessary that I should show that all of these are false—I shall perhaps never arrive at this end. But inasmuch as reason already persuades me that I ought no less carefully to withhold my assent from matters which are not entirely certain and indubitable than from those which appear to me manifestly to be false, if I am able to find in each one some reason to doubt, this will suffice to justify my rejecting the whole. And for that end it will not be requisite that I should examine each in particular, which would be an endless undertaking; for owing to the fact that the destruction of the foundations of necessity brings with it the downfall of the rest of the edifice, I shall only in the first place attack those principles upon which all my former opinions rested.

The first set of principles to be doubted is that "common-sense" set of beliefs that relies upon the senses—seeing, hearing, tasting, smelling, touching. Descartes argues that, despite our common-sense reliance on these, it is nevertheless possible that we could be deceived by our senses.

> All that up to the present time I have accepted as most true and certain I have learned either from the senses or through the senses; but it is sometimes proved to me that these senses are deceptive, and it is wiser not to trust entirely to any thing by which we have once been deceived.
>
> But it may be that although the senses sometimes deceive us concerning things which are hardly perceptible, or very far away, there are yet many others to be met with as to which we cannot reasonably have any doubt, although we recognise them by their means. For example, there is the fact that I am here, seated by the fire, attired in a dressing gown, having this paper in my hands and other similar matters. And how could I deny that these hands and this body are mine, were it not perhaps that I compare myself to certain persons, devoid of sense, whose cerebella are so troubled and clouded by the violent vapours of black bile, that they constantly assure us that they think they are kings when they are really quite poor, or that they are clothed in purple when they are really without covering, or who imagine that they have an earthenware head or are nothing but pumpkins or are made of glass. But they are mad, and I should not be any the less insane were I to follow examples so extravagant.

Now Descartes makes one of his most famous philosophical moves: He wonders whether he could possibly be dreaming all of his experience; for in a dream, as we all know, it is possible that everything can still seem perfectly real, as if we were actually awake:

> At the same time I must remember that I am a man, and that consequently I am in the habit of sleeping, and in my dreams representing to myself the same things or sometimes even less probable things, than do those who are insane in their waking moments. How often has it happened to me that in the night I dreamt that I found myself in this particular place, that I was dressed and seated near the fire, whilst in reality I was lying undressed in bed! At this moment it does indeed seem to me that it is with eyes awake that I am looking at this paper; that this head which I move is not asleep, that it is deliberately and of set purpose that I extend my hand and perceive it; what happens in sleep does not appear so clear nor so distinct as does all this. But in thinking over this I remind myself that on many occasions I have in sleep been deceived by similar illusions, and in dwelling carefully on this reflection I see so manifestly that there are no certain indications by which we may clearly distinguish wakefulness from sleep that I am lost in astonishment. And my astonishment is such that it is almost capable of persuading me that I now dream.

Thus Descartes has brought himself to the point where he doubts the existence of the whole of nature, even the existence of his own body. After all, one can dream that one's body has changed grotesquely, and on rare occasions it is even possible to dream that one leaves one's body altogether. So isn't it possible, according to this strict method of doubt, to wonder whether one does indeed have a body, just as it is possible to wonder how one knows of the existence of the "external world" in general?

But there is one sphere of knowledge that would seem to be immune even to Descartes's radical doubting — the principles of arithmetic and geometry:

> Arithmetic, Geometry and other sciences of that kind which only treat of things that are very simple and very general, without taking great trouble to ascertain whether they are actually existent or not, contain some measure of certainty and an element of the indubitable. For whether I am awake or asleep, two and three together always form five, and the square can never have more than four sides, and it does not seem possible that truths so clear and apparent can be suspected of any falsity [or uncertainty].

But these can be doubted, too. To do so, Descartes turns his attention to God, his Creator, and asks whether God might be able to deceive him even about these apparently certain principles:

> Nevertheless I have long had fixed in my mind the belief that an all-powerful God existed by whom I have been created such as I am. But how do I know that He has not brought it to pass that there is no earth, no heaven, no extended body, no magnitude, no place, and that nevertheless [I possess the perceptions of all these things and that] they seem to me to exist just exactly as I now see them? And, besides, as I sometimes imagine

that others deceive themselves in the things which they think they know best, how do I know that I am not deceived every time that I add two and three, or count the sides of a square, or judge of things yet simpler, if anything simpler can be imagined? But possibly God has not desired that I should be thus deceived, for He is said to be supremely good. If, however, it is contrary to His goodness to have made me such that I constantly deceive myself, it would also appear to be contrary to His goodness to permit me to be sometimes deceived, and nevertheless I cannot doubt that He does permit this.

Descartes's argument, which he .will use again later in his *Meditations,* is that God is good and would not deceive him. But suppose, just suppose, that God did not exist?

There may indeed be those who would prefer to deny the existence of a God so powerful, rather than believe that all other things are uncertain. But let us not oppose them for the present, and grant that all that is here said of a God is a fable; nevertheless in whatever way they suppose that I have arrived at the state of being that I have reached—whether they attribute it to fate or to accident, or make out that it is by a continual succession of antecedents, or by some other method—since to err and deceive oneself is a defect, it is clear that the greater will be the probability of my being so imperfect as to deceive myself ever, as is the Author to whom they assign my origin the less powerful. To these reasons I have certainly nothing to reply, but at the end I feel constrained to confess that there is nothing in all that I formerly believed to be true, of which I cannot in some measure doubt, and that not merely through want of thought or through levity, but for reasons which are very powerful and maturely considered; so that henceforth I ought not the less carefully to refrain from giving credence to these opinions than to that which is manifestly false, if I desire to arrive at any certainty [in the sciences].

To bring his method to its extreme conclusion, Descartes now introduces a drastic supposition, namely, that not a good God but an evil genius, a malicious demon, is constantly deceiving him, even about those things of which he seems to be most certain:

I shall then suppose, not that God who is supremely good and the fountain of truth, but some evil genius not less powerful than deceitful, has employed his whole energies in deceiving me; I shall consider that the heavens, the earth, colours, figures, sound, and all other external things are nought but the illusions and dreams of which this genius has availed himself in order to lay traps for my credulity; I shall consider myself as having no hands, no eyes, no flesh, no blood, nor any senses, yet falsely believing myself to possess all these things; I shall remain obstinately attached to this idea, and if by this means it is not in my power to arrive at the knowledge of any truth, I may at least do what is in my power [i.e. suspend my judgment], and with firm purpose avoid giving credence to any false thing, or being imposed upon by this arch deceiver, however powerful and deceptive he may be. But this task is a laborious one, and insensibly a certain lassitude leads me into the course of my ordinary life. And just as a captive who in sleep enjoys an imaginary liberty, when he begins to suspect that his liberty is but a dream, fears to awaken, and conspires with these agreeable illusions that the deception may be prolonged, so insensibly of my own accord I fall back into my former opinions, and I dread awakening from this slumber, lest the laborious wakefulness which would follow the tranquility of this repose should have to be spent not in daylight, but in the excessive darkness of the difficulties which have just been discussed.[3]

Descartes has taken his doubt as far as he can possibly go; he now doubts everything, until, that is, he finds the one principle that is beyond all doubt and perfectly certain. That principle is the fact of his own existence. That he cannot doubt, for if he doubts it, he still knows that he must exist to doubt. Which means that he can be certain of one thing, at least, that he himself exists. And from this first principle, Descartes proceeds, through the "Meditations" that follow, to reestablish his confidence in other things he believes as well — the existence of God, the existence of the "external world," and the existence of his own body.

Many philosophers have challenged the extremity of Descartes's method and have often objected that once you begin to doubt things so thoroughly, you will never again be able to argue your way back to certainty. One way of making this objection is to ask, how can Descartes possibly get rid of an "evil genius" who is deceiving him about everything once he has introduced this possibility? Indeed, the supposition of an evil genius was so extreme that even Descartes, in the years that followed the publication and many disputes about his *Meditations*, insisted that no one should take his argument too seriously. But in the "Meditations" themselves, he tried to show that we could indeed get rid of the evil genius. Having watched Descartes work his way into the depths of Plato's cave, let us now watch him work his way out again.

from *Meditation II*, by Descartes

Of the nature of the human mind; and
that it is more easily known than the body

The Meditation of yesterday filled my mind with so many doubts that it is no longer in my power to forget them. And yet I do not see in what manner I can resolve them; and, just as if I had all of a sudden fallen into very deep water, I am so disconcerted that I can neither make certain of setting my feet on the bottom, nor can I swim and so support myself on the surface. I shall nevertheless make an effort and follow anew the same path

---

[3]Descartes, *Meditations on First Philosophy*, in *The Philosophical Works of Descartes*, trans. Elizabeth S. Haldane and G. R. T. Ross (Cambridge: Cambridge University Press, 1911). All subsequent "Meditations" by Descartes are from this edition.

as that on which I yesterday entered, i.e. I shall proceed by setting aside all that in which the least doubt could be supposed to exist, just as if I had discovered that it was absolutely false; and I shall ever follow in this road until I have met with something which is certain, or at least, if I can do nothing else, until I have learned for certain that there is nothing in the world that is certain. Archimedes, in order that he might draw the terrestrial globe out of its place, and transport it elsewhere, demanded only that one point should be fixed and immovable; in the same way I shall have the right to conceive high hopes if I am happy enough to discover one thing only which is certain and indubitable.

I suppose, then, that all the things that I see are false; I persuade myself that nothing has ever existed of all that my fallacious memory represents to me. I consider that I possess no senses; I imagine that body, figure, extension, movement and place are but the fictions of my mind. What, then, can be esteemed as true? Perhaps nothing at all, unless that there is nothing in the world that is certain.

But how can I know there is not something different from those things that I have just considered, of which one cannot have the slightest doubt? Is there not some God, or some other being by whatever name we call it, who puts these reflections into my mind? That is not necessary, for is it not possible that I am capable of producing them myself? I myself, am I not at least something? But I have already denied that I had senses and body. Yet I hesitate, for what follows from that? Am I so dependent on body and senses that I cannot exist without these? But I was persuaded that there was nothing in all the world, that there was no heaven, no earth, that there were no minds, nor any bodies: was I not then likewise persuaded that I did not exist? Not at all; of a surety I myself did exist since I persuaded myself of something [or merely because I thought of something]. But there is some deceiver or other, very powerful and very cunning, who ever employs his ingenuity in deceiving me. Then without doubt I exist also if he deceives me, and let him deceive me as much as he will, he can never cause me to be nothing so long as I think that I am something. So that after having reflected well and carefully examined all things, we must come to the definite conclusion that this proposition: I am, I exist, is necessarily true each time that I pronounce it, or that I mentally conceive it.

Here it is, the one, certain truth that Descartes needs to start his argument. The more famous formulation of this truth, *cogito, ergo sum,* "I think, therefore I am," occurs in his earlier *Discourse on Method* (1637). (It may be worth pointing out that a similar argument appears in St. Augustine, over one thousand years earlier.)

But now that Descartes knows that he exists, what is he? His answer: "a thing which thinks."

But I do not yet know clearly enough what I am, I who am certain that I am; and hence I must be careful to see that I do not imprudently take some other object in place of myself, and thus that I do not go astray in respect of this knowledge that I hold to be the most certain and most evident of all that I have formerly learned. That is why I shall now consider anew what I believed myself to be before I embarked upon these last reflections; and of my former opinions I shall withdraw all that might even in a small degree be invalidated by the reasons which I have just brought forward, in order that there may be nothing at all left beyond what is absolutely certain and indubitable.

What then did I formerly believe myself to be? Undoubtedly I believed myself to be a man. But what is a man? Shall I say a reasonable animal? Certainly not; for then I should have to inquire what an animal is, and what is reasonable; and thus from a single question I should insensibly fall into an infinitude of others more difficult; and I should not wish to waste the little time and leisure remaining to me in trying to unravel subtleties like these. But I shall rather stop here to consider the thoughts which of themselves spring up in my mind, and which were not inspired by anything beyond my own nature alone when I applied myself to the consideration of my being. In the first place, then, I considered myself as having a face, hands, arms, and all that system of members composed of bones and flesh as seen in a corpse which I designated by the name of body. In addition to this I considered that I was nourished, that I walked, that I felt, and that I thought, and I referred all these actions to the soul: but I did not stop to consider what the soul was, or if I did stop, I imagined that it was something extremely rare and subtle like a wind, a flame, or an ether, which was spread throughout my grosser parts. As to body I had no manner of doubt about its nature, but thought I had a very clear knowledge of it; and if I had desired to explain it according to the notions that I had then formed of it, I should have described it thus: By the body I understand all that which can be defined by a certain figure: something which can be confined in a certain place, and which can fill a given space in such a way that every other body will be excluded from it; which can be perceived either by touch, or by sight, or by hearing, or by taste, or by smell: which can be moved in many ways not, in truth, by itself, but by something which is foreign to it, by which it is touched [and from which it receives impressions]: for to have the power of self-movement, as also of feeling or of thinking, I did not consider to appertain to the nature of body: on the contrary, I was rather astonished to find that faculties similar to them existed in some bodies.

But what am I, now that I suppose that there is a certain genius which is extremely powerful, and, if I may say so, malicious, who employs all his powers in deceiving me? Can I affirm that I possess the least of all those things which I have just said pertain to the nature of body? I pause to consider, I revolve all these things in my mind, and I find none of which I can say that it pertains to me. It would be tedious to stop to enumerate them. Let us pass to the attributes of soul and see if there is any one which is in me? What of nutrition or walking [the first mentioned]? But if it is so that I have no body it is also true that I can neither walk nor take nourishment. Another attribute is sensation. But one cannot feel without body, and besides I have thought I perceived many things during sleep that I recognized in my waking moments as not having been experienced at all. What of thinking? I find here that thought is an attribute that belongs to me; it alone cannot be separated from me. I am, I exist, that is certain. But how often? Just when I think; for it might possibly be the case if I ceased entirely to think, that I should likewise cease altogether to exist. I do not now admit anything which is not necessarily true: to speak accurately I am not more than a thing which thinks, that is to say a mind or a soul, or an understanding, or a reason, which are terms whose significance was formerly unknown to me. I am, however, a real thing and really exist; but what thing? I have answered: a thing which thinks. . . . What is a thing which thinks? It is a thing which doubts, understands, [conceives], affirms, denies, wills, refuses, which also imagines and feels.

In other words, Descartes cannot know for certain that he has a body, much less a particular kind of body, since the evil genius could fool him about that. The only thing that the evil genius could not possibly fool him about is his own thinking, and therefore, the "I" that he knows to exist can only be a thinking "I", not a person or a man in the more usual sense. Later on, this will cause Descartes to raise a gigantic problem, namely, how to explain the connection between this thinking self and the body with which it is associated. But for now, we are more interested in the way he will use his discovery of a single, certain truth. (His discussion of the "mind-body" connection occurs in "Meditation VI," which we shall discuss in Chapter 8, pp. 365–418.)

Descartes has his premise, the fact of his own existence as a "thinking thing." What must follow, then, is the use of this premise in an argument that will "prove" the beliefs he began by doubting: the existence of his own body, the existence of the "external" world, and the existence of God. And, finally, he must somehow get rid of his tentative supposition of the evil demon. But first, he raises once again the old metaphysical question of substance. In a famous example from "Meditation II" he argues:

Let us begin by considering the commonest matters, those which we believe to be the most distinctly comprehended, to wit, the bodies which we touch and see; not indeed bodies in general, for these general ideas are usually a little more confused, but let us consider one body in particular. Let us take, for example, this piece of wax: it has been taken quite freshly from the hive, and it has not yet lost the sweetness of the honey which it contains; it still retains somewhat of the odour of the flowers from which it has been culled; its colour, its figure, its size are apparent; it is hard, cold, easily handled, and if you strike it with the finger, it will emit a sound. Finally all the things which are requisite to cause us distinctly to recognize a body, are met with in it. But notice that while I speak and approach the fire what remained of the taste is exhaled, the smell evaporates, the colour alters, the figure is destroyed, the size increases, it becomes liquid, it heats, scarcely can one handle it, and when one strikes it, no sound is emitted. Does the same wax remain after this change? We must confess that it remains; none would judge otherwise. What then did I know so distinctly in this piece of wax? It could certainly be nothing of all that the senses brought to my notice, since all these things which fall under taste, smell, sight, touch, and hearing, are found to be changed, and yet the same wax remains.

Perhaps it was what I now think, viz. that this wax was not that sweetness of honey, nor that agreeable scent of flowers, nor that particular whiteness, nor that figure, nor that sound, but simply a body which a little while before appeared to me as perceptible under these forms, and which is now perceptible under others. But what, precisely, is it that I imagine when I form such conceptions? Let us attentively consider this, and, abstracting from all that does not belong to the wax, let us see what remains. Certainly nothing remains excepting a certain extended thing which is flexible and movable. But what is the meaning of flexible and movable? Is it not that I imagine that this piece of wax being round is capable of becoming square and of passing from a square to a triangular figure? No, certainly it is not that, since I imagine it admits of an infinitude of similar changes, and I nevertheless do not know how to compass the infinitude of my imagination, and consequently this conception which I have of the wax is not brought about by the faculty of imagination. What now is this extension? Is it not also unknown? For it becomes greater when the wax is melted, greater when it is boiled, and greater still when the heat increases; and I should not conceive [clearly] according to truth what wax is, if I did not think that even this piece that we are considering is capable of receiving more variations in extension than I have ever imagined. We must then grant that I could not even understand through the imagination what this piece of wax is, and that it is my mind alone which perceives it. I say this piece of wax in particular, for as to wax in general it is yet clearer. But what is this piece of wax which cannot be understood excepting by the [understanding or] mind? It is certainly the same that I see, touch, imagine, and finally it is the same which I have always believed it to be from the beginning. But what must particularly be observed is that its perception is neither an act of vision, nor of touch, nor of imagination, and has never been such although it may have appeared formerly to be so, but only an intuition of the mind, which may be imperfect and confused as it was formerly, or clear and distinct as it is at present, according as my attention is more or less directed to the elements which are found in it, and of which it is composed.

This "intuition of mind" is the key to all rationalist thinking. Intuition is where the rationalist obtains his premises, from which he argues to all other conclusions. And the difference between the rationalist and the empiricist, at least in what they say that they are doing, is the rationalist's heavy reliance on non-empirical intuition. Both would agree on the legitimacy of the deductions that follow; it is the source of the premises that is in dispute. And intuition, according to the rationalists, has its source in reason alone. (Notice that "reason" refers not only to the activity of reasoning but to unreasoned intuitions and insights as well.) Accordingly it is this source of intuition that will be the center of the dispute rather than the actual arguments that Descartes then uses to "prove" his other beliefs. The strategy of Descartes's argument is as follows. First, there is the premise, which you have seen,

I exist (as a thinking thing).

Then (in "Meditation III"), Descartes uses this premise to prove the existence of God. This is the second key move in the argument. (The first is the establishment of the premise, "I exist.") The argument itself is a version of two arguments called "the cosmological argument" and "the ontological argument for God's existence." We will discuss them in detail in Chapter 6 ("Religion") but the basic logic of both arguments is this: if a finite, dependent, and merely contingent being like myself can even think of an infinite, independent, and necessary being, then such a being must exist. The details of these arguments, however, are not so much the concern of epistemology or the theory of knowledge as they are of the special logical considerations necessary when talking about the Supreme Being. For now, therefore, let us simply grant Descartes his second step, with the promissory note that the proofs will be explained in the later chapter on the philosophy of religion. So, we have

I exist (as a thinking thing). (premise)
God exists (because I could not exist without Him).

Now we can say that, by His very nature (another intuition), God is good, in fact, perfectly good. And so, as Descartes says in "Meditation VI,"

from *Meditation VI*, by Descartes

Since He has given me a very strong inclination to believe that these ideas (of trees, houses, etc.) arise from corporeal objects, I do not see how He could be vindicated from the charge of deceit, if in truth they proceeded from any other source, or were produced by other causes than corporeal things? [For example, by the evil demon, or in dreams.]

Therefore:

We cannot be deceived [whether by the evil demon or whatever else.]

... I cannot doubt but that there is in me a certain passive faculty of perception, that is, of receiving and taking knowledge of the ideas of sensible things; but this would be useless to me, if there did not also exist in me, or in some other thing, another active faculty capable of forming and producing those ideas. But this active faculty cannot be in me [in as far as I am but a thinking thing], seeing that it does not presuppose thought, and also that those ideas are frequently produced in my mind without my contributing to it in any way, and even frequently contrary to my will. This faculty must therefore exist in some substance different from me, in which all the objective reality of the ideas that are produced by this faculty is contained formally or eminently, as I before remarked: and this substance is either a body, that is to say, a corporeal nature in which is contained formally [and in effect] all that is objectively [and by representation] in those ideas; or it is God himself, or some other creature, of a rank superior to body, in which the same is contained eminently. But as God is no deceiver, it is manifest that he does not of himself and immediately communicate those ideas to me, nor even by the intervention of any creature in which their objective reality is not formally, but only eminently, contained. For as he has given me no faculty whereby I can discover this to be the case, but, on the contrary, a very strong inclination to believe that those ideas arise from corporeal objects, I do not see how he could be vindicated from the charge of deceit, if in truth they proceeded from any other source, or were produced by other causes than corporeal things: and accordingly it must be concluded, that corporeal objects exist. Nevertheless they are not perhaps exactly such as we perceive by the senses, for their comprehension by the senses is, in many instances, very obscure and confused; but it is at least necessary to admit that all which I clearly and distinctly conceive as in them, that is, generally speaking, all that is comprehended in the object of speculative geometry, really exists external to me.

The argument is not convincing, as Descartes's critics were quick to point out. Where does Descartes get his confidence in reason to begin with, such that he feels confident in his own abilities to prove God's existence? Descartes's answer is that we get that confidence from God Himself. But with this answer he has begged the question; that is, he has presumed the existence of God in order to get the confidence with which he then proves God's existence. (This circularity of argument is often called "the Cartesian Circle.") Another way of criticizing the same strategy is to say that, having once introduced the evil demon, Descartes has no way of getting rid of him, since that supposition undermines his confidence in his own reason just as thoroughly as his confidence in God bolsters it.

Our primary concern, however, is with Descartes's claim that certain beliefs are self-evident or "clear and distinct" on the basis of intuition and reason alone. These are beliefs that we don't have to learn — in fact, couldn't learn — from experience. It is not just Descartes's "I exist" premise that is such a belief; all of the rules of inference, which he uses in his arguments, are also beliefs of this kind. And, ultimately, his confidence in reason itself is one, too. But how does one defend these beliefs, for not every philosopher agrees with them. In particular, John Locke, in his disillusionment with metaphysics, begins his philosophy with an assault on the very idea of knowledge that is independent of experience. Thus he begins with an attack on the heart of the rationalist methodology.

CONCERNING HUMAN UNDERSTANDING: JOHN LOCKE

Regarding metaphysics, John Locke is reported to have commented to a friend, "you and I have had enough of this kind of fiddling." Against the sometimes fantastic claims of the metaphysicians, Locke sought a restoration of common sense.[4] Just as Aristotle had acted as a critic of Plato's extravagant two-worlds view, Locke acted as a corrective to the metaphysical enthusiasm of the medieval and modern worlds. He accepted Descartes's method of tentative skepticism, but he questioned his French predecessor's urge to metaphysics as well as his confidence in the insights of pure reason. He rejected the unsupportable "intuitions" that provided Descartes with his rules and his premises, and he turned instead to the data of experience as the ultimate source of all knowledge. He therefore rejected Descartes's exclusively deductive method and supplanted it with a method appropriate to generalizations from experience, or **induction.** In inductive reasoning, the conclusion always goes beyond the premises and therefore, unlike deduction, is always less certain than they are. (For example, from the observed fact that all the philosophy professors that you have met have been absent-minded [the premise] you conclude by **inductive generalization** that all philosophy professors are probably absent-minded.) Accordingly, Locke also modified Descartes's demand for "perfect certainty" and allowed for probability and "degrees of assent." But it must not be thought that Locke therefore rejected reason as such. He still accepted the certainty of mathematical reasoning and the validity of deductive inferences; but he also expanded the concept of rationality to include inductive reasoning and probability as well as deduction and certainty.

Locke's *Essay Concerning Human Understanding* (1689) is built on a single premise, namely, that all our knowledge comes from experience. This means, in his view, that there cannot possibly be ideas that are prior to experience, ideas that are "born into" us, as suggested so vividly by Plato. In other words, Locke refuses to accept the notion of innate ideas, by which he means not only those ideas that are literally "born into us" but all ideas that are derived without appeal to experience. This includes, in his opinion, Descartes's "clear and distinct ideas," Spinoza's "adequate ideas," and Leibniz's "truths of reason."

from *An Essay Concerning Human Understanding,* by John Locke

1. *The way shown how we come by any knowledge, sufficient to prove it not innate.* — It is an established opinion among some men, that there are in the understanding certain innate principles; some primary notions, κοιναί ἔννοιαι, characters, as it were, stamped upon the mind of man which the soul receives in its very first being, and brings into the world with it. It would be sufficient to convince unprejudiced readers of the falseness of this supposition, if I should only show (as I hope I shall in the following parts of this discourse) how men, barely by the use of their natural faculties, may attain to all the knowledge they have, without the help of any innate

---

[4]British empiricism has traditionally considered itself the defender of "common sense" against the excesses of metaphysics. This was even true of Berkeley and Hume, who reached conclusions more outrageous than any metaphysician. And it is also true of Bertrand Russell and G. E. Moore in this century.

impressions, and may arrive at certainty, without any such original notions or principles. . . .

2. *General Assent the great Argument.* — There is nothing more commonly taken for granted, than that there are certain principles, both speculative and practical (for they speak of both), universally agreed upon by all mankind, which therefore, they argue, must needs be constant impressions which the souls of men receive in their first beings, and which they bring into the world with them, as necessarily and really as they do any of their inherent faculties.

3. *Universal Consent proves nothing innate.* — This argument, drawn from universal consent, has this misfortune in it, that if it were true in matter of fact that there were certain truths wherein all mankind agreed, it would not prove them innate, if there can by any other way shown how men may come to that universal agreement in the things they do consent in, which I presume may be done.

4. *"What is, is," and "it is impossible for the same Thing to be and not to be," not universally assented to.* — But, which is worse, this argument of universal consent, which is made use of to prove innate principles, seems to me a demonstration that there are none such; because there are none to which all mankind give an universal assent. I shall begin with the speculative, and instance in those magnified principles of demonstration, "Whatsoever is, is," and "It is impossible for the same thing to be, and not to be"; which, of all others, I think, have the most allowed title to innate. These have so settled a reputation of maxims universally received that it will no doubt be thought strange if anyone should seem to question it. But yet I take liberty to say that these propositions are so far from having an universal assent that there are a great part of mankind to whom they are not so much as known.

5. *Not on the Mind naturally imprinted, because not known to Children, Idiots, &c.* — For, first, it is evident that all children and idiots have not the least apprehension or thought of them; and the want of that is enough to destroy that universal assent which must needs be the necessary concomitant of all innate truths: it seeming to me near a contradiction to say that there are truths imprinted on the soul which it perceives or understands not; imprinting, if it signify anything, being nothing else but the making certain truths to be perceived. For to imprint anything on the mind without the mind's perceiving it, seems to me hardly intelligible. If therefore children and idiots have souls, have minds, with those impressions upon them, they must unavoidably perceive them, and necessarily know and assent to these truths; which since they do not, it is evident that there are no such impressions. For if they are not notions naturally imprinted, how can they be innate, And if they are notions imprinted, how can they be unkown? To say a notion is imprinted on the mind, and yet at the same time to say that the mind is ignorant of it, and never yet took notice of it, is to make this impression nothing. No proposition can be said to be in the mind which it never yet knew, which it was never yet conscious of.[5]

---

[5]John Locke, *An Essay Concerning Human Understanding*, ed. A. C. Fraser (Oxford: Clarendon Press, 1894). All subsequent quotations from Locke are from this edition.

The argument is straightforward; there is, in fact, no universal agreement regarding supposedly "innate" principles, and even if there were, that would not prove their "innateness." Rather, he argues:

> Let us suppose the mind to be, as we say, a blank tablet *(tabula rasa)* of white paper, void of all characters, without any ideas; how comes it to be furnished? Whence comes it by that vast store, which the busy and boundless fancy of man has painted on it with almost endless variety? Whence has it all the materials of reason and knowledge? To this I answer in one word, from *experience*: in that all our knowledge is founded, and from that it ultimately derives itself.

It is this premise that Locke is concerned to defend and use, and his attack on innate ideas is by way of introduction. But Locke fails to succeed in proving that the human mind does not have inborn potentials and limitations, and more importantly, he fails to recognize that inference from experience might itself require principles that are not drawn from experience. In fact, Leibniz, one of the chief targets of Locke's attack, was not long in providing what we might call "the rationalist's reply." Turning Locke against himself, Leibniz argued that, by his own principles, he could not attack the concept of innate ideas.

Leibniz's Rebuttal, from *New Essays on the Human Understanding*, by Gottfried von Leibniz

... The question at issue is whether the soul in itself is entirely empty, like the tablet upon which nothing has yet been written [*tabula rasa*], as is the view of Aristotle and the author of the *Essay* [Locke], and whether all that is traced on it comes solely from the senses and from experience; or whether the soul contains originally the principles of various notions and doctrines which external objects merely awaken from time to time, as I believe, with Plato and even with the Schoolmen, and with all those who take in this sense the passage of St. Paul (Romans, 2:15) where he remarks that the law of God is written in the heart.... From this there arises another question, whether all truths depend on experience, that is to say, on induction and examples, or whether there are some that have some other basis. For if some events can be foreseen before any trial has been made of them, it is clear that we must here contribute something of our own. The senses, although necessary for all our actual knowledge, are not sufficient to give us the whole of it, since the senses never give anything except examples, that is to say, particular or individual truths. All examples which confirm a general truth, however numerous they may be, are not enough to establish the universal necessity of this same truth; for it does not follow that what has happened will happen again in the same way.

... It would seem that necessary truths, such as are found in pure mathematics, and especially in arithmetic and in geometry, must have principles the proof of which does not depend on examples, nor, consequently, on the testimony of the senses, although without the senses it would never have occurred to us to think of them. This ought to be well recognised; Euclid has so well understood it that he often demonstrates by reason what is obvious enough through experience and by sensible images. Logic also, together with metaphysics and ethics, one of which forms natural theology and the other natural jurisprudence, are full of such truths; and consequently their proof can only come from internal principles, which are called innate. It is true that we must not imagine that these eternal laws of the reason can be read in the soul as in an open book, as the edict of the praetor can be read in his *album* without difficulty or research; but it is enough that they can be discovered in us by dint of attention, for which opportunities are given by the senses. The success of experiments serves also as confirmation of the reason, very much as proofs serve in arithmetic for better avoiding error of reckoning when the reasoning is long. . . .

It seems that our able author claims that there is nothing potential in us and nothing even of which we are not at any time actually conscious; but he cannot mean this strictly, or his opinion would be too paradoxical; for acquired habits and the contents of our memory are not always consciously perceived and do not even always come to our aid at need, although we often easily bring them back to mind on some slight occasion which makes us remember them, just as we need only the beginning of a song to remember the song. Also he modifies his assertion in other places by saying that there is nothing in us of which we have not been at least formerly conscious. But besides the fact that no one can be sure by reason alone how far our past apperceptions, which we may have forgotten, may have gone, especially in view of the Platonic doctrine of reminiscence, which, mythical as it is, is not, in part at least, incompatible with bare reason; in addition to this, I say, why is it necessary that everything should be acquired by us through the perceptions of external things, and that nothing can be unearthed in ourselves? Is our soul, then, such a blank that, besides the images borrowed from without, it is nothing? . . . there are a thousand indications that lead us to think that there are at every moment numberless perceptions in us, but without apperception and without reflections; that is to say, changes in the soul itself of which we are not conscious, because the impressions are either too slight and too numerous, or too even, so that they have nothing sufficient to distinguish them one from the other; but, joined to others, they do not fail to produce their effect and to make themselves felt at least confusedly in the mass. . . .[6]

Locke himself did not continue the debate; he was already convinced of his own position and had more urgent problems to worry about (the political chaos in London following the "Glorious Revolution" of 1688). But the debate continued in different forms. The rise of anthropology in the nineteenth century, with the discoveries of societies whose basic ideas were radically different from our own, seemed to support Locke's claim that no one will believe in innate universal principles if they "ever look beyond the smoke of their own chimneys." But in the nineteenth century, there were also a great many philosophers who still

[6]Gottfried von Leibniz, *New Essays on the Human Understanding*, trans. A. G. Langley (La Salle, Ill.: Open Court, 1949).

argued for the existence of universal principles not learned through experience. (Immanuel Kant did this in a very powerful set of arguments that we will view in the next several chapters.) In the early twentieth century, opinion was in general accord with Locke, but recently it has taken another swing back to Leibniz, this time, ironically, supported by anthropology. A major movement in the social sciences, usually called structuralism (whose main proponent is Claude Levi-Strauss in France), has argued that underneath the many superficial differences between very different societies there are certain basic "structures" that are universal and innate. And in America, the notion of innate ideas has appeared once again in the work of the well-known linguist Noam Chomsky. According to Chomsky, certain capacities for language are built into us from birth, and this allows him to explain not only the similarities of human thinking (which was the view that Locke attacked) but also the enormous capacity for learning different languages quickly. (The average three-year-old learns a language in six months.) The Locke-Leibniz debate is still very much alive.

THE EMPIRICIST THEORY OF KNOWLEDGE

The *tabula rasa* or "blank tablet" view of the mind is Locke's most famous epistemological concept. Leaving aside those special concerns that involve only "the relations between ideas" (as in mathematics, logic, and trivial conceptual truths such as "a horse is an animal"), all of our ideas are derived from experience. Epistemology (and philosophy in general) now became a kind of psychology (indeed, the two disciplines were not yet distinguished), a study of the history of our common experiences in order to discover where we get our ideas, particularly such ideas as substance, God, and our various conceptions of reality. In his theory, Locke uses three familiar terms: **sensation** (or what more modern empiricists call sense-data), **ideas** (not in the Platonic sense but simply "the immediate object of perception, thought, or understanding"), and **quality** (or what we have so far been calling property, for example, being red, being round, being heavy).

from *Essay*,
by Locke

1. Concerning the simple ideas of Sensation, it is to be considered — that whatsoever is so constituted in nature as to be able, by affecting our senses, to cause any perception in the mind, doth thereby produce in the understanding a simple idea; which, whatever be the external cause of it, when it comes to be taken notice of by our discerning faculty, it is by the mind looked on and considered there to be a real positive idea in the understanding, as much as any other whatsoever; though, perhaps, the cause of it be but a privation of the subject.

2. Thus the ideas of heat and cold, light and darkness, white and black, motion and rest, are equally clear and positive ideas in the mind; though

perhaps, some of the causes which produce them are barely privations, in those subjects from whence our senses derive those ideas. These the understanding, in its view of them, considers all as distinct positive ideas, without taking notice of the causes that produce them: which is an inquiry not belonging to the idea, as it is in the understanding, but to the nature of the things existing without us. These are two very different things, and carefully to be distinguished; it being one thing to perceive and know the idea of white or black, and quite another to examine what kind of particles they must be, and how ranged in the superficies, to make any object appear white or black. . . .

7. To discover the nature of our *ideas* the better, and to discourse of them intelligibly, it will be convenient to distinguish them *as they are ideas or perceptions in our minds;* and *as they are modifications of matter in the bodies that cause such perceptions in us:* that so we may not think (as perhaps usually is done) that they are exactly the images and resemblances of something inherent in the subject; most of those of sensation being in the mind no more the likeness of something existing without us, than the names that stand for them are the likeness of our ideas, which yet upon hearing they are apt to excite in us.

8. Whatsoever the mind perceives *in itself,* or is the immediate object of perception, thought, or understanding, that I call *idea;* and the power to produce any idea in our mind, I call *quality* of the subject wherein that power is. Thus a snowball having the power to produce in us the ideas of white, cold, and round, — the power to produce those ideas in us, as they are in the snowball, I call qualities; and as they are sensations or perceptions in our understandings, I call them ideas; which *ideas,* if I speak of sometimes as in the things themselves, I would be understood to mean those qualities in the objects which produce them in us.

Notice that the basis of Locke's theory is the "common sense" distinction between physical objects in the world and sensations and ideas in our minds. Accordingly, we may talk of the qualities or properties inherent in the objects in the world, such as size and shape, and the qualities or properties they merely appear to have, such as color or texture, but that do not exist independently of the objects' effects on our sense organs. Locke refers to those properties of the objects themselves as **primary qualities;** he calls those "properties" of the objects which we merely see them as having, **secondary qualities.**

Primary qualities:
Qualities thus considered in bodies are, *First,* such as are utterly inseparable from the body, in what state soever it be; and such as in all the alterations and changes it suffers, all the force can be used upon it, it constantly keeps; and such as sense constantly finds in every particle of matter which has bulk enough to be perceived; and the mind finds inseparable from every particle of matter, though less than to make itself singly be perceived by our senses: e.g. Take a grain of wheat, divide it into two parts; each part has still solidity, extension, figure, and mobility: divide it again, and it retains still the same qualities; and so divide it on, till the parts become insensible;

they must retain still each of them all those qualities. For division (which is all that a mill, or pestle, or any other body, does upon another, in reducing it to insensible parts) can never take away either solidity, extension, figure, or mobility from any body, but only makes two or more distinct separate masses of matter, of that which was but one before; all which distinct masses, reckoned as so many distinct bodies, after division, make a certain number. These I call *original* or *primary qualities* of body, which I think we may observe to produce simple ideas in us, viz. solidity, extension, figure, motion or rest, and number.

Secondary qualities:
   Secondly, such qualities which in truth are nothing in the objects themselves but powers to produce various sensations in us by their primary qualities, i.e. by the bulk, figure, texture, and motion of their insensible parts, as colours, sounds, tastes, &c. These I call *secondary qualities*. To these might be added a *third* sort, which are allowed to be barely powers; though they are as much real qualities in the subject as those which I, to comply with the common way of speaking, call qualities, but for distinction, secondary qualities. For the power in fire to produce a new colour, or consistency, in *wax* or *clay*, — by its primary qualities, is as much a quality in fire, as the power it has to produce in *me* a new idea or sensation of warmth or burning, which I felt not before, — by the same primary qualities, viz. the bulk, texture, and motion of its insensible parts.

   The question, then, is how physical objects cause us to have sensations and ideas. Locke's answer (which, like his theory as a whole, is very strongly influenced by the physical theories of his contemporary Isaac Newton) is, by impulse. This might not seem illuminating until you try to think of the Newtonian theory of force as a product of particles and masses in motion. And on this model, Locke develops what is now called his "Causal Theory of Perception." First, for the primary qualities:

   If then external objects be not united to our minds when they produce ideas therein; and yet we perceive these *original* qualities in such of them as singly fall under our senses, it is evident that some motion must be thence continued by our nerves, or animal spirits, by some parts of our bodies, to the brains or the seat of sensation, there to produce in our minds the particular ideas we have of them. And since the extension, figure, number, and motion of bodies of an observable bigness, may be perceived at a distance by the sight, it is evident some singly imperceptible bodies must come from them to the eyes, and thereby convey to the brain some motion; which produces these ideas which we have of them in us.

Then, for secondary qualities:

   After the same manner that the ideas of these original qualities are produced in us, we may conceive that the ideas of *secondary* qualities are also produced, viz. by the operation of insensible particles on our senses. For, it

being manifest that there are bodies and good store of bodies, each whereof
are so small, that we cannot by any of our senses discover either their bulk,
figure, or motion, — as is evident in the particles of the air and water, and
others extremely smaller than those; perhaps as much smaller than the particles of air and water, as the particles of air and water are smaller than peas
or hail-stones; — let us suppose at present that the different motions and figures, bulk and number, of such particles, affecting the several organs of our
senses, produce in us those different sensations which we have from the
colours and smells of bodies; e.g. that a violet, by the impulse of such insensible particles of matter, of peculiar figures and bulks, and in different
degrees and modifications of their motions, causes the ideas of the blue colour, and sweet scent of that flower to be produced in our minds. It being no
more impossible to conceive that God should annex such ideas to such
motions, with which they have no similitude, than that he should annex
the idea of pain to the motion of a piece of steel dividing our flesh, with
which that idea hath no resemblance.

What I have said concerning colours and smells may be understood also
of tastes and sounds, and other the like sensible qualities; which, whatever
reality we by mistake attribute to them, are in truth nothing in the objects
themselves, but powers to produce various sensations in us; and depend on
those primary qualities, viz. bulk, figure, texture, and motion of parts [as I
have said.]

Therefore:

I think it easy to draw this observation, — that the ideas of primary qualities of bodies are resemblances of them, and their patterns do really exist
in the bodies themselves, but the ideas produced in us by these secondary
qualities have no resemblance of them at all. There is nothing like our
ideas, existing in the bodies themselves. They are, in the bodies we denom-
inate from them, only a power to produce those sensations in us: and what
is sweet, blue, or warm in idea, is but the certain bulk, figure, and motion
of the insensible parts, in the bodies themselves, which we call so.

Flame is denominated hot and light; snow, white and cold; and manna,
white and sweet, from the ideas they produce in us. Which qualities are
commonly thought to be the same in those bodies that those ideas are in
us, the one the perfect resemblance of the other, as they are in a mirror,
and it would by most men be judged very extravagant if one should say
otherwise. And yet he that will consider that the same fire that, at one
distance produces in us the sensation of warmth, does, at a nearer approach,
produce in us the far different sensation of pain, ought to bethink himself
what reason he has to say — that this idea of warmth, which was produced
in him by the fire, is *actually in the fire*; and his idea of pain, which the
same fire produced in him the same way, is *not* in the fire. Why are whiteness and coldness in snow, and pain not, when it produces the one and the
other idea in us; and can do neither, but by the bulk, figure, number, and
motion of its solid parts?

The particular bulk, number, figure, and motion of the parts of fire or
snow are really in them, — whether any one's senses perceive them or no:
and therefore they may be called *real* qualities, because they really exist in

those bodies. But light, heat, whiteness, or coldness, are no more really in them then sickness or pain is in manna. Take away the sensation of them; let not the eyes see light or colours, nor the ears hear sounds; let the palate not taste, nor the nose smell, and all colours, tastes, odours, and sounds, *as they are such particular ideas*, vanish and cease, and are reduced to their causes, i.e. bulk, figure, and motion of parts.

This is the basic theory. Its logical consequences, as we shall see when we study Berkeley and Hume, are not nearly so palatable. But how does the "causal theory of perception" allow Locke to approach the traditional questions of metaphysics? Significantly, the first two steps in the argument are identical with those we traced in Descartes—one's own existence and the existence of God—and Locke even includes the problematic notion of "intuition."

1. The knowledge of our own being we have by intuition. The existence of God, reason clearly makes known to us.

But then, the strict empiricist reemerges and insists.

The knowledge of the existence of *any other thing* we can have only by *sensation:* for there being no necessary connexion of real existence with any *idea* a man hath in his memory; nor of any other existence but that of God with the existence of any particular man: no particular man can know the existence of any other being, but only when, by actual operating upon him, it makes itself perceived by him. For, the having the idea of anything in our mind, no more proves the existence of that thing, than the picture of a man evidences his being in the world, or the visions of a dream make thereby a true history.

2. It is therefore the *actual receiving* of ideas from without that gives us notice of the existence of other things, and makes us know, that something doth exist at that time without us, which causes that idea in us; though perhaps we neither know nor consider how it does it. For it takes not from the certainty of our senses, and the ideas we receive by them, that we know not the manner wherein they are produced: e.g. whilst I write this, I have, by the paper affecting my eyes, that idea produced in my mind, which, whatever object causes, I call *white;* by which I know that that quality or accident (i.e. whose appearance before my eyes always causes that idea) doth really exist, and hath a being without me. And of this, the greatest assurance I can possibly have, and to which my faculties can attain, is the testimony of my eyes, which are the proper and sole judges of this thing; whose testimony I have reason to rely on as so certain, that I can no more doubt, whilst I write this, that I see white and black, and that something really exists that causes that sensation in me, than that I write or move my hand; which is a certainty as great as human nature is capable of, concerning the existence of anything, but a man's self alone, and of God.

And here Locke asserts his alternative to the strict Cartesian limitation of knowledge to matters of certainty and deduction:

3. The notice we have by our senses of the existing of things without us, though it be not altogether so certain as our intuitive knowledge, or the deductions of our reason employed about the clear abstract ideas of our own minds; yet it is an assurance that deserves the name of *knowledge*. If we persuade ourselves that our faculties act and inform us right concerning the existence of those objects that affect them, it cannot pass for an ill-grounded confidence: for I think nobody can, in earnest, be so sceptical as to be uncertain of the existence of those things which he sees and feels. At least, he that can doubt so far, (whatever he may have with his own thoughts,) will never have any controversy with me; since he can never be sure I say anything contrary to his own opinion. As to myself, I think God has given me assurance enough of the existence of things without me: since, by their different application, I can produce in myself both pleasure and pain, which is one great concernment of my present state. This is certain: the confidence that our faculties do not herein deceive us, is the greatest assurance we are capable of concerning the existence of material beings. For we cannot act anything but by our faculties; nor talk of knowledge itself, but by the help of those faculties which are fitted to apprehend even what knowledge is.

Experience has its own supports:

> ... besides the assurance we have from our senses themselves, that they do not err in the information they give us of the existence of things without us, when they are affected by them, we are further confirmed in this assurance by other concurrent reasons: —
>
> 4. I. It is plain those perceptions are produced in us by exterior causes affecting our senses: because those that want the *organs* of any sense, never can have the ideas belonging to that sense produced in their minds. This is too evident to be doubted: and therefore we cannot but be assured that they come in by the organs of that sense, and no other way. The organs themselves, it is plain, do not produce them: for then the eyes of a man in the dark would produce colours, and his nose smell roses in the winter: but we see nobody gets the relish of a pineapple, till he goes to the Indies, where it is, and tastes it.
>
> 5. II. Because sometimes I find that *I cannot avoid having those ideas produced in my mind.* For though, when my eyes are shut, or windows fast, I can at pleasure recall to my mind the ideas of light, or the sun, which former sensations had lodged in my memory; so I can at pleasure lay by *that* idea, and take into my view that of the smell of a rose, or taste of sugar. But, if I turn my eyes at noon towards the sun, I cannot avoid the ideas which the light or sun then produces in me. So that there is a manifest difference between the ideas laid up in my memory, (over which, if they were there only, I should have constantly the same power to dispose of them and lay them by at pleasure,) and those which force themselves upon me, and I cannot avoid having. And therefore it must needs be some exterior cause, and the brisk acting of some objects without me, whose efficacy I cannot resist, that produces those ideas in my mind, whether I will or no. Besides, there is nobody who doth not perceive the difference in himself between contemplating the sun, as he hath the idea of it in his memory, and actually looking upon it: of which two, his perception is so distinct,

that few of his ideas are more distinguishable one from another. And therefore he hath certain knowledge that they are not *both* memory, or the
actions of his mind, and fancies only within him; but that actual seeing
hath a cause without.

6. III. Add to this, that many of those ideas are *produced in us with pain*,
which afterwards we remember without the least offence. Thus, the pain
of heat or cold, when the idea of it is revived in our minds, gives us no
disturbance; which, when felt, was very troublesome; and is again, when
actually repeated: which is occasioned by the disorder the external object
causes in our bodies when applied to them: and we remember the pains of
hunger, thirst, or the headache, without any pain at all; which would either
never disturb us, or else constantly do it, as often as we thought of it, were
there nothing more but ideas floating in our minds, and appearance entertaining our fancies, without the real existence of things affecting us from
abroad. The same may be said of *pleasure*, accompanying several actual sensations. And though mathematical demonstration depends not upon sense,
yet the examining them by diagrams gives great credit to the evidence of
our sight, and seems to give it a certainty approaching to that of demonstration itself. For, it would be very strange, that a man should allow it for an
undeniable truth, that two angles of a figure, which he measures by lines
and angles of a diagram, should be bigger one than the other, and yet doubt
of the existence of those lines and angles, which by looking on he makes
use of to measure that by.

7. IV. Our *senses* in many cases *bear witness to the truth of each other's
report*, concerning the existence of sensible things without us. He that *sees*
a fire, may, if he doubt whether it be anything more than a bare fancy, *feel*
it too; and be convinced, by putting his hand in it. Which certainly could
never be put into such exquisite pain by a bare idea or phantom, unless that
the pain be a fancy too: which yet he cannot, when the burn is well, by
raising the idea of it, bring upon himself again.

Thus I see, whilst I write this, I can change the appearance of the paper;
and by designing the letters, tell *beforehand* what new idea it shall exhibit
the very next moment, by barely drawing my pen over it: which will neither appear (let me fancy as much as I will) if my hands stand still; or
though I move my pen, if my eyes be shut: nor, when those characters are
once made on the paper, can I choose afterwards but see them as they are;
that is, have the ideas of such letters as I have made. Whence it is manifest,
that they are not barely the sport and play of my own imagination, when
I find that the characters that were made at the pleasure of my own
thoughts, do not obey them; nor yet cease to be, whenever I shall fancy it,
but continue to affect my senses constantly and regularly, according to the
figures I made them. To which if we will add, that the sight of those shall,
from another man, draw such sounds as I beforehand design they shall
stand for, there will be little reason left to doubt that those words I write
do really exist without me, when they cause a long series of regular sounds
to affect my ears, which could not be the effect of my imagination, nor
could my memory retain them in that order.

8. But yet, if after all this any one will be so sceptical as to distrust his
senses, and to affirm that all we see and hear, feel and taste, think and do,
during our whole being, is but the series and deluding appearance of a long

dream, whereof there is no reality; and therefore will question the existence of all things, or our knowledge of anything. I must desire him to consider, that, if all be a dream, then he doth but dream that he makes the question, and so it is not much matter that a waking man should answer him. But yet, if he pleases, he may dream that I make him this answer, That the certainty of things existing in *rerum natura* when we have the testimony of our senses for it is not only as great as our frame can attain to, but as our condition needs. For, our faculties being suited not to the full extent of being, nor to a perfect, clear, comprehensive knowledge of things free from all doubt and scruple; but to the preservation of us, in whom they are; and accommodated to the use of life: they serve to our purpose well enough, if they will but give us certain notice of those things, which are convenient or inconvenient to us. For he that sees a candle burning, and hath experimented the force of its flame by putting his finger in it, will little doubt that this is something existing without him, which does him harm, and puts him to great pain: which is assurance enough, when no man requires greater certainty to govern his actions by than what is as certain as his actions themselves. And if our dreamer pleases to try whether the glowing heat of a glass furnance be barely a wandering imagination in a drowsy man's fancy, by putting his hand into it, he may perhaps be wakened into a certainty greater than he could wish, that it is something more than bare imagination. So that this evidence is as great as we can desire, being as certain to us as our pleasure or pain, i.e. happiness or misery; beyond which we have no concernment, either of knowing or being. Such an assurance of the existence of things without us is sufficient to direct us in the attaining the good and avoiding the evil which is caused by them, which is the important concernment we have of being made acquainted with them.

9. In summary, then, when our senses do actually convey into our understanding any idea, we cannot but be satisfied that there doth something *at that time* really exist without us, which doth affect our senses, and by them give notice of itself to our apprehensive faculties, and actually produce that idea which we then perceive.

We are now ready to return to the traditional metaphysical notion of substance — that which underlies both the primary and the secondary qualities of a thing.

1. *Ideas of Substances, how made.* — The mind being, as I have declared, furnished with a great number of the simple ideas conveyed in by the senses, as they are found in exterior things, or by reflection on its own operations, takes notice, also, that a certain number of these simple ideas go constantly together; which being presumed to belong to one thing, and words being suited to common apprehensions, and made use of for quick dispatch, are called, so united in one subject, by one name; which, by inadvertency, we are apt afterward to talk of and consider as one simple idea, which indeed is a complication of many ideas together: because, as I have said, not imagining how these simple ideas can subsist by themselves, we accustom ourselves to suppose some substratum wherein they do subsist, and from which they do result; which therefore we call "substance."

2. *Our Idea of Substance in general.* — So that if anyone will examine himself concerning his notion of pure substance in general, he will find he has no other idea of it at all, but only a supposition of he knows not what support of such qualities which are capable of producing simple ideas in us; which qualities are commonly called "accidents." If anyone should be asked, "What is the subject wherein colour or weight inheres?" he would have nothing to say but, "The solid extended parts." And if he were demanded "What is it that solidity and extension inhere in?" he would not be in a much better case than the Indian before mentioned, who, saying that the world was supported by a great elephant, was asked what the elephant rested on? to which his answer was, "A great tortoise"; but being again pressed to know what gave support to the broad-backed tortoise, replied — something, he knew not what. And thus here, as in all other cases where we use words without having clear and distinct ideas, we talk like children, who, being questioned what such a thing is which they know not, readily give this satisfactory answer, that it is something, which in truth signifies no more, when so used, either by children or men, but that they know not what; and that the thing they pretend to know and talk of is what they have no distinct idea of at all, and so are perfectly ignorant of it, and in the dark. The idea, then, we have, to which we give the general name "substance" being nothing but the supposed, but unknown, support of those qualities we find existing, which we imagine cannot subsist *sine re substante,* "without something to support them," we call that support *substantia;* which, according to the true import of the word, is, in plain English, "standing under," or "upholding."

. . . . .

Hence, when we talk or think of any particular sort of corporeal substances, as horse, stone, &c., though the idea we have of either of them be but the complication or collection of those several simple ideas of sensible qualities which we used to find united in the thing called "horse" or "stone"; yet because we cannot conceive how they should subsist alone, nor one in another, we suppose them existing in, and supported by, some common subject; which support we denote by the name "substance," though it be certain we have no clear or distinct idea of that thing we suppose a support.

Substance is "we know not what." Yet Locke hesitates to reject the notion, for he cannot escape the suspicion that talk of "qualities" makes no sense unless the qualities are the qualities of something. But this suspicion is dispensable according to Locke's own principles. And so, it turns out, is his central distinction between primary and secondary qualities, as Bishop Berkeley is soon to point out. And the consequence of these simple, technical moves will be shocking, to say the least.

COMMON SENSE UNDONE: BISHOP BERKELEY

Beginning from John Locke's common-sense philosophy, Bishop Berkeley developed the most provocative thesis in all of philosophy. Berkeley's thesis is called **subjective idealism.** It is the doctrine that there are no material substances, no physical objects, only minds and ideas in minds. (His concept of "idea" comes directly from Locke.) This surprising position emerges directly from Locke's thesis by three simple steps. First, it accepts the argument that we have no idea whatsoever what a substance might be, and it agrees that all that we can ever know of a thing are its sensible properties (or "qualities"). Second, it is shown that the distinction between primary and secondary qualities cannot be, as Locke had argued, a distinction between properties inherent in the objects themselves as opposed to properties which the objects simply cause in us. And third, once one has agreed that all knowledge of the world (except for knowledge of one's own existence and of God) must be based upon experience, the question becomes why we should ever think that there is anything other than our experiences. Locke had argued that our experiences were caused by the physical objects; but how could this claim be justified by experience? Since we have no experience of either the objects themselves or their causation, but only of their effects (that is, the ideas they cause in us) a consistent empiricist must give up not only the causal theory of perception but the notion of physical objects as well.

Bishop Berkeley is an exceptionally clear writer, and the following excerpts from his *Treatise Concerning the Principles of Human Knowledge* (1710) should not be difficult to understand:

from *The Principles of Human Knowledge,* by Berkeley

1. It is evident to anyone who takes a survey of the objects of human knowledge, that they are either ideas (1) actually imprinted on the senses, or else such as are (2) perceived by attending to the passions and operations of the mind, or lastly (3) ideas formed by help of memory and imagination, either compounding, dividing, or barely representing those originally perceived in the aforesaid ways. By sight I have the ideas of lights and colors, with their several degrees and variations. By touch I perceive hard and soft, heat and cold, motion and resistance, and of all these more and less either as to quantity or degree. Smelling furnishes me with odors, the palate with tastes, and hearing conveys sounds to the mind in all their variety of tone and composition. And as several of these are observed to accompany each other, they come to be marked by one name, and so to be reputed as one thing. Thus, for example, a certain color, taste, smell, figure, and consistence, having been observed to go together, are accounted one distinct thing, signified by the name "apple." Other collections of ideas constitute a stone, a tree, a book, and the like sensible things; which, as they are pleasing or disagreeable, excite the passions of love, hatred, joy, grief, and so forth.

2. But besides all that endless variety of ideas or objects of knowledge, there is likewise something which knows or perceives them, and exercises divers operations, as willing, imagining, remembering, about them. This perceiving, active being is what I call *mind, spirit, soul,* or *myself.* By which words I do not denote any one of my ideas, but a thing entirely distinct from them wherein they exist, or, which is the same thing, whereby they are perceived, for the existence of an idea consists in being perceived.

3. That neither our thoughts, nor passions, nor ideas formed by the imagination, exist without the mind, is what everybody will allow. And it seems no less evident that the various sensations or ideas imprinted on the sense, however blended or combined together (that is, whatever objects they compose), cannot exist otherwise than in a mind perceiving them. I think an intuitive knowledge may be obtained of this by anyone that shall attend to what is meant by the term "exist" when applied to sensible things. The table I write on I say exists—that is, I see and feel it; and if I were out of my study I should say it existed—meaning thereby that if I was in my study I might perceive it, or that some other spirit actually does perceive it. There was an odor, that is, it was smelt; there was a sound, that is, it was heard; a color or figure, and it was perceived by sight or touch. This is all that I can understand by these and the like expressions. For as to what is said of the absolute existence of unthinking things without any relation to their being perceived, that seems perfectly unintelligible. Their *esse* is *percipi*,[7] nor is it possible they should have any existence out of the minds or thinking things which perceive them.

4. It is indeed an opinion strangely prevailing amongst men, that houses, mountains, rivers, and in a word all sensible objects, have an existence, natural or real, distinct from their being perceived by the understanding. But with how great an assurance and acquiescence so ever this principle may be entertained in the world, yet whoever shall find in his heart to call it in question may, if I mistake not, perceive it to involve a manifest contradiction. For what are the forementioned objects but the things we perceive by sense? and what do we perceive *besides our own ideas or sensations?* and is it not plainly repugnant that any one of these, or any combination of them, should exist unperceived?

5. If we thoroughly examine this tenet it will perhaps be found at bottom to depend on the doctrine of *abstract ideas.* For can there be a nicer strain of abstraction than to distinguish the existence of sensible objects from their being perceived, so as to conceive them existing unperceived? Light and colors, heat and cold, extension and figures—in a word the things we see and feel—what are they but so many sensations, notions, ideas, or impressions on the sense? And is it possible to separate, even in thought, any of these from perception? For my part, I might as easily divide a thing from itself. I may, indeed, divide in my thoughts, or conceive apart from each other, those things which perhaps I never perceived by sense so divided. Thus I imagine the trunk of a human body without the limbs, or conceive the smell of a rose without thinking on the rose itself. So far, I will not deny, I can abstract, if that may properly be called abstraction which extends only to the conceiving separately such objects as it is possible may really exist or be actually perceived asunder. But my conceiving or imagining power does not extend beyond the possibility of real existence or perception. Hence, as it is impossible for me to see or feel anything without an actual sensation of that thing, so it is impossible for me to conceive in my thoughts any sensible thing or object distinct from the sensation or perception of it.

[7] *to be* is *to be perceived*

6. Some truths there are so near and obvious to the mind that a man need only open his eyes to see them. Such I take this important one to be, to wit, that all the choir of heaven and furniture of the earth, in a word all those bodies which compose the mighty frame of the world, have not any subsistence without a mind, that their *being* is to be perceived or known; that consequently so long as they are not actually perceived by me, or do not exist in my mind or that of any other created spirit, they must either have no existence at all, or else subsist in the mind of some Eternal Spirit; it being perfectly unintelligible, and involving all the absurdity of abstraction, to attribute to any single part of them an existence independent of a spirit. To be convinced of which, the reader need only reflect and try to separate in his own thoughts the *being* of a sensible thing from its *being perceived.*

7. From what has been said it follows there is not any other substance than *spirit*, or that which perceives. But for the fuller proof of this point, let it be considered the sensible qualities are color, figure, motion, smell, taste, etc. — that is, the ideas perceived by sense. Now, for an idea to exist in an unperceiving thing is a manifest contradiction, for to have an idea is all one as to perceive; that therefore wherein color, figure, and the like qualities exist must perceive them; hence it is clear there can be no unthinking substance or *substratum* of those ideas.

8. But, say you, though the ideas themselves do not exist without the mind, yet there may be things *like* them, whereof they are copies or resemblances, which things exist without the mind in an unthinking substance. I answer, an idea can be like nothing but an idea; a color or figure can be like nothing but another color or figure. If we look but never so little into our thoughts, we shall find it impossible for us to conceive a likeness except only between our ideas. Again, I ask whether those supposed originals or external things, of which our ideas are the pictures or representations, be themselves perceivable or no? If they are, then they are ideas and we have gained our point; but if you say they are not, I appeal to anyone whether it be sense to assert a color is like something which is invisible, hard or soft, like something which is intangible; and so of the rest.

9. Some there are who make a distinction betwixt *primary* and *secondary* qualities. By the former they mean extension, figure, motion, rest, solidity or impenetrability, and number; by the latter they denote all other sensible qualities, as colors, sounds, tastes, and so forth. The ideas we have of these they acknowledge not to be the resemblances of anything existing without the mind, or unperceived, but they will have our ideas of the primary qualities to be patterns or images of things which exist without the mind, in an unthinking substance which they call *matter*. By *matter*, therefore, we are to understand an inert, senseless substance, in which extension, figure, and motion do actually subsist. But it is evident from what we have already shown, that extension, figure, and motion are only ideas existing in the mind, and that an idea can be like nothing but another idea, and that consequently neither they nor their archetypes can exist in an unperceiving substance. Hence, it is plain that the very notion of what is called *matter*, or *corporeal substance*, involves a contradiction in it.

10. They who assert that figure, motion, and the rest of the primary or original qualities do exist without the mind in unthinking substances, do

at the same time acknowledge that color, sounds, heat, cold, and suchlike secondary qualities, do not; which they tell us are sensations existing in the mind alone, that depend on and are occasioned by the different size, texture, and motion of the minute particles of matter. This they take for an undoubted truth, which they can demonstrate beyond all exception. Now, if it be certain that those original qualities are inseparably united with the other sensible qualities, and not, even in thought, capable of being abstracted from them, it plainly follows that they exist only in the mind. But I desire anyone to reflect and try whether he can, by any abstraction of thought, conceive the extension and motion of a body without all other sensible qualities. For my own part, I see evidently that it is not in my power to frame an idea of a body extended and moving, but I must withal give it some color or other sensible quality which is acknowledged to exist only in the mind. In short, extension, figure, and motion, abstracted from all other qualities, are inconceivable. Where therefore the other sensible qualities are, there must these be also, to wit, in the mind and nowhere else. . . .

14. I shall farther add that, after the same manner as modern philosophers prove certain sensible qualities to have no existence in matter, or without the mind, the same thing may be likewise proved of all other sensible qualities whatsoever. Thus, for instance, it is said that heat and cold are affections only of the mind, and not at all patterns of real beings, existing in the corporeal substances which excite them, for that the same body which appears cold to one hand seems warm to another. Now, why may we not as well argue that figure and extension are not patterns or resemblances of qualities existing in matter, because to the same eye at different stations, or eyes of a different texture at the same station, they appear various, and cannot therefore be the images of anything settled and determinate without the mind? Again, it is proved that sweetness is not really in the sapid thing, because the thing remaining unaltered the sweetness is changed into bitter, as in case of a fever or otherwise vitiated palate. Is it not as reasonable to say that motion is not without the mind, since if the succession of ideas in the mind become swifter, the motion, it is acknowledged, shall appear slower without any alteration in any external object?

15. In short, let anyone consider those arguments which are thought manifestly to prove that colors and taste exist only in the mind, and he shall find they may with equal force be brought to prove the same thing of extension, figure, and motion—though it must be confessed this method of arguing does not so much prove that there is no extension or color in an outward object, as that we do not know by sense which is the true extension or color of the object. But the arguments foregoing plainly show it to be impossible that any color or extension at all, or other sensible quality whatsoever, should exist in an unthinking subject without the mind, or in truth, that there should be any such thing as an outward object.

16. But let us examine a little the received opinion. It is said extension is a mode or accident of matter, and that matter is the *substratum* that supports it. Now I desire that you would explain to me what is meant by matter's *supporting* extension. Say you, I have no idea of matter and therefore cannot explain it. I answer, though you have no positive, yet, if you have any meaning at all, you must at least have a relative idea of matter; though

you know not what it is, yet you must be supposed to know what relation it bears to accidents, and what is meant by its supporting them. It is evident "support" cannot here be taken in its usual or literal sense — as when we say that pillars support a building; in what sense therefore must it be taken?

17. If we inquire into what the most accurate philosophers declare themselves to mean by *material substance*, we shall find them acknowledge they have no other meaning annexed to those sounds but the idea of *Being in general*, together with the relative notion of its supporting accidents. The general idea of Being appeareth to me the most abstract and incomprehensible of all other; and as for its supporting accidents, this, as we have just now observed, cannot be understood in the common sense of those words; it must therefore be taken in some other sense, but what that is they do not explain. So that when I consider the two parts or branches which make the signification of the words *material substance*, I am convinced there is no distinct meaning annexed to them. But why should we trouble ourselves any farther, in discussing this material *substratum* or support of figure and motion, and other sensible qualities? Does it not suppose they have an existence without the mind? And is not this a direct repugnancy, and altogether inconceivable?

18. But though it were possible that solid, figured, movable substances may exist without the mind, corresponding to the ideas we have of bodies, yet how is it possible for us to know this? Either we must know it by sense or by reason. As for our senses, by them we have the knowledge only of our sensations, ideas, or those things that are immediately perceived by sense, call them what you will; but they do not inform us that things exist without the mind, or unperceived, like to those which are perceived. This the materialists[8] themselves acknowledge. It remains therefore that if we have any knowledge at all of external things, it must be by reason, inferring their existence from what is immediately perceived by sense. But what reason can induce us to believe the existence of bodies without the mind, from what we perceive, since the very patrons of matter themselves do not pretend there is any necessary connection betwixt them and our ideas? I say it is granted on all hands (and what happens in dreams, frenzies, and the like, puts it beyond dispute) that *it is possible we might be affected with all the ideas we have now, though there were no bodies existing without, resembling them.* Hence, it is evident the supposition of external bodies is not necessary for the producing our ideas; since it is granted they are produced sometimes, and might possibly be produced always in the same order we see them in at present, without their concurrence.

19. But, though we might possibly have all our sensations without them, yet perhaps it may be thought easier to conceive and explain the manner of their production by supposing external bodies in their likeness rather than otherwise; and so it might be at least probable there are such things as bodies that excite their ideas in our minds. But neither can this be said; for though we give the materialists their external bodies, they by their own confession are never the nearer knowing how our ideas are produced, since they own themselves unable to comprehend in what manner body can act

[8]Berkeley uses "materialists" to refer to those who believe in the existence of matter, not to those who believe in only matter, its usual meaning.

upon spirit, or how it is possible it should imprint any idea in the mind. Hence it is evident the production of ideas or sensations in our minds can be no reason why we should suppose matter or corporeal substances, since that is acknowledged to remain equally inexplicable with or without this supposition. If therefore it were possible for bodies to exist without the mind, yet to hold they do so, must needs be a very precarious opinion; since it is to suppose, without any reason at all, that God has created innumerable things that are entirely useless, and serve to no manner of purpose.

20. In short, if there were external bodies, it is impossible we should ever come to know it; and if there were not, we might have the very same reasons to think there were that we have now. Suppose (what no one can deny possible) an intelligence without the help of external bodies, to be affected with the same train of sensations or ideas that you are, imprinted in the same order and with like vividness in his mind. I ask whether that intelligence hath not all the reason to believe the existence of corporeal substances, represented by his ideas, and exciting them in his mind, that you can possibly have for believing the same thing? Of this there can be no question; which one consideration were enough to make any reasonable person suspect the strength of whatever arguments he may think himself to have for the existence of bodies without the mind. . . .

23. But, say you, surely there is nothing easier than for me to imagine trees, for instance, in a park, or books existing in a closet, and nobody by to perceive them. I answer, you may so, there is no difficulty in it; but what is all this, I beseech you, more than framing in your mind certain ideas which you call books and trees, and the same time omitting to frame the idea of anyone that may perceive them? But do not you yourself perceive or think of them all the while? This therefore is nothing to the purpose; it only shews you have the power of imagining or forming ideas in your mind: but it doth not shew that you can conceive it possible the objects of your thought may exist without the mind. To make out this, it is necessary that you conceive them existing unconceived or unthought of, which is a manifest repugnancy. When we do our utmost to conceive the existence of external bodies, we are all the while only contemplating our own ideas.[9]

But what, then, can explain the fact that we cannot simply "think" things into existence by imagining them? And how can we say that a thing exists when no one is there to perceive it? ("If a tree falls in the forest, and there's no one there to hear it, does it make a sound?") It is here that God enters the picture as a matter of necessity.

29. But, whatever power I may have over my own thoughts, I find the ideas actually perceived by Sense have not a like dependence on my will. When in broad daylight I open my eyes, it is not in my power to choose whether I shall see or no, or to determine what particular objects shall present themselves to my view; and so likewise as to the hearing and other senses, the ideas imprinted on them are not creatures of my will. There is therefore some *other* Will or Spirit that produces them.

---

[9]George Berkeley, *Treatise Concerning the Principles of Human Knowledge* (New York: Bobbs-Merrill, 1957).

30. The ideas of Sense are more strong, lively, and distinct than those of the Imagination; they have likewise a steadiness, order, and coherence, and are not excited at random, as those which are the effects of human wills often are, but in a regular train or series — the admirable connexion whereof sufficiently testifies the wisdom and benevolence of its Author. Now the set rules or established methods wherein the Mind we depend on excites in us the ideas of sense, are called the *laws of nature;* and these we learn by experience, which teaches us that such and such ideas are attended with such and such other ideas, in the ordinary course of things.

31. This gives us a sort of foresight which enables us to regulate our actions for the benefit of life. And without this we should be eternally at a loss; we could not know how to act anything that might procure us the least pleasure, or remove the least pain of sense. That food nourishes, sleep refreshes, and fire warms us; that to sow in the seedtime is the way to reap in the harvest; and in general that to obtain such or such ends, such or such means are conducive — all this we know, not by discovering any *necessary connexion* between our ideas, but only by the *observation* of the settled laws of nature, without which we should be all in uncertainty and confusion, and a grown man no more know how to manage himself in the affairs of life than an infant just born. . . .

33. The ideas imprinted on the senses by the Author of nature are called *real things;* and those excited in the imagination, being less regular, vivid, and constant, are more properly termed *ideas,* or *images of things,* which they copy and represent. But then our sensations, be they never so vivid and distinct, are nevertheless ideas, that is, they exist in the mind, or are perceived by it, as truly as the ideas of its own framing. The ideas of sense are allowed to have more reality in them, that is, to be more strong, orderly, and coherent than the creatures of the mind; but this is no argument that they exist without the mind. They are also less dependent on the spirit, or thinking substance which perceives them, in that they are excited by the will of another and more powerful spirit; yet still they are *ideas,* and certainly no idea, whether faint or strong, can exist otherwise than in a mind perceiving it.[10]

---

[10]This final formulation, that the things of the world are nothing other than ideas in the mind of God, is the subject of a limerick by Ronald Knox, quoted for us by Bertrand Russell.

> There was a young man who said, "God
> Must think it exceedingly odd
>   If he finds that this tree
>   Continues to be
> When there's no one about in the Quad."

> REPLY

> Dear Sir:
>   Your astonishment's odd:
> *I* am always about in the Quad.
>   And that's why the tree
>   Will continue to be,
> Since observed by
>   *Yours faithfully,*
>   GOD.

And finally, the defense against common sense:

> 38. But after all, say you, it sounds very harsh to say we eat and drink ideas, and are clothed with ideas. I acknowledge it does so; the word "idea" not being used in common discourse to signify the several combinations of sensible qualities which are called "things"; and it is certain that any expression which varies from the familiar use of language will seem harsh and ridiculous. But this doth not concern the truth of the proposition, which in other words is no more than to say, we are fed and clothed with those things which we perceive immediately by our senses.
>
> 39. If it be demanded why I make use of the word "idea," and do not rather in compliance with custom call them "thing"; I answer, I do it for two reasons: — first, because the term "thing" in contradistinction to "idea," is generally supposed to denote somewhat existing without the mind; secondly, because "thing" hath a more comprehensive signification than "idea," including spirit or thinking things as well as ideas. Since therefore the objects of sense exist only in the mind, and are withal thoughtless and inactive, I chose to mark them by the word "idea," which implies those properties.[11]

Is this where Locke was leading us? If so, it looks as if the "new metaphysics" is every bit as fantastic as the old ones. But the controversial development of Locke's empiricism has still another step to go.

THE CONGENIAL SKEPTIC: DAVID HUME

It isn't very far from Berkeley's subjective idealism to David Hume's outrageous, but seemingly irrefutable, skepticism. Bertrand Russell, writing about Hume two hundred years later (1945), says,

> To refute him has been, ever since he wrote, a favorite pastime among metaphysicians. For my part, I find none of their refutations convincing; nevertheless, I cannot but hope that something less skeptical than Hume's system may be discoverable.

and

> Hume's skeptical conclusions ... are equally difficult to refute and to accept. The result was a challenge to philosophers, which, in my opinion, has still not been adequately met.[12]

There have been many philosophers who have said — or feared — that Hume's skepticism is the last word in philosophy. But in any case, it is one of those positions that no philosophy student can avoid taking seriously.

[11]Berkeley, *Treatise Concerning the Principles of Human Knowledge.*
[12]Bertrand Russell, *A History of Western Philosophy* (New York: Simon and Schuster, 1945).

Hume's *Treatise of Human Nature* (1739) was written when he was in his early twenties; his ambition was no less than to be the Isaac Newton of philosophy and psychology, following but outdoing John Locke. The book failed to attract attention (he said "it fell stillborn from the press"), and Hume turned his attention to other matters, making himself famous as a historian. Later, in 1748, he wrote a more popular version of his earlier *Treatise,* which he called *An Enquiry Concerning Human Understanding.* It was extremely successful, and Hume became widely known as a "devil's advocate" during his lifetime, a position he generally enjoyed. Both the *Treatise* and the *Enquiry* are firmly committed to Locke's empiricist methodology, but where Locke was generous with doubtful ideas with no clear experiential basis (notably, substance and God), Hume was ruthless. In a famous threatening passage, he had bellowed,

> When we run over libraries, persuaded of these [empiricist] principles, what havoc must we make? If we take in our hand any volume of divinity or school metaphysics, for instance, let us ask, Does it contain any abstract reasoning concerning quantity or number? No. Does it contain any experimental reasoning concerning matter of fact and existence? No, Commit it to the flames, for it can contain nothing but sophistry and illusion.[13]

In this unveiled threat to traditional metaphysics we can see in a glance Hume's formidable tactics — the insistence that every justifiable belief must be either a "relation of ideas," for example, a statement of mathematics, logic, or a trivial conceptual truth, or a "matter of fact," which can be confirmed by appeal to our experience. (This "either-or" is sometimes called "Hume's fork.") Of course, most of the modern philosophers we have discussed shared this insistence upon justifiability either by reason ("relation of ideas") or by experience. But it is only Hume who realizes the severity of this demand and the embarrassing number of our fundamental beliefs that do not allow justification either by reason or experience.

Like his empiricist predecessor, Hume insists that all knowledge begins with basic units of sensory experience. Hume's "impressions" (Locke's "sensations") are these basic units (what we would still call "sensations" or "sense-data").

from *A Treatise of Human Nature,* by David Hume

ALL the perceptions of the human mind resolve themselves into two distinct kinds, which I shall call IMPRESSIONS and IDEAS. The difference betwixt these consists in the degrees of force and liveliness with which they strike upon the mind, and make their way into our thought or consciousness. Those perceptions, which enter with most force and violence, we may name

[13]David Hume, *An Enquiry Concerning Human Understanding,* 2nd ed., ed. L. A. Selby-Bigge (Oxford: Oxford University Press, 1902). All subsequent quotations from Hume's *Enquiry* are from this edition unless otherwise noted.

impressions; and under this name I comprehend all our sensations, passions and emotions, as they make their first appearance in the soul. By *ideas* I mean the faint images of these in thinking and reasoning; such as, for instance, are all the perceptions excited by the present discourse, excepting only, those which arise from the sight and touch, and excepting the immediate pleasure or uneasiness it may occasion. I believe it will not be very necessary to employ many words in explaining this distinction. Every one of himself will readily perceive the difference betwixt feeling and thinking. The common degrees of these are easily distinguished; tho' it is not impossible but in particular instances they may very nearly approach to each other. Thus in sleep, in a fever, in madness, or in any very violent emotions of soul, our ideas may approach to our impressions: As on the other hand it sometimes happens, that our impressions are so faint and low, that we cannot distinguish them from our ideas. But notwithstanding this near resemblance in a few instances, they are in general so very different, that no-one can make a scruple to rank them under distinct heads, and assign to each a peculiar name to mark the difference.

There is another division of our perceptions, which it will be convenient to observe, and which extends itself both to our impressions and ideas. This division is into Simple and Complex. Simple perceptions or impressions and ideas are such as admit of no distinction nor separation. The complex are the contrary to these, and may be distinguished into parts. Tho' a particular colour, taste, and smell are qualities all united together in this apple, 'tis easy to perceive they are not the same, but are at least distinguishable from each other.

Having by these divisions given an order and arrangement to our objects, we may now apply ourselves to consider with the more accuracy their qualities and relations. The first circumstance, that strikes my eye, is the great resemblance betwixt our impressions and ideas in every other particular, except their degree of force and vivacity. The one seem to be in a manner the reflexion of the other; so that all the perceptions of the mind are double, and appear both as impressions and ideas. When I shut my eyes and think of my chamber, the ideas I form are exact representations of the impressions I felt, nor is there any circumstance of the one, which is not to be found in the other. In running over my other perceptions, I find still the same resemblance and representation. Ideas and impressions appear always to correspond to each other. This circumstance seems to me remarkable, and engages my attention for a moment.

Upon a more accurate survey I find I have been carried away too far by the first appearance, and that I must make use of the distinction of perceptions into *simple and complex,* to limit this general decision, *that all our ideas and impressions are resembling.* I observe, that many of our complex ideas never had impressions, that corresponded to them, and that many of our complex impressions never are exactly copied in ideas. I can imagine to myself such a city as the *New Jerusalem,* whose pavement is gold and walls are rubies, tho' I never saw any such. I have seen *Paris;* but shall I affirm I can form such an idea of that city, as will perfectly represent all its streets and houses in their real and just proportions?

I perceive, therefore, that tho' there is in general a great resemblance betwixt our *complex* impressions and ideas, yet the rule is not universally true, that they are exact copies of each other. We may next consider how the case stands with our *simple* perceptions. After the most accurate examination, of which I am capable, I venture to affirm, that the rule here holds without any exception, and that every simple idea has a simple impression, which resembles it; and every simple impression a correspondent idea. That idea of red, which we form in the dark, and that impression, which strikes our eyes in sun-shine, differ only in degree, not in nature. That the case is the same with all our simple impressions and ideas, 'tis impossible to prove by a particular enumeration of them. Every one may satisfy himself in this point by running over as many as he pleases. But if any one should deny this universal resemblance, I know of no way of convincing him, but by desiring him to shew a simple impression that has not a correspondent idea, or a simple idea, that has not a correspondent impression. If he does not answer this challenge, as 'tis certain he cannot, we may from his silence and our own observation establish our conclusion.

Thus we find, that all simple ideas and impressions resemble each other; and as the complex are formed from them, we may affirm in general, that these two species of perception are exactly correspondent. Having discover'd this relation, which requires no farther examination, I am curious to find some other of their qualities. Let us consider how they stand with regard to their existence, and which of the impressions and ideas are causes, and which effects.

The *full* examination of this question is the subject of the present treatise; and therefore we shall here content ourselves with establishing one general proposition. *That all our simple ideas in their first appearance are deriv'd from simple impressions, which are correspondent to them, and which they exactly represent.*

According to Hume, simple ideas are derived from simple impressions. A simple idea would be something like a red, round image; the simple impression would be seeing a red, round image. More complex ideas, for example, the idea of an apple, are complex arrangements and associations of simple ideas. To justify a belief as knowledge, therefore, we must break up its complex ideas into simple ideas and then find the impressions upon which those ideas are based. If I claim to see an apple, for example, I analyze my experience; my idea that there is an apple out there depends upon my seeing several red, round images from different angles, feeling something smooth, tasting something fruity and tart, and so on. If I claim that there are objects of a certain kind (apples, for example), I must identify the simple ideas and impressions upon which my supposed knowledge is based. And if I make a metaphysical claim, about the existence of God or substances, I must either be prepared to identify the ideas and impressions upon which such a claim is based, or I must show that it is nothing other than a "relation of ideas"; otherwise, the claim cannot be justified ("commit it to the flames").

But, to the embarrassment of most metaphysical doctrines, they cannot be defended by either of the methods allowed by Hume. They are, by their very nature, about things beyond everyday experience (for example, God, substance) and so are not based upon "impressions"; nor are they "relations of ideas" that can be demonstrated by a simple logical or mathematical proof. Therefore, they cannot be justified. The problem, however, is that the same argument extends far beyond the debatable claims of metaphysics and undermines some of the beliefs that are most essential to our everyday experiences as well. In Hume's philosophy, three such beliefs in particular are singled out for analysis. On the one hand, they are so fundamental to our daily experience and common knowledge that no sane man or woman could possibly doubt them; but, on the other hand, they are completely without justification. As Hume argues, first, there is our idea of **causation** (or causality), of one event bringing about or causing another event. From this idea, which provides what Hume calls "the strongest connections" of our experience and, elsewhere, "the cement of the universe," we derive a most important principle, the principle of universal causation, which states that every event has its **cause** (or causes). It is evident that we invoke such a principle every time we explain anything; for example, the car won't start. We search for the cause, but everything seems to check out—the carburetor, the electrical system, and so on. Now we might search for hours without finding the cause, but there is one thing that we know for certain, and that is that there must be a cause somewhere—even if it is a very complex cause. What is not possible is that there be no cause. Presupposed in our everyday thinking is this principle, that every event has its cause. (You may recognize this principle as a version of Leibniz's Principle of Sufficient Reason, but substituting the more Newtonian notion of "cause" for the notion of "reason.")

Second, because of our presupposed belief in causation and its universal applicability, we are able to think beyond our immediate "ideas" and predict the future and explain the past. But to do so, we must also believe that our observations of the present will have some relevance in the future, that we can in fact draw valid inductive generalizations from our experience. Of course, we do so all of the time; for example, when I wake up at 6:00 in the morning, I expect the sun to rise within the hour. Why? Because it has always done so, because it is February 26th and the almanac says it will. In making every such prediction, we presuppose a **principle of induction,** that is, that the laws of nature that have always held in the past will continue to hold in the future. The principle of induction is sometimes summarized as "the future will be like the past," which is all right only so long as it is not taken too literally; for of course the future is never just like the past (you are now fifteen seconds older, for example, and have added a whole new expression to your knowledge, and, [unless you are eating while you read] lost a tiny bit of weight as well). But the laws of nature, at least, do not change from moment to moment.

And third, there is our belief in the "external world," that is, a physical or material world that exists independently of our impressions and ideas, which it presumably causes in us. Bishop Berkeley had already done Hume's work for him here. Hume, following Berkeley, also rejects all notions of substance as unintelligible, including even that minimal "we know not what" of John Locke. But where Berkeley turned the rejection of matter and substance into a metaphysics (namely, his subjective idealism) and used it to defend the existence of God, Hume rejects this idealist metaphysics as well and remains wholly skeptical, refusing to accept the existence of God. He remains firm in his insistence that our belief in the existence of anything is no different from "the idea of what we conceive to be existent."

We can see that these three basic beliefs are intimately tied together; it is the notion of cause that supports the principle of induction,[14] and it is the causal theory of perception that supports our belief in the "external world." Accordingly, Hume takes causation to be the central idea of all reasoning,[15] that is, all attempts to connect separate ideas together in a single belief. Hume's arguments are both elegant and simple to follow. He refutes both the principle of universal causation and the principle of induction by showing that neither can be defended either as a "relation of ideas" or as a "matter of fact." He begins with a statement that all human knowledge must be one or the other, explains what he means by "relations of ideas" and "matters of fact," shows how it is that "cause and effect" are the basis of all reasoning, and then proceeds to show that such reasoning can be neither a relation of ideas nor a simple matter of fact.

from the *Treatise,* by Hume

All the objects of human reason or enquiry may naturally be divided into two kinds, to wit, *Relations of Ideas,* and *Matters of Fact.* Of the first kind are the sciences of Geometry, Algebra, and Arithmetic; and in short, every affirmation which is either intuitively or demonstratively certain. *That the square of the hypothenuse is equal to the square of the two sides,* is a proposition which expresses a relation between these figures. *That three times five is equal to the half of thirty,* expresses a relation between these numbers. Propositions of this kind are discoverable by the mere operation of thought, without dependence on what is anywhere existent in the universe. Though there never were a circle or triangle in nature, the truths demonstrated by Euclid would for ever retain their certainty and evidence.

Matters of fact, which are the second objects of human reason, are not ascertained in the same manner; nor is our evidence of their truth, however great, of a like nature with the foregoing. The contrary of every matter of fact is still possible; because it can never imply a contradiction, and is conceived by the mind with the same facility and distinctness, as if ever so conformable to reality. *That the sun will not rise to-morrow* is no less intelligible a proposition, and implies no more contradiction than the affirmation, *that it will rise.* We should in vain, therefore, attempt to demonstrate

---

[14]Modern philosophers have given a great deal of attention to inductive inferences that are not based upon any obvious causes, for example, statistical probabilities (as in genetics or gambling).

[15]It is important to remember that Hume, like Locke, models his philosophy-psychology after Newton's physics. So even if he rejects Locke's "causal theory of perception," the Newtonian model, in which causality is central, remains at the heart of his theories.

its falsehood. Were it demonstratively false, it would imply a contradiction, and could never be distinctly conceived by the mind.

It may, therefore, be a subject worthy of curiosity, to enquire what is the nature of that evidence which assures us of any real existence and matter of fact, beyond the present testimony of our senses, or the records of our memory. This part of philosophy, it is observable, has been little cultivated, either by the ancients or moderns; and therefore our doubts and errors, in the prosecution of so important an enquiry, may be the more excusable; while we march through such difficult paths without any guide or direction. They may even prove useful, by exciting curiosity, and destroying that implicit faith and security, which is the bane of all reasoning and free enquiry. The discovery of defects in the common philosophy, if any such there be, will not, I presume, be a discouragement, but rather an incitement, as is usual, to attempt something more full and satisfactory than has yet been proposed to the public.

All reasonings concerning matter of fact seem to be founded on the relation of *Cause and Effect*. By means of that relation alone we can go beyond the evidence of our memory and senses. If you were to ask a man, why he believes any matter of fact, which is absent; for instance, that his friend is in the country, or in France; he would give you a reason; and this reason would be some other fact; as a letter received from him, or the knowledge of his former resolutions and promises. A man finding a watch or any other machine in a desert island, would conclude that there had once been men in that island. All our reasonings concerning fact are of the same nature. And here it is constantly supposed that there is a connexion between the present fact and that which is inferred from it. Were there nothing to bind them together, the inference would be entirely precarious. The hearing of an articulate voice and rational discourse in the dark assures us of the presence of some person: Why? because these are the effects of the human make and fabric, and closely connected with it. If we anatomize all the other reasonings of this nature, we shall find that they are founded on the relation of cause and effect, and that this relation is either near or remote, direct or collateral. Heat and light are collateral effects of fire, and the one effect may justly be inferred from the other.

Hume's argument, which we shall see again and again, is that we explain our experiences and events by appeal to other experiences and events. If I burn my finger and wonder how, I look down and see that I have just placed my hand too near the stove-top burner. I explain that the heat of the burner is the cause and the burn is the effect of the hot burner. Indeed, we are perplexed whenever we cannot find some such causal explanation, and the suggestion that there might not be one ("there was no cause; you just burned yourself, that's all") is all but unintelligible to us. But now, Hume asks, where do we get this knowledge of causes and effects?

If we would satisfy ourselves, therefore, concerning the nature of that evidence, which assures us of matters of fact, we must enquire how we arrive at the knowledge of cause and effect.

I shall venture to affirm, as a general proposition, which admits of no exception, that the knowledge of this relation is not, in any instance, attained by reasonings *a priori;* but arises entirely from experience, when we find that any particular objects are constantly conjoined with each other. Let an object be presented to a man of ever so strong natural reason and abilities; if that object be entirely new to him, he will not be able, by the most accurate examination of its sensible qualities, to discover any of its causes or effects. Adam, though his rational faculties be supposed, at the very first, entirely perfect, could not have inferred from the fluidity and transparency of water that it would suffocate him, or from the light and warmth of fire that it would consume him. No object ever discovers, by the qualities which appear to the senses, either the causes which produced it, or the effects which will arise from it; nor can our reason, unassisted by experience, ever draw any inference concerning real existence and matter of fact.

This proposition, *that causes and effects are discoverable, not by reason but by experience,* will readily be admitted with regard to such objects, as we remember to have once been altogether unknown to us; since we must be conscious of the utter inability, which we then lay under, of foretelling what would arise from them. Present two smooth pieces of marble to a man who has no tincture of natural philosophy; he will never discover that they will adhere together in such a manner as to require great force to separate them in a direct line, while they make so small a resistance to a lateral pressure. Such events, as bear little analogy to the common course of nature, are also readily confessed to be known only by experience; nor does any man imagine that the explosion of gunpowder, or the attraction of a lodestone, could ever be discovered by arguments *a priori.* In like manner, when an effect is supposed to depend upon an intricate machinery or secret structure of parts, we make no difficulty in attributing all our knowledge of it to experience. Who will assert that he can give the ultimate reason, why milk or bread is proper nourishment for a man, not for a lion or a tiger?

But the same truth may not appear, at first sight, to have the same evidence with regard to events, which have become familiar to us from our first appearance in the world, which bear a close analogy to the whole course of nature, and which are supposed to depend on the simple qualities of objects, without any secret structure of parts. We are apt to imagine that we could discover these effects by the mere operation of our reason, without experience. We fancy, that were we brought on a sudden into this world, we could at first have inferred that one Billiard-ball would communicate motion to another upon impulse; and that we needed not to have waited for the event, in order to pronounce with certainty concerning it. Such is the influence of custom, that, where it is strongest, it not only covers our natural ignorance, but even conceals itself, and seems not to take place, merely because it is found in the highest degree.

But to convince us that all the laws of nature, and all the operations of bodies without exception, are known only by experience, the following reflections may, perhaps, suffice. Were any object presented to us, and were we required to pronounce concerning the effect, which will result from it, without consulting past observation; after what manner, I beseech you, must the mind proceed in this operation? It must invent or imagine some event, which it ascribes to the object as its effect; and it is plain that this invention must be entirely arbitrary. The mind can never possibly find the effect in the supposed cause, by the most accurate scrutiny and examination. For the effect is totally different from the cause, and consequently can never be discovered in it. Motion in the second Billiard-ball is a quite distinct event from motion in the first; nor is there anything in the one to suggest the smallest hint of the other. A stone or piece of metal raised into the air, and left without any support, immediately falls: but to consider the matter *a priori*, is there anything we discover in this situation which can beget the idea of a downward, rather than an upward, or any other motion in the stone or metal?

And as the first imagination or invention of a particular effect, in all natural operations, is arbitrary, where we consult not experience; so must we also esteem the supposed tie or connexion between the cause and effect, which binds them together, and renders it impossible that any other effect could result from the operation of that cause. When I see, for instance, a Billiard-ball moving in a straight line towards another; even suppose motion in the second ball should by accident be suggested to me, as the result of their contact or impulse; may I not conceive, that a hundred different events might as well follow from that cause? May not both these balls remain at absolute rest? May not the first ball return in a straight line, or leap off from the second in any line or direction? All these suppositions are consistent and conceivable. Why then should we give the preference to one, which is no more consistent or conceivable than the rest? All our reasonings *a priori* will never be able to show us any foundation for this preference.

Hume's argument so far is that we do not know particular causes and effects through reason, but only through experience. Because you have seen it so many times, you know that a billiard ball moving toward and striking another billiard ball sets the second in motion on a predictable path. But if you had never seen anything like it before — perhaps if you were Adam or Eve (pool tables were not created until the eighth day of creation) — you would not have any idea what to expect. Both balls might stop dead. Both might explode. The second might start a law suit. Prediction of cause and effect, in other words, depends upon prior experience, and no amount of mere reasoning will suffice by itself.

In a word, then, every effect is a distinct event from its cause. It could not, therefore, be discovered in the cause, and the first invention or conception of it, *a priori*, must be entirely arbitrary. And even after it is suggested, the conjunction of it with the cause must appear equally arbitrary; since there are always many other effects, which, to reason, must seem fully as consistent and natural. In vain, therefore, should we pretend to determine any single event, or infer any cause or effect, without the assistance of observation and experience.

. . . . .

When we reason *a priori*, and consider merely any object or cause, as it appears to the mind, independent of all observation, it never could suggest to us the notion of any distinct object, such as its effect; much less, show us the inseparable and inviolable connexion between them. A man must be very sagacious who could discover by reasoning that crystal is the effect of heat, and ice of cold, without being previously acquainted with the operation of these qualities.

In this argument, we see Hume applying the first half of his "fork" to the idea of causation. The idea of cause and effect cannot be a relation of ideas because, no matter how closely we examine, for example, the idea of fire we will never discover the idea of its causing gunpowder to explode. Reasoning alone cannot reveal the causes or effects of particular events. At the outset of this argument, Hume also suggests that the idea of causation is not discoverable through perception either: Although we perceive many different qualities of fire, we never perceive its power to cause gunpowder to explode. Hume concludes that the idea of cause and effect must be derived from our experience of the constant conjunction of two events. We observe, for example, that every time we set a match to gunpowder it explodes; and because we expect the future to be like the past, we infer that the application of fire is the cause of the gunpowder's exploding. In short, our knowledge of causes is arrived at through induction from past experiences.

Hume's argument against induction, and in particular against the inductive principle that the future will be like the past, takes exactly the same form. Again he begins with his "fork" between "relations of ideas" and "matters of fact," and again he proves that one of the basic assumptions of all of our thinking, the principle of induction, cannot be established either way:

> But we have not yet attained any tolerable satisfaction with regard to the question first proposed. Each solution still gives rise to a new question as difficult as the foregoing, and leads us on to farther enquiries. When it is asked, *What is the nature of all our reasonings concerning matter of fact?* the proper answer seems to be, that they are founded on the relation of cause and effect. When again it is asked, *What is the foundation of all our reasonings and conclusions concerning that relation?* it may be replied in one word, Experience. But if we still carry on our sifting humour, and ask, *What is the foundation of all conclusions from experience?* this implies a new question, which may be of more difficult solution and explication. Philosophers, that give themselves airs of superior wisdom and sufficiency, have a hard task when they encounter persons of inquisitive dispositions, who push them from every corner to which they retreat, and who are sure at last to bring them to some dangerous dilemma. The best expedient to prevent this confusion, is to be modest in our pretensions; and even to discover the difficulty ourselves before it is objected to us. By this means, we may make a kind of merit of our very ignorance.
>
> I shall content myself, in this section, with an easy task, and shall pretend only to give a negative answer to the question here proposed. I say then, that, even after we have experience of the operations of cause and effect, our conclusions from that experience are *not* founded on reasoning,

or any process of the understanding. This answer we must endeavour both to explain and to defend.

It must certainly be allowed, that nature has kept us at a great distance from all her secrets, and has afforded us only the knowledge of a few superficial qualities of objects; while she conceals from us those powers and principles on which the influence of those objects entirely depends. Our senses inform us of the colour, weight, and consistence of bread; but neither sense nor reason can ever inform us of those qualities which fit it for the nourishment and support of a human body. Sight or feeling conveys an idea of the actual motion of bodies; but as to that wonderful force or power, which would carry on a moving body for ever in a continued change of place, and which bodies never lose but by communicating it to others; of this we cannot form the most distant conception. But notwithstanding this ignorance of natural powers and principles, we always presume, when we see like sensible qualities, that they have like secret powers, and expect that effects, similar to those which we have experienced, will follow from them. If a body of like colour and consistence with that bread, which we have formerly eat, be presented to us, we make no scruple of repeating the experiment, and foresee, with certainty, like nourishment and support. Now this is a process of the mind or thought, of which I would willingly know the foundation. It is allowed on all hands that there is no known connexion between the sensible qualities and the secret powers; and consequently, that the mind is not led to form such a conclusion concerning their constant and regular conjunction, by anything which it knows of their nature. As to past *Experience*, it can be allowed to give *direct* and *certain* information of those precise objects only, and that precise period of time, which fell under its cognizance: but why this experience should be extended to future times, and to other objects, which for aught we know, may be only in appearance similar; this is the main question on which I would insist. The bread, which I formerly eat, nourished me; that is, a body of such sensible qualities was, at that time, endued with such secret powers: but does it follow, that other bread must also nourish me at another time, and that like sensible qualities must always be attended with like secret powers? The consequence seems nowise necessary. At least, it must be acknowledged that there is here a consequence drawn by the mind; that there is a certain step taken; a process of thought, and an inference, which wants to be explained. These two propositions are far from being the same, *I have found that such an object has always been attended with such an effect*, and *I foresee, that other objects, which are, in appearance, similar, will be attended with similar effects.*

The argument so far is just like the argument regarding cause and effect, namely, that it is only from experience that we know the properties and effects of things and events, that moving bodies cause others to move, for instance, or that eating bread gives me nourishment. But now Hume distinguishes two propositions: (1) I have recognized a certain cause and effect relationship in my past experience, and (2) I predict that a similar cause and effect relationship will hold in the future also. The inference is surely reasonable, Hume says, but again he forces us to say why such an inference is reasonable, and he argues that we cannot do so.

I shall allow, if you please, that the one proposition may justly be inferred from the other: I know, in fact, that it always is inferred. But if you insist that the inference is made by a chain of reasoning, I desire you to produce that reasoning. The connexion between these propositions is not intuitive. There is required a medium, which may enable the mind to draw such an inference, if indeed it be drawn by reasoning and argument. What that medium is, I must confess, passes my comprehension; and it is incumbent on those to produce it, who assert that it really exists, and is the origin of all our conclusions concerning matter of fact.

This negative argument must certainly, in process of time, become altogether convincing, if many penetrating and able philosophers shall turn their enquiries this way and no one be ever able to discover any connecting proposition or intermediate step, which supports the understanding in this conclusion. But as the question is yet new, every reader may not trust so far to his own penetration, as to conclude, because an argument escapes his enquiry, that therefore it does not really exist. For this reason it may be requisite to venture upon a more difficult task; and enumerating all the branches of human knowledge, endeavour to show that none of them can afford such an argument.

Here is "Hume's fork"; the division of all knowledge into reasoning about relations of ideas (which he here calls "demonstrative") and reasoning about matters of fact (which he here calls "moral"). He says that it is clear from the above arguments that no demonstrative reasoning is available to justify our predictions of the future. But then he goes on to argue that no reasoning about matters of fact — no appeal to experience — can justify our propensity to make predictions either, for in order to justify our belief that the future will resemble the past on the basis of our experience, we would in effect be arguing that we know that the future will be like the past because in the past the future has always been like the past, and this is "begging the question" and a "vicious circle" in which one defends a proposition by referring it back to itself. (Like asking a suspected liar, "Are you lying to me?") Therefore our propensity for predicting can't be justified by appealing to experience either, which leaves us without any justification at all.

All reasonings may be divided into two kinds, namely, demonstrative reasoning, or that concerning relations of ideas, and moral reasoning, or that concerning matter of fact and existence. That there are no demonstrative arguments in the case seems evident; since it implies no contradiction that the course of nature may change, and that an object, seemingly like those which we have experienced, may be attended with different or contrary effects. May I not clearly and distinctly conceive that a body, falling from the clouds, and which, in all other respects, resembles snow, has yet the taste of salt or feeling of fire? Is there any more intelligible proposition than to affirm, that all the trees will flourish in December and January, and decay in May and June? Now whatever is intelligible, and can be distinctly conceived, implies no contradiction, and can never be proved false by any demonstrative argument or abstract reasoning *a priori.*

If we be, therefore, engaged by arguments to put trust in past experience, and make it the standard of our future judgement, these arguments must be probable only, or such as regard matter of fact and real existence, according to the division above mentioned. But that there is no argument of this kind, must appear, if our explication of that species of reasoning be admitted as solid and satisfactory. We have said that all arguments concerning existence are founded on the relation of cause and effect; that our knowledge of that relation is derived entirely from experience; and that all our experimental conclusions proceed upon the supposition that the future will be conformable to the past. To endeavour, therefore, the proof of this last supposition by probable arguments, or arguments regarding existence, must be evidently going in a circle, and taking that for granted, which is the very point in question.

When a man says, *I have found, in all past instances, such sensible qualities conjoined with such secret powers:* And when he says, *Similar sensible qualities will always be conjoined with similar secret powers,* he is not guilty of tautology, nor are these propositions in any respect the same. You say that the one proposition is an inference from the other. But you must confess that the inference is not intuitive; neither is it demonstrative: Of what nature is it, then? To say it is experimental, is begging the question. For all inferences from experience suppose, as their foundation, that the future will resemble the past, and that similar powers will be conjoined with similar sensible qualities. If there be any suspicion that the course of nature may change, and that the past may be no rule for the future, all experience becomes useless, and can give rise to no inference or conclusion. It is impossible, therefore, that any arguments from experience can prove this resemblance of the past to the future; since all these arguments are founded on the supposition of that resemblance. Let the course of things be allowed hitherto ever so regular; that alone, without some new argument or inference, proves not that, for the future, it will continue so. In vain do you pretend to have learned the nature of bodies from your past experience. Their secret nature, and consequently all their effects and influence, may change, without any change in their sensible qualities. This happens sometimes, and with regard to some objects: Why may it not happen always, and with regard to all objects? What logic, what process of argument secures you against this position? My practice, you say, refutes my doubts. But you mistake the purport of my question. As an agent, I am quite satisfied in the point; but as a philosopher, who has some share of curiosity, I will not say scepticism, I want to learn the foundation of this inference. No reading, no enquiry has yet been able to remove my difficulty, or give me satisfaction in a matter of such importance. Can I do better than propose the difficulty to the public, even though, perhaps, I have small hopes of obtaining a solution? We shall at least, by this means, be sensible of our ignorance, if we do not augment our knowledge.

Hume's arguments against the principle of universal causation and the principle of induction are also arguments against rationalism in general. What he is saying is that reasoning alone, without information from experience, cannot tell us any-thing whatever about the world. Reasoning *a priori*, that is, thinking without any appeal to experience, is incapable of proving any of those theorems so impor-tant to the rationalists, such as the existence of substances, a God, and causes, as well as the conformity of future events to past ones. His arguments are at the same time skeptical ones, since he reasons that even an appeal to experience can-not prove the reality of any of these things.

What is the solution to these skeptical doubts? If we seek a justification or defense, there is none, according to Hume. But in everyday life, such philosoph-ical doubts need have no effect at all, for though there is no justification of our beliefs, we can yet remain confident that at least there is an explanation for them.

Suppose a person, though endowed with the strongest faculties of reason and reflection, to be brought on a sudden into this world; he would, indeed, immediately observe a continual succession of objects and one event follow-ing another, but he would not be able to discover anything further. He would not at first, by any reasoning, be able to reach the idea of cause and effect, since the particular powers by which all natural operations are per-formed never appear to the senses; nor is it reasonable to conclude, merely because one event in one instance precedes another, that therefore the one is the cause, the other the effect. The conjunction may be arbitrary and casual. There may be no reason to infer the existence of one from the appearance of the other: and, in a word, such a person without more expe-rience could never employ his conjecture or reasoning concerning any mat-ter of fact or be assured of anything beyond what was immediately present to his memory or senses.

Suppose again that he has acquired more experience and has lived so long in the world as to have observed similar objects or events to be constantly conjoined together — what is the consequence of this experience? He imme-diately infers the existence of one object from the appearance of the other, yet he has not, by all his experience, acquired any idea or knowledge of the secret power by which the one object produces the other, nor is it by any process of reasoning he is engaged to draw this inference; but still he finds himself determined to draw it, and though he should be convinced that his understanding has no part in the operation, he would nevertheless continue in the same course of thinking. There is some other principle which deter-mines him to form such a conclusion.

This principle is *custom* or *habit*. For wherever the repetition of any particular act or operation produces a propensity to renew the same act or operation without being impelled by any reasoning or process of the under-standing, we always say that this propensity is the effect of *custom*. By employing that word we pretend not to have given the ultimate reason of such a propensity. We only point out a principle of human nature which is universally acknowledged, and which is well known by its effects. Per-haps we can push our inquiries no further or pretend to give the cause of this cause, but must rest contented with it as the ultimate principle which we can assign of all our conclusions from experience. It is sufficient satis-faction that we can go so far without repining at the narrowness of our faculties, because they will carry us no further. And it is certain we here advance a very intelligible proposition at least, if not a true one, when we assert that after the constant conjunction of two objects, heat and flame, for instance, weight and solidity, we are determined by custom alone to expect the one from the appearance of the other. This hypothesis seems even the only one which explains the difficulty why we draw from a thousand instances an inference which we are not able to draw from one instance that is in no respect different from them. Reason is incapable of any such variation. The conclusions which it draws from considering one circle are the same which it would form upon surveying all the circles in the universe. But no man, having seen only one body move after being impelled by another, could infer that every other body will move after a like impulse. All inferences from experience, therefore, are effects of custom, not of reasoning.

In other words, there is no "solution to these skeptical doubts," but, at most, what Hume calls "a skeptical solution." It means an end, not only to philosophy, but to all rational inquiry and all claims that we can know anything (even that the sun will rise tomorrow, or that there is a typewriter now in front of me). You might think that such conclusions would have driven Hume mad or caused him such confusion that he would have been incapable of coping with the most everyday chores. Yet we know that he was the most practical and jolliest sort of fellow. As a philosopher, he has been driven right up against the wall of Plato's Cave. But he remains unperturbed. In a famous passage at the end of the *Treatise*, he simply remarks:

> Most fortunately it happens, that since reason is incapable of dispelling these clouds, nature herself suffices to that purpose, and cures me of this philosophical melancholy and delirium, either by relaxing this bent of mind, or by some avocation, and lively impression of my senses, which obliterate all these chimeras. I dine, I play a game of back-gammon, I converse, and am merry with my friends; and when after three or four hours' amusement, I wou'd return to these speculations, they appear so cold, and strain'd, and ridiculous, that I cannot find in my heart to enter into them any farther.[16]

Perhaps you too find "these speculations cold, strained and ridiculous." If so, however, this is not the time to run off to dinner and an evening of games and conversation. Something has gone very wrong. The empiricist attempt to restore common sense to philosophy has ended in the least commonsensical philosophy imaginable. A person who really believed that there might be no material world, or that the future will not resemble the past (and therefore, having been hit by a truck last week, steps into the street unconvinced that it will not happen again)

---

[16]David Hume, *Treatise of Human Nature*, ed. L. A. Selby-Bigge (Oxford: Oxford University Press, 1888).

would be crazy! How can our intellects be so out of joint with our experience? or our philosophy so far away from practical life? How serious is Hume's skepticism.

SUMMARY AND CONCLUSION

Epistemology is the study of human knowledge—what we can know, how we can know it, and what we cannot know. In this sense, epistemology and metaphysics are complementary disciplines. Epistemology becomes the method or approach to the knowledge of the way the world really is. For some philosophers, for example, Descartes, this approach places its primary trust in reason; accordingly, they are called rationalists. For other philosophers, for example, Locke, the preferred approach is to trust the senses and experience; they are called empiricists. The problem for both the rationalists and the empiricists is to get beyond the mere appearance of things to the reality behind them. The rationalist tries to do this by appealing to intuition and certain principles from which he can deduce the way the world really is. The empiricist, on the other hand, appeals to his experiences, trying to find there his evidence for the nature of reality. For both views, however, the danger is that their methods do not always seem to achieve as much as they would like. Rationalists disagree about which principles to start with and which intuitions to trust. Empiricists find that their own method of experience makes it impossible to say anything about what lies beyond experience. Thus Bishop Berkeley argues that only our ideas and the minds that have these ideas exist (including God), and David Hume concludes that we can never know anything about reality, but only about our own associations of ideas. Epistemologists are still working on more satisfactory answers to the questions of knowledge, and still trying to defeat once and for all the skeptical conclusions so brilliantly argued by Hume two centuries ago.

GLOSSARY

appearance: the way something seems to us, through our senses. Usually philosophers worry about something's being a mere appearance, such that it bears no faithful resemblance to the reality of which it is the appearance.

a priori (knowledge): "before experience," or more accurately, independent of all experience. *A priori* knowledge is always necessary, for there can be no imaginable instances that would refute it and no intelligible doubting of it. One might come to know something *a priori* through experience (for example, you might find out that no parallel lines ever touch each other by drawing tens of thousands of parallel lines) but what is essential to *a priori* knowledge is that no such experience is needed. Knowledge is *a priori* if it can be proven independently of experience. The most obvious examples of *a priori* knowledge are analytic sentences, such as " a horse is an animal." and "if all men are mammals and Socrates is a man, then Socrates is a mammal."

association of ideas: a central idea of empiricist psychology, according to which all knowledge is composed of separate ideas that are connected by their resemblance to one another (e.g., "this one looks exactly like that one"), by their contiguity in space and time (e.g., "every time I see this, I see that as well") and causality (e.g., "every time a thing of that sort happens it is followed by something of this sort"). (The three different "associations" here are Hume's.)

causation *or* **causality:** the relation of cause and effect, one event's bringing about another according to natural law. In Hume, (1) one event's following another necessarily (or so it seems to us); (2) one type of event regularly following another (See *association of ideas* above).

cause: that which produces an effect; an event (or state of affairs, object, act, or person) that brings about another event.

causal theory of perception: the view that our experience (our sensations and ideas) are the effects of physical objects acting upon our sense organs (which are thereby the causes).

cogito, ergo sum: or "I think, therefore I am" is Descartes's only principle that he finds "beyond doubt" and "perfectly certain." ("Think" here refers to any kind of idea or experience in the mind, not just what we would call "thinking.") It is the premise of his entire philosophy.

datum: Latin, literally, "what is given." (plural, *data*)

empiricism: the philosophy that demands that all knowledge, except for certain logical truths and principles of mathematics, comes from experience. British empiricism is often used to refer specifically to the three philosophers Locke, Berkeley, and Hume. It is still very much an alive movement, however, and includes Bertrand Russell in our own century and a great many philosophers of the past forty years who have called themselves "logical empiricists" (better known as logical positivists).

epistemology: the study of human knowledge, its nature, its sources, its justification.

explanation: an account—usually a causal account—of something; it is opposed to *justification*, which also defends. One can, for example, explain one's action (say, by claiming that he or she was drunk) without thereby justifying it, that is, showing it to be right. Hume ultimately explains our knowledge but does not justify it.

generalization from experience *or* **inductive generalization:** inference from observation, experience, and experiment to a generalization about all members of a certain class. For example, in a laboratory, a researcher finds that certain experiments on tobacco plants always have the same result. He or she generalizes, through induction, from experimental observations to a claim (or *hypothesis*) about all tobacco plants. But notice that this generalization is never certain (like the generalization in geometry from a proof of a theorem about this triangle to a theorem about all triangles). It might always turn out that there was a fluke in the experiment or that he/she chose a peculiar sample of plants.

Hume's fork: Hume's insistence that every belief be justified either as a "relation between ideas" or as a "matter of fact."

idea: in epistemology, almost any mental phenomenon (not, as in Plato, with existence independent of individual minds). The terminology varies slightly; Locke uses "idea" to refer to virtually any "mental content"; Hume reserves "idea" for those mental atoms that are derived by the mind from impressions.

impression: Hume's word for sensations or sense-data, that which is given to the mind through the senses.

induction; inductive reasoning; inductive generalization: induction is the process of inferring general conclusions (for example, "all swans are white") from a sufficiently large sample of particular observations ("this swan is white, that swan is white, and that one, and that one, and that one . . ."). It is usually contrasted with *deduction* (see Ch. 1), in that, while deductive reasoning guarantees that the conclusion shall be as certain as the premises, induction never gives us a conclusion as certain as the premises. Its conclusions are, at most, merely probable. (There might always be some black swan somewhere; and there are, in Western Australia.) (See "Logic," pp. 18–37.)

innate ideas: literally, ideas that are "born into the mind." Locke's famous attack on such ideas took them to be literally ideas that all men share from birth. The rationalist philosophers he was supposedly attacking, however, held a much more sophisticated notion; they did not believe that ideas were literally "born into us," but they did believe that we are born with certain "innate" capacities and dispositions, which will develop with proper education (and mental health). And these ideas, most importantly, can be defended or justified without appeal to any particular experiences or experiments. This is the claim that Locke ultimately rejected.

intuition: immediate knowledge, without the aid of reasoning or inference. It must be stressed, however, that intuition is often (even usually) argued to be a function of reason, and capable of rational insights even if they are, by their very nature, not defensible by any arguments.

justification: an attempt to defend a position or an act, to show that it is correct (or at least reasonable). (Cf. *explanation* above.)

primary qualities: in Locke, those properties ("qualities") that inhere in the object.

principle of induction: the belief that the laws of nature will continue to hold in the future as they have in the past. (Crudely, "the future will be like the past.")

principle of universal causation: the belief that every event has its cause (or causes). In scientific circles, it is usually added, "its sufficient natural cause," in order to eliminate the possibility of miracles and divine intervention (which are allowed in Leibniz's similar but broader Principle of Sufficient Reason).

probable: likely; or supported by the evidence (but not conclusively). The empiricist's middle step between the extremities of certainty and doubt. (Probability is the measure of how probable something is.)

quality: in Locke (and other authors), a property.

rationalism: the philosophy that is characterized by its confidence in reason, and intuition in particular, to know reality independently of experience. (See *reason* and *intuition*.) Continental rationalism is usually reserved for the three great European philosophers, Descartes, Spinoza, and Leibniz.

reason: in rationalism the faculty that allows us to know reality, through intuition. In empiricism, simply the ability to recognize certain principles that are "relations of ideas," for example, trivial truths ("a cat is an animal") and, more complicated, principles of arithmetic and geometry. Empiricists deny that reason allows us special insight into reality, however; it tells us only relations between ideas.

relations of ideas: in empiricism, knowledge that is restricted to the logical and conceptual connections between ideas, not to the correspondence of those ideas to experience or to reality.

secondary qualities: in Locke, those properties ("qualities") that are caused in us by objects, but do not inhere in the objects themselves (for example, color).

sensation: the experimental result of the stimulation of a sense organ, for example, *seeing* red, *hearing* a ringing noise, *smelling* something burning. The simplest of mental phenomena.

sense-data: that which is given to the senses, prior to any reasoning or organization on our part.

skepticism: the philosophical belief (or fear) that knowledge is not possible, and that no rational arguments will succeed in overcoming our doubts.

subjective idealism: the view that only ideas and mind exist, and that there are no substances, matter, or material objects. In particular, the philosophy of Bishop Berkeley.

tabula rasa: in Locke's philosophy, the "blank tablet" metaphor of the mind, in opposition to the doctrine that there are innate ideas. In other words, the mind is a "blank" at birth, and everything we know must be "stamped in" through experience.

4

Truth

*Necessary judgments must be believed to be true for the
sake of the preservation of such creatures as ourselves; though
they might, of course, be* false *judgments for all that.*

Friedrich Nietzsche

We turned from metaphysics to epistemology because we began to question our ability to know "the way the world really is." Hence, we thought we should first find out what we can know. But then after Hume, it seemed that not only were we incapable of doing metaphysics but we could not justify even the most ordinary and obvious principles of our everyday lives. If we can't even know with certainty that there is an "external" world, then how can we claim to know anything — except, perhaps, our own isolated and limited experiences? But then, what is the *truth?* Surely it cannot be solely a function of our ideas. If it is true that there is a bald-headed man in the governor's mansion, then there must *be* a bald-headed man in the governor's mansion, not just our impression or idea of him. Furthermore, if our knowledge of reality is colored by our ideas and "habits" of understanding and interpretation, could it be possible that reality will be different for different people, who have different ideas and different intellectual and perceptual habits? Did Aristotle and the ancient animists live in the same world as John Locke and modern scientists? Or were their ideas about the world so different that the worlds they lived in were different as well? Is there, in that case, any such thing as "the Truth"? Or does it make sense to say that what is true for one person might nevertheless be false for someone else?

The problem of truth has always been central to philosophy. In asking "what is reality *really* like?" the ancient philosophers were trying to ascertain the truth behind the appearances of reality, and some of them — like Parmenides and

Plato—quite clearly distinguished between the True World—or simply "the Truth"—and the world of our everyday experiences. Descartes and John Locke were both looking for the truth, but in different ways, and the difference in their approaches signified a difference in their sense of what the truth should be. But they both believed that there was such a thing as the Truth, that their preferred philosophical methods would get them the truth. It is with the skeptics—and Hume in particular—that this assurance has broken down.

The view of the Truth as "out there," in the world, is the basis of both common sense and the whole history of philosophy. Even Bishop Berkeley, who argued that the world consists of ideas, insisted that these ideas were caused by God, Who is the Truth. But skepticism challenges God as Truth just as it challenges our assumption that most of what we know is the Truth. The idea that the Truth is outside of us becomes no longer a matter of common sense but the source of serious paradoxes. If it is outside of us, how will we ever know it? If it is not outside of us, is there anything at all to know?

What now comes into question are the very assumptions that have ruled metaphysics and common sense since the time of the first philosophers. First of all, there is Plato's "two-worlds" view: "the world of Being," which is the true world, and the "world of Becoming," the world of our daily experience that, though perhaps not unreal, is less real than the world of Being. Now, the actual model Plato uses (the real world as the world of Forms, our world as the world of material objects and change) has not been accepted by all modern philosophers, and it is certainly out of line with common sense. Many philosophers, especially empiricists, *have* accepted the distinction between appearance and reality. Ironically, this view is precisely the reverse of Plato's view. According to empiricism, it is the material world that becomes the real world, and the world of ideas—our mental "ideas" and experiences—becomes the less real world. And the problem, in Descartes, Locke, Hume, and Russell, is always how to know that our "ideas" or experiences in fact match up to the real world. The fact that Descartes is confident that he can know that his experiences "match up," while Hume believes that we can never know even if there is such a world, must not hide from us the "two-worlds" model that both of them presuppose: reality (if there is one) on the one side, our experience on the other. How do we move from experience to reality?

Second, there are the two assumptions we mentioned in Chapter 2, common not only to Plato and Aristotle but to most modern thinkers as well, Spinoza and Leibniz, for example. They were: (1) faith in our language to capture the structures of reality and the idea that the world in itself is intelligible to us, and (2) the idea that all knowledge of reality (that is, metaphysical knowledge) must consist of necessary truths. The first assumption seems to presuppose the "two-worlds" model in some sense, because something (our language) can't be "faithful" unless it is faithful to something else, outside of itself (reality). But it also assumes that the language we (or the Greeks) use to express ourselves is also adequate to describe the world without distortion. Is that so obviously the case? For example, could the words we use to pick out individual objects in fact distort the truth for us, forcing certain things into categories not natural to them and making impossible the identification of other things for which we do not have a word? And could it be that different languages (English and ancient Greek, for example) actually interpret the world in different ways?

This very difficult question—which raises the problem that many philosophers call **relativism**—is also a problem that infects the assumption that knowledge of reality consists of necessary truths. (We will discuss necessary truth in detail in Chapter 5.) Relativism is the thesis that Truth varies from context to context; truth is *relative to* a language, a culture, a way of looking at the world. (But what, then, is "the world," if there are only so many ways of looking at it?) But to say that knowledge consists of necessary truths is to insist that knowledge *could not be mistaken*. But is this a fact about the world, or is it rather an inability on our part to see through the common assumptions that are, perhaps, built right into our language? How do we know that what we believe to be necessary—because of the structure of our language—is not just necessary for us, and not true of reality at all? So we have to ask, "Are we trapped inside our language? Is it impossible for us to know anything about reality that we have not ourselves imposed through language?"

The assumption that knowledge consists of necessary truths has already begun to bother us, since John Locke and his empiricist followers insisted that all of our knowledge of the world must consist of truths based upon experience, and since, by the very nature of inductive arguments from experience, we could not actually be certain of anything. Descartes had insisted that any belief worth the honorific title "knowledge" had to be certain ("perfectly certain," he said). But now, let us ask, wasn't he demanding a bit too much? In fact, much too much! Surely I have the right to say that I know that I'm not dreaming right now, even if it's true that I might be wrong. In other words, it is time to weaken our demands. Perhaps it will be enough if we believe what is **rational** to believe, even if it is not certain and even if it does not "match up" with some unexperienceable reality. You might even say, "perhaps it is not necessary to believe what is true," but notice that you would already have presupposed that what makes our belief true is some reality beyond our experience. It is just this notion of truth we must examine in this chapter.

WHAT IS TRUTH?

That familiar question was raised by Pontius Pilate as he dismissed Christ's case from his court. He was just a politician; he did not take the question seriously. Philosophers do. It is their business to find the truth, to expose fraudulent beliefs and superstitions, and to assure us that we can know, at least most of the time, what is true from what is false.

What indeed is truth? Should we say, as we have so far, that our beliefs are true if and only if they "match up" with reality? Or, in accordance with our present suspicions, should we not perhaps hold out for some different conception of "truth," one that does not place such emphasis on "matching up" and the separation of reality on the one hand from our beliefs and experiences on the other?

The proper philosophical name for this notion of "matching up" our beliefs and experiences with reality is the **correspondence theory of truth.** On the one hand, it is an obvious truism: for example, when I tell you "there is beer in the refrigerator," what I tell you is true if and only if there is in fact beer in the refrigerator. So obvious is this "correspondence" criterion of truth — that a belief or a statement is true if and only if it "corresponds" to the facts — that no one would have thought of calling it a "theory" at all until recently. In his *Metaphysics*, Aristotle dismissed the whole "problem of truth" in a single sentence: "To say of what is that it is not, or of what is not that it is, is false, while to say of what is that it is, or of what is not that it is not, is true." As long as philosophers (and everyone else) believed themselves unquestionably capable of knowing reality as such, this common-sense platitude was as appropriate for the investigations of metaphysics as it was for the daily task of checking to see whether or not there was beer in the refrigerator. But as empiricism and Hume's skepticism grew in persuasiveness and the confidence that we could know reality was thrown into question, the platitude became a problem.

For Descartes, the correspondence between our ideas and reality had to be demonstrated. Locke expressed his doubts; Berkeley rejected the "external world" altogether, leaving only God (and other minds like Berkeley's own); and Hume left us with the seemingly irrefutable argument that we could never know reality outside of us, or even if there was a reality to be known. Hume had given us a *reductio ad absurdum* argument; one of his premises — perhaps not an explicit one — has brought us to the absurdity of not being able to defend the most common-sense beliefs. But all of these philosophers presuppose the correspondence theory of truth, the idea that knowledge is the correspondence of our ideas to reality and that the only knowledge worthy of the name is our being certain of this correspondence. It is here that Kant returns to the beginnings of Hume's arguments, and everyone else's, and roots out the correspondence theory of truth as the implicit premise that is the cause of all the trouble.

Now it will probably seem odd to you to even question something so obviously "true" as the correspondence theory of truth. Of course, we cannot deny that "there is beer in the refrigerator" is true if and only if there is beer in the refrigerator. But let us note immediately that the correspondence theory is not so obviously adequate for all true statements. What does "two plus two equals four" correspond to that makes it true? One might suggest that it corresponds to all combinations in the world of two things (walnuts, elephants, acres, or apples) and two other things of the same kind. "Two plus two equals four" would still be true even if there were no such combinations in the universe. A tautology such as "either it is snowing or it is not snowing" does not correspond to anything; it "tells us nothing about the world." A conceptual truth such as "blue is a color" tells us only about the meanings of the words in our language. A rule of inference tells us how to think. But none of these "correspond" to anything. So, at most, we shall have to say that the correspondence theory is good as an account of empirical knowledge only! (This is the conclusion of most empiricists, including more contemporary "logical positivists.")

But there are more serious problems, even within the domain of empirical knowledge. Let's look again at the truism, "'there's beer in the refrigerator' is true if and only if there is beer in the refrigerator." Let's ask, first of all, in what sense the noises you utter (the sounds, "there's beer . . .") correspond to the fact that there is beer in the refrigerator. If you think of one thing corresponding to another, you might think of a map corresponding to the terrain it is a map of: smaller scale with many omissions, but at least it is the same shape, same proportions, and has representations of things in that terrain that you can recognize. But how do those sounds coming out of your mouth (which, now that you listen to them, might sound strange indeed) "correspond" to that six-pack of Schlitz in the kitchen? Now you will say that it is not merely "the sounds" that correspond but rather what you are saying or meaning. And, of course, this is correct. But notice that what those words mean is not a matter of their use in this particular instance; they depend upon their role in a language (American English), which you happen to speak. (If you spoke only Eskimo and pronounced the same sounds, it would be a remarkable coincidence, but wouldn't mean anything.) And the "correspondence" between those words with their meanings and the fact that there is beer in the refrigerator depends not only on the whole American-English language and your knowledge of it but also on a set of conventions that both you and your friend must understand as referring to the beer in the refrigerator. In class, for example, your teacher says, "there is beer in the refrigerator" as an example of an English sentence. But you do not get up and look for a refrigerator. You know that although your teacher has said the same words that you say to your friend when offering a beer he or she is not directly referring to anything. And the statement does not "correspond" to a fact that there is beer in the refrigerator. It is clear that what you've said (and the same is true of what you've thought) cannot correspond to anything by itself. In a sense, you might say that what corresponds to the fact that there is beer in the refrigerator when you offer your friend a beer is the whole of the English language, with all of its conventions and everything that you and your friend know that is relevant to the meaning of your statement in this particular case.

And from the other side of this "correspondence" matters are no less complicated. What is "the fact" that there is beer in the refrigerator? Sounds like an easy question. The answer is—that there is beer in the refrigerator! But how do we pick out this fact, except by using our language to distinguish this fact from any number of others. Suppose, instead of saying anything, you were simply to point toward the refrigerator for your friend. Now, of course, knowing you, your friend knows what you mean. In this case, the pointing is shorthand for the statement, and presupposes it. But suppose your friend is a New Guinea headhunter who had no idea what a refrigerator was, or a beer for that matter? Would he pick out the right "fact"? How would he know whether you were pointing to the kitchen, to the door of the refrigerator, or to its contents? And which contents? Even if you point to the beer, is it the can or the contents? Is the "beer" to be drunk or to be poured on one's feet? How do we even understand the pointing gesture? (When I point my finger toward the cat food, my cats smell my finger!) So, if it seems obvious to you that "the facts" are simply there, waiting to be corresponded to by our verbal or gestural pointing, think again. One distinguishes the facts of the world only by picking them out by language. The language then can't be said to "correspond" to the world, for it is language that "carves up" our world into those individually identifiable "facts."

Now none of this is to say that your statement, "there's beer in the refrigerator" isn't true if and only if there is beer in the refrigerator. It is rather to say that this simple "correspondence" is possible only because of the enormous number of systematic assumptions we share within our language and about the world and about the way we refer to particular "facts" in the world by use of certain statements. In everyday life we don't have to think about such things. But in philosophy, they make us marvel at what complex and clever creatures we are. Bertrand Russell, certainly one of the smartest among us, spent forty years trying to make sense out of the "common sense" correspondence theory. He never did. He never succeeded in formulating an adequate defense of the idea that some single unit of language could "correspond" to discrete "facts" in the world. And today, most philosophers would agree, no matter what kind of method they follow, that the correspondence theory — no matter how commonsensical — cannot make sense of the notion of truth. A statement means something only within a language, and a "fact" is "corresponded to" only after it has been picked out by language. And that means that truth can't be correspondence.

And so, the seemingly simple act of "saying what is true" turns out to be enormously complicated. And against the "correspondence theory of truth," there are three telling arguments:

1) It is, at best, limited. All cases of necessary truth, and perhaps some others, cannot be accounted for by it at all.
2) There is no such thing as a statement or a belief that by itself is capable of "corresponding" to anything.
3) There is no such thing as a "fact" that can be picked out independently of the language used to describe it.

Next time you say or think that there is beer in the refrigerator, you might marvel at the complex that has just come into action. That won't, unfortunately, guarantee that your statement or thought will be true. For despite all this sophisticated, intellectual apparatus we still occasionally forget to buy the beer.

THEORIES OF TRUTH

Now what? We find ourselves with some ill-defined complex in which our language and reality are tied together and mutually depend on each other. But what we have been leading up to, finally, is that we need something more than the naive common sense "correspondence theory of truth," one which takes into account this complexity of interrelations. Three such theories have achieved prominence in this century, although all three of them were anticipated by Immanuel Kant, whom we shall meet later in this chapter. The three theories are:

1) **The coherence theory of truth:** which says that a statement or a belief is true if and only if it "coheres" or ties in with other statements and beliefs.

2) **The pragmatic theory of truth:** which says that a statement or a belief is true if and only if "it works," if it allows us to predict certain results, if it allows us to function effectively in everyday life, and if it encourages further inquiry or helps us lead better lives.

3) **The semantic theory of truth:** which says that a statement or a belief is true because the rules of our language set up a correspondence between certain statements and "the facts" that our language picks out in the world. Superficially this theory looks like the correspondence theory, but it is very different. The correspondence theory accepts facts as "already there," independent of our language. The semantic theory explains this apparent correspondence by telling us that it is our language that sets it up in the first place.

The Coherence Theory

The coherence theory of truth does not necessarily oppose the common sense idea that true statements "correspond" to facts in the world, but it does shift the focus of the discussion away from this correspondence — if there is one — to the interdependence of the statements themselves. In other words, it seizes on the observation made above, in our discussion of the correspondence theory, that a simple statement of fact ("there's beer in the refrigerator") involves, in some sense, the whole English language. The words in that simple sentence would not mean much if they did not also have the same meaning in an unlimited number of other sentences, and their ability to refer to the world therefore depends on their role in a language. Furthermore, when we try to ascertain the truth of a statement, how do we do it? By ascertaining the truth of other statements and arguing, deductively or inductively, for the consequent truth of this one. Thus the coherence theory places its emphasis on the ways in which we find out the truth, and it rightly points out that knowledge is not just a matter of establishing the truth of one statement after another; it is a matter of getting more and more statements to cohere in a unified body of knowledge. And it is this coherence that makes them true, whether or not there is some metaphysical sense in which they cohere because, in fact, they are true.

To represent the coherence theory, here is a selection from the American philosopher, Brand Blanshard.

on the Coherence Theory,
by Brand Blanshard

To think is to seek understanding. And to seek understanding is an activity of mind that is marked off from all other activities by a highly distinctive aim. This aim . . . is to achieve systematic vision, so to apprehend what is now unknown to us as to relate it, and relate it necessarily, to what we know already.

. . . . .

But may it not be that what satisfies thought fails to conform to the real world? Where is the guarantee that when I have brought my ideas into the form my ideal requires, they should be *true?* . . . In our long struggle with the relation of thought to reality we saw that if thought and things are conceived as related only externally, then knowledge is luck; there is no necessity whatever that what satisfies intelligence should coincide with what really is. It may do so, or it may not; on the principle that there are many misses to one bull's-eye, it more probably does not. But if we get rid of the misleading analogies through which this relation has been conceived, of copy and original, stimulus and organism, lantern and screen, and go to thought itself with the question what reference to an object means, we get a different and more hopeful answer. To think of a thing is to get that thing itself in some degree within the mind. To think of a color or an emotion is to have that within us which if it *were developed and completed,* would identify itself with the object. In short, if we accept its own report, thought is related to reality as the partial to the perfect fulfillment of a purpose. The more adequate its grasp the more nearly does it approximate, the more fully does it realize in itself, the nature and relations of its objects.

. . . . .

. . . We may look at the growth of knowledge, individual or social, either as an attempt by our own minds to return to union with things as they are in their ordered wholeness, or the affirmation through our minds of the ordered whole itself. And if we take this view, our notion of truth is marked out for us. Truth is the approximation of thought to reality. It is thought on its way home. Its measure is the distance thought has travelled, under guidance of its inner compass, toward that intelligible system which unites its ultimate object with its ultimate end. Hence at any given time the degree of truth in our experience as a whole is the degree of system it has achieved. The degree of truth of a particular proposition is to be judged in the first instance by its coherence with experience as a whole, ultimately by its coherence with that further whole, all-comprehensive and fully articulated, in which thought can come to rest.[1]

The coherence theory of truth, according to Blanshard, begins with the observation that we test the truth of a belief by seeing its implications and other logically connected beliefs. But the theory is not confined to this test. Truth itself,

---

[1] Brand Blanshard, *The Nature of Thought* (New York: Macmillan, 1941).

he insists, is nothing other than the interconnectedness of our various beliefs. The truth of a particular belief is nothing other than how well it fits in with everything else that we believe.

The Pragmatic Theory

Pragmatism is the one major philosophical movement to originate and remain more or less completely in America. The three philosophers most easily identified with this movement are Charles Peirce, William James, and John Dewey, all of them Americans (Peirce and James in Massachusetts, Dewey in Chicago and New York). We shall see more of pragmatism later in this chapter, but for now, what is important to us is the pragmatists' theory or theories of truth (for they did not entirely agree with one another). As one might expect, both from the name "pragmatism" and the characteristic American concern for what is "practical," and pragmatic theory of truth begins with a certain impatience for the abstractions and obscurities of traditional metaphysics and epistemology. In particular, the inadequacies of the correspondence theory of truth struck them not just as a philosophical dilemma, but as a genuine source of scandal. How is it possible, they asked, that the traditional theories of truth ended up in skepticism?

Charles Peirce found the traditional discussions absurd just because they tried to conceive of truth without any concern or reference whatsoever to the practical circumstances in which we worry about the truth. Truth is not a relationship between sentences and the world, nor is it a complex relationship among sentences. Truth is the answer to questions that we ask, because we are uncertain, because we have doubts. The truth is what we all, eventually, agree upon. According to Peirce, "The opinion which is fated to be ultimately agreed to by all who investigate, is what we mean by the truth." The emphasis thus gets shifted from truth as a property of sentences and beliefs and their relationships to facts and each other to truth as a function of asking questions, carrying on investigations, and clearing up actual mysteries and disagreements. The test of truth is neither correspondence nor coherence but agreement, what in fact solves our problems and answers our inquiries.

Peirce was deeply concerned with the practices of scientific investigation, and his theory of truth was aimed primarily at questions of truth in science, where experimentation and observation should lead, eventually, to agreement on one hypothesis or theory or another. William James, on the other hand, had much broader interests in philosophy. While he was interested in science (and, indeed, was one of America's leading physicians and psychologists), he was also interested in the less scientific aspects of human life, in which truth was also a critical issue. For example, he wrote extensively on the topic of religious belief in which questions of experimentation and observation play virtually no role at all. (One of his best known essays is included in Chapter 6.) Accordingly, James places very little emphasis on agreement as the test of truth. However appropriate this might be in science, it is surely not even plausible in the subject of religion. Instead, he stressed the advantages of a certain belief in life. By "practical," James meant the concrete, the effective, not that which leads to scientific agreement. Thus a religious belief can be said to be true, for example, according to its effects on us. Believing in a good, just God makes us optimistic and happy; believing that life is meaningless makes us miserable. Thus truth refers to what significance a belief has in our lives, not correspondence, coherence or, we can add, the limited success of scientific hypotheses and theories. Scientific truth still has its place in James's philosophy, of course. But that kind of truth is defined by the restricted context of an investigation; it should not be generalized as a concept of truth in all contexts. (It should be noted that Peirce so radically disagreed with James's generalization of his theory that he actually changed the name of his philosophy, from "pragmatism" to "pragmaticism," which he noted was a word "sufficiently ugly" to avoid popularization.)

John Dewey returned the pragmatic theory to its narrower focus. He did not restrict truth to scientific truth, but he did restrict it to *experiential* truth. But whereas James would include, for example, religious experience, Dewey insists that the only meaningful notion of "experience" must be limited to empirically verifiable matters. That eliminates questions of theology. And like Peirce, Dewey emphasizes the context of investigation, in particular, the intellectually painful experience of doubt. Like James and unlike Peirce, Dewey does not emphasize the notion of general agreement as the test of truth so much as he emphasizes its efficacy in ending doubts and closing an investigation. A police case, for example, comes to an end when "all the pieces fall into place." But that is not a matter of coherence so much as it is a matter of resolving doubts and "tying together loose ends," satisfying all of our questions and quieting critics and skeptics. A scientific hypothesis is said to be true when all attempts to falsify it have failed and every attempt to confirm it comes out successfully. Again, it is an end to the inquiry, a solution to the problem. Where traditional philosophy gets into trouble is in trying to understand "truth" in a vacuum, without reference to any inquiry or investigation, without any reference to the context in which truth makes a difference.

The following selections are from Charles Peirce, "How to Make Our Ideas Clear" and William James, *Pragmatism:*

from "How to Make Our Ideas Clear," by Charles Peirce

Let us now approach the subject of logic, and consider a conception which particularly concerns it, that of *reality*. Taking clearness in the sense of familiarity, no idea could be clearer than this. Every child uses it with perfect confidence, never dreaming that he does not understand it. As for clearness in its second grade, however, it would probably puzzle most men, even among those of a reflective turn of mind, to give an abstract definition of the real. Yet such a definition may perhaps be reached by considering the points of difference between reality and its opposite, fiction. A figment is a product of somebody's imagination; it has such characters as his thought impresses upon it. That those characters are independent of how you or I think is an external reality. There are, however, phenomena within our own minds, dependent upon our thought, which are at the same time real in the sense that we really think them. But though their characters depend on how we think, they do not depend on what we think those characters to be. Thus, a dream has a real existence as a mental phenomenon, if somebody has really dreamt it; that he dreamt so and so, does not depend on what anybody thinks was dreamt, but is completely independent of all opinion on the subject. On the other hand, considering, not the fact of dreaming, but the thing dreamt, it retains its peculiarities by virture of no other fact than that it was dreamt to possess them. Thus we may define the real as that whose characters are independent of what anybody may think them to be.

But, however satisfactory such a definition may be found, it would be a great mistake to suppose that it makes the idea of reality perfectly clear. Here, then, let us apply our rules. According to them, reality, like every other quality, consists in the peculiar, sensible effects which things partaking of it produce. The only effect which real things have is to cause belief, for all the sensations which they excite emerge into consciousness in the form of beliefs. The question, therefore, is, how is true belief (or belief in the real) distinguished from false belief (or belief in fiction). Now, as we have seen in the former paper, the ideas of truth and falsehood, in their full development, appertain exclusively to the scientific method of settling opinion. A person who arbitrarily chooses the propositions which he will adopt can use the word truth only to emphasize the expression of his determination to hold on to his choice. Of course, the method of tenacity never prevailed exclusively; reason is too natural to men for that. But in the literature of the Dark Ages we find some fine examples of it. When Scotus Erigena is commenting upon a poetical passage in which hellebore is spoken of as having caused the death of Socrates, he does not hesitate to inform the inquiring reader that Helleborus and Socrates were two eminent Greek philosophers, and that the latter having been overcome in argument by the former took the matter to heart and died of it! What sort of an idea of truth could a man have who could adopt and teach, without the qualification of a "perhaps," an opinion taken so entirely at random? The real spirit of Socrates, who I hope would have been delighted to have been "overcome in argument," because he would have learned something by it, is in curious contrast with the naïve idea of the glossist, for whom (as for the "born missionary" of today) discussion would seem to have been simply a struggle. When philosophy began to awake from its long slumber, and before theology completely dominated it, the practice seems to have been for each professor to seize upon any philosophical position he found unoccupied and which seemed a strong one, to intrench himself in it, and to sally forth from time to time to give battle to the others. Thus, even the scanty records we possess of those disputes enable us to make out a dozen or more opinions held by different teachers at one time concerning the question of nominalism and realism. Read the opening part of the *Historia Calamitatum* of Abélard, who was certainly as philosophical as any of his contemporaries, and see the spirit of combat which it breathes. For him, the truth is simply his particular stronghold. When the method of authority prevailed, the truth meant little more than the Catholic faith. All the efforts of the scholastic doctors are directed toward harmonizing their faith in Aristotle and their faith in the Church, and one may search their ponderous folios through without finding an argument which goes any further. It is noticeable that where different faiths flourish side by side, renegades are looked upon with contempt even by the party whose belief they adopt; so completely has the idea of loyalty replaced that of truth-seeking. Since the time of Descartes, the defect in the conception of truth has been less apparent. Still, it will sometimes strike a scientific man that the philosophers have been less intent on finding out what the facts are than on inquiring what belief is most in harmony with their system. It is hard to convince a follower of the *a priori* method by adducing facts; but show him that an opinion he is defending is inconsistent with what he has laid down elsewhere, and he will be very apt to retract it. These minds do not seem to believe that disputation is ever to cease; they seem to think that the opinion which is natural for one man is not so for another, and that belief will, consequently, never be settled. In contenting themselves with fixing their own opinions by a method which would lead another man to a different result, they betray their feeble hold of the conception of what truth is.

On the other hand, all the followers of science are fully persuaded that the processes of investigation, if only pushed far enough, will give one certain solution to each question to which they can be applied. One man may investigate the velocity of light by studying the transits of Venus and the aberration of the stars; another by the oppositions of Mars and the eclipses of Jupiter's satellites; a third by the method of Fizeau; a fourth by that of Foucault; a fifth by the motions of the curves of Lissajous; a sixth, a seventh, an eighth, and a ninth, may follow the different methods of comparing the measures of statical and dynamical electricity. They may at first obtain different results, but, as each perfects his method and his processes, the results will move steadily together toward a destined center. So with all scientific research. Different minds may set out with the most antagonistic views, but the progress of investigation carries them by a force outside of themselves to one and the same conclusion. This activity of thought by which we are carried, not where we wish, but to a foreordained goal, is like the operation of destiny. No modification of the point of view taken, no selection of other facts for study, no natural bent of mind even, can enable a man to escape the predestinate opinion. This great law is embodied in the conception of truth and reality. The opinion which is fated[2] to be ultimately agreed to by all who investigate is what we mean by the truth, and the object represented in this opinion is real. That is the way I would explain reality.

But it may be said that this view is directly opposed to the abstract definition which we have given of reality, inasmuch as it makes the characters of the real depend on what is ultimately thought about them. But the answer to this is that, on the one hand, reality is independent, not neces-

---

[2]Fate means merely that which is sure to come true, and cannot be avoided. It is a superstition to suppose that a certain sort of events are ever fated, and it is another to suppose that the word "fate" can never be freed from its superstitious taint. We are all fated to die.

sarily of thought in general, but only of what you or I or any finite number of men may think about it; and that, on the other hand, though the object of the final opinion depends on what that opinion is, yet what that opinion is does not depend on what you or I or any man thinks. Our perversity and that of others may indefinitely postpone the settlement of opinion; it might even conceivably cause an arbitrary proposition to be universally accepted as long as the human race should last. Yet even that would not change the nature of the belief, which alone could be the result of investigation carried sufficiently far; and if, after the extinction of our race, another should arise with faculties and disposition for investigation, that true opinion must be the one which they would ultimately come to. "Truth crushed to earth shall rise again," and the opinion which would finally result from investigation does not depend on how anybody may actually think. But the reality of that which is real does depend on the real fact that investigation is destined to lead, at last, if continued long enough, to a belief in it.[3]

on the Pragmatic Theory,
by William James

I fully expect to see the pragmatist view of truth run through the classic stages of a theories career. First, you know, a new theory is attacked as absurd; then it is admitted to be true, but obvious and insignificant; finally it is seen to be so important that its adversaries claim that they themselves discovered it. Our doctrine of truth is at present in the first of these three stages, with symptoms of the second stage having begun in certain quarters. ... Truth, as any dictionary will tell you, is a property of certain of our ideas. It means their "agreement," as falsity means their disagreement, with "reality." Pragmatism and intellectualists both accept this definition as a matter of course. They begin to quarrel only after the question is raised as to what may precisely be meant by the term "agreement," and what by the term "reality," when reality is taken as something for our ideas to agree with.

In answering these questions the pragmatists are more analytic and painstaking, the intellectualists more offhand and irreflective. The popular notion is that a true idea must copy its reality. Like other popular views, this one follows the analogy of the most usual experience. Our true ideas of sensible things do indeed copy them. Shut your eyes and think of yonder clock on the wall, and you get just such a true picture or copy of its dial. But your idea of its "works" (unless you are a clock-maker) is much less of a copy, yet it passes muster, for it in no way clashes with the reality. Even though it should shrink to the mere word "works," that word still serves you truly; and when you speak of the "time-keeping function" of the clock, or of its spring's "elasticity," it is hard to see exactly what your ideas can copy.

You perceive that there is a problem here. Where our ideas cannot copy definitely their object, what does agreement with that object mean? Some idealists seem to say that they are true whenever they are what God means that we ought to think about that object. Other hold the copy-view all

[3]Charles S. Peirce, "How to Make Our Ideas Clear," *Popular Science Monthly* 12 (Jan. 1878).

through, and speak as if our ideas possessed truth just in proportion as they approach to being copies of the Absolute's eternal way of thinking.

These views, you see, invite pragmatistic discussion. But the great assumption of the intellectualists is that truth means essentially an inert static relation. When you've got your true idea of anything, there's and end of the matter. You're in possession: you *know*; you have fulfilled your thinking destiny. You are where you ought to be mentally; you have obeyed your categorical imperative; and nothing more need follow on that climax of your rational destiny. Epistemologically you are in stable equilibrium.

Pragmatism, on the other hand, asks its usual question, "Grant an idea or belief to be true," it says, "what concrete difference will its being true make in any one's actual life? How will the truth be realized? What experiences will be different from those which would obtain if the belief were false? What, in short, is the truth's cash-value in experiential terms?"

The moment pragmatism asks this question, it sees the answer: *True ideas are those that we can assimilate, validate, corroborate and verify. False ideas are those that we can not.* That is the practical difference it makes to us to have true ideas; that therefore, is the meaning of truth, for it is all that truth is known as.

This thesis is what I have to defend. The truth of an idea is not a stagnant property inherent in it. Truth *happens* to an idea. It *becomes* true, is *made* true by events. Its verity *is* in fact an event, a process: the process namely of its verifying itself, its veri-*fication*. Its validity is the process of its valid-*ation*.

But what do the words verification and validation themselves pragmatically mean? They again signify certain practical consequences of the verified and validated idea. It is hard to find any one phrase that characterizes these consequences better than the ordinary agreement-formula—just such consequences being what we have in mind whenever we say that our ideas "agree" with reality. They lead us, namely, through the acts and other ideas which they instigate, into or up to, or towards, other parts of experience with which we feel all the while—such feeling being among our potentialities—that the original ideas remain in agreement. The connexions and transitions come to us from point to point as being progressive, harmonious, satisfactory. This function of agreeable leading is what we mean by an idea's verification. Such an account is vague and it sounds at first quite trivial, but it has results which it will take the rest of my hour to explain.

Let me begin by reminding you of the fact that the possession of true thoughts means everywhere the possession of invaluable instruments of action; and that our duty to gain truth, so far from being a blank command from out of the blue, or a "stunt" self-imposed by our intellect, can account for itself by excellent practical reasons.

The importance to human life of having true beliefs about matters of fact is a thing too notorious. We live in a world of realities that can be infinitely useful or infinitely harmful. Ideas that tell us which of them to expect count as the true ideas in all this primary sphere of verification, and the pursuit of such ideas is a primary human duty. The possession of truth, so far from being here an end in itself, is only a preliminary means towards other vital satisfactions. If I am lost in the woods and starved, and find what looks like a cow-path, it is of the utmost importance that I should think of a human habitation at the end of it, for if I do so and follow it, I save myself. The true thought is useful here because the house which is its object is useful. The practical value of true ideas is thus primarily derived from the practical importance of their objects to us. Their objects are, indeed, not important at all times. I may on another occasion have no use for the house; and then my idea of it, however verifiable, will be practically irrelevant, and had better remain latent. Yet since almost any object may some day become temporarily important, the advantage of having a general stock of *extra* truths, of ideas that shall be true of merely possible situations, is obvious. We store such extra truths away in our memories, and with the overflow we fill our books of reference. Whenever such an extra truth becomes practically relevant to one of our emergencies, it passes from cold-storage to do work in the world and our belief in it grows active. You can say of it then either that "it is useful because it is true" or that "it is true because it is useful." Both these phrases mean exactly the same thing, namely that here is an idea that gets fulfilled and can be verified. True is the name for whatever idea starts the verification-process, useful is the name for its completed function in experience. True ideas would never have been singled out as such, would never have acquired a class-name, least of all a name suggesting value, unless they had been useful from the outset in this way.

·   ·   ·   ·   ·

To 'agree' in the widest sense with a reality *can only mean to be guided either straight up to it or into its surroundings, or to be put into such working touch with it as to handle either it or something connected with it better than if we disagreed.*

·   ·   ·   ·   ·

'The true,' to put it very briefly, *is only the expedient in the way of our thinking, just as 'the right' is only the expedient way of our behaving.*[4]

In other words, truth, according to the pragmatic theory, is what allows us to handle situations better, what is expedient, what "works." This includes, however, not isolated tasks (in which a "false" belief might occasionally work better) but the entire process of scientific verification, so that the truth of a belief depends not only on its workability on some particular occasion, but, as in the coherence theory, on its connection with scientific testing and the whole of our lives.

The Semantic Theory

The semantic theory is most difficult of all, partly because of its misleading superficial resemblance to the correspondence theory, but mainly because it has been a purely formal theory. That is, it concerns only the artificial systems of the logician and not ordinary, "natural" languages (for example, English or French). In a

---

[4]William James, *Pragmatism: A New Name for Some Old Ways of Thinking* (New York: Longmans, Green, 1907).

sense, it is a theory that has been developing in many ways since the Kantian turn in philosophy. In its formal "semantic" version, however, it is generally credited to the American logician Alfred Tarski.

from "The Semantic Theory of Truth," by Alfred Tarski

. . . we must always relate the notion of truth, like that of a sentence, to a specific language; for it is obvious that the same expression which is a true sentence in one language can be false or meaningless in another.

Let us start with a concrete example. Consider the sentence *"snow is white."* We ask the question under what conditions this sentence is true or false. It seems clear that if we base ourselves on the classical conception of truth, we shall say that the sentence is true if snow is white, and that it is false if snow is not white. Thus, if the definition of truth is to conform to our conception, it must imply the following equivalence:

The sentence "snow is white" is true, if, and only if, snow is white.

We shall now generalize the procedure which we have applied above. Let us consider an arbitrary sentence; we shall replace it by the letter *"p."* We form the name of this sentence and we replace it by another letter, say *"X."* We ask now what is the logical relation between the two sentences *"X is true"* and *"p."* It is clear that from the point of view of our basic conception of truth these sentences are equivalent. In other words, the following equivalence holds:

(T)   *X is true if, and only if, p.*

We shall call any such equivalence (with *"p"* replaced by any sentence of the language to which the word *"true"* refers, and *"X"* replaced by a name of this sentence) an *"equivalence of the form* (T)."

Now at last we are able to put into a precise form the conditions under which we will consider the usage and the definition of the term *"true"* as adequate from the material point of view: we wish to use the term *"true"* in such a way that all equivalences of the form (T) can be asserted, and *we shall call a definition of truth "adequate" if all these equivalences follow from it.*

I should like to propose the name *"the semantic conception of truth"* for the conception of truth which has just been discussed.

Semantics is a discipline which, speaking loosely, *deals with certain relations between expressions of a language and the objects* (or "states of affairs") *"referred to"* by those expressions. As typical examples of semantic concepts we may mention the concepts of *designation, satisfaction,* and *definition* as these occur in the following examples:

> the expression *"the father of his country" designates (denotes) George Washington;*
> snow satisfies the sentential function (the condition) "x is white";
> the equation "2 · x = 1" defines (uniquely determines) the number ½

While the words *"designates,"* *"satisfies,"* and *"defines"* express relations (between certain expressions and the objects "referred to" by these expressions), the word *"true"* is of a different logical nature: it expresses a property (or denotes a class) of certain expressions, viz., of sentences. However, it is easily seen that all the formulations which were given earlier and which aimed at the meaning of this word ("true") referred not only to sentences themselves, but also to objects "talked about" by these sentences, or possibly to "states of affairs" described by them.... A definition of truth can be obtained in a very simple way from that of another semantic notion, namely, of the notion of *satisfaction.*[5]

Very simply explained, Tarski's semantic theory picks out a "class" of "individuals" (objects, states of affairs, or "facts") and specifies, for every sentence in the language, which individuals will or will not "satisfy" it, that is, make it "true" or not. But since the logician must "set up" each pair of sentences and individuals that will satisfy it, it is obvious that this formula will work only for a relatively small number of basic sentences with a manageable class of individuals. Here is the problem in extending the theory to natural languages (such as American English), which have a potentially infinite number of sentences and have to deal with an indefinite number of individuals. (This extension is being attempted today, however, by several leading philosophers, particularly Donald Davidson.) But for our purposes, the theory comes to this: We must set up the rules of satisfaction according to which our sentences become true or false. "Correspondence" is not a relation for which we supply only the appropriate sentences. In developing a language, we must also specify the relation of the language to the world, and thus "set up" the world to correspond to our language.

The semantic theory certainly resembles the correspondence theory. (Some philosophers, such as Karl Popper, have insisted that it *is* a version of the correspondence theory.) But in the development of the semantic theory of truth, Tarski and his followers have avoided traditional talk of "facts"; indeed facts are in disfavor. Instead, the emphasis is on the sematic conception of "satisfaction" (and the related notion of "reference"). *Something* outside of the language makes statements true — that is, satisfies them, but the semantic theory, unlike the traditional correspondence theory, does not insist or suggest that this "something" consists of already discrete and complete units of reality. The "something" too is defined through language by its stipulative role in our statements. (It is an open question, for the semantic theory, whether the same references, the same *something's*, are available in every language or whether reference and satisfaction are limited to particular languages; in other words, it is still being argued — vigorously — whether or not the semantic theory leads to relativism.)

Taken individually, each of these theories has its opponents. We have attacked the correspondence theory sufficiently. Against the coherence theory, other phi-

---

[5]Alfred Tarski, "The Semantic Theory of Truth," in *Philosophy and Phenomenological Research,* Vol. 4, No. 3, March 1944.

losophers have objected that a system of statements and beliefs can be "coherent" but yet not be true. For example, take a simple system of true beliefs and deny them all. They will still form a coherent system, but they will all be false. Similarly, we said in Chapter 1 that an argument can be valid (which makes it coherent) but yet have false premises and false conclusions.

Two opposed systems of statements and beliefs can be equally "coherent," but surely both cannot be true, for they claim opposite things about the world. (Think of the metaphysical systems of Spinoza and Leibniz.) So, truth must be more than mere coherence.

Against the pragmatic theory, philosophers have objected that a belief might "work" but not be true. Scientists have often made great headway with false hypotheses. Political demagogues have often obtained great power and even achieved positive results with lies. And false beliefs often make us happier than the truth. ("What you don't know won't hurt you" and "the truth hurts.") The reason some beliefs "work" better than others, it has been argued (for example, by Bertrand Russell), is that they are true. They are true, therefore, not because they "work," but they work because they are true to the facts.

And against the semantic theory, philosophers have objected that ultimately, it is still a restatement of the correspondence theory ("'snow is white' is true if and only if snow is white"). Although the semantic theory is an improvement because it emphasizes the role of language in picking out the facts that make our statements true, it still leaves the nature of the "picking out" as obscure as ever. We are not in the position of a logician, who can make up his semantic models and languages at will. (Consider the following silly but profoundly philosophical joke: Eve says to Adam: "Let's call that one a hippopotamus." Adam: "Why 'hippopotamus'?" Eve: "Because it looks more like a hippopotamus than anything else we've seen so far.")

An adequate semantic theory of truth must be far more than merely formal. It must specify how such a theory would apply to natural (unformalized and open-ended) languages. Truth cannot be only formally defined. If the semantic theory is true, then translations between languages are impossible since the rules of satisfaction are unique to each language.

The debate between these theories continues, but the likeliest outcome is usually a combination of theories rather than the exclusive victory of any particular one. Each makes up for the deficiencies in the others. But one of the most important consequences of this debate, ironically, has been the loss of interest in the very concept of Truth (with a capital "T"). In everyday contexts, of course, philosophers, like everyone else, will talk about statements and beliefs being "true" and "false" on the basis of a primitive "correspondence" notion, that is, "correspondence to the facts." But philosophically, the power of the word "Truth" has always dwelled in its strong metaphysical linkage to "the way the world really is." And having given up on that grandiose conception of Truth, many philosophers are sometimes inclined to give up the word "truth" altogether. They concern themselves only with what we ordinarily mean when we say that a statement is "true."[6] Other philosophers, however, refuse to give up the traditional search for truth, and new and improved versions of the traditional and newer theories are still appearing.

KANT'S REVOLUTION

What, then, is truth? It seems that either it is "out there," independent of us but perhaps therefore unknowable, or else it is, in some sense, "in us" — in the language we speak or the practical concerns we bring to our inquiries. The correspondence and semantic theories of truth accept this dualism of language and world; the coherence and pragmatic theories challenge it but, however hesitantly, find themselves uneasy about denying correspondence altogether, and with it, "the real world." But there is another tradition — one of which the coherence theory and the pragmatic theory are partial heirs — in which this very distinction between language and world, between us and Truth, is rejected. The prime mover of this other tradition is the German philosopher Immanuel Kant.

Immanuel Kant is considered by a great many philosophers to be the greatest thinker since Plato and Aristotle. He stands at the beginning of almost every modern movement in philosophy in America and Europe, as an inspiration and as a kind of founder. Existentialism would not be possible without him; nor would phenomenology, pragmatism, or many of the varieties of linguistic philosophy that have dominated English and American philosophy for most of this century. He brings together the often opposed threads of rationalism and empiricism and weaves them into a single, monumental philosophical system, which he published primarily in three "critiques" (*The Critique of Pure Reason, The Critique of Practical Reason,* and *The Critique of Judgment*) in the last two decades of the eighteenth century. His writing is notoriously difficult, but it is possible for even a beginning philosophy student to appreciate the main theme of his self-proclaimed "revolution" in philosophy. It is, in one sense, a total reorientation of what we mean when we talk about Truth.

Ever since the ancient Greeks, almost all philosophers had accepted the idea that there is a reality "out there," which we could come to know through reason, through experience, or perhaps which we could not come to know at all, according to a sceptic like David Hume. The idea of an "external world" seemed innocent enough, until metaphysicians began to find that their contradictory views about this world could not be reconciled. This dilemma prompted John Locke to turn away from metaphysics and pay more attention to the way we acquire knowledge. The shift of attention to knowledge led Hume to argue that we

---

[6]J. L. Austin, for example, begins an essay on "Truth" by declaring, "*In vino veritas,* ('in wine, truth') perhaps, but in a sober symposium, *verum* ('true')."

couldn't even know that the sun would rise tomorrow, or that one billiard ball in fact causes the movement of another, or that there is indeed a world outside of our own ideas.

This sceptical conclusion seemed utterly absurd to Kant, who was, in his own words, "awakened from his dogmatic slumbers" by Hume. Kant had been a metaphysician (a follower of Leibniz), but reading Hume convinced him that there was a serious problem, not only for metaphysics, but for our claims to know the world at all. And Kant, who was also a scientist and an enthusiastic supporter of Isaac Newton and the new physics, saw that he had to refute Hume if he was going to keep claiming that scientists (and everyone else) could know anything at all. But the problem, as he diagnosed it, turned out to be the unquestioned idea that there was a distinction to be made between our beliefs and experience of the world, on the one hand, and the world itself, Reality or Truth, on the other.

What Kant suspected, and what many philosophers believe today, is that our "ideas" — our concepts and our language — do not just correspond to reality but in some sense "set up" the world, impose upon the world the structures we experience. We see material objects instead of just patterns of light and colors (as seen perhaps by a newborn baby), and this is our contribution to experience. We experience events in a cause and effect relationship, instead of as mere sequences of events, and this is not because of experience alone, but because we *make* our experience conform to causal rules. We expect certain events in the future on the basis of what we have experienced in the past; and this too is not mere habit, but a set of rules we impose necessarily on every experience. According to Kant, space and time do not exist "out there," independent of our experience; we impose the forms of three-dimensional space and one-dimensional time on our experience, and through these forms come to know the world. So too, Kant argues, all of our knowledge of the world is in part a product of the various forms and rules that we impose upon, or use to "set up," our experience. The word Kant uses for "set up" is "constitutes." A "constitution" sets up a government, provides it with its rules and structures. We **constitute** our own experience in the sense that we provide the rules and structures according to which we experience objects, as objects in space and time, as governed by the laws of nature and the relations of cause and effect. Kant writes, "the understanding does not derive its laws from, but prescribes them to, nature."

According to Kant's philosophy, reality has no existence that we can understand except as we constitute it through our basic concepts. Kant took these concepts — or what he called "categories" — to be the basic rules of the human mind as such, common to all peoples in all places at all times. Today, many philosophers would rather say that these concepts through which we constitute the world are part of a language, which raises the intriguing but controversial possibility that the world might be quite different for people who speak different languages. (Kant himself did not believe this.) Truth, in other words, is a function of our concepts. It is not correspondence; it is not mere coherence. And it is not just a matter of what "works" or satisfies our investigations. Kant's revolution rejects the very idea of an external Reality and instead looks to the concepts through which we "constitute" Reality. Thus there is no point to wondering whether our concepts match up to Reality, since there would be no Reality without our concepts. Our concepts not only cohere with each other; they "set up" a corresponding reality as well. And of course those concepts "work"—it is as if someone were to wonder how it is that a ceramic mold exactly fits a piece of jewelry, when the mold gave shape to the jewelry in the first place.

Previous philosophers had asked, "How can we know that our ideas correspond with the way the world really is?" Kant rejected that question. Instead, he asked, *"How do our ideas constitute the world?"* "What is the structure and what are the rules (the *concepts* or *categories*) of the human mind according to which we 'set up' our world, the world of our experience?" The project of Kant's *Critique of Pure Reason* is to analyze and prove the necessity of these concepts, which we can know *a priori*—independently of all experience and with certainty, just because they are the rules within which all of our knowledge is possible. Think of it this way: you take a number of pieces of wood and a checkerboard and "set up" the game by making up rules about what can be moved where, how, and when. Then, within the game, you are free to make any number of moves, some brilliant, some stupid, but you are always bound by the rules that you yourself have "set up." And since you yourself have established these rules, it would be absurd to wonder whether or not they are "true."

Kant's revolution changed our conception of truth, and, along with it, our conception of reality, our conception of knowledge, and, most importantly, our conception of ourselves. Truth is no longer correspondence between our ideas and reality, but our own system of rules (concepts or categories) by which we constitute our reality. Knowledge, accordingly, is no longer the comprehending of a reality beyond our experience, but knowledge of our experience. But this does not mean knowledge of experience, distinct from knowledge of objects, for the objects of our experience are all there is to reality. Moreover, in making this move, Kant gives the philosophers something which they thought they had lost, a renewed ideal of certainty, for, he argued, we can be certain of the rules of our own experience. Kant defended the necessity of the truths of arithmetic and geometry as those rules that have to do with the *a priori* forms of our intuitions of space and time. According to Kant's philosophy in general, reality is the world of our experience, as we constitute it through the concepts of our understanding. Therefore, we can know it with certainty, for truth, in general, is our own construction.

You might at first think that there is some trick here, as if Kant is saying, "well if we can't have knowledge in the hard sense, then I'll simply redefine the words 'knowledge,' 'reality,' and 'truth.'" But what he has done is to point to the difficulty of the picture that other philosophers had accepted; he has shown that what we normally mean by "truth," "knowledge," and "reality" is not an insatiable appeal to a world beyond our experience. My everyday statement, "there's beer in the refrigerator" is true, whatever any philosopher might say, if there is beer in the refrigerator — if I can go and look, see it, pick it up, open the can, and drink it. As for some beer beyond my experience that is the real beer, what kind of absurdity is that? Underneath Kant's spectacular pronouncements, there is, once again, a return to common sense. This world, the one I stand in, touch, and see, is the real world. But what makes it real, according to Kant, is not just that I stand in, touch, and see it, but that I actively constitute it as the way it is, apply my own rules for understanding it, and structure it through my own experience.

In 1781 Kant already anticipated the three "theories of truth" that would become so powerful in the twentieth century. In his emphasis on our constitution of reality through interconnected rules and concepts, Kant anticipates the coherence theory of truth, which stresses precisely these interconnections. In his emphasis on the workability of these rules, he anticipates the pragmatic theory. And in his theory that it is our concepts and rules that "set up" reality, Kant anticipates Tarski's semantic theory. But what is of equal importance is that Kant does not endorse any single one of these theories, but embraces them all.

Kant gives us a general way of giving an account of all those truths that metaphysicians have always argued about. Using Kant's terminology, we can say they are forms of *synthetic a priori* knowledge. Such knowledge is, briefly characterized, knowledge of our own rules with which we (necessarily) constitute reality. If a truth is not true because of our experiences, nor is it true because of the grammar or meanings of the sentences of our language, how else could it be defended? This was Hume's dilemma, and with his two-test system of justification, he eliminated many of our most important beliefs as "unjustifiable," as neither "truths of reason" nor "matters of fact." But now, we have our third way: A belief can be true, necessarily true, if it is one of those rules that we impose to constitute our experience. Thus we saw that Kant defended the truths of arithmetic and geometry by showing that they were the "*(a priori)* forms of intuition," the ways in which we must experience our world. So too will he defend all of those truths that Hume had claimed to be unjustifiable. The principle of universal causation is neither a generalization from experience nor an analytic truth, but rather a *rule* for "setting up" our world. And that rule is, "Always look for regular (or 'lawlike') connections between events, so that you can explain an event as an *effect* of previous events, and therefore predict future events as well." Like a rule in chess, this is not a move within the game but one of those rules that defines the game. So too with the principle of induction; it is neither based upon experience nor a trivial truth but a rule with which we govern all of our experience. And so too for our belief in the "external" or material world, which Berkeley and Hume found so problematic. Our experience alone will not tell us whether we are dreaming or not, and the idea of the material ("external") world is not a tautology or a conceptual truth. It too is one of the rules that we use to constitute our experience, namely, that we shall *always* interpret our experience of objects in space as external to us and as material or *substantial*. But notice, our metaphysical notion of substance is no longer that which is, by definition, outside of our experience. It is now part of the rules by which we set up our experience.

from *Prolegomena*
to *Any Future Metaphysics*,
by Immanuel Kant

My purpose is to persuade all those who think metaphysics worth study-ing that it is absolutely necessary to pause a moment and, regarding all that has been done as though undone, to propose first the preliminary question, "Whether such a thing as metaphysics be even possible at all?"

If it be science, how is it that it cannot, like other sciences, obtain uni-versal and lasting recognition? If not, how can it maintain its pretensions and keep the human mind in suspense with hopes never ceasing, yet never fulfilled? Whether then we demonstrate our knowledge or our ignorance in this field, we must come once and for all to a definite conclusion respecting the nature of this so-called science, which cannot possibly remain on its present footing. It seems almost ridiculous, while every other science is con-tinually advancing, that in this, which pretends to be wisdom incarnate, for whose oracle everyone inquires, we should constantly move round the same spot, without gaining a single step. An so its votaries having melted away, we do not find men confident of their ability to shine in other sciences venturing their reputation here, where everybody, however ignorant in other matters, presumes to deliver a final verdict, because in this domain there is actually as yet no standard weight and measure to distinguish sound knowledge from shallow talk.

. . . . .

Hume started chiefly from a single but important concept in metaphys-ics, namely, that of the connection of cause and effect (including its deriv-atives force and action, and so on). He challenged reason, which pretends to have given birth to this concept of herself, to answer him by what right she thinks anything could be so constituted that if that thing be posited, something else also must necessarily be posited; for this is the meaning of the concept of cause. He demonstrated irrefutably that it was perfectly impossible for reason to think *a priori* and by means of concepts such a combination, for it implies necessity. We cannot at all see why, in conse-quence of the existence of one thing, another must necessarily exist or how the concept of such a combination can arise *a priori*. Hence he inferred that reason was altogether deluded with reference to this concept, which she erroneously considered as one of her own children, whereas in reality it was nothing but a bastard of imagination, impregnated by experience, which subsumed certain representations under the law of association and mistook a subjective necessity (habit) for an objective necessity arising from insight. Hence he inferred that reason had no power to think such combinations, even in general, because her concepts would then be purely fictitious and all her pretended *a priori* cognitions nothing but common experiences marked with a false stamp. In plain language, this means that there is not and cannot be any such thing as metaphysics at all.

. . . . .

I openly confess my recollection of David Hume was the very thing which many years ago first interrupted my dogmatic slumber and gave my investigations in the field of speculative philosophy a quite new direction.

I was far from following him in the conclusions at which he arrived by regarding, not the whole of his problem, but a part, which by itself can give us no information. If we start from a well-founded, but undeveloped, thought which another has bequeathed to us, we may well hope by continued reflection to advance farther than the acute man to whom we owe the first spark of light.

I therefore first tried whether Hume's objection could not be put into a general form, and soon found that the concept of the connection of cause and effect was by no means the only concept by which the understanding thinks the connection of things *a priori*, but rather that metaphysics consists altogether of such concepts. I sought to ascertain their number; and when I had satisfactorily succeeded in this by starting from a single principle, I proceeded to the deduction of these concepts, which I was now certain were not derived from experience, as Hume had attempted to derive them, but sprang from the pure understanding. This deduction (which seemed impossible to my acute predecessor, which had never even occurred to anyone else, though no one had hesitated to use the concepts without investigating the basis of their objective validity) was the most difficult task which ever could have been undertaken in the service of metaphysics; and the worst was that metaphysics, such as it is, could not assist me in the least because this deduction alone can render metaphysics possible. But as soon as I had succeeded in solving Hume's problem, not merely in a particular case, but with respect to the whole faculty of pure reason, I could proceed safely, though slowly, to determine the whole sphere of pure reason completely and from universal principles, in its boundaries as well as in its contents. This was required for metaphysics in order to construct its system according to a safe plan.[7]

Kant gives us a way of resolving the age-old disputes of metaphysics — questions concerning reality as such. Since the claims of the metaphysicians are all synthetic *a priori*, Kant provides us with the following policy:

1. Those claims that are rules by which we must interpret our experience are true — necessarily true.
2. Those claims that contradict rules by which we must interpret our experience are false — necessarily false.
3. Those that are not rules by which we must interpret our experience are either analytic, contingently true, or contingently false.
4. Finally, those claims that cannot be decided by appeal to the rules of our experience and make no difference to our experience one way or the other, are to be rejected as possible topics of knowledge.

The logical positivists in this century took this last part of Kant's policy as a program for a devastating attack on metaphysics in general. Although the logical positivists, as empiricists in the tradition of David Hume, did not accept much of

---

[7]Immanuel Kant, *Prolegomena to Any Future Metaphysics*, trans. Lewis White Beck (New York: Bobbs-Merrill, 1950).

Kant's theory, they wholeheartedly endorsed his rejection of claims that made no difference whatever to our experience. They said that any claim that makes no difference to our experience — that cannot be tested in any way — is meaningless.

Some of the metaphysician's claims will be upheld. For example, Kant saves Newton's (and Spinoza's) determinism in his rule of causality, thus rejecting Leibniz's "pre-established harmony" view as necessarily false. With some revisions, he accepts a large part of Leibniz's view of space and time as relative, that is, relative to our experience. He saves the notion of substance because he says that one of the most important rules of our experience is that we see objects as substantial (that is, as "real"). But he does not accept the view that substance is something independent of human experience, for such a view, by definition, means that substance would be irrelevant to our experience. Nor does he accept the central dispute between Spinoza and Leibniz, whether there is but one substance or many, for no rule of our experience is concerned one way or another. It makes no difference to our experience. It is a metaphysician's game and not a possible topic for knowledge.

Kant's revolution is the elimination of "reality" and "truth" as external to ourselves. Since Kant, many philosophers no longer view human knowledge as the passive reception of sensations or intuitions. And, needless to say, the problems of philosophy have become radically changed.

Kant destroyed the old problems, resolved the old disputes, and answered Hume's skepticism, at least for a while. In rejecting the correspondence theory of truth and the idea of an "external" reality, he eliminated the basis of those problems, disputes, and doubts. But I expect that you can already see a new and even more virulent version of those problems, disputes, and doubts on the horizon. By denying us our anchor in reality, Kant launches philosophy in a bold new direction, and he creates the dilemma that still defines philosophy today: If we supply our own rules for our experience, is there any uniquely correct way of describing the way the world is?

The basis of Kant's theory is that we supply the rules according to which we constitute our experience. Truth can be talked about only within our experience and according to those rules. But you can see what happens when we raise the following question: What about people (or creatures) who are very different from us? Will they use the same rules? Will they have the same experiences? And, if we do differ from them, who is "right"? Whose rules are "better"? Whose experience is "true"? You can see here the problems of the coherence theory of truth coming to haunt Kant's philosophy. Suppose there are two (or more) sets of rules, equally coherent? Can they both be "true"? And the problems of the semantic theory, too: What if there are different languages with different basic concepts or categories, constituting different "facts"? Are they all "true"? You can appreciate how easily the German Romantic philosophers who immediately followed Kant replaced his notion of "constitution" with the more exciting notion of "creation." We create our realities, they announced. We are all artists, building our worlds. And notice the words "reali*ties*" and "worlds"; there is no longer confidence, much less a guarantee, that there is only one reality or one world.

Kant's most immediate follower, a German named Johann Gottlieb Fichte, used the pragmatic theory of truth to come to the same conclusion; the truth is, according to him, that which is most practical, most conducive to the good life, and the evaluation of different realities depends wholly on the practical consequences. (He said, in his most famous dictum: "the kind of philosophy a man chooses depends upon the kind of man he is.") With Kant's revolution, the Truth seems destined to be replaced by many truths.

But before we go on to explore these intriguing complications, let us make it clear that Kant himself never accepted a word of all this. According to him, there was still but one possible set of rules, and therefore only one way of constituting our experience, whoever we are, wherever we're from, and no matter what kind of conscious creature we happen to be. And this means: one world, one science, one reality, and one truth. Kant tries to prove this in the central section of his *Critique of Pure Reason*, in a formidable argument that he calls a "transcendental deduction."

Like so much philosophical jargon, Kant's term is easily explained, and is used often enough to make it worth explaining. You already know what a deduction is, an inference from one statement to another according to a set of rules of inference. In this case, Kant attempts to infer from various statements that we believe, the basic rules (concepts, categories) of human experience. And this is what "transcendental" means, the basic rules of human experience. But a transcendental deduction is not satisfied with simply deducing some such rules; it also proves that they are the *only* rules that we are able to use to constitute our experience. That is why it is so important to Kant. It allows him his revolution without its anarchist consequences.

The argument itself is enormously complicated and scholars who have studied it for half their lives still do not agree what it is or whether it is a valid argument. So, obviously, we won't try to summarize it for you here. What can and must be said is this, however: Kant believed that such a transcendental deduction would prove that, although it is we ourselves who supply the rules of our experience and determine what can be true for us, we don't have a choice in the matter. There still is only one truth for all of us.

Philosophers are still arguing whether any such transcendental argument (Kant's or not) might succeed. If one does, then people must, in their basic rules, all agree. (Of course, they will always disagree about particular matters; no two chess players make all the same moves.) But if there is no successful transcendental argument, then there need be no such universal agreement. It then makes sense to talk about different truths for different people. This, we may say, is the dominant battle of twentieth-century philosophy in America and in Europe.[8]

---

[8]It is important to recognize that there are many possible perspectives from which to summarize the more recent developments in philosophy since the turn of the nineteenth century and this is one of them. The dual purpose of this chapter is (1) to bring into the present day one of the most controversial aspects of the entire history of Western metaphysics and epistemology discussed in the preceding chapters, and (2) to give a brief survey of some of the major movements in recent philosophy.

Those who believe that there is only one set of rules and one truth are often called **absolutists** (though many philosophers find that name repulsive because it sounds so dogmatic). Others, who believe that there are different rules for different people and therefore different "truths," are called **relativists.** Kant was an absolutist. Most of his followers were relativists. (This is obscured by the confusing fact that many of them talked about "the Absolute" all the time. But, they were still relativists, and to avoid confusion, we shall not talk about "the Absolute" at all in this book.)

THE BATTLE IN EUROPE AFTER KANT: RELATIVISM AND ABSOLUTISM

The story of philosophy in Europe since Kant is largely the story of a war between relativism and absolutism, in which even the politics and arts of the times play a continuing role. The philosophers immediately following Kant, as we have already mentioned, pursued relativism with a relish, developing alternative systems of philosophy as fast as they could find publishers. The philosopher Friedrich Schelling, for example, produced about one system a year at the turn of the century. He became the best-known "Romantic" philosopher of a large group of "Romantic" intellectuals, poets, and critics throughout Europe who turned to the virtual worship of individual "genius" and competed for the most extravagant and creative views of the world.

The virtually undisputed winner of this contest, however, was not Schelling but one of his schoolmates, Georg Wilhelm Friedrich Hegel. Hegel developed in his first book one of the most colossal systems of thought since Plato, perhaps outdoing even Leibniz and Spinoza. But where Leibniz and Spinoza were telling us "the way the world really is," Hegel gave us a long series of alternative ways of viewing (and living in) the world. He called these different views "forms of consciousness," and the series itself a "phenomenology of spirit," that is, the long road over which human consciousness has traveled in its adoption of one view of the world (or "form of consciousness") and then another.

Starting from a clearly Kantian perspective, Hegel taught that we have to stop talking about "true" and "false" philosophies, and "true" and "false" religions, political systems, societies, scientific theories, and values. There are only different "forms of consciousness," some more sophisticated and perspicacious than others, but none wholly true (or false) to the exclusion of others. Hegel wholly endorsed the Kantian thesis that the world is nothing other than the way in which we constitute it. Or rather, the ways, for Hegel no longer believes that there is only one. And that means that seemingly opposed philosophies are not really contradictory; they are just alternative views of reality. But, didn't we just claim that there is a reality that exists independently of these various "views" of it? Not at all, according to Hegel. "Reality" is nothing other than the totality of these different human views of it, that comprehensive consciousness that sees not just this view or that view but sees them all as bits and pieces of the truth. And what is that "truth"? Just that there is no reality other than the reality we constitute with our concepts.

Hegel had his own favorite world-views, which were in themselves extravagant and admirable creations. For example, he developed a conception he called *Geist* (the German word for "Spirit" in the title of his *Phenomenology*), which was his view of a God who could not be distinguished from mankind. (You will recognize a heavy debt to Spinoza here.) He also argued, as Napoleon was marching across Europe, for the importance of internationalism. He was an arch enemy of what he considered vulgar individualism (for example, in his friends, the Romantics) and defended a sense of community spirit, which very strongly influenced Karl Marx, and formed the philosophical foundations of both socialism and fascism. But most famously, he developed the old idea of **dialectic** (which we found in Socrates), and suggested that the various "forms of consciousness" he catalogued were linked to one another in a progressive logical chain. He resurrected the old Aristotelian animism with a picture of the universe that, through human consciousness, was evolving towards a goal. But like Heraclitus, to whom the concept of "dialectic" is often attributed, Hegel believed that this evolution was anything but a smooth progression: It was violent, depending on a constant battle of opposites and reconciliations that would last only a moment, until the next battle. It is from this notion of dialectic that Marx develops his powerful and influential view of history as class conflict, replacing Hegel's abstract "forms of consciousness" with the day-to-day battles of wages, jobs, exploitation, and profits.[9]

After Hegel, relativism became ever more sophisticated. In Marx, differences in philosophical world views were explained in terms of different economic and social circumstances. The question was no longer "which view of the world was true?" but rather, "what circumstances would make a person believe that?" A few years later, a similar view was defended by the eccentric but brilliant iconoclast, Friedrich Nietzsche. He too attacked the traditional notions of truth with a vengeance and argued that there could be as many equally "true" (or equally "false"—it doesn't matter) world views as there were creative people and societies. He also urged that every person adopt for himself or herself as many different world-views as possible, at one time or another, as a matter of "experiment." And, like Marx, he replaced the old question, "which view of the world is true?" with a question of circumstances. But Nietzsche was not interested in economic or social circumstances so much as psychological factors. And so he asked, "what kind of personality would need to believe that?" Truth is no longer even an issue. In fact, even rationality is starting to feel the threat of relativism. For, with Nietzsche, not only is truth out the window, but coherence and pragmatism are forced to take second place as well. What comes first? Excitement, adventure, heroism, creativity, and what Nietzsche generally calls "the will to power." Of

---

[9]The familiar doctrine of Hegel's dialectic is often known only in terms of "thesis-antithesis-synthesis." In fact these categories are rarely used by either Hegel or Marx.

course, one must still act rationally if one is to achieve these things, but thinking, in Nietzsche's view, plays at most a secondary role in our lives.

The turn of this century saw the introduction of a powerful doctrine that is still immensely influential in Europe and, to a lesser degree, in the United States. It is called **historicism,** and the man who is best known for defending it is a philosopher named Wilhelm Dilthey. Historicism is Hegel's dialectic of forms of consciousness, pinned down to precise social and historical periods. It is the thesis, simply, that truth and rationality are relative to particular peoples at particular times in history and that overall comparison of them, with the intention of finding out which is "true," is totally mistaken. It is, obviously, a very strong relativist doctrine, so strong and so influential that the absolutists in philosophy, who had had much less publicity and success than the relativists for the last century, started looking around for a champion. They found him in the "phenomenologist" Edmund Husserl.

Phenomenology is a self-consciously "scientific" and "rigorous" discipline, modeled after mathematics (as it was for Descartes and the ancient Greeks). Phenomenology is the study of the esssential structures of the human mind, and because these are essential, they can be known to be true, universally and necessarily. (We shall see more of Husserl and phenomenology in Chapter 5.) Husserl was a new kind of rationalist, who believed that the truths of arithmetic and geometry are known — and known with certainty — by appeal to a certain kind of intuition, which he called "essential" intuition. Believing that such intuitions are adequate for arithmetic and geometry, Husserl turned his theory elsewhere, to philosophy in general. Husserl, as much as any philosopher of his time (the early twentieth century), was horrified by what he saw as rampant relativism. He saw it, in fact, not only as a crisis in philosophy but as "a crisis in European civilization." And so he turned his phenomenology to attack it. Turning against Dilthey, for example, he argued that:

> Historicism takes its position in the factual sphere of the empirical life of the spirit. To the extent that it posits this latter absolutely, without exactly naturalizing it (the specific sense of nature in particular lies far from historical thinking and in any event does not influence it by determining it in general), there arises a relativism that has a close affinity to naturalistic psychologism and runs into similar sceptical difficulties.
>
> ... In view of this constant change in scientific views we would actually have no right to speak of sciences as objectively valid unities instead of merely as cultural formations. It is easy to see that historicism, if consistently carried through, carries over into extreme sceptical subjectivism. The ideas of truth, theory, and science would then, like all ideas, lose their absolute validity. That an idea has validity would mean that it is a factual construction of spirit which is held as valid and which in its contingent validity determines thought. There would be no unqualified validity, or validity-in-itself, which is what it is even if no one has achieved it and though no historical humanity will ever achieve it. Thus too there would then be no validity to the principle of contradiction nor to any logic, which latter is nevertheless still in full vigor in our time. The result, perhaps, will be that

the logical principles of noncontradiction will be transformed into their opposites.[10]

Using both Kant's terminology and his absolutist intentions, Husserl attacked all forms of relativism and attempted to develop a *transcendental phenomenology*, in other words, a phenomenology that discovers the basic rules of all experience (just as he had discovered them for arithmetic and geometry before). And because these rules (or "ideal laws") were discovered to be essential, they were, Husserl concluded, the only rules possible. In Husserl as in Kant, the word "transcendental" means the basic and the only rules with which we "constitute" our world. (Husserl used the notion of "constitution" also, with much the same meaning that Kant did.) But what is *phenomenology*? It is the study of human consciousness. These essential rules of experience, in other words, were to be found in consciousness, not in a mysterious Platonic "world of being" nor simply in our language. Consciousness itself, with the objects of its own constitution, becomes our new anchor.

Husserl's battle, from beginning to end, was a battle against relativism, against all of those philosophies that held that there can be different equally true or equally rational world-views. And it must be said that his phenomenology, for all of its internal struggles, was immensely successful and still attracts the attention of a great many philosophers today. But phenomenology was not the solution to relativism. Husserl thought that phenomenology could be transcendental and prove that certain rules were basic and essential to all human thinking. But just as Kant opened the door to relativism with his view that we constitute our world, Husserl opened it wider with his view that a study of consciousness was the way to do philosophy. For were there not, his followers asked, many different forms of consciousness? (Thus returning to Hegel rather than Kant.) And phenomenology as it developed in France, rather than Germany, became the source of a new relativism, which is extremely fashionable today.

HERMENEUTICS: THE NEW QUEST FOR UNDERSTANDING

Absolutism seems to deny the obvious fact that people are different and disagree, not only in superficial ways but in terms of their most basic beliefs. Relativism, on the other hand, seems to imply that we will never be able to understand one another—or find the truth—at all. One attempt to bridge the gap between dogmatic absolutism and solipsistic relativism is **hermeneutics.**

"Hermeneutics" is an old name for "interpretation," with an eye to getting at the Truth. For many centuries, this formidable word was applied exclusively to the interpretation of the Bible, with the aim of understanding the Word of God.

---

[10]Edmund Husserl, "Philosophy as Rigorous Science," in *Phenomenology and the Crisis of Philosophy*, trans. Quentin Lauer (New York: Harper & Row, 1965).

Today, however, the term has a much broader meaning. It is often used in literary criticism to talk about the interpretation of texts—any text and not only the Bible. But it is now used in philosophy too to refer to the discipline of interpreting and understanding the world, which becomes, in effect, our text.

The modern father of hermeneutics is the German "historicist" Wilhelm Dilthey, whom we encountered in the previous section. Dilthey came to realize that the methods of the physical sciences were not very successful when applied to the "human sciences," in part because history played such enormous importance in human life. He also realized that there was a very real danger in the Kantian attempt to overcome traditional philosophical distinctions between appearance and reality, subjectivity, and objective truth. While his historicism lent itself to relativism, Dilthey himself was vehemently anti-relativist. The problem, he argued, was to develop a method for **understanding** human differences.

Contemporary hermeneutics is just this attempt to provide a way of understanding viewpoints other than our own. It is simply dogmatic to insist—as Kant and many other philosophers have insisted—that the structures of the human mind are everywhere the same and, consequently, that we all share a common basis of knowledge. But it is simple-minded, on the other hand, to insist that we are all different and have different truths, since there is at least enough overlap for us to understand that we do disagree. For example, the medievals saw God and the earth as the spiritual and spatial centers of the universe. How can a twentieth century scientist understand them? Well, not just by dismissing their views as nonsense, nor can we sensibly say, "Well, they have their opinions and we have ours." Hermeneutics is just this attempt to step into someone else's shoes (but without taking off our own shoes first).

In this century, hermeneutics has been turned into a powerful style of philosophizing by the German metaphysician Martin Heidegger. It was Heidegger, in his monumental book, **Being and Time** (1928) who suggested that life is like a text, and the purpose of our lives is to understand that text. Heidegger was a student of Husserl, and thus a phenomenologist. But in his hermeneutical phenomenology he tries to "uncover" the hidden meanings in our experience. He rejects the scientific tone of Husserl's phenomenology and prefers to talk about the structures of life itself, including our profound sense of history, which defines human life.

The most important proponent of hermeneutics, however, is a student of Heidegger's, Hans Georg Gadamer. In fact, Gadamer is so wary of the fact that method—and not only scientific method—may distort our understanding that he insists that hermeneutics must resist the temptation to become another method. It is rather the attempt to overcome methods, to dispense with the overemphasis on proofs and arguments and the quest for certainty and emphasize instead the shared understandings that we already have with one another. The substance of philosophy then becomes dialogue rather than individual phenomenology or abstract proofs. Interpretation thus becomes not an abstract function of the intellect but a process that permeates our every activity. The following is an account of Gadamer's **Truth and Method** by Alasdair MacIntyre:

on Gadamer's
Truth and Method,
by Alasdair MacIntyre

Ever since Bacon and Descartes the dominant intellectual tradition has connected truth and method. Let us only discover the appropriate method of enquiry and truth will lie plain before us. It is not only in the mythological belief in *the* scientific method or in those graveyards of the mind, the social scientists' textbooks on methodology (the transition from "method" to "methodology" is itself a symptom of cultural sickness), that this seventeenth-century faith is still evident. It is presupposed in the very forms of professionalized graduate education, in what intellectual sophistication is generally taken to be in academic life.

But suppose that method does not yield truth; suppose that it is not sophistication that we need but the right kind of naïveté; suppose that what we need to reflect upon to move toward the truth is what we already (in some sense) know; suppose that if truth is hidden, it is not because it requires searching out by some device of method, but because it is so plainly before our eyes in our everday activities and conversations that we cannot perceive it. At the very end of his book Gadamer invites us to reflect on certain types of conversation. When I am engrossed in a stimulating conversational exchange I do not pick my words with care, as I might under cross-examination, or recite already constructed sentences, like an actor. I speak spontaneously and in speaking formulate thoughts, often enough for the very first time. So that I learn what I think at the same moment that my hearer learns it too. And often enough my hearer discovers that his questions or comment or objection which evoked my new thoughts had a meaning which he had not recognized in the act of speaking. The conversation takes on a life which transcends the previous intentions and experiences of the speakers. Conversation is thus a dramatic form in which I am caught up and by which I am transformed.

At the same time no conversation is an isolated episode. Each of the participants brings with him an inherited mode of interpretation which leads him to construe both what others say and what he himself says in one way rather than another. The hearer has to translate what the speaker says; and this unacknowledged act of translation confers a determinacy on what is heard, which is in part the work of the hearer. Notice that conversation is in general purposeless; the question "What are you having that conversation for?" is misleading except in certain special cases. Conversation is rather the medium within which purposes are developed, criticized, modified and abandoned. It is a form of activity which individuals sustain, but do not create; and it is a form of activity such that in it the whole weight of an historical tradition is present, although usually unperceived.

This conception of language is primarily not a set of instruments to serve purposes, but as the medium presupposed by any application of concepts such as purpose, Gadamer owes to Heidegger. But he uses it in ways that are very different from Heidegger's. For he uses it to undermine any concept of method, by showing that prior to the application of any methodological rules, there must have been acts of interpretation and understanding which rendered into appropriate form the materials to which the methodological rules were to be applied; and that these acts of interpretation and understanding already involve the use of criteria of truth. So Gadamer inverts the received view of the relationship of truth to method; method is not the path to truth, but a prior grasp of the place of truth in human understanding is a prerequisite for any fruitful method.

.   .   .   .   .

This brings us . . . to Gadamer's restoration of the concept of *mimesis* — representation, if you like, as Gadamer's English translators like — so central to most pre-Kantian theories. To understand Gadamer's concept it is crucial to distinguish between what I shall call "external representation" and what I shall call "internal representation." External representation is the relationship which holds between a passport photograph and its subject; one can inspect the two items independently and enquire as to the degree of resemblance between them. It is quite otherwise with internal representation; here the key features of that which is represented can only be identified by means of the representation. It is by means of the representation that we learn to see what is represented. So Rembrandt teaches us to see in the human face what we could not — and perhaps did not want to — see before; the officers of the *Night Watch* who objected to paying for their group portrait took it to be a bad composite passport photograph. But, as Gadamer writes, "The world which appears in the play of representation does not stand like a copy next to the real world, but is the latter in the heightened truth of its being. . . . The concept of mimesis . . . did not mean a copy so much as the appearance of what is represented". . . .

Some philosophers have tried to elucidate truth as a relationship between statements or sentences (taken to be linguistic items) on the one hand and facts or states of affairs (taken to be non-linguistic items) on the other. The unsolved problem for any such view lies in saying of any particular alleged non-linguistic item what it is; for the moment we say what it is, it appears that it can only be captured by means of language. The same problem holds for those accounts of the truth (or falsity) of scientific theories which try to compare theories (taken to be linguistic items) with facts or states of affairs (taken to be non-linguistic items). For every characterization of the facts is itself to some degree theory-laden. It turns out that we are not, in asserting truth or falsity, asserting or denying some relationship between part of language and a non-linguistic feature of the world; we are always comparing one linguistic characterization with another. Truth is a property of internal as much or more than of external representation, elsewhere just as in art.

.   .   .   .   .

Philosophers who interpret the world with the acuteness with which Gadamer has interpreted it must learn that they cannot evade the accusation that they have thereby also changed it. We inhabit an interpreted world in which reinterpretation is the most fundamental form of change.[11]

[11] Alasdair MacIntyre, "Contexts of Interpretation," *Boston University Journal*, vol. XXIV, no. 1, 1976.

Gadamer's hermeneutics does not reject the notion of truth, but it does give up entirely the idea that there is a Truth wholly outside of us which we need a method (rationalism, empiricism, scientific psychology) to discover. Like the coherence theorist and the pragmatist, he gives up the idea of secure *foundations* for our knowledge—such as the raw experiences or "sense data" discussed by some empiricists, or the *a priori* principles defended by Kant. But where both the coherence theorist and the pragmatist tend to interpret truth as a function of the present—coherence of beliefs and workability, respectively—the hermeneuticist insists that truth must be understood *historically*, in terms of a *tradition*. Thus the philosophical tradition, ironically, has tended to ignore the importance of its own tradition and look for strictly eternal truths. Gadamer's hermeneutics hold rather that it is only within a tradition, and by looking at our tradition, that philosophical truth is possible at all. Does this mean that we must accept whatever our tradition may be, even if it is wrong? But what would it be, Gadamer asks, for a tradition to be wrong? We can criticize ourselves, of course, and that is just the point of hermeneutics. But does it mean that we must also justify ourselves and what we have always believed? "Do we need to justify," he asks rhetorically, "that which has always supported us?"

RELATIVISM RECONSIDERED

Does relativism mean that there can be no truth? Does relativism apply only to philosophical views, not to *real* theories? Could there be *really* different views of the world—and different worlds? But does it even make sense to talk about relative truth, that is, a truth that is only "true for" one person or group and not another?

If such a phrase even makes sense, it must mean that a statement is true for a person or group by virtue of the scheme or conceptual framework they employ; thus it is true for a certain society that the witchdoctor embodies the power of the devil, but true for another society that the powers of the so-called witchdoctor are nothing but the combination of natural pharmaceuticals plus the power of suggestion. But what must not be the case—if we are to continue using the word "truth"at all—is that a statement or a belief is true just by virtue of its being believed, if there is, in other words, no possibility that a person or a group can believe what is false (or, not believe some statement that is nevertheless true). Furthermore, as in hermeneutics, it is essential that we do not close off the possibility that one truth might be understandable—perhaps in different terms—by those who believe another, apparently contradictory truth.

In the following essay, philosopher Chris Swoyer discusses the intelligibility of "relative truth"—the idea that a statement might be true in one conceptual framework but not in another.

"Relative Truth,"
by Chris Swoyer

Over two thousand years ago Protagoras declared that man is the measure of all things, and philosophers have been debating the merits of various relativistic claims ever since. Discussions of relativism are often vague and impressionistic, partly because explicit characterizations of relativism are most often found in the writings of opponents of the doctrine who sketch the view perfunctorily in order to have a target for criticism. Such writers have had the day largely because the label "relativistic" is widely regarded as pejorative, and few philosophers have been willing to mount an explicit defense of relativism. Consequently, although relativistic themes abound in recent writings, the authors in whose work they appear often spend much of their time trying to avoid the seemingly relativistic consequences of their views. . . .

Relativism is less a unified view than a family of themes united by their claim that some feature of thought or experience is relative to a culture, language, historical period or, to use a more general term (explained below), to a *conceptual framework*. For a claim about relativism to be of much philosophical interest, this feature should be something that is often taken to be absolute and invariant across all populations, for instance: truth, moral principles, fundamental concepts, modes of perception, or standards for reasoning.

Generalizing a distinction found in many discussions of ethical relativism, we may distinguish descriptive relativism and normative relativism with respect to any such feature. Descriptive relativism about features like moral or logical principles are empirical claims to the effect that different groups of people in fact have different moral or logical principles. The corresponding versions of normative relativism tell us that there is no objective fact about which moral or logical principles are correct and that at best they can be said to be *correct for*, or *relative to*, a given population.

I shall focus on normative relativism with respect to truth or, for short, on the *doctrine of relative truth*. Truth provides a useful starting point for a discussion of relativism for several reasons. In the first place, opponents of relativism usually concentrate on truth. Moreover, although those attracted by relativism may begin with considerations about concepts, perception, or moral principles, their views often *appear* to lead rather naturally to the conclusion that truth is relative. Finally, despite the existence of well-known arguments against the claim that truth is relative, a number of able thinkers have been drawn to the view that it is, and it is important to try to see why this is so. . . .

CONCEPTS AND EXPERIENCE

Many forms of relativism can be viewed in terms of a fairly simple model which — despite differences in their interests, terminology, and the tradition in which they work — may be found in the writings of a number of important thinkers. The first step in the defense of this model owes an obvious debt to Kant and a less obvious one to Hume. According to this tradition, knowledge and perception are *constructive processes*. Far from the mind's being a blank tablet on which perception records a story about the world, knowledge and experience are possible only if the mind organizes or conceptualizes some sort of "input," This input may be construed in a variety of ways, ranging from Hume's "impressions" or Kant's "manifold of empirical intuitions" to physical stimulations of our sensory receptors. The input may be viewed as some sort of uninterpreted, unconceptualized element in experience — "the given," as some philosophers have called it — though it need not be. The critical point is just that knowledge requires that we *do* something to this input.

Early philosophers saw our contribution in terms of the psychological activity of association, while more recent thinkers have viewed it in terms of the application of concepts and principles of classification. The latter philosophers often added that since *all* thought requires the use of concepts, there can be no vantage point from which we can survey the world as it is "in itself" — as it is entirely apart from the way we think about it. We cannot say, for instance, that our classifications are based on objective similarities to be found in the input or, for that matter, to be found out there in a mind-independent world. For what counts as similar to what depends on how things are classified, and our practices of classification depend on the concepts we employ. And since our concepts cannot be "read off"or abstracted from the world, they must be supplied by us.

Kant believed that a handful of concepts like causation and substance were indispensable for thought. Many later thinkers rejected this claim, but even if it is correct, it seems reasonable to suppose that — with the exception of a few examples like Kant's — interestingly different sets of concepts are possible. We have at least many of the concepts that we do because of the interests and concerns that we have, and perhaps we have others because of the sort of biological makeup that we have (if we were color blind, we might not have the concept chartreuse). Moreover, it is almost a truism that members of different cultures often employ different systems of classification, even for such mundane things as colors or the weather — to say nothing about more abstruse matters like religion and politics. And even within our own culture once well-entrenched scientific and everyday concepts and beliefs have changed, sometimes in quite dramatic ways. Furthermore, differences in beliefs, expectations, and the like can even influence how we perceive things, as is demonstrated by phenomena connected with various perceptual illusions.

Such facts show that knowledge and reality are not connected in the simple way that we might naively have supposed them to be. Taken by themselves, however, the facts that different cultures or species might (or, perhaps, actually do) think about the world in radically different ways and that we cannot think about the world without using our concepts, do not show that any radical sort of normative relativism is correct. It may be that all but one way of thinking abut the world is wrong — that only one way matches up with the way things really are. Or it may be that there are a variety of equally correct ways of thinking about the world, in the unexciting sense that there are several different ways to think about a single, objective, mind-independent world.

CONCEPTS AND REALITY

Suppose, as seems reasonable, that alternative sets of concepts are possible and that we can't compare our concepts and beliefs with an unconceptualized reality. What more is needed to support the more radical forms of relativism? This is one of the most important questions one can ask about relativism, but when we press the relativist on this point, we are typically greeted with a flood of metaphors, slogans, and calls to arms, rather than with a detailed answer. This is no accident, for it turns out to be very difficult to find a non-trivial *and* half-way clear statement of just what it is the relativist's view here is.

We can gain some insight, though, by noting that at this point relativists frequently attack the correspondence theory of truth — the view that a belief or sentence is true just in case it matches up with the facts "out there" in a mind-independent world. For, they aver, the notion of correspondence is hopelessly elusive and, since there is no neutral access to facts untinged by thought, talk about such facts to which our beliefs could correspond is empty. The facts as we know them are correlative with the set of concepts that we happen to employ. Hence the world as we know it and experience it — and this (we are told) is the *only* notion of the world that is not entirely empty and useless — depends in part on the way we think about it. Indeed, our modes of thought somehow structure or even constitute the world.

The problem, of course, is to explain the sense in which concepts of thought could constitute the world or the objects in it. No one believes that the world is literally composed of concepts, but perhaps the relativist could give sense to the claim that our concepts and beliefs somehow structure a rather formless input from the world as we know it. At all events, it is clear that the relativist thinks that the world and the things in it are not independent of minds, even though he may concede that the exact sense in which this is so is not easy to explain. (This is equally a problem for the relativist's arch foe, the realist, since his chief concern is to deny that the world is dependent on thought in the sense that the relativist holds that it is.) But at the very least, we can say that the relativist wants to hold that the familiar world of mountains and forests and lakes would not have existed if there had been no thinkers. . . .

RELATIVE TO WHAT?

In a moment we will turn to truth, but first something needs to be said about our notion of a *conceptual framework* or *world view. . . .*

While such things as truth, concepts, moral principles, and standards of rationality have been viewed by relativists as determined by conceptual frameworks, frameworks are in turn thought to be determined by something else. For generality, we may view frameworks as the dependent variable and construe different relativistic positions as offering different candidates for the independent variables. For example, it has been argued that different cultures or different historical periods give rise to different conceptual frameworks (views often labeled *cultural relativism* and *historicism respectively).* Others, following the lead of thinkers like Cassirer, Whorf, and Winch, have contended that fundamental differences between languages bring with them differences in frameworks. It may even be that economic and social factors, religion, or scientific views play some role in shaping one's thought, as is suggested by Marx, Durkheim, and Kuhn respectively. Finally, it has been suggested that all human beings have pretty much the same conceptual framework and that it is grounded in the biological makeup of the species. . . . Few actual relativistic positions involve a Protagorean realtivism in which *each individual* is the measure of things. Instead, conceptual frameworks are typically regarded as the common property of those who share a language, culture, or location in history. . . .

My strategy is to begin with some reasonable clear examples, real or imaginary, of putative cases of conceptual frameworks different from our own — for example, with such frequently discussed examples as the Hopi Indians as interpreted by linguist Benjaman Whorf or the Azande as characterized by the social anthropologist E. E. Evans-Pritchard. Thus Whorf tells us that the Hopi view time as a relation between events rather than in terms of duration, that they think of the world as containing events rather than enduring objects, that they believe it possible to influence objects in the external world merely by thinking about them, and so on. . . .

Such examples involve beliefs and concepts different from our own. But clearly not just *any* difference in beliefs or concepts justifies talk of different world-views. Some differences matter more than others, but which? Without attempting to define the notions, let us say that such examples involve differences in *basic beliefs* and *central concepts.* Basicness and centrality clearly are matters of degree, but some fairly clear examples can be given which cast light on the two notions. Central concepts have much in common with the items on traditional lists of categories: among our central concepts are those of object, cause, and person. And a basic belief is one that is so fundamental that a person could not abandon it without surrendering many other beliefs as well. Such beliefs may be quite specific; the beliefs that most events have causes, that others have minds, and that some things which aren't actual are possible, are basic for us. But basic beliefs may also involve general standards for explanation and intelligibility, e.g., that induction is a reasonable way to gather evidence or that certain sorts of general claims are confirmed by their instances. . . .

TRUTH AND FRAMEWORKS

The above considerations are often connected with the doctrine of relative truth by the claim that things are not simply or absolutely true but that they are only true *relative to a conceptual framework.* Most versions of relativism involve claims about the actual situation of existing groups of people, and so the force of this view is that a person's beliefs — including yours or mine — can be true only relative to his conceptual framework. Since the relativist's claim is one about *our* notion of truth, he will want to be able to explain as many of our platitudes about truth as he can (though he may well give some of them a rather novel and surprising interpretation). Thus the serious relativist will grant that something can be true (relative to a framework) even if none whose framework it is believed it to be true and, indeed, even if they all believe it to be false. For example, nearly all sixteenth-century Western Europeans believed that the earth was flat, but the relativist can maintain that their belief was false, even relative to their framework. The discovery that the earth wasn't flat led them to revise one of their beliefs. We do not have to conclude that it changed their conceptual framework, however, since it was the concepts and standards of evidence of that framework that led them to revise their belief about the earth's shape. At least the serious relativist *wants* to say that their original belief was false relative to their framework, but exactly how can he account for this fact?

Although the above model of relativism involving differing sets of concepts does not force us to adopt a doctrine of relative truth, it has often been thought to support such a doctrine in the following way. The relativist believes that our concepts, language, or patterns of classification somehow constitute the world as we know it *and* that any notion of *the world* that is entirely independent of the way we know it is empty and useless. If this is correct, then it is natural to think of truth as correspondence to the world — but now since the only world we can talk or think or know about is partly constituted by our concepts, it can only be correspondence to a world associated wth some conceptual framework. On this account, a sentence like 'snow is white' is true in our conceptual framework becasue it corresponds to the world of our framework, where this means something like this: we organize input under concepts like *snow* and *white* and the input is such that what is singled out and marked off as snow is also one of the things that is singled out and marked off as being white.

The serious relativist wants to explain how there can be objectivity *within* a framework, and this is one reason why he needs a picture of some sort of input that provides the raw material for conceptual thinking. We have noted that this input can be construed in a variety of ways, but the important point here is that although the input does not force us to think about it in any particular way, it nevertheless places constraints on our experience and thought; it somehow guides our application of concepts. Like Aristotle's prime matter or Kant's thing-in-itself, such a notion is nearly empty, for by the relativist's own lights it cannot be experienced or described in any neutral way. It is a limiting notion, entering into experience only as mediated by concepts or language. But the relativist's hope is that it is enough to allow him to say that, *given* a battery of concepts and a certain input, there *will* be a correct way to classify the latter. To be sure, one of the chief tasks facing the relativist is to make this claim intelligible to us. But something of this sort must be postulated if the relativist's picture is to avoid the slide into subjective idealism. Without some sort of input, there would be virtually no constraints on experience at all, and the relativist would be unable to account for the possibility of intra-framework communication and objectivity.

The relativist also needs a notion that we might call *collateral commitment* if he is to explain how something can be true relative to a framework even if none of its users believe it to be true. The basic beliefs and concepts of a framework involve a collateral commitment to additional truths in the framework. Some of these commitments may be hypothetical, to the effect that if future experience is of a certain sort, then such and such is the case. Among other things, collateral commitments may involve logical and evidential relations. For example, if a given sentence S is true in a framework, then any sentence that is a logical consequence (according to the logic of that framework) of S will also be true in that framework.

This picture explains why a person's (or a group's) believing something is neither necessary nor sufficient for its being true for him (or them), and it does so without abandoning the claim that truth is relative. I think that this sketch conveys the general flavor of a wide variety of relativistic accounts. We could go on to develop it further, but I shall not do so here, since it turns out that no matter how one fills in the details, it is very hard to defend any very interesting doctrine of relative truth. In a moment we will see why this is so, but first it will be useful to see how the relativist might respond to the most common objection to the doctrine of relative truth, namely the charge that it is self-refuting.

SELF-REFUTATION?

At least since the time of Plato, it has been objected that the relativist's claim undermines itself in the following way. Either the claim is true absolutely (i.e., true in a non-relative sense) or else it is only true relative to the relativist's own conceptual framework. If it is true absolutely, then obviously at least one truth is not true merely relative to a conceptual framework. Not only is this sufficient to refute the relativist's general claim, but once we allow this exception to his doctrine, it is difficult to find a principled way to rule out other exceptions. On the other hand, if the relativist's claim that truth is relative is true only relative to *his* conceptual framework, then it appears that his claim needn't be true in other frameworks — and perhaps it is even false in some. This may seem calamitous, but the consistent relativist really cannot avoid this conclusion. What he can do is try to minimize the calamity by arguing that any actual critic — any would-be objectivist he faces — shares the relativist's framework.

The relativist's hope here is to convince the would-be objectivist that the latter's *seemingly* objective concepts and beliefs in fact presuppose the same framework as the relativist's and then to argue for relativisim in the context of the framework that they share. If the relativist can make such a position plausible, he can add that his claims about relative truth are no more shaky than most of the other things that we take to be true. And if relativism's claims are as secure as the myriad claims that are on solid ground for us normally, what more could be demanded? The project of showing the objectivist that his beliefs about objectivity depend upon a set of beliefs and standards according to which relativism is correct may not be an easy one to carry out, of course, but then no one ever said that relativism was an easy position to defend.

RELATIVE TRUTH

The doctrine of relative truth need not be self-refuting, but that doesn't mean that it is free of problems. If different conceptual frameworks are couched in different languages, then since sentences in one language are typically not to be found in another, a given *sentence* is not likely to be true relative to one framework and false relative to another. Still, perhaps a sentence could be true in a framework while its *translation* into the language of a second framework was false in the second. Suppose that there are Martians and that their conceptual framework is so different from ours that it is in principle impossible to translate between Martianese and English. Let us say that in cases like this truth is relative in the *weak sense*, where this means that at least many truths of one framework are inexpressible (and so neither true nor false) in the other. In this situation truth would not be relative in the *strong sense* that something was true relative to one framework and false relative to another. There are many interesting questions that might be asked about the claim that truth could be relative in the weak sense; for example, we might wonder whether there are things that can be expressed in some natural languages but not in others. The doctrine of weak relative truth does not bear on deeper questions concerning objectivity and justification as directly as the doctrine of strong relative truth does, however, and so I shall set the former aside to concentrate on the latter.

For truth to be relative in the *strong* sense, it must be possible for *some one thing* to be true in one framework and false in another. For example, we might say that a sentence of one language and its translation into another language express (at least roughly) the same "meaning" or "proposition." If a *single* proposition is to be true relative to one framework and false relative to another, then surely the worlds correlated with the two frameworks will have to be quite different. But if they are, it is difficult to see how a sentence of the language associated with one framework can mean even roughly the same thing as a sentence associated with (that of) another. In a nutshell, the problem is that the sentences associated with the respective frameworks are *about* very different worlds, and any move from the language of one framework to that of the other seems only to involve a change of subject rather than the retention of any proposition that is true in one framework and false in the other.

We can sharpen the point in the following way. To begin with a simple case, suppose that we have a pair of subject-predicate sentences. The relativist is not concerned with different but similar languages where we have different words like the German's *"Tisch"* and our "table" that stand for the same things in a shared world. In the relativist's example, the subject terms of the two sentences will refer to things in "different worlds, and the predicates will stand for properties in different worlds." More generally, it is unclear how there could be an overlap in the references or extensions of terms in the two languages, even an overlap of a very complicated sort, for they are not about things in a common world. Unlike the case where two languages involve a common framework, we can no longer even speak of two languages categorizing things in *the* world differently, for by the relativist's own lights, the worlds themselves differ. . . .

The relativist seems unable to tell a convincing story about *what it is* that can be realtively true in the strong sense. The problem arises because the relativist wants to maintain that two frameworks can be sufficiently different for something to be true in one while false in the other and at the same time he wants to hold that they can be sufficiently alike to share something which could vary in truth value in this way. If the frameworks are radically different, however, they deal with different worlds, and so have little subject matter in common. As we imagine the frameworks' evolving to become more like one another, we can make more sense of their containing resources for expressing the same thing—but less sense of their assigning it different truth values. Put another way, a strong version of relativism is most naturally stated as a pair of claims: *first*, that something can be shared by different frameworks and, *second*, that this something can receive different truth-values in those frameworks. But there is a strong tension between these two claims for the very picture that lends plausibility to talk of relative truth leaves little room for anything that can be shared by different frameworks in a way that satisfies the first.

THE UPSHOT

Our brief discussion is only an introduction to questions about relativism, but I think that we have gotten a good enough view of the terrain to see that even if the relativist is right in claiming that our knowledge of the world is colored by our concepts, that at least many of our concepts might have been different, and, indeed, even that our concepts somehow help to "constitute" the world, it does not follow that truth is relative in a strong sense. Moreover, if it is not, then the relativist's doctrine of relative truth could not be true relative to one conceptual framework and false relative to another. But on the other hand, a number of relativistic themes receive a partial vindication by being dissociated from the extremely problematic doctrine of strongly relative truth.[12]

SUMMARY AND CONCLUSION

Philosophers have always seen their main business as the search for truth. But the notion of truth has itself become a problem and several competing theories of truth have emerged. The traditional theory is the correspondence theory of truth, which claims that a belief (or statement) is true if it "matches up" or corresponds to the facts of reality. But there have been many arguments to show that

[12]Written especially for this edition by the author, on the basis of a more detailed essay entitled, "True For," in M. Krausz & J. Meiland, eds., *Relativism: Cognitive and Moral* (Notre Dame, Ind.: Univ. of Notre Dame Press, 1982).

this view is inadequate. Accordingly, philosophers have defended the coherence theory of truth, which says that a belief or statement is true if it is logically connected to other beliefs and statements; the pragmatic theory of truth, which says that a belief or statement is true if it helps us in practice with our work and our lives; and a semantic theory of truth, which says that truth is a function of our language as well as a question about the "facts" of the world.

Since the writings of Immanuel Kant, truth is sometimes discussed in terms of our "constitution" of reality, but this also tends to lead to "relativism," the view that there is no reality — no truth — independent of our consciousness and "constitution" of the world.

GLOSSARY

absolutism: the thesis that there is but one correct view of reality. Opposed to *relativism*.

analytic philosophy: the movement in twentieth-century philosophy, particularly in America and Britain, that focuses its primary attention on language and linguistic analysis. Also called "linguistic philosophy."

categories: Kant's word (borrowed from Aristotle) for those most basic and *a priori* concepts of human knowledge, for example, "causality," "substance."

coherence theory of truth: a statement or a belief is true if and only if it "coheres" with a system of statements or beliefs. A truth of mathematics is "true" because it forms part of the nexus in the complex of mathematical truths. A geometrical theorem is "true" because it can be proven from other theorems (axioms, definitions) of the geometrical system. A "factual" statement is "true" insofar as other "factual" statements, including general statements about experience that are logically relevant to the original statement, support it. Since we can never get "outside" our experience, the only sense in saying that a belief is true (according to this theory) is that it "coheres" with the rest of our experience.

constitute: to put together, "set up," or synthesize experience through categories or concepts. First used by Kant, later by Husserl.

correspondence theory of truth: a statement or belief is true if and only if it "corresponds" with "the facts." Even when restricting our attention to statements of fact, however, this commonsensical "theory" gets into trouble as soon as it tries to pick out what corresponds to what. How can we identify a "fact," for example, apart from the language we use to identify it? And what does it mean to say that a statement "corresponds" to a fact?

dialectic: a "logic" developed by Hegel in which different forms or philosophies are arranged according to increasing sophistication and scope. The "logic" is a development from one form, whose inadequacies are demonstrated, to another, which corrects these inadequacies, and so on. Marx borrows this "dialectic" and gives it a social interpretation. (The "logic" need not be anything like the form "thesis-antithesis-synthesis.")

essence or essential intuition: in Husserl, those ideal objects and laws that constitute necessary truths. The term "essence" is borrowed from Aristotle (and the medieval philosophers) and used in much the same way, except that Husserl's notion of essence is always tied to "intuition" and consciousness.

hermeneutics: the discipline of interpretation of texts. Broadly conceived (as by Heidegger, Gadamer) it is the "uncovering" of meanings in everyday life, the attempt to understand the signs and symbols of one's culture and tradition in juxtaposition with other cultures and traditions.

historicism: a philosophy that localizes truth and different views of reality to particular times, places, and peoples in history. It is generally linked to a very strong relativist thesis as well, that there is no truth apart from these various historical commitments.

phenomenology: a contemporary European philosophy, founded by the German-Czech philosopher Edmund Husserl, that begins with a "pure description of consciousness." Originally developed as an answer to certain questions of necessary truth in the foundations of arithmetic, it was later expanded to answer more general philosophical questions and, in the hands of its later practitioners, it became a "philosophy of man" as well as a theory of knowledge.

pragmatic theory of truth: a statement or a belief is true if and only if it "works," that is, if it allows us to predict certain results and function effectively in everyday life, and if it encourages further inquiry and helps us lead better lives.

pragmatism: a distinctly American philosophical movement founded by Charles Sanders Pierce at the turn of this century and popularized by William James and John Dewey. Its central thesis is obvious in its name, that truth (etc.) is always to be determined by reference to practical (pragmatic) considerations. Only those metaphysical distinctions that make some difference in practice are worth considering. And the only ultimate defense of any belief is that "it works."

rational: in accordance with the rules of effective thought: coherence, consistency, practicability, simplicity, comprehensiveness, looking at the evidence and weighing it carefully, not jumping to conclusions, etc. Rationality may not guarantee truth; all of the evidence and everything we believe may point to one conclusion, while later generations, who know things that we do not, may see that our conclusion was incorrect. Yet it would still be, for us, the rational conclusion. Rationality points to the manner of thinking rather than its ultimate conclusions. Philosophically, the stress on rationality takes the emphasis off reality and places it on our manner of philosophizing.

realism: the thesis that reality exists in itself and it is independent of our consciousness of it.

relativism: the thesis that there is no single correct view of reality, no single truth. Relativists often talk about the possibility of "different conceptual frameworks," "alternative lifestyles," and various "forms of consciousness." They are opposed, often violently, to realists and absolutists.

semantics: the meanings of a sentence and its various components. Also, the study of those meanings. (So, we can talk about the semantics of a sentence, and we can talk about doing semantics.) "Merely semantic" is a nasty way of referring to conceptual truths, analytic sentences that are true just by virtue of meanings.

semantic theory of truth: a formal theory, best known from the work of Alfred Tarski, that defines "true" in terms of a technical notion of *satisfaction*. According to the theory, every sentence in the language is either satisfied or not by a distinct class of individuals. This is adequate, however, only for artificially constructed languages. Generalizing the theory to natural languages (for example, American English), we can say that the theory suggests that we (but not each of us personally) set up the rules according to which our sentences do or do not "correspond with the facts" of the world.

transcendental: referring to the basic rules of human knowledge, usually with an absolutist suggestion that there can be but a single set of such basic rules. Thus Kant's
"transcendental deduction" attempted to deduce the one possible set of basic rules
for human understanding, and Husserl's transcendental phenomenology attempted
to lay bare the one set of basic ("essential") laws of human consciousness. Contemporary philosophers sometimes talk about "the transcendental turn" in philosophy,
in other words, the attempt to move beyond claims that might apply only to ourselves and our way of viewing things to the way that things must be viewed.

transcendental deduction: Kant's elaborate attempt to prove that there is but one set
of categories (basic rules or *a priori* concepts) that all rational creatures must use in
constituting their experience.

5

Necessity

The limits of my language mean the limits of my world.

Ludwig Wittgenstein

Surely there are some things that we can know with certainty! Even Hume, for example, granted that some of our beliefs are beyond the range of his skeptical doubts, namely, those which he calls "relations of ideas," such as the basic principles of arithmetic. Nothing could make us doubt that two plus two equals four. Descartes may have suggested that it was possible that an evil demon was fooling him about even this; but what would it mean to be "fooled" about such matters? How could he have been wrong about that? Of course, he could always say that he might be wrong about two plus two equalling four, just as we could always say that two plus two equals five. But what could we possibly mean by that? We can understand what it would be like to be wrong about some factual belief, such as "there are no Chinese paratroopers in Cuba"; perhaps it even makes sense, however implausible, to suggest that we might be dreaming right now. But one can't even imagine, no matter how hard one tries, what it would be for "two plus two equals four" to be false.

Beliefs that we cannot even imagine being false and that lie beyond the range of all possible doubt and refutation are called **necessary truths.** In short, they must be true. Necessary truth is contrasted with **contingent truth,** which is a belief that is in fact true but might not have been. It is true, for example, that I am now wearing a sweater, but we can easily imagine what it would be for me not to wear one. That is a contingent truth. Necessary truths, because we cannot even imagine what it would be like for them to be false, are always "perfectly certain"; contingent truths, because we can always imagine that they might be false (and that we are possibly fooled or misled in believing them) are never "perfectly certain" but always merely probable. We can always think of some way, no matter how implausible, in which we might be wrong. (I might be dreaming that I'm wearing a sweater, for example.) But one cannot be mistaken about a necessary truth. (There is a curious but important exception to this distinction that is already familiar to you: Descartes's "I exist" is both necessary [it can't be intelligibly doubted] and contingent [since it is possible that he might not have existed].)

A partial distinction between necessary truth and contingent truth is this: Contingent truths are based upon experience and necessary truths are not. Accordingly, contingent truths allow for some further experience that would change our minds. We may be sure that there are no armadillos on the upper east side of Manhattan, but because that is a contingent truth, it is always possible that we shall see an armadillo crossing 86th Street, and thereby have to give up our belief. Because of this essential link between contingent truths and experience, philosophers often refer to our knowledge of them as **empirical knowledge.** Necessary truths, on the other hand, are not based upon experience, and there is no possible experience — real or imagined — that could change our minds about them. For this reason, philosophers talk about these truths as being prior to experience or *a priori* and knowledge of them is also considered to be *a priori*, in other words, to be knowledge that is independent of experience. It is important to stress that the word "prior" which means "before," does not mean "earlier in time." For example, it does not mean that we know *a priori* that "two plus two equals four" before we ever have experience of two things adding up with two other things to give us four things. It means rather that the justification of *a priori* knowledge does not depend on any possible experience. You cannot refute "two plus two equals four" through experience. But neither can you justify it through experience. You could spend a year adding up different pairs of things: walnuts, elephants, pieces of chalk, people, and scoops of ice cream. You would then have the general claim that "whenever I add two things to two things I get four things," but you would fail to prove the necessity of that truth.

There are philosophers, as we have seen, who do take *a priori* to mean literally "before"; that is, those philosophers who believe in innate ideas believe that we actually do have certain knowledge before we have any experience at all. We are born with it, and that would explain, if you accept this theory, how it is that *a priori* knowledge is possible. But it is important to emphasize that the belief in innate ideas is not essential to the notion of either necessary truth or *a priori* knowledge, and most philosophers talk about the latter without ever mentioning the former.

What then, is the source of *a priori* knowledge? For those philosophers who believe in innate ideas, the answer is that we are born with it. But even this is not enough, for it is necessary to say how it is that we are born with such knowledge. Even if it is "stamped in our minds by God," as some philosophers have held, how do we recognize it? The traditional answer, for those who believe in innate ideas and for those who do not, is through reason. In fact, reason is traditionally defined (for example, by Plato, Aristotle, Spinoza, and Leibniz) as our ability to know necessary truths. But our account is circular; we are told that we can know necessary truths because of reason, but reason is defined as our ability to know necessary truths. So, in this chapter we must ask, what is this ability? How do we have it? How is *a priori* knowledge possible?

Although we shall be exclusively concerned with necessary and contingent truths, it is important to say that there is a similar distinction between necessary and contingent falsehoods. "Every triangle has at least five sides" is a necessary falsehood — it could not possibly be true. "There are no eagles in America" is a contingent falsehood — it is in fact false, but we can (too easily) imagine that it might be true.

We will divide our discussion of necessary truths into three parts:

1) *Analytic truths* or *logical truths:* these are, for example, trivial statements such as "either it is raining or it is not raining" and "a horse is an animal." Analytic truths can be known to be true by analyzing the form of the statement and the meanings of the words of the statement.

2) *Truths of arithmetic and geometry:* many philosophers, following Kant, have insisted that these are not analytic, that is, known to be true just because of the form of the statement or the meanings of its component terms. "413 plus 2785 = 3198," for example does not seem to be true because of the meanings of the terms, "413," "2785," etc., yet this would seem to be a necessary truth if anything is. The same would be true of "the internal angles of a triangle equal two right angles." Are these analytic, or something else?

3) *Truths of metaphysics:* these are the principles of metaphysics formulated by the great metaphysicians (Plato, Aristotle, Leibniz, Spinoza), which were claimed to be necessary truths. It has also been suggested that the principles Hume claimed could not be justified, the principle of universal causation and the principle of induction, are necessary truths. (You can guess that this category of necessary truths will be far more controversial than the first two.)

ANALYTIC TRUTHS

Consider the utterly trivial statement, "all bachelors are unmarried." Not very interesting, to be sure, but it is, obviously, a necessary truth. We can be perfectly certain that this statement is true, and we know in advance that no study of bachelors could possibly turn up an instance of one who was married. We cannot even imagine a situation in which this statement would be false, and there is no sense in wondering "well, we've only looked at the bachelors in our neighborhood, what about the bachelors in southern California?" All we have to know to know that "all bachelors are unmarried" is the meaning of the English sentence, nothing else.

Now consider the contingent claim, "all bachelors are happy." Of course, in order to find out whether that is true or not you have to know the meanings of the words, but you cannot tell whether or not it is true just by looking at the words. This statement raises an empirical question. That is, in order to know whether or not it is true you have to go out into the world and interview bachelors. To falsify the claim that all bachelors are happy, you would have to find only one unhappy bachelor. But even if you never found one, you could never be perfectly certain of the truth of the claim. There might always be one unhappy bachelor, living in a cave off the coast of Madagascar. A contingent claim, therefore, is never perfectly certain. One can always at least imagine some circumstance that would prove it to be false, even if it seems, on the basis of the present evidence, to be true.

The example, "all bachelors are unmarried" is an analytic truth: its truth can be demonstrated just by referring to the meanings of the words in the sentence. This particular example is what we referred to in earlier chapters as a conceptual truth (such as, "a horse is an animal"). **Conceptual truths** are a special class of analytic truths. Aristotle discussed such truths in terms of essences. He would say that "the essence of a bachelor is to be unmarried." More modern philosophers would talk about concepts. They would say that "the concept 'bachelor' includes the concept of being unmarried." Today most philosophers would rather say that "bachelor means unmarried person." But these different formulations all point to the same fact, that conceptual truths are necessary truths because of the meanings of the words in the sentence.

Not all analytic truths are conceptual truths, however. Consider the statement, "either it is raining or it is not raining." Now obviously you don't have to look out the window to see whether this is true or not. It is true just because of the form of the sentence, which is "*P* or not *P*." Such sentences are called **tautologies.** They are true by virtue of the form of the sentence alone, and it doesn't matter what phrase you substitute for *P*. For example, you know that "either there are exactly 7,500 comets in our galaxy or there are not," even if you don't know anything about astronomy, or exactly what a "comet" or a "galaxy" is. ("*P* or not *P*" is called the **law of the excluded middle** — either a sentence or its denial must be true.)

Tautologies are not very interesting. They are the most boring and uninformative sentences in our language, but they are also very important. Every tautology gives us what we called (in the Introduction) a **rule of inference,** one of those basic rules that we use in all our thinking. (This is true even for people who claim "not to be logical" or actually attack logic.) It is according to these rules of inference that we define the validity of our arguments. But here a problem arises. How can we defend a rule of inference itself? We cannot say that it is valid, since we have to use such rules in order to say that anything is valid. And you can't use a rule to prove itself. (That would be the same as appointing a magistrate to judge his or her own alleged corruption.) To answer this question, many philosophers appeal to **intuition** as a defense of our fundamental rules of inference. Rationalists feel comfortable with this since they have confidence in reason to show us such basic truths through intuition. Empiricists tend to feel very uncomfortable, however, for they would rather either that these rules are based upon experience (but they are not) or that they are matters of reasoning (but this can't be either, since they are the foundation of all reasoning). So what empiricists try to do is find as small a set of basic rules as possible, from which they can derive all of the others. The problem then becomes, how do you defend that basic set of rules?

The most fundamental of these rules is called the **law of contradiction.** That law says: a statement and its denial cannot both be true. For example, it cannot be true that it is raining and that it is not raining at the same place at the same time. This law has been used by many philosophers (for example, Leibniz and Hume) to define analytic truths in general. They say that a statement is analytic if when you deny it you get a contradiction. The recognition of the importance of this law, however, goes as far back as Aristotle, who worried about this law and what makes it true. After considerable thought, he concluded:

from *Metaphysics,*
by Aristotle

This is the most certain of all principles, for it is impossible for anyone to suppose that the same thing is and is not . . . then clearly it is impossible for the same man to suppose at the same time that the same thing is and is not; for the man who made this error would entertain two contrary opinions at the same time. Hence all men who are demonstrating anything refer back to this as an ultimate belief; for it is by nature the starting-point of all the other axioms as well.

. . . . .

Some, indeed, demand to have the law proved, but this is because they lack education; for it shows lack of education not to know of what we should require proof, and of what we should not. For it is quite impossible that everything should have a proof; the process would go on to infinity, so that even so there would be no proof. If on the other hand there are some things of which no proof need be sought, they cannot say what principle they think to be more self-evident. Even in the case of this law, however, we can demonstrate the impossibility of refutation, if only our opponent makes some statement. If he makes none, it is absurd to seek for an argument against one who has no arguments of his own about anything, in so far as he has none; for such a person, in so far as he is such, is really no better than a vegetable.[1]

Aristotle's answer is still accepted by most philosophers. This one principle, at least, cannot be defended except to say that it would be utterly absurd to deny it. Even if a philosopher will not accept the appeal to intuition in any other case, it seems that he must at least in this one.

There are many other kinds of analytic truths, but it would take a course in logic to adequately discuss them. But what they all have in common is that they

---

[1]Aristotle, *Metaphysics*, Bk. IV, trans. Hugh Tredennick (Cambridge, Mass.: Harvard University Press, 1933).

are necessary truths that can be known simply by the analysis of the form of the sentence or the meanings of the words within the sentence. But will this account of analytic truths cover all cases of necessary truths? For example, will it work for the truths of arithmetic and geometry too?

THE TRUTHS OF ARITHMETIC AND GEOMETRY

Since ancient times, the principles of arithmetic and geometry have been considered necessary truths. The explanations of them varied, from religious laws of the cosmos (as in Pythagoras and many ancient cults of astrology) to Plato's theory of ideal forms. But this much has seemed obvious to almost everyone who has thought about the nature of these principles: no stretch of the imagination could describe a circumstance in which they would not be true. No matter how the world changed, and no matter what else people came to believe, two plus two would still equal four, and the principles of Euclidean geometry would still be true.

Think for a moment about the simple truth of arithmetic, "two plus two equals four." It is not the case that two things plus two things of the same kind always result in four things: two drops of ink added to two more drops of ink give you one big drop, not four. But this doesn't give us a counter-example to the laws of arithmetic, since the volume of the large drop would still have to equal the total volume of the two plus two smaller drops. Similarly, you can draw a triangle whose interior angles do not equal two right angles, as Euclid shows they must, by drawing the triangle on the curved surface of a globe. But this does not show that Euclid's principles, which are specifically concerned with figures drawn on a flat surface, could possibly be false. In general, people have believed that, even if there are apparent counter-examples to the truths of arithmetic and geometry, those truths themselves are absolutely necessary and cannot be challenged.

The defense of this necessary truth, however, and all such truths of mathematics, Euclidean geometry and arithmetic, does not simply appeal to the meanings of the words involved. The truth of "two plus two equals four" does not depend on replacing one synonym with another, as in "all bachelors are unmarried." The number four, for example, can be described in many ways, as "two plus two," as "one plus three," as "the number following three" or "the number preceding five," as "the number that is the first nonprime," and as "the square root of sixteen." This list could be extended indefinitely (for example, "one half of eight," "one third of twelve," "one fourth of sixteen"). Consequently, it is difficult to see how "two plus two equals four" is true just because the meaning of "four" is "two plus two." If the symbolic system that we call arithmetic makes its principles necessarily true by some system of interconnected definitions, they would have to be infinitely more complicated than any of the analytic truths we have seen thus far.

There is another consideration, however, that has often been argued as a reason for thinking that the truths of arithmetic and geometry cannot be merely analytic. The argument was originally formulated by Immanuel Kant. He pointed out, against Hume and his other predecessors who so glibly spoke of "relations of ideas" and "truths of reason," that the truths of arithmetic and geometry are not just abstract formulas that we accept as true because we accept the overall system of which they are a part. We also apply these principles to the world in concrete ways, to give us new knowledge of things. For example, we count things, "one, two, three . . ." and this means that our number system must be linked up with the world of experience as well as being a self-contained system of necessary truths. (Logicians refer to any logical system of abstract symbols as a **calculus;** a system that is applied to the world, such as arithmetic, is an *interpreted calculus.*) Analytic truths, as we have described them, do not tell us anything about the world; logical principles tell us how we reason, but they say nothing of what we reason about. Conceptual truths tell us something about the meanings of words, but (except for teaching young children the categories to which things belong, as for example, "a horse is an animal, but a tree is a plant") they too tell us nothing about the world itself. But arithmetic and geometry, it seems, give us new information that we did not have before. This is obviously true of the principles of physics and of "higher" mathematics. Perhaps it is also true of the simplest truths of arithmetic.

In elementary education, there are some problems that we learn to calculate, given the basic principles of arithmetic. "Long" division, for example, presupposes the simple truths of "short" division, multiplication, and subtraction. These simple truths, however, like the simple truths of multiplication, subtraction, and addition "tables," are not calculated but memorized. The important question, then, is whether these basic principles can themselves be proved or calculated, or whether they can only be memorized. How do we defend these basic truths? Can we only say, "by intuition"? Further, there are some evident truths of arithmetic that no mathematicians have ever been able to prove. There is now a general proof, developed only a few years ago by a contemporary logician named Kurt Gödel, which shows that there can never be a system of proofs that can succeed in proving all the truths of arithmetic without proving some false claims as well. The same is true in Euclidean geometry. You may remember from high school that problematic theorem, that one and only one line can be drawn through a point parallel to a given line. It is obviously true, necessarily true, but no one can develop a valid proof for it.

The Empiricist Argument

The basic principles of arithmetic would seem to be necessary truths if anything is. But are they logical truths, true by virtue of their logical form? or conceptual truths, true by virtue of their symbolic meanings? It is here that the arguments about the nature of necessary truth become most violent and most brilliant. Once again, the rationalist need not be particularly disturbed, for his confidence in reason allows him to agreeably accept the idea that certain nonanalytic truths may yet be necessary and known by intuition. For him, it is enough to say, along with

Plato, Descartes, and Leibniz, that certain principles of mathematics are "self-evident," "intuitively obvious," or even "innate ideas." But for the empiricist, who insists that all knowledge is based upon either experience or analytic sentences, the foundations of arithmetic prove to be an embarrassing problem. It is worth noting that all three traditional empiricists, Locke, Berkeley, and Hume, simply accepted the idea that the truths of arithmetic were "relations of ideas," without looking any further. Modern empiricists, however, have not been so negligent. The most famous of the British "logical positivists," A. J. Ayer, for example, states the empiricist problem in the following way:

from *Language, Truth and Logic,* by A. J. Ayer

Where the empiricist does encounter difficulty is in connection with the truths of formal logic and mathematics. For whereas a scientific generalization is readily admitted to be fallible, the truths of mathematics and logic appear to everyone to be necessary and certain. But if empiricism is correct no proposition which has a factual content can be necessary or certain. Accordingly the empiricist must deal with the truths of logic and mathematics in one of the two following ways: he must say either that they are not necessary truths, in which case he must account for the universal conviction that they are; or he must say that they have no factual content, and then he must explain how a proposition which is empty of all factual content can be true and useful and surprising.

If neither of these courses proves satisfactory, we shall be obliged to give way to rationalism. We shall be obliged to admit that there are some truths about the world which we can know independently of experience; that there are some properties which we can ascribe to all objects, even though we cannot conceivably observe that all objects have them. And we shall have to accept it as a mysterious inexplicable fact that our thought has this power to reveal to us authoritatively the nature of objects which we have never observed. . . . It is vital, therefore, for us to be able to show that one or other of the empiricist accounts of the propositions of logic and mathematics is correct. If we are successful in this, we shall have destroyed the foundations of rationalism. For the fundamental tenet of rationalism is that thought is an independent source of knowledge, and is moreover a more trustworthy source of knowledge than experience; indeed some rationalists have gone so far as to say that thought is the only source of knowledge. And the ground for this view is simply that the only necessary truths about the world which are known to us are known through thought and not through experience. So that if we can show either that the truths in question are not necessary or that they are not "truths about the world," we shall be taking away the support on which rationalism rests. We shall be making good the empiricist contention that there are no "truths of reason" which refer to matters of fact.[2]

[2]A. J. Ayer, *Language, Truth and Logic,* 2nd ed. (London: Victor Gollancz, 1936; rpt. New York: Dover, 1946).

The alternatives are few, but the variety of ways in which they have been developed is dazzling. One possibility is to simply deny what we have seemingly accepted as obvious all along, namely, that the truths of arithmetic are necessary truths. The fact that they are not analytic does not therefore appear as a problem. They are rather, according to this empiricist position, well-confirmed matters of fact (and therefore not "relations of ideas" at all). John Stuart Mill, the most famous British philosopher of the nineteenth century, argued this position as follows:

from *A System of Logic*, by J. S. Mill

Why are mathematics by almost all philosophers, and (by some) even those branches of natural philosophy which, through the medium of mathematics, have been converted into deductive sciences, considered to be independent of the evidence of experience and observation, and characterized as systems of Necessary Truth?

The answer I conceive to be, that this character of necessity, ascribed to the truths of mathematics, and (even with some reservations to be hereafter made) the peculiar certainty attributed to them, is an illusion; in order to sustain which, it is necessary to suppose that those truths relate to, and express the properties of, purely imaginary objects. It is acknowledged that the conclusions of geometry are deduced, partly at least, from the so-called Definitions, and that those definitions are assumed to be correct representations, as far as they go, of the objects with which geometry is conversant. Now we have pointed out that, from a definition as such, no proposition, unless it be one concerning the meaning of a word, can ever follow; and that what apparently follows from a definition, follows in reality from an implied assumption that there exists a real thing conformable thereto. This assumption, in the case of the definitions of geometry, is not strictly true: there exist no real things exactly conformable to the definitions. There exist no points without magnitude; no lines without breadth, nor perfectly straight; no circles with all their radii exactly equal, nor squares with all their angles perfectly right. It will perhaps be said that the assumption does not extend to the actual, but only to the possible, existence of such things. I answer that, according to any test we have of possibility, they are not even possible. Their existence, so far as we can form any judgment, would seem to be inconsistent with the physical constitution of our planet at least, if not of the universe. To get rid of this difficulty, and at the same time to save the credit of the supposed system of necessary truth, it is customary to say that the points, lines, circles, and squares which are the subject of geometry, exist in our conceptions merely, and are part of our minds; which minds, by working on their own materials, construct an *a priori* science, the evidence of which is purely mental, and has nothing whatever to do with outward experience. By howsoever high authorities this doctrine may have been sanctioned, it appears to me psychologically incorrect. The points, lines, circles, and squares which any one has in his mind, are (I apprehend) simply copies of the points, lines, circles, and squares which he has known in his experience. Our idea of a point, I apprehend to be simply our idea of the *minimum visible,* the smallest portion of surface which we can see. A line, as defined by geometers, is wholly inconceivable. We can reason about a line as if it had no breadth; because we have a power, which is the foundation of all the control we can exercise over the operations of our minds; the power, when a perception is present to our senses, or a conception to our intellects, of *attending* to a part only of that perception or conception, instead of the whole. But we can not *conceive* a line without breadth; we can form no mental picture of such a line: all the lines which we have in our minds are lines possessing breadth. If any one doubts this, we may refer him to his own experience. I much question if any one who fancies that he can conceive what is called a mathematical line, thinks so from the evidence of his consciousness: I suspect it is rather because he supposes that unless such a conception were possible, mathematics could not exist as a science: a supposition which there will be no difficulty in showing to be entirely groundless.

Since, then, neither in nature, nor in the human mind, do there exist any objects exactly corresponding to the definitions of geometry, while yet that science can not be supposed to be conversant about nonentities; nothing remains but to consider geometry as conversant with such lines, angles, and figures, as really exist; and the definitions, as they are called, must be regarded as some of our first and most obvious generalizations concerning those natural objects. The correctness of those generalizations, *as* generalizations, is without a flaw: the equality of all the radii of a circle is true of all circles, so far as it is true of any one: but it is not exactly true of any circle; it is only nearly true; so nearly that no error of any importance in practice will be incurred by feigning it to be exactly true. . . .

When, therefore, it is affirmed that the conclusions of geometry are necessary truths, the necessity consists in reality only in this, that they correctly follow from the suppositions from which they are deduced. Those suppositions are so far from being necessary, that they are not even true; they purposely depart, more or less widely, from the truth. The only sense in which necessity can be ascribed to the conclusions of any scientific investigation, is that of legitimately following from some assumption, which, by the conditions of the inquiry, is not to be questioned. In this relation, of course, the derivative truths of every deductive science must stand to the inductions, or assumptions, on which the science is founded, and which, whether true or untrue, certain or doubtful in themselves, are always supposed certain for the purposes of the particular science. . . .

From these considerations it would appear that Deductive or Demonstrative Sciences are all, without exception, Inductive Sciences; that their evidence is that of experience.

. . . . .

One theory attempts to solve the difficulty apparently inherent in the case, by representing the propositions of the science of numbers as merely verbal, and its processes as simple transformations of language, substitutions of one expression for another. The proposition, Two and one is equal to three, according to these writers, is not a truth, is not the assertion of a really existing fact, but a definition of the word three; a statement that mankind have agreed to use the name three as a sign exactly equivalent to two and one; to call by the former name whatever is called by the other more clumsy phrase. According to this doctrine, the longest process in algebra is but a succession of changes in terminology, by which equivalent expressions are substituted one for another; a series of translations of the same fact, from one into another language; though how, after such a series of translations, the fact itself comes out changed (as when we demonstrate a new geometrical theorem by algebra), they have not explained; and it is a difficulty which is fatal to their theory.

It must be acknowledged that there are peculiarities in the processes of arithmetic and algebra which render the theory in question very plausible, and have not unnaturally made those sciences the stronghold of Nominalism. The doctrine that we can discover facts, detect the hidden processes of nature, by an artful manipulation of language, is so contrary to common sense, that a person must have made some advances in philosophy to believe it: men fly to so paradoxical a belief to avoid, as they think, some even greater difficulty, which the vulgar do not see. What has led many to believe that reasoning is a mere verbal process is, that no other theory seemed reconcilable with the nature of the Science of Numbers. For we do not carry any ideas along with us when we use the symbols of arithmetic or of algebra. In a geometrical demonstration we have a mental diagram, if not one on paper; AB, AC, are present to our imagination as lines, intersecting other lines, forming an angle with one another, and the like; but not so *a* and *b*. These may represent lines or any other magnitudes, but those magnitudes are never thought of; nothing is realized in our imagination but *a* and *b*. The ideas which, on the particular occasion, they happen to represent, are banished from the mind during every intermediate part of the process, between the beginning, when the premises are translated from things into signs, and the end, when the conclusion is translated back from signs into things. Nothing, then, being in the reasoner's mind but the symbols, what can seem more inadmissible than to contend that the reasoning process has to do with any thing more?

Nevertheless, it will appear on consideration, that this apparently so decisive instance is no instance at all; that there is in every step of an arithmetical or algebraical calculation a real induction, a real inference of facts from facts; and that what disguises the induction is simply its comprehensive nature, and the consequent extreme generality of the language. All numbers must be numbers of something; there are no such things as numbers in the abstract. *Ten* must mean ten bodies, or ten sounds, or ten beatings of the pulse. But though numbers must be numbers of something, they may be numbers of any thing. Propositions, therefore, concerning numbers, have the remarkable peculiarity that they are propositions concerning all things whatever; all objects, all existences of every kind, known to our experience. All things possess quantity; consist of parts which can be numbered; and in that character possess all the properties which are called properties of numbers. That half of four is two, must be true whatever the word four represents, whether four hours, four miles, or four pounds weight. We need only conceive a thing divided into four equal parts (and all things may be conceived as so divided), to be able to predicate of it every property of the number four, that is, every arithmetical proposition in which the number four stands on one side of the equation.

. . . . .

There is another circumstance, which still more than that which we have now mentioned, gives plausibility to the notion that the propositions of arithmetic and algebra are merely verbal. That is, that when considered as propositions respecting Things, they all have the appearance of being identical propositions. The assertion, Two and one is equal to three, considered as an assertion respecting objects, as for instance, "Two pebbles and one pebble are equal to three pebbles," does not affirm equality between two collections of pebbles, but absolute identity. It affirms that if we put one pebble to two pebbles, those very pebbles are three. The objects, therefore, being the very same, and the mere assertion that "objects are themselves" being insignificant, it seems but natural to consider the proposition, Two and one is equal to three, as asserting mere identity of signification between the two names.

This, however, though it looks so plausible, will not bear examination. The expression "two pebbles and one pebble," and the expression "three pebbles," stand indeed for the same aggregation of objects, but they by no means stand for the same physical fact. They are names of the same objects, but of those objects in two different states: though they *de*note the same things, their *con*notation is different. Three pebbles in two separate parcels, and three pebbles in one parcel, do not make the same impression on our senses; and the assertion that the very same pebbles may by an alteration of place and arrangement be made to produce either the one set of sensations or the other, though a very familiar proposition, is not an identical one. It is a truth known to us by early and constant experience: an inductive truth; and such truths are the foundation of the science of Number. The fundamental truths of that science all rest on the evidence of sense; they are proved by showing to our eyes and our fingers that any given number of objects — ten balls, for example — may by separation and re-arrangement exhibit to our senses all the different sets of numbers the sums of which is equal to ten. All the improved methods of teaching arithmetic to children proceed on a knowledge of this fact. All who wish to carry the child's *mind* along with them in learning arithmetic; all who wish to teach numbers, and not mere ciphers — now teach it through the evidence of the senses, in the manner we have described.

We may, if we please, call the proposition, "Three is two and one," a definition of the number three, and assert that arithmetic, as it has been asserted that geometry, is a science founded on definitions. But they are definitions in the geometrical sense, not the logical; asserting not the meaning of a term only, but along with it an observed matter of fact. The proposition, "A circle is a figure bounded by a line which has all its points equally distant from a point within it," is called the definition of a circle; but the proposition from which so many consequences follow, and which is really a first principle in geometry, is, that figures answering to this description exist. And thus we may call "Three is two and one" a definition of three; but the calculations which depend on that proposition do not follow from the definition itself, but from an arithmetical theorem presupposed in it, namely, that collections of objects exist, which while they impress the senses thus, o o o, may be separated into two parts, thus, o o   o. This proposition being granted, we term all such parcels Threes, after which the enunciation of the above-mentioned physical fact will serve also for a definition of the word Three.

The Science of Number is thus no exception to the conclusion we previously arrived at, that the processes even of deductive sciences are altogether inductive, and that their first principles are generalizations from experience.[3]

In this selection, John Stuart Mill challenges what has been one of the best established beliefs in the history of Western thought, the belief that arithmetical and geometrical truths are necessary and could not be otherwise. He argues that these truths, like all truths, are nothing other than generalizations from experience and that they differ only in the degree of confirmation, not in kind. He uses the Kantian argument that arithmetic is never simply abstract calculation, but also applicable to the world. And this means, according to Mill (but not according to Kant), that there must always be some inference from facts about the world. Numbers are never simply numbers, he argues, they are always numbers of something, and this means that the meaning of a number (for example, "four") always extends beyond the language of arithmetic alone. The truths of arithmetic and geometry, in other words, are just like the truths of science — generalizations about the world.

Most empiricists, however, have not taken Mill's alternative of arguing that these truths are not necessary. Like A. J. Ayer, they have generally agreed that the principles of arithmetic and geometry are indeed necessary truths, and therefore, they conclude, they must be analytic. Mill refers to several such attempts in his own day. The problem, however, is to show how these truths are derivable either from principles of logic or from the meanings of arithmetical or geometrical terms. The attempt to derive arithmetic from logic was begun by Gottlob Frege in Germany, who attacked the defenders of Mill's empirical interpretation in his own country. The project was fully developed in England by Bertrand Russell and Alfred North Whitehead in their *Principia Mathematica*. In what has been called the most brilliant single philosophical campaign in the twentieth century, they proved that the principles of arithmetic could be deduced from a small set of axioms (developed by an Italian mathematician named Giuseppe Peano), which could in turn be defined and defended in logical terms alone.

In what follows, the basic empiricist position is presented by the contemporary American philosopher C. G. Hempel. Hempel argues that mathematical truths are necessary and analytic, but he employs some of the very sophisticated logical machinery that had been developed by Peano, Frege, Russell, and Whitehead. He goes beyond Ayer in trying to show how mathematical truths can be derived from simpler logical rules, thus demonstrating their analyticity. He begins, how-

---

[3]John Stuart Mill, *A System of Logic*, 8th ed. (New York: Harper & Row, 1874).

ever, by first attacking the rationalist's belief that mathematical truths are "self-evident" as well as Mill's belief that mathematics is a form of empirical knowledge. He then goes on to show how mathematical truths can be derived by logical inference from a limited number of axioms.

from "On the Nature of Mathematical Truth," by C. G. Hempel

ARE THE PROPOSITIONS OF MATHEMATICS SELF-EVIDENT TRUTHS?

One of the several answers which have been given to our problem asserts that the truths of mathematics, in contradistinction to the hypotheses of empirical science, require neither factual evidence nor any other justification because they are "self-evident." This view, however, which ultimately relegates decisions as to mathematical truth to a feeling of self-evidence, encounters various difficulties. First of all, many mathematical theorems are so hard to establish that even to the specialist in the particular field they appear as anything but self-evident. Secondly, it is well known that some of the most interesting results of mathematics — especially in such fields as abstract set theory and topology — run counter to deeply ingrained intuitions and the customary kind of feeling of self-evidence. Thirdly, the existence of mathematical conjectures such as those of Goldbach and of Fermat, which are quite elementary in content and yet undecided up to this day, certainly shows that not all mathematical truths can be self-evident. And finally, even if self-evidence were attributed only to the basic postulates of mathematics, from which all other mathematical propositions can be deduced, it would be pertinent to remark that judgments as to what may be considered as self-evident are subjective; they may vary from person to person and certainly cannot constitute an adequate basis for decisions as to the objective validity of mathematical propositions.

IS MATHEMATICS THE MOST GENERAL EMPIRICAL SCIENCE?

According to another view, advocated especially by John Stuart Mill, mathematics is itself an empirical science which differs from the other branches such as astronomy, physics, chemistry, etc., mainly in two respects: its subject matter is more general than that of any other field of scientific research, and its propositions have been tested and confirmed to a greater extent than those of even the most firmly established sections of astronomy or physics. Indeed, according to this view, the degree to which the laws of mathematics have been borne out by the past experiences of mankind is so overwhelming that — unjustifiably — we have come to think of mathematical theorems as qualitatively different from the well-confirmed hypotheses or theories of other branches of science: we consider them as certain, while other theories are thought of as at best "very probable" or very highly confirmed.

But this view, too, is open to serious objections. From a hypothesis which is empirical in character — such as, for example, Newton's law of gravitation — it is possible to derive predictions to the effect that under certain specified conditions certain specified observable phenomena will occur. The actual occurrence of these phenomena constitutes confirming evidence, their nonoccurrence disconfirming evidence for the hypothesis. It follows in particular that an empirical hypothesis is theoretically disconfirmable; i.e., it is possible to indicate what kind of evidence, if actually encountered, would disconfirm the hypothesis. In the light of this remark, consider now a simple "hypothesis" from arithmetic: $3 + 2 = 5$. If this is actually an empirical generalization of past experiences, then it must be possible to state what kind of evidence would oblige us to concede the hypothesis was not generally true after all. If any disconfirming evidence for the given proposition can be thought of, the following illustration might well be typical of it: We place some microbes on a slide, putting down first three of them and then another two. Afterwards we count all the microbes to test whether in this instance 3 and 2 actually added up to 5. Suppose now that we counted 6 microbes altogether. Would we consider this as an empirical disconfirmation of the given proposition, or at least as a proof that it does not apply to microbes? Clearly not; rather, we would assume we had made a mistake in counting or that one of the microbes had split in two between the first and the second count. But under no circumstances could the phenomenon just described invalidate the arithmetical proposition in question; for the latter asserts nothing whatever about the behavior of microbes; it merely states that any set consisting of $3 + 2$ objects may also be said to consist of 5 objects. And this is so because the symbols "$3 + 2$" and "5" denote the same number: they are synonymous by virtue of the fact that the symbols "2," "3," "5," and "$+$" are *defined* (or tacitly understood) in such a way that the above identity holds as a consequence of the meaning attached to the concepts involved in it.

THE ANALYTIC CHARACTER OF MATHEMATICAL PROPOSITIONS

The statement that $3 + 2 = 5$, then, is true for similar reasons as, say, the assertion that no sexagenarian is 45 years of age. Both are true simply by virtue of definitions or of similar stipulations which determine the meaning of key terms involved. Statements of this kind share certain important characteristics: Their validation naturally requires no empirical evidence; they can be shown to be true by a mere analysis of the meaning attached to the terms which occur in them. In the language of logic, sentences of this kind are called analytic or true *a priori*, which is to indicate that their truth is logically independent of, or logically prior to, any experiential evidence. And while the statements of empirical science, which are synthetic and can be validated only *a posteriori*, are constantly subject to revision in the light of new evidence, the truth of an analytic statement can be established definitely, once and for all. However, this characteristic "theoretical certainty" of analytic propositions has to be paid for at a high price: An analytic statement conveys no factual information. Our statement about sexagenarians, for example, asserts nothing that could possibly conflict with any factual evidence: it has no factual implications, no empirical content; and it is precisely for this reason that the statement can be validated without recourse to empirical evidence.

Let us illustrate this view of the nature of mathematical propositions by reference to another, frequently cited, example of a mathematical — or rather logical — truth, namely the proposition that whenever $a = b$ and $b = c$ then $a = c$. On what grounds can this so-called "transitivity of identity" be asserted? Is it of an empirical nature and hence at least theoretically disconfirmable by empirical evidence? Suppose, for example, that a, b, c, are certain shades of green, and that as far as we can see, $a = b$ and $b = c$, but clearly $a \neq c$. This phenomenon actually occurs under certain conditions; do we consider it as disconfirming evidence for the proposition under consideration? Undoubtedly not; we would argue that if $a \neq c$, it is impossible that $a = b$ and also $b = c$; between the terms of at least one of these latter pairs, there must obtain a difference, though perhaps only a subliminal one. And we would dismiss the possibility of empirical disconfirmation, and indeed the idea that an empirical test should be relevant here, on the grounds that identity is a transitive relation by virtue of its definition or by virtue of the basic postulates governing it. Hence, the principle in question is true *a priori.*

. . . . .

. . . the following conclusion is obtained, which is also known as *the thesis of logicism concerning the nature of mathematics:*

Mathematics is a branch of logic. It can be derived from logic in the following sense:

a. All the concepts of mathematics, i.e., of arithmetic, algebra, and analysis, can be defined in terms of four concepts of pure logic.

b. All the theorems of mathematics can be deduced from those definitions by means of the principles of logic (including the axioms of infinity and choice.)[4]

The Rationalist Response

What kinds of truths are the truths of arithmetic and geometry? We just watched various empiricists try to show that (1) the truths of mathematics are not necessary and not analytic and therefore not known *a priori* (Mill), and (2) they are necessary and analytic and therefore known *a priori* (Ayer, Hempel).

Against both of these empiricist views, the rationalist continues to insist that the truths of arithmetic and mathematics are neither empirical nor analytic, but matters of necessity in some other way. Traditionally, particularly in the philosophy of Descartes, this other way is through "intuition," the anathema of the empiricist. The empiricist does not trust the appeal to intuition, for, by its very

[4]C. G. Hempel, "On the Nature of Mathematical Truth," in *American Mathematical Monthly*, Vol. 52, 1945.

nature, it cannot be defended either by rational argument or by appeal to ordinary experience.

The last two centuries have seen a great many rationalist attempts to work out the problematic notion of "intuition" and to display the viability of confidence in human reason. In this chapter, we shall mention only two of them. One is by Immanuel Kant, the man whom most contemporary philosophers would call the greatest philosopher since Plato and Aristotle. The other, which emerged only in this century, is called **phenomenology.** It was invented by the German-Czech philosopher-mathematician Edmund Husserl, and it is a philosophy that has enormous influence in both Europe and the United States.

Of course, even the empiricist may be eventually forced back to intuition, if there is no further justification of ultimate principles and "relations of ideas." But unlike the traditional rationalist, the empiricist believes that such intuition follows from our use of language or our adopting a certain logic. We can only intuit analytic truths. If the rationalist is right, we can also intuit truths that are necessary but not analytic. What kind of truth could this be?

KANT AND SYNTHETIC *A PRIORI* KNOWLEDGE   In historical terms, the discovery of a third alternative (a truth that is neither analytic nor empirical) precedes the empiricist attempts of the nineteenth and twentieth centuries (by Mill and later by Frege, Russell, Whitehead, Hempel, and Ayer). It was discovered by Immanuel Kant in the 1770s as an answer to both the traditional rationalists and the empiricists. He found their theories all unacceptable. Both Leibniz and Hume, for example, had simply distinguished necessary from contingent truths, without further distinction. And we so far have done the same thing, only using more sophisticated terminology. But are all necessary truths analytic, known by analysis of the sentence alone? Or might there be some *a priori* knowledge of the world rather than just of language? The rationalist believes that there is, and Kant, a new kind of rationalist, shows what it would be.

It is one thing to say that knowledge is either *a priori* or *empirical*. It is quite another to say that sentences are either analytic or not analytic. The first distinguishes two kinds of knowledge; the second distinguishes two kinds of sentences. The term Kant used for "not analytic" is **synthetic;** so we have two sets of distinctions, *a priori* versus empirical and analytic versus synthetic.

We have been talking as if all *a priori* knowledge were based on analytic sentences. But then, we have also been talking as if only empirical knowledge could be stated in nontrivial or synthetic sentences: for example, "not all trees are green all year." But isn't it possible that there might be synthetic sentences whose truth can be known *a priori*? Kant thinks that there can be, and he calls such knowledge *synthetic a priori knowledge.* Arithmetic and geometry are his most important examples, but he also uses this notion of "the synthetic *a priori*" to provide a generally new conception of the problems and principles of philosophy.

So far, we haven't resolved anything. You remember (in our discussion of Plato's word "participation") that we insisted we must always be careful not to mistake a new word for an explanation, and, so far, that's all that we have. The words "synthetic *a priori*," though very impressive, only tell us that the truths of arithmetic are neither analytic nor empirical. In other words, it is a restatement of the problem, which still remains. How does one justify synthetic *a priori* principles?

In what follows, Kant makes his distinctions between *a priori* and empirical (*a posteriori*) knowledge and between analytic and synthetic sentences (or "judgments"). Then he introduces the idea of synthetic *a priori* knowledge. And, finally, he gives us his radically new way of defending the truths of arithmetic and geometry.

from *The Critique of Pure Reason*, by Kant

THE DISTINCTION BETWEEN PURE *(A PRIORI)* AND EMPIRICAL *(A POSTERIORI)* KNOWLEDGE

That all our knowledge begins with experience there can be no doubt. For how should the faculty of knowledge be called into activity, if not by objects which affect our senses, and which either produce representations by themselves, or rouse the activity of our understanding to compare, to connect, or to separate them, and thus to convert the raw material of our sensuous impressions into a knowledge of objects, which we call experience? In respect of time, therefore, no knowledge within us is antecedent to experience, but all knowledge begins with it.

But although all our knowledge begins with experience, it does not follow that it arises from experience. For it is quite possible that even our empirical experience is a compound of that which we receive through impressions, and of that which our own faculty of knowledge (incited only by sensuous impressions), supplies from itself, a supplement which we do not distinguish from that raw material, until long practice has roused our attention and rendered us capable of separating one from the other.

It is therefore a question which deserves at least closer investigation, and cannot be disposed of at first sight, whether there exists a knowledge independent of experience, and even of all impressions of the senses? Such *knowledge* is called *a priori*, and distinguished from *empirical* knowledge, which has its sources *a posteriori*, that is, in experience.

The idea that our "faculty of knowledge supplies from itself a supplement" to our experience is the key to Kant's theory of necessity. *A priori* knowledge, according to Kant, is possessed by everyone everywhere at all times precisely because these are the rules that consciousness imposes upon every experience; indeed, these are the rules that make our experience possible. Kant will answer Hume's skepticism by insisting that our knowledge of necessary principles is knowledge of the workings of the mind itself.

The distinction between *analytic* and *synthetic* judgments is the key to Kant's argument. He defines an analytic judgment as one whose predicate is "contained" in the concept of the subject. His example is "all bodies are extended" (that is, take up space), since the idea of "taking up space" is already "contained in" the concept of a physical body. On the other hand, the judgment "all bodies are heavy" would not be analytic, but rather synthetic, since "the predicate is quite different from anything I think in the mere concept of body in general, and the addition of such a predicate therefore yields a synthetic judgment."

Judgments of experience, Kant tells us, are all synthetic. But not all synthetic judgments are merely empirical. Synthetic *a priori* judgments are not derived from experience but rather precede every experience, and these in turn provide all of those necessary truths that are not merely analytic, not merely tautologies and logical truths.

The most notorious deviation that Kant makes in his attempt to defend what other philosophers called "truths of reason" is his inclusion of the judgments of mathematics as synthetic, rather than *a priori*. Here he disagrees with all the empiricists who preceded him and followed him, too. "All mathematical judgments, without exception, are synthetic." These are necessary and not derived from experience, but they are not mere tautologies or logical truths, and not, Kant thinks, reducible to, or derivable from, any set of merely logical principles.

> At first sight one might suppose indeed that the proposition $7 + 5 = 12$ is merely analytical, following, according to the principle of contradiction, from the concept of a sum of 7 and 5. But, if we look more closely, we shall find that the concept of the sum of 7 and 5 contains nothing beyond the union of both sums into one, whereby nothing is told us as to what this single number may be which combines both. We by no means arrive at a concept of Twelve, by thinking that union of Seven and Five; and we may analyse our concept of such a possible sum as long as we will, still we shall never discover in it the concept of Twelve. We must go beyond these concepts, and call in the assistance of the intuition corresponding to one of the two, for instance, our five fingers, or, as Segner does in his arithmetic, five points, and so by degrees add the units of the Five, given in intuition, to the concept of the Seven. For I first take the number 7, and taking the intuition of the fingers of my hand, in order to form with it the concept of the 5, I gradually add the units, which I before took together, to make up the number 5, by means of the image of my hand, to the number 7, and I thus see the number 12 arising before me. That 5 should be added to 7 was no doubt implied in my concept of a sum $7 + 5$, but not that that sum should be equal to 12. An arithmetical proposition is, therefore, always synthetical, which is seen more easily still by taking larger numbers, where we clearly perceive that, turn and twist our conceptions as we may, we could never, by means of the mere analysis of our concepts and without the help of intuition, arrive at the sum that is wanted.
>
> Nor is any proposition of pure geometry analytical. That the straight line between two points is the shortest, is a synthetical proposition. For my concept of *straight* contains nothing of magnitude (quantity), but a quality only. The concept of the *shortest* is, therefore, purely adventitious, and cannot be deduced from the concept of the straight line by any analysis whatsoever. The aid of intuition, therefore, must be called in, by which alone the synthesis is possible.

It is true that some few propositions, presupposed by the geometrician, are really analytical, and depend on the principle of contradiction: but then they serve only, like identical propositions, to form the chain of the method, and not as principles.[5]

Mathematics, according to Kant as well as the empiricists, is a product of human reason. However, he also argued that it is entirely synthetic; "how then," he asks, "is it possible for human reason to produce such knowledge entirely *a priori?*" His answer lies in the notion of "intuition"; mathematics (and geometry) are representations of the "pure forms of sensibility," in particular, our intuitions of space and time.

from *Prolegomena,* by Kant

. . . We find that all mathematical cognition has this peculiarity: it must first exhibit its concept in intuition and indeed *a priori;* therefore in an intuition which is not empirical but pure. Without this mathematics cannot take a single step; hence its judgments are always intuitive. . . . In one way only can my intuition anticipate the actuality of the object, and be a cognition *a priori,* namely: *if my intuition contains nothing but the form of sensibility, antedating in my mind all the actual impressions through which I am affected by objects.*

.   .   .   .   .

Now, the intuitions which pure mathematics lays at the foundation of all its cognitions and judgments which appear at once apodictic and necessary are space and time. For mathematics must first present all its concepts in intuition, and pure mathematics in pure intuition; that is, it must construct them. If it proceeded in any other way, it would be impossible to take a single step; for mathematics proceeds, not analytically by dissection of concepts, but synthetically, and if pure intuition be wanting there is nothing in which the matter for synthetical judgments *a priori* can be given. Geometry is based upon the pure intuition of space. Arithmetic achieves its concept of number by the successive addition of units in time, and pure mechanics cannot attain its concepts of motion without employing the representation of time. Both representations, however, are only intuitions; for if we omit from the empirical intuitions of bodies and their alterations (motion) everything empirical, that is, belonging to sensation, space and time still remain, which are therefore pure intuitions that lie *a priori* at the basis of the empirical.

.   .   .   .   .

The problem of the present section is therefore solved. Pure mathematics, as synthetical cognition *a priori,* is possible only by referring to no other objects than those of the senses. At the basis of their empirical intuition lies a pure intuition (of space and of time) which is *a priori,* because the latter

---

[5]Immanuel Kant, *The Critique of Pure Reason,* rev. 2nd ed., trans. Max Müller (London: Macmillan, 1927).

intuition is nothing but the mere form of sensibility, which precedes the actual appearance of the objects, since in fact it makes them possible. Yet this faculty of intuiting *a priori* affects not the matter of the phenomenon (that is, the sensation in it, for this constitutes that which is empirical), but its form, namely, space and time. . . . Consequently, the basis of mathematics actually is pure intuitions, which make its synthetical and apodictically valid propositions possible.[6]

Kant's solution to the problem of mathematical truth is colossal. He is defending the claim that the truths of arithmetic depend upon certain intuitions which can give us *a priori* knowledge. But, for Kant, these intuitions are nothing other than the forms of space and time, by which we organize our perceptual experiences; geometry is nothing other than a formalized set of descriptions about the way we must experience space, and the same is true of arithmetic and time. Now notice two things about this theory. First, in addition to explaining something about the nature of arithmetic and geometry, it also provides a middle way between Newton and Leibniz's theories of space and time, which we mentioned in Chapter 2 (p. 99). In agreement with Newton, Kant says that space and time are absolute, but he also agrees with Leibniz that they don't exist outside of experience. But second, and much more important, here is an example of Kant's philosophical strategy, which is basic to carry out his revolution in philosophy. What he is saying, in effect, is that the necessary truths of arithmetic and geometry are true because they describe the *essential structures of the human mind*, in this case, the ways in which we are aware of space and time.

HUSSERL AND PHENOMENOLOGY   Husserl was also a rationalist. He began as a mathematician, and his first theory (and his first book) was a defense of the empiricist approach of John Stuart Mill. That is, he thought that the truths of arithmetic and geometry were simply well-confirmed empirical generalizations. An argument with Frege changed his mind, and he turned to the position that such truths must be what they seem to be, namely necessary. But he refused to accept the idea that they were also trivial analytic truths, true by linguistic convention or derivable from basic logical truths, the positions defended during his lifetime by Frege, Russell, and Whitehead. He held, like Kant before him, that such truths were synthetic *a priori*. And he held that these truths were known through a special kind of *intuition*. Husserl spent his life, and many tens of thousands of pages, trying to say precisely what this special kind of "intuition" amounted to.

The heart of Husserl's phenomenology is that there are two very different kinds of "experience": (1) ordinary "experience," which he calls "individual intuition," such as my present awareness that there are three bananas and two cats on my desk, and (2) a special kind of intuition, which Husserl calls *essential* (or, when he uses the Greek, *eidetic*) *intuition*. In this second kind of intuition, we do not see particular things but rather universal truths, or essences (the Greek

---

[6]Immanuel Kant, *Prolegomena to Any Future Metaphysics*, trans. Lewis White Beck (New York: Bobbs-Merrill, 1950).

here is *eidos*). Now this theory, and even its Greek terminology, ought to seem very familiar to you. From where? From Plato and Aristotle. Husserl is revising a very old theory, in which such things as numbers and triangles and the various truths of arithmetic and geometry are ideal objects and laws, like Plato's Forms. (The word Plato uses is also *Eidos*, and the title of Husserl's best-known work is *Ideas*.) But Husserl, unlike Plato, does not believe that these special entities have an existence independent of human consciousness. Here he shares Aristotle's criticisms of Plato. These essences, such as numbers and triangles and the laws of arithmetic and geometry, are "in consciousness," and *phenomenology* is the attempt to study consciousness in order to determine what these essences are.

What Husserl is doing, then, is to give an overall theory of the rationalist's important appeal to intuition. And how can we defend this appeal to intuition? Phenomenologists still don't agree on the defense of intuition. Well, at least this much is clear: We can reject a claim based on intuition if not everyone shares that intuition, since the most important characteristic of rational intuitions and essences is that everyone shares them. Properly described, everyone in the world will agree about a rational intuition. But here we recall Locke's argument, that even universal agreement among men would not prove that an idea was *necessarily* common to all men. And the phenomenologist must respond again to this old argument. You can see that these are still very much living issues, now formulated in more sophisticated language, but still much the same as they were when Leibniz and Locke debated them centuries ago.

Husserl is a notoriously difficult author, but it is important to include at least a sample of his work. What follows is from *Ideas* (Vol. I) and outlines his distinction between two kinds of intuition: "individual" (contingent and particular) and "essential" (necessary and universal).

from *Ideas,* by Husserl

Individual Being of every kind is, to speak quite generally, *"accidental."* It is so-and-so, but essentially it could be other than it is. . . . But the import of this contingency, which is there called matter-of-factness, is limited in this respect that the contingency is correlative to a *necessity* which does not carry the mere actuality-status of a valid rule of connexion obtaining between temporo-spatial facts, but has the character of *essential necessity*, and therewith a relation to *essential universality*. Now when we stated that every fact could be "essentially" other than it is, we were already expressing thereby *that it belongs to the meaning of everything contingent that it should have essential being and therewith an Eidos to be apprehended in all its purity;* and this Eidos comes under *essential truths of varying degrees of universality.*

ESSENTIAL INSIGHT AND INDIVIDUAL INTUITION

At first "essence" indicated that which in the intimate self-being of an individual discloses to us *"what"* it is. But every such What can be "set out as Ideas." *Empirical or individual intuition* can be transformed into *essen-*

tial insight (ideation) — a possibility which is itself not to be understood as empirical but as essential possibility. The object of such insight is then the corresponding *pure* essence or eidos, whether it be the highest category or one of its specializations, right down to the fully "concrete."

Of whatever kind the individual intuition may be, whether adequate or not, it can pass off into essential intuition, and the latter, whether correspondingly adequate or not, has the character of a dator act. And this means that —

The essence (Eidos) is an object of a new type. Just as the datum of individual or empirical intuition is an individual object, so the datum of essential intuition is a pure essence.

Here we have not a mere superficial analogy, but a radical community of nature. *Essential insight is still intuition,* just as the eidetic object is still an object. . . . It is an intuition of a fundamentally *unique* and *novel* kind, namely in contrast to the types of intuition which belong as correlatives to the object-matters of other categories, and more specifically to intuition in the ordinary narrow sense, that is, individual intuition.

It lies undoubtedly in the intrinsic nature of essential intuition that it should rest on what is a chief factor of individual intuition, namely the striving for this, the visible presence of individual fact, though it does not, to be sure, presuppose any apprehension of the individual or any recognition of its reality. Consequently it is certain that no essential intuition is possible without the free possibility of directing one's glance to an individual *counterpart* and of shaping an illustration; just as contrariwise no individual intuition is possible without the free possibility of carrying out an act of ideation and therein directing one's glance upon the corresponding essence which exemplifies itself in something individually visible; but that does not alter the fact that *the two kinds of intuition differ in principle,* and in assertions of the kind we have just been making it is only the essential relations between them that declare themselves. Thus, to the essential differences of the intuitions correspond the essential relations between "existence" (here clearly in the sense of individual concrete being) and "essence," between *fact* and *eidos.*[7]

Husserl begins with the very old distinction, taken from Aristotle and medieval philosophers, between "essence" and "accident." An "accident," according to this usage, could possibly be other than it is, an essence could not. For example, it is possible that some particular triangle might have been drawn acute rather than isosceles, but it is not possible that it could have been drawn as a triangle with five angles. Having three angles is essential to being a triangle, being isosceles is not. This essence is what Husserl calls the *eidos,* and an *eidos,* within a certain description ("various degrees of universality") provides us with a necessary truth. Thus the *eidos* of this particular figure drawn as a triangle includes having three angles. Its *eidos* as a geometric figure, however, does not include having any particular number of angles, but it does require that it consist of lines on a plane. Husserl insists that the essence or *eidos* makes something "what" it is; in other words, it defines it as a certain kind of thing. The distinction between

[7] Edmund Husserl, *Ideas,* trans. W. R. Boyce Gibson (New York: Collier, Macmillan, 1962).

individual intuition and essential intuition is then a difference between (1) *particular* things, which might be different or might not exist at all, and (2) essence
or *eidos*, which enables us to talk about a *kind* of thing (for example, centaurs or
unicorns) even if they do not, never have, and never will, exist.

The most important claim of Husserl's argument is his insistence that the
eidos is itself "an object of a new type." In other words, it is something which
can be intuited itself, apart from particular examples of it. (In medieval philosophy and since, these entities which represent "kinds of things" are called "universals." The problems of necessary truth are sometimes called "the problem of
universals.") A geometer can talk about the properties of a right triangle, for
example, without using or thinking of any particular right triangle. He is talking
about the type, about the *eidos*. And Husserl's central claim is that, through phenomenology, we learn to recognize the essence or *eidos* by special sorts of intuition. It is such intuitions that make necessary truths possible. In other words,
where Kant insisted that it is the form of our intuitions (as space and time) that
makes the principles of arithmetic and geometry necessarily true, Husserl says
that it is the content of our intuitions that makes these principles true. That
content is what he calls the *eidos* or essence. This is his way of developing the
rationalist's belief that necessary truths can be known by intuition. It is also the
basis of what he calls **phenomenology.**

from "An Introduction
to Phenomenology,"
by Husserl

INTRODUCTION

The term 'phenomenology' designates two things: a new kind of descriptive method which made a breakthrough in philosophy at the turn of the
century, and an a priori science derived from it; a science which is intended
to supply the basic instrument *(Organon)* for a rigorously scientific philosophy and, in its consequent application, to make possible a methodical
reform of all the sciences. Together with this philosophical phenomenology, but not yet separated from it, however, there also came into being a
new psychological discipline parallel to it in method and content: the a
priori pure or "phenomenological" psychology, which raises the reforma-
tional claim to being the basic methodological foundation on which alone
a scientifically rigorous empirical psychology can be established. An outline
of this psychological phenomenology, standing nearer to our natural thinking, is well suited to serve as a preliminary step that will lead up to an
understanding of philosophical phenomenology.

· · · · ·

*2. The Purely Psychical in Self-experience and Community Experience.
The Universal Description of Intentional Experiences.*

To establish and unfold this guiding idea, the first thing that is necessary
is a clarification of what is peculiar to experience, and especially to the pure
experience of the psychical—and specifically the purely psychical that
experience reveals, which is to become the theme of a pure psychology. It

is natural and appropriate that precedence will be accorded to the most immediate types of experience, which in each case reveal to us our own psychic being.

Focusing our experiencing gaze on our own psychic life necessarily takes place as reflection, as a turning about of a glance which had previously been directed elsewhere. Every experience can be subject to such reflection, as can indeed every manner in which we occupy ourselves with any real or ideal objects — for instance, thinking, or in the modes of feeling and will, valuing and striving. So when we are fully engaged in conscious activity, we focus exclusively on the specific things, thoughts, values, goals, or means involved, but not on the psychical experience as such, in which these things are known *as* such. Only reflection reveals this to us. Through reflection, instead of grasping simply the matter straight-out — the values, goals, and instrumentalities — we grasp the corresponding subjective experiences in which we become "conscious" of them, in which (in the broadest sense) they "appear." For this reason, they are called "phenomena," and their most general essential character is to exist as the "consciousness-of" or "appearance-of" the specific things, thoughts (judged states of affairs, grounds, conclusions), plans, decisions, hopes, and so forth. This relatedness [of the appearing to the object of appearance] resides in the meaning of all expressions in the vernacular languages which relate to psychic experience — for instance, perception *of* something, recalling *of* something, thinking *of* something, hoping *for* something, fearing something, striving *for* something, deciding on something, and so on. If this realm of what we call "phenomena" proves to be the possible field for a pure psychological discipline related exclusively to phenomena, we can understand the designation of it as *phenomenological psychology*. The terminological expression, deriving from Scholasticism, for designating the basic character of being as consciousness, as consciousness of something, is *intentionality*. In unreflective holding of some object or other in consciousness, we are turned or directed towards it: our "*intentio*" goes out towards it. The phenomenological reversal of our gaze shows that this "being directed" [*Gerichtetsein*] is really an immanent essential feature of the respective experiences involved; they are "intentional" experiences.

. . . . .

3. The Self-contained Field of the Purely Psychical.—Phenomenological Reduction and True Inner Experience.

The idea of a phenomenological psychology encompasses the whole range of tasks arising out of the experience of self and the experience of the other founded on it. But it is not yet clear whether phenomenological experience, followed through in exclusiveness and consistency, really provides us with a kind of closed-off field of being, out of which a science can grow which is exclusively focused on it and completely free of everything psychophysical. Here [in fact] difficulties do exist, which have hidden from psychologists the possibility of such a purely phenomenological psychology even after Brentano's discovery of intentionality. They are relevant already to the construction of a really pure self-experience, and therewith of a really pure psychic datum. A particular method of access is required for the pure phenomenological field: the method of "phenomenological reduction."

This *method of "phenomenological reduction"* is thus the foundational method of pure psychology and the presupposition of all its specifically theoretical methods. Ultimately the great difficulty rests on the way that already the self-experience of the psychologist is everywhere intertwined with external experience, with that of extra-psychical real things. The experienced "exterior" does not belong to one's intentional interiority, although certainly the experience itself belongs to it as experience — *of* the exterior. Exactly this same thing is true of every kind of awareness directed at something out there in the world. A consistent epoche of the phenomenologist is required, if he wishes to break through to his own consciousness as pure phenomenon or as the totality of his purely mental processes.

4. *Eidetic Reduction and Phenomenological Psychology as an Eidetic Science.*

To what extent does the unity of the field of phenomenological experience assure the possibility of a psychology exclusively based on it, thus a pure phenomenological psychology? It does not automatically assure an empirically pure science of *facts* from which everything psychophysical is abstracted. But this situation is quite different with an a priori science. In it, every self-enclosed field of possible experience permits *eo ipso* the all-embracing transition from the factual to the essential form, the *eidos.* So here, too. If the phenomenological actual fact as such becomes irrelevant; if, rather, it serves only as an example and as the foundation for a free but intuitive variation of the factual mind and communities of minds *into* the a priori possible (thinkable) ones; and if now the theoretical eye directs itself to the necessarily enduring invariant in the variation; then there will arise with this systematic way of proceeding a realm of its own, of the "a priori." There emerges therewith the eidetically necessary typical form, the *eidos;* this *eidos* must manifest itself throughout all the potential forms of mental being in particular cases, must be present in all the synthetic combinations and self-enclosed wholes, if it is to be at all "thinkable," that is, intuitively conceivable. Phenomenological psychology in this manner undoubtedly must be established as an "eidetic phenomenology"; it is then exclusively directed toward the invariant essential forms. . . . If the phenomenological reduction contrived a means of access to the phenomenon of real and also potential inner experience, the method founded in it of "eidetic reduction" provides the means of access to the invariant essential structures of the total sphere of pure mental process.[8]

THE TRUTHS OF METAPHYSICS

Because the principles of metaphysics are so very basic to all human thought and experience, it has often been argued that they too, like the principles of logic and mathematics, must be necessary truths. As the foundation principles of all of our

[8]Edmund Husserl, "An Introduction to Phenomenology," in F. Elliston and M. McCormick, eds., *Husserl: Shorter Works* (Notre Dame, Ind.: Univ. of Notre Dame Press, 1981).

knowledge, they must have as much certainty as possible, just as a building must have the strongest foundations possible. Without such foundations, everything built on top will be rickety and uncertain. Furthermore, traditional rationalists have claimed that the way in which we come to understand these basic principles, namely, through reason, guarantees us precisely this certainty. The principles of reason, unlike principles drawn from experience, are by their very nature necessary truths.

The various principles of metaphysics advanced by Plato, Aristotle, Spinoza, and Leibniz were all supposed to be necessary truths by virtue of reason. Spinoza's argument that there can only be one substance, for instance, was based upon definitions and axioms that were necessarily true by virtue of reason and derived in the form of theorems (or "propositions") in much the same way that geometrical theorems are derived from the definitions and axioms of Euclidean geometry. The idea that there could be but one substance was not drawn from experience and was not intended to be merely a hypothesis or a viewpoint. It had to be true in exactly the same sense that the principles of arithmetic had to be true, as necessary truths.

But if Spinoza's principle is a necessary truth, then how is it possible that Leibniz, using a similar set of definitions and a similar deductive method, arrived at the very opposite conclusion, that there are many substances? He too claimed this as a necessary truth about the universe. But obviously these cannot both be true; either there is only one substance or there is more than one substance. There cannot be both only one and more than one. But this means (assuming that the systems of Spinoza and Leibniz are consistent within themselves) that either one of them is wrong and the other right, or else that they have each given us a view of the world without giving us necessary truths at all. Each is giving us a possible, not a necessary, principle, nothing more. How can one decide which of these great philosophers is correct? Or should we rather say that neither of them has in fact given us a necessary truth and that each has given us an elegant but only speculative idea about the way the world really is? Reason alone seems not to be enough.

The problem of justifying supposedly necessary truths of metaphysics arises even in those cases in which there is no such direct disagreement. The basic principles of our knowledge (for example, the principle of universal causation, which states that every event has its cause, or the principle of induction, which asserts that the future will be like the past) display the same problem of justification. The problem here is not so much whether or not we should accept these principles (although a few philosophers might reject them, as Leibniz rejects the first principle). We do in fact accept them and use them virtually every moment of our lives. The problem is showing that they are necessarily true and not merely habitual or useful to us. Yet it is clear, as David Hume argued, that such principles can be neither analytic ("relations of ideas") nor straightforward "matters of fact," since it is upon these principles that all "matters of fact" are based. Because of this, Hume suggested that such principles were only matters of habit and custom, that we had become so accustomed to using these principles that we now assumed (wrongly) that they were necessary. But because they could not be defended either as principles of reason—as analytic truths or as principles like those of arithmetic and geometry—or as principles drawn from experience, they could not be justified at all. It is largely against Hume, therefore, that modern metaphysics has had to defend itself.

There is a sense in which the entire history of metaphysics, from Plato to the present day, revolves around the various attempts to establish metaphysical principles as necessary truths based on a foundation that is certain. Traditionally, confidence in reason itself, as divinely inspired and capable of grasping necessary truths, was sufficient to justify confidence in metaphysics. In modern times, this tradition is continued by many rationalists, but it has also been subjected to critical scrutiny and rejected by a great many empiricists and others. This critical scrutiny reaches its extremes with Hume, who dismisses not only the whole of traditional metaphysics and theology as "sophistry and illusion" but the basic principles of all human knowledge as unjustifiable as well. It is at this point in history that Kant steps into the picture, attempting to reestablish the traditional claims of metaphysicians to be able to provide necessary truths. This is not to say that he accepts all the suggestions of the metaphysicians in the past. It is clear that he prefers Leibniz to Spinoza on many issues, for example. Moreover, there are some metaphysical disputes, such as the dispute between Leibniz and Spinoza about whether there can be only one substance or more than one, which he dismisses as irresolvable and useless. There are still other metaphysical principles, for example, belief in God and the immortality of the human soul, which he defends as necessary, but as necessary on practical grounds, not as necessary truths or necessary knowledge. But at least some of the principles that Hume rejected as unjustifiable are defended by Kant in his unique way as synthetic *a priori* truths, truths that are neither analytic nor empirical (as Hume had also argued) but that are nevertheless necessary truths (which Hume had denied). Kant argued that these principles are, like the principles of arithmetic and geometry, basic to the structure of the human mind. What makes them necessarily true, therefore, is just the fact that they represent the only possible way in which we can conceive and perceive the world. Here is a third way of defending metaphysical claims that earlier philosophers had not anticipated. By showing that such principles as the principle of universal causation and the principle of induction are necessary for any human knowledge whatever, Kant succeeds in providing a new way of looking at metaphysics and a new way of defending its principles as necessary truths.

SUMMARY AND CONCLUSION

Do we know some things for certain, for example, the basic principles of logic and arithmetic and geometry? The answer isn't as sure as we would like. On the one hand, it is clear that we can't even imagine what it would be like for such necessary truths to be false or for us to be mistaken about them. But on the other hand, it is not clear how these truths can be justified. We can appeal to intuition, but can we absolutely trust our intuitions? We can deduce some of these truths from other truths, but then how do we justify the truths that act as premises? And then some philosophers (for example, Mill) argue that these are not necessary truths at all, but only well-confirmed generalizations from experience, which could possibly (but not likely) turn out to be false.

Although philosophers do not agree about how to justify the basic principles of logic and arithmetic and geometry, most would agree that they are the most certain principles of our knowledge. A much more difficult problem arises with the necessary truths of metaphysics, however. Everyone agrees that two plus two equals four, even if they don't agree about why they so confidently agree. But not everyone agrees that there is only one substance, or that God exists, or that human acts are free from causal determination. In this chapter, we have discussed the difficulties that are involved in defending even those necessary truths that we all agree about. In later chapters, we shall find it even more difficult to defend those claims that people don't agree about. Yet they would still argue that what they believe is necessarily true.

GLOSSARY

analytic (of a sentence or truth): demonstrably true (and necessarily true) by virtue of the logical form or the meanings of the component words. The concept was introduced by Kant, who defined it in terms of a sentence (he called it a "judgment") in which the "predicate was contained in the subject" and "added nothing to it." For example, in "a horse is an animal," he would say that the concept of "horse" already includes the concept of being an animal; we would say that "horse" means "an animal which . . ." and thus "is an animal" adds nothing to what we already know just from "horse." Kant also says that the *criterion* or test for analytic sentences (or *analyticity*) is the principle of contradiction; an analytic sentence is one whose denial yields a self-contradiction.

a posteriori (knowledge): "after experience," or empirical. (See *empirical.*)

a priori (knowledge): independent of all experience. *A priori* knowledge is always necessary, for there can be no imaginable instances that would refute it and no intelligible doubting of it. One might come to know something *a priori* through experience (for example, you might find out that no parallel lines ever touch each other by drawing tens of thousands of parallel lines) but what is essential to *a priori* knowledge is that no such experience is needed. Knowledge is *a priori* if it can be proven independently of experience. The most obvious examples of *a priori* knowledge are analytic sentences, such as "a horse is an animal" and "if all men are mammals and Socrates is a man, then Socrates is a mammal."

calculus: any logical system of abstract symbols, whether interpreted or not.

conceptual truth: an analytic sentence that is true by virtue of the meanings of its component words, or concepts. The example, "a horse is an animal," is a conceptual truth because part of the definition of the word "horse" is "an animal." "All sisters are females" is a conceptual truth because part of the meaning of "sister" is "female."

contingent (truth): dependent on the facts; neither logically necessary nor logically impossible. A contingent state of affairs could have been otherwise. One test to see if a state of affairs is contingent is to see if it is conceivable that it could be other than it is. It is contingent, for example, that heavy objects fall towards the earth, since it is easily imaginable what it would be like if they did not. This is so even though, in another sense, we say that it is (physically) necessary that heavy objects fall. The philosophical terms, "contingent" and "necessary," refer to logical possibility, not to the factual question whether a statement is true or not.

definition: a statement which gives the meaning of a word or phrase. Some definitions, called stipulative definitions, actually introduce the meaning of a word with rigor and distinct boundaries (for example, the logician's definition of "validity"). But, most of the time, a definition is an attempt to capture the not very exact ways in which we ordinarily use a word. In conceptual truths, we can say that they are true "by definition," that is, they are true by virtue of the meanings of the component words, for one word (the subject) contains another (the predicate) in its definition; for example, "a cow is an animal" and the definition of "cow" is "the female *animal* of the genus *Bos*."

eidos: (in Husserl), see *essence*.

empirical (knowledge): derived from and to be defended by appeal to experience. Empirical knowledge can only be so derived and so defended (as opposed to *a priori* knowledge, which need not be).

essence: (in Husserl), an ideal object (for example, a number) or an ideal law (of arithmetic).

hypothesis: a provisional suggestion that must be confirmed (or falsified) through experience. Hypotheses are the bulwark of all empirical knowledge and the end point of all inductive reasoning.

intuition: immediate knowledge of the truth, without the aid of any reasoning and without appeal to experience. Intuition, as rational intuition (there are other kinds), is a central concern of the rationalist philosophers, who consider intuition one of the main functions of reason. But because of its very nature, intuition cannot be argued for, nor can it be defended by experience. Accordingly, many philosophers, especially empiricists, reject the notion of intuition and accept it only when absolutely unavoidable. In this century, Edmund Husserl has defended the appeal to intuition in his phenomenology.

law of contradiction: that basic rule of logic that demands that a sentence and its denial cannot both be true. "Not (*P* and not *P*)." This law is used by many philosophers (Kant, Leibniz, and Hume, for example) as a criterion for analyticity or analytic truth.

law of the excluded middle: that rule of logic that says that either a sentence or its denial must be true: "Either *P* or not *P*." In formal logic, this law, together with the law of contradiction, forms the basis of a great many arguments (for example, that form of *reductio ad absurdum* argument in which the consequences of one premise are shown to be absurd, and therefore its denial is accepted. Many logicians are now reconsidering this law, for it is becoming evident that not all sentences are either true or false. For example, consider Russell's famous example, "the King of France is bald" (when there is no king of France); is that true or false? It surely isn't true, but neither can it be false, for there is no king of France who is not bald. Or what of, "green ideas sleep furiously"? Many philosophers would say that these are neither true nor false, thus rejecting the law of the excluded middle.

logic: that part of philosophy which studies the rules of valid inference and (we now add) the rules of inductive generalization. It is also, however, the study of the form of sentences, their grammar or syntax, or logical form. More loosely, "logic" sometimes means simply "order."

logical truth: a sentence that can be shown to be true by virtue of its logical form alone (by virtue of the connectives, "and," "or," etc.).

logicism: the thesis that all necessary truths are reducible to logical or analytic truths.

matter of fact: (in Hume), an empirical claim, to be confirmed or falsified through experience.

necessary (truth): cannot be otherwise and cannot be imagined to be otherwise. In philosophy, it is not enough that something be "necessary" according to physical laws (for example, the law of gravity), or "necessary" according to custom or habit (for example, the "necessity" of laws against rape, or the felt necessity of having a cigarette after dinner). Necessary allows for not even imaginary counter-examples; thus it is a necessary truth that two plus two equals four. Not only do we believe this with certainty and find ourselves incapable of intelligibly doubting it, but we cannot even suggest what it might be for it to be false, no matter how wild our imaginations.

necessity: in accordance with a necessary truth.

phenomenology: the philosophy of Edmund Husserl, a twentieth-century rationalism that defends appeals to intuition in the defense of necessary truths.

relation of ideas: in traditional empiricist philosophy, analytic truths, which can be demonstrated without appeal to experience. Arithmetic and geometry were taken to be paradigm examples of "relations of ideas."

rules of inference: those rules of logic according to which validity is defined. All such rules are analytic, but there is considerable disagreement whether all are so by virtue of their own logical form or whether some are so because they are derived from other, more basic rules. There is also the following question: given that these rules define correct logical form, how is it possible to say that they have correct logical form?

synonym: "meaning the same." Two words are synonymous if they are interchangeable in a sentence, without losing the meaning of the sentence. For example, "criminal" and "felon" are synonyms in most contexts. The test of a supposedly conceptual truth is to replace certain words with synonyms, and then see if its denial yields a self-contradiction. In other words, substituting synonyms turns a conceptual truth into an analytic truth. For example, "ferns are plants"; substituting for "fern" its synonym (or, in this case, also its definition) "a primitive plant that bears spores, etc." we have "a plant is a plant," whose denial is a contradiction ("a plant is not a plant") and thus is analytic.

synthetic (statement): a non-contradictory proposition in which the predicate is not entailed by the subject, for example, "horses are generally obstinate." ("Synthetic" is opposed, in this sense, to "analytic.") A synthetic sentence cannot be shown to be true by appeal to the logical form or the meanings of the component words. Kant defined a "synthetic" sentence as one that "adds an idea to the subject which is not already contained in it." For example, "a horse is the source of a large income for some people" is a strictly synthetic sentence. No appeal to the meaning of "horse" will help you find out whether it is true or not, and its denial surely does not result in self-contradiction. But, according to Kant, it must not be concluded that all synthetic sentences can be shown to be true solely by appeal to experience. Some, he claimed, are known *a priori*.

synthetic a priori (knowledge): knowledge that is necessary and known independently of experience (and thus *a priori*), but that does not derive its truth from the logic or meaning of sentences (thus synthetic). This is the focal concept of Kant's philosophy.

tautology: a trivial truth that is true by virtue of logical form alone and tells us nothing about the world. (Popularly, a bit of repetitive nonsense, for example, "a rose is a rose is a rose." Technically, [in logic] a sentence that can be shown to be true no matter what the truth or falsity of its component parts.)

truth of reason: in traditional rationalism, a belief that can be justified solely by appeal to intuition or deduction from premises based upon intuition. Arithmetic and geometry were, for the rationalists as for the empiricists, a paradigm case of such truths. They disagreed mainly on the scope of such truths, and the restrictions to be placed on the problematic appeal to intuition.

6

Religion

Now faith is the substance of things hoped for, the evidence of things not seen.

Hebrews 11:1

The age-old efforts of metaphysicians to know the way the world really is have rarely been motivated by curiosity or the scientific spirit alone. Most often, metaphysics and philosophy in general have been motivated by religious devotion. The search for truth and the concern with what we can know have often been tied to the very personal concern about the nature of God and our relationship to Him. For many people, there is no more powerful an experience than the religious experience, and they have no more important beliefs than their religious beliefs. Religion defines their lives, and their religious views define reality. Although religion is philosophically within the domain of metaphysics and epistemology, its importance demands special attention. It involves experiences of a kind that are not common to other ontological and cosmological concerns. Religious beliefs involve emotions that are not relevant to the technical concerns with substance and science. And it is this emotional involvement in religion that has inspired some of the greatest art, the bloodiest wars, and the most brilliant philosophy in Western history.

THE TRADITIONAL CONCEPTION OF GOD

There have been many conceptions of God and many different gods in the history of religion. But whatever the variations in belief and however broad modern interest in religion has become, our dominant conception of God is inherited from the Old and New Testaments and the Jewish and Christian religions. This is not to say that the dominant conception is final or "the best" or even that it is a single conception rather than a summary of a great many conceptions. But it is necessarily the starting point of virtually any discussion of God and religion in our culture.

The power of religious experience does not mean that one cannot be rational and philosophical where religious matters are concerned. Some of the greatest philosophical thought in history can be found in the devoted rationalism of the medieval philosophers, especially in their attempts to understand religious experience and clarify the Christian conception of God. Their rationalism and analysis in no way interfered with their piety. Examination of our religious beliefs clearly does not necessarily entail a change in those beliefs. A moment's reflection reveals that our beliefs, no matter how personal, have much in common and require examination. The God of Judaism and Christianity has many characteristics that must be identified for our understanding. Most importantly, it is generally believed that God is an independent being, the creator of the universe, and distinct from the universe He created. It is generally agreed that God is the supremely rational and moral being with concern for human justice and human suffering. It is agreed that He is all-powerful **(omnipotent)**, all-knowing **(omniscient)**, and that He is everywhere at once **(omnipresent)**. In the Old Testament, it is made evident that God has emotions; for example, we read of God as "a jealous God" and we hear of "the wrath of God." It is also worth noting that we traditionally think of God as male, as in "God the Father," who created man (Adam, not Eve) "in His own image," but this whole interpretation is now under serious reconsideration, even to the point of re-translating the Bible into sex-neutral language. It is the attempt to understand the being who has these characteristics that defines Western theology and a great deal of Western metaphysics.

To insist that God is an independent being, the creator of the universe but distinct from that universe is of the utmost importance for traditional Western religion. You will appreciate why this belief is so important if you recall Spinoza's pantheism, in which he argues that God is nothing other than the universe. When people try to reinterpret God so that He is nothing other than some universal quality, as in "God is love," or "God is ultimate force," or "God is life," or "God is the universe," there is a very real possibility that they are actually denying that God exists as an independent being. One can say "God is love" as shorthand for "God loves us and wants us to love each other" without this danger. But if one believes that God simply is identical to people's loving one another, then it is evident that this belief is no different from that of a person who might not believe in God at all but just believes in love. Similarly, it is one thing to believe that God is a "force," among other things, who created the universe; but if you believe that God is nothing other than a force that created the universe, without consciousness or concern, then your belief does not differ from that of someone who also believes that some force created the universe but does not believe in God. Of course, there are alternative conceptions of God, some of which we shall discuss in this chapter. But in traditional Western religion, the independence of

God from the universe He created is an all-important belief. Philosophers and theologians refer to this independence as the **transcendence** of God. (Don't confuse this word with the adjective "transcendental" we used in Chapter 4.) We say that God "transcends" the universe and mankind. We also say that He "transcends" all human experience. It is this notion of transcendence that raises an immediate epistemological problem. If God transcends our experience, how can we know that He exists at all? If He is outside of our every possible experience, if we cannot see, hear, or touch Him, what possible evidence can we have for His existence? And how would we have any way of knowing what He must be like?

In some ancient religions, gods and goddesses were very much like human beings. They were usually stronger and perhaps smarter. They lived forever and had powers of special kinds (for example, they could change into animals at will, or cause changes in the weather with a snap of their fingers). The Greek and Roman gods, for example, were like this. They took sides and even fought in the Trojan War; they often misbehaved and became jealous or furious at one another. Philosophers use the word **anthropomorphism** when they refer to the perception of gods as more or less human. It is quite natural, when people try to envision their deities, that they should endow them with those characteristics they understand best, human characteristics.

The God of Judaism and Christianity is much less anthropomorphic than the gods and goddesses of ancient Greece and Rome. But it would be a mistake to deny that God is conceived in certain anthropomorphic ways as well. The God of the Hebrews frequently took their side in battle in the Old Testament, helping them to fell the walls of Jericho, keeping the sun still for extra hours, or holding apart the waters of the Red Sea. The God of the Old Testament has many human emotions: He becomes jealous or angry when His commands are not carried out, having people swallowed by whales and sometimes destroying whole cities. Even the notion that God is a loving God carries with it anthropomorphism. It is often said that these are mere approximations, based on the fact that we can never really know or understand what God is like. (For example, it is said that we cannot understand divine love and use our all too human conception of love as the only example we can find.) But it must also be said that such anthropomorphic projections are in no way an objection to a belief in God; it is only to be expected that people will try to understand religion in those terms they know best. The biblical emphasis on God's sense of justice and His concern for mankind also demonstrates anthropomorphic characteristics, even if it is true, as we are so often told, that God's conception of justice may be very different from our own. And these characteristics are so important that if a person does not believe that God is a merciful and concerned being with a strong sense of justice, then that person probably does not believe in God at all. (For example, a person might believe in something like Aristotle's "prime mover," a first force that gets the universe moving, but it is highly debatable whether that should count as a "belief in God.") Prayer is meaningful only on the assumption that God listens to us and understands us; faith is intelligible only on the assumption that God cares about us. Without these characteristics, God would not be a moral force in our lives.

The traditional conception of God has been varied in so many ways that we can't even begin to consider them. The differences between the God of the Old Testament and the God of the New Testament have been often discussed. Then there are the obvious differences between the various sects of Judaism and Christianity. And the differences between the Judeo-Christian God and other gods (Zeus, Krishna, Isis) are so enormous that traditional Christians and Jews would hesitate to call these "God" at all. Furthermore, there are religions that do not have any god at all. But for our purposes in this chapter, it will be more than enough to stay within the bounds of our own traditions. (At the end of this chapter, we shall briefly discuss two alternative conceptions of God, in Hinduism and Buddhism.) Without considering the more modern variations of Judaism and Christianity or the sometimes considerable differences among their various sects, let us say that a person who believes in God with our previously enumerated characteristics (an independent Being, who is the Creator of the universe, all-powerful and all-knowing, and is rational, moral, concerned for man, with a perfect sense of justice) is a **theist,** a believer, whether Jewish, Catholic, Protestant, or Muslim. To refuse to believe in God is to be an **atheist.** (Spinoza was treated as an atheist in his time even though he believed in something he called "God," because it lacked most of the characteristics just described.) To admit one's ignorance, and simply accept the fact that one does not know and perhaps has no way of knowing whether there is such a being or not, is to be an **agnostic.**

CAN WE KNOW THAT GOD EXISTS?

It is one thing to be taught that there is a God; it is another to believe in God for good reason, rationally, and to know what one believes. Of course, there have been many people who have insisted that belief in God is not a matter of rationality or knowledge at all but only of faith. But the turn to faith logically comes after attempts to know. The early Jews and Christians would not talk simply of "faith"; they claimed to know. So before we turn to examine faith, let us ask whether or not we can know that God exists.

The problem is a familiar one. Since God by definition transcends our experience, how can we have evidence for His existence? It is the same problem we faced with substance (and it is for that reason that God and substance are so easily interchanged in metaphysics, as for example, in Spinoza). There are people who claim to have been direct witnesses to miracles or to have heard God's own voice. But, assuming that none of us is one of them, our problem remains: Should we believe their reports? Might they have been victims of imagination or hallucination? Is there any evidence in our experience that would allow us to know of God's existence? And if not, what reasons can we give for a belief in God?

In the long history of Christian theology, three major sets of "proofs" have emerged as attempts to demonstrate God's existence. Each has received various formulations, and all are still being discussed today. They are called, (1) the *ontological argument*, (2) the *cosmological argument*, and (3) the *teleological argument*.

The Ontological Argument

The **ontological argument** is the most difficult, for it is a purely logical proof; it attempts to argue from the idea of God to His necessary existence. It is this argument that Descartes used in his *Meditations* to prove God's existence from the idea that he (Descartes) had of Him. Similar arguments were to be found in both Spinoza and Leibniz. But the man who is generally credited with the invention of the argument is an eleventh-century monk named Saint Anselm. Because the argument depends wholly on the idea of God's existence, it is called *ontological.* Here is how Anselm presents it:

the Ontological Argument, by Saint Anselm

Some time ago, at the urgent request of some of my brethren, I published a brief work, as an example of meditation on the grounds of faith. I wrote it in the role of one who seeks, by silent reasoning with himself, to learn what he does not know. But when I reflected on this little book, and saw that it was put together as a long chain of arguments, I began to ask myself whether *one* argument might possibly be found, resting on no other argument for its proof, but sufficient in itself to prove that God truly exists, and that he is the supreme good, needing nothing outside himself, but needful for the being and well-being of all things. I often turned my earnest attention to this problem, and at times I believed that I could put my finger on what I was looking for, but at other times it completely escaped my mind's eye, until finally, in despair, I decided to give up searching for something that seemed impossible to find. But when I tried to put the whole question out of my mind, so as to avoid crowding out other matters, with which I might make some progress, by this useless preoccupation, then, despite my unwillingness and resistance, it began to force itself on me more persistently than ever. Then, one day, when I was worn out by my vigorous resistance to the obsession, the solution I had ceased to hope for presented itself to me, in the very turmoil of my thoughts, so that I enthusiastically embraced the idea which in my disquiet, I had spurned.

· · · · ·

GOD TRULY IS

And so, O Lord, since thou givest understanding to faith, give me to understand — as far as thou knowest it to be good for me — that thou dost exist, as we believe, and that thou art what we believe thee to be. Now we believe that thou art a being than which none greater can be thought. Or can it be that there is no such being, since "the fool hath said in his heart, 'There is no God'"? But when this same fool hears what I am saying — "A being than which none greater can be thought" — he understands what he hears, and what he understands is in his understanding, even if he does not understand that it exists. For it is one thing for an object to be in the understanding, and another thing to understand that it exists. When a painter considers beforehand what he is going to paint, he has it in his understanding, but he does not suppose that what he has not yet painted already exists. But when he has painted it, he both has it in his understanding and understands that what he has now produced exists. Even the fool, then, must be convinced that a being than which none greater can be thought exists at least in his understanding, since when he hears this he understands it, and whatever is understood is in the understanding. But clearly that than which a greater cannot be thought cannot exist in the understanding alone. For if it is actually in the understanding alone, it can be thought of as existing also in reality, and this is greater. Therefore, if that than which a greater cannot be thought is in the understanding alone, this same thing than which a greater cannot be thought is that than which a greater can be thought. But obviously this is impossible. Without doubt, therefore, there exists, both in the understanding and in reality, something than which a greater cannot be thought.

GOD CANNOT BE THOUGHT OF AS NONEXISTENT

And certainly it exists so truly that it cannot be thought of as nonexistent. For something can be thought of as existing, which cannot be thought of as not existing, and this is greater than that which *can* be thought of as not existing. Thus, if that than which a greater cannot be thought can be thought of as not existing, this very thing than which a greater cannot be thought is *not* that than which a greater cannot be thought. But this is contradictory. So, then, there truly is a being than which a greater cannot be thought — so truly that it cannot even be thought of as not existing.

And *thou* art this being, O Lord our God. Thou so truly are, then, O Lord my God, that thou canst not even be thought of as not existing. And this is right. For if some mind could think of something better than thou, the creature would rise above the Creator and judge its Creator; but this is altogether absurd. And indeed, whatever is, except thyself alone, can be thought of as not existing. Thou alone, therefore, of all beings, has being in the truest and highest sense, since no other being so truly exists, and thus every other being has less being. Why, then, has "the fool said in his heart, 'There is no God,'" when it is so obvious to the rational mind that, of all beings, thou dost exist supremely? Why indeed, unless it is that he is a stupid fool?

HOW THE FOOL HAS SAID IN HIS HEART
WHAT CANNOT BE THOUGHT

But how did he manage to say in his heart what he could not think? Or how is it that he was unable to think what he said in his heart? After all, to say in one's heart and to think are the same thing. Now if it is true — or, rather, since it is true — that he thought it, because he said it in his heart, but did not say it in his heart, since he could not think it, it is clear that something can be said in one's heart or thought in more than one way. For we think of a thing, in one sense, when we think of the word that signifies it, and in another sense, when we understand the very thing itself. Thus, in the first sense God can be thought of as nonexistent, but in the second sense this is quite impossible. For no one who understands what God is can think that God does not exist, even though he says these words in his heart — perhaps without any meaning, perhaps with some quite extraneous meaning. For God is that than which a greater cannot be thought, and whoever understands this rightly must understand that he exists in such a way that he cannot be nonexistent even in thought. He, therefore, who understands that God thus exists cannot think of him as nonexistent.

Thanks be to thee, good Lord, thanks be to thee, because I now understand by thy light what I formerly believed by thy gift, so that even if I were to refuse to believe in thy existence, I could not fail to understand its truth.[1]

The logic of the argument is deceptively simple: God is defined, innocently enough, as "a being greater than which none can be thought." Then, Anselm asks, "which would be greater, a being who is merely thought, or a being who actually exists?" The answer, of course, is a being who actually exists. But since God is, by definition, the greatest being who can be thought, He must therefore exist. "God cannot be nonexistent even in thought." Anselm goes on to argue that the idea of an eternal being who either does not yet exist or no longer exists is self-contradictory, so that the very idea we have of such a being requires existence. It is worth noting that, while formulating the ontological argument, Anselm was also putting into place some of the final ingredients in the Christian conception of God, as not only a perfect or even the most perfect being but rather as the greatest (most perfect) *conceivable* being.

The argument has had a long, influential history, and logicians are still arguing about it. The argument was not seriously altered for five centuries, when Descartes took up Anselm's argument and gave it its modern formulation. In the seventeenth century, Descartes (in his *Meditations*) made explicit the presupposition of the argument, that existence is a property which, like color, shape, weight, and charm, a thing may either have or not have. Some properties, however, are essential to a thing: three angles are essential to a triangle, spots are essential to a dalmation. So too, Descartes suggests, perfection is essential to the most perfect being, and existence is a perfection. One can no more conceive of a most perfect being without existence than one can a triangle without three angles or a dalmation without spots.

the Ontological Argument, by Descartes

But now, if just because I can draw the idea of something from my thought, it follows that all which I know clearly and distinctly as pertaining to this object does really belong to it, may I not derive from this an argument demonstrating the existence of God? It is certain that I no less find the idea of God, that is to say, the idea of a supremely perfect Being, in me,

---

[1]St. Anselm, *Proslogion*, in *A Scholastic Miscellany*, Vol. 10, The Library of Christian Classics, ed. and trans. Eugene R. Fairweather (Philadelphia: Westminster Press, 1956).

than that of any figure or number whatever it is; and I do not know any less clearly and distinctly that an [actual and] eternal existence pertains to this nature than I know that all that which I-am able to demonstrate of some figure or number truly pertains to the nature of this figure or number, and therefore, although all that I concluded in the preceding Meditations were found to be false, the existence of God would pass with me as at least as certain as I have ever held the truths of mathematics (which concern only numbers and figures) to be.

This indeed is not at first manifest, since it would seem to present some appearance of being a sophism. For being accustomed in all other things to make a distinction between existence and essence, I easily persuade myself that the existence can be separated from the essence of God, and that we can thus conceive God as not actually existing. But, nevertheless, when I think of it with more attention, I clearly see that existence can no more be separated from the essence of God than can its having its three angles equal to two right angles be separated from the essence of a [rectilinear] triangle, or the idea of a mountain from the idea of a valley; and so there is not any less repugnance to our conceiving a God (that is, a Being supremely perfect) to whom existence is lacking (that is to say, to whom a certain perfection is lacking), than to conceive of a mountain which has no valley.

But although I cannot really conceive of a God without existence any more than a mountain without a valley, still from the fact that I conceive of a mountain with a valley, it does not follow that there is such a mountain in the world; similarly although I conceive of God as possessing existence, it would seem that it does not follow that there is a God which exists; for my thought does not impose any necessity upon things, and just as I may imagine a winged horse, although no horse with wings exists, so I could perhaps attribute existence to God, although no God existed.

But a sophism is concealed in this objection; for from the fact that I cannot conceive a mountain without a valley, it does not follow that there is any mountain or any valley in existence, but only that the mountain and the valley, whether they exist or do not exist, cannot in any way be separated one from the other. While from the fact that I cannot conceive God without existence, it follows that existence is inseparable from Him, and hence that He really exists; not that my thought can bring this to pass, or impose any necessity on things, but, on the contrary, because the necessity which lies in the thing itself, i.e. the necessity of the existence of God determines me to think in this way. For it is not within my power to think of God without existence (that is of a supremely perfect Being devoid of a supreme perfection) though it is in my power to imagine a horse either with wings or without wings.

And we must not here object that it is in truth necessary for me to assert that God exists after having presupposed that He possesses every sort of perfection, since existence is one of these, but that as a matter of fact my original supposition was not necessary, just as it is not necessary to consider that all quadrilateral figures can be inscribed in the circle; for supposing I thought of this, I should be constrained to admit that the rhombus might be inscribed in the circle since it is a quadrilateral figure, which, however, is manifestly false. Although it is not necessary that I should at any time entertain the notion of God, nevertheless whenever it happens that I think of a first and a sovereign Being, and, so to speak, derive the idea of Him from the storehouse of my mind, it is necessary that I should attribute to Him every sort of perfection, although I do not get so far as to enumerate them all, or to apply my mind to each one in particular. And this necessity suffices to make me conclude (after having recognised that existence is a perfection) that this first and sovereign Being really exists; just as though it is not necessary for me ever to imagine any triangle, yet, whenever I wish to consider a rectilinear figure composed only of three angles, it is absolutely essential that I should attribute to it all those properties which serve to bring about the conclusion that its three angles are not greater than two right angles, even although I may not then be considering this point in particular. But when I consider which figures are capable of being inscribed in the circle, it is in no way necessary that I should think that all quadrilateral figures are of this number; on the contrary, I cannot even pretend that this is the case, so long as I do not desire to accept anything which I cannot conceive clearly and distinctly. And in consequence there is a great difference between the false suppositions such as this, and the true ideas born within me, the first and principal of which is that of God. For really I discern in many ways that this idea is not something factitious, and depending solely on my thought, but that it is the image of a true and immutable nature; first of all, because I cannot conceive anything but God himself to whose essence existence [necessarily] pertains; in the second place because it is not possible for me to conceive two or more Gods in this same position; and, granted that there is one such God who now exists, I see clearly that it is necessary that He should have existed from all eternity, and that He must exist eternally; and finally, because I know an infinitude of other properties in God, none of which I can either diminish or change.[2]

Descartes's version is

> I cannot conceive of a God without the property of existence.
> ("His existence cannot be separated from His essence.")
> Therefore, God exists.

and then he adds

> My conception of God is such that He has every sort of perfection.
> Existence is a perfection.
> Therefore, God necessarily exists.

These arguments are valid as stated, but are they also sound? Consider the following argument, which has been proposed in the same form as the above arguments. Define a "grenlin" as "the greenest imaginable creature." Now,

---

[2]René Descartes, "Meditation IV," in *Meditations on First Philosophy*, in *The Philosophical Works of Descartes*, trans. Elizabeth S. Haldane and G. R. T. Ross (Cambridge: Cambridge University Press, 1911).

which is greener, a green creature that does exist, or one that does not? Obviously the one that exists. Therefore, at least one grenlin exists.

It is worth noting that this objection had been raised against Anselm too, by Gaunilo of Marmoutier, who suggested the existence of an island more perfect than any other, on the same grounds that it would be contradictory for the most perfect island not to exist. Anselm replied that the argument cannot be applied to islands (or grenlins) or anything else whose nonexistence is even conceivable. The question, then, is what it means for nonexistence to be conceivable, or for existence to be a necessary property of a thing.

Descartes faced a similar challenge to his formulation when a critic attacked his analogy with triangles and insisted that, while it may be true that *if* a triangle exists, then it must have three angles, it does not follow that triangles must exist, or that any in fact do exist. Descartes' answer is similar to Anselm's response to his critic: the essence of triangle does not include the perfection of existence, as God's surely does.

The ontological argument makes a special case for God, because He is the only "greatest conceivable" or "most perfect" being. Nevertheless, the argument has made many believers uneasy, and has been dismissed as a clever trick by nonbelievers. But, whatever our unease, the argument is clearly valid. The form of Descartes' version:

$$G =_{df} \text{(the being with all perfections)}$$

or

(x)(Gx ⊃ Px)(If anything is God then it has all perfections)
(x)(Px ⊃ Ex) (If something has all perfections, then it has existence)
Therefore, (x)(Gx ⊃ Ex) (If anything is God, He exists)

The argument is a straightforward syllogism of the "All men are mortal/ Socrates is a man/ Socrates is mortal" type, the only real (but significant) difference being that, while there can be any number of men, there can be only one God, one "most perfect" being. But what we have so far taken for granted in the above presentations of the argument is the presupposition that existence is a property, like a color or a shape. One way of attacking the logic of the argument, even while accepting its validity, is to challenge this presupposition, and thus the soundness of the argument. Should we be allowed to write, in our second premise, "Ex"? In other words, is "exists" a predicate, like "barks" and "is green"? Or is it rather (as we saw in the symbolization of quantificational logic, p. 21) one of the quantifiers, like "all" and "none" and "some" (which is, essentially, "there exists at least one . . .")? The objection that "existence is not a predicate" was formulated against the ontological argument by Immanuel Kant.

The great philosopher Kant suggested that the problem lies in the central idea, shared by the ontological argument and the unacceptable arguments that follow the same form, that existence is one of the essential properties, that is, part of the definition of a thing. But existence, Kant argues, is not a property and cannot be part of a definition. In an often quoted passage of his *Critique of Pure Reason*, he argues

against the Ontological Argument, by Immanuel Kant

I answer: — Even in introducing into the concept of a thing, which you wish to think in its possibility only, the concept of its existence, under whatever disguise it may be, you have been guilty of a contradiction. If you were allowed to do this, you would apparently have carried your point; but in reality you have achieved nothing, but have only committed a tautology. I simply ask you, whether the proposition, that *this or that thing* (which, whatever it may be, I grant you as possible) *exists*, is an analytical or a synthetical proposition? If the former, then by its existence you add nothing to your thought of the thing; but in that case, either the thought within you would be the thing itself, or you have presupposed existence, as belonging to possibility, and have according to your own showing deduced existence from internal possibility, which is nothing but a miserable tautology. The mere word *reality*, which in the concept of a thing sounds different from existence in the concept of the predicate, can make no difference. For if you call all accepting or positing (without determining what it is) reality, you have placed a thing, with all its predicates, within the concept of the subject, and accepted it as real, and you do nothing but repeat it in the predicate. If, on the contrary, you admit, as every sensible man must do, that every proposition involving existence is synthetical, how can you say that the predicate of existence does not admit of removal without contradiction, a distinguishing property which is peculiar to analytical propositions only, the very character of which depends on it?

I might have hoped to put an end to this subtle argumentation, without many words, and simply by an accurate definition of the concept of existence, if I had not seen that the illusion, in mistaking a logical predicate for a real one (that is the predicate which determines a thing), resists all correction. Everything can become a *logical predicate*, even the subject itself may be predicated of itself, because logic makes no account of any contents of concepts. *Determination*, however, is a predicate, added to the concept of the subject, and enlarging it, and it must not therefore be contained in it.

Being is evidently not a real predicate, or a concept of something that can be added to the concept of a thing. It is merely the admission of a thing, and of certain determinations in it. Logically, it is merely the copula of a judgment. The proposition, *God is almighty*, contains two concepts, each having its object, namely, God and almightiness. The small word *is*, is not an additional predicate, but only serves to put the predicate *in relation* to the subject. If, then, I take the subject (God) with all its predicates (including that of almightiness), and say, *God is*, or there is a God, I do not put a new predicate to the concept of God, but I only put the subject by itself, with all its predicates, in relation to my concept, as its object. Both must contain exactly the same kind of thing, and nothing can have been added to the concept, which expresses possibility only, by my thinking its object as simply given and saying, it is. And thus the real does not contain more than the possible. A hundred real dollars do not contain a penny more than a hundred possible dollars. For as the latter signify the concept, the former the object and its position by itself, it is clear that, in case the former contained more than the latter, my concept would not express the whole object, and would not therefore be its adequate concept. In my financial position no doubt there exists more by one hundred real dollars, than by their concept only (that is their possibility), because in reality the object is not only contained analytically in my concept, but is added to my concept (which is a determination of my state), synthetically; but the conceived hundred dollars are not in the least increased through the existence which is outside my concept.[3]

What Kant is arguing is that the existence of a thing can never be merely a matter of logic. (This is what he means when he says that the proposition that a thing exists cannot be analytic.) "Existence" or "being," he argues, isn't a "real predicate" (though it is a grammatical predicate) because it does not tell us anything more about whatever is said to have existence or being. In other words, there is something odd about the statement, "this apple is red, round, ripe, and exists." What is odd is that "exists" does not give a characteristic of the apple but rather says that there is an apple with these characteristics. The proper characterization of God, therefore, includes the various characteristics we discussed earlier in this chapter, but it should not include, according to Kant, any characteristic that implies God's existence. It is one thing to say that God, if He exists, has such-and-such characteristics; it is something more to say that such a God exists. (This is what Kant means by his example about the one hundred real versus one hundred possible dollars; they both have exactly the same number of cents, but only the one hundred real dollars are worth anything.)

Many contemporary philosophers agree with Kant's argument, but many do not. Furthermore, contemporary logicians have developed versions of the ontological argument that can even dispense with this controversial notion of existence as a property. For example, with just the seemingly innocent premise "if God exists, then He necessarily exists," some logicians have recently argued according to the sophisticated rules of modern logic that the conclusion that "God exists" does follow. The premise is innocent because you can grant that "if God exists" without in any way admitting that God in fact exists. Charles Hartshorne, for example, has argued that, if our concept of God is of a being who is eternal and self-existent then the question of God's existence cannot be a contingent matter but must be a matter of logical necessity (or impossibility). An existent being, but one which we can imagine not existing, could not be God, for, following Anselm, God is the being of whom it must be said (by definition) that nothing greater is conceivable. But instead of employing the objectionable presupposition — that existence is a predicate, Hartshorne's argument simply goes on to demonstrate that there is nothing self-contradictory in the concept of such a being, and therefore we must conclude that God necessarily exists. (The presupposition here is that either a most perfect being necessarily exists or he necessarily does not exist — what logicians call "the law of the excluded middle"; in other words, there are no other possibilities.)

---

[3]Immanuel Kant, *The Critique of Pure Reason*, rev. 2nd ed., trans. Max Müller (London: Macmillan).

Whether or not the argument succeeds in its classical form, it can be understood in another way, which clearly distinguishes it from all the absurd arguments that apparently have the same form. If you believe in God, then the argument might be taken in a very different way, not as a "proof" but as an attempt to articulate your belief. The theologian Karl Barth has argued that this is what Anselm's argument really tries to do, and as you read over his argument a second or third time it becomes clear that he is expressing his faith as much as he is offering a logical proof. In general, the "proofs" of God's existence have been such articulations and expressions as well as proper logical arguments. And even if they fail as proofs, they often succeed in this other, and perhaps more important, function.

It is clear that, considered simply as a logical argument, the ontological argument does not have the power to convert nonbelievers into believers. Or if you are a believer, it is clear that an objection to the "proof" is not going to shake your faith in any way whatsoever. So the significance of the proof is ambiguous; as a logical exercise it is brilliant, as an expression of faith it may be edifying, but as an actual proof that God exists or as a means of converting atheists it seems to have no power at all.

The Cosmological Argument

The second "proof" of God's existence is a set of arguments that date back to Aristotle's argument for the prime mover. The basis of all these arguments is the intolerability if not the unthinkability of an infinite regress and the need for some ultimate explanation. Together they are called the **cosmological argument,** and their best-known formulation is by Saint Thomas Aquinas as the first three of his "five ways" of proving God's existence.

the Cosmological Argument, by Saint Thomas Aquinas

The first and more manifest way is the argument from motion. It is certain, and evident to our senses, that in the world some things are in motion. Now whatever is moved is moved by another, for nothing can be moved except it is in potentiality to that towards which it is moved whereas a thing moves inasmuch as it is in act. For motion is nothing else than the reduction of something from potentiality to actuality. But nothing can be reduced from potentiality to actuality, except by something in a state of actuality. Thus that which is actually hot, as fire, makes wood, which is potentially hot, to be actually hot, and thereby moves and changes it. Now it is not possible that the same thing should be at once in actuality and potentiality in the same respect, but only in different respects. For what is actually hot cannot simultaneously be potentially hot; but it is simultaneously potentially cold. It is therefore impossible that in the same respect and in the same way a thing should be both mover and moved, i.e., that it should move itself. Therefore, whatever is moved must be moved by another. If that by which it is moved be itself moved, then this also must needs be moved by another, and that by another again. But this cannot go on to infinity, because then there would be no first mover, and consequently, no other mover, seeing that subsequent movers move only inasmuch as they are moved by the first mover, as the staff moves only because it is moved by the hand. Therefore, it is necessary to arrive at a first mover, moved by no other; and this everyone understands to be God.

The second way is from the nature of efficient cause.[4] In the world of sensible things we find there is an order of efficient causes. There is no case known (neither is it, indeed, possible) in which a thing is found to be the efficient cause of itself; for so it would be prior to itself, which is impossible. Now in efficient causes it is not possible to go on to infinity, because in all efficient causes following in order, the first is the cause of the intermediate cause, and the intermediate is the cause of the ultimate cause, whether the intermediate cause be several, or one only. Now to take away the cause is to take away the effect. Therefore, if there be no first cause among efficient causes, there will be no ultimate, nor any intermediate, cause. But if in efficient causes it is possible to go on to infinity, there will be no first efficient cause, neither will there be an ultimate effect, nor any intermediate efficient causes; all of which is plainly false. Therefore it is necessary to admit a first efficient cause, to which everyone gives the name of God.

The third way is taken from possibility and necessity, and runs thus. We find in nature things that are possible to be and not to be, since they are found to be generated, and to be corrupted, and consequently, it is possible for them to be and not to be. But it is impossible for these always to exist, for that which can not-be at some time is not. Therefore, if everything can not-be, then at one time there was nothing in existence. Now if this were true, even now there would be nothing in existence, because that which does not exist begins to exist only through something already existing. Therefore, if at one time nothing was in existence, it would have been impossible for anything to have begun to exist; and thus even now nothing would be in existence—which is absurd. Therefore, not all beings are merely possible, but there must exist something the existence of which is necessary. But every necessary thing either has its necessity caused by another, or not. Now it is impossible to go on to infinity in necessary things which have their necessity caused by another, as has been already proved in regard to efficient causes. Therefore we cannot but admit the existence of some being having of itself its own necessity, and not receiving it from another, but rather causing in others their necessity. This all men speak of as God.

And in his "fourth way," Aquinas combines the form of the cosmological argument with some of the ideas from the ontological argument:

The fourth way is taken from the gradation to be found in things. Among beings there are some more and some less good, true, noble, and the

---

[4]An *efficient cause* is an event (or an agent) that brings something about. The term comes from Aristotle. See glossary to Chapter 2, "cause."

like. But *more* and *less* are predicated of different things according as they resemble in their different ways something which is the maximum, as a thing is said to be hotter according as it more nearly resembles that which is hottest; so that there is something which is truest, something best, something noblest, and, consequently, something which is most being, for those things that are greatest in truth are greatest in being, as it is written in [Aristotle's] *Metaphysics*. . . . Now the maximum in any genus is the cause of all in that genus, as fire, which is the maximum of heat, is the cause of all hot things, as is said in the same book. Therefore, there must also be something which is to all beings the cause of their being, goodness, and every other perfection; and this we call God.[5]

The cosmological argument, in all of these versions, is also both an attempt at "proof" and an expression of one's belief in God. Accordingly, it must be appreciated for its role in articulating the concept of God in traditional Christianity and evaluated as a logical argument. As a logical argument, there are two modern objections that seem to have considerable weight. First, even if the argument is formally valid, it proves only that there is some "first mover" or "first cause" or "necessary being." It does not prove that this being has all of the other attributes that allow us to recognize God. (Aquinas's fourth "way," however, includes moral attributes of perfection as well.) Taken at face value, the first three versions of the cosmological argument are similar to Aristotle's argument for the "prime mover" (Chapter 1) except that Aquinas takes the "first cause" to be an "efficient" as well as "final" cause, that is, as the creator as well as the meaning of the universe. Furthermore, Aristotle (in his *Physics*) allows that there might be several prime movers, while Aquinas is clear that there can be only one. Nevertheless, one might accept the argument and believe only in a "first cause" and deny the existence of God. Or if it is accepted that there must be a first cause, why could the universe itself not be its own cause? In current physics, scientists would argue that this idea is just as plausible as the idea that there must have been something else that caused our universe to exist. And this leads us to the second objection, which would have been unthinkable to Aquinas (or Aristotle), but is generally accepted today. The idea of an "infinite regress," that the universe did not have a beginning but has always existed, seemed like an obvious absurdity until the last century. But now, even though scientists and mathematicians talk about the beginning of the universe and the relativity of time, they no longer consider an infinite regress as necessarily impossible. And without the idea that every infinite regress is an absurdity, the cosmological argument loses its main premise.

In fact, Aquinas admits that there is no valid argument against the claim that God and the universe existed for all eternity, but he has another argument to help him here. He says that the beginning of the universe required an *act*, which means that the universe could not have been the cause of itself. Furthermore,

---

[5]St. Thomas Aquinas, *Summa Theologica*, trans. Fathers of the English Dominican Province (New York: Benziger, Bruce & Glencoe, 1948).

even if the universe existed eternally, it would still require a prime mover to keep it in motion. Therefore, he concludes, God must exist even if the infinite regress argument by itself does not prove this.

The Teleological Argument

The third "proof" of God's existence is the one that is probably most familiar to you. It is usually called "the argument from design." Immanuel Kant called it the **teleological argument.** It is often the most universally appealing of the three arguments because it depends as much on our emotions and our sense of wonder as it does on logical principles. The classical form of the argument goes like this. Suppose you are walking across a deserted beach and come across a watch, lying in the sand. You immediately conclude, "people have been here." Why? Because it is highly unlikely that a mechanism as intricately designed as a watch might be thrown together by the chance forces of nature. A pebble on the beach might be curiously shaped, but anything approaching the complexity of a tool or a piece of sculpture, much less a complex mechanism, would strike us as proof of some intelligent being. Now, looking at the universe, it is easy to wonder at its complexity, the intricate workings of the heavens or even a single-celled organism and the grand variety and interconnection of all living things. And from this, one concludes that the universe as a whole must have been rationally designed. No less a scientist than Albert Einstein, for example, has argued that it is this religious awe and appreciation for the complex regularities and "design" of nature that has spawned the great efforts of science to understand it.

on the Design of the Universe, by Albert Einstein

It is easy to see why the churches have always fought science and per-secuted its devotees. On the other hand, I maintain that the cosmic religious feeling is the strongest and noblest motive for scientific research. Only those who realize the immense efforts and, above all, the devotion without which pioneer work in theoretical science cannot be achieved are able to grasp the strength of the emotion out of which alone such work, remote as it is from the immediate realities of life, can issue. What a deep conviction of the rationality of the universe and what a yearning to understand, were it but a feeble reflection of the mind revealed in this world, Kepler and Newton must have had to enable them to spend years of solitary labor in disentan-gling the principles of celestial mechanics! Those whose acquaintance with scientific research is derived chiefly from its practical results easily develop a completely false notion of the mentality of the men who, surrounded by a skeptical world, have shown the way to kindred spirits scattered wide through the world and the centuries. Only one who has devoted his life to similar ends can have a vivid realization of what has inspired these men and given them the strength to remain true to their purpose in spite of countless failures. It is cosmic religious feeling that gives a man such strength. A contemporary has said, not unjustly, that in this materialistic age of ours the serious scientific workers are the only profoundly religious people.[6]

Einstein's statement of scientific faith is particularly important in times when science and religion seem once again at each other's throats. Current controversies over "Creation" versus "evolution," for example, have made it seem as if science and religion are utterly irreconcilable, with completely opposed visions of the world. One of the great advantages of the teleological argument or "argument from design," therefore, is the fact that it uses the discoveries of science as support for religious belief, and at the same time encourages scientists with the assurance that the world really is divinely designed in marvelous ways. Consider in much the same vein some recent remarks by Cambridge physicist Stephen Hawking, who is at the forefront of new investigations into the origins of the universe:

on God and the Universe, by Stephen Hawking

Hawking once told an interviewer that he wanted to know why the universe exists at all and why it is as it is. I quote that back to him and ask if his search has a religious component. "I suppose so. But I would have thought that everyone would want to know that." Is the search in competition with religion? "If one took that attitude," he replies, "then Newton"—a very religious man—"would not have discovered the law of gravity."

"The whole history of human thought has been to try to understand what the universe was like. I think you can do that without prejudice as to the idea that God exists. Even if God created the universe, we want to know what it is like." I start to ask a clarifying question, but he interrupts me. "One attitude would be that God set up the universe in a completely arbitrary way, with all that anyone can say about anything is that it is just the will of God. But in fact, the more we examine the universe, we find it is not arbitrary at all but obeys certain well-defined laws that operate in different areas. It seems very reasonable to suppose that there may be some unifying principles, so that all laws are part of some bigger law. So what we are trying to find out is whether there is some bigger law from which all other laws can be derived. I think you can ask that question whether or not you believe in God."

For some people, I remind him, the existence of God is a satisfactory answer to all the questions he is dealing with. "Yes, but it is certainly not to me. I don't think that it answers anything. Whether you say that God created the universe does not really make any difference. I would regard it as a very meaningless statement, unless you're going to attach some other

[6]Albert Einstein, "Religion and Science," in *Ideas and Opinions*, trans. Sonia Bargmann (New York: Crown, 1954).

attributes to God. I'm not sure that I believe anything else about God. If that is the only attribute, then it is an unnecessary concept, because it doesn't have any consequences."

Yet man does need to explain the Beginning, the First Cause. How did it all start — and what existed to make a start possible? Science has not achieved that explanation, and the theoretical physicists are still searching. "I have an idea that people would feel happier with the idea of a big bang than of a universe that existed forever and ever," says Hawking. "The big bang may not be very like Genesis, but at least you can regard it as a creation, and you can invoke God as the creator. But if you had a universe that existed forever, people might feel there was not much room for God. I was at a conference on cosmology at the Vatican last year, and the Roman Catholic Church seems to be very happy with the idea of the big bang."[7]

And, classically, the teleological argument is Aquinas's "fifth way":

the "Fifth Way,"
by Saint Thomas Aquinas

The fifth way is taken from the governance of the world. We see that things which lack knowledge, such as natural bodies, act for an end, and this is evident from their acting always, or nearly always in the same way, so as to obtain the best result. Hence it is plain that they achieve their end, not fortuitously, but designedly. Now whatever lacks knowledge cannot move towards an end, unless it be directed by some being endowed with knowledge and intelligence; as the arrow is directed by the archer. Therefore some intelligent being exists by whom all natural things are directed to their end; and this being we call God.[8]

The argument is powerful psychologically, but it too has its problems. Like the earlier two arguments, it may prove much less about God than the theist needs to be proven. The God who has rationally designed the universe need not have the slightest concern for humankind, for example. He may well consider us just one of those little curiosities of evolution that, for a few thousand years, interfered with His other interests. But there are other problems peculiar to this argument. It is easily mocked, and Voltaire, who was around when the argument was most popular, parodied its logic in *Candide* (by suggesting that, among other things, it was marvelous that God gave us noses so that we can wear eye-glasses.) About the same time, the German Enlightenment writer Georg Christoph Lichtenberg commented that it was clever of God to put holes in the cat's skin right where his eyes are. These nonsensical comments make an important point, however. The "design" in nature appears as such only to one who is already predisposed to believe in a designer. This is most powerfully presented by David Hume in his blasphemous (and therefore posthumous) *Dialogues on Natural Religion*:

[7]From *The New York Times*, Jan. 23, 1983.
[8]Aquinas, *Summa Theologica*.

an Imperfect Universe,
by David Hume

In a word, Cleanthes, a man who follows your hypothesis is able, perhaps, to assert or conjecture that the universe sometime arose from something like design; but beyond that position he cannot ascertain one single circumstance and is left afterwards to fix every point of his theology by the utmost license of fancy and hypothesis. This world, for aught he knows, is very faulty and imperfect compared to a superior standard and was only the first rude essay of some infant deity who afterwards abandoned it, ashamed of his lame performance; it is the work only of some dependent, inferior deity and is the object of derision to his superiors; it is the production of old age and dotage in some superannuated deity and, ever since his death, has run on at adventures from the first impulse and active force which it received from him.[9]

Hume's argument is, quite simply, that this is not a perfect world, which means that the God who supposedly designed it cannot be perfect either. And one can even wonder whether a universe that has been so badly designed has been designed at all. But Cleanthes replies that he rejects both the suppositions and the tone of these sarcastic remarks and even insists that the argument that the universe is badly designed presupposes a designer. There are more powerful replies, however: that the world is in fact designed as well as it could possibly be, or else that it is a design that has not yet been fully realized and has not yet come to its full perfection.

The credibility of the argument from design has suffered enormously (but perhaps needlessly) from the shock of Darwin's theory of evolution. Accordingly, the Christian Church has combatted the latter with all of the resources at its command. But the battle has been largely unnecessary and, if anything, has falsely overemphasized the conflict between science and religion, weakening the credibility of the Church. For evolution does not deny the argument from design. It only changes the argument from the traditional idea that God created the universe all at once (though even in Genesis, He spread it out over several days) to the idea that He created it over a long period of time, using "natural selection" as one of His tools.

But the logic of evolution does undermine the appeal of the argument from design in a more subtle way. The power of the argument is, boiled down to essentials, "Isn't it marvelous that things are as they are!" But our "marvel" depends on our putting some premium on "the way things are." We place a high premium on "the way things are" because according to the laws of probability (or chance) the odds against this way are enormous. Now consider the following analogy: you are playing cards, stud poker, and the dealer gives you excellent hands twice in a row. You would be suspicious. The odds are against it. And, particularly if you

---

[9]David Hume, *Dialogues on Natural Religion*, ed. Norman Kemp Smith (Oxford: Oxford University Press, 1935).

lose both times, you will be certain that some "design" (namely, the dealer's) is behind it. But now, why would you not have the same suspicions given any two consecutive hands, for the odds are exactly the same against any combination of cards? (The odds against receiving any one hand of five cards twice are 2.6 million to one.) The answer, of course, has nothing to do with the "likelihood" of getting one set of hands rather than another but with the significance you place on the one combination rather than the other. So too, with the argument from design. Evolution has given the world many different "ways that things are" and will give it many more. The reason for our marveling at this particular "way that things are" is that we suppose that the odds against it are uniquely high. But they are not. They are equally high against every other possible "way that things are," and so this "way" seems to deserve no special explanation. This does not deny "design," of course; it only emphasizes the importance of a certain way of seeing the world, a way shared by science and nature-lovers as well as theists.

Wittgenstein summed up this view towards the argument from design in a phrase: "What is remarkable is not how things are, but that they are at all." (This turns us back to the cosmological argument.) Or consider the following parable by one of Wittgenstein's students, John Wisdom:

from "Gods," by John Wisdom

Two people return to their long neglected garden and find among the weeds a few of the old plants surprisingly vigorous. One says to the other "It must be that a gardener has been coming and doing something about these plants." Upon inquiry they find that no neighbor has ever seen anyone at work in their garden. The first man says to the other "He must have worked while people slept." The other says "No, someone would have heard him and besides, anybody who cared about the plants would have kept down these weeds." The first man says "Look at the way these are arranged. There is purpose and a feeling for beauty here. I believe that someone comes, someone invisible to mortal eyes. I believe that the more carefully we look the more we shall find confirmation of this." They examine the garden ever so carefully and sometimes they come on new things suggesting that a gardener comes and sometimes they come on new things suggesting the contrary and even that a malicious person has been at work. Besides examining the garden carefully they also study what happens to gardens left without attention. Each learns all the other learns about this and about the garden. Consequently, when after all this, one says "I still believe a gardener comes" while the other says "I don't" their different words now reflect no difference as to what they have found in the garden, no difference as to what they would find in the garden if they looked further, and no difference about how fast untended gardens fall into disorder. At this stage, in this context, the gardener hypothesis has ceased to be experimental; the difference between one who accepts and one who rejects it is now not a matter of the one expecting something the other does not expect. What is the difference between them? The one says: "A gardener comes unseen and unheard. He is manifested only in his works with which we are all familiar." The other says "There is no gardener." And with this difference in what they say about the gardener goes a difference in how they feel toward the garden, in spite of the fact that neither expects anything of it which the other does not expect.

But is this the whole difference between them — that the one calls the garden by one name and feels one way toward it, while the other calls it by another name and feels in another way toward it? And if this is what the difference has become, then is it any longer appropriate to ask "Which is right?" or "Which is reasonable?"[10]

WHAT IS RELIGIOUS BELIEF?

Like the other two classical arguments, the teleological argument may not be a proper "proof" of God's existence so much as an expression of belief in Him. So considered, the argument may be extremely important even if it is not formally valid. In fact, it may not be the case that religious beliefs are best construed as assertions about the nature of the world at all. In a now famous symposium of thirty years ago, three British philosophers argued about just this problem. The three philosophers are Antony Flew, who pursues an argument derived from Hume; R. M. Hare (also following Hume), who argues that the attempt to explain the universe may not be the point of religion and that it doesn't matter if nothing could count against religions beliefs; and Basil Mitchell, who also argues that explanation is not primary to religion, but rather that the key ingredient must be "faith."

ANTONY FLEW

Let us begin with a parable. It is a parable developed from a tale told by John Wisdom in his haunting and revelatory article 'Gods.' Once upon a time two explorers came upon a clearing in the jungle. In the clearing were growing many flowers and many weeds. One explorer says, 'Some gardener must tend this plot.' The other disagrees, 'There is no gardener.' So they pitch their tents and set a watch. No gardener is ever seen. 'But perhaps he is an invisible gardener.' So they set up a barbed-wire fence. They electrify it. They patrol with bloodhounds. (For they remember how H. G. Wells's *The Invisible Man* could be both smelt and touched though he could not be seen.) But no shrieks ever suggest that some intruder has received a shock. No movements of the wire ever betray an invisible climber. The bloodhounds never give cry. Yet still the Believer is not convinced. 'But there is a gardener, invisible, intangible, insensible to electric shocks, a gardener who has no scent and makes no sound, a gardener who comes secretly to look after the garden which he loves.' At last the Sceptic despairs, 'But what remains of your original assertion? Just how does what you call an

[10]John Wisdom, "Gods," in *Proceedings of the Aristotelean Society*, XLV (London: Harrison & Sons, 1944–45).

invisible, intangible, eternally elusive gardener differ from an imaginary gardener or even from no gardener at all?'

In this parable we can see how what starts as an assertion, that something exists or that there is some analogy between certain complexes of phenomena, may be reduced step by step to an altogether different status, to an expression perhaps of a 'picture preference.' The Sceptic says there is no gardener. The Believer says there is a gardener (but invisible, etc.). One man talks about sexual behaviour. Another man prefers to talk of Aphrodite (but knows that there is not really a superhuman person additional to, and somehow responsible for, all sexual phenomena). The process of qualification may be checked at any point before the original assertion is completely withdrawn and something of that first assertion will remain (Tautology). Mr. Wells's invisible man could not, admittedly, be seen, but in all other respects he was a man like the rest of us. But though the process of qualification may be, and of course usually is, checked in time, it is not always judiciously so halted. Someone may dissipate his assertion completely without noticing that he has done so. A fine brash hypothesis may thus be killed by inches, the death by a thousand qualifications.

And in this, it seems to me, lies the peculiar danger, the endemic evil, of theological utterance. Take such utterances as 'God has a plan,' 'God created the world,' 'God loves us as a father loves his children.' They look at first sight very much like assertions, vast cosmological assertions. Of course, this is no sure sign that they either are, or are intended to be, assertions. But let us confine ourselves to the cases where those who utter such sentences intend them to express assertions. (Merely remarking parenthetically that those who intend or interpret such utterances as crypto-commands, expressions of wishes, disguised ejaculations, concealed ethics, or as anything else but assertions, are unlikely to succeed in making them either properly orthodox or practically effective.)

Now to assert that such and such is the case is necessarily equivalent to denying that such and such is not the case. Suppose then that we are in doubt as to what someone who gives vent to an utterance is asserting, or suppose that, more radically, we are sceptical as to whether he is really asserting anything at all, one way of trying to understand (or perhaps it will be to expose) his utterance is to attempt to find what he would regard as counting against, or as being incompatible with, its truth. For if the utterance is indeed an assertion, it will necessarily be equivalent to a denial of the negation of that assertion. And anything which would count against the assertion, or which would induce the speaker to withdraw it and to admit that it had been mistaken, must be part of (or the whole of) the meaning of the negation of that assertion. And to know the meaning of the negation of an assertion, is as near as makes no matter, to know the meaning of that assertion. And if there is nothing which a putative assertion denies then there is nothing which it asserts either: and so it is not really an assertion. When the Sceptic in the parable asked the Believer, 'Just how does what you call an invisible, intangible, eternally elusive gardener differ from an imaginary gardener or even from no gardener at all?' he was suggesting that the Believer's earlier statement had been so eroded by qualification that it was no longer an assertion at all.

Now it often seems to people who are not religious as if there was no conceivable event or series of events the occurrence of which would be admitted by sophisticated religious people to be a sufficient reason for conceding 'there wasn't a God after all' or 'God does not really love us then.' Someone tells us that God loves us as a father loves his children. We are reassured. But then we see a child dying of inoperable cancer of the throat. His earthly father is driven frantic in his efforts to help, but his Heavenly Father reveals no obvious sign of concern. Some qualification is made — God's love is 'not a merely human love' or it is 'an unscrutable love,' perhaps — and we realize that such sufferings are quite compatible with the truth of the assertion that 'God loves us as a father (but, of course, ...).' We are reassured again. But then perhaps we ask: what is this assurance of God's (appropriately qualified) love worth, what is this apparent guarantee really a guarantee against? Just what would have to happen not merely (morally and wrongly) to tempt but also (logically and rightly) to entitle us to say 'God does not love us' or even 'God does not exist'? I therefore put to the succeeding symposiasts the simple central questions, 'What would have to occur or to have occurred to constitute for you a disproof of the love of, or of the existence of, God?'

R. M. HARE

I wish to make it clear that I shall not try to defend Christianity in particular, but religion in general — not because I do not believe in Christianity, but because you cannot understand what Christianity is, until you have understood what religion is.

I must begin by confessing that, on the ground marked out by Flew, he seems to me to be completely victorious. I therefore shift my ground by relating another parable. A certain lunatic is convinced that all dons want to murder him. His friends introduce him to all the mildest and most respectable dons that they can find, and after each of them has retired, they say, 'You see, he doesn't really want to murder you; he spoke to you in the most cordial manner; surely you are convinced now?' But the lunatic replies, 'Yes, but that was only his diabolical cunning; he's really plotting against me the whole time, like the rest of them; I know it I tell you.' However many kindly dons are produced, the reaction is still the same.

Now we say that such a person is deluded. But what is he deluded about? About the truth or falsity of an assertion? Let us apply Flew's test to him. There is no behaviour of dons that can be enacted which he will accept as counting against his theory; and therefore his theory, on this test, asserts nothing. But it does not follow that there is no difference between what he thinks about dons and what most of us think about them — otherwise we should not call him a lunatic and ourselves sane, and dons would have no reason to feel uneasy about his presence in Oxford.

Let us call that in which we differ from the lunatic, our respective *bliks*. He has an insane *blik* about dons; we have a sane one. It is important to realize that we have a sane one, not no *blik* at all; for there must be two sides to any argument — if he has a wrong *blik*, then those who are right about dons must have a right one. Flew has shown that a *blik* does not consist in an assertion or system of them; but nevertheless it is very important to have the right *blik*.

Let us try to imagine what it would be like to have different *bliks* about other things than dons. When I am driving my car, it sometimes occurs to me to wonder whether my movements of the steering-wheel will always continue to be followed by corresponding alterations in the direction of the car. I have never had a steering failure, though I have had skids, which must be similar. Moreover, I know enough about how the steering of my car is made, to know the sort of thing that would have to go wrong for the steering to fail—steel joints would have to part, or steel rods break, or something—but how do I know that this won't happen? The truth is, I don't know; I just have a *blik* about steel and its properties, so that normally I trust the steering of my car; but I find it not at all difficult to imagine what it would be like to lose this *blik* and acquire the opposite one. People would say I was silly about steel; but there would be no mistaking the reality of the difference between our respective *bliks*—for example, I should never go in a motorcar. Yet I should hesitate to say that the difference between us was the difference between contradictory assertions. No amount of safe arrivals or bench-tests will remove my *blik* and restore the normal one; for my *blik* is compatible with any finite number of such tests.

It was Hume who taught us that our whole commerce with the world depends upon our *blik* about the world; and that difference between *bliks* about the world cannot be settled by observation of what happens in the world. That was why, having performed the interesting experiment of doubting the ordinary man's *blik* about the world, and showing that no proof could be given to make us adopt one *blik* rather than another, he turned to backgammon to take his mind off the problem. It seems, indeed, to be impossible even to formulate as an assertion the normal *blik* about the world which makes me put my confidence in the future reliability of steel joints, in the continued ability of the road to support my car, and not gape beneath it revealing nothing below; in the general non-homicidal tendencies of dons; in my own continued well-being (in some sense of that word that I may not now fully understand) if I continue to do what is right according to my lights; in the general likelihood of people like Hitler coming to a bad end. But perhaps a formulation less inadequate than most is to be found in the Psalms: 'The earth is weak and all the inhabiters thereof: I bear up the pillars of it.'

The mistake of the position which Flew selects for attack is to regard this kind of talk as some sort of *explanation*, as scientists are accustomed to use the word. As such, it would obviously be ludicrous. We no longer believe in God as an Atlas—*nous n'avons pas besoin de cette hypothèse*. But it is nevertheless true to say that, as Hume saw, without a *blik* there can be no explanation; for it is by our *bliks* that we decide what is and what is not an explanation. Suppose we believe that everything that happened, happened by pure chance. This would not of course be an assertion; for it is compatible with anything happening or not happening, and so, incidentally, is its contradictory. But if we had this belief, we should not be able to explain or predict or plan anything. Thus, although we should not be *asserting* anything different from those of a more normal belief, there would be a great difference between us; and this is the sort of difference that there is between those who really believe in God and those who really disbelieve in him.

The word 'really' is important, and may excite suspicion. I put it in, because when people have had a good Christian upbringing, as have most of those who now profess not to believe in any sort of religion, it is very hard to discover what they really believe. The reason why they find it so easy to think that they are not religious, is that they have never got into the frame of mind of one who suffers from the doubts to which religion is the answer. Not for them the terrors of the primitive jungle. Having abandoned some of the more picturesque fringes of religion, they think that they have abandoned the whole thing — whereas in fact they still have got, and could not live without, a religion of a comfortably substantial, albeit highly sophisticated, kind, which differs from that of many 'religious people' in little more than this, that 'religious people' like to sing Psalms about theirs — a very natural and proper thing to do. But nevertheless there may be a big difference lying behind — the difference between two people who, though side by side, are walking in different directions. I do not know in what direction Flew is walking; perhaps he does not know either. But we have had some examples recently of various ways in which one can walk away from Christianity, and there are any number of possibilities. After all, man has not changed biologically since primitive times; it is his religion that has changed, and it can easily change again. And if you do not think that such changes make a difference, get acquainted with some Sikhs and some Mussulmans of the same Punjabi stock; you will find them quite different sorts of people.

There is an important difference between Flew's parable and my own which we have not yet noticed. The explorers do not *mind* about their garden; they discuss it with interest, but not with concern. But my lunatic, poor fellow, minds about dons; and I mind about the steering of my car; it often has people in it that I care for. It is because I mind very much about what goes on in the garden in which I find myself, that I am unable to share the explorers' detachment.

BASIL MITCHELL

Flew's article is searching and perceptive, but there is, I think, something odd about his conduct of the theologian's case. The theologian surely would not deny that the fact of pain counts against the assertion that God loves men. This very incompatibility generates the most intractable of theological problems — the problem of evil. So the theologian *does* recognize the fact of pain as counting against Christian doctrine. But it is true that he will not allow it — or anything — to count decisively against it; for he is committed by his faith to trust in God. His attitude is not that of the detached observer, but of the believer.

Perhaps this can be brought out by yet another parable. In time of war in an occupied country, a member of the resistance meets one night a stranger who deeply impresses him. They spend that night together in conversation. The Stranger tells the partisan that he himself is on the side of the resistance — indeed that he is in command of it, and urges the partisan to have faith in him no matter what happens. The partisan is utterly convinced at that meeting of the Stranger's sincerity and constancy and undertakes to trust him.

They never meet in conditions of intimacy again. But sometimes the Stranger is seen helping members of the resistance, and the partisan is grateful and says to his friends, 'He is on our side.'

Sometimes he is seen in the uniform of the police handing over patriots to the occupying power. On these occasions his friends murmur against him: but the partisan still says, 'He is on our side.' He still believes that, in spite of appearances, the Stranger did not deceive him. Sometimes he asks the Stranger for help and receives it. He is then thankful. Sometimes he asks and does not receive it. Then he says, 'The Stranger knows best.' Sometimes his friends, in exasperation, say 'Well, what *would* he have to do for you to admit that you were wrong and that he is not on our side?' But the partisan refuses to answer. He will not consent to put the Stranger to the test. And sometimes his friends complain, 'Well, if *that's* what you mean by his being on our side, the sooner he goes over to the other side the better.'

The partisan of the parable does not allow anything to count decisively against the proposition 'The Stranger is on our side.' This is because he has committed himself to trust the Stranger. But he of course recognizes that the Stranger's ambiguous behaviour *does* count against what he believes about him. It is precisely this situation which constitutes the trial of his faith.

When the partisan asks for help and doesn't get it, what can he do? He can (a) conclude that the Stranger is not on our side or; (b) maintain that he is on our side, but that he has reasons for withholding help.

The first he will refuse to do. How long can he uphold the second position without its becoming just silly?

I don't think one can say in advance. It will depend on the nature of the impression created by the Stranger in the first place. It will depend, too, on the manner in which he takes the Stranger's behavior. If he blandly dismisses it as of no consequence, as having no bearing upon his belief, it will be assumed that he is thoughtless or insane. And it quite obviously won't do for him to say easily, 'Oh, when used of the Stranger the phrase "is on our side" *means* ambiguous behaviour of this sort.' In that case he would be like the religious man who says blandly of a terrible disaster 'It is God's will.' No, he will only be regarded as sane and reasonable in his belief, if he experiences in himself the full force of the conflict.

It is here that my parable differs from Hare's. The partisan admits that many things may and do count against his belief: whereas Hare's lunatic who has a *blik* about dons doesn't admit that anything counts against his *blik*. Nothing *can* count against *bliks*. Also the partisan has a reason for having in the first instance committed himself, viz, the character of the Stranger; whereas the lunatic has no reason for his *blik* about dons — because, of course, you can't have reasons for *bliks*.

This means that I agree with Flew that theological utterances must be assertions. The partisan is making an assertion when he says, 'The Stranger is on our side.'

Do I want to say that the partisan's belief about the Stranger is, in any sense, an explanation? I think I do. It explains and makes sense of the Stranger's behaviour: it helps to explain also the resistance movement in the context of which he appears. In each case it differs from the interpretation which the others put upon the same facts.

'God loves men' resembles 'the Stranger is on our side' (and many other significant statements, e.g. historical ones) in not being conclusively falsifiable. They can both be treated in at least three different ways: (1) As provisional hypotheses to be discarded if experience tells against them; (2) As significant articles of faith; (3) As vacuous formulae (expressing, perhaps, a desire for reassurance) to which experience makes no difference and which make no difference to life.

The Christian, once he has committed himself, is precluded by his faith from taking up the first attitude: 'Thou shalt not tempt the Lord thy God.' He is in constant danger, as Flew has observed, of slipping into the third. But he need not; and, if he does, it is a failure in faith as well as in logic.

ANTONY FLEW

The challenge, it will be remembered, ran like this. Some theological utterances seem to, and are intended to, provide explanations or express assertions. Now an assertion, to be an assertion at all, must claim that things stand thus and thus; *and not otherwise.* Similarly an explanation, to be an explanation at all, must explain why this particular thing occurs; *and not something else.* Those last clauses are crucial. And yet sophisticated religious people — or so it seemed to me — are apt to overlook this, and tend to refuse to allow, not merely that anything actually does occur, but that anything conceivably could occur, which would count against their theological assertions and explanations. But in so far as they do this their supposed explanations are actually bogus, and their seeming assertions are really vacuous.

Mitchell's response to this challenge is admirably direct, straightforward, and understanding. He agrees 'that theological utterances must be assertions.' He agrees that if they are to be assertions, there must be something that would count against their truth. He agrees, too, that believers are in constant danger of transforming their would-be assertions into 'vacuous formulae.' But he takes me to task for an oddity in my 'conduct of the theologian's case. The theologian surely would not deny that the fact of pain counts against the assertion that God loves men. This very incompatibility generates the most intractable of theological problems, the problem of evil.' I think he is right. I should have made a distinction between two very different ways of dealing with what looks like evidence against the love of God: the way I stressed was the expedient of qualifying the original assertion; the way the theologian usually takes, at first, is to admit that it looks bad but to insist that there is — there must be — some explanation which will show that, in spite of appearances, there really is a God who loves us. His difficulty, it seems to me, is that he has given God attributes which rule out all possible saving explanations. In Mitchell's parable of the Stranger it is easy for the believer to find plausible excuses for ambiguous behaviour: for the Stranger is a man. But suppose the Stranger is God. We cannot say that he would like to help but cannot: God is omnipotent. We cannot say that he would help if he only knew: God is omniscient. We cannot say that he is not responsible for the wickedness of others: God creates those others. Indeed an omnipotent, omniscient God must be an accessory before (and during) the fact to every human misdeed; as well as being responsible for every non-moral defect in the universe. So, though I entirely concede that Mitchell was absolutely right to insist against me that the theologian's first move is to look for an *explanation,* I still think that in the end, if relentlessly pursued, he will have to resort to the avoiding action of *qualification.* And there lies the danger of that death by a thousand qualifications, which would, I agree, constitute 'a failure in faith as well as in logic.'

Hare's approach is fresh and bold. He confesses that 'on the ground marked out by Flew, he seems to me to be completely victorious.' He therefore introduces the concept of *blik.* But while I think that there is room for some such concept in philosophy, and that philosophers should be grateful to Hare for his invention, I nevertheless want to insist that any attempt to analyse Christian religious utterances as expressions or affirmations of a *blik* rather than as (at least would-be) assertions about the cosmos is fundamentally misguided. *First,* because thus interpreted they would be entirely unorthodox. If Hare's religion really is a *blik,* involving no cosmological assertions about the nature and activities of a supposed personal creator, then surely he is not a Christian at all? *Second,* because thus interpreted, they could scarcely do the job they do. If they were not even intended as assertions then many religious activities would become fraudulent, or merely silly. If 'You ought *because* it is God's will' asserts no more than 'You ought,' then the person who prefers the former phraseology is not really giving a reason, but a fraudulent substitute for one, a dialectical dud cheque. . . . Religious utterances may indeed express false or even bogus assertions: but I simply do not believe that they are not both intended and interpreted to be or at any rate to presuppose assertions, at least in the context of religious practice; whatever shifts may be demanded, in another context, by the exigencies of theological apologetic.[11]

KNOWLEDGE AND FAITH

Can we know that God exists? The three traditional forms of "proof" don't seem to be adequate as literal proofs. In order to accept any of them, it looks as if one has to *begin* by believing in God. Moreover, what each of them proves is not the existence of *God* but at most the existence of something; something that is defined by its existence, something that is a first cause, or something that is an

[11]Antony Flew, R. M. Hare, and Basil Mitchell, "Theology and Falsification," *University,* 1950–51; rpt. *New Essays in Philosophical Theology,* eds. A. Flew and A. MacIntyre (New York: Macmillan, 1955).

intelligent "designer." But there is a very different view of God, defended, for example, by Immanuel Kant. On this view, the most important attribute of the traditional Western God—the reason why men and women have worshipped Him, prayed to Him, feared Him, fought wars and died for Him—is their belief in God's divine justice. Thus the most important attributes of God in Western religion are His moral qualities. Without them, our belief in God would be very different than it is.

According to this view, the importance of God in Western thought is His role as the source of our moral laws, as the judge of our actions and feelings, and as the sanction that stands behind those laws and judgments. The preceding "proofs" of God's existence are not wholly convincing, even if they are valid, just because they leave out this all-important moral aspect of belief in God. What distinguishes theists from atheists is not a matter of mere theory or argument ("a mere hypothesis," the French philosopher La Place called it), but a difference in lifestyle and confidence. The theist believes in a divine source of morality, in a judgment of his actions that transcends everyday life, and the promise of reward (or threat of punishment) after death. The atheist also believes in morality, but not in divine morality, and he believes that all judgments of our actions and all rewards and punishments must take place in this life, or not at all. Accordingly, the question of our knowledge of God's existence has a distinctly moral dimension.

Immanuel Kant, after attempting to refute all three of the traditional arguments for God's existence, offered one of his own. He no longer tried to "prove" God's existence as such and even said that, strictly speaking, we could have no knowledge of God at all, since God, as transcendent, cannot be the object of any possible experience. So Kant, following a long tradition in Christianity, said that belief in God is a matter of faith. But this does not mean, as people so often take it to mean, that it was an irrational belief. Quite to the contrary, Kant insisted that it was the most rational belief of all. For without it, we would not have the anchor for our morality, nor would we have any reason to suppose that our good deeds would in fact be eventually rewarded or evil deeds punished. For it was obvious to Kant, as it has been to every person with his or her eyes open since ancient times, that justice is not always delivered in this life. Innocent children are butchered in wars; evil men live grand lives well into old age. Therefore, according to Kant, it was rational to believe in God, rational to have faith, even if faith was not, strictly speaking, a matter of knowledge. It is, he says, a "Postulate of Practical Reason."

on God and Morality, by Immanuel Kant

The moral law led, in the foregoing analysis, to a practical problem which is assigned solely by pure reason and without any concurrence of sensuous incentives. It is the problem of the completeness of the first and principal part of the highest good, viz., morality; since this problem can be solved only in eternity, it led to the postulate of immortality. The same law must also lead us to affirm the possibility of the second element of the highest good, i.e., happiness proportional to that morality; it must do so just as disinterestedly as heretofore, by a purely impartial reason. This it can do on the supposition of the existence of a cause adequate to this effect, i.e., it must postulate the existence of God as necessarily belonging to the possibility of the highest good (the object of our will which is necessarily connected with the moral legislation of pure reason). We proceed to exhibit this connection in a convincing manner.

Happiness is the condition of a rational being in the world, in whose whole existence everything goes according to wish and will. It thus rests on the harmony of nature with his entire end and with the essential determining ground of his will. But the moral law commands as a law of freedom through motives wholly independent of nature and of its harmony with our faculty of desire (as incentives). Still, the acting rational being in the world is not at the same time the cause of the world and of nature itself. Hence there is not the slightest ground in the moral law for a necessary connection between the morality and proportionate happiness of a being which belongs to the world as one of its parts and as thus dependent on it. Not being nature's cause, his will cannot by its own strength bring nature, as it touches on his happiness, into complete harmony with his practical principles. Nevertheless, in the practical task of pure reason, i.e., in the necessary endeavor after the highest good, such a connection is postulated as necessary: we *should* seek to further the highest good (which therefore must be at least possible). Therefore also the existence is postulated of a cause of the whole of nature, itself distinct from nature, which contains the ground of the exact coincidence of happiness with morality. This supreme cause, however, must contain the ground of the agreement of nature not merely with a law of the will of rational beings but with the idea of this law so far as they make it the supreme ground of determination of the will. Thus it contains the ground of the agreement of nature not merely with actions moral in their form but also with their morality as the motives to such actions, i.e., with their moral intention. Therefore, the highest good is possible in the world only on the supposition of a supreme cause of nature which has a causality corresponding to the moral intention. Now a being which is capable of actions by the idea of laws is an intelligence (a rational being), and the causality of such a being according to this idea of laws is his will. Therefore, the supreme cause of nature, in so far as it must be presupposed for the highest good, is a being which is the cause (and consequently the author) of nature through understanding and will, i.e., God. As a consequence, the postulate of the possibility of a highest derived good (the best world) is at the same time the postulate of the reality of a highest original good, namely, the existence of God. Now it was our duty to promote the highest good; and it is not merely our privilege but a necessity connected with duty as a requisite to presuppose the possibility of this highest good. This presupposition is made only under the condition of the existence of God, and this condition inseparably connects this supposition with duty. Therefore, it is morally necessary to assume the existence of God.[12]

---

[12]Immanuel Kant, *Critique of Practical Reason*, trans. Lewis White Beck (New York: Bobbs-Merrill, 1956).

The key to Kant's argument is the obvious fact that good deeds are not always rewarded in this life and evil deeds are often not punished. Why then, he asks, should a person be moral and do what is right? If we are to rationally decide to be moral, therefore, we must also believe that happiness and morality will be in harmony (what Kant calls "the highest good"), that good people will be rewarded with happiness and evil people will be punished. But if this does not happen in this life, then we must believe that it happens in another life (" . . . this problem can be solved only in eternity"). Further, we must believe in some ultimate source of justice, a divine judge who will weigh good against evil and make certain that eternal happiness and punishment are meted out fairly. This argument is at one and the same time a defense of the Christian belief in the immortality of the human soul and in God. It is necessary to believe in both, according to Kant, in order to sustain our willingness to be moral. "Therefore, it is morally necessary to assume the existence of God."

A similar position was argued more recently by the pragmatist William James. His position is a "pragmatic" one; that is, believing in God is "rational" insofar as it doesn't conflict with our other beliefs (for example, our beliefs in science, a matter that Kant stressed also) and if it tends to make us lead better lives. He argues:

from "The Will to Believe," by William James

Science says things are; morality says some things are better than other things; and religion says essentially two things.

First, she says that the best things are the more eternal things, the overlapping things, the things in the universe that throw the last stone, so to speak, and say the final word. "Perfection is eternal"—this phrase of Charles Secrétan seems a good way of putting this first affirmation of religion, an affirmation which obviously cannot yet be verified scientifically at all.

The second affirmation of religion is that we are better off even now if we believe her first affirmation to be true.

Now, let us consider what the logical elements of this situation are *in case the religious hypothesis in both its branches be really true.* (Of course, we must admit that possibility at the outset. If we are to discuss the question at all, it must involve a living option. If for any of you religion be a hypothesis that cannot, by any living possibility be true, then you need go no farther. I speak to the "saving remnant" alone.) So proceeding, we see, first, that religion offers itself as a *momentous* option. We are supposed to gain, even now, by our belief, and to lose by our nonbelief, a certain vital good. Secondly, religion is a *forced* option, so far as that good goes. We cannot escape the issue by remaining sceptical and waiting for more light, because, although we do avoid error in that way *if religion be untrue*, we lose the good, *if it be true*, just as certainly as if we positively chose to disbelieve. It is as if a man should hesitate indefinitely to ask a certain woman to marry him because he was not perfectly sure that she would prove an angel after he brought her home. Would he not cut himself off from that particular angel-possibility as decisively as if he went and married someone else? Scepticism, then, is not avoidance of option; it is option of a certain particular kind of risk. *Better risk loss of truth than chance of error*—that is your faith-vetoer's exact position. He is actively playing his stake as much as the believer is; he is backing the field against the religious hypothesis, just as the believer is backing the religious hypothesis against the field. To preach scepticism to us as a duty until "sufficient evidence" for religion be found, is tantamount therefore to telling us, when in presence of the religious hypothesis, that to yield to our fear of its being error is wiser and better than to yield to our hope that it may be true. It is not intellect against all passions, then; it is only intellect with one passion laying down its law. And by what, forsooth, is the supreme wisdom of this passion warranted? Dupery for dupery, what proof is there that dupery through hope is so much worse than dupery through fear? I, for one, can see no proof; and I simply refuse obedience to the scientist's command to imitate his kind of option, in a case where my own stake is important enough to give me the right to choose my own form of risk. If religion be true and the evidence for it be still insufficient, I do not wish, by putting your extinguisher upon my nature (which feels to me as if it had after all some business in this matter), to forfeit my sole chance in life of getting upon the winning side — that chance depending, of course, on my willingness to run the risk of acting as if my passional need of taking the world religiously might be prophetic and right.

All this is on the supposition that it really may be prophetic and right, and that, even to us who are discussing the matter, religion is a live hypothesis which may be true. Now, to most of us religion comes in a still further way that makes a veto on our active faith even more illogical. The more perfect and more eternal aspect of the universe is represented in our religions as having personal form. The universe is no longer a mere *It* to us, but a *Thou*, if we are religious; and any relation that may be possible from person to person might be possible here. For instance, although in one sense we are passive portions of the universe, in another we show a curious autonomy, as if we were small active centres on our own account. We feel, too, as if the appeal of religion to us were made to our own active good-will, as if evidence might be forever withheld from us unless we met the hypothesis half-way. To take a trivial illustration: just as a man who in a company of gentlemen made no advances, asked a warrant for every concession, and believed no one's word without proof, would cut himself off by such churlishness from all the social rewards that a more trusting spirit would earn — so here, one who should shut himself up in snarling logicality and try to make the gods extort his recognition willy-nilly, or not get it at all, might cut himself off forever from his only opportunity of making the gods' acquaintance. This feeling, forced on us we know not whence, that by obstinately believing that there are gods (although not to do so would be so easy both for our logic and our life) we are doing the universe the deepest service we can, seems part of the living essence of the religious hypothesis. If the hypothesis *were* true in all its parts, including this one, then pure intellectualism, with its veto on our making willing advances, would be an absurdity; and some participation of our sympathetic nature would be logically required. I, therefore, for one, cannot see my way to accepting the agnostic rules of truth-seeking, or willfully agree to keep my willing nature out of the game. I cannot do so for this plain reason, that *a rule of thinking which would absolutely prevent me from acknowledging certain kinds of truth if those kinds of truth were really there, would be an irrational rule.* That for me is the long and short of the formal logic of the situation, no matter what the kinds of truth might materially be.[13]

This "practical" argument for belief in God ruled philosophy from the time of Kant until the present century. It has its origins in a short but brilliant argument by the French philosopher Blaise Pascal. Pascal offered an argument that he called a wager, literally a bet about God. It isn't a proof of God's existence in any sense; in fact, one of its explicit terms is the fact that we can't know whether God exists or not. But then, he says, if God exists, and we believe in Him, we are entitled to an infinite reward. If He exists and we don't believe in Him, on the other hand, we are really in for it—eternal damnation. Even if He doesn't exist, we are still better off believing in God because of the qualities faith brings to life in us. In support of the decision to believe, Pascal asks:

> Now, what harm will befall you in taking this side? You will be faithful, honest, humble, grateful, generous, a sincere friend, truthful. Certainly you will not have those poisonous pleasures, glory and luxury; but will you not have others? I will tell you that you will thereby gain in this life, and that, at each step you take on this road, you will see so great certainty of gain, so much nothingness in what you risk, that you will at last recognize that you have wagered for something certain and infinite, for which you have given nothing.[14]

So, if we treat this as a betting situation, in which our option is simply to believe or not believe, our betting odds look like this:

"Pascal's Wager"

IF WE BELIEVE	AND GOD EXISTS Then eternal reward	AND GOD DOESN'T EXIST We've wasted a little piety but perhaps been better people.
IF WE DON'T BELIEVE	Then eternal damnation	No reward, no punishment.

Looking at the odds as a betting person, it is obvious which option we ought to choose. The risk of eternal damnation overwhelms the promise of a few "poi-

[13]William James, "The Will to Believe," in *The Will to Believe and Other Essays in Popular Philosophy* (New York: Longmans, Green, 1896).
[14]Blaise Pascal, *Pensees,* # 233 (New York: Modern Library, 1941).

sonous" pleasures; and the promise of eternal reward is well worth the risk that we may be wrong, considering what is gained even in this life. The conclusion, then, on strictly practical grounds, is that we ought to believe in God.

All three of these arguments by Kant, James, and Pascal are based on the same all-important assumption that "God is good." On the basis of this assumption, they then argue that it is rational to believe in God, even if it is not possible to prove (or even know) that He exists. Accordingly, belief in God is a matter of faith, but this faith can be argued and justified as rational belief. Just because it is faith and not knowledge, it does not follow that it is "blind faith" or irrational, beyond argument or arbitrary. To insist that belief in God is a matter of faith, therefore, is not to say that it is beyond the reach of philosophy or rational consideration.

The Problem of Evil

These "moral" arguments for believing in God are sound only as long as we accept the assumption that "God is good." There have been few theists who have actually denied this, of course, but there have been a great many, particularly in modern times, who have worried about it considerably. The problem is called "the problem of evil." It can be stated very simply, but the solution, if you believe in God, is not simple at all. The problem is this: If God is all-powerful (omnipotent), all-knowing (omniscient), and just, then how is it possible that there is so much unearned suffering and unpunished wickedness in the world? Or simply, if God exists, how can the world be so full of evil? It cannot be that He does not know of these misfortunes, for He is all-knowing. Nor can it be that He is unable to do anything about them, for He is all-powerful. And if He is just and has concern for human beings, then He must care about protecting the innocent and punishing or preventing evil.

The problem of evil is a problem because no theist is willing to give up any of these vital attributes of God. The idea that God is not all-powerful, or that He doesn't know what is going on, or that He is not wholly just, is intolerable to traditional Christianity. So the problem is to show how there can be evil in the world without denying God any of his essential attributes. A partial solution is this: Since God created men and women with "free will" and thereby the power to choose between good and evil, the evil and suffering in the world is not due to God's inability to do anything about it or His lack of knowledge or any injustice on His part. It is the fault of people who misuse their freedom and create their own hardships. Having given humanity the freedom of choice, it is argued, there is no reason why God should be blamed for human mistakes resulting from that freedom. It can even be argued that, having once given people the freedom of choice, God ought not to interfere with their choices. Accordingly, evil is explained and the problem of evil seems solved, at least partially.

The following excerpt is from Saint Augustine's Confessions:

from Confessions,
by Saint Augustine

But although I declared and firmly believed that you, our Lord God, the true God who made not only our souls but also our bodies and not only our souls and bodies but all things, living and inanimate, as well, although I believed that you were free from corruption or mutation or any degree of change, I still could not find a clear explanation, without complications, of the cause of evil. Whatever the cause might be, I saw that it was not to be found in any theory that would oblige me to believe that the immutable God was mutable. If I believed this, I should myself become a cause of evil, the very thing which I was trying to discover. So I continued the search with some sense of relief, because I was quite sure that the theories of the Manichees were wrong. I repudiated these people with all my heart, because I could see that while they were inquiring into the origin of evil they were full of evil themselves, since they preferred to think that yours was a substance that could suffer evil rather than that theirs was capable of committing it.

I was told that we do evil because we choose to do so of our own free will, and suffer it because your justice rightly demands that we should. I did my best to understand this, but I could not see it clearly. I tried to raise my mental perceptions out of the abyss which engulfed them, but I sank back into it once more. Again and again I tried, but always I sank back. One thing lifted me up into the light of your day. It was that I knew that I had a will, as surely as I knew that there was life in me. When I chose to do something or not to do it, I was quite certain that it was my own self, and not some other person, who made this act of will, so that I was on the point of understanding that herein lay the cause of my sin. If I did anything against my will, it seemed to me to be something which happened to me rather than something which I did, and I looked upon it not as a fault, but as a punishment. And because I thought of you as a just God, I admitted at once that your punishments were not unjust.

But then I would ask myself once more: "Who made me? Surely it was my God, who is not only good but Goodness itself. How, then, do I come to possess a will that can choose to do wrong and refuse to do good, thereby providing a just reason why I should be punished? Who put this will into me? Who sowed this seed of bitterness in me, when all that I am was made by my God, who is Sweetness itself? If it was the devil who put it there, who made the devil? If he was a good angel who became a devil because of his own wicked will, how did he come to possess the wicked will which made him a devil, when the Creator, who is entirely good, made him a good angel and nothing else?"

These thoughts swept me back again into the gulf where I was being stifled. But I did not sink as far as that hell of error where no one confesses to you his own guilt, choosing to believe that you suffer evil rather than that man does it.

· · · · ·

"Where then is evil? What is its origin? How did it steal into the world? What is the root or seed from which it grew? Can it be that there simply is no evil? If so, why do we fear and guard against something which is not there? If our fear is unfounded, it is itself an evil, because it stabs and wrings our hearts for nothing. In fact the evil is all the greater if we are afraid when there is nothing to fear. Therefore, either there is evil and we fear it, or the fear itself is evil.

"Where then does evil come from, if God made all things and, because he is good, made them good too? It is true that he is the supreme Good, that he is himself a greater Good than these lesser goods which he created. But the Creator and all his creation are both good. Where then does evil come from?

"Can it be that there was something evil in the matter from which he made the universe? When he shaped this matter and fitted it to his purpose, did he leave in it some part which he did not convert to good? But why should he have done this? Are we to believe that, although he is omnipotent, he had not the power to convert the whole of this matter to good and change it so that no evil remained in it? Why, indeed, did he will to make anything of it at all? Why did he not instead, by this same omnipotence, destroy it utterly and entirely? Could it have existed against his will? If it had existed from eternity, why did he allow it to exist in that state through the infinite ages of the past and then, after so long a time, decide to make something of it? If he suddenly determined to act, would it not be more likely that he would use his almighty power to abolish this evil matter, so that nothing should exist besides himself, the total, true, supreme, and infinite Good? Or, if it was not good that a God who was good should not also create and establish something good, could he not have removed and annihilated the evil matter and replaced it with good, of which he could create all things? For he would not be omnipotent if he could not create something good without the help of matter which he had not created himself."

These were the thoughts which I turned over and over in my unhappy mind, and my anxiety was all the more galling for the fear that death might come before I had found the truth. But my heart clung firmly to the faith in Christ your Son, our Lord and Saviour, which it had received in the Catholic Church. There were many questions on which my beliefs were still indefinite and wavered from the strict rule of doctrine, yet my mind never relinquished the faith but drank it in more deeply day by day.

10

. . . Under your guidance I entered into the depths of my soul, and this I was able to do because *your aid befriended me.* I entered, and with the eye of my soul, such as it was, I saw the Light that never changes casting its rays over the same eye of my soul, over my mind. It was not the common light of day that is seen by the eye of every living thing of flesh and blood, nor was it some more spacious light of the same sort, as if the light of day were to shine far, far brighter than it does and fill all space with a vast brilliance. What I saw was something quite, quite different from any light we know on earth. It shone above my mind, but not in the way that oil floats above water or the sky hangs over the earth. It was above me because it was itself the Light that made me, and I was below because I was made by it. All who know the truth know this Light, and all who know this Light know eternity. It is the Light that charity knows.

Eternal Truth, true Love, beloved Eternity—all this, my God, you are, and it is to you that I sigh by night and day. When first I knew you, you raised me up so that I could see that there was something to be seen, but also that I was not yet able to see it. I gazed on you with eyes too weak to resist the dazzle of your splendour. Your light shone upon me in its brilliance, and I thrilled with love and dread alike. I realized that I was far away from you. It was as though I were in a land where all is different from your own and I heard your voice calling from on high, saying "I am the food of full-grown men. Grow and you shall feed on me. But you shall not change me into your own substance, as you do with the food of your body. Instead you shall be changed into me." I realized too that you have chastened man for his sins; you made my life melt away like gossamer, and I asked myself "Is truth then nothing at all, simply because it has no extension in space, with or without limits?" And, far off, I heard your voice saying *I am the God who IS.* I heard your voice, as we hear voices that speak to our hearts, and at once I had no cause to doubt. I might more easily have doubted that I was alive than that Truth had being. For we catch sight of the Truth, as he is known through his creation.

11

Also I considered all the other things that are of a lower order than yourself, and I saw that they have not absolute being in themselves, nor are they entirely without being. They are real in so far as they have their being from you, but unreal in the sense that they are not what you are. For it is only that which remains in being without change that truly is. As for me, *I know no other content but clinging to God*, because unless my being remains in him, it cannot remain in me. But *himself ever unchanged, he makes all things new. I own him as my God; he has no need of aught that is mine.*

12

It was made clear to me also that even those things which are subject to decay are good. If they were of the supreme order of goodness, they could not become corrupt; but neither could they become corrupt unless they were in some way good. For if they were supremely good, it would not be possible for them to be corrupted. On the other hand, if they were entirely without good, there would be nothing in them that could become corrupt. For corruption is harmful, but unless it diminished what is good, it could do no harm. The conclusion then must be either that corruption does no harm—which is not possible; or that everything which is corrupted is deprived of good—which is beyond doubt. But if they are deprived of all good, they will not exist at all. For if they still exist but can no longer be corrupted, they will be better than they were before, because they now continue their existence in an incorruptible state. But could anything be more preposterous than to say that things are made better by being deprived of all good?

So we must conclude that if things are deprived of all good, they cease altogether to be; and this means that as long as they are, they are good. Therefore, whatever is, is good; and evil, the origin of which I was trying to find, is not a substance, because if it were a substance, it would be good. For either it would be an incorruptible substance of the supreme order of goodness, or it would be a corruptible substance which would not be corruptible unless it were good. So it became obvious to me that all that you have made is good, and that there are no substances whatsoever that were not made by you. And because you did not make them all equal, each single thing is good and collectively they are very good, for our God made his whole creation *very good.*

13

For you evil does not exist, and not only for you but for the whole of your creation as well, because there is nothing outside it which could invade it and break down the order which you have imposed on it. Yet in the separate parts of your creation there are some things which we think of as evil because they are at variance with other things. But there are other things again with which they are in accord, and then they are good. In themselves, too, they are good. And all these things which are at variance with one another are in accord with the lower part of creation which we call the earth. The sky, which is cloudy and windy, suits the earth to which it belongs. So it would be wrong for me to wish that these earthly things did not exist, for even if I saw nothing but them, I might wish for something better, but still I ought to praise you for them alone. For all things *give praise to the Lord on earth, monsters of the sea and all its depths; fire and hail, snow and mist, and the storm-wind that executes his decree; all you mountains and hills, all you fruit trees and cedars; all you wild beasts and cattle, creeping things and birds that fly in air; all you kings and peoples of the world, all you that are princes and judges on earth; young men and maids, old men and boys together; let them all give praise to the Lord's name.* The heavens, too, ring with your praises, O God, for you are the god of us all. *Give praise to the Lord in heaven; praise him, all that dwells on high. Praise him, all you angels of his, praise him, all his armies. Praise him, sun and moon; praise him, every star that shines. Praise him, you highest heavens, you waters beyond the heavens. Let all these praise the Lord.* And since this is so, I no longer wished for a better world, because I was thinking of the whole of creation, and in the light of this clearer discernment I had come to see that though the higher things are better than the lower, the sum of all creation is better than the higher things alone.[15]

---

[15]St. Augustine, *Confessions,* Book VII, trans. R. S. Pine-Coffin (Harmondsworth, England: Penguin Books, 1961), pp. 136–49.

The problem arises once again, however, if we ask, "how could God have given people free will, knowing — as He must have — that they would misuse it so badly?" Would everyone be much better off if we had a bit less "free will," or at least if we would have more desires to do good and fewer impulses to cause trouble and suffering? There are several traditional responses to this. One is that God has allowed us moral latitude to provide a test of our virtue, for if we were all "naturally" good, there would be little question of good versus evil or salvation versus damnation. But it is open to question whether these distinctions are themselves desirable; wouldn't it have been better for humanity to have stayed in the Garden of Eden? Why did God have to create temptation, and what would have been lost from the world if Adam and Eve had been created with a bit more fortitude and obedience? And then there is the familiar defense, "but doesn't the world need some evil, in order that we recognize the good?" But it isn't at all obvious that we need anything like the amount of evil and suffering we have in the world in order to recognize what is good. You can see that the argument has a great many familiar defenses and rejoinders, and it would take at least a long chapter to spell out the various objections and replies to this "free will" solution to the problem of evil. But even if we were to agree on this "free will" defense of the traditional conception of God as omnipotent, omniscient, and perfectly just, laying the blame for suffering to people's own choices, that would not solve the problem of evil. This is why we said that the "free will" defense is, at best, a partial solution. For the obvious truth of the matter is that not all human hardships and sufferings are our own doing and that much of the evil in the world does not depend on human action in any way.

During the Enlightenment, the European world found itself in a state of theological confusion because of a monstrous earthquake that killed thousands of people, including many children, in Lisbon, Portugal. And to make matters worse, the earthquake struck on a Sunday morning, just as people were in church worshipping, so that the pious people were more likely to be killed than the atheists who had drunken themselves to sleep on the beach. And today theists are forced to ask the same question after every such "natural" disaster: "Does it even make sense to say that God is punishing us or testing our faith?" What could justify a punishment that killed innocent children and spared the guilty? And what could justify a "test" in which people are killed just to see if they are still faithful? (The Job story is relevant here too. In general, ask yourself if the same actions would even be tolerable on a human scale. For example, what would we say of a father who punished his youngest child when the older children got into trouble? And what would we say of a father who spanked his children just to "test" their loyalty to him?)

No one, perhaps, has felt and written more incisively from within this tension than the pivotal French Enlightenment figure Pierre Bayle. With the Huguenot (French Protestants) persecution under Louis XIV, Bayle lost his teaching position (1681), was forced into exile in Holland and later suffered the loss of his brother, a Protestant cleric still in France. These losses, compounded with his expulsion from a Rotterdam teaching post (1693) for "sedition," put Bayle at the experiential center of the religious controversies racking his age. With all of his formidable scholarship, theological training, and personal losses, this "Christian Sceptic" brings the problem of evil to its absolute pitch in the article on the Paulicians in his *Historical and Critical Dictionary* (1697). In this selection from *Paulicians* (Armenian Manicheans — who believed good and evil to be equally original and world-governing principles), Bayle exposes the insufficiency of reason to resolve the dilemma using either the "free will" defense or denying God's foreknowledge of events.

on the Problem of Evil, by Pierre Bayle

Their fundamental doctrine was that of the two co-eternal principles which were independent one from another. This dogma inspires horror at first, and consequently it is strange that the Manichean sect was able to deceive so many people. On the other hand, it is so difficult to answer its objections concerning the origin of evil that it is not astonishing that the hypothesis of the two principles, one good and the other evil, dazzled several ancient philosophers and found so many disciples in Christianity where the doctrine which teaches the enmity of the devils to the true God is always accompanied by the doctrine which teaches the rebellion and fall of one part of the good angels. . . . According to the Scripture there is only one principle of good, and nonetheless moral and physical evil found their way into the human race. It is therefore not against the nature of the good principle both to permit the introduction of moral evil and to punish crime, for it is not more evident that four and four are eight than it is evident that an event is possible if it has happened. *Ab actu ad potentiam valet consequentia* is one of the clearest and most incontestable axioms of all metaphysics. Now here we find an invulnerable rampart, and that is sufficient to insure the victory of the orthodox even though their *a priori* reasons might be refuted. But it is true that they can be refuted? I will answer, "Yes," for the way in which evil was introduced into the world under the dominion of a Supreme Being who is infinitely good, all wise, and all powerful is not only inexplicable but even incomprehensible. Therefore, when we undertake to explain why this Being permitted evil, we are confronted on every side with objections which are more in accord with our natural light of understanding and with our ideas of order than is our explanation.

Reason is incapable of unraveling the question.

If upon strictly unscriptural and rational grounds we undertake to ascertain the reasons for which sin entered into the world, we will find ourselves opposed by other reasons which have a greater appearance of truth and harmony with our ideas of order, no matter how good our own reasons might be. For example, if you say that God permitted sin in order to manifest His wisdom, which is more resplendent in the midst of the disorders which the evil of men produces every day than it would be in a state of innocence, you will be answered that one might as well compare the Godhead with a father who had let the legs of his children be broken in order to display before an entire city the skill which he has in setting bones; or with a monarch who would allow strife and seditions to spring up throughout his kingdom in order to aquire the glory of having put an end to them. The conduct of this father and of this monarch is so contrary to the clear and distinct ideas which we have of goodness and wisdom, and in general, of all the duties of a father and a king, that our reason cannot understand that God should act as they do. "But," you will say, "the ways of God are not our ways" I will say, "Go no further. Hold to this text of the Scripture (Isaiah 55:8) and make no further pretense to reasoning." Give up trying to tell us or convince us that without the fall of the first man the justice and mercy of God would have remained unknown, for we will answer you that there was nothing easier than to make known these two attributes to man. Nothing more than the idea of the sovereignly perfect Being makes known very clearly to sinful man that God possesses all of the virtues which are worthy in every way of an infinite nature. How much more then would this idea have made known to innocent man that God is infinitely just? Could it be that if man had remained innocent, God could not have punished anyone and therefore could not have exercised His justice? No, we cannot make this supposition, because if no one would have been worthy of punishment God could have exercised his attribute of justice perpetually by refraining from punishing anyone. Tell me what you think of two princes, one of which lets his subjects fall into abject wretchedness in order that he may deliver them after they have groaned in their misery for some time, and the other who preserves his subjects in a continual state of prosperity. Is not the latter better and more merciful than the first? Those who teach the Immaculate Conception of the Holy Virgin prove demonstratively that God shed forth upon her His mercy and redemptive grace more than upon other humans. But one does not have to be deeply versed in metaphysics to know, as does the veriest villager, that it is a greater goodness to prevent a man from falling into a ditch than to let him fall in it and then pull him out after an hour, and that it is better to keep a murderer from killing someone than to torture him on the rack for the murders that he has been permitted to commit. All of this warns us that we should not enter into dispute with the Manicheans without establishing first of all the dogma of "the elevation of faith and the abasement of reason."

The doctrine of free agency cannot account for the presence of evil in the world.

There are those who say that God permitted sin because He could not have prevented it without compromising the free agency of man, which was the best gift that He had given him. But they leave themselves open to many objections. The reason they give is fine enough and has a certain dazzling quality to it, and one even finds a certain grandeur in it; but even so, it can be opposed by reasons which are more within the reach of all men and founded more solidly upon common sense and our ideas of order.

Without having read the fine treatise of Seneca upon blessings, we know by the natural light of our intelligence that it is in the essence of a benefactor to refrain from giving any gift which he knows would be the ruin of the recipient. If this were not so, there would be no enemy so bitter that he would not heap gifts upon his adversary. We also know that it is the essence of a benefactor to go to any lengths to assure that his gifts will procure the happiness of the person whom he is honoring. If he could confer upon the recipient of his gifts the ability to use these gifts well and then refused to do so, we would say that he did not long retain the characteristics of a benefactor, and our opinion of him would not be any better if he could prevent his beneficiary from making ill-usage of his gifts and did not do so by curing him of all of his evil inclinations. These are ideas which are as well known to the common people as to the philosophers. I admit that one would not be obliged to prevent the ill-usage of a gift if the only way to do so were to break the arms and legs of its recipient, or to cast him into the bottom of a dungeon in irons, but in that case, it would be much better not to give the gift. However, if one could prevent an ill-usage of it by changing the disposition of the heart and in giving the recipient an inclination toward good, one should do it. Now this is what God could have done easily if He had willed it . . .

If humans acted as God is said to have done, they would be condemned.

There is no good mother who, having given permission to her daughters to go to a ball, would not revoke this permission if she were assured that they would there succumb to gallant enticings and part company with their virginity. Moreover, any mother who knowing most assuredly that this unfortunate event would infallibly take place and who would nonetheless let her daughters go to the ball after simply exhorting them to virtue and threatening them with disgrace if they returned home deflowered, would draw upon herself at least the merited condemnation of having loved neither her daughters nor chastity. No matter how hard she tried to justify her conduct by saying that she did not wish to infringe upon the liberty of her daughters, neither to show any lack of confidence in them, people would nonetheless answer her that her great circumspection was not called for and more befitted a spiteful stepdame than a mother. They would add that it would have been better to keep her daughters under her eye than to give them such a privilege of liberty or such marks of confidence so inappropriately.

This example shows the temerity of those who tell us that God permitted sin so as not to infringe upon the free agency of the first man. It is better to believe and be silent than to advance reasons which can be refuted by the examples which I have just given. . . .

Free agency was not a good gift.

With these reasons it is easy to show that the free agency of the first man was not a good gift, since it was given to him inviolable in circumstances where he would use it for his own ruin, the ruin of the human race, the eternal damnation of the greater part of his descendants, and the introduction into the world of a dreadful deluge of moral and physical evils. We will never be able to understand how this gift could have been preserved in man because of God's goodness and because of His love of holiness. Again, those who say that there had to be free beings in order for God to be loved with a love freely chosen, feel in their conscience that this hypothesis does not satisfy the demands of reason, for when it is foreseen that these free beings will choose, not the love of good but the love of sin, it is easily seen that the intended purpose is frustrated, and thus it is not at all necessary to preserve free agency.

Providence is not exonerated by denying Divine foreknowledge.

In addition, if you agree with those who come the closest to exonerating Providence and say that God did not foresee the fall of Adam, you gain very little. For He at least knew most certainly that the first man would run the risk of losing his innocence and introducing into the world all of the evils of pain and guilt which followed his revolt. Neither His goodness, His holiness, nor His wisdom could have permitted Him to run the risk of these events. Our reason convinces us most clearly that when a mother would let her daughters go to a ball knowing very certainly that they would run a great risk with respect to their honor, she would witness that she loved neither her daughters nor chastity. Furthermore, if we suppose that she has an infallible preservative against all temptations and does not give it to her daughters in sending them to the ball, we can be most assured that she is guilty and cares very little about the virginity of her daughters.

Let us carry this comparison a little further. Suppose that this mother herself went to the ball and happened to see through a window that one of her daughters was defending herself very feebly in some secluded corner against the pleadings of some young gallant. If she then saw that her daughter had only one step to take to acquiesce to the desires of the tempter and then did not rush to her aid to keep her from this pitfall, would we not justly say that she was acting as a cruel stepdame and that she would be capable of selling the honor of her own daughter?

. . . . .

Howsoever this be explained, it follows plainly, that God was willing that man should sin, and that he preferred this to the perpetual duration of innocence, which it was so easy for him to procure and ordain. Reconcile this if you can with the goodness he ought to have for his creatures, and the infinite love he ought to have for holiness.[16]

A popular response at this point is to refer to "God's mysterious ways" and to argue that we cannot possibly understand God's ultimate purposes. This response does succeed in answering the problem of evil, but only at considerable cost. In all of the arguments we have considered so far, and in most of the history of Western religion, belief in God, and belief in God's omnipotence, omniscience, and perfect justice, has been a matter of rational belief (whether or not it was considered a matter of knowledge or of faith). But with the reference to "God's mysterious ways," we mark a major breach with this rational tradition, and we

---

[16]From Pierre Bayle, "Paulicans" in *Historical and Critical Dictionary* (London: Harper, 1710).

admit that not only can we not know about God, but we cannot even understand or rationally argue these matters. In other words, the phrase "God's mysterious ways" solves the problem of evil only at the cost of ending discussion altogether.

There are many philosophers and religious people who do not object to this costly consequence. It is costly, they would argue, only to the interests of those who insist on arguing and understanding these religious matters; it need have no effect on religious belief itself. In the next section, we shall discuss some of these nonrational alternatives to the philosophy of religion. But it is first important to appreciate that there is a long history of efforts to solve the problem of evil, and save a more or less traditional conception of God, that do not take this drastic alternative. Spinoza's **pantheism,** for example, is one of these many attempts to save at least a nominal belief in God while getting around the problem of evil, in this case, by denying that God is just and by denying that He has any moral characteristics at all. On Spinoza's theory, God is identical to the universe. He is not its creator and so is not responsible for the existence of evil in it. He is not a moral agent, so He has neither concern nor ability for the misfortunes and suffering of the world. He has no special concern for people and no concern for justice. And since Spinoza defends a strict determinism in which no one — not even God — has "free will," questions of moral responsibility, reward, and punishment are irrelevant, a matter of human vanity, nothing more.

This way of avoiding the problem of evil was quite common in the Enlightenment, in that period of Western thought in which people were rebelling against medieval authority. The best example of this attitude was the French genius Voltaire. He was a vehement opponent of Christianity. ("I have heard enough how it took only twelve men to establish Christianity; I should like to prove that only one can destroy it.") But he wouldn't give up God, so he invented a new religion (that he in many ways borrowed from the English), which sheered the concept of God of all His moral attributes, thus avoiding the problem of evil by denying God His attribute of "justice." "It makes no more sense to say that God is just or unjust than it does to say that he is blue or green." For Voltaire, God was just a "hypothesis," the creator who turned on the giant Newtonian machine but then left it to go on its own. This peculiarly truncated version of theism is usually called **deism.** It believes in God, but not much of one. It is essentially an appeal to the cosmological argument; and it is satisfied with a minimal deity, which stops far short of our traditional conception of God. Needless to say, Voltaire despised the "argument from design" with all of its hidden moralizing. The world is full of evil, Voltaire insisted, and there is no denying it. And since there is evil, there cannot be an all-powerful, all-knowing God who is also just. And there can be no appeal to His "mysterious ways." He has no "mysterious ways"; in fact, He has no "ways" at all.

But these abstract answers to the problem of evil do not easily stand up to a well-described single instance of evil. The happy phrase "best of all possible worlds" may warm our hearts in the comfort of a church or a seminar room, but it quickly becomes cold when confronting real tragedy. Thus Voltaire made his point against Leibniz and his "best of all possible worlds" hypothesis by imagining a whole book full of disasters and tragedies and evils of the most sadistic sort, all greeted rather foolishly by a Leibnizian character named Doctor Pangloss. The book was called *Candide*, and it remains one of the classics of Western literature.

The problem of evil also haunted the great Russian novelist, Fyodor Dostoevsky. Dostoevsky was a devout Christian whose faith had been shaken many times, not least by the cruelty that he often witnessed and (he was occasionally the victim) in feudal Tsarist Russia. In his novel, *The Brothers Karamazov*, he portrays a conversation between two of the three Karamazov brothers, Ivan — who like the author is wracked with doubts — and Alyosha — who has joined a monastery and aspires to be a true Christian. Ivan presents us with a vivid picture of the problem of evil, especially for someone who wants desperately to believe in God.

on *the Problem of Evil,*
by Dostoevsky

"It will reduce the scope of my argument to about a tenth of the total, but I still prefer to restrict myself to the subject of children. Not that that restriction is to my advantage. But, in the first place, it *is* possible to love children, at close quarters, even if they are dirty, even if they have ugly faces, although to me a child's face is never really ugly. In the second place, I also will not speak of adults at the moment, because, besides being disgusting and undeserving of love, they have something to compensate them for their suffering: they have eaten their apple of knowledge, they know about good and evil and are like gods themselves. And they keep eating the apple. But little children haven't eaten it. They're not yet guilty of anything. Do you like small children, Alyosha? I know you do and that you'll understand why I have chosen to speak exclusively of them. Well then, if they suffer here in this world, it's because they're paying for the sins of their fathers who ate the apple. But that is the reasoning of another world and it's incomprehensible to the human heart here on earth. No innocent should be made to suffer for another man's sins, especially innocents such as these!

. . . . . .

"Do you understand this . . . my dear friend, my brother, you gentle novice who is so eager to spend his life in the service of God? Tell me, do you understand the purpose of this absurdity? Who needs it and why was it created? They say that man could not do without it on earth, for otherwise he would not be able to learn the difference between good and evil. But I say I'd rather not know about their damned good and evil than pay such a terrible price for it. I feel that all universal knowledge is not worth that child's tears when she was begging 'gentle Jesus' to help her! I'm not even talking about the sufferings of adults: they, at least, have eaten their apple of knowledge, so the hell with them. But it's different when it comes to children. It seems I'm hurting you, Alyosha, my boy. You don't look very well. I won't go on if you don't want me to."

"Never mind. I want to suffer too," Alyosha mumbled.

"One more little sketch then, the last, and that only because it's a rather curious little story and a very typical one.

"Well, this happened early in our nineteenth century, during the darkest days of serfdom — and, by the way, long live our Tsar Alexander II, the Liberator of the People! Well then, at the turn of this century, there lived a retired general, a man with the highest connections, a big landowner, one of those, you know (although even at that time there were only a few such left), who, upon retiring from the service of their country, feel sure that they have earned the right of life and death over those subjected to them. Yes, there used to be such people then. This general lived on his estate, which had two thousand serfs. He strutted around, feeling immensely important, and bullying his lesser neighbors as if they were hangers-on and clowns obliged to amuse him. He had hundreds of hounds and just about as many kennel attendants, all dressed in special livery and every one of them mounted.

"It so happened that one day an eight-year-old boy, playing in the courtyard, threw a stone and inadvertently hit the General's favorite hound in the leg, injuring it. 'Why is my favorite hound limping?' the General demanded, and he was informed that the boy had hit it with a stone. 'So it was you,' the General said, looking the boy up and down. 'Lock him up.' They took the boy away from his mother and locked him up in the guardroom for the whole night. The next day, at dawn, the General rode out to the hunt in full dress, surrounded by his obsequious neighbors, hounds, kennel attendants, huntsmen, every one of them on horseback. All the serfs of the estate were summoned too, for their edification, and so was the boy's mother. They brought the boy out of the guardroom. It was a bleak, foggy, raw day — an ideal day for hunting. The General ordered the boy stripped naked. The boy was shivering. He seemed paralyzed with fear. He didn't dare utter a sound. 'Off with him now, chase him!' 'Hey, you, run, run!' a flunkey yelled, and the boy started to run. 'Sic 'im!' the General roared. The whole pack was set on the boy and the hounds tore him to pieces before his mother's eyes. I believe that, as a result of this, the General was later declared incompetent to administer his own estates without an appointed supervisory body. . . . But perhaps you could tell me what should have been done in this case? Perhaps he ought to have been shot, to satisfy the moral indignation that such an act arouses in us? Well, speak up, my boy, go on!"

"Yes, shot . . ." Alyosha murmured, raising his eyes to his brother with a strange, faint, twisted grin.

"Good!" Ivan cried with affected delight. "Now, if you say so, it really shows that . . . Ah, you little novice, so there is that devil lurking in your heart too, you wicked Alyosha Karamazov, you!"

"What I said was pretty stupid, but. . . . "

"Yes, that 'but' is just the thing!" Ivan cried. "I want you to know, novice, that absurdity is very much needed on this earth of ours. Indeed, the whole universe is founded on absurdity, and, perhaps, without absurdity there would be nothing at all. There are a few things we do know, after all."

.   .   .   .   .

Ivan remained silent for a moment and suddenly his face grew very sad.

"I want you to understand me," he said. "I spoke only of small children to make my point more obvious. I didn't mention the other human tears with which our earth is soaked from crust to core, because I was deliberately narrowing the subject. I'm nothing but a bug and I most humbly admit that it's quite beyond me why things are arranged the way they are. I suppose that men themselves are to blame for it: they were given a paradise on earth, but they wanted freedom and they stole fire from heaven, although they knew that it would bring them unhappiness. So there's no reason to be sorry for them. All that my puny, Euclidean, earthling's mind can grasp is that there is such a thing as suffering, that no one can be blamed for it, that quite uncomplicatedly cause precedes effect, that everything that flows finds its proper level — but then all that is just Euclidean gibberish, and, being aware of that fact, I cannot agree to live by it! What good does it do me to know that no one is to blame, that every effect is determined by a cause, which itself is an effect of some other cause, and so on, and that, therefore, no one should ever be blamed for anything? For, even though I may know it, I still need retribution. Without it I'd rather destroy myself. And I must have that retribution not somewhere far off in infinity but here, on earth. I want to see it myself. I believe in justice and I want to see justice done with my own eyes; if I should be dead by that time, I want to be brought back to life, because the idea that, when justice finally does triumph, I won't even be there to witness it is too abhorrent to me. No, I want to see with my own eyes the lamb lie down with the lion and the resurrected victim rise and embrace his murderer. I want to be here when everyone understands why the world has been arranged the way it is. It is on that craving for understanding that all human religions are founded, so I am a believer. But then, what about the children? How will we ever account for their sufferings? For the hundredth time I repeat, there are many questions that could be asked, but I ask you only one — about the children — because I believe it conveys fully and clearly what I am trying to tell you. Listen, even if we assume that every person must suffer because his suffering is necessary to pay for eternal harmony, still do tell me, for God's sake, where the children come in. If the suffering of little children is needed to complete the sum total of suffering required to pay for the truth, I don't want that truth, and I declare in advance that all the truth in the world is not worth the price! And finally, I don't really want to see the mother of the little boy embrace the man who set the hounds on him to tear him apart! She won't be able to forgive him. If she wants to, she may forgive him for herself, for having caused her, the mother, infinite suffering. But she has no right to forgive him for her child torn to pieces. She may not forgive him, even if the child chooses to forgive him himself. And if I am right, if they cannot forgive, what harmony can there be? Is there one single creature in the whole world who could forgive or would have the right to do so? No, I want no part of any harmony; I don't want it, out of love for mankind. I prefer to remain with my unavenged suffering and my unappeased anger — *even if I happen to be wrong.* I feel, moreover, that such harmony is rather overpriced. We cannot afford to pay so much for a ticket. And so I hasten to return the ticket I've been sent. If I'm honest, it is my duty to return it as long as possible before the show. And that's just what I'm trying to do, Alyosha. It isn't that I reject God; I am simply returning Him most respectfully the ticket that would entitle me to a seat."

"That's rebellion," Alyosha said softly, lowering his eyes.

"Rebellion? I wish you hadn't used that word," Ivan said feelingly. "I don't believe it's possible to live in rebellion, and I want to live! Tell me yourself — I challenge you: let's assume that you were called upon to build the edifice of human destiny so that men would finally be happy and would find peace and tranquility. If you knew that, in order to attain this, you would have to torture just one single creature, let's say the little girl who beat her chest so desperately in the outhouse, and that on her unavenged tears you could build that edifice, would you agree to do it? Tell me and don't lie!"

"No, I would not," Alyosha said softly.[17]

The number of alternative religions during this intellectually creative period in our history was truly astounding. But virtually all had approximately the same purpose: to continue to believe in God, at least nominally, but to avoid the problem of evil by cutting out at least one of God's traditional attributes. It was during this period that Kant invented his "moral proof," attempting to plug up the problem of evil by postponing all judgments of justice until some indefinite future date. It was also during this period that many of the still popular formulas, "God is the energy of the universe," "God is life," and "God is universal love," became influential and respectable. The problem with these moves is already familiar: It is not clear whether they are, as they seem, revisions of the concept of God or rather subtle denials of God's existence. Many people have doubts about their religion at one time or another, but very few people are willing to jump immediately from theism to atheism (although people often jump from atheism to theism in a single "revelation"). Accordingly, people who are torn between religious belief on the one hand and arguments against such belief on the other often adopt an ambiguous intermediary position, holding onto the name of God explicitly but sometimes giving up much of the substance of their traditional belief. And just as this is an important crisis in individual lives, it is also a crisis in history. The Enlightenment was one such period in history. The outcome is by no means inevitably atheism; it might just as well be a renewed commitment to religion. But at least, such crises require rigorous thinking and a renewed attempt to understand and justify beliefs that were once taken for granted.

Faith and Irrationality

Whenever you can defend your belief rationally, it is obviously desirable to do so. The move from rationality to irrationality in the defense of religion, therefore, is a serious step. Kant, who defended belief in God as a matter of faith, nevertheless defended this belief as rational. But there have always been religious people who have defended faith against reason, emphasizing the impossibility of rational justification and the irrelevance of the usual forms of understanding and knowledge where religion is concerned. In some cases, particularly in modern times,

[17] Fyodor Dostoevsky, *The Brothers Karamozov*, trans. Andrew R. MacAndrew (New York: Bantam, 1970).

this step away from rationality may be a convenient escape from arguments and doubts that have become too overpowering. But it is not always, or even usually, taken for this reason. Instead, there has always been an enthusiastic movement within the sometimes overly formal confines of organized religion and dogma to emphasize the experience of religious belief. Such experience may well be indescribable and incommunicable. (Philosophers would thereby say it is **ineffable**.) But it is precisely the fact that it defies description and contradicts our everyday rational beliefs that makes such experiences so important to those who have had them.

Among the ancient Hebrews, there were already a considerable number of mystics who rejected the solid and conscientiously rational teachings of the religion in favor of its more mysterious and less describable experiences. And Christianity has always been powerfully motivated by its mystics; some were burned as heretics, others have been celebrated as saints. The history of Western religion has always had its nonrational side, in which faith depended upon passion and experience rather than argument and reason, even through those many centuries in which theism was generally accepted as the rational thing to believe and when the justification of this belief as knowledge had not yet been seriously challenged.

GOD AS EXPERIENCE   In earlier chapters, we discussed the rationalist notion of intuition, a special kind of experience that allows us to know some things for certain without argument and without abstraction from experience in the usual sense. According to the rationalists, we know the basic principles of logic and arithmetic in this way, and perhaps the basic principles of metaphysics as well. But when we introduced intuition, however, we emphasized that not everyone believed that intuition was part of rationality. In addition to rational insight, there may also be, according to most religious mystics, extra-rational or even irrational insight. Their epistemology is often ambiguous at this point. On the one hand, mystics want to deny the rational nature of their intuitions. But at the same time, they want to insist that what they experience is true. You can see how this will generate considerable confusion. When the mystic insists that his experience is true, he has made a claim that is on a par with the rationalist's claim (whether they agree or disagree in their conclusions). If they disagree, that is, if the mystic insists that there is a God (perhaps he has even "seen" Him) and the rationalist denies it, it should be obvious to you that there will be little room for constructive argument. The mystic considers the rationalist's arguments irrelevant; the rationalist considers the mystic obstinate and unwilling to argue rationally. It is at this point that, assuming the discussion does not degenerate to name-calling and fisticuffs, the rationalist will probably storm out of the room in frustration and the mystic, like a Zen master, may just shrug his shoulders. In such a case, that is probably the most rational response for both of them.

The mystic need not argue that what he has experienced is true, however. He might insist only that what he has "seen" is extremely important to him personally. And if he does so, it is clear that he need have no disagreement whatsoever with the rationalist, either in conclusions or in methods. They are different, of course, but not at odds. The mystic may simply be satisfied with saying that his experience is what it is and not be concerned with claims about the nature of reality. This is rare, of course, since it is a rare person indeed who does not yield to the temptation to insist that his or her experience is the truth about reality as well. But whether the mystical experience is an intuition of the (more-or-less) traditional Judeo-Christian God, whether it is a vision of the Virgin or simply a "feeling of oneness with the universe," whether the experience is the result of twenty years of prayer and meditation or induced in an evening with peyote or mescaline, the philosophical question that follows is always one of interpretation. Without denying the reality of the experience, the question is always whether one ought to interpret the experience as the knowledge of reality. Is it just an experience? perhaps beautiful, worth repeating, even worth building your life around? But it is very different to claim that the experience is true, a breakthrough in our normal perceptions (or, perhaps, our everyday illusions) to the reality behind them. This is not to say that the mystic must be wrong. It is only to say that, given the impossibility of argument, there is no way to decide the issue. Just because the mystic is "irrational" doesn't mean that he is wrong.

The retreat to personal experience was the natural strategy for those many believers who saw the substance of their beliefs hard to defend against rational criticism. Following the Enlightenment, particularly in Germany, religion took a dramatic swing to the subjective. Attempts at rational defense were given up entirely. The German Romantic philosopher Friedrich Schliermacher insisted that religion was simply a matter of intense feelings of dependence, nothing more. (His contemporary, Hegel, wryly commented that this would make a dog a better Christian than most of us.) Other philosophers turned to modernized mysticism, including very contemporary experiments with drug-induced experiences, in an attempt to save their religion from rational criticism. The American philosopher William James, for example, wrote about mysticism in his book *The Varieties of Religious Experience* and defended the idea that personal religious experience has a central place in religion and that mysticism is the root of such experience. He too insists that mystical experiences are essentially "ineffable," that is, impossible to describe to anyone else, and he compares this experience with the experience of listening to a symphony or being in love. But he also insists that mystical experiences provide us with knowledge, "states of insight into depths of truth unplumbed by the discursive intellect." And so James concludes that "the existence of mystical states absolutely overthrows the pretension of non-mystical states to be the sole and ultimate dictators of what we may believe." "The mystic," he writes, "is *invulnerable*, and must be left, whether we like it or not, in undisturbed enjoyment of his creed."[18]

THE LEAP OF FAITH   The best and most famous of all of these "new" Christians was an eccentric Danish philosopher, Søren Kierkegaard, who is often considered the father of both the "new" Christianity and that nonreligious philosophy called "existentialism." Kierkegaard was born into a society in which everyone was a

---

[18]William James, "The Varieties of Religious Experience," in *The Writings of William James*, ed. John J. McDermott (New York: Random House, 1967).

Christian; they all believed the same dogmas, without thinking about them. They all went to the same (Lutheran) churches for Sunday services and Friday afternoon bingo games and enjoyed these social gatherings immensely. They were all entitled to call themselves "Christians" just by virtue of the fact that they had been born of certain parents, brought as children to certain churches, and continued to mouth certain doctrines that they didn't understand or care to understand in the slightest. What they all lacked was passion. Their religion and they themselves, according to Kierkegaard, were boring through and through. Whatever happened to the phrase "the fear of God in their hearts"? These people felt no "fear," just the security of a comfortable and self-righteous society and the warm swill of beer in their bellies, he complained. And Kierkegaard, who had been brought up in an unusually devout Lutheran home, was disgusted with them. This isn't Christianity, he insisted, and the sophisticated disputes over doctrine and dogma had nothing more to do with being religious than the calculations of an accountant at tax time.

Accordingly, Kierkegaard offered his alternative — a new (in fact, very old) way of seeing oneself as a Christian. Rational argument was irrelevant. The doctrines of Christianity, he admitted, were absolutely absurd. But that didn't matter. In fact, it was the very absurdity of these beliefs that made the passion of Christianity possible. After all, if it were simply a matter of accepting some proposition, why should we feel anything? And "proofs" of God's existence, needless to say, were as irrelevant — in fact, offensive — as you could imagine. "Christianity is passion!" he insisted. "Religion is feeling and commitment." No talk of "truth" — unless you mean simply subjective truth, truth for me alone. No talk of "proof" and no talk of "rationality." There is simply, to use his most famous phrase, *the leap of faith,* across the borders of rationality and thinking to the passion-filled life of old-fashioned Christian fear and awe of God. "My only analogy is Socrates. My task is a Socratic task — to revise the conception of what it means to be a Christian."

Kierkegaard's move away from rationality is characterized as a rejection of "objectivity." Being a Christian, he says, is not a matter of "objective faith" (consisting of reason, doctrines, and "proofs") but of subjectivity, passion, and "inwardness."

on Subjective Truth, by Kierkegaard

... The objective faith, what does that mean? It means a sum of doctrinal propositions. But suppose Christianity were nothing of the kind; suppose on the contrary it were inwardness, and hence also the paradox, so as to thrust the individual away objectively, in order to obtain significance for the existing individual in the inwardness of his existence, in order to place him as decisively as no judge can place an accused person, between time and eternity in time, between heaven and hell in the time of salvation. The objective faith — it is as if Christianity also had been promulgated as a little system, if not quite so good as the Hegelian; it is as if Christ — aye, I speak without offense — it is as if Christ were a professor, and as if the Apostles had formed a little scientific society. Verily, if it was once difficult to become a Christian, now I believe it becomes increasingly difficult year by year, because it has now become so easy that the only ambition which stirs any competition is that of becoming a speculative philosopher. And yet the speculative philosopher is perhaps at the farthest possible remove from Christianity, and it is perhaps far preferable to be an offended individual who nevertheless sustains a relation to Christianity than a speculative philosopher who assumes to have understood it.

. . . . .

Suppose, on the other hand, that subjectivity is the truth, and that subjectivity is an existing subjectivity, then, if I may so express myself, Christianity fits perfectly into the picture. Subjectivity culminates in passion, Christianity is the paradox, paradox and passion are a mutual fit, and the paradox is altogether suited to one whose situation is, to be in the extremity of existence. Aye, never in all the world could there be found two lovers so wholly suited to one another as paradox and passion, and the strife between them is like the strife between lovers, when the dispute is about whether he first aroused her passion, or she his. And so it is here; the existing individual has by means of the paradox itself come to be placed in the extremity of existence. And what can be more splendid for lovers than that they are permitted a long time together without any alteration in the relationship between them, except that it becomes more intensive in inwardness?[19]

Religion is a confrontation with the unknown, not something knowable.

But what is this unknown something with which the Reason collides when inspired by its paradoxical passion, with the result of unsettling even man's knowledge of himself? It is the Unknown. It is not a human being, in so far as we know what man is; nor is it any other known thing. So let us call this unknown something: *the God*. It is nothing more than a name we assign to it. The idea of demonstrating that this unknown something (the God) exists, could scarcely suggest itself to the Reason. For if the God does not exist it would of course be impossible to prove it; and if he does exist it would be folly to attempt it. For at the very outset, in beginning my proof, I would have presupposed it, not as doubtful but as certain (a presupposition is never doubtful, for the very reason that it is a presupposition), since otherwise I would not begin, readily understanding that the whole would be impossible if he did not exist. But if when I speak of proving the God's existence I mean that I propose to prove that the Unknown, which exists, is the God, then I express myself unfortunately. For in that case I do not prove anything, least of all an existence, but merely develop the content of a conception. Generally speaking, it is a difficult matter to prove that anything exists; and what is still worse for the intrepid souls who undertake the venture, the difficulty is such that fame scarcely awaits those who concern themselves with it. The entire demonstration always turns into something very different and becomes an additional development of the consequences that flow from my having assumed that the object in question exists. Thus I always reason from existence, not toward existence, whether

[19]Søren Kierkegaard, *Concluding Unscientific Postscript*, trans. David F. Swenson and Walter Lowrie (Princeton, N.J.: Princeton University Press, 1941).

I move in the sphere of palpable sensible fact or in the realm of thought. I do not for example prove that a stone exists, but that some existing thing is a stone. The procedure in a court of justice does not prove that a criminal exists, but that the accused, whose existence is given, is a criminal. Whether we call existence an *accessorium* [something predicated] or the eternal *prius* [first given or assumed], it is never subject to demonstration. Let us take ample time for consideration. We have no such reason for haste as have those who from concern for themselves or for the God or for some other thing, must make haste to get existence demonstrated. Under such circumstances there may indeed be need for haste, especially if the prover sincerely seeks to appreciate the danger that he himself, or the thing in question, may be nonexistent unless the proof is finished and does not surreptitiously entertain the thought that it exists whether he succeeds in proving it or not.

If it were proposed to prove Napoleon's existence from Napoleon's deeds, would it not be a most curious proceeding? His existence does indeed explain his deeds, but the deeds do not prove *his* existence, unless I have already understood the word "his" so as thereby to have assumed his existence. But Napoleon is only an individual, and in so far there exists no absolute relationship between him and his deeds; some other person might have performed the same deeds. Perhaps this is the reason why I cannot pass from the deeds to existence. If I call these deeds the deeds of Napoleon the proof becomes superfluous, since I have already named him; if I ignore this, I can never prove from the deeds that they are Napoleon's, but only in a purely ideal manner that such deeds are the deeds of a great general, and so forth. But between the God and his works there is an absolute relationship; God is not a name but a concept. Is this perhaps the reason that his *essentia involvit existentiam* [essence entails existence]? The works of God are such that only the God can perform them. Just so, but where then are the works of the God? The works from which I would deduce his existence are not directly and immediately given. The wisdom in nature, the goodness, the wisdom in the governance of the world — are all these manifest, perhaps, upon the very face of things? Are we not here confronted with the most terrible temptations to doubt, and is it not impossible finally to dispose of all these doubts? But from such an order of things I will surely not attempt to prove God's existence; and even if I began I would never finish, and would in addition have to live constantly in suspense, lest something so terrible should suddenly happen that my bit of proof would be demolished. From what works then do I propose to derive the proof? From the works as apprehended through an ideal interpretation, i.e., such as they do not immediately reveal themselves. But in that case it is not from the works that I make the proof; I merely develop the ideality I have presupposed, and because of my confidence in *this* I make so bold as to defy all objections, even those that have not yet been made. In beginning my proof I presuppose the ideal interpretation, and also that I will be successful in carrying it through; but what else is this but to presuppose that the God exists, so that I really begin by virtue of confidence in him?[20]

---

[20]Søren Kierkegaard, *Philosophical Fragments*, trans. David Swenson (Princeton, N.J.: Princeton University Press, 1936).

You can see how little Kierkegaard thinks of the ingenious "proofs" of God's existence, as well as all attempts to "know" Him. The point of religion, he says, is precisely not to know, but rather to feel. And it is the absurdity and the irrationality of Christian doctrines, he insists, that makes this rare intensity of feeling possible.

> . . . The absurd is precisely by its objective repulsion the measure of the intensity of faith in inwardness. Suppose a man who wishes to acquire faith; let the comedy begin. He wishes to have faith, but he wishes also to safeguard himself by means of an objective inquiry and its approximation-process. What happens? With the help of the approximation-process the absurd becomes something different; it becomes probable, it becomes increasingly probable, it becomes extremely and emphatically probable. Now he is ready to believe it, and he ventures to claim for himself that he does not believe as shoemakers and tailors and simple folk believe, but only after long deliberation. Now he is ready to believe it; and lo, now it has become precisely impossible to believe it. Anything that is almost probable, or probable, or extremely and emphatically probable, is something he can almost know, or as good as know, or extremely and emphatically almost *know* — but it is impossible to *believe*. For the absurd is the object of faith, and the only object that can be believed.[21]

Christianity, Kierkegaard concludes, is suffering, the suffering that comes with the anticipation of our own death and our feeling of smallness and insignificance when we consider the eternal order of things. And for those who try to minimize this suffering through professional "understanding" and knowledge, Kierkegaard has little but sarcasm: *"The two ways.* One is to suffer; the other is to become a professor of the fact that another suffered."

GOD AS ULTIMATE CONCERN   Following Kierkegaard, Christian "irrationalism" changed the complexion of Western religion and gave faith a meaning that is not vulnerable to rational arguments. Recently Paul Tillich proposed an extremely powerful form of Christianity that also gives up the traditional view of God and moves the focus of the religion to purely personal concerns and commitments. These are our religion, and we don't need anything more.

the Ultimate Concern, by Paul Tillich

RELIGIOUS SYMBOLS

We have discussed the meaning of symbols generally because, as we said, man's ultimate concern must be expressed symbolically! One may ask: Why can it not be expressed directly and properly? If money, success, or the nation is someone's ultimate concern, can this not be said in a direct

[21]Kierkegaard, *Concluding Unscientific Postscript.*

way without symbolic language? Is it not only in those cases in which the content of the ultimate concern is called "God" that we are in the realm of symbols? The answer is that everything which is a matter of unconditional concern is made into a god. If the nation is someone's ultimate concern, the name of the nation becomes a sacred name and the nation receives divine qualities which far surpass the reality of the being and functioning of the nation. The nation then stands for and symbolizes the true ultimate, but in an idolatrous way. Success as ultimate concern is not the natural desire of actualizing potentialities, but is readiness to sacrifice all other values of life for the sake of a position of power and social predominance. The anxiety about not being a success is an idolatrous form of the anxiety about divine condemnation. Success is grace; lack of success, ultimate judgment. In this way concepts designating ordinary realities become idolatrous symbols of ultimate concern.

The reason for this transformation of concepts into symbols is the character of ultimacy and the nature of faith. That which is the true ultimate transcends the realm of finite reality infinitely. Therefore, no finite reality can express it directly and properly. Religiously speaking, God transcends his own name. This is why the use of his name easily becomes an abuse or a blasphemy. Whatever we say about that which concerns us ultimately, whether or not we call it God, has a symbolic meaning. It points beyond itself while participating in that to which it points. In no other way can faith express itself adequately. The language of faith is the language of symbols. If faith were what we have shown that it is not, such an assertion could not be made. But faith, understood as the state of being ultimately concerned, has no language other than symbols. When saying this I always expect the question: Only a symbol? He who asks this question shows that he has not understood the difference between signs and symbols nor the power of symbolic language, which surpasses in quality and strength the power of any nonsymbolic language. One should never say "only a symbol," but one should say "not less than a symbol." With this in mind we can now describe the different kinds of symbols of faith.

The fundamental symbol of our ultimate concern is God. It is always present in any act of faith, even if the act of faith includes the denial of God. Where there is ultimate concern, God can be denied only in the name of God. One God can deny the other one. Ultimate concern cannot deny its own character as ultimate. Therefore, it affirms what is meant by the word "God." Atheism, consequently, can only mean the attempt to remove any ultimate concern — to remain unconcerned about the meaning of one's existence. Indifference toward the ultimate question is the only imaginable form of atheism. Whether it is possible is a problem which must remain unsolved at this point. In any case, he who denies God as a matter of ultimate concern affirms God, because he affirms ultimacy in his concern. God is the fundamental symbol for what concerns us ultimately. Again it would be completely wrong to ask: So God is nothing but a symbol? Because the next question has to be: A symbol for what? And then the answer would be: For God! God is symbol for God. This means that in the person of God we must distinguish two elements: the element of ultimacy, which is a matter of immediate experience and not symbolic in itself, and the element of concreteness, which is taken from our ordinary experience and symbolically applied to God. The man whose ultimate concern is a sacred tree has both the ultimacy of concern and the concreteness of the tree which symbolizes his relation to the ultimate. The man who adores Apollo is ultimately concerned, but not in an abstract way. His ultimate concern is symbolized in the divine figure of Apollo. The man who glorifies Jahweh, the God of the Old Testament, has both an ultimate concern and a concrete image of what concerns him ultimately. This is the meaning of the seemingly cryptic statement that God is the symbol of God. In this qualified sense God is the fundamental and universal content of faith.

It is obvious that such an understanding of the meaning of God makes the discussions about the existence or nonexistence of God meaningless. It is meaningless to question the ultimacy of an ultimate concern. This element in the idea of God is in itself certain. The symbolic expression of this element varies endlessly through the whole history of mankind. Here again it would be meaningless to ask whether one or another of the figures in which an ultimate concern is symbolized does "exist." If "existence" refers to something which can be found within the whole of reality, no divine being exists. The question is not this, but: Which of the innumerable symbols of faith is most adequate to the meaning of faith? In other words, which symbol of ultimacy expresses the ultimate without idolatrous elements? This is the problem, and not the so-called "existence of God"—which is in itself an impossible combination of words. God as the ultimate in man's ultimate concern is more certain than any other certainty, even that of oneself. God as symbolized in a divine figure is a matter of daring faith, of courage and risk.

God is the basic symbol of faith, but not the only one. All the qualities we attribute to him, power, love, justice, are taken from finite experiences and applied symbolically to that which is beyond finitude and infinity. If faith calls God "almighty," it uses the human experience of power in order to symbolize the content of its infinite concern, but it does not describe a highest being who can do as he pleases. So it is with all the other qualities and with all the actions, past, present, and future, which men attribute to God. They are symbols taken from our daily experience, and not information about what God did once upon a time or will do sometime in the future. Faith is not the belief in such stories, but it is the acceptance of symbols that express our ultimate concern in terms of divine actions.

Another group of symbols of faith are manifestations of the divine in things and events, in persons and communities, in words and documents. This whole realm of sacred objects is a treasure of symbols. Holy things are not holy in themselves, but they point beyond themselves to the source of all holiness, that which is of ultimate concern.[22]

Notice how far Tillich has moved from the traditional Judeo-Christian conception of God. Yet he is still a theist and a Christian. But "God" for him does

---

[22]Paul Tillich, *Dynamics of Faith* (New York: Harper & Row and London: George Allen and Unwin, 1957).

not mean that divine being discussed in the Old and New Testaments but a symbol of "ultimate concern." The belief in God is now expanded to represent the fact that one finds his or her life meaningful. Tillich says that this "makes the discussions about the existence or nonexistence of God meaningless." It also undercuts the traditional idea that God is a single kind of being with precisely the characteristics we discussed in the beginning of this chapter. God is whatever concerns us ultimately, whatever is most important in our lives. This is even true, Tillich says, when one denies the existence of God. "Where there is ultimate concern, God can be denied only in the name of God."

OTHER GODS

We have limited our attention to the traditional conception of God in Judaism and Christianity. We have said very little about the third great monotheistic religion — Islam. It is appropriate, perhaps, to end this chapter on religion with a glimpse at Islam, and at two very different religions that have histories and influence just as impressive as our own. Buddhism and Hinduism have dominated the religious beliefs of millions of people in Asia and elsewhere. The following selections are brief descriptions of Islam and then of the Buddhist and Hindu conceptions of God by an American religious philosopher, Huston Smith.

Islam

The basic theological concepts of Islam as outlined in the sweeping strokes of the Koran are at most points identical with those of Judaism and Christianity, its neighbors. We shall confine our attention in this section to the most important four: Allah, Creation, Man, and the Day of Judgment.

As in other high religions, everything in Islam centers in the primal fact of God or Allah. To begin with, Allah is immaterial and hence invisible. For the Arabs this cast no doubt on his reality for they had never learned the art of ignoring everything but what could be seen. As desert dwellers, the notion of invisible hands that drove the blasts that swept the desert and formed the deceptive mirages that lured the traveler to his destruction was always with them.

The Koran did not introduce the Arab to the unseen world of the spirit. What it did by way of innovation was to focus the divine in a single God, a unified Personal Will who overshadows the entire universe with his power and grace. The indelible contribution of Islam to Arabic religion was monotheism.

To the Muslim, we must add, monotheism is Islam's contribution not simply to Arabic religion but to the religion of man in its entirety. Hinduism's prolific images he takes as obvious proof that this religion has never really approached the worship of one God only. Judaism, standing in the tradition the Koran culminates, was correctly instructed in its great *Shema:*

"Hear O Israel, the Lord our God, the Lord is One." Alas, from the Muslim perspective the Jews prior to Muhammed's reminder departed tragically from this truth. They reverted to the worship of household gods and golden calves, episodes that figure far more frequently in the Koran than in the Old Testament; in the persons of the Scribes and Pharisees they approached idolatry in their worship of the Law. Christians, for their part, have in Islam's eyes compromised their monotheism by deifying Christ. Islam honors Jesus as a true prophet of God. It even accepts the Christian doctrine of his virgin birth. But at the doctrine of the Incarnation and Trinity it draws the line, seeing these as concessions to man's inclination to seek a compromise between the human and the divine. In the words of the Koran: "They say the God of mercy hath gotten to himself a son. Now have ye uttered a grievous thing. . . . It is not meet for God to have children" (iii:78, xix:93). When Jesus claimed to be the Son of God, He was thinking of God's Fatherhood as embracing all mankind. Every human being was to him a child of God. The accretions of councils and theologies have carried Christian doctrine a long way from the simple purity of the Nazarene.

Against all these apostasies the Muslim sees the Koran taking its stand as the grand advocate of God's unity. The strength of the Arab's arms was to wax and wane but again and again the Prophet's vision of a single God triumphed over peoples like the Mongols and the Turks who would subdue his followers in physical combat. Almost every page of the Koran cries out with burning fervor: "Your God is one God. . . . There is no God but He — the Living, the Eternal" (ii:158, 255).

Islam is so well known for its recognition of the majesty and might of its one God that this point needs little documentation. Allah is almighty, omnipotent, Lord of the worlds, the Author of heaven and earth, the Creator of life and death in whose hand is dominion and irresistible power. Where the outsider has often misjudged Allah is in picturing him as domineering and ruthless; "a pitiless tyrant, who plays with humanity as on a chess-board, and works out His game without regard to the sacrifice of the pieces" is one not atypical Western characterization. Muslims see him otherwise. He who is Lord of the worlds is also

the Holy, the Peaceful, the Faithful, the Guardian over His servants, the Shelterer of the orphan, the Guide of the erring, the Deliverer from every affliction, the Friend of the bereaved, the Consoler of the afflicted; in His hand is good, and He is the generous Lord, the Gracious, the Hearer, the Near-at-Hand, the Compassionate, the Merciful, the Very-forgiving, whose love for man is more tender than that of the mother-bird for her young.

Because of Allah's grace the world of the Koran, despite its heavy warnings to the unrighteous, is a world of joy. There is air and sun and a confidence not only in ultimate justice but also in help along the way and pardon for the contrite.

By the noonday brightness, and by the night when it darkeneth, thy Lord hath not forsaken thee, neither hath He been displeased. Surely the future shall be better for thee than the past; and in the end He shall be bounteous to thee, and thou shalt be satisfied. Did He not find thee an orphan, and give thee a home; erring, and guided thee; needy, and enriched thee (xciii).

Standing beneath God's gracious skies, the Muslim can at any moment lift his heart directly into the divine presence, there to receive both strength and guidance for the living of his days. He has such ready access to the divine because between man and Allah stands nothing.

Is He not closer than the vein of thy neck? Thou needest not raise thy voice, for He knoweth the secret whisper, and what is yet more hidden. . . . He knows what is in the land and in the sea; no leaf falleth but He knoweth it; nor is there a grain in the darkness under the earth, nor a thing, green or sere, but it is recorded (vi:12,59).

Allah, then, is one, immaterial, all-powerful, all-pervading, and benevolent. He is also creator, which brings us to the second basic concept in Islam. In the Islamic conception the world did not emerge, as the Hindus would have it, by some process of unconscious emanation from the divine. It was created by a deliberate act of God's will: "He hath created the heavens and the earth" (xvi:3). This fact carries two important consequences. First, the world of matter is completely real. It is dependent to be sure on God as its creator, but once originated it is as real as anything there is. Herein lies the basis of Muslim science which during Europe's Dark Age flourished in the Near East as nowhere else. Second, being the handiwork of a God who is both great and good, the world of matter must likewise be basically good. "No defect canst thou see in the creation of the God of mercy; repeat the gaze, seest thou a single flaw" (lxvii:4). Here we meet a confidence in the material aspects of life and existence which we shall find pervading the other two semitically originated religions, Judaism and Christianity, as well.

Wonderful as is Allah's material creation — and the Koran abounds in lyric descriptions of the majesties of heaven and earth — God's supreme accomplishment lies in the fact that "He hath created man" (xvi:3). . . . The most important thing to note about the Muslim view of man is its appreciation of both the ultimacy and value of individuality. In the religions of the Far East, the indivisible, all-encompassing cosmic spirit is the primary fact and the fleeting expressions of individuality have no permanence or value. But for Islam individuality is not only fully real but also good in principle. As expressed in the human soul it is also eternal, for once created the soul lives forever. Value, virtue, goodness, and spiritual fulfillment come by expressing one's unique self by virtue of which one is different from anyone or anything else. As a great Muslim philosopher has written, "This inexplicable finite centre of experience is the fundamental fact of the universe. All life is individual; there is no such thing as universal life. God Himself is an individual: He is the most unique individual."

So intense and vivid is the Koran's feel for Allah's power and sovereign will that some interpreters have concluded that it eclipses man's freedom. That there is in Islam a problem of reconciling man's free will with God's omnipotence no Muslim will deny. What he does deny is, first, that the problem is more acute in Islam than in any other developed theology, and second, that it lands the Muslim in fatalism. In the final analysis man is master of his conduct and completely responsible for the decisions he makes. "Whoever gets to himself a sin, gets it solely on his own responsibility" (iv:111). "Whoever goes astray, he himself bears the whole responsibility of wandering" (x:103).

This belief in man's freedom and responsibility leads directly to Islam's doctrine of the afterlife. For the Muslim life on earth is the seedbed of an eternal future. It will be followed by a day of reckoning which is foreshadowed in the most awesome terms. "When the sun shall be folded up, and the stars shall fall, and when the mountains shall be set in motion. . . . and the seas shall boil. . . . then shall every soul know what it hath done" (lxxxi). On that day of judgment each individual will be accountable for the way he has lived. "Every man's actions have we hung round his neck, and on the last day shall be laid before him a wide-open Book" (xvii:13).

Depending on how it fares in this accounting the soul will then repair either to Heaven or Hell. In the Koran these conditions are described with all the vividness of Eastern imagery. Heaven abounds in deep rivers of cool, crystal water, lush fruit and vegetation, boundless fertility, and beautiful mansions with gracious attendants. Hell's portrayal is at times equally graphic with its account of molten metal, boiling liquids, and the fire that splits everything to pieces. Conservative Muslims take these descriptions literally; others as symbolically as modernist Christians read New Testament passages about pearly gates and streets of gold. In defense of their allegorical interpretation, these liberal Muslims quote the Koran itself: "Some of the signs are firm — these are the basis of the book — and others are figurative" (iii:5). Also supporting the non-materialistic interpretation of paradise is Muhammed's statement that for the favored of God, to "see his Lord's face night and morning [is] a felicity which will surpass all the pleasures of the body, as the ocean surpasses a drop of sweat." From this view, the joy of joys consists in the beatific vision in which the veil which divides man from Allah will be rent forever and his heavenly glory disclosed to the soul untrammeled by its earthly raiments. In the midst of these subtleties of interpretation, the belief that unites all Muslims concerning the afterlife is that each soul will be held accountable for his actions on earth with his happiness or misery thereafter dependent upon how well he has observed God's laws.

God, Creation, Man, and the Day of Judgment — these are the chief theological pegs on which all the Koran's teachings are hung. In spite of their crucial importance, however, the Koran, as Muhammad Iqbal tells us, is "a book which emphasizes deed rather than idea."[23]

Buddhism

We may begin with the concept of Nirvana. Etymologically the word means "to bow out," or "to extinguish," not transitively but as a fire ceases to draw. Deprived of fuel the fire goes out. This is Nirvana. From this imagery it has been widely supposed that the extinction to which Buddhism points is total, an absolute annihilation. If this were so, if absolute

---

[23]Huston Smith, *The Religions of Man* (New York: Harper & Row, 1958).

non-existence were the highest goal to which Buddhism could point for man, there would indeed be grounds for the oft-repeated accusation that Buddhism is life-denying and pessimistic. As it is, scholarship of the last thirty years has exploded this view. Nirvana is the highest destiny of the human spirit and its literal meaning is extinction. But we must be precise as to what is to be extinguished; it is the boundary of the finite self. It does not follow that what is left will be nothing. Negatively Nirvana is the state in which the faggots of private desire have been completely consumed and everything that restricts the boundless life has died. Affirmatively it is that boundless life itself. Buddha parried every request for a positive description of the condition insisting that it was "incomprehensible, indescribable, inconceivable, unutterable," for after we eliminate every aspect of the only consciousness we now know, how can we speak of what is left. An early disciple, Nagasena, preserves his point in the following dialogue. Asked "What is Nirvana like?" he answered with a counterquestion: "Is there, sir, what is called wind?"

"Yes, revered sir."

"Please, sir, show the wind by its color or configuration or as thin or thick or long or short."

"But it is not possible, revered Nagasena, for the wind to be shown; for the wind cannot be grasped in the hand or touched; but yet there is the wind."

"If, sir, it is not possible for the wind to be shown, well then, there is no wind."

"I, revered Nagasena, know that there is wind; I am convinced of it, but I am not able to show the wind."

"Even so, sir, there is Nirvana; but it is not possible to show Nirvana." Our final ignorance is to imagine that our final destiny is presently conceivable. All we can know is that it is a condition beyond — beyond the limitations of mind, thought, feelings, and will, all these as well as bodily things being confinements. Buddha would venture only one affirmative characterization: "Bliss, yes bliss, my friends is Nirvana."

Is Nirvana God? When answered in the negative, this question has led to amusingly contrary conclusions. Some concluded that since original Buddhism knew not God it could not be a religion; others, that since Buddhism obviously was a religion, belief in God is not essential to religion. Both conclusions seem so strained as to force a reconsideration of the initial assumption that Nirvana is not God.

The question, "Is Nirvana God?" has no simple answer because the word God has no single meaning. Two meanings at least must be distinguished before any sort of satisfactory answer can be even hoped for.

One accepted meaning of God is that of a personal being who created the universe by a deliberate act of will. If defined in this sense, Nirvana is not God. Buddha did not consider it personal because personality requires definition which is precisely what Nirvana excludes. And while he did not expressly deny creation, he seemed clearly not to have saddled Nirvana with responsibility for it, tracing it instead to primordial ignorance and willfulness which got started no one knows how. If indifference to a personal creator is atheism, Buddha was indeed an atheist.

There is, however, a second meaning of God which to distinguish it from the first we may call the Godhead. The idea of personality is not part of this concept which is strong in the mystical traditions of a number of religions including Christianity. When Buddha comes forward with his decisive declaration, "There is O monks, an Unborn, neither become nor created nor formed. . . . Were there not there would be no deliverance from the born, the made, the compounded" he seems to be speaking precisely in this tradition. Impressed by the similarities between Nirvana and the Godhead, Edward Conze has compiled from Buddhist texts a series of attributes that apply to both. We are told

that Nirvana is permanent, stable, imperishable, immovable, ageless, deathless, unborn, and unbecome, that it is power, bliss and happiness, the secure refuge, the shelter, and the place of unassailable safety; that it is the real Truth and the supreme Reality; that it is the Good, the supreme goal and the one and only consummation of our life, the eternal, hidden and incomprehensible Peace.

We may conclude with Mr. Conze that Nirvana is not God defined as personal creator but stands sufficiently close to the concept of God as Godhead to warrant the name in this sense.

The most startling thing Buddha said about man was that he has no soul. This *anatta* (no soul) doctrine has again caused Buddhism to look like a peculiar religion, if indeed deserving of the name at all. But once more the word in question must be used with the greatest possible care. What was the *atta* (Pali for the Sanskrit *atman*) or soul which Buddha denied? In Buddha's day it had come to signify (1) a spiritual substance which in accord with the dualistic outlook in Hinduism (2) retained its separateness throughout eternity.

Buddha denied both elements in this concept of soul. His denial of soul as a spiritual substance — a sort of miniature self in the head — appears to have been the chief point that distinguished his concept of transmigration from prevailing Hindu interpretations. Authentic child of India, he never doubted that reincarnation in some sense was a fact, but he was openly uncomfortable over the way his Brahmanic contemporaries were interpreting the concept. The crux of his discontent may be gathered from the clearest description he gave of his own view on the subject. The image he used was a flame being passed from candle to candle. As it is difficult to think of the flame on the last candle as being in any meaningful sense the same as the original flame, the connection would seem instead to be a causal one in which influence was transmitted by chain reaction but not substance.

When to this image of the flame we add Buddha's acceptance of *karma*, we have before us the clearest statements Buddha made on the subject of transmigration. From them, the best summary of his views we can construct would run something like this: (1) There is a chain of causation threading each life to those which have led up to it and others which will follow. That is to say, each life is in the condition it is in because of the way the lives which have led into it were lived. (2) In the midst of this causal sequence, man's will remains free. Though the orderliness of the world sees to it that up to a point acts will be followed by predictable consequences, these consequences never shackle man's will or determine completely what he must do. Man remains a free agent, always at liberty to do something to effect his destiny. (3) Though these points assume the importance of causal connections in life, none of them requires the notion of a lump of mental substance that is passed on from life to life. Impressions, ideas, feelings, "streams of consciousness," "present moments," — these are all that we find, no underlying spiritual substrata. Hume and James were right; if there be an enduring self, subject always, never object, it cannot be found.

We can repeat these three ingredients in Buddha's combined views of reincarnation and *karma* by way of an analogy. In the realm of ideas, (1) the thoughts that fill my mind have not appeared by accident. They have definite histories. Apart from the conditioning impact which the minds of my teachers, my parents, and the molders of Western civilization have exerted upon me, they could not possibly have come into being. (2) This fact, however, does not mean that I must pass on unchanged the ideas that have thus come my way. By altering and adding to them I can definitely affect the ongoing current of thought which we call civilization. (3) Neither the continuity nor the freedom claimed by the above two points requires that ideas be regarded as entities, things, mental substances that are in any way physically transmitted. Catching the idea of justice from my father did not mean that in the act of transmission some substance, however dematerialized or spiritual, leapt from his mind into mine.

This denial of spiritual substance was only an aspect of Buddha's wider denial of substance of every sort. Substance carries two connotations. In its precise philosophical meaning it refers to something relatively permanent that persists throughout changes in the surface variations of the things in question; in its cruder interpretations it proposes that this more basic feature of things is matter. The psychologist in Buddha rebelled against this second notion, for to him mind was far more basic in man and nature than matter. The empiricist in him, for its part, challenged the implications of permanence contained in the idea of substance. It is impossible to read much Buddhist literature without catching its sense of the transitoriness of all things finite, its profound acknowledgment of the perpetual perishing of every natural object. It is this that gives Buddhist descriptions of the natural world their poignancy and melancholy.[24]

Buddhism, in other words, conceives of God (or *Nirvana*) in terms that are very different from our own traditional conception of God. The Buddhist God is not a creator; He has no personality, unlike the God of the Old and New Testaments. In Hinduism, the notion of God is even more confused by the fact that He (She) can take on many different contradictory forms as well.

Hinduism

"HE BEFORE WHOM ALL WORDS RECOIL"

Arnold Toynbee tells of criticizing his mother for omitting a foreground detail in the landscape she was drawing. She replied that in sketching the first principle is what to leave out.

[24]Smith, *The Religions of Man*.

This is also the first principle to be learned in speaking of God, the Hindus would insist. Man is forever trying to lay hold of Reality with words, only in the end to find mystery rebuking his speech and his syllables swallowed by silence. The problem is not that our minds are not bright enough. The problem lies deeper. Our minds, taken in their conscious, surface sense, are the wrong kind of instrument for the undertaking. The effect, as a result, is like trying to ladle the ocean with a net or lasso the wind with rope. The awe-inspiring prayer of Shankara, the St. Thomas Aquinas of Hinduism, begins with the invocation, "Oh Thou, before whom all words recoil."

Man's mind has been evolved to facilitate his survival in this natural world. It is adapted to deal with finite objects. God, on the contrary, is infinite and of a completely different order of being from what our minds can grasp. To expect man to corner the infinite with his finite mind is like asking a dog to understand Einstein's equation with his nose. This analogy becomes misleading if, pressed in a different direction, it suggests that man can never know the Abysmal God. The *yogas*, as we saw, are roads to precisely such knowledge. But the knowledge to which they lead transcends the knowledge of the rational mind, rising to the deep yet dazzling darkness of the mystical consciousness. The only literally accurate description of the Unsearchable of which man's surface mind is capable is *neti . . . neti*. If you go throughout the length and breadth of the universe saying of everything you can see and conceive, "not this . . . not this," what remains will be God.

Still, words and concepts cannot be avoided. Being the only equipment at our mind's disposal, any conscious progress toward God must be made with their aid. Though concepts can never carry the mind to its destination, they can point in the right direction.

We may begin simply with a name to give our thoughts focus. The name the Hindus give to the supreme reality is *Brahman*, from the root *brih* meaning "to be great." The chief attributes to be linked with this name are *sat, chit* and *ananda;* God is being, awareness, and bliss. Utter Reality, utterly conscious, and utterly beyond all possibility of frustration, this is the basic Hindu view of God. Even these words cannot claim to describe him literally, however, for the meanings they carry for us are radically unlike the senses in which they apply to God. What pure being would be like, being infinite with absolutely nothing excluded, of this we have scarcely an inkling. Similarly with awareness and joy. As Spinoza would say, God's nature resembles our words here about as much as the dog star resembles a dog. The most that can be said for these words is that they are pointers; our minds do better to move in their direction than in their opposite. God lies on the further side of being as we understand it, not nothingness; beyond minds as we know them, not mindless clay; beyond ecstasy not agony.

This is as far as some minds need go in their vision of God: infinite being, infinite consciousness, infinite bliss, all else is at best commentary, at worst detraction. There are sages who can live in this austere, conceptually thin atmosphere of the spirit and find it invigorating — with Shankara they can understand that "the sun shines even without objects to shine upon." Most persons, however, cannot be gripped by such high-order abstractions. That C. S. Lewis of Oxford University is among their number is proof that their minds are not inferior, only different. Professor Lewis tells us that while he was a child his parents kept admonishing him not to think of God in terms of any form, for these could only limit his infinity. He tried his best to heed their instructions, but the closest he could come to the idea of a formless God was an infinite sea of grey tapioca.

This anecdote, the Hindus would say, points up perfectly the circumstance of the man or woman whose mind must bite into something concrete and representational if it is to find life-sustaining meaning. Most persons find it impossible to conceive, much less be motivated by, anything that is removed very far from what they directly experience. Hinduism advises such persons not to try to think of God as the supreme instance of abstractions like being or consciousness but instead to think of him as the archetype of the noblest reality they actually encounter in this natural world. This means thinking of him as the supreme person (*Ishwara* or *Bhagavan*), for persons are nature's noblest crown. Our discussion of *bhakti yoga*, the path to God through love and devotion, has already introduced us to God conceived in this way. He is, to use Pascal's Western idiom, the God of Abraham, Isaac, and Jacob, not the God of the philosophers. He is God the Father, lovingly merciful, omniscient, almighty, our eternal contemporary, the great companion who understands.

God so conceived is called *Saguna Brahman* or God-with-attributes to distinguish him from the philosophers' more abstract *Nirguna Brahman* or God-without-attributes. *Nirguna Brahman* is the ocean without wave or ripple; *Saguna Brahman* is the same ocean cloven with foaming waves. In the language of theology, the distinction is between impersonal and personal conceptions of God. Hinduism has included superb champions of each view, notably Shankara of the impersonal and Ramanuja of the personal, but the conclusion that does most justice to Indian history as a whole and has its own explicit champions like Ramakrishna is that both are equally correct. At first blush this may look like a glaring violation of the law of the excluded middle. God may be either personal or not, we are likely to insist; both he cannot be. But is this so? What the disjunction forgets, India argues, is the distance our rational minds are from God however we define him. As he is in himself, God may not be capable of being two contradictory things—we say may not because logic itself may melt in the full blast of the divine incandescence. But concepts of God contain so much alloy to begin with that two contradictory ones may be true from different points of view, as both waves and particles may be equally accurate heuristic devices for describing the nature of light. On the whole, India has been content to encourage the devotee to conceive of Brahman as either personal or impersonal depending on which carries the most exalted meaning for his particular mind set. The exaltedness is what is true, the symbols through which it comes garbed are but runways that can get the spirit into the air even though they point in different directions. Take care, therefore, in denouncing contradictories: they may be somebody's truth.

God's relation to the world likewise varies with the way in which he is conceived. If he is thought of as personal he will stand in relation to the world as an artist to his handiwork. He will be Creator *(Brahma)*, Preserver *(Vishnu)*, and Destroyer *(Shiva)* who in the end resolves all finite forms back into the primordial nature from which they emerged. If, on the other hand, he is conceived impersonally, he will stand above the struggle, aloof from the finite in every respect. "As the sun does not tremble, although its image trembles when you shake the cup filled with water in which the sun's light is reflected; thus the Lord also is not affected by pain, although pain be felt by that part of him which is called the individual soul." The world will still depend on him. It will have emerged in some unfathomable way from the plenitude of his being and be sustained by his power. "He shining, the sun, the moon and the stars shine after Him; by His light all is lighted. . . . He is the Ear of the ear, the Mind of the mind, the Speech of the speech, the Life of life, and the Eye of the eye." But he will not have intentionally willed the world nor be affected by its inherent ambiguity, imperfections, and finitude.

The personalist will see little religious availability in this idea of a God who is so far removed from our predicaments that he is not even aware of us as his children. Is it not religion's death to despoil man's heart of its final treasure, the diamond of God's love? The answer is that for the impersonalist God serves an entirely different function, equally important, equally religious, but different. If one is struggling against a current it is a comfort to have a master swimmer by one's side. It is equally important that there be a bank, solid and serene, that stands beyond the struggle as the terminus of all one's splashings. The impersonalist has become so possessed by the goal that he cannot bring his interest back to himself even to ask if he will make it or if there is a friend cheering him on from the further shore.[25]

DOUBT

One can be an atheist and still be religious. A Zen Buddhist, for example, may be extremely religious, but he or she does not believe in God. One can be religious as a humanist — as a lover of humanity — and not believe in God. Religion, in general, is the sense that something, at least, is sacred. But, in the context of traditional Western religion, being an *atheist* means one thing in particular, not believing in God. For some, atheism is not merely an intellectual position, it is a tragedy. For others, it is simply the logical conclusion of contemporary rationality and a proper antidote for centuries of superstition. In the following two selections, we will see the difference between these views. The first is another selection from the Russian novelist Fyodor Dostoevsky, who found himself facing unwelcome and terrifying doubts about Christianity. He reflects his despair in all of his works. His doubts began with the problem of evil but now develop to such a pitch that he begins to wonder whether the whole of Christianity has been nothing

[25]Smith, *The Religions of Man.*

more than a sham, so much so that if Christ were to return as promised, He would be burned as a heretic.

Here again is Dostoevsky:

[Ivan to Alyosha] ... "do you find acceptable the idea that those for whom you are building that edifice should gratefully receive a happiness that rests on the blood of a tortured child and, having received it, should continue to enjoy it eternally?"

"No, I do not find that acceptable," Alyosha said and his eyes suddenly flared up. "But a moment ago you asked whether there was in the world 'a single creature who could forgive.' Well, there is. And He can forgive everyone for everything, because He Himself gave His innocent blood for everyone's sins and for everyone's sake. You forgot to mention Him, although it is on Him that the edifice must be founded, it is to Him that they will sing, 'You were right, O Lord, for Your ways have now been revealed to us!'"

"You mean 'the one without sin' and His blood! No, Alyosha, I hadn't forgotten about Him. Indeed, I was wondering how long it would take you to bring Him into our discussion, because the people on your side usually make use of Him above all else in their arguments. You know — well, don't laugh now — about a year or so ago I composed a sort of poem and, if you're willing to waste, say, another ten minutes with me, I could recite it to you."

"You? You wrote a poem?"

"Why should an author forego even one listener, after all?" Ivan said with a grin. "So, are you willing to hear it?"

"I'm listening attentively."

"My poem is called 'The Grand Inquisitor.' It's a ridiculous piece really, but I'd like you to hear it."

THE GRAND INQUISITOR

"Fifteen centuries have passed since He promised to come in His glory, fifteen centuries since His prophet wrote, 'Behold, I come quickly.' 'Of that day and hour knoweth no man, neither the Son, but the Father,' as He Himself announced when He was still on earth. But men still wait for Him with the same faith, with the same love. Nay, with even greater faith, for fifteen centuries have passed without a sign from heaven to mankind.

" ... He decided to show Himself, if only for a moment, to His people, long-suffering, tormented, sinful people who loved Him with a child-like love. My story takes place in Spain, in Seville, during the grimmest days of the Inquisition, when throughout the country fires were burning endlessly to the greater glory of God and

> In autos-da-fé resplendent
> Wicked heretics were burned.

"Of course, this was not the coming in which He had promised to appear in all His heavenly glory at the end of time and which would be as sudden as a bolt of lightning cutting the sky from east to west. No, He wanted to come only for a moment to visit His children and He chose to appear where the fires were crackling under the heretics.

"In His infinite mercy He came among men in human form, just as He had walked among them fifteen centuries before. He came down to that sunbaked Southern city the day after nearly a hundred heretics had been burned all at once *ad majorem gloriam Dei*, in a resplendent auto-da-fé by the order of the Cardinal, the Grand Inquisitor, and in the presence of the King, the royal court, knights, beautiful ladies-in-waiting, and the entire population of Seville.

"He came unobserved and moved about silently but, strangely enough, those who saw Him recognized Him at once. This might, perhaps, be the best part of my poem — I mean if I could explain what made them recognize Him ... People are drawn to Him by an irresistible force, they gather around Him, follow Him, and soon there is a crowd. He walks among them in silence, a gentle smile of infinite compassion on His lips. The sun of love burns in His heart; light, understanding, and spiritual power flow from His eyes and set people's hearts vibrating with love for Him. He holds His hands out to them, blesses them, and just from touching Him, or even His clothes, comes a healing power. An old man who has been blind from childhood suddenly cries out to Him: 'Cure me, O Lord, so that I may see You too!' And it is as if scales had fallen from his eyes, and the blind man sees Him. People weep and kiss the ground on which He walks. Children scatter flowers in His path and cry out to Him, 'Hosannah!' 'It is He, He Himself!' people keep saying. 'Who else could it be!' He stops on the steps of the cathedral of Seville at a moment when a small white coffin is carried into the church by weeping bearers. In it lies a girl of seven, the only daughter of a prominent man. She lies there amidst flowers. 'He will raise your child from the dead!' people shout to the weeping mother. The priest, who has come out of the cathedral to meet the procession, looks perplexed and frowns. But now the mother of the dead child throws herself at His feet, wailing, 'If it is truly You, give me back my child!' and she stretches out her hands to Him. The procession stops. They put the coffin down at His feet. He looks down with compassion, His lips form the words '*Talitha cumi*' — arise, maiden — and the maiden arises. The little girl sits up in her coffin, opens her little eyes, looks around in surprise, and smiles. She holds the white roses that had been placed in her hand when they had laid her in the coffin. There is confusion among the people, shouting and weeping . . .

"Just at that moment, the Cardinal, the Grand Inquisitor himself, crosses the cathedral square. He is a man of almost ninety, tall and erect. His face is drawn, his eyes are sunken, but they still glow as though a spark smoldered in them. Oh, now he is not wearing his magnificent cardinal's robes in which he paraded before the crowds the day before, when they were burning the enemies of the Roman Church; no, today he is wearing just the coarse cassock of an ordinary monk. He is followed by his grisly assistants, his slaves, his 'holy guard.' He sees the crowd gathered, stops, and watches from a distance. He sees everything: the placing of the coffin at His feet and the girl rising from it. His face darkens. He knits his thick white brows; his eyes flash with an ominous fire. He points his finger and orders his guards to seize Him.

"The Grand Inquisitor's power is so great and the people are so submissive and tremblingly obedient to him that they immediately open up a passage for the guards. A death-like silence descends upon the square and in that silence the guards lay hands on Him and lead Him away.

"Then everyone in the crowd, to a man, prostrates himself before the Grand Inquisitor. The old man blesses them in silence and passes on.

"The guards take their prisoner to an old building of the Holy Inquisition and lock Him up there in a dark, narrow, vaulted prison cell. The day declines and is replaced by the stifling, black Southern night of Seville. The air is fragrant with laurel and lemon.

"Suddenly, in the complete darkness, the iron gate of the cell opens and there stands the Grand Inquisitor himself, holding a light in his hand. The old man enters the cell alone and, when he is inside, the door closes behind him. He stops and for a long time — one or even two minutes — he looks at Him. At last he sets the light down on the table and says: "You? Is it really You?' Receiving no answer, he continues in great haste:

"'You need not answer me. Say nothing. I know only too well what You could tell me now. Besides, You have no right to add anything to what You said before. Why did You come here, to interfere and make things difficult for us? For You came to interfere — You know it. But shall I tell You what will happen tomorrow? Well, I do not know who You really are, nor do I want to know whether You are really He or just a likeness of Him, but no later than tomorrow I shall pronounce You the wickedest of all heretics and sentence You to be burned at the stake, and the very people who today were kissing Your feet will tomorrow, at a sign of my hand, hasten to Your stake to rake the coals. Don't You know it? Oh yes, I suppose You do,' he added, deeply immersed in thought, his eyes fixed for a moment on his prisoner."

"And the prisoner — He just looks at him and says nothing?"

"Why, yes," Ivan laughed once more, "and that's as it should be in any case. Besides, the old man himself reminds Him that He may not add a single word to what He has said before. I might add that this may be the most crucial feature of Roman Catholicism, at least the way I see it. It's as if the Grand Inquisitor said to Him: 'You have transmitted all Your authority to the Pope and now he wields it. As to You, You had better stay away or, at any rate, not interfere with us for the time being.' They don't just say that, they even have it in writing, at least the Jesuits have. I've read it myself in the works of their theologians.

"'Do You think You have the right to reveal even a single mystery of the world from which You come?' the Grand Inquisitor asks Him and then answers himself: 'No, You do not, for You may not add anything to what has been said before and You may not deprive men of the freedom You defended so strongly when You were on earth. Anything new that You might reveal to them now would encroach upon the freedom of their faith, for it would come to them as a miracle, and fifteen centuries ago it was freely given faith that was most important to You. Didn't You often tell them then that You wanted to make them free. Well, then,' the old man adds with a grin, 'so now You have seen *free* men. Yes, that business cost us a great deal,' he continues, looking sternly at Him, 'but at last, in Your name, we saw it through. For fifteen hundred years we were pestered by that notion of freedom, but in the end we succeeded in getting rid of it, and now we are rid of it for good. You don't believe that we got rid of it, do You? You look at me so gently, and You do not even consider me worthy of Your anger? I want You to know, though, that on this very day men are convinced that they are freer than they have ever been, although they themselves brought us their freedom and put it meekly at our feet. This is what we have achieved, but was it really what You wanted, was this the freedom that You wanted to bring them?'"

"I'm afraid I'm lost again," Alyosha interrupted Ivan, "is he being sarcastic? Is he laughing at Him?"

"He certainly is not. Indeed, he is claiming for himself and his church the credit for having done away with freedom and having thus given happiness to mankind.

"'It is only now,' he says, obviously thinking of the Inquisition, 'that it has become possible, for the first time, to think of men's happiness. Man is a rebel by nature and how can a rebel be happy? You were warned,' he says to Him. 'There was no lack of warnings and signs, but You chose to ignore them. You spurned the only way that could have brought happiness to men. Fortunately, though, You allowed us to take over from You when You left. You made commitments to us, You sealed them with Your word, You gave us the right to loosen and to bind their shackles, and, of course, You cannot think of depriving us of that right now.'"

And then, the most troublesome doubt of all: Jesus leans over and kisses the Grand Inquisitor. Is this a sign that He is willing to forgive absolutely anyone? Or does it mean that God loves most those who rebel against Him?

Alyosha blurted out: "You don't really believe in God." He had the impression that his brother was looking at him sarcastically; he lowered his eyes and asked: "Does it have an ending, your poem, or is that how it ends?"

"Here's how I propose to end, it," Ivan said, continuing.

"The Grand Inquisitor falls silent and waits for some time for the prisoner to answer. The prisoner's silence has weighed on him. He has watched Him; He listened to him intently, looking gently into his eyes, and apparently unwilling to speak. The old man longs for Him to say something, however painful and terrifying. But instead, He suddenly goes over to the old man and kisses him gently on his old, bloodless lips. And that is His only answer. The old man is startled and shudders. The corners of his lips seem to quiver slightly. He walks to the door, opens it, and says to Him, 'Go now, and do not come back ... ever. You must never, never come again!' And he lets the prisoner out into the dark streets of the city. The prisoner leaves."

"And what about the old man?"

"The kiss glows in his heart ... But the old man sticks to his old idea."

"And you too, you stick to it?" Alyosha cried out bitterly. Ivan laughed.

"You know what," he said, "it's all nonsense really, a meaningless poem by a scatter-brained student who's never written two lines of poetry in his life. Why must you take it so seriously?"[26]

IS RELIGION NONSENSE?

Dostoevsky was torn by doubt. Not so the British logical positivist A. J. Ayer. In the cool and logical style of his positivism, Ayer dismantles religion like a piece of old machinery that has never worked correctly. Belief in God is nonsense, he tells us. And so too is belief that God does not exist, and so too are doubts about whether He does or doesn't. In other words, Ayer says, the whole issue is *meaningless*, not a matter of proof or disproof, nor even of uncertainty.

"God" Is Meaningless,
by A. J. Ayer

It is now generally admitted, at any rate by philosophers, that the existence of a being having the attributes which define the god of any non-animistic religion cannot be demonstratively proved. To see that this is so, we have only to ask ourselves what are the premises from which the existence of such a god could be deduced. If the conclusion that a god exists is to be demonstratively certain, then these premises must be certain; for, as the conclusion of a deductive argument is already contained in the premises, any uncertainty there may be about the truth of the premises is necessarily shared by it. But we know that no empirical proposition can ever be anything more than probable. It is only *a priori* propositions that are logically certain. But we cannot deduce the existence of a god from an *a priori* proposition. For we know that the reason why *a priori* propositions are certain is that they are tautologies. And from a set of tautologies nothing but a further tautology can be validly deduced. It follows that there is no possibility of demonstrating the existence of a god.

What is not so generally recognised is that there can be no way of proving that the existence of a god, such as the God of Christianity, is even probable. Yet this also is easily shown. For if the existence of such a god were probable, then the proposition that he existed would be an empirical hypothesis. And in that case it would be possible to deduce from it, and other empirical hypotheses, certain experiential propositions which were not deducible from those other hypotheses alone. But in fact this is not possible. It is sometimes claimed, indeed, that the existence of a certain sort of regularity in nature constitutes sufficient evidence for the existence of a

[26]Fyodor Dostoevsky, *The Brothers Karamazov*, trans. Andrew R. MacAndrew (New York: Bantam, 1970).

god. But if the sentence "God exists" entails no more than that certain types of phenomena occur in certain sequences, then to assert the existence of a god will be simply equivalent to asserting that there is the requisite regularity in nature; and no religious man would admit that this was all he intended to assert in asserting the existence of a god. He would say that in talking about God, he was talking about a transcendent being who might be known through certain empirical manifestations, but certainly could not be defined in terms of those manifestations. But in that case, the term "god" is a metaphysical term. And if "god" is a metaphysical term, then it cannot be even probable that a god exists. For to say that "God exists" is to make a metaphysical utterance which cannot be either true or false. And by the same criterion, no sentence which purports to describe the nature of a transcendent god can possess any literal significance.

It is important not to confuse this view of religious assertions with the view that is adopted by atheists, or agnostics. For it is characteristic of an agnostic to hold that the existence of a god is a possibility in which there is no good reason either to believe or disbelieve; and it is characteristic of an atheist to hold that it is at least probable that no god exists. And our view that all utterances about the nature of God are nonsensical, so far from being identical with, or even lending any support to, either of these familiar contentions, is actually incompatible with them. For if the assertion that there is a god is nonsensical, then the atheist's assertion that there is no god is equally nonsensical, since it is only a significant proposition that can be significantly contradicted. As for the agnostic, although he refrains from saying either that there is or that there is not a god, he does not deny that the question whether a transcendent god exists is a genuine question. He does not deny that the two sentences "There is a transcendent god" and "There is no transcendent god" express propositions one of which is actually true and the other false. All he says is that we have no means of telling which of them is true, and therefore ought not to commit ourselves to either. But we have seen that the sentences in question do not express propositions at all. And this means that agnosticism is also ruled out.

Thus we offer the theist the same comfort as we gave to the moralist. His assertions cannot possibly be valid, but they cannot be invalid either. As he says nothing at all about the world, he cannot justly be accused of saying something false, or anything for which he has insufficient grounds. It is only when the theist claims that in asserting the existence of a transcendent god be in expressing a genuine proposition that we are entitled to disagree with him.

It is to be remarked that in cases where deities are identified with natural objects, assertions concerning them may be allowed to be significant. If, for example, a man tells me that the occurrence of thunder is alone both necessary and sufficient to establish the truth of the proposition that Jehovah is angry, we may conclude that, in his usage of words, the sentence "Jehovah is angry" is equivalent to "It is thundering." But in sophisticated religions, though they may be to some extent based on men's awe of natural processes which they cannot sufficiently understand, the "person" who is supposed to control the empirical world is not himself located in it; he is held to be superior to the empirical world, and so outside it; and he is endowed with super-empirical attributes. But the notion of a person whose essential attributes are non-empirical is not an intelligible notion at all. We may have a word which is used as if it named this "person," but, unless the sentences in which it occurs express propositions which are empirically verifiable, it cannot be said to symbolise anything. And this is the case with regard to the word "god," in the usage in which it is intended to refer to a transcendent object. The mere existence of the noun is enough to foster the illusion that there is a real, or at any rate a possible entity corresponding to it. It is only when we inquire what God's attributes are that we discover that "God," in this usage, is not a genuine name.

It is common to find belief in a transcendent god conjoined with belief in an after-life. But, in the form which it usually takes, the content of this belief is not a genuine hypothesis. To say that men do not ever die, or that the state of death is merely a state of prolonged insensibility, is indeed to express a significant proposition, though all the available evidence goes to show that it is false. But to say that there is something imperceptible inside a man, which is his soul or his real self, and that it goes on living after he is dead, is to make a metaphysical assertion which has no more factual content than the assertion that there is a transcendent god.

It is worth mentioning that, according to the account which we have given of religious assertions, there is no logical ground for antagonism between religion and natural science. As far as the question of truth or falsehood is concerned, there is no opposition between the natural scientist and the theist who believes in a transcendent god. For since the religious utterances of the theist are not genuine propositions at all, they cannot stand in any logical relation to the propositions of science. Such antagonism as there is between religion and science appears to consist in the fact that science takes away one of the motives which make men religious. For it is acknowledged that one of the ultimate sources of religious feeling lies in the inability of men to determine their own destiny; and science tends to destroy the feeling of awe with which men regard an alien world, by making them believe that they can understand and anticipate the course of natural phenomena, and even to some extent control it. The fact that it has recently become fashionable for physicists themselves to be sympathetic towards religion is a point in favour of this hypothesis. For this sympathy towards religion marks the physicists' own lack of confidence in the validity of their hypotheses, which is a reaction on their part from the antireligious dogmatism of nineteenth-century scientists, and a natural outcome of the crisis through which physics has just passed.

It is not within the scope of this enquiry to enter more deeply into the causes of religious feeling, or to discuss the probability of the continuance of religious belief. We are concerned only to answer those questions which arise out of our discussion of the possibility of religious knowledge. The point which we wish to establish is that there cannot be any transcendent truths of religion. For the sentences which the theist uses to express such "truths" are not literally significant.

An interesting feature of this conclusion is that it accords with what many theists are accustomed to say themselves. For we are often told that the nature of God is a mystery which transcends the human understanding. But to say that something transcends the human understanding is to say that it is unintelligible. And what is unintelligible cannot significantly be described. Again, we are told that God is not an object of reason but an object of faith. This may be nothing more than an admission that the existence of God must be taken on trust, since it cannot be proved. But it may also be an assertion that God is the object of a purely mystical intuition, and cannot therefore be defined in terms which are intelligible to the reason. And I think there are many theists who would assert this. But if one allows that it is impossible to define God in intelligible terms, then one is allowing that it is impossible for a sentence both to be significant and to be about God. If a mystic admits that the object of his vision is something which cannot be described, then he must also admit that he is bound to talk nonsense when he describes it.

For his part, the mystic may protest that his intuition does reveal truths to him, even though he cannot explain to others what these truths are; and that we who do not possess this faculty of intuition can have no ground for denying that it is a cognitive faculty. For we can hardly maintain *a priori* that there are no ways of discovering true propositions except those which we ourselves employ. The answer is that we set no limit to the number of ways in which one may come to formulate a true proposition. We do not in any way deny that a synthetic truth may be discovered by purely intuitive methods as well as by the rational method of induction. But we do say that every synthetic proposition, however it may have been arrived at, must be subject to the test of actual experience. We do not deny *a priori* that the mystic is able to discover truths by his own special methods. We wait to hear what are the propositions which embody his discoveries, in order to see whether they are verified or confuted by our empirical observations. But the mystic, so far from producing propositions which are empirically verified, is unable to produce any intelligible propositions at all. And therefore we say that his intuition has not revealed to him any facts. It is no use his saying that he has apprehended facts but is unable to express them. For we know that if he really had acquired any information, he would be able to express it. He would be able to indicate in some way or other how the genuineness of his discovery might be empirically determined. The fact that he cannot reveal what he "knows," or even himself devise an empirical test to validate his "knowledge," shows that his state of mystical intuition is not a genuinely cognitive state. So that in describing his vision the mystic does not give us any information about the external world; he merely gives us indirect information about the condition of his own mind.

These considerations dispose of the argument from religious experience which many philosophers still regard as a valid argument in favour of the existence of a god. They say that it is logically possible for men to be immediately acquainted with God, as they are immediately acquainted with a sense content, and that there is no reason why one should be prepared to believe a man when he says that he is seeing a yellow patch, and refuse to believe him when he says that he is seeing God. The answer to this is that if the man who asserts that he is seeing God is merely asserting that he is experiencing a peculiar kind of sense-content, then we do not for a moment deny that his assertion may be true. But, ordinarily, the man who says that he is seeing God is saying not merely that he is experiencing a religious emotion, but also that there exists a transcendent being who is the object of this emotion; just as the man who says that he sees a yellow patch is ordinarily saying not merely that his visual sense-field contains a yellow sense-content, but also that there exists a yellow object to which the sense-content belongs. And it is not irrational to be prepared to believe a man when he asserts the existence of a yellow object, and to refuse to believe him when he asserts the existence of a transcendent god. For whereas the sentence "There exists here a yellow-coloured material thing" expresses a genuine synthetic proposition which could be empirically verified, the sentence "There exists a transcendent god" has, as we have seen, no literal significance.

We conclude, therefore, that the argument from religious experience is altogether fallacious. The fact that people have religious experiences is interesting from the psychological point of view, but it does not in any way imply that there is such a thing as religious knowledge, any more than our having moral experiences implies that there is such a thing as moral knowledge. The theist, like the moralist may believe that his experiences are cognitive experiences, but, unless he can formulate his "knowledge" in propositions that are empirically verifiable, we may be sure that he is deceiving himself. It follows that those philosophers who fill their books with assertions that they intuitively "know" this or that moral or religious "truth" are merely providing material for the psycho-analyst. For no act of intuition can be said to reveal a truth about any matter of fact unless it issues in verifiable propositions. And all such propositions are to be incorporated in the system of empirical propositions which constitutes science.[27]

It is important to notice that neither of these positions is "atheist" in the literal sense — neither denies the existence of God as such. Dostoevsky's character Ivan speaks for his author in what might be called an extremely sentimental and traumatic agnosticism, filled with the doubts that arise from the problem of evil and from a general cynicism about humanity. "If there is not God," he worries, "then everything is permitted." But even if there is God, the Grand Inquisitor tells us, the purpose of religion has little to do with Him. It is instead an instrument of unfreedom and a way to keep people ignorant and hopeful. Ayer explicitly rejects atheism as well as theism, but he does this not as an agnostic (that is, one who does not know) but as a philosopher who claims that the very notion of "God" is ultimately meaningless. This too is atheism, if by that word we mean not believing in God. What Ayer rejects under that name is the assertion that something with certain characteristics that might exist does indeed exist. Ayer insists that there is no sense even in suggesting that God might exist. Notice the difference

[27] A. J. Ayer, *Language, Truth and Logic*, 2nd ed. (London: Victor Gollancz, 1936 and New York: Dover, 1946).

between Ayer and Tillich however. For Ayer, the notion that it makes no sense to discuss the existence of God is an argument for atheism; for Tillich the same notion is an argument for theism.

THE ATTACK ON RELIGION:
MARX, NIETZSCHE, AND FREUD

But even if religion is a matter of personal viewpoint, beyond rational argument and mere passion or "experience," this is not to say that it is immune from attack. The truth and falsity of religious doctrines may not be subject to rational scrutiny, but the motivation of religious thinking might be. Why do people turn to religion? Is it just for edification? or to give them hope? or as a rationalization for the lack of justice in this world? Or is it an escape, a kind of irresponsible reaction to a world we cannot cope with, perhaps a childish unwillingness to give up an illusion of security we ought to have outgrown in adolescence?

Karl Marx is often quoted for his incisive critique of religion. His point is simple, and he makes it powerfully. Humans invent religion to escape their intolerable social conditions. And once we see this, we should reject religion as an escape and turn instead to the correction of those conditions that make such an escape necessary.

The basis of irreligious criticism is this: *man makes religion; religion does not make man.* Religion is indeed man's self-consciousness and self-awareness so long as he has not found himself or has lost himself again. But *man* is not an abstract being, squatting outside the world. Man is *the human world,* the state, society. This state, this society, produce religion which is an *inverted world consciousness,* because they are an *inverted world.* Religion is the general theory of this world, its encyclopedic compendium, its logic in popular form, its spiritual *point d'honneur,* its enthusiasm, its moral sanction, its solemn complement, its general basis of consolation and justification. It is *the fantastic realization* of the human being inasmuch as the *human being* possesses no true reality. The struggle against religion is, therefore, indirectly a struggle against *that world* whose spiritual *aroma* is religion.

Religious suffering is at the same time an *expression* of real suffering and a *protest* against real suffering. Religion is the sigh of the oppressed creature, the sentiment of a heartless world, and the soul of soulless conditions. It is the *opium* of the people.

The abolition of religion as the *illusory* happiness of men, is a demand for their *real* happiness. The call to abandon their illusions about their condition is a *call to abandon a condition which requires illusions.* The criticism of religion is, therefore, *the embryonic criticism of this vale of tears* of which religion is the *halo.*

Criticism has plucked the imaginary flowers from the chain, not in order that man shall bear the chain without caprice or consolation but so that he shall cast off the chain and pluck the living flower. The criticism of religion disillusions man so that he will think, act and fashion his reality as a man who has lost his illusions and regained his reason; so that he will revolve about himself as his own true sun. Religion is only the illusory sun about which man revolves so long as he does not revolve about himself.

.   .   .   .   .   .

It is clear that the arm of criticism cannot replace the criticism of arms. Material force can only be overthrown by material force; but theory itself becomes a material force when it has seized the masses. Theory is capable of seizing the masses when it demonstrates *ad hominem*, and it demonstrates *ad hominem* as soon as it becomes radical. To be radical is to grasp things by the root. But for man the root is man himself. What proves beyond doubt the radicalism of German theory, and thus its practical energy, is that it begins from the resolute *positive* abolition of religion. The criticism of religion ends with the doctrine that *man is the supreme being for man*. It ends, therefore, with the *categorical imperative to overthrow all those conditions* in which man is an abased, enslaved, abandoned, contemptible being — conditions which can hardly be better described than in the exclamation of a Frenchman on the occasion of a proposed tax upon dogs: "Wretched dogs! They want to treat you like men!"[28]

Fifty years later, Friedrich Nietzsche opened an even more blistering attack on religion in general, on Christianity in particular. Christianity is accused of being nothing other than rationalizations for impotence, an expression of everything that is most contemptible in human nature.

In the Jewish "Old Testament," the book of divine justice, there are men, things, and speeches in so grand a style that Greek and Indian literature have nothing to compare with it. One stands in awe and reverence before these tremendous remnants of what man once was, and sad thoughts come to one about ancient Asia and its jutting peninsula, Europe, which wants so definitely to signify, as against Asia, the "progress of man." Of course, those who are merely wretched tame domestic animals and know only the wants of domestic animals (like our cultivated people of today, including the Christians of "cultivated" Christianity) need neither be amazed nor even sorry when faced with these ruins: the taste for the Old Testament is a touchstone of "greatness" and "smallness." Perhaps they will even find the New Testament, the book of grace, more to their taste (it is full of the odor of the real, effeminate, stupid canter and petty soul). To have glued this New Testament, a kind of rococo of taste in every respect, to the Old Testament to form one book — the "Bible," *the* book — that is perhaps the great-

---

[28]Karl Marx, *Critique of Hegel's Philosophy of Right*, in *Early Writings*, trans. T. Bottomore (New York: McGraw-Hill, 1963).

est audacity and "sin against the spirit" which literary Europe has on its conscience.[29]

. . . . .

Christianity should not be beautified and embellished: it has waged deadly war against this higher type of man; it has placed all the basic instincts of this type under the ban; and out of these instincts it has distilled evil and the Evil One: the strong man as the typically reprehensible man, the "reprobate." Christianity has sided with all that is weak and base, with all failures; it has made an ideal of what *contradicts* the instinct of the strong life to preserve itself; it has corrupted the reason even of those strongest in spirit . . . it has in fear of them bred the opposite type—the domestic animal, the herd animal, the sick human animal—the Christian.

As long as the priest is considered a *higher* type of man—this *professional* negator, slanderer, and poisoner of life—there is no answer to the question: what *is* truth? For truth has been stood on its head when the conscious advocate of nothingness and negation is accepted as the representative of "truth."

In Christianity neither morality nor religion has even a single point of contact with reality. Nothing but imaginary *causes* ("God," "soul," "ego," "spirit," "free will"—for that matter, "unfree will"), nothing but imaginary *effects* ("sin," "redemption," "grace," "punishment," "forgiveness of sins"). Intercourse between imaginary *beings* ("God," "spirits," "souls"); an imaginary *natural* science (anthropocentric; no trace of any concept of natural causes); an imaginary *psychology* (nothing but self-misunderstandings, interpretations of agreeable or disagreeable general feelings—for example, of the states of the *nervus sympathicus*—with the aid of the sign language of the religio-moral idiosyncrasy: "repentance," "pangs of conscience," "temptation by the devil," "the presence of God"); an imaginary *teleology* ("the kingdom of God," "the Last Judgment," "eternal life").

This *world of pure fiction* is vastly inferior to the world of dreams insofar as the latter *mirrors* reality, whereas the former falsifies, devalues, and negates reality. Once the concept of "nature" had been invented as the opposite of "God," "natural" had to become a synonym of "reprehensible": this whole world of fiction is rooted in *hatred* of the natural (of reality!); it is the expression of a profound vexation at the sight of reality.

But this explains everything. Who alone has good reason to lie his way out of reality? He who suffers from it. But to suffer from reality is to be a piece of reality that has come to grief. The preponderance of feelings of displeasure over feelings of pleasure is the cause of this fictitious morality and religion; but such a preponderance provides the very formula for decadence.

. . . . .

The deity of decadence, gelded in his most virile virtues and instincts, becomes of necessity the god of the physiologically retrograde, of the weak.

---

[29]Friedrich Nietzsche, *Beyond Good and Evil*, trans. Walter Kaufmann (New York: Random House, 1966).

Of course, they do not *call* themselves the weak; they call themselves "the good."

.   .   .   .   .

The Christian conception of God — God as god of the sick, God as a spider, God as spirit — is one of the most corrupt conceptions of the divine ever attained on earth. It may even represent the low-water mark in the descending development of divine types. God degenerated into the *contradiction* of life, instead of being its transfiguration and eternal Yes! God as the declaration of war against life, against nature, against the will to live! God — the formula for every slander against "this world," for every lie about the "beyond"! God — the deification of nothingness, the will to nothingness pronounced holy!

.   .   .   .   .

This pitiful god of Christian monotono-theism! This hybrid product of decay, this mixture of zero, concept, and contradiction, in which all the instincts of decadence, all cowardices and wearinesses of the soul, find their sanction![30]

Not surprisingly, Nietzsche sees the decline of Christianity, and religion in general, with great enthusiasm. It is Nietzsche who popularized the old Lutheran phrase, "God is dead," but with an antireligious twist and a shout of delight that declared open war on all remaining forms of religious "weaknesses."

The most important of more recent events — that "God is dead," that the belief in the Christian God has become unworthy of belief — already begins to cast its first shadows over Europe. To the few at least whose eye, whose *suspecting* glance, is strong enough and subtle enough for this drama, some sun seems to have set, some old, profound confidence seems to have changed into doubt: our old world must seem to them daily more darksome, distrustful, strange and "old." In the main, however, one may say that the event itself is far too great, too remote, too much beyond most people's power of apprehension, for one to suppose that so much as the report of it could have *reached* them; not to speak of many who already knew *what* had taken place, and what must all collapse now that this belief had been undermined — because so much was built upon it, so much rested on it, and had become one with it: for example, our entire European morality. This lengthy, vast and uninterrupted process of crumbling, destruction, ruin and overthrow which is now imminent: who has realised it sufficiently to-day to have to stand up as the teacher and herald of such a tremendous logic of terror, as the prophet of a period of gloom and eclipse, the like of which has probably never taken place on earth before? . . . Even we, the born riddle-readers, who wait as it were on the mountains posted 'twixt to-day and to-morrow, and engirt by their contradiction, we, the firstlings and premature

---

[30]Friedrich Nietzsche, *The Antichrist*, in *The Portable Nietzsche*, ed. and trans. Walter Kaufmann (New York: Viking, 1954).

children of the coming century, into whose sight especially the shadows which must forthwith envelop Europe *should* already have come — how it is that even we, without genuine sympathy for this period of gloom, contemplate its advent without any *personal solicitude or fear?* Are we still, perhaps, too much under the *immediate effects* of the event — and are these effects, especially as regards *ourselves,* perhaps the reverse of what was to be expected — not at all sad and depressing, but rather like a new and indescribable variety of light, happiness, relief, enlivenment, encouragement, and dawning day? ... In fact, we philosophers and "free spirits" feel ourselves irradiated as by a new dawn by the report that the "old God is dead"; our hearts overflow with gratitude, astonishment, presentiment and expectation. At last the horizon seems open once more, granting even that it is not bright; our ships can at last put out to sea in face of every danger; every hazard is again permitted to the discerner; the sea, *our* sea, again lies open before us; perhaps never before did such an "open sea" exist. — [31]

Finally, in our own century, the attack has been given a psychoanalytic foundation by Sigmund Freud, who also reduces the grand aspirations of religion to mere illusions, but, even worse, the illusions of an insecure child who has never properly grown up. In *The Future of an Illusion,* he says

... if we turn our attention to the psychical origin of religious ideas. These, which are given out as teachings, are not precipitates of experience or end results of thinking: they are illusions, fulfilments of the oldest, strongest and most urgent wishes of mankind. The secret of their strength lies in the strength of those wishes. As we already know, the terrifying impression of helplessness in childhood aroused the need for protection — for protection through love — which was provided by the father; and the recognition that this helplessness lasts throughout life made it necessary to cling to the existence of a father, but this time a more powerful one. Thus the benevolent rule of a divine Providence allays our fear of the dangers of life; the establishment of a moral world-order ensures the fulfilment of the demands of justice, which have so often remained unfulfilled in human civilization; and the prolongation of earthly existence in a future life provides the local and temporal framework in which these wish-fulfilments shall take place. Answers to the riddles that tempt the curiosity of man, such as how the universe began or what the relation is between body and mind, are developed in conformity with the underlying assumptions of this system. It is an enormous relief to the individual psyche if the conflicts of its childhood arising from the father-complex — conflicts which it has never wholly overcome — are removed from it and brought to a solution which is universally accepted.

When I say that these things are all illusions, I must define the meaning of the word. An illusion is not the same thing as an error; nor it is necessarily an error. Aristotle's belief that vermin are developed out of dung (a

[31]Friedrich Nietzsche, *The Joyful Wisdom,* trans. Thomas Common, in *The Complete Works of Friedrich Nietzsche,* Oscar Levy, General Editor (1909–11) (New York: Russell & Russell, 1964).

belief to which ignorant people still cling) was an error; so was the belief of a former generation of doctors that *tabes dorsalis* is the result of sexual excess. It would be incorrect to call these errors illusions. On the other hand, it was an illusion of Columbus's that he had discovered a new sea-route to the Indies. The part played by his wish in this error is very clear. One may describe as an illusion the assertion made by certain nationalists that the Indo-Germanic race is the only one capable of civilization; or the belief, which was only destroyed by psycho-analysis, that children are creatures without sexuality. What is characteristic of illusions is that they are derived from human wishes. In this respect they come near to psychiatric delusions. But they differ from them, too, apart from the more complicated structure of delusions. In the case of delusions, we emphasize as essential their being in contradiction with reality. Illusions need not necessarily be false — that is to say, unrealizable or in contradiction to reality. . . . Thus we call a belief an illusion when a wish-fulfilment is a prominent factor in its motivation, and in doing so we disregard its relations to reality, just as the illusion itself sets no store by verification.[32]

In conclusion, Freud agrees with Marx and Nietzsche that the only proper concern of man is humanity. But is this necessarily an indictment of religion? Freud was fascinated by Jewish mysticism, and Nietzsche offered extravagant praise of Buddhism. There have been many Christians, Muslims, and Jews who have used their religion as a metaphysical support for concerted social activism and humanism (as well as "holy" wars), and there are many people for whom religion is an emotional support without which they could not even function as human beings. The balance is precarious. No one can deny that there have been thousands of atrocities — to both spirit and body — in the name of religion. But neither has it been proved that such cruelty is necessary for religion nor that religion is as easily dispensable as some of its critics have suggested. (Even Nietzsche had his serious doubts.)

SUMMARY AND CONCLUSION

Religion is one of the most important, and therefore one of the most controversial and sensitive parts of our lives. It is therefore also one of the most important, controversial, and sensitive areas of philosophy. Initially, religion seems to be part of metaphysics, an examination of the way the world really is, and the answer of religion is that reality is, in a word, divine. But we have seen that religion is much more than a search for knowledge; it is also a search for meaning, for morality, for ultimate justice, and for a type of experience that is like no other. Philosophy of religion begins as a metaphysical discipline, attempting to define a supreme

[32]Sigmund Freud, *The Future of An Illusion*, ed. and trans. James Strachey (New York: Norton, 1961).

entity of a certain type (God) and to demonstrate His existence through rational arguments and proofs. But many philosophers and religious people deny that such a metaphysical approach is either possible or appropriate. Some philosophers deny that we can *know* God but insist that it is necessary to have faith. But while some philosophers interpret this faith as a form of rationality, others claim that it is strictly an emotional commitment beyond the domain of rational argument and understanding.

These various approaches to the philosophy of religion are all very much alive, and so too are the doubts that accompany each approach. Those who believe that we can know God are at odds with those who deny that we can know Him. Those who insist on faith disagree among themselves whether this faith can be or ought to be justified. There are those who want to believe in God but find that certain problems (for example, the problem of evil) make it difficult or impossible for them to do so. There are those who see belief in God as an outmoded belief, left over from the inadequate science and metaphysics of previous centuries. And there are those who attack religion as not only outmoded but as insidious, as a symptom of decadence, weakness, or immaturity. But in the face of these various doubts and attacks, the traditional religious beliefs of Judaism and Christianity seem to be barely disturbed. Religion is humanity's oldest philosophy, and it is still the most controversial area of philosophical concern.

GLOSSARY

agnosticism: the refusal to believe either that God exists or that He does not exist, usually on the grounds that there can be no sufficient evidence for either belief.

anthropomorphic: human-like. An anthropomorphic conception of God ascribes human attributes to Him.

argument from design: see *teleological argument.*

atheism: the belief that there is no God. A person who believes that there is no God is an *atheist.*

cosmological argument: an argument (or set of arguments) that undertakes to "prove" that God exists on the basis of the idea that there must have been a first cause or an ultimate reason for the existence of the universe (the cosmos).

deism: a variation of the Judeo-Christian religion that was extremely popular in the science-minded eighteenth century. Deism holds that God must have existed to create the universe with all of its laws (and thereby usually accepts some form of the cosmological argument) but also holds that there is no justification for our belief that God has any special concern for man, any concern for justice, or any of those anthropomorphic attributes for which we worship Him, pray to Him, and believe in biblical stories about Him.

faith: in the popular sense, believing in something for which you have inadequate evidence or little good reason. In theology, faith usually refers to the trust that a believer should have in God's ultimate grace and fairness. Sometimes, faith is defended as a rational belief in God (for example, in Kant). More often, faith is defended against rationality (as in Kierkegaard).

God: in traditional Judeo-Christian theology, that being who created the universe and exists independently of it, who is all-powerful, all-knowing, everywhere at once, and concerned with justice and the ultimate welfare of humankind. When spelled with a small "g" the word refers to any supernatural being worthy of worship or at least extraordinary respect.

illusion: a false belief motivated by intense wishes. According to Marx, religion is an illusion that is intended to compensate for an intolerable social situation. According to Freud, religion is an illusion that attempts to hold onto our childhood desires for fatherly protection and security.

ineffable: indescribable.

mysticism: the belief that one can come to grasp certain fundamental religious truths (the existence of God, the oneness of the universe) through direct experience, but of a very special kind, different from ordinary understanding and often at odds with reason.

omnipotent: all-powerful, usually said of God.

omnipresent: everywhere at once, usually said of God.

omniscient: all-knowing, usually said of God.

ontological argument: an argument (or set of arguments) that tries to "prove" the existence of God from the very concept of "God." For example, "God," by definition, is that being with all possible perfection; existence is a perfection; therefore, God exists.

pantheism: the belief that God is identical to the universe as a whole. Spinoza, for example, was a pantheist. Hinduism is a form of pantheism in that it includes a conception of the divine in all things, rather than as a separate Creator.

problem of evil: the dilemma that emerges from trying to reconcile the belief that God is omnipotent, omniscient, and just with the suffering and evil in the world.

teleological argument (for God's existence): an argument that attempts to "prove" that God exists because of the intricacy and "design" of nature. It is sometimes called the "argument from design," since the basis of the argument is that, since the universe is evidently designed, it must have a designer. The analogy most often used is our inference from finding a complex mechanism on the beach (for example, a watch) that there must have been some intelligent being who created it.

theism: belief in God.

transcendent: independent of. In the philosophy of religion, a *transcendent God* is one who is distinct and separate from the universe he created. This is contrasted with the concept of an immanent God, for example, in pantheism, where God is identical with his creation, or, to take a different example, in certain forms of humanism, in which God is identical with humankind. (Hegel argued such a thesis.)

PART TWO

Knowing Oneself, and Acting

7

Self-identity

"I'm not myself today, you see," Alice said to the caterpillar.
"I don't see," said the caterpillar.

Lewis Carroll

"Just be yourself!" How often have you heard that? What is it to be a "self"? And what does it mean to be a particular self? In the abstract, the question seems to be obscure. But in everything that we do, we adopt some conception of our identity, whether we are called upon to articulate it or not. You walk into a classroom with certain conceptions of your own abilities and intelligence, your status among other students, your role vis-à-vis the professor, the haunting memory of a previous embarrassment, and a certain vanity about your looks, your grades, or just your new pair of shoes.

If you had to identify yourself as an individual, describe what makes you you, how would you do it? What features are essential to being the person you are and what features distinguish you from other persons? Think for a moment of yourself in an office, applying for a job or a scholarship for professional school or just filling out one of those dozens of forms that bombard you during the year. You dutifully fill in your birthdate, where you were born, your grades in school, your service in the army if any, awards you have received, arrests and other troubles, whether you're married or not, male or female, perhaps your race and religion. This list of facts about yourself would be one way of identifying "you." But at some point, I am sure you have felt that sense of absurdity and rebellion, "this isn't me!" or "this is all irrelevant!" What may seem more relevant to your self-identity are your political views, your tastes in art and music, your favorite books and movies, your loves and hates, habits and beliefs. These more personal features as well as the "cold facts" about yourself are important for identifying what makes you the person you are as well as for identifying you as an individual different from other individuals. In one sense, then, your *self-identity* is the way you characterize yourself as an individual. The philosophical problem of self-identity is thus concerned in part with what these characterizing qualities are. Are they just concerned with status and roles among other people? Or is there something that can truly be called "your self," without reference to anyone else? Should we think of ourselves as individuals? Or should we rather see ourselves as components of a larger organism, society, or perhaps, humanity? How should we identify ourselves?

There is, however, another sense in which we might talk about a person's self-identity. You may know someone who has experienced a religious conversion, or who has just undergone treatment for alcoholism, or perhaps just someone you see again after a long time and who says, "I'm not the same person." What does this mean? And how is it possible to say you are not the same person? When someone says, "I'm not the same person I was," he is pointing to the fact that some significant aspects of himself have changed; he has a new self-identity. And yet, in another sense, he is still the same person; the old identity and the new identity are both identities of the same person. So we have a second sense of "self-identity." Here your *self-identity* is what makes you the same person over time. Thus, the second philosophical problem, which is the one that has most concerned philosophers, is how to identify an individual as the *same* individual over time. What is it about you without which you wouldn't be you? Presumably you would still be you if you changed your religious beliefs or tastes in music. But what if you had a sex change operation? Or what if you completely lost your memory, all recollection of your family and friends? Or what if you physically disappeared altogether, remaining only a wispy consciousness, a spirit, or a ghost without a body? Would it then make sense to say that you are still you?

In this chapter, we shall explore a number of different questions and conceptions about self-identity. We will begin with the question of what makes you the same person over time, in spite of changes in tastes, habits, beliefs, and so on. An all-important and still influential tradition in philosophy, from Descartes and Locke to Hume and Kant, focuses on self-consciousness as the sole key to this sort of personal identity. Then we will return to the first conception of self-identity (what makes you you), asking whether self-identity is a matter of personal choice or whether certain facts, factors, or other people define our identity for us? And finally, we will look at a number of general questions: Whether each person can have only one self or whether a single "person" might in fact have several or many selves? Whether there is a self at all? Or, as many Eastern philosophers have argued, whether the self is an illusion and the ideal self-identity is rather self-lessness? And whether we ought to conceive of ourselves as individuals or instead as organic components of a larger community or society?

THE ENDURING SELF AND SELF-CONSCIOUSNESS: FROM DESCARTES TO KANT

Sometimes we act out our identities without being aware of it at all. At other times, particularly when we talk about ourselves or are placed in a situation where we are forced to "look at ourselves as others see us," we are very much aware — even painfully aware — of our identities. At such times we say we are self-conscious. In general, most modern philosophers and psychologists would argue that you can't have a concept of who you are unless you are also sometimes (not necessarily always) self-conscious. Conversely, you can't ever be self-conscious unless you have some sense of identity, no matter how crude. The two concepts, in other words, go hand in hand and cannot be separated from each other.

Many philosophers have argued that not only is self-consciousness crucial to having a concept of one's own individuality, but it is also crucial for establishing that one is an enduring self, that is, the same person over time. Descartes is an example. Remember how he characterized himself:

> But what then am I? A thing which thinks. What is a thing which thinks? It is a thing which doubts, understands, affirms, denies, wills, refuses, which also imagines and feels.

And, he goes on to say, I am a thing with desires, who perceives light and noise and feels heat. But he also shows, by his method of doubt, that all of this might be so even if he were not to have a body at all. Perhaps, he argues, I am fooled about my "having" a body just as I might be fooled about all sorts of other things. Therefore, he concludes, it is not my body that provides me with an identity or with the self from which I begin my philosophy. It follows from this that the particular aspects of my body — whether I am male or female, black or white, tall or short, handsome or ugly, strong or weak — cannot be essential to my identity either. My self-identity is in my mind, in my thinking, doubting, feeling, perceiving, imagining, and desiring. I am, essentially, "a thing which thinks."

from "Meditation VI,"
by Descartes

And first of all, because I know that all things which I apprehend clearly and distinctly can be created by God as I apprehend them, it suffices that I am able to apprehend one thing apart from another clearly and distinctly in order to be certain that the one is different from the other, since they may be made to exist in separation at least by the omnipotence of God; and it does not signify by what power this separation is made in order to compel me to judge them to be different: and, therefore, just because I know certainly that I exist, and that meanwhile I do not remark that any other thing necessarily pertains to my nature or essence, excepting that I am a thinking thing, I rightly conclude that my essence consists solely in the fact that I am a thinking thing [or a substance whose whole essence or nature is to think]. And although possibly (or rather certainly, as I shall say in a moment) I possess a body with which I am very intimately conjoined, yet because, on the one side, I have a clear and distinct idea of myself inasmuch as I am only a thinking and unextended thing, and as, on the other, I possess a distinct idea of body, inasmuch as it is only an extended and unthinking thing, it is certain that this I [that is to say, my soul by which I am what I am], is entirely and absolutely distinct from my body, and can exist without it. . . .[1]

It is important to appreciate the kind of step Descartes has taken here. What he is saying is that self-identity depends on self-consciousness: We are conscious of being the same thinking substance. Because our identity does not depend in any way on our body remaining the same, human identity is different from the identity of anything else in the world.

John Locke, like Descartes, sees self-consciousness as the key to self-identity. But unlike Descartes, he argues that this identity does not depend on our remaining the same thinking substance, that is, on our having the same soul. Indeed, in the course of our life our soul might be replaced with new souls just as in the course of a tree's growth its cells are replaced with new cells. What makes the tree the same tree is the fact that the same life is present in spite of changes in its physical structure; and what makes a person the same person is that the same *consciousness* and memories are present. Thus Locke differs from Descartes in distinguishing between the soul (a substance) and consciousness. It is our consciousness that we call our "self." In *An Essay Concerning Human Understanding*, Locke argues:

on Personal Identity, by John Locke

To find wherein personal identity consists, we must consider what *person* stands for;—which, I think, is a thinking intelligent being, that has reason and reflection, and can consider itself as itself, the same thinking thing, in different times and places; which it does only by that consciousness which is inseparable from thinking, and, as it seems to me, essential to it: it being impossible for any one to perceive without *perceiving* that he does perceive. When we see, hear, smell, taste, feel, meditate, or will anything, we know that we do so. Thus it is always as to our present sensations and perceptions: and by this every one is to himself that which he calls *self:*—it not being considered, in this case, whether the same self be continued in the same or divers substances. For, since consciousness always accompanies thinking, and it is that which makes every one to be what he calls self, and thereby distinguishes himself from all other thinking things, in this alone consists personal identity, i.e. the sameness of a rational being: and as far as this consciousness can be extended backwards to any past action or thought, so far reaches the identity of that person; it is the same self now it was then; and it is by the same self with this present one that now reflects on it, that that action was done.

Consciousness makes personal Identity.—But it is further inquired,

---

[1]René Descartes, "Meditation VI," in *Meditations on First Philosophy*, in *The Philosophical Works of Descartes*, trans. Elizabeth S. Haldane and G. R. T. Ross (Cambridge: Cambridge University Press, 1911).

whether it be the same identical substance. This few[2] would think they had reason to doubt of, if these perceptions, with their consciousness, always remained present in the mind, whereby the same thinking thing would be always consciously present, and, as would be thought, evidently the same to itself. But that which seems to make the difficulty is this, that this consciousness being interrupted always by forgetfulness, there being no moment of our lives wherein we have the whole train of all our past actions before our eyes in one view, but even the best memories losing the sight of one part whilst they are viewing another; and we sometimes, and that the greatest part of our lives, not reflecting on our past selves, being intent on our present thoughts, and in sound sleep having no thoughts at all, or at least none with that consciousness which remarks our waking thoughts, — I say, in all these cases, our consciousness being interrupted, and we losing the sight of our past selves, doubts are raised whether we are the same thinking thing, i.e. the same *substance* or no. Which, however reasonable or unreasonable, concerns not *personal* identity at all. The question being what makes the same person; and not whether it be the same identical substance, which always thinks in the same person, which, in this case, matters not at all: different substances, by the same consciousness (where they do partake in it) being united into one person, as well as different bodies by the same life are united into one animal, whose identity is preserved in that change of substances by the unity of one continued life. For, it being the same consciousness that makes a man be himself to himself, personal identity depends on that only, whether it be annexed solely to one individual substance, or can be continued in a succession of several substances. For as far as any intelligent being *can* repeat the idea of any past action with the same consciousness it had of it at first, and with the same consciousness it has of any present action; so far it is the same personal self. For it is by the consciousness it has of its present thoughts and actions, that it is *self to itself* now, and so will be the same self, as far as the same consciousness can extend to actions past or to come; and would be by distance of time, or change of substance, no more two persons, than a man be two men by wearing other clothes to-day than he did yesterday, with a long or a short sleep between: the same consciousness uniting those distant actions into the same person, whatever substances contributed to their production.

Personal Identity in Change of Substance. — That this is so, we have some kind of evidence in our very bodies, all whose particles, whilst vitally united to this same thinking conscious self, so that *we feel* when they are touched, and are affected by, and conscious of good or harm that happens to them, are a part of ourselves; i.e. of our thinking conscious self. Thus, the limbs of his body are to every one a part of himself; he sympathizes and is concerned for them. Cut off a hand, and thereby separate it from that consciousness he had of its heat, cold, and other affections, and it is then no longer a part of that which is himself, any more than the remotest part of matter. Thus, we see the *substance* whereof personal self consisted at one time may be varied at another, without the change of personal identity;

[2]Locke refers here to Descartes.

there being no question about the same person, though the limbs which but now were a part of it, be cut off.

· · · · ·

If the same consciousness (which, as has been shown, is quite a different thing from the same numerical figure or motion in body) can be transferred from one thinking substance to another, it will be possible that two thinking substances may make but one person. For the same consciousness being preserved, whether in the same or different substances, the personal identity is preserved. Whether the same immaterial being, being conscious of the action of its past duration, may be wholly stripped of all the consciousness of its past existence, and lose it beyond the power of ever retrieving it again: and so as it were beginning a new account from a new period, have a consciousness that *cannot* reach beyond this new state. All those who hold pre-existence are evidently of this mind; since they allow the soul to have no remaining consciousness of what it did in the pre-existing state, either wholly separate from body, or informing any other body; and if they should not, it is plain experience would be against them. So that personal identity, reaching no further than consciousness reaches, a pre-existent spirit not having continued so many ages in a state of silence, must needs make different persons. Suppose a Christian Platonist or a Pythagorean should, upon God's having ended all his works of creation the seventh day, think his soul hath existed ever since; and should imagine it has revolved in several human bodies; as I once met with one, who was persuaded his had been the *soul* of Socrates (how reasonably I will not dispute; this I know, that in the post he filled, which was no inconsiderable one, he passed for a very rational man, and the press has shown that he wanted not parts or learning;) — would any one say, that he, being not conscious of any of Socrates's actions or thoughts, could be the same *person* with Socrates? Let any one reflect upon himself, and conclude that he has in himself an immaterial spirit, which is that which thinks in him, and, in the constant change of his body keeps him the same: and is that which he calls *himself.*

The body, as well as the soul, goes to the making of a Man. — And thus may we be able, without any difficulty, to conceive the same person at the resurrection, though in a body not exactly in make or parts the same which he had here, — the same consciousness going along with the soul that inhabits it. But yet the soul alone, in the change of bodies, would scarce to any one but to him that makes the soul the man, be enough to make the same man. For should the soul of a prince, carrying with it the consciousness of the prince's past life, enter and inform the body of a cobbler, as soon as deserted by his own soul, every one sees he would be the same *person* with the prince, accountable only for the prince's actions: but who would say it was the same *man?* The body too goes to the making the man, and would, I guess, to everybody determine the man in this case, wherein the soul, with all its princely thoughts about it, would not make another man: but he would be the same cobbler to every one besides himself. I know that, in the ordinary way of speaking, the same person, and the same man, stand for one and the same thing.

Consciousness alone unites actions into the same Person. — But though the same immaterial substance or soul does not alone, wherever it be, and in whatsoever state, make the same *man;* yet it is plain, consciousness, as far as ever it can be extended — should it be to ages past — unites existences and actions very remote in time into the same *person*, as well as it does the existences and actions of the immediately preceding moment: so that whatever has the consciousness of present and past actions, is the same person to whom they both belong. Had I the same consciousness that I saw the ark and Noah's flood, as that I saw an overflowing of the Thames last winter, or as that I write now, I could no more doubt that I who write this now, that saw the Thames overflowed last winter, and that viewed the flood at the general deluge, was the same *self*, — place that self in what *substance* you please — than that I who write this am the same *myself* now whilst I write (whether I consist of all the same substance, material or immaterial, or no) that I was yesterday. For as to this point of being the same self, it matters not whether this present self be made up of the same or other substances — I being as much concerned, and as justly accountable for any action that was done a thousand years since, appropriated to me now by this self-consciousness, as I am for what I did the last moment.

Self depends on Consciousness, not on Substance. — Self is that conscious thinking thing, — whatever substance made up of, (whether spiritual or material, simple or compounded, it matters not) — which is sensible or conscious of pleasure and pain, capable of happiness or misery, and so is concerned for itself, as far as that consciousness extends. Thus every one finds that, whilst comprehended under that consciousness, the little finger is a much a part of himself as what is most so. Upon separation of this little finger, should this consciousness go along with the little finger, and leave the rest of the body, it is evident the little finger would be the person, the same person; and self then would have nothing to do with the rest of the body. As in this case it is the consciousness that goes along with the substance, when one part is separate from another, which makes the same person, and constitutes this inseparable self: so it is in reference to substances remote in time. That with which the consciousness of this present thinking thing *can* join itself, makes the same person, and is one self with it, and with nothing else; and so attributes to itself, and owns all the actions of that thing, as its own, as far as that consciousness reaches, and no further.[3]

The main thesis of Locke's argument is this: Personal self-identity is based upon self-consciousness, in particular, upon memories about one's former experiences. In this, he argues, man is different from animals, whose identity (that is, "the same dog" or "the same horse") is based on the continuity of the body, just as you would say that you have had "the same car" for ten years even if almost every part except the chassis has been replaced during that time. The identity of a "person," that is, "personal" identity, depends on self-consciousness.

Locke's idea that memory is what constitutes self-identity is inspired by the distinctly Cartesian notion that a person's relationship to her own thoughts is unique. You cannot think my thoughts and I cannot think yours. (Compare p.

[3]John Locke, *An Essay Concerning Human Understanding*, ed. A. C. Fraser (Oxford: Clarendon Press, 1894).

372 for a discussion of privileged access.) Since memory is a species of thought, it follows that you cannot remember my experiences, nor I yours. For example, you may remember your first day of school. Because *you* are remembering that experience as one that happened to *you*, you are self-identical to the person who had the earlier experience. According to Locke, then, memory provides an infallible link between what we might call different "stages" of a person. Memory seems to guarantee the identity of the person who is now remembering with the person who was then having the experience.

While Locke's theory has the advantage over Descartes's of allowing us to understand self-identity in terms of consciousness without requiring that we posit the existence of a persisting immaterial soul, it is not without its own difficulties. First, much of what we experience, we later forget. Do you remember everything that has ever happened to you? Undoubtedly, the answer is "no." Even a person who has a very good memory does not remember being born, learning to walk, or what he had for breakfast on June 3, 1972. Probably there are some fairly long stretches of your past that you have completely forgotten. Does it follow that *you* did not exist during those stretches? According to Locke's theory, it is not clear that you did.

Second, our memories are not always accurate. Sometimes we remember things that never happened. For example, you might remember very clearly lending your copy of *Introducing Philosophy* to a friend, only to find later that you had, in fact, been using it as a doorstop. Even more disturbing, though fortunately less frequent, cases of inaccurate memory occur when a person sincerely remembers experiences which, in fact, happened, but didn't happen to him. There are people who now remember delivering the Gettysburg Address, discovering radium, or singing "I wanna hold your hand" with George, John, Paul, and Ringo at Carnegie Hall. What are we to say of the memories of the deluded and the deranged? They are not *genuine* memories, but are only *apparent* memories. Clearly, Locke did not intend merely apparent memories to count among those which guarantee identity. We must, then, find a way to distinguish between those cases in which a memory is genuine and those cases in which it is not. But to do this, it seems that we would have to say that the memories are in fact the correct memories *of that person*. If this is so, it would appear that the Memory Theory is circular.

A genuine memory, as opposed to a merely apparent one, is, of course, a memory of an experience actually had by the rememberer. The person who is having the memory must be the person who had the experience. Now you can see that in distinguishing genuine from apparent memory, we have presupposed the existence of a persisting, self-identical person. That would be all very well were it not for the fact that the concept of self-identity is precisely what we are trying to explain. We cannot use the concept of memory to explain self-identity and then use the concept of self-identity to explain memory. Moreover, once we reflect on the nature of genuine memory, we can see that Locke was, indeed, putting the cart before the horse. When a person says, "I remember when I learned to ride my bike," the truth of his statement presupposes, rather than establishes, that he is self-identical to the little boy with the scabby knees.

Nevertheless, modern theories of personal identity have by and large appealed to some notion of memory, self-consciousness or psychological continuity. It is worth mentioning that ancient philosophers, Aristotle for example, did not believe this and probably would not even have understood much of what Descartes and Locke were arguing about. For Aristotle, self-identity was essentially bodily identity, without any particular reference to self-consciousness. But neither must it be thought that the modern thesis has been without its critics, in fact, its devastating critics.

Hume completely undercuts Descartes's and Locke's view of self-identity. Relying on his belief that any idea must be derived from an impression, Hume argues that when we are self-conscious we are only aware of fleeting thoughts, feelings, and perceptions; we do not have an impression of the self or a thinking substance. He concludes that the idea of the self is simply a fiction. Moreover, since we are never aware of any enduring self, we are never justified in claiming we are the same person we were a year or a minute ago.

"There is *No Self*," by David Hume

There are some philosophers, who imagine we are every moment intimately conscious of what we call our SELF; that we feel its existence and its continuance in existence and are certain, beyond the evidence of a demonstration, both of its perfect identity and simplicity. The strongest sensation, the most violent passion, say they, instead of distracting us from this view, only fix it the more intensely, and make us consider their influence on *self* either by their pain or pleasure. To attempt a farther proof of this were to weaken its evidence; since no proof can be deriv'd from any fact, of which we are so intimately conscious; nor is there any thing, of which we can be certain, if we doubt of this.

Unluckily all these positive assertions are contrary to that very experience, which is pleaded for them, nor have we any idea of *self*, after the manner it is here explain'd. For from what impression cou'd this idea be deriv'd? This question 'tis impossible to answer without a manifest contradiction, and absurdity; and yet 'tis a question, which must necessarily be answer'd, if we wou'd have the idea of self pass for clear and intelligible. It must be some one impression, that gives rise to every real idea. But self or person is not any one impression, but that to which our several impressions and ideas are suppos'd to have a reference. If any impression gives rise to the idea of self, that impression must continue invariably the same, thro' the whole course of our lives; since self is suppos'd to exist after that manner. But there is no impression constant and invariable. Pain and pleasure, grief and joy, passions and sensations succeed each other, and never all exist at the same time. It cannot, therefore, be from any of these impressions, or from any other, that the idea of self is deriv'd; and consequently there is no such idea.

But farther, what must become of all our particular perceptions upon this hypothesis? All these are different, and distinguishable, and separable from each other and may be separately consider'd, and may exist separately, and have no need of any thing to support their existence. After what manner, therefore, do they belong to self and how are they connected with it? For my part, when I enter most intimately into what I call *myself*, I always stumble on some particular perception or other, of heat or cold, light or shade, love or hatred, pain or pleasure. I never can catch *myself* at any time without a perception, and never can observe any thing but the perception. When my perceptions are remov'd for any time, as by sound sleep; so long am I insensible of myself, and may truly be said not to exist. And were all my perceptions remov'd by death, and cou'd I neither think, nor feel, nor see, nor love, nor hate after the dissolution of my body, I shou'd be entirely annihilated, nor do I conceive what is further requisite to make me a perfect non-entity. If any one upon serious and unprejudiced reflexion, thinks he has a different notion of *himself*, I must confess I can reason no longer with him. All I can allow him is, that he may be in the right as well as I, and that we are essentially different in this particular. He may, perhaps, perceive something simple and continu'd, which he calls *himself*; tho' I am certain there is no such principle in me.

But setting aside some metaphysicians of this kind, I may venture to affirm of the rest of mankind, that they are nothing but a bundle or collection of different perceptions, which succeed each other with an inconceivable rapidity, and are in a perpetual flux and movement. Our eyes cannot turn in their sockets without varying our perceptions. Our thought is still more variable than our sight; and all our other senses and faculties contribute to this change; nor is there any single power of the soul, which remains unalterably the same, perhaps for one moment. The mind is a kind of theatre, where several perceptions successively make their appearance; pass, repass, glide away, and mingle in an infinite variety of postures and situations. There is properly no *simplicity* in it at one time, nor *identity* in different; whatever natural propension we may have to imagine that simplicity and identity. The comparison of the theatre must not mislead us. They are the successive perceptions only, that constitute the mind: nor have we the most distant notion of the place, where these scenes are represented, or of the materials, of which it is compos'd.

What then gives us so great a propension to ascribe an identity to these successive perceptions, and to suppose ourselves possest of any invariable and uninterrupted existence thro' the whole course of our lives?[4]

To answer this question, Hume draws an analogy between the fictitious identity we ascribe to persons and the equally fictitious identity we ascribe to things. Just as we can never find an impression of the self that will explain human identity, so we can never find an impression of an object or substance to explain the identity of plants, animals, and things. According to Hume, then, we are never justified in claiming that, for example, a tree we see now is the same tree we saw five years ago or even five minutes ago. The cells and parts of the tree are continuously being replaced so that at no time is it ever literally the same tree. But

---

[4]David Hume, *A Treatise of Human Nature*, ed. L. A. Selby-Bigge (Oxford: Oxford University Press, 1888).

Hume's argument goes further than this; even if that were not so, we would still have no way of justifying our belief that this tree is the same one we saw some time ago, rather than another, reasonably similar to it, but yet different. How do we know, for example, that someone has not come along and replaced it with another?

The temptation to ascribe identity to things and persons, Hume thinks, arises in part from the spatio-temporal continuity of the thing; the tree is in the same place at different times. People, however, have the troublesome habit of moving around, going to Europe for the summer or college for the semester; we still see the continuity of his or her movement, receive postcards from the appropriate places at the appropriate times, and so we conclude that it is the same person. In addition to spatio-temporal continuity, we ordinarily rely on resemblance as a criterion of identity. We tolerate small changes, a haircut or a new scar, perhaps even a lost leg or a bit of plastic surgery. As long as there is a strong resemblance between two individuals, for example before and after a haircut, we think of them as the same. Only when there is a great change, as from Dr. Jekyll to Mr. Hyde, do we question the identity of the two individuals.

Hume, however, argues that spatio-temporal continuity and resemblance do not in fact guarantee identity:

> The identity, which we ascribe to the mind of man, is only a fictitious one, and of a like kind with that which we ascribe to vegetables and animal bodies. It cannot, therefore, have a different origin, but must proceed from a like operation of the imagination upon his objects.
>
> We have a distinct idea of an object, that remains invariable and uninterrupted thro' a suppos'd variation of time; and this idea we call that of *identity* or *sameness*. We have also a distinct idea of several different objects existing in succession, and connected together by a close relation; and this to an accurate view affords as perfect a notion of *diversity*, as if there was no manner of relation among the objects. But tho' these two ideas of identity, and a succession of related objects be in themselves perfectly distinct, and even contrary, yet 'tis certain, that in our common way of thinking they are generally confounded with each other. That action of the imagination, by which we consider the uninterrupted and invariable object, and that by which we reflect on the succession of related objects, are almost the same to the feeling, nor is there much more effort to thought requir'd in the latter case than in the former. The relation facilitates the transition of the mind from one object to another, and renders its passage as smooth as if it contemplated one continu'd object. This resemblance is the cause of the confusion and mistake, and makes us substitute the notion of identity, instead of that of related objects.
>
> Our last resource is to . . . boldly assert that these different related objects are in effect the same, however interrupted and variable. In order to justify to ourselves this absurdity, we often feign some new and unintelligible principle, that connects the objects together, and prevents their interruption or variation. Thus we feign the continu'd existence of the perceptions of our senses, to remove the interruption; and run into the notion of a *soul*, and

self, and *substance*, to disguise the variation. But we may farther observe, that where we do not give rise to such a fiction, our propension to confound identity with relation is so great, that we are apt to imagine something unknown and mysterious connecting the parts, beside their relation; and this I take to be the case with regard to the identity we ascribe to plants and vegetables. And even when this does not take place, we still feel a propensity to confound these ideas, tho' we are not able fully to satisfy ourselves in that particular, nor find any thing invariable and uninterrupted to justify our notion of identity. . . .

Suppose any mass of matter, of which the parts are contiguous and connected, to be plac'd before us; 'tis plain we must attribute a perfect identity to this mass, provided all the parts continue uninterruptedly and invariably the same, whatever motion or change of place we may observe either in the whole or in any of the parts. But supposing some very *small* or *inconsiderable* part to be added to the mass, or subtracted from it; tho' this absolutely destroys the identity of the whole, strictly speaking; yet as we seldom think so accurately, we scruple not to pronounce a mass of matter the same, where we find so trivial an alteration. The passage of the thought from the object before the change to the object after it, is so smooth and easy, that we scarce perceive the transition, and are apt to imagine, that 'tis nothing but a continu'd survey, of the same object.[5]

Hume's argument is familiar to us from our discussion of empiricism in Chapter 3. All we perceive, he says, is a sequence of impressions, and nowhere do we encounter an impression either of a substance (an enduring object) or of the self. What right do we have, therefore, to identify the object of this impression with the object of another? What right do we have to identify the person we are now with someone in the past?

But Hume's argument that "I never can catch myself . . ." suffers from a peculiar but obvious form of self-contradiction. He can't even deny that there is a self without in some sense pointing to himself in order to do it. This point was not missed by Kant. Kant agrees with Hume that the enduring self is not to be found in self-consciousness. The enduring self is not an object of experience — Hume was right on this point and both Descartes and Locke were mistaken. In Kant's words, the enduring self is not empirical. It is transcendental.

By "transcendental" Kant means what is a necessary condition for the possibility of *any* experience. Kant saw that if there were a different self at each moment of consciousness, we would not be able to perceive anything. In order to experience an object, we must be able to combine our various impressions of it in a unified consciousness. Thus, if we do in fact experience objects, we must assume that we have a unified consciousness that combines these impressions into the perception of an object. Or, to take a different example, Hume talks of different sorts of relations of impressions, for example, succession. In order for an individual to perceive two impressions as successive, these impressions must have been perceived by the *same* consciousness.

[5]Hume, *A Treatise of Human Nature*.

The self or "I" for Kant, then, is the necessary logical subject of any thought, perception, feeling, and so on. It is not an object of experience but transcends and is presupposed by all experience.

Hume's error, as in other matters, was in confusing the supposed experience of self-consciousness with the transcendental rules with which we tie these various experiences together. Accordingly, Kant argues, Descartes and Locke are both correct in equating self-identity and self-consciousness, but it must not be thought that the self is therefore a "thing" (as Descartes said) that we find in experience.

According to Kant, the self is the activity of consciousness, in particular the activity of organizing our various experiences. Kant borrows Hume's argument, but he turns it toward the opposite conclusion: True, I never find a self "in" my experiences, but I can always find myself in that "I" that has the experience. Kant's "self," in other words, is the act of having experiences rather than anything that we experience itself. But for Kant this self is not merely the passive recipient of experiences, and here is where the notion of self as activity becomes all-important. The self is the activity of applying the rules by which we organize our experience. Moreover, Kant argues that one of the most basic rules of this activity is that the self organize its experience as its own experience. The rule is that we must always "synthesize" our various experiences into a unity, for we could not come to have any knowledge whatever of a scattering of various impressions and sensations without this synthesis. (Think, for example, of the slightly painful and generally meaningless sensations you have when someone sets off a camera flashbulb in your eyes.) This basic rule of synthesis allows Kant to say that not only is the self the activity that applies the various rules to experience but its existence as a unified self with a unified synthesis of experiences is itself a rule. Kant gives this curious idea of the self as a rule a formidable name, "the transcendental unity of apperception." What is important in this concept is that the self for Kant is indeed essential to self-consciousness, but it is not "in" self-consciousness. Metaphorically, it is often said that it is "behind" self-consciousness, that is, it is the activity of bringing our various experiences together in accordance with the basic rules of our experience. Accordingly, Kant refers to this self as the **transcendental ego,** "transcendental" because, as we discussed in Chapter 5, it is basic and necessary for all possible human experience. The difference between Hume and Kant is sometimes illustrated in this way: Hume looks for the self among our experiences and doesn't find it. Kant agrees with Hume but argues that he looked in the wrong place. The self, Kant says, is the thread that ties together our various experiences. Accordingly, the self is not in the bundle of our experiences; it is rather the "transcendental" thread that holds them all together and is as real as any experience.

Kant returns to Descartes and challenges his main theses, even while agreeing with parts of them. First, while Descartes thought that we had to be self-conscious all the time, Kant insists that it is only necessary for "the 'I think' to be able to accompany all experiences." It is not necessary to be always conscious of our selves but only to be, at any point in our experience, capable of becoming self-conscious; we can turn our attention when we want to from whatever we are doing and watch ourselves doing what we are doing. This is an important point: our concern with self-consciousness is given impetus just because we are often not self-conscious. In fact, there have been several philosophers (and many mystics) who have argued that self-consciousness is bad, a useless thing, and should be avoided as much as possible. According to Descartes, this is not possible, for to exist at all as a human being is to exist self-consciously. According to Kant, on the other hand, to exist as a human being is "to be able" to be self-conscious.

Second, Kant objects to Descartes's belief that the thinking self is a thinking thing. He objects to this, first of all, because of his insistence (as a result of Hume's argument) that the self (or "transcendental ego") is not in our experience but rather "behind" it and responsible for it. More literally, he says that the self must be thought of as an activity. You can see what a radical move this is when you recall the traditional doctrine of the soul in Plato, in Christianity, and in much of modern thought. The soul, quite simply, is the self conceived of as a thing, an enduring thing that can survive the death of the body. By saying that the self is an activity, Kant undermines (as Hume had intended to undermine) the traditional concept of soul.[6]

Against the Soul,
by Immanuel Kant

Pure reason requires us to seek for every predicate of a thing its own subject, and for this subject, which is itself necessarily nothing but a predicate, its subject, and so on indefinitely (or as far as we can reach). But hence it follows that we must not hold anything at which we can arrive to be an ultimate subject.

Now we appear to have this substance in the consciousness of ourselves (in the thinking subject), and indeed in an immediate intuition; for all the predicates of an internal sense refer to the *ego*, as a subject, and I cannot conceive myself as the predicate of any other subject. Hence completeness in the reference of the given concepts as predicates to a subject — not merely an Idea, but an object — that is, the absolute subject itself, seems to be given in experience. But this expectation is disappointed. For the ego is not a concept, but only the indication of the object of the inner sense, so far as we know it by no further predicate. Consequently it cannot indeed be itself a predicate of any other thing; but just as little can it be a definite concept of an absolute subject, but is, as in all other cases, only the reference of the inner phenomena to their unknown subject. Yet this idea (which serves very well as a regulative principle totally to destroy all materialistic explanations of the internal phenomena of the soul) occasions by a very natural misunderstanding a very specious argument, which infers its nature from this supposed knowledge of the substance of our thinking being. This is

---

[6]It is worth mentioning, however, that Kant held onto the Christian concept of soul; but to do so, he could defend it only as a "postulate of practical reason," in other words, as a strictly moral claim, much as he had defended his belief in God. Later philosophers borrowed Kant's arguments to get rid of the soul altogether.

specious so far as the knowledge of it falls quite without the complex of experience.

But though we may call this thinking self (the soul) "substance," as being the ultimate subject of thinking which cannot be further represented as the predicate of another thing, it remains quite empty and without significance if permanence — the quality which renders the concept of substances in experience fruitful — cannot be proved of it.

But permanence can never be proved of the concept of a substance as a thing in itself, but for the purposes of experience only.

If, therefore, from the concept of the soul as a substance we would infer its permanence, this can hold good as regards possible experience only, not of the soul as a thing in itself and beyond all possible experience. Life is the subjective condition of all our possible experience; consequently we can only infer the permanence of the soul in life, for the death of a man is the end of all experience which concerns the soul as an object of experience, except the contrary be proved — which is the very question in hand. The permanence of the soul can therefore only be proved (and no one cares to do that) during the life of man, but not, as we desire to do, after death. The reason for this is that the concept of substance, so far as it is to be considered necessarily with the concept of permanence, can be so combined only according to the principles of possible experience, and therefore for the purposes of experience only.[7]

Third, Kant argued that we need two very different conceptions of self. He saw that this conception of self as self-consciousness was not sufficient to do the whole job that philosophers had wanted it to do. One part of Descartes's enterprise was to find out what was essential to his existence, what could not be doubted and so could serve as a first premise for his *Meditations.* So too Locke and Hume had tried to find (though Locke did and Hume didn't) that self that defined us through our various changes, which identified Jekyll and Hyde and identifies us from year to year, day to day, and mood to mood. But the function of the self was also to serve as a way of identifying ourselves in distinction from other people and other things. Thus Descartes's concept of the self as a thinking thing was not sufficient to tell us what made one person different from another, and he found it necessary to supplement his concept of self with an account of how a person was composed of a self and a body in some special way. Similarly, Locke distinguishes between personal identity and identity as a man (that is, as a biological example of the species *homo sapiens*) and tells us that both are necessary for us

---

[7]Immanuel Kant, *Prolegomena to Any Future Metaphysics,* trans. Lewis White Beck (New York: Bobbs-Merrill, 1950). Ludwig Wittgenstein, for example, used a Kantian thesis to deny the existence of the subject altogether. In his *Tractatus Logico-Philosophicus,* he tells us:

> The thinking, presenting subject — there is no such thing. *In an important sense* there is no subject. The subject does not belong to the world, but is a limit of the world. There is [therefore] really a sense in which in philosophy we can talk non-psychologically of the I. The I occurs in philosophy through the fact that the 'world is my world.' The philosophical I is not the man, not the human body, or the human soul of which psychology treats, but the metaphysical subject, the limit — not a part of the world.

to understand how one particular person is different from another particular person. We can now clearly see that the question of self-identity divides into two questions: (1) What is essential to being a self? and (2) What is essential to being a particular self? Kant's conception of self as that which has experiences, the transcendental self, only answers the first question. There is nothing in the notion of transcendental self that allows us to distinguish between different people and tell them apart. Accordingly, he identifies another "self" that he calls the **empirical ego,** which includes all of those particular things about us that make us different people. Differences in our bodies, our looks, our size, our strength would be such differences. So too would our different personalities, our different thoughts and memories. It is the empirical self that identifies us as individual persons. It is the transcendental self that makes us human.

These have been the traditional answers to the philosophical problem of self-identity. What is it that makes one "the same person" from moment to moment and year to year? The spatio-temporal **continuity** of the body would seem to be a part of the answer. But philosophers since (and before) Descartes have seen quite clearly that this is never enough, that it is also self-consciousness that provides the key to self-identity. But even this has not solved the problem. To see this, consider the following two bizarre but illuminating examples:

Jones has an emergency brain operation. His own brain is removed and replaced by the brain of Brown (who is recently deceased). "Jones" still looks like Jones, still carries the same driver's license, and lives in the same house, but all of his memories and personality traits are those of Brown. Is he still Jones? Or is he Brown in Jones's body? Suppose you had been (or are?) Brown, could you claim to be still alive in Jones's body?

Smith undergoes a personality split of the most radical kind imaginable. Like the one-celled animal, the amoeba, Smith splits, head to toe, each half of him forming an exact duplicate of the original, same memories and personality, same habits, knowledge, likes and dislikes, skills, and so on. Which of the two is Smith? Does it make any sense to say that both are? Suppose you are now one of the two resultant Smiths: Would you — could you — intelligibly say that the other Smith is also you? That would surely violate the concept of the transcendental self, which must always be oneself. It would also violate common sense. But, given your common origins and exact similarities, could you say that the other Smith was merely someone else?

To consider these bizarre complications, here is Massachusetts philosopher Meredith Michaels, who writes extensively on the problems of personal identity:

"Personal Identity," by Meredith Michaels

While they are illuminating, particularly in relation to one another, these traditional answers to the philosophical problem of self-identity raise as many questions as they answer. To see this, let us travel to a not very distant make-believe world.

One night, after a serious bout with the library, you and your best friend Wanda Bagg (or Walter, if you prefer) decide to indulge yourselves at the College Haven. Before you can stop her, Wanda steps out in front of a steamroller that happens to be moving down Main Street. Wanda is crushed. Witnessing the horror of the accident, you have a stroke. Fortunately, Dr. Hagendaas, the famous neurosurgeon who has been visiting the campus, is also on the way to the College Haven. Taking charge, he rushes you and Wanda to the Health Center, where he performs a "body transplant." He takes Wanda's brain, which miraculously escaped the impact of the steamroller, and puts it in the place of yours, which was, of course, severely damaged by the stroke. After several days, the following battle ensues: Wanda's parents claim that they are under no obligation to continue paying tuition. After all, Wanda was killed by a steamroller. Your parents claim that they are under no obligation to continue paying tuition. After all, you died of a stroke. It is clear, then, that a basic question is in need of an answer: who is the person lying in bed in the Health Center? Is it Wanda? Is it you? Is it someone else altogether? For the sake of discussion, let us call the person lying in the bed Schwanda. What reasons do we have for believing that Schwanda is Wanda? Given that one's self-consciousness, one's thoughts, beliefs and feelings are all mental phenomena, we might naturally conclude that a person goes wherever her brain goes (on the assumption that our mental characteristics are more likely "located" in the brain than in, say, our smallest left toe). Schwanda will remember having set off for the College Haven with you; she will remember receiving the college acceptance letter addressed: "Dear Wanda, We are happy to inform you that . . ."; she'll remember being hugged by Wanda's mother on the afternoon of her first day of school. That is, Schwanda will *believe* that she's Wanda.

Nevertheless, the fact that Schwanda believes herself to be Wanda does not in itself guarantee that she is. Do we have any basis for insisting that Schwanda is Wanda and not someone who is *deluded* into thinking that she's Wanda? How can we determine whether Schwanda's Wanda memories are genuine and not merely apparent? As we came to realize in our discussion of Locke's Memory Theory, it is not legitimate at this point to appeal to the self-identity of Schwanda and Wanda, since that is precisely what we're trying to determine. In other words, in attempting to establish that Schwanda's Wanda memories are genuine memories, we cannot argue that they are genuine on the grounds that Schwanda *is* Wanda.

Perhaps it is possible to stop short of circularity. Why couldn't we say that Schwanda's Wanda memories are genuine because the *brain* that is remembering is the same as the brain that had the original experiences. Thus, the experiences are preserved in the very organ that underwent them. Though there is an initial plausibility to this response, it fails to solve our problem. Suppose that Schwanda is Wanda — remembering the experience of learning to ride a bicycle. Though the brain in question is indeed the same, it is nonetheless clear to all of us that brains alone do not learn to ride bicycles. Nor, indeed, do brains alone remember having done so. *People* learn to ride bicycles and *people* remember having done so. And the question we are trying to answer is whether Schwanda (who is remembering) is the same person as Wanda (who did the bicycling). The appeal to the fact that the same brain is involved in each event does not provide us with a way out of the Lockean circle.

It is at this point that philsophers begin to reconsider the Aristotelian position, mentioned earlier, that self-identity is essentially *bodily* identity. If the Body Theory of Personal Identity is true, then the person lying in bed at the Health Center is you, deluded into believing that you are Wanda. That is, Schwanda is self-identical to you.

You might wonder, at this point, whether there are any positive reasons for endorsing the Body Theory, or whether it is simply a place to which one retreats only in defeat? The following case is designed to persuade you that there is at least *some* plausibility to the Body Theory. Suppose that an evil scientist, Dr. Nefarious, has selected you as his prime subject for a horrible experiment. You are dragged into his office. He says, "Tomorrow at 5:00, you will be subjected to the most terrible tortures. Your nails will be pulled out one by one. Rats will be caged around your head. Burning oil will drip slowly on your back. The remainder I leave as a surprise."

Are you worried about what will happen to you at 5:00 tomorrow? If you have any sense, you are. You think of the excruciating pain and suffering you will undergo and would surely do just about anything to avoid it.

But now, Dr. Nefarious says, "Tomorrow at 4:55, I will use my Dememorizer to erase your memory of this conversation." Are you still anxious about what is going to happen to you tomorrow at 5:00? Surely you are. After all the fact that you won't, between 4:55 and 5:00, be anticipating your torture doesn't entail that the torture itself will be any less painful. When you forget that your Calculus professor told the class there would be a test on Friday, you aren't thereby spared the experience of taking the test (in fact, in that case the experience is made worse by your not having had the opportunity to anticipate it).

Now, Dr. Nefarious says, "Tomorrow at 4:57, I will use my Dememorizer to erase *all* of your memories." Are you still anxious about what will happen tomorrow at 5:00? Isn't it natural to describe the situation as one in which you will undergo horrible torture, though you won't know who you are or why this is happening to you? *You* will still experience *your* fingernails being pulled out, *your* back being burned, *your* face being eaten up by rats. Surely, those experiences are ones you would like to avoid.

Finally, Dr. Nefarious says to you, "Tomorrow at 4:58, I am going to use my Rememorizer to implant in your brain all of Ronald Regan's memories." Though this may not please you for personal or political reasons, the relevant question remains this: are you still worried about what is going to happen tomorrow at 5:00? Isn't it again perfectly natural to describe the situation as one in which you will undergo horrible torture, all the while believing that you are Ronald Reagan. Do you not *now* remain concerned that *you* will experience excruciating pain and intolerable suffering? Look at your fingernails while you consider your answer to this question.

What this story demonstrates is not the conclusive superiority of the Body Theory over the Memory (or Brain) Theory, but rather the importance of our bodies to our self-identity. This is something that tends to get lost in the traditional conceptions of personal identity. Furthermore, returning to the case of Schwanda, we can now see that it is not altogether preposterous to argue that Schwanda is indeed you, deluded into believing that she is Wanda. In other words, anyone who wishes to dismiss that possibility must also dismiss the possibility that the person who undergoes the torture is indeed you, deluded into believing that you are Ronald Reagan.

While it is true that we tend to identify ourselves with and by our thoughts, beliefs, inclinations and feelings, our discussion of the Body Theory should remind us that there are reasons for believing that our bodies are, at the very least, important to who we are. Some philosophers would argue that our bodies *are* who we are, that self-identity *is* bodily identity.

In considering these admittedly fanciful problem cases, we have seen that we lack a concept of self-identity that allows us to predict when we would or wouldn't persist through time. This might suggest to us that our concept of self-identity is not an all-or-nothing one, that, in fact, our concept is one which admits of degrees. If so, we are no longer talking about identity *per se*, which is an all-or-nothing concept, but rather about some other relation of psychological and physical connectedness. Nevertheless, we can now see first, that the answer to the question "Who ought to pay Schwanda's tuition?" will depend upon which theory of personal identity we are inclined to endorse and second, that the answer may not be as clear and unequivocal as we would like it to be.[8]

None of the traditional answers would seem to provide us with satisfactory answers to such puzzles. Granting that the examples are strange, they still show us that our traditional conceptions of personal self-identity are not as adequate as they might be. And given the increasing possibility of such examples in real life with some of the advances in modern science, we must expect that our conceptions of personal identity may well change in the near future just in order to make sense of these cases.

FACTS AND FANTASIES: EXISTENTIALISM AND BEYOND

It is one thing to be *a* self. It is something else to be a *particular* self. Let's return to common experience again. You are once again filling out one of those many forms that ask for the facts about you — age, place of birth, marital status, grades, and such. And you are once again experiencing that familiar sense of revolt and disgust that says, "this is all irrelevant." But is it? What are you, if anything, over and above all the facts about you? Of course job and scholarship applications rarely ask what is more personal about you. They won't dare ask about your sexual exploits and drinking habits, what you dream about, or how you like your pizza. But suppose you were to supply all of that information too. Would that be you?

[8]This essay was written by Meredith Michaels especially for this edition.

This problem of concrete self-identity has always been a practical problem for self-conscious people. Who am I? It isn't enough to say that a person is the sum total of facts about him or her. Surely some such "facts" are simply irrelevant, like the fact that you had a mole on your knee when you were three or the fact that, in last week's chemistry exam, you got number 18 wrong but luckily guessed number 23 correctly. So we want to say that some facts are more essential than others. The fact that you are "devastatingly good looking" is probably much more important to you than the fact that you own exactly fourteen kitchen forks; or the fact that you are a straight "A" student is far more essential to your self-identity than the fact that you once failed a driving test. But what of other facts? Is the fact that you are white, or black, or Chinese, or congenitally bald, or male, or female an essential fact about you? Does it also constitute your identity, the way you essentially think about yourself? Do you think it should? Or do you think it is irrelevant, like the number of forks in your kitchen or the fact that you happened to be born in a taxicab?

This problem has long troubled European philosophers. In the Middle Ages, Christian philosophers argued forcefully that all of this, except for one's individual religious attitudes and the soul, was irrelevant. One's identity was or should be simply a soul seeking salvation before God. Contemporary philosophers, enamored by the growth of science, often talked as if our ultimate self-identity was or should be what we know. The self was considered nothing other than the locus of knowledge; other things — our looks, athletic abilities, enjoyments, and actions — might be amusing or curious distractions but not the essence of self-identity. It is not at all unusual for people who are exceptional in one area rather than another to use their own abilities or vanities as a standard for everyone; athletes tend to admire athletes, intellectuals tend to admire intellectuals. But there is nothing necessary about this, or even desirable. The problem of self-identity, both in each individual case and as a general problem, is the problem of deciding which of the many possible characteristics (not necessarily one) should be chosen as our own standards for self-identity.

What difference does it make? Well, it makes an enormous difference. A self-identity isn't simply a label you throw on yourself in the casual discussion of a philosophy class. It is a mask and a role that you wear in every social encounter (though perhaps slightly different masks and roles for significantly different encounters). It is the way you think of yourself and the standards by which you judge yourself in every moment of reflection and self-evaluation. It is the self-image you follow in every action, when you decide that one thing is "worth doing" more than another or when you decide how to act in a given circumstance. Because of it, you feel proud, guilty, ashamed, or delighted after you have done something. The problem of self-identity is not just a problem for philosophers; it is a problem we all face, either explicitly or implicitly, every self-conscious minute of our lives.

But, you might say, why make it sound as if there is a correct self-identity? The way in which a contemporary Chinese farmer will think of himself and judge himself is very different from that of a contemporary American college student. And a very handsome but stupendously dumb bully type will surely have a very different conception of self-identity than an extremely intelligent and talented coed studying art in college. This will not stop the medieval scholastic, for he will immediately declare all of that irrelevant, and insist that "before God" all of us are the same, and our identities are to be judged accordingly. And most of us, despite the glib relativism we usually defend, would insist on a category that transcends all such individual considerations; we call it "being a good person." Ultimately we would judge the dumb bully and the budding young artist according to the same criterion, and, in doing so, we would think that they should share the criterion "being a good person." Even where cultural differences would seem to demand entirely different conceptions of self-identity, we might still insist on applying the same criterion. For example, a South Sea Islander might well think of himself or herself in terms that would be wholly unacceptable to us, but we can always reduce any variance from our norms to mere "accidental differences," insisting that we are essentially the same. Of course people are different and think differently of themselves; but it does not follow that those differences are essential, nor does it follow that relativism is true. Ultimately when you say that all people are "essentially the same," then you believe that there are, indeed, universal criteria for self-identity and that the differences between people, though we need not deny them, are merely superficial.

One of the most powerful schools of contemporary thought, however, has been dedicated to the idea that self-identity, in every case, is a matter of individual choice. This school, which we have briefly met before, is **existentialism.** Its most powerful contemporary advocate is the French philosopher Jean-Paul Sartre. According to Sartre, there are no set standards for self-identity, either for individuals or for people in general. There is, he argues, no such thing as "human nature," and what we are — and what it means to be a human being — are always matters of decision. There is no correct choice; there are only choices. In a well-known essay from the late 1940s, he argues:

on Existentialism, by Jean-Paul Sartre

What existentialists have in common is simply the fact that they believe that *existence* comes before *essence* — or, if you will, that we must begin from the subjective. What exactly do we mean by that?

If one considers an article of manufacture — as, for example, a book or paper-knife — one sees that it has been made by an artisan who had a conception of it; and he has paid attention, equally, to the conception of a paper-knife and to the pre-existent technique of production which is a part of that conception and is, at bottom, a formula. Thus the paper-knife is at the same time an article producible in a certain manner and one which, on the other hand, serves a definite purpose, for one cannot suppose that a man would produce a paper-knife without knowing what it was for. Let us say, then, of the paper-knife that its essence — that is to say the sum of the formulae and the qualities which made its production and its definition possible — precedes it existence. The presence of such-and-such a paper-knife or book is thus determined before my eyes. Here, then, we are viewing the world from a technical standpoint, and we say that production precedes existence.

When we think of God as the creator, we are thinking of him, most of the time, as a supernal artisan. Whatever doctrine we may be considering, whether it be a doctrine like that of Descartes, or of Leibnitz himself, we always imply that the will follows, more or less, from the understanding or at least accompanies it, so that when God creates he knows precisely what he is creating. Thus, the conception of man in the mind of God is comparable to that of the paper-knife in the mind of the artisan: God makes man according to a procedure and a conception, exactly as the artisan manufactures a paper-knife, following a definition and a formula. Thus each individual man is the realisation of a certain conception which dwells in the divine understanding. In the philosophic atheism of the eighteenth century, the notion of God is suppressed, but not, for all that, the idea that essence is prior to existence; something of that idea we still find everywhere, in Diderot, in Voltaire and even in Kant. Man possesses a human nature; that "human nature," which is the conception of human being, is found in every man; which means that each man is a particular example of an universal conception, the conception of Man. In Kant, this universality goes so far that the wild man of the woods, man in the state of nature and the bourgeois are all contained in the same definition and have the same fundamental qualities. Here again, the essence of man precedes that historic existence which we confront in experience

. . . . .

What do we mean by saying that existence precedes essence? We mean that man first of all exists, encounters himself, surges up in the world—and defines himself afterwards. If man as the existentialist sees him is not definable, it is because to begin with he is nothing. He will not be anything until later, and then he will be what he makes of himself. Thus, there is no human nature, because there is no God to have a conception of it. Man simply is. Not that he is simply what he conceives himself to be, but he is what he wills, and as he conceives himself after already existing—as he wills to be after that leap towards existence. Man is nothing else but that which he makes of himself. That is the first principle of existentialism. And this is what people call its "subjectivity," using the word as a reproach against us. But what do we mean to say by this, but that man is of a greater dignity than a stone or a table? For we mean to say that man primarily exists—that man is, before all else, something which propels itself towards a future and is aware that it is doing so. Man is, indeed, a project which possesses a subjective life, instead of being a kind of moss, or a fungus or a cauliflower. Before that projection of the self nothing exists; not even in the heaven of intelligence: man will only attain existence when he is what he purposes to be. Not, however, what he may wish to be. For what we usually understand by wishing or willing is a conscious decision taken—much more often than not—after we have made ourselves what we are. I may wish to join a party, to write a book or to marry—but in such a case what is usually called my will is probably a manifestation of a prior and more spontaneous decision. If, however, it is true that existence is prior to essence, man is responsible for what he is. Thus, the first effect of existentialism is that it puts every man in possession of himself as he is, and places the entire responsibility for his existence squarely upon his own shoulders. And, when we say that man is responsible for himself, we do not mean that he is responsible only for his own individuality, but that he is responsible for all men.

When we say that man chooses himself, we do mean that every one of us must choose himself; but by that we also mean that in choosing for himself he chooses for all men. For in effect, of all the actions a man may take in order to create himself as he wills to be, there is not one which is not creative, at the same time, of an image of man such as he believes he ought to be.[9]

But this existentialist doctrine of choice doesn't make the problem of self-identity any easier. In fact, it complicates it enormously. Earlier in this section, we began by asking whether the facts about a person are sufficient to determine his or her identity. And we said surely not all of them are necessary, some are more essential than others. But this isn't yet an answer to the question, for it may be that all the essential facts are still not sufficient to determine a person's identity. According to the existentialist, this is made even more complex by the fact that a person chooses which facts are to be considered as essential. Are the facts alone ever sufficient to determine our identity? Sartre's answer, which he adapted from a German existentialist follower of Husserl named Martin Heidegger, is "never!" The facts that are true of a person are always, at least so long as a person is alive, only indicative of what a person has been and done so far. In judging a person's identity, we must always consider more than the facts that are true of him or her (which Sartre and Heidegger collectively name, somewhat technically, a person's **facticity**); we must also consider their projections into the future, their ambitions, plans, intentions, hopes, and fantasies. (Sartre calls these considerations a person's **transcendence.** Notice that this is the third different way in which "transcendence" has been used, so be careful.) This way of viewing the person makes the question of self-identity impossibly complex, in fact, irresolvable. For example, consider Sartre's example of what he calls "bad faith" in one of his most important works, *Being and Nothingness* (1943).

Bad faith, quite simply, is refusing to accept yourself.[10] And this can happen in two different ways. Either you can refuse to accept the fact that your actions establish your self-identity (for example, denying that your repeated cowardly behavior establishes your identity as a coward). Or you can go too far in the opposite direction, believing that your actions conclusively and unalterably establish your self-identity (for example, denying that you could ever alter your cowardly self-identity through an act of heroism).

---

[9]Jean-Paul Sartre, *Existentialism As a Humanism*, trans. Philip Mairet (New York: Philosophical Library, 1949).

[10]This is, however, the main concept of *Being and Nothingness* and takes well over seven hundred pages to analyze correctly.

on Bad Faith,
by Sartre

Let us take an example: A homosexual frequently has an intolerable feeling of guilt, and his whole existence is determined in relation to this feeling. One will readily foresee that he is in bad faith. In fact it frequently happens that this man, while recognizing his homosexual inclination, while avowing each and every particular misdeed which he has committed, refuses with all his strength to consider himself "*a homosexual*." His case is always "different," peculiar; there enters into it something of a game, of chance, of bad luck; the mistakes are all in the past; they are explained by a certain conception of the beautiful which women cannot satisfy; we should see in them the results of a restless search, rather than the manifestations of a deeply rooted tendency, *etc., etc.* Here is assuredly a man in bad faith who borders on the comic since, acknowledging all the facts which are imputed to him, he refuses to draw from them the conclusion which they impose. His friend, who is his most severe critic, becomes irritated with this duplicity. The critic asks only one thing — and perhaps then he will show himself indulgent: that the guilty one recognize himself as guilty, that the homosexual declare frankly — whether humbly or boastfully matters little — "I am a homosexual." We ask here: Who is in bad faith? The homosexual or the champion of sincerity?

The homosexual recognizes his faults, but he struggles with all his strength against the crushing view that his mistakes constitute for him a *destiny*. He does not wish to let himself be considered as a thing. He has an obscure but strong feeling that a homosexual is not a homosexual as this table is a table or as this red-haired man is red-haired. It seems to him that he has escaped from each mistake as soon as he has posited it and recognized it; he even feels that the psychic duration by itself cleanses him from each misdeed, constitutes for him an undetermined future, causes him to be born anew. Is he wrong? Does he not recognize in himself the peculiar, irreducible character of human reality? His attitude includes then an undeniable comprehension of truth. But at the same time he needs this perpetual rebirth, this constant escape in order to live; he must constantly put himself beyond reach in order to avoid the terrible judgment of collectivity. Thus he plays on the word *being*. He would be right actually if he understood the phrase "I am not a homosexual" in the sense of "I am not what I am." That is, if he declared to himself, "To the extent that a pattern of conduct is defined as the conduct of a paederast and to the extent that I have adopted this conduct, I am a homosexual. But to the extent that human reality cannot be finally defined by patterns of conduct, I am not one." But instead he slides surreptitiously toward a different connotation of the word "being." He understands "not being" in the sense of "not-being-in-itself." He lays claim to "not being a homosexual" in the sense in which this table *is not* an inkwell. He is in bad faith.[11]

---

[11]Jean-Paul Sartre, *Being and Nothingness*, trans. Hazel E. Barnes (New York: Philosophical Library, 1956).

And then, Sartre lays bare the heart of his theory. Bad faith points to the most important single fact about personal self-identity — there isn't any. In somewhat paradoxical terminology, Sartre tells us, "one is what one is not, and one is not what one is." In other words, whatever the facts about you, you are always something more than those facts. The homosexual in Sartre's example *is* a homosexual to the extent that all his past actions and desires are those of a homosexual. He falls into bad faith by refusing to see that his past actions point to his having a self-identity as a homosexual. Yet at the same time, there is a genuine sense in which he is *not* a homosexual: In the future, he may radically alter his lifestyle. It would, then, also be bad faith were he to totally accept his self-identity as a homosexual, denying that he could be anything else. As long as a person is alive, he or she is identified by intentions, plans, dreams, and hopes as much as by what is already true by virtue of the facts. And given this complexity, the problem of deciding "who I am" takes on dramatic and extravagant complications. Consider the following scene from Sartre's famous play, *No Exit*, in which one of the characters (now dead and "living" in hell) tries to justify his image of himself as a hero, despite the facts of his life, which would indicate that he was a coward.

from *No Exit*, by Sartre

GARCIN. They shot me.

ESTELLE. I know. Because you refused to fight. Well, why shouldn't you?

GARCIN. I — I didn't exactly refuse. [*In a far-away voice*] I must say he talks well, he makes out a good case against me, but he never says what I should have done instead. Should I have gone to the general and said: "General, I decline to fight"? A mug's game; they'd have promptly locked me up. But I wanted to show my colors, my true colors, do you understand? I wasn't going to be silenced. [*To* ESTELLE] So I — I took the train. . . . They caught me at the frontier.

ESTELLE. Where were you trying to go?

GARCIN. To Mexico. I meant to launch a pacifist newspaper down there. [*A short silence.*] Well, why don't you speak?

ESTELLE. What could I say? You acted quite rightly, as you didn't want to fight. [GARCIN *makes a fretful gesture.*] But, darling, how on earth can I guess what you want me to answer?

INEZ. Can't you guess? Well, *I* can. He wants you to tell him that he bolted like a lion. For "bolt" he did, and that's what's biting him.

GARCIN. "Bolted," "went away" — we won't quarrel over words.

ESTELLE. But you *had* to run away. If you'd stayed they'd have sent you to jail, wouldn't they?

GARCIN. Of course. [*A pause.*] Well, Estelle, am I a coward?

ESTELLE. How can I say? Don't be so unreasonable, darling. I can't put myself in your skin. You must decide that for yourself.

GARCIN [*wearily*]. I can't decide.

ESTELLE. Anyhow, you must remember. You must have had reasons for act-
    ing as you did.

GARCIN. I had.

ESTELLE. Well?

GARCIN. But were they the real reasons?

ESTELLE. You've a twisted mind, that's your trouble. Plaguing yourself over
    such trifles!

GARCIN. I'd thought it all out, and I wanted to make a stand. But was that
    my real motive?

INEZ. Exactly. That's the question. Was that your real motive? No doubt
    you argued it out with yourself, you weighed the pros and cons, you
    found good reasons for what you did. But fear and hatred and all the
    dirty little instincts one keeps dark — they're motives too. So carry on,
    Mr. Garcin, and try to be honest with yourself — for once.

GARCIN. Do I need you to tell me that? Day and night I paced my cell, from
    the window to the door, from the door to the window. I pried into my
    heart, I sleuthed myself like a detective. By the end of it I felt as if I'd
    given my whole life to introspection. But always I harked back to the
    one thing certain — that I had acted as I did, I'd taken that train to the
    frontier. But why? Why? Finally I thought: My death will settle it. If I
    face death courageously, I'll prove I am no coward.

INEZ. And how did you face death?

GARCIN. Miserably. Rottenly. [INEZ *laughs.*] Oh, it was only a physical
    lapse — that might happen to anyone; I'm not ashamed of it. Only
    everything's been left in suspense, forever. [*To* ESTELLE] Come here,
    Estelle. Look at me. I want to feel someone looking at me while they're
    talking about me on earth. . . . I like green eyes.

INEZ. Green eyes! Just hark to him! And you, Estelle, do you like cowards?

ESTELLE. If you knew how little I care! Coward or hero, it's all one — provided
    he kisses well.

GARCIN. There they are, slumped in their chairs, sucking at their cigars.
    Bored they look. Half-asleep. They're thinking: "Garcin's a coward."
    But only vaguely, dreamily. One's got to think of something. "That
    chap Garcin was a coward." That's what they've decided, those dear
    friends of mine. In six months' time they'll be saying: "Cowardly as
    that skunk Garcin." You're lucky, you two; no one on earth is giving
    you another thought. But I — I'm long in dying.

·   ·   ·   ·   ·

GARCIN [*putting his hands on* (INEZ'S) *shoulders*]. Listen! Each man has an
    aim in life, a leading motive; that's so, isn't it? Well, I didn't give a
    damn for wealth, or for love. I aimed at being a real man. A tough, as
    they say. I staked everything on the same horse. . . . Can one possibly
    be a coward when one's deliberately courted danger at every turn? And
    can one judge a life by a single action?

INEZ. Why not? For thirty years you dreamt you were a hero, and condoned a thousand petty lapses — because a hero, of course, can do no wrong. An easy method obviously. Then a day came when you were up against it, the red light of real danger — and you took the train to Mexico.

GARCIN. I "dreamt," you say. It was no dream. When I chose that hardest path, I made my choice deliberately. A man is what he wills himself to be.

INEZ. Prove it. Prove it was no dream. It's what one does, and nothing else, that shows the stuff one's made of.

GARCIN. I died too soon. I wasn't allowed time to — to do my deeds.

INEZ. One always dies too soon — or too late. And yet one's whole life is complete at that moment, with a line drawn neatly under it, ready for the summing up. You are — your life, and nothing else.[12]

ONE SELF? ANY SELF?: THE EASTERN ALTERNATIVE

So, "who am I"? How does one decide? It looks like one of those questions that, on the one hand, we can't ever avoid asking, but at the same time, we can never succeed in answering. It gets more complicated yet. So far, we have talked as if, even if it is a matter of personal choice, self-identity is something singular, a unified set of ideals and characteristics according to which one identifies himself or herself. There are, however, other ways of viewing the self. In his novel *Steppenwolf*, Hermann Hesse argues a very different ideal, one taken from the Orient. It is not the ideal of selflessness but rather the ideal of the *multiple* or *pluralistic* self, the self as a collection of "selves," with no one of them "real" or "essential." The "hero" of *Steppenwolf* (Harry Haller) is a man of extraordinary talents, but he is immensely unhappy. Like many of us, he lives with the myth of "two selves," one human, rational, and well behaved, the other beastly, wild, and wolf-like. He is torn between the two. But, Hesse tells us, Harry's unhappiness is not, as he thinks, a result of this "war between the selves" at all but rather of an oversimplified notion of self. "The Steppenwolf is a fiction," writes Hesse, a "mythological simplification." The idea of two selves, one wolf, one man, is as old as the Christian division between the body and the soul — even older, in fact, dating back to Pythagoras and Plato. It had been expressed in a classic line in Goethe's *Faust*, where the great poet bemoans, "two souls, alas, inhabit my breast," and it could be found in Nietzsche, who greatly influenced Hesse, in his view of man as a bridge between "the beast and the *übermensch*" (the "superman"). Hesse's argument is that this simple self is a strictly "bourgeois convention," a middle-class argument for the simplicity and unity of the self; indeed, Harry is unhappy because of the tension and complexity of only two selves: the

---

[12]Jean-Paul Sartre, *No Exit*, trans. Stuart Gilbert (New York: Vintage, 1948).

"human" who has culture and cultivated thoughts and feelings and the "wolf" who is savage and cruel, the dark world of Freud's unconscious instincts and raw, untamed nature. Hesse argues:

from *Steppenwolf*, by Hermann Hesse

Suppose that Harry tried to ascertain in any single moment of his life, any single act, what part the man had in it and what part the wolf, he would find himself at once in a dilemma, and his whole beautiful wolf theory would go to pieces. For there is not a single human being . . . not even the idiot, who is so conveniently simple that his being can be explained as the sum of two or three principal elements; and to explain so complex a man as Harry by the artless division into wolf and man is a hopelessly childish attempt. Harry consists of a hundred or a thousand selves, not of two. His life oscillates, as everyone's does, not merely between two poles, such as the body and the spirit, the saint and the sinner, but between thousand and thousands.

Why is it, Hesse asks, that we all seem to have this need to think of ourselves in such deceptive terms and regard the self as a single unit? Because, he suggests, we are deluded by an analogy; since each of us has but one body, it is assumed that each of us has a single soul too. From this analogy, we assume that there must be one self within each body. But it is here that Hesse contrasts our view with the views of ancient India and notes with admiration that there is no trace of such a notion in the poems of the ancient Asiatics. He then offers us his own analogy:

Man is an onion made up of a hundred integuments, a texture made up of many threads. The ancient Asiatics knew this well enough, and in the Buddhist Yoga an exact technique was devised for unmasking the illusion of the personality. The human merry-go-round sees many changes: The illusion that cost India the efforts of thousands of years to unmask is the same illusion that the West has labored just as hard to maintain and strengthen.[13]

Hesse refers to Buddhist concepts of the self with praise. Although he remains entrenched in Western ideas as well, Hesse is already more than halfway to a very Eastern conception of self, which is essentially a denial of the self as we think of it. The Buddhist says, "give up your self-identity," "give up your self-consciousness," and finally, "give up your self." This is a familiar refrain among many Eastern mystics, although Zen Buddhists have been the best-known advocates of selflessness in recent years in America. It may also be an ideal secular aspiration, however, for example, in contemporary China, and it is the goal of a large variety of ancient and contemporary forms of meditation.

Buddha says (notice a certain similarity to Hume):

[13]Hermann Hesse, *Steppenwolf*, trans. Basil Creighton and rev. Joseph Mileck (New York: Holt, Rinehart and Winston, 1929).

from *The Teachings of the Buddha*

Though both body and mind appear because of cooperating causes, it does not follow that there is an ego-personality. As the body of flesh is an aggregate of elements, it is, therefore, impermanent.

If the body were an ego-personality, it could do this and that as it would determine.

A king has the power to praise or punish as he wishes, but he becomes ill despite his intent and desire, he comes to old age unwillingly, and his fortune and his wishes often have little to do with each other.

Neither is the mind the ego-personality. The human mind is also an aggregate of causes and conditions. It is in constant change.

If the mind were an ego-personality it could do this and that as it would determine, but the mind often flies from what it knows is right and chases after evil unwillingly. Nothing seems to happen exactly as the ego desires.

If one is asked whether the body is constant or impermanent, he will be obliged to answer "impermanent."

If one is asked whether impermanent existence is happiness or suffering, he will generally have to answer "suffering."

If a man believes that such an impermanent thing, so changeable and replete with suffering is the ego-personality, it is a serious mistake.

The human mind is also impermanent and suffering; it has nothing that can be called an ego-personality.

Therefore, both body and mind, which make up an individual life, and the external world which seems to surround it, are far apart from both the conceptions of "me" and "mine."

It is simply the mind clouded over by impure desires, and impervious to wisdom, that obstinately persists in thinking of "me" and "mine."

Since both body and its surroundings are originated by cooperating causes and conditions, they are continually changing and never can come to an end.

The human mind, in its never-ending changes, is like the moving water of a river, or the burning flame of a candle; like an ape, it is forever jumping about, not ceasing for even a moment.

A wise man, seeing and hearing such, should break away from any attachment to body or mind, if he is ever to attain Enlightenment.

. . . . .

. . . there is nothing that can be called an "ego," and there is no such thing as "mine" in all the world.

. . . everything is impermanent and passing and egoless. . . .

But even this call to "selflessness" is not simply a negative teaching. It has a positive counterpart called "Buddha-nature."

We have been speaking of Buddha-nature as though it were something that could be described, as though it were similar to the "soul" of other teachings, but it is not.

The concept of an "ego-personality" is something that has been imagined by a discriminating mind which first grasped it and then became attached to it, but which must abandon it. On the contrary, Buddha-nature is something indescribable that must first be discovered. In one sense, it resembles an "ego-personality" but it is not the "ego" in the sense of "I am" or "mine."

To believe in the existence of an ego is an erroneous belief, that supposes non-existence; to deny Buddha-nature is wrong, for it supposes that existence is non-existence.

This can be explained in a parable. A mother took her sick child to a doctor. The doctor gave the child medicine and instructed the mother not to nurse the child until the medicine was digested.

The mother anointed her breast with something bitter so that the child would keep away from her of his own volition. After the medicine had time enough to be digested, the mother cleansed her breast and let the child suck her. The mother took this method of saving her child out of kindness because she loved the child.

Like the mother in the parable, Buddha, in order to remove misunderstanding and to break up attachments to an ego-personality, denies the existence of an ego; and when the misunderstanding and attachments are done away with, then He explains the reality of the true mind that is Buddha-nature.

Attachment to an ego-personality leads people into delusions, but faith in their Buddha-nature leads them to Enlightenment.

It is like the woman in a story, to whom a chest was bequeathed. Not knowing that the chest contained gold, she continued to live in poverty until another person opened it and showed her the gold. Buddha opens the minds of people and shows them the purity of their Buddha-nature.[14]

The Buddhist position offers us a paradoxical answer to the question of self-identity. On the one hand, it denies that there is a self and rejects the views of self-identity that have become so familiar in Western philosophy, on the other, this too is a conception of self-identity. That is, if self-identity is a way of conceiving of oneself, then a denial that one has a self, a denial that one ought to think of oneself as a self, and a denial that one ought to see oneself as an individual rather than as part of Universal Mind is itself a form of self-identity. In the next section, we shall see that the concept of self need not be a concept of individual self. In Buddhism, the concept of self is expanded to the point at which it includes everything. (There have been similar moves in Western thought, for example, in the work of the German philosopher Hegel, whom we shall discuss in the following section.) The paradoxical answer of the Buddhist is the denial of self as individual self on the one hand and the expansion of the concept of self to include everything. We may seriously disagree whether or not this should still be called a "self" at all. But its importance in any discussion of self-identity is beyond argument. To deny the self is as important an option as to define the self in the individualistic ways we discussed in Descartes, Locke, and Kant.

The Buddhist conception of self introduces another very important alternative to our usual Western conceptions. Our Western conceptions are typically con-

---

[14]*The Teaching of Buddha*, rev. ed. (Tokyo: Bukkyo Deudo Kyokai, 1976).

cerned with striving and ambition, status and planning for the future, "making something of yourself." Existentialism is one form of this conception. The American dream and the Protestant and capitalist ethics in general are another. But from the Buddhist conception of self comes a very different picture — of unqualified acceptance of things as they are rather than struggling to change them, which involves a rejection of such notions as "status" and "making something of yourself."

Once again we must not confuse this rejection of traditional Western conceptions of the self with a rejection of the philosophical question of self-identity. "Who am I?" is as important a question for the Buddhist as it is for the Western philosopher. It is just that his answer to the question is radically different. Does it make sense to say that the one is more "correct" than the other? This too is part of the question of self-identity. Must there be a single "correct" answer for everyone?

THE INDIVIDUAL AND THE COMMUNITY

In Buddhism, we saw a concept of self that was not, like everything else we have been discussing, an individual self. But even within discussions of the individual self, it becomes evident that the individual self is largely, if not entirely, a social product and a self defined by society. We have all had the experience of finding ourselves in company in which we "could not be ourselves" or, even worse, in which we acted according to an identity that was wholly imposed upon us by other people. When going to school, for example, we long played the role of "student," ingratiating and oppressed, much before we started to recognize that it is a role, and not a very pleasant one at that. Now we see it as a role that has been formulated solely for the advantage of other people — teachers, administrators, parents — so that we could be forced to "behave." Have you started to wonder how many other aspects of your identity have been similarly imposed upon you, not chosen at all, much less created by you? How much of your behavior has been "programmed" or "conditioned" by parents, society, television, movies, friends, and schoolmates? The suspicion deepens. And soon you start to see a split developing in your thinking about yourself: First, there is your conception of your own identity; second, there is the identity that has been imposed upon you. The two drift apart like boat and dock, and you find yourself falling between. No wonder, then, that one of the leading psychiatrists of our times, R. D. Laing, has looked at this problem not only as the basis of much of our everyday unhappiness but as the cause of some of our most serious psychological breakdowns as well. Laing describes what he calls "ontological insecurity" as just this split between your awareness of yourself by yourself and the awareness that is imposed upon yourself as an object of other people's attention. Guilt is an example of this split; in excess (as Freud often argued) such emotions tend to be pathological. Guilt is a kind of self-consciousness that is caught between the need for approval and recognition by others and the feeling that you must be "yourself." Thus we tend to get the idea of a "true self" that lies concealed behind the masks that we present in public, even to our closest friends. We get the sense that our real selves are known only to ourselves, but at the same time we do not really exist except with other people.

But this is an extremely negative view of a tension that is in fact central to our whole Western notion of self, the tension between individuality and social self-identity. In most societies, Plato and Aristotle's Greece, for example, a person would always see his or her own identity in terms of the society of which one was a member. The idea of a self that was antagonistic to society would have been completely foreign to them. (Consider, for instance, Socrates' speech in the *Crito*, in our Introduction, in which he says, in effect, that he cannot serve his own interests against the state without betraying himself.) And yet our own idea of self-identity has become so individualistic that the very idea that self-identity is really social-identity flies in the face of that whole Cartesian tradition — and much of Western thinking — that begins with the autonomy of the self and self-consciousness. Nietzsche, for example, goes so far as to suggest that self-consciousness is simply superfluous.

on the Dispensability of Consciousness, by Friedrich Nietzsche

The *"Genius of the Species."* — The problem of consciousness (or more correctly: of becoming conscious of oneself) meets us only when we begin to perceive in what measure we could dispense with it: and it is at the beginning of this perception that we are now placed by physiology and zoology (which have thus required two centuries to overtake the hint thrown out in advance by Leibnitz). For we could in fact think, feel, will and recollect, we could likewise "act" in every sense of the term, and nevertheless nothing of it all need necessarily "come into consciousness" (as one says metaphorically). The whole of life would be possible without its seeing itself as it were in a mirror: as in fact even at present the far greater part of our life still goes on without this mirroring, — and even our thinking, feeling, volitional life as well, however painful this statement may sound to an older philosopher. *What* then is *the purpose* of consciousness generally, when it is in the main *superfluous?* — Now it seems to me, if you will hear my answer and its perhaps extravagant supposition, that the subtlety and strength of consciousness are always in proportion to the *capacity for communication* of a man (or an animal), the capacity for communication in its turn being in proportion to the *necessity for communication:* the latter not to be understood as if precisely the individual himself who is master in the art of communicating and making known his necessities would at the same time have to be most dependent upon others for his necessities. It seems to me, however, to be so in relation to whole races and successions of generations: where necessity and need have long compelled men to communicate with their fellows and understand one another rapidly and subtly, a surplus of the power and art of communication is at last acquired, as if it were a fortune which had gradually accumulated, and now waited for an heir to squander it prodigally (the so-called artists are these heirs, in like manner the orators, preachers and authors: all of them men who come at the end of a long succession, "late-born" always, in the best sense of the word, and as has been said, *squanderers* by their very nature). Granted that this obser- vation is correct, I may proceed further to the conjecture that *consciousness generally has only been developed under the pressure of the necessity for communication,* — that from the first it has been necessary and useful only between man and man (especially between those commanding and those obeying), and has only developed in proportion to its utility. Consciousness is properly only a connecting network between man and man, — it is only as such that it has had to develop; the recluse and wild-beast species of men would not have needed it. The very fact that our actions, thoughts, feelings and motions come within the range of our consciousness — at least a part of them — is the result of a terrible, prolonged "must" ruling man's destiny: as the most endangered animal he *needed* help and protection; he needed his fellows, he was obliged to express his distress, he had to know how to make himself understood — and for all this he needed "consciousness" first of all: he had to "know" himself what he lacked, to "know" how he felt, and to "know" what he thought. For, to repeat it once more, man, like every living creature, thinks unceasingly, but does not know it; the thinking which is becoming *conscious of itself* is only the smallest part thereof, we may say, the most superficial part, the worst part: — for this conscious thinking alone *is done in words, that is to say, in the symbols for communication,* by means of which the origin of consciousness is revealed. In short, the devel- opment of speech and the development of consciousness (not of reason, but of reason becoming self-conscious) go hand in hand. Let it be further accepted that it is not only speech that serves as a bridge between man and man, but also looks, the pressure and the gestures; our becoming conscious of our sense impressions, our power of being able to fix them, and as it were to locate them outside of ourselves, has increased in proportion as the neces- sity has increased for communicating them to *others* by means of signs. The sign-inventing man is at the same time the man who is always more acutely self-conscious; it is only as a social animal that man has learned to become conscious of himself, — he is doing so still, and doing so more and more. — As is obvious, my idea is that consciousness does not properly belong to the individual existence of man, but rather to the social and gregarious nature in him; that, as follows therefrom, it is only in relation to communal and gregarious utility that it is finely developed; and that consequently each of us, in spite of the best intention of *understanding* himself as individually as possible, and of "knowing himself," will always just call into conscious- ness the non-individual in him, namely, his "averageness"; — that our thought itself is continuously as it were *outvoted* by the character of con- sciousness — by the imperious "genius of the species" therein — and is trans- lated back into the perspective of the herd. Fundamentally our actions are in an incomparable manner altogether personal, unique, and absolutely individual — there is no doubt about it; but as soon as we translate them into consciousness, they *do not appear so any longer.* . . . This is the proper phe- nomenalism and perspectivism as I understand it: the nature of *animal con- sciousness* involves the notion that the world of which we can become conscious is only a superficial and symbolic world, a generalised and vulgarised world; — that everything which becomes conscious *becomes* just thereby shallow, meagre, relatively stupid, — a generalisation, a symbol, a characteristic of the herd; that with the evolving of consciousness there is always combined a great, radical perversion, falsification, superficialisation and generalisation. Finally, the growing consciousness is a danger, and whoever lives among the most conscious European knows even that it is a disease. As may be conjectured, it is not the antithesis of subject and object with which I am here concerned: I leave that distinction to the epistemologists who have remained entangled in the toils of grammar (popular metaphysics). It is still less the antithesis of "thing in itself" and phenomenon, for we do not "know" enough to be entitled even to *make such a distinction*. Indeed, we have not any organ at all for *knowing*, or for "truth": we "know" (or believe, or fancy) just as much as may be of *use* in the interest of the human herd, the species; and even what is here called "usefulness" is ultimately only a belief, a fancy, and perhaps precisely the most fatal stupidity by which we shall one day be ruined.

Our response to this split between what some philosophers call the "self for itself" and the "self for others" has been varied. For some, particularly those who have been called existentialists, the response has been wholesale rebellion, the demand that we break away from "the masses" and our given social identities and create our selves. Nietzsche, for example, attacks what he calls "the herd" in the above passage and urges us to develop ourselves as unique individuals. Indeed, this is the main point of Nietzsche's entire philosophy and underlies his attack on religion and morality.

"Herd Instinct," by Nietzsche

Herd-Instinct. — Wherever we meet with a morality we find a valuation and order of rank of the human impulses and activities. These valuations and orders of rank are always the expression of the needs of a community or herd: that which is in the first place to *its* advantage — and in the second place and third place — is also the authoritative standard for the worth of every individual. By morality the individual is taught to become a function of the herd, and to ascribe to himself value only as a function. As the conditions for the maintenance of one community have been very different from those of another community, there have been very different moralities; and in respect to the future essential transformations of herds and communities, states and societies, one can prophesy that there will still be very divergent moralities. Morality is the herd-instinct in the individual.[15]

A similar attempt at individual rebellion was attempted even earlier by Kierkegaard, the religious philosopher who has often been called the father of exis-

[15]Friedrich Nietzsche, *The Joyful Wisdom*, trans. Thomas Common, in *The Complete Works of Friedrich Nietzsche*, Oscar Levy, General Editor (1909–11) (New York: Russell & Russell, 1964).

tentialism. Like Nietzsche, he deplores what he sarcastically calls "the public" and urges an end to collective identity and social roles in favor of renewed respect for the individual.

on "The Public," by Kierkegaard

In spite of all his exertion the subjective thinker enjoys only a meager reward. The more the collective idea comes to dominate even the ordinary consciousness, the more forbidding seems the transition to becoming a particular existing human being instead of losing oneself in the race, and saying "we," "our age," "the nineteenth century." That it is a little thing merely to be a particular existing human being is not to be denied; but for this very reason it requires considerable resignation not to make light of it. For what does a mere individual count for? Our age knows only too well how little it is, but here also lies the specific immorality of the age. Each age has its own characteristic depravity. Ours is perhaps not pleasure or indulgence or sensuality, but rather a dissolute pantheistic contempt for the individual man. In the midst of all our exultation over the achievements of the age and the nineteenth century, there sounds a note of poorly conceived contempt for the individual man; in the midst of the self-importance of the contemporary generation there is revealed a sense of despair over being human. Everything must attach itself so as to be a part of some movement; men are determined to lose themselves in the totality of things, in world-history, fascinated and deceived by a magic witchery; no one wants to be an individual human being.

In fact, so adamant is Kierkegaard on this issue that he argues that a person who "follows the crowd" and does not choose his or her own identity and live passionately as an individual cannot even be said to really exist.

on Self and Passion, by Kierkegaard

It is impossible to exist without passion, unless we understand the word "exist" in the loose sense of a so-called existence. Every Greek thinker was therefore essentially a passionate thinker. I have often reflected how one might bring a man into a state of passion. I have thought in this connection that if I could get him seated on a horse and the horse made to take fright and gallop wildly, or better still, for the sake of bringing the passion out, if I could take a man who wanted to arrive at a certain place as quickly as possible, and hence already had some passion, and could set him astride a horse that can scarcely walk—and yet this is what existence is like if one is to become consciously aware of it. Or if a driver were otherwise not especially inclined toward passion, if someone hitched a team of horses to a wagon for him, one of them a Pegasus and the other a worn-out jade, and told him to drive—I think one might succeed. And it is just this that it means to exist, if one is to become conscious of it. Eternity is the winged horse, infinitely fast, and time is a worn-out jade; the existing individual is the driver. That is to say, he is such a driver when his mode of existence is not an existence loosely so called; for then he is no driver, but a drunken peasant who lies asleep in the wagon and lets the horses take care of themselves. To be sure, he also drives and is a driver; and so there are perhaps many who — also exist.[16]

And in this century, borrowing from both Kierkegaard and Nietzsche, the German existentialist Martin Heidegger has argued against collective social identity in terms of what he (also ironically) calls *das Man*, an extremely useful German expression that roughly translates as "they" in "*they* say that garlic cures colds." Who are "they"? No one at all, Heidegger says, just an anonymous no one. In extremely dense philosophical prose,[17] he argues

"Dasein" and the "They," by Martin Heidegger

Dasein, as everyday Being-with-one-another, stands in *subjection* to Others. It itself *is* not; its Being has been taken away by the Others. Dasein's everyday possibilities of Being are for the Others to dispose of as they please. These Others, moreover, are not *definite* Others. On the contrary, any Other can represent them. What is decisive is just that inconspicuous domination by Others which has already been taken over unawares from Dasein as Being-with. One belongs to the Others oneself and enhances their power. 'The Others' whom one thus designates in order to cover up the fact of one's belonging to them essentially oneself, are those who proximally and for the most part '*are there*' in everyday Being-with-one-another. The "who" is not this one, not that one, not oneself, not some people, and not the sum of them all. The 'who' is the neuter, *the* "they" [*das Man*].

⋅ ⋅ ⋅ ⋅ ⋅

Everyone is the other, and no one is himself. The "*they*," which supplies the answer to the question of the "*who*" of everyday Dasein, is the "*nobody*" to whom every Dasein has already surrendered itself in Being-among-one-other.

And against this "surrender," Heidegger urges us to "take hold of ourselves" as individuals and find our "authentic" selves.

The Self of everyday Dasein is the *they-self*, which we distinguish from the *authentic Self* — that is, from the Self which has been taken hold of in its own way.[18]

This individualist movement is not unique to existentialism; it is in the mainstream of Western thinking, from ancient Socrates through Reformation Chris-

---

[16]Søren Kierkegaard, *Concluding Unscientific Postscript*, trans. David F. Swenson and Walter Lowrie (Princeton, N.J.: Princeton University Press, 1941).

[17]For "Dasein," read "individual human being"; for "Being-with," read "being around other people."

[18]Martin Heidegger, *Being and Time*, trans. J. MacQuarrie and E. Robinson (New York: Harper & Row, 1962).

tianity to contemporary capitalism. Socrates' rebellion was, in a very important way, an existential rebellion. He stood up for his principles against the opinions of the age. And Luther's Reformation was, among other things, very much a reassertion of the individual (individual conscience, individual actions) against the all-embracing spirit of the Catholic Church. And today, virtually every American would agree that every individual deserves at least some individual rights and respect. But individualism has always had its doubters. Individualism arises largely as a reaction against the awareness of how socially conditioned we really are. As an instrument of personal growth and as a defense against excessive socialization (to the point, for example, where individual rights and.values are no longer meaningful), individualism is extremely valuable. But when individualism becomes so powerful that personal interests eclipse the interests of everyone else and individual values begin to destroy the community, then it may be time to bring the limits of individualism into question as well. Furthermore, there are limits to the degree to which we can challenge the values and customs of our upbringing. Some rebellion is required for growth and change of the society as well as of the individual. But too much rebellion can be self-destructive as well as destructive to the community. For our self-identities, no matter how hard we try to think of ourselves as total individuals, are inextricably tied to the communities and values in which we were raised.

The American sociologist David Reisman looks again at individualism in the light of these considerations and defends it as follows:

on Individualism,
by David Reisman

Social science has helped us become more aware of the extent to which individuals, great and little, are the creatures of their cultural conditioning; and so we neither blame the little nor exalt the great. But the same wisdom has sometimes led us to the fallacy that, since all men have their being in culture and as the result of the culture, they owe a debt to that culture which even a lifetime of altruism could not repay. (One might as well argue, and in fact many societies in effect do, that since we are born of parents, we must feel guilt whenever we transcend their limitations!) Sometimes the point is pushed to the virtual denial of individuality: since we arise in society, it is assumed with a ferocious determinism that we can never transcend it. All such concepts are useful correctives of an earlier solipsism. But if they are extended to hold that conformity with society is not only a necessity but also a duty, they destroy that margin of freedom which gives life its savor and its endless possibility for advance.[19]

But the argument for individualism is often stated as a form of mutual conflict (as in the existentialists and Reisman), which many philosophers would not accept. Why need there be a conflict? Kant, for example, while very much the champion of individual autonomy, insisted that the only individuality worth defending was the ability of the individual to participate in universal morality.

[19]David Reisman, *Individualism Reconsidered* (New York: Doubleday, 1954).

The same argument is to be found in Socrates, Plato, and Aristotle. And in more recent times, this argument has found a large following among thinkers who have seen the disastrous results of overly-individual thinking (what Reisman refers to as "solipsism"). The German philosopher Hegel, for example, writing in the midst of the great international movements of the early nineteenth century, argued:

"Spirit" and the Individual, by Hegel

... at a time when the universal nature of spiritual life has become so very much emphasized and strengthened, and the mere individual aspect has become, as it should be, correspondingly a matter of indifference, when, too, that universal aspect holds, by the entire range of its substance, the full measure of the wealth it has built up, and lays claim to it all, the share in the total work of mind that falls to the activity of any particular individual can only be very small. Because this is so, the individual must all the more forget himself, as in fact the very nature of science implies and requires that he should; and he must, moreover, become and do what he can. But all the less must be demanded of him, just as he can expect the less from himself, and may ask the less for himself.[20]

And elsewhere, in a famous passage, he argues that individuals in history are significant only insofar as they contribute to movements far greater than themselves:

... in contemplating history as the slaughter-bench at which the happiness of peoples, the wisdom of states, and the virtue of individuals have been sacrificed, a question necessarily arises: To what principle, to what final purpose, have these monstrous sacrifices been offered?

... human agents have before them limited aims, special interests. But they are also intelligent, thinking beings. Their purposes are interwoven with general and essential considerations of law, the good, duty, etc. For mere desire, volition in its raw and savage form, falls outside the scene and sphere of world history. These general considerations, which at the same time form norms for directing purposes and actions, have a definite content. For such empty abstractions as "good for its own sake" have no place in living actuality.

... Each individual has his position; he knows, on the whole, what a lawful and honorable course of conduct is. To assert in ordinary private relations that it is difficult to choose the right and good, and to regard it as mark of an exalted morality to find difficulties and raise scruples on that score indicates an evil and perverse will. It indicates a will that seeks to evade obvious duties or, at least, a petty will that gives its mind too little to

[20]G. W. F. Hegel, *The Phenomenology of Spirit*, trans. A. N. Miller (Oxford: Oxford Univ. Press, 1977).

do. The mind, then, in idle reflection, busies itself with itself and indulges in moral smugness.

> ... *each individual is also the child of a people at a definite stage of its development. One cannot skip over the spirit of his people any more than one can skip over the earth. The earth is the center of gravity; a body imagined as leaving this center can only be imagined as exploding into the air. So it is with an individual. But only through his own effort can he be in harmony with his substance; he must bring the will demanded by his people to his own consciousness, to articulation. The individual does not invent his own content; he is what he is by acting out the universal as his own content.*
>
> *In the course of history two factors are important. One is the preservation of a people, a state, of the well-ordered spheres of life. This is the activity of individuals participating in the common effort and helping to bring about its particular manifestations. It is the preservation of ethical life. The other important factor, however, is the decline of a state. The existence of a national spirit is broken when it has used up and exhausted itself. World history, the World Spirit, continues on its course.*
>
> .   .   .   .   .
>
> This universal is an essential phase in the development of the creating Idea, of truth striving and urging toward itself. The historical men, *world-historical individuals*, are those [*who grasp just such a higher universal, make it their own purpose, and realize this purpose in accordance with the higher law of the spirit*].[21]

In the midst of the international upheavals led by Napoleon, you can appreciate the appropriateness of such a brutal philosophy. "The slaughter-bench of history" is not a pleasant concept! And the idea that each of us is virtually insignificant in our tiny place in history also hurts our grander conceptions of ourselves. But Hegel argues that no other view of ourselves is defensible. Even the greatest among us is nothing more than an expression of the "universal," the monumental forces of society and humankind as a whole (these are what Hegel refers to as "the Creating Idea" and elsewhere as "the cunning of Reason").

But however appropriate in times of international warfare, Hegel's conception is bound to raise hackles among the individualists in peacetime. Consider Kierkegaard's ironic retort to Hegel's philosophy:

A Retort by Kierkegaard

Hence perhaps the many attempts to continue clinging to Hegel, even by men who have reached an insight into the questionable character of his philosophy. It is a fear that if they were to become particular existing human beings, they would vanish tracelessly, so that not even the daily press would be able to discover them, still less critical journals, to say nothing at all of speculative philosophers immersed in world-history. As particular human beings they fear that they will be doomed to a more isolated

[21]G. W. F. Hegel, *Reason in History*, trans. Robert S. Hartman (New York: Bobbs-Merrill, 1953).

and forgotten existence than that of a man in the country; for if a man lets go of Hegel he will not even be in a position to have a letter addressed to him.[22]

Karl Marx was a student of Hegel's philosophy. In his "early writings" of 1844, he too argues for a view of self as essentially social, a part of a community, a "species-being":

on the Social Self,
by Karl Marx

It follows from the character of this relationship [the human family] how far *man* has become, and has understood himself as, a *species-being*, a *human being*.

. . . . .

Activity and mind are social in their content as well as in their *origin*; they are *social* activity and social mind.

. . . . .

It is above all necessary to avoid postulating "society" once again as an abstraction confronting the individual. The individual *is* the *social being*. The manifestation of his life — even when it does not appear directly in the form of a communal manifestation, accomplished in association with other men — is, therefore, a manifestation and affirmation of *social life*. Individual human life and species-life are not different things, even though the mode of existence of individual life is necessarily either a more *specific* or a more *general* mode of species-life, or that of species-life a *specific* or more *general* mode of individual life.

In his *species-consciousness* man confirms his real *social life*, and reproduces his real existence in thought; while conversely, species-life confirms itself in species-consciousness and exists for itself in its universality as a thinking being. Though man is a unique individual — and it is just his particularity which makes him an individual, a really *individual* communal being — he is equally the *whole*, the ideal whole, the subjective existence of society as thought and experienced. He exists in reality as the representation and the real mind of social existence, and as the sum of human manifestations of life.[23]

It is important to emphasize that neither Marx nor Hegel (nor Socrates nor Kant) is actually denying the individual, or individual respect or individual rights. They are, however, insisting that an individual deserves such respect or such rights only insofar as he or she is a member of a community. This does not mean that a person cannot be eccentric, like the weirdo artist or the spaced-out rock musician, but it does mean that even their eccentricity, as well as their talents, must be viewed as social contributions. What they are denying, in other words, is what has sometimes been called "vulgar individualism," that form of self-identity that denies all social relevance and social obligations.

[22]Kierkegaard, *Concluding Unscientific Postscript.*
[23]Karl Marx, *Early Writings*, trans. T. Bottomore (New York: McGraw-Hill, 1963).

SUMMARY AND CONCLUSION

Self-identity is a question of essential properties: What is it about you that makes you a particular person and the same person over time? In this chapter we have reviewed a series of different answers to this question. The tradition from Descartes and Locke to Kant stresses the importance of consciousness in our conception of ourselves. (Even Hume, who denies that there is a self, is part of this tradition.) Then there is the general question, how much is the self something that we can choose, and how much is it something that is determined for us? Does each person have just one self, one set of essential properties, or might a single "person" be several people, with several selves? Or might there really be no self at all, as argued by Hume and Sartre, and in a very different way by several influential Eastern philosophies? And how much should we conceive of ourselves as individuals, and how much as organic components of a larger community? None of these questions have any firmly agreed upon answers, but all of us adopt one view or another, even if just for a short time, every time we attempt to define ourselves or just "be ourselves."

GLOSSARY

bad faith: Sartre's characterization of a person's refusal to accept himself or herself; this sometimes means not accepting the facts that are true about you. More often, it means accepting the facts about you as conclusive about your identity, as in the statement "Oh, I couldn't do that, I'm too shy."

continuity (spatio-temporal continuity): the uninterrupted identifiability of an object over time in the same location or in a sequence of tangent locations.

criterion: test or standard.

empirical ego: all those characteristics of a person that can be discovered through experience and that distinguish each of us from other persons qualitatively; that which makes each of us a particular man or woman and gives us a particular "character." Compare *transcendental ego.*

essence: that which is necessary for something to be what it is. The essence of a person is that without which we would not say one is *that* particular person (Fred rather than Mary, for example).

existentialism: in Sartre's terms, the philosophy that teaches that "man's existence precedes his essence." That is, people have no given self-identity, they have to choose their identities and work for them through their actions. (Neglect and omission, however, are also actions. One can be a certain type of person just by not bothering to do the appropriate activities.)

facticity: Sartre's term (borrowed from Heidegger) for the totality of facts that are true of a person at any given time.

resemblance: having the same features. All people resemble each other (or at least most do) in having one and only one head; you resemble yourself five years ago in (perhaps) having the same texture hair, the same color eyes, the same fear of spiders, and the same skill at chess.

self-consciousness: being aware of oneself, whether "as others see you" (looking in a mirror or "watching yourself play a role" at a party) or just "looking into yourself" (as when you reflect on your goals in life or wonder, in a moment of philosophical perversity, whether you really exist or not). Self-consciousness requires having some concept of your "self." Accordingly, it is logically tied to questions of self-identity.

self-identity: the way you characterize yourself, either in general (as a human being, as a man or as a woman, as a creature before God or as one among many animals) or in particular (as the person who can run the fastest mile, as an all-"C" student, or as the worst-dressed slob in your class). Self-identity, on this characterization, requires self-consciousness. The self-identity of a person, in other words, is not merely the same as the identity of a "thing," for example, the identity of a human body.

transcendence: Sartre's term for a person's plans, ambitions, intentions, and hopes for the future. (Do not confuse this use of the word with those introduced in Chapters 4 and 6.)

transcendental ego: the bare, logical fact of one's own self-consciousness: Descartes's "I think"; the self "behind" all of our experiences; the mental activity that unifies our various thoughts and sensations. (The term comes from Kant's *Critique of Pure Reason*.)

8

Mind and Body

*It is certain that I (that is, my mind, by which I am what I am) is
entirely and truly distinct from my body, and may exist without it.*

René Descartes

Whatever our attempts to answer the problems of self-identity, they begin with
a single "fact," our own consciousness. This was the logical beginning for Descartes, who used the fact of his own consciousness as the starting point for his
whole philosophy. It was true for Locke, who argued that our identity is to be
found in the continuity of our consciousness rather than in the continuity of our
bodies. It was even used by Hume, who used his own consciousness as the basis
of his denial that there was any such thing as the self. It was the starting point
of Kant's philosophy; his transcendental ego, like Descartes's "I think," gave him
the basis for the rest of his philosophy. And even those philosophers who have
not been interested in these logical arguments — Buddhists, Marxists, and existentialists — have begun with at least one of a variety of considerations of consciousness; the fact of our own self-consciousness, the facts of consciousness, or just the
fact that only people seem capable of or interested in asking the question "Who
am I?" But now what is this "consciousness"? As soon as we ask the question, we
find ourselves once again up to our eyeballs in the labyrinth of traditional
metaphysics.

WHAT IS CONSCIOUSNESS?

We can begin to appreciate the problems of consciousness by returning to the
attempts of the eighteenth-century rationalist metaphysicians to be clear about
their notion of "substance." Descartes said that there were two different kinds of

substances: mind or mental substance, and body or physical substance. Accordingly, he is usually called a *dualist* and the position, in general, that mind and body are different substances is called **Cartesian dualism.**[1] You remember that Descartes insisted that his identity was as a "thinking thing," in other words, a mental substance. But now, what of his body? We have seen that he believed that he could intelligibly doubt the existence of his body but not of his mind. But what is so special about this body that, unlike other bodies (the chair in front of him, the body of the king), was so intimately connected to his mind? It moved when he willed it to move, it walked when he decided to walk, it wrote what he wanted to write. In the last of his six *Meditations*, he returns to this problem.

from "Meditation VI," by Descartes

Firstly, then, I perceived that I had a head, hands, feet, and other members composing that body which I considered as part, or perhaps even as the whole, of myself. I perceived further, that that body was placed among many others, by which it was capable of being affected in diverse ways, both beneficial and hurtful; and what was beneficial I remarked by a certain sensation of pleasure, and what was hurtful by a sensation of pain. And, besides this pleasure and pain, I was likewise conscious of hunger, thirst, and other appetites, as well as certain corporeal inclinations towards joy, sadness, anger, and similar passions.

. . . . .

Nor was I altogether wrong in likewise believing that that body which, by a special right, I called my own, pertained to me more properly and strictly than any of the others; for in truth, I could never be separated from it as from other bodies: I felt in it and on account of it all my appetites and affections, and in fine I was affected in its parts by pain and the titillation of pleasure, and not in the parts of the other bodies that were separated from it. But when I inquired into the reason why, from this I know not what sensation of pain, sadness of mind should follow, and why from the sensation of pleasure joy should arise, or why this indescribable twitching of the stomach, which I call hunger, should put me in mind of taking food, and the parchedness of the throat of drink, and so in other cases, I was unable to give any explanation, unless that I was so taught by nature; for there is assuredly no affinity, at least none that I am able to comprehend, between this irritation of the stomach and the desire of food, any more than between the perception of an object that causes pain and the consciousness of sadness which springs from the perception. And in the same way it seemed to me that all the other judgments I had formed regarding the objects of sense, were dictates of nature; because I remarked that those judgments were formed in me, before I had leisure to weigh and consider the reasons that might constrain me to form them.

---

[1]Named after Descartes. As a matter of fact, Descartes believed that there were three kinds of substances, the third being God. But we need not worry about that third substance at this point. For our purposes, he is simply a dualist.

But, afterwards, a wide experience by degrees sapped the faith I had reposed in my senses; for I frequently observed that towers, which at a distance seemed round, appeared square when more closely viewed, and that colossal figures, raised on the summits of these towers, looked like small statues, when viewed from the bottom of them; and, in other instances without number, I also discovered error in judgments founded on the external senses; and not only in those founded on the external, but even in those that rested on the internal senses; for is there aught more internal than pain? and yet I have sometimes been informed by parties whose arm or leg had been amputated, that they still occasionally seemed to feel pain in that part of the body which they had lost, — a circumstance that led me to think that I could not be quite certain even that any one of my members was affected when I felt pain in it. And to these grounds of doubt I shortly afterwards also added two others of very wide generality: the first of them was that I believed I never perceived anything when awake which I could not occasionally think I also perceived when asleep, and as I do not believe that the ideas I seem to perceive in my sleep proceed from objects external to me, I did not any more observe any ground for believing this of such as I seem to perceive when awake; the second was that since I was as yet ignorant of the author of my being, or at least supposed myself to be so, I saw nothing to prevent my having been so constituted by nature as that I should be deceived even in matters that appeared to me to possess the greatest truth.

. . . . .

But now that I begin to know myself better, and to discover more clearly the author of my being, I do not, indeed, think that I ought rashly to admit all which the senses seem to teach, nor, on the other hand, is it my conviction that I ought to doubt in general of their teachings.

And, firstly, because I know that all which I clearly and distinctly conceive can be produced by God exactly as I conceive it, it is sufficient that I am able clearly and distinctly to conceive one thing apart from another, in order to be certain that the one is different from the other, seeing they may at least be made to exist separately, by the omnipotence of God; and it matters not by what power this separation is made, in order to be compelled to judge them different; and, therefore, merely because I know with certitude that I exist, and because, in the meantime, I do not observe that aught necessarily belongs to my nature or essence beyond my being a thinking thing, I rightly conclude that my essence consists only in my being a thinking thing [or a substance whose whole essence or nature is merely thinking]. And although I may, or rather, as I will shortly say, although I certainly do possess a body with which I am very closely conjoined; nevertheless, because, on the one hand, I have a clear and distinct idea of myself, in as far as I am only a thinking and unextended thing, and as, on the other hand, I possess a distinct idea of body, in as far as it is only an extended and unthinking thing, it is certain that I [that is, my mind, by which I am what I am] is entirely and truly distinct from my body, and may exist without it.

Then comes Descartes's proof that, in general, he could not be fooled about the existence of bodies "outside" of him.

But there is nothing which that nature teaches me more expressly [or more sensibly] than that I have a body which is ill affected when I feel pain, and stands in need of food and drink when I experience the sensations of hunger and thirst, etc. And therefore I ought not to doubt but that there is some truth in these informations.

Nature likewise teaches me by these sensations of pain, hunger, thirst, etc., that I am not only lodged in my body as a pilot in a vessel, but that I am besides so intimately conjoined, and as it were intermixed with it, that my mind and body compose a certain unity. For if this were not the case, I should not feel pain when my body is hurt, seeing I am merely a thinking thing, but should perceive the wound by the understanding alone, just as a pilot perceives by sight when any part of his vessel is damaged; and when my body has need of food or drink, I should have a clear knowledge of this, and not be made aware of it by the confused sensations of hunger and thirst: for, in truth, all these sensations of hunger, thirst, pain, etc., are nothing more than certain confused modes of thinking, arising from the union and apparent fusion of mind and body.

Besides this, nature teaches me that my own body is surrounded by many other bodies. . . . some are agreeable, and others disagreeable, there can be no doubt that my body, or rather my entire self, in as far as I am composed of body and mind, may be variously affected, both beneficially and hurtfully, by surrounding bodies.[2]

But how can two different substances, particularly two such different kinds of substances, interact? We know what it is for two bodies to interact, but how can a body make contact with a mind, which seems so intangible and "ghostly"? Descartes never answers this problem to his or to his critics' satisfaction. Spinoza, seeing Descartes's troubles, insists that there is only one substance and that body and mind are but different "attributes" of that one substance. That avoids the metaphysical problem, for there is no problem about interaction within a substance. But it still leaves a sizable problem, namely, how these two attributes are coordinated. That is a problem Spinoza never answers. And Leibniz, attacking the same problem, finds it preferable to deny the reality of physical substance altogether. There are only mental substances, monads, each locked into its own experience. The extravagance of these two solutions should give you some idea of the difficulty of the problem.

We can get a more specific clue to the mysterious quality of "consciousness" if we consider the following. Descartes, Spinoza, and Leibniz, you recall, define mind as "unextended," that is, unextended in space. (Bodies, on the other hand, are defined as extended in space.) In other words, it is essential that minds, unlike bodies, cannot be said to be "this large" or to be located in such and such a place. But despite this definition, notice how much of our talk about consciousness consists of metaphors of a spatial form; we talk about something being "in" our

[2]René Descartes, "Meditation VI," in *Meditations on First Philosophy*, in *The Philosophical Works of Descartes*, trans. Elizabeth S. Haldane and G. R. T. Ross (Cambridge: Cambridge University Press, 1911).

minds. We talk about something "slipping (out of) our minds." Philosophers often talk about the "contents" of consciousness, and a popular phrase from William James is the "stream of consciousness." Now we might say, "those are just metaphors"; but why are such metaphors necessary?

How would you answer the question "What is it to be conscious?" You might say something about "awareness" or "feelings," but that only restates the problem with different words. When we try to describe an image we do so in terms appropriate to physical things (namely, what it is an image *of*). We try to describe a pain and come out with metaphors ("it's as if a vice were closing on my head") or comparisons ("it feels the same as when . . ."). The retreat to spatial metaphors reflects this difficulty. We talk about our experiences as if we were describing other things but then qualify our descriptions by saying that they are "in" consciousness rather than in the world.

How can we describe consciousness itself? There is a further difficulty: if I can talk about my mind only with difficulty, how can I talk about your mind at all? I can experience only what is "in" my mind. I can't feel your pain. Even if I feel "sympathy pains" with you, it is my pain I feel. So I can't describe your mind at all, and evidently I have difficulty describing my mind as well. Therefore, how can we talk about "mind" at all? Not surprisingly, many psychologists and philosophers have rejected the idea of "mind" altogether, preferring to talk only about what is mutually observable and "extended" in physical space (for example, neurology and overt behavior).

We shall later consider some of these attempts to reject the idea of "mind" altogether. But what should seem fairly obvious to you is that this idea can be rejected only with reference to other people, not with reference to ourselves. Why? Because of Descartes's first premise, to put it bluntly. The same logic that allows him to assert with certainty "I am thinking" and "I exist as a thinking thing" now forces us to admit that "I am not thinking" and "I am not a thinking thing" are utterly absurd and unintelligible statements. They are self-refuting in exactly the same sense that "I am thinking" is self-confirming. (This isn't to say that you are thinking clearly, or well, or enjoying it; only that, in some minimal sense, you are thinking.) And, therefore, you must have a mind. In one's own case, the fact that a person is conscious is the last thing one could ever deny.

"INCORRIGIBILITY" AS THE MARK OF THE MENTAL

The special relationship we have to our own consciousness has been the subject of considerable debate among philosophers, as you can well imagine. In their various attempts to get clear about the nature of consciousness, they have used this special relationship as a way of defining what they mean by "mind." Descartes claimed that he knew what was going on in his mind with an immediate certainty that he could never have about what was going on in the world "outside" him. In his first "Meditation," he talks about his seeming to be sitting in front of the fire and the fact that he might be wrong (if he were in bed asleep at the time). But what he could not be wrong about is his seeming to be sitting in front of the fire. Similarly, you think you see a friend walking across the street. You are wrong, for your friend is in fact in Alaska this week. But you can still be certain that you thought that you saw him, even if you didn't. Philosophers often refer to this special kind of "immediate" certainty in the case of our own conscious experiences as **incorrigibility.** You might make a mistake in any factual claim about the world, for you might be hallucinating, or dreaming, or simply fooled by circumstances. But nothing could lead you to suspect that you might be mistaken about your own experiences. Given enough evidence against you, you might be willing to change from "but I know that I saw it" to "well, I thought I saw it." But nothing could convince you that you were wrong in thinking that you saw whatever it was. That claim, the claim about your experience, is incorrigible. Your claim about what you saw, however, is always open to further questioning.

For many years, this notion of incorrigibility served as part of the definition of "mind"; whatever was mental could be described incorrigibly. But doubts have begun to creep in recently. Part of the problem was Freud's introduction of the notion of "the unconscious." According to his famous "psychoanalytic" theory, not everything mental is knowable, and therefore surely not everything "in the mind" can be described incorrigibly. In a famous passage from his "Introductory Lectures," Freud says:

on The Unconscious, by Sigmund Freud

There is no need to discuss what is to be called conscious: it is removed from all doubt. The oldest and best meaning of the word 'unconscious' is the descriptive one; we call a psychical process unconscious whose existence we are obliged to assume — for some such reason as that we infer it from its effects —, but of which we know nothing. In that case we have the same relation to it as we have to a physical process in another person, except that it is in fact one of our own. If we want to be still more correct, we shall modify our assertion by saying that we call a process unconscious if we are obliged to assume that it is being activated *at the moment* though *at the moment* we know nothing about it. This qualification makes us reflect that the majority of conscious processes are conscious only for a short time; very soon they become *latent*, but can easily become conscious again. We might also say that they had become unconscious, if it were at all certain that in the condition of latency they are still something psychical. So far we should have learnt nothing new; nor should we have acquired the right to introduce the concept of an unconscious into psychology. But then comes the new observation that we were already able to make in parapraxes. In order to explain a slip of the tongue, for instance, we find ourselves obliged to assume that the intention to make a particular remark was present in the subject. We infer it with certainty from the interference with his remark which has occurred; but the intention did not put itself through and was thus unconscious. If, when we subsequently put it before the speaker, he recognizes it as one familiar to him, then it was only temporarily unconscious to him; but if he repudiates it as something foreign to him, then it was permanently unconscious. From this experience we retrospectively obtain the right also to pronounce as something unconscious what had been described as latent. A consideration of these dynamic relations permits us now to distinguish two kinds of unconscious — one which is easily, under frequently occurring circumstances, transformed into something conscious, and another with which this transformation is difficult and takes place only subject to a considerable expenditure of effort or possibly never at all. In order to escape the ambiguity as to whether we mean the one or the other unconscious, whether we are using the word in the descriptive or in the dynamic sense, we make use of a permissible and simple way out. We call the unconscious which is only latent, and thus easily becomes conscious, the 'preconscious' and retain the term 'unconscious' for the other. We now have three terms, 'conscious,' 'preconscious' and 'unconscious,' with which we can get along in our description of mental phenomena. Once again: the preconscious is also unconscious in the purely descriptive sense, but we do not give it that name, except in talking loosely or when we have to make a defence of the existence in mental life of unconscious processes in general.[3]

Notice that Freud starts from a Cartesian position, the idea that "conscious is removed from all doubt." But then he suggests what no Cartesian can tolerate, the idea that there are ideas (experiences, intentions) in our minds that we do not and sometimes cannot know, much less know with certainty. And if we accept this notion of "the unconscious" (or even the weaker notion of "preconscious"), the traditional notion of the "incorrigibility" of the mental is seriously challenged.

The argument, however, cuts both ways. Many philosophers have rejected Freud just because his notion of "the unconscious" goes against the notion of incorrigibility. "If it isn't knowable incorrigibly," these philosophers have said, "then it can't be mental at all." And even Freud himself was forced to admit that his theory flew in the face of our normal "manner of speaking." And the debate continues. Can you be wrong about what is going on in your own mind? For a long time, it was generally agreed that you could not be. Now we aren't so sure. You are certain that you are over an old love affair, but, without too much difficulty, a friend or a psychologist convinces you that you have been thinking about it constantly. You are certain that you are angry, but on closer examination, and in retrospect, you decide that you really felt guilty. You thought that you were thinking about your professor, when suddenly you realize that in fact it was the face of your father!

Can you be wrong about what you feel? Can you be wrong about what is going on in your own mind? It isn't clear. We now admit (as few philosophers had

[3]Sigmund Freud, *New Introductory Lectures on Psychoanalysis*, ed. and trans. James Strachey (New York: Norton, 1964).

before) that at least there are some things we can be wrong about. Is there anything about which we could not be mistaken? What of those basic bits of data
that the empiricists talked about — sensations or impressions? Could we possibly
be wrong in our confidence that "right now, I am experiencing a cold feeling in
my hand"? The empiricists assumed that one could not be wrong about this, for
it was on the basis of such certainties that we were able to construct, through
inductive reasoning, our theories about the world. Could we be wrong even about
our own sensations? Consider this example (it comes from Bishop Berkeley): A
mischievous friend tells you that he is going to touch your hand with a very hot
spoon. When you aren't looking, he touches you with a piece of ice. You scream
and claim, with seeming certainty, that he has given you an uncomfortable sensation of heat. But you're wrong. What you felt was cold. What you seemed to
feel was heat. But even your "seeming," in this case, was mistaken.

Philosophers have also pointed out that what is unique to mind as opposed to
body is the fact that one and only one person can (and must) experience what is
going on. I can (and must) feel only my pains, I can't experience your pains.
Philosophers have referred to this as **privileged access,** sometimes as the
privacy of mental events. The "privilege" is the fact that, whatever is going on
in your mind, you are not only the first but the only one to know of it directly.
The "privacy" refers to the fact that if you decide not to tell anyone or betray
yourself (through your facial expressions or your behavior), no one else need ever
know. If you have a wart on your thigh, you can keep it contingently "private"
by choosing suitable clothing. But if you have a "dirty little secret" in your mind,
you have a logical guarantee of its privacy — it is private necessarily.

"Incorrigible" means "beyond correction"; "privileged access" means "known
in a special way." (These concepts must be kept separate.) Because of privileged
access and the "privacy" of consciousness, our states of mind have the very peculiar status of being always knowable to ourselves (though whether or not we want
to say "knowable with certainty" depends on our views about incorrigibility) and
yet possibly unknowable to anyone else. That is why, as you learned in grade
school, you could always fake a headache to stay home for the day but you
couldn't fake a fever or a sore. As long as it was purely mental, it was also purely
private. Your success depended wholly upon how good (or bad) an actor you were.
But when it came to your body, you were in no privileged position. It was the
thermometer, not your opinions, that told whether you had a fever or not. And
it was the doctor, not you, who decided how serious your sore really was. But
when it came to your own consciousness, you were in a truly privileged and
irrefutable position.

THE PROBLEM OF DUALISM

Defining consciousness is not easy, but what is even more difficult is giving any
plausible account of how consciousness is connected to your body. You decide to
raise your hand, and your hand goes up. You formulate an answer to your friend's

question, and it comes out of your mouth. How does what takes place "in your mind" determine what happens with your body? A familiar image, borrowed from untold numbers of cartoons, is the little man (or woman) in your head, operating your body as a construction worker operates a giant steam shovel. But this is no answer at all. First, there is no little man. But even if there were, the same problem would then focus on him (or her). How does he or she move a body by making certain mental decisions? The same problem arises in the other direction, from body to mind. A friend steps on your toe — your physiology teacher can explain to you what happens — nerves are pinched and signals are sent through your central nervous system into that huge complex of fat cells called your brain. But then, at some point, there is something else, the feeling, the pain. How does this happen? How does a feeling emerge from that complex and still unknown network of neurological reactions going on in your body?

You can see that this problem of mind-body interaction is no longer just a technical metaphysical problem having to do with the special notion of substance. The problem of "interaction" is the same for Spinoza with his one substance as it is for Descartes with his dualism. And even if you don't want to talk of substances at all, there is still the problem of explaining how your mind affects your body and how your body affects your mind. For whether or not you accept the special problems of the eighteenth-century metaphysicians, you have to admit that your mind is very different from your body. And that is the source of the trickiest of all modern philosophy problems, the "mind-body problem." How are mind and body related?

The human body, like any other physical body, can be described in terms of its size, weight, chemical composition, and movements in space. The workings of the human nervous system, although very complex and not yet adequately understood, can be described just like any other biological reaction, in terms of the changes in cell membranes and chemical reactions, the procession of chemo-electric nerve "impulses," and the computer-like network of different nerve components that are stimulated at any given time. The human brain can be seen as a complex machine, like a gooey computer. The human mind, however, is not to be characterized in any such spatial or chemical terms. The mind is not the same as the brain. It has no shape, no weight, and has the awkward property of being observable — in any particular case — by one and only one person. (Anyone can see my brain if they can get inside my skull.) We can understand how a body might interact with another body, even when the "forces" involved are hard to picture (for example, the gravitational attraction between two distant planets). But how does a body interact with something that has none of the crucial characteristics of a body? You might think of "energy" here, for energy would seem to have at least some of the intangible and "unextended" features of mind. It too, in a very limited sense, "has no size or weight." But energy is a function of physical bodies, force is a function of mass and acceleration. They are not, like our experiences, "private": a lightning bolt is observable to anyone who looks. And no one has ever claimed that descriptions of energy states, like descriptions of our ideas, are incorrigible. And while it has often been demonstrated (by Einstein) that energy and mass are interconvertible, any such "interconvertibility" of mind and matter is still at the highly speculative stage, limited to freak performances by a few isolated and not wholly dependable "psychics" and such. We may well talk about "mental energy," but it is far from clear what we mean. (And the fact that transcendental meditation gives us more of "whatever it is" only proves that we don't yet know what meditation is either.)

How can something so different as ideas and sensations interact with nervous systems and brain cells? Philosophers have proposed a number of solutions, all of them controversial and none of them yet satisfactory. But even before we look at some of them, it is important to stress the following point: The "mind-body problem" is not simply a matter of how little we still know about the human nervous system. No matter how our knowledge develops, we will still be faced with that mysterious gap between the last known neurological occurrence and the experience. Right now we can trace our neural impulses only so far, and the "last known neurological occurrence" is not very far along. But even when we have complete "brain maps" and can say for every mental occurrence what is going on in the brain at the same time, the problem will still remain: How are the two related?[4]

The classic attempt to resolve the problem of dualism is by Descartes. The following selection is from his essay "The Passions of the Soul":

from "The Soul and the Body," by Descartes

But in order to understand all these things more perfectly, we must know that the soul is really joined to the whole body, and that we cannot, properly speaking, say that it exists in any one of its parts to the exclusion of the others, because it is one and in some manner indivisible, owing to the disposition of its organs, which are so related to one another that when any one of them is removed, that renders the whole body defective; and because it is of a nature which has no relation to extension, nor dimensions, nor other properties of the matter of which the body is composed, but only to the whole conglomerate of its organs, as appears from the fact that we could not in any way conceive of the half or the third of a soul, nor of the space it occupies, and because it does not become smaller owing to the cutting off of some portion of the body, but separates itself from it entirely when the union of its assembled organs is dissolved.

It is likewise necessary to know that although the soul is joined to the whole body, there is yet in that a certain part in which it exercises its functions more particularly than in all the others; and it is usually believed that this part is the brain, or possibly the heart: the brain, because it is with it that the organs of sense are connected, and the heart because it is apparently in it that we experience the passions. But, in examining the matter with

[4]Scientific research could show, although it is extremely unlikely, that the brain and our mind have very little to do with each other, that the presumed coordination between the two does not exist. It once was thought, for example, that the heart had to do with emotions (Aristotle and Descartes, for example). Science has proved them wrong. But science cannot do more than lay the ground for the problem. It cannot solve it.

care, it seems as though I had clearly ascertained that the part of the body in which the soul exercises its functions immediately is in nowise the heart, nor the whole of the brain, but merely the most inward of all its parts, to wit, a certain very small gland which is situated in the middle of its substance and so suspended above the duct whereby the animal spirits in its anterior cavities have communication with those in the posterior, that the slightest movements which take place in it may alter very greatly the course of these spirits; and reciprocally that the smallest changes which occur in the course of the spirits may do much to change the movements of this gland.[5]

Let us then conceive here that the soul has its principal seat in the little gland which exists in the middle of the brain, from whence it radiates forth through all the remainder of the body by means of the animal spirits, nerves, and even the blood, which, participating in the impressions of the spirits, can carry them by the arteries into all the members. And recollecting what has been said above about the machine of our body, i.e. that the little filaments of our nerves are so distributed in all its parts, that on the occasion of the diverse movements which are there excited by sensible objects, they open in diverse ways the pores of the brain, which causes the animal spirits contained in these cavities to enter in diverse ways into the muscles, by which means they can move the members in all the different ways in which they are capable of being moved; and also that all the other causes which are capable of moving the spirits in diverse ways suffice to conduct them into diverse muscles; let us here add that the small gland which is the main seat of the soul is so suspended between the cavities which contain the spirits that it can be moved by them in as many different ways as there are sensible diversities in the object, but that it may also be moved in diverse ways by the soul, whose nature is such that it receives in itself as many diverse impressions, that is to say, that it possesses as many diverse perceptions as there are diverse movements in this gland. Reciprocally, likewise, the machine of the body is so formed that from the simple fact that this gland is diversely moved by the soul, or by such other cause, whatever it is, it thrusts the spirits which surround it towards the pores of the brain, which conduct them by the nerves into the muscles, by which means it causes them to move the limbs.[6]

The technical name given to this theory is **causal interactionism,** in other words, mental changes cause bodily changes and vice versa. Descartes did not take as seriously as his followers the problem of separate substances or radically different changes causally affecting one another. He apparently felt satisfied, if not exactly comfortable, with such a causal account. He was vigorously attacked in this by most of his immediate followers, including Spinoza, Leibniz,

---

[5]The gland Descartes is referring to is what is now called the Pineal Gland, a small endocrine gland at the base of the brain. It had only recently been discovered in Descartes's time, and its functions are still not adequately understood. It is currently hypothesized that it controls mating cycles in higher animals and possibly any number of other activity cycles.

[6]René Descartes, "The Passions of the Soul," in *The Philosophical Works of Descartes.*

and many of the empiricists. "Different substances cannot interact," they insisted. Or, in more modern dress, they argued that only physical bodies can causally interact, not anything so different as physical bodies and minds. Yet one thing remains obvious. And that is that the familiar coordination of our mental activities and the movements of our bodies must be accounted for. And to do so, without bringing in causal interaction, required considerable ingenuity on the part of Descartes's critics.

We have already seen the two metaphysical alternatives that immediately followed Descartes. The first was formulated by Leibniz as part of his overall theory of monads. He insisted that there could be no causal interaction between monads, and specifically, there could be no sense made out of the claim that mental substances interacted with anything that we call "physical bodies." So what could he suggest as an alternative? His answer to the problem was that God, who had created monads in the first place, had also "programmed" them in such a way that our mental activities and what we call our bodily activities are exactly coordinated. Leaving aside the rest of Leibniz's theory and looking just at the mind-body problem, we can restate his solution as a form of what is called **parallelism.** His "pre-established harmony" between monads can now be viewed as the somewhat strange theory that our mental lives and the movements of our bodies are exactly coordinated (so that I feel pain when you step on my toe and so that my hand goes up just when I "decide" that it should). Yet there is no causal interaction between them whatsoever. It is like the sound and visual tracks of a movie film, moving along exactly parallel but never in fact interacting. (That is, the character who appears to be talking in the movie does not cause the sounds that you hear as if he or she were producing them. The sounds are actually produced separately and would continue even if the projector bulb burned out and the figure on the screen disappeared altogether.) Of course, to accept this theory you must also accept the considerable metaphysical and theological supports that it requires. If you don't believe in a God who could set up this complex system, there is absolutely no way of explaining the remarkable coordination of mind and body. And even if you do believe in God, you may well think that the mind-body problem requires some more plausible and secular solution.

Spinoza's theory need not be kept in the "one substance" metaphysics that he used to present it. In fact, much the same theory was defended only a few years ago by Bertrand Russell, without reference to the metaphysical notion of substance at all. Russell said, as Spinoza had said centuries before, that mind and body, mental events and physical changes, were different aspects of one and the same "something." For Spinoza, the "something" was "the one substance" and the aspects were what he called "attributes." Russell claimed only that our experiences and ideas were one aspect of some events or activities of which the various chemical reactions of the brain were another aspect. Accordingly, the theory has often been called the **dual aspect theory,** whether or not it is specifically addressed to the problem of substances and their attributes. Since we are now talking about two "aspects" of the same thing rather than two different things, the problem of interaction doesn't arise. But, as we complained before, this only hides the problem rather than solves it. What is this mysterious "something" of which mind and body are merely "aspects"? It is neither brain nor mind, so what could it be? By the nature of the case, we can't find out. And it leaves us with the equally embarrassing question, "How could one and the same thing have such different aspects?" You might say, "Well, a hot coal has both 'aspects' of being heavy and being hot." But that we can explain. What are we to say of a "something" that is neither brain nor mind but both?

THE REJECTION OF DUALISM

If the problem is dualism, then perhaps the answer is the rejection of dualism. Of course, we still have to account for the obvious facts of the case: that we feel something when certain things happen to our bodies, that we do something when we mentally decide to. But philosophers of recent years — and nearly all psychologists — have taken a dim view towards dualism in all of the above forms.

A first, still timid step towards eliminating dualism consists of minimizing, though not rejecting, the mental side of dualism. This theory is usually called **epiphenomenalism** and William James was one of its best-known defenders. Epiphenomenalism allows for causal interaction, but only in one direction. Bodies and changes in bodies cause mental events. You might think of a boiler system or automobile engine equipped with various gauges to tell us how the machine is functioning at any given time. The machine works on, registering certain results on the attached gauges. But notice that the gauge is relatively unimportant to the working of the machine. In fact, the gauge can break and the machine can function for years. What is the significance of such a theory? Many philosophers and psychologists are interested primarily in the continuity of physical and physiological laws without the problematic disruption of mysterious "mental causes." For them, such a theory allows them to concentrate wholly on the physical side of the matter and ignore "the mind" completely. If an objection is raised one can always insist: "Oh, I'm not denying that you feel something too." But this is an unimportant detail, a side-product, an epiphenomenon, that need not be taken all that seriously.

Radical Behaviorism

Epiphenomenalism is a timid rejection of dualism. It doesn't actually reject dualism, but it minimizes one half the duality. Other forms of attack are not so timid. In psychology, it has long been accepted by many authors that all talk of "the mental" is a hopeless tangle of confusions that, by the nature of the case, cannot be resolved through any experiment whatsoever. (That is, only one person could observe the results of the experiment in any given case, and the very nature of a scientific experiment is that it must be observable by anyone.) Accordingly, many psychologists have followed the American theorist John Watson in practicing what they call **behaviorism.** Today the best-known behaviorist is the Harvard psychologist B. F. Skinner. Behaviorism, as a form of science, refuses to even consider any events that cannot be publicly witnessed, and that immediately and logically excludes mental events. Behaviorism is primarily a scientific method and need not deny the existence of mental events. Most behaviorists, however, have gone beyond the method—which only says that they will not scientifically study such events—and have done a bit of metaphysics as well: They also deny that there can be any mental events. Watson, for example, goes so far as to suggest that belief in consciousness goes back to the ancient days of superstition and magic. He insists that any good behaviorist can catch the average undergraduate student in a mess of tongue-tied contradictions but concludes from this not that our concept of consciousness is complicated and confused but rather that there could not possibly be any such thing. His argument is self-consciously "scientific," the alternative to which is being a mere "savage and still believing in magic." His test is simply whether the soul (philosophers and psychologists often shift too easily between "soul" and "consciousness") can be experienced; "no one has ever touched a soul, or seen one in a test tube, or has in any other way come into relationship with it as he has with the other objects of his daily experience."[7] Thus Watson shifts from his view as a scientist, able to write about only what he can measure and observe, to a view as a metaphysician, insisting that there cannot be any such thing as consciousness and that no rational person should believe that there is.

Logical Behaviorism

Philosophers too have turned to behaviorism as a way of escaping the problems of Cartesian dualism. Oxford philosopher Gilbert Ryle, following some suggestions by Ludwig Wittgenstein, established a new form of behaviorism—*logical* behaviorism—in his book *The Concept of Mind* (1949). Its first chapter is appropriately called "Descartes' Myth." First he describes what he calls "the official doctrine":

"Descartes' Myth," by Gilbert Ryle

There is a doctrine about the nature and place of minds which is so prevalent among theorists and even among laymen that it deserves to be described as the official theory. Most philosophers, psychologists and religious teachers subscribe, with minor reservations, to its main articles and, although they admit certain theoretical difficulties in it, they tend to assume that these can be overcome without serious modifications being made to the architecture of the theory. It will be argued here that the cen-

[7]John Watson, *Behaviorism* (New York: Norton, 1930).

tral principles of the doctrine are unsound and conflict with the whole body of what we know about minds when we are not speculating about them.

The official doctrine, which hails chiefly from Descartes, is something like this. With the doubtful exceptions of idiots and infants in arms every human being has both a body and a mind. Some would prefer to say that every human being is both a body and a mind. His body and his mind are ordinarily harnessed together, but after the death of the body his mind may continue to exist and function.

Human bodies are in space and are subject to the mechanical laws which govern all other bodies in space. Bodily processes and states can be inspected by external observers. So a man's bodily life is as much a public affair as are the lives of animals and reptiles and even as the careers of trees, crystals and planets.

But minds are not in space, nor are their operations subject to mechanical laws. The workings of one mind are not witnessable by other observers; its career is private. Only I can take direct cognisance of the states and processes of my own mind. A person therefore lives through two collateral histories, one consisting of what happens in and to his body, the other consisting of what happens in and to his mind. The first is public, the second private. The events in the first history are events in the physical world, those in the second are events in the mental world.

It has been disputed whether a person does or can directly monitor all or only some of the episodes of his own private history; but, according to the official doctrine, of at least some of these episodes he has direct and unchallengeable cognisance. In consciousness, self-consciousness and introspection he is directly and authentically apprised of the present states and operations of his mind. He may have great or small uncertainties about concurrent and adjacent episodes in the physical world, but he can have none about at least part of what is momentarily occupying his mind.

It is customary to express this bifurcation of his two lives and of his two worlds by saying that the things and events which belong to the physical world, including his own body, are external, while the workings of his own mind are internal. This antithesis of outer and inner is of course meant to be construed as a metaphor, since minds, not being in space, could not be described as being spatially inside anything else, or as having things going on spatially inside themselves. But relapses from this good intention are common and theorists are found speculating how stimuli, the physical sources of which are yards or miles outside a person's skin, can generate mental responses inside his skull, or how decisions framed inside his cranium can set going movements of his extremities.

Even when 'inner' and 'outer' are construed as metaphors, the problem how a person's mind and body influence one another is notoriously charged with theoretical difficulties. What the mind wills, the legs, arms and the tongue execute; what affects the ear and the eye has something to do with what the mind perceives; grimaces and smiles betray the mind's moods and bodily castigations lead, it is hoped, to moral improvement. But the actual transactions between the episodes of the private history and those of the public history remain mysterious, since by definition they can belong to neither series. They could not be reported among the happenings described in a person's autobiography of his inner life, but nor could they be reported among those described in someone else's biography of that person's overt career. They can be inspected neither by introspection nor by laboratory experiment. They are theoretical shuttlecocks which are forever being bandied from the physiologist back to the psychologist and from the psychologist back to the physiologist.

Underlying this partly metaphorical representation of the bifurcation of a person's two lives there is a seemingly more profound and philosophical assumption. It is assumed that there are two different kinds of existence or status. What exists or happens may have the status of physical existence, or it may have the status of mental existence. Somewhat as the faces of coins are either heads or tails, or somewhat as living creatures are either male or female, so, it is supposed, some existing is physical existing, other existing is mental existing. It is a necessary feature of what has physical existence that it is in space and time; it is a necessary feature of what has mental existence that it is in time but not in space. What has physical existence is composed of matter, or else is a function of matter; what has mental existence consists of consciousness, or else is a function of consciousness.

.　.　.　.　.

What sort of knowledge can be secured of the workings of a mind? On the one side, according to the official theory, a person has direct knowledge of the best imaginable kind of the workings of his own mind. Mental states and processes are (or are normally) conscious states and processes, and the consciousness which irradiates them can engender no illusions and leaves the door open for no doubts. A person's present thinkings, feelings and willings, his perceivings, rememberings and imaginings are intrinsically 'phosphorescent'; their existence and their nature are inevitably betrayed to their owner. The inner life is a stream of consciousness of such a sort that it would be absurd to suggest that the mind whose life is that stream might be unaware of what is passing down it.

.　.　.　.　.

On the other side, one person has no direct access of any sort to the events of the inner life of another. He cannot do better than make problematic inferences from the observed behaviour of the other person's body to the states of mind which, by analogy from his own conduct, he supposes to be signalised by that behaviour. Direct access to the workings of a mind is the privilege of that mind itself; in default of such privileged access, the workings of one mind are inevitably occult to everyone else. For the supposed arguments from bodily movements similar to their own to mental workings similar to their own would lack any possibility of observational corroboration. Not unnaturally, therefore, an adherent of the official theory finds it difficult to resist this consequence of his premises, that he has no good reason to believe that there do exist minds other than his own. Even if he prefers to believe that to other human bodies there are harnessed minds not unlike his own, he cannot claim to be able to discover their individual characteristics, or the particular things that they undergo and do. Absolute solitude is on this showing the ineluctable destiny of the soul. Only our bodies can meet.

Then, in section 2, Ryle argues that the "official doctrine" is "absurd" and is based upon what he calls "a category mistake":

> Such in outline is the official theory. I shall often speak of it, with deliberate abusiveness, as 'the dogma of the Ghost in the Machine'. I hope to prove that it is entirely false, and false not in detail but in principle. It is not merely an assemblage of particular mistakes. It is one big mistake and a mistake of a special kind. It is, namely, a category-mistake. It represents the facts of mental life as if they belonged to one logical type or category (or range of types or categories), when they actually belong to another. The dogma is therefore a philosopher's myth. In attempting to explode the myth I shall probably be taken to be denying well-known facts about the mental life of human beings, and my plea that I aim at doing nothing more than rectify the logic of mental-conduct concepts will probably be disallowed as mere subterfuge.
>
> I must first indicate what is meant by the phrase 'Category-mistake.' This I do in a series of illustrations.
>
> A foreigner visiting Oxford or Cambridge for the first time is shown a number of colleges, libraries, playing fields, museums, scientific departments and administrative offices. He then asks 'But where is the university? I have seen where the members of the Colleges live, where the Registrar works, where the scientists experiment and the rest. But I have not yet seen the University in which reside and work the members of your University.' It has then to be explained to him that the University is not another collateral institution, some ulterior counterpart to the colleges, laboratories and offices which he has seen. The University is just the way in which all that he has already seen is organized. When they are seen and when their coordination is understood, the University has been seen. His mistake lay in his innocent assumption that it was correct to speak of Christ Church, the Bodleian Library, the Ashmolean Museum *and* the University, to speak, that is, as if 'the University' stood for an extra member of the class of which these other units are members. He was mistakenly allocating the University to the same category as that to which the other institutions belong. . . .
>
> One more illustration. A foreigner watching his first game of cricket learns what are the functions of the bowlers, the batsmen, the fielders, the umpires and the scorers. He then says 'But there is no one left on the field to contribute the famous element of team-spirit. I see who does the bowling, the batting and the wicket-keeping; but I do not see whose role it is to exercise *esprit de corps.*' Once more, it would have to be explained that he was looking for the wrong type of thing. Team-spirit is not another cricketing-operation supplementary to all of the other special tasks. It is, roughly, the keenness with which each of the special tasks is performed, and performing a task keenly is not performing two tasks. Certainly exhibiting team-spirit is not the same thing as bowling or catching, but nor is it a third thing such that we can say that the bowler first bowls *and* then exhibits team-spirit or that a fielder is at a given moment *either* catching *or* displaying *esprit de corps.*

These illustrations of category-mistakes have a common feature which must be noticed. The mistakes were made by people who did not know how to wield the concepts *University* . . . and *team-spirit*. Their puzzles arose from inability to use certain items in the English vocabulary.[8]

A *category mistake*, in general, is mistaking one *type* of thing for another. For example, it would be a category mistake to ask, "what color is the number 3?" The philosophically interesting mistakes, of course, are neither so obvious nor so silly as the above examples. They are mistakes made when we try to think abstractly. Most important are the category mistakes that philosophers make when they talk about "the mind":

> My destructive purpose is to show that a family of radical category-mistakes is the source of the double-life theory. The representation of a person as a ghost mysteriously ensconced in a machine derives from this argument. Because, as is true, a person's thinking, feeling and purposive doing cannot be described solely in the idioms of physics, chemistry and physiology, therefore they must be described in counterpart idioms. As the human body is a complex organised unit, so the human mind must be another complex organized unit, though one made of a different sort of stuff and with a different sort of structure. Or, again, as the human body, like any other parcel of matter, is a field of causes and effects, so the mind must be another field of causes and effects, though not (Heaven be praised) mechanical causes and effects.

This disastrous category mistake, which Ryle attributes primarily to Descartes, is thinking that "the mind" and its events are some strange and mysteriously private sort of *thing* behind our behavior, when, in fact, mind is the *pattern* of our behavior and not "behind" behavior at all.

> When two terms belong to the same category, it is proper to construct conjunctive propositions embodying them. Thus a purchaser may say that he bought a left-hand glove and a right-hand glove, but not that he bought a left-hand glove, a right-hand glove and a pair of gloves. 'She came home in a flood of tears and a sedan-chair' is a well-known joke based on the absurdity of conjoining terms of different types. It would have been equally ridiculous to construct the disjunction 'She came home either in a flood of tears or else in a sedan-chair'. Now the dogma of the Ghost in the Machine does just this. It maintains that there exist both bodies and minds; that there occur physical processes and mental processes; that there are mechanical causes of corporeal movements and mental causes of corporeal movements. I shall argue that these and other analogous conjunctions are absurd; but, it must be noticed, the argument will not show that either of the illegitimately conjoined propositions is absurd in itself. I am not, for example,

[8]Gilbert Ryle, *The Concept of Mind* (New York: Barnes & Noble, 1949).

denying that there occur mental processes. Doing long division is a mental process and so is making a joke. But I am saying that the phrase 'there occur mental processes' does not mean the same sort of thing as 'there occur physical processes', and, therefore, that it makes no sense to conjoin or disjoin the two.[9]

The key to Ryle's analysis is what he calls a disposition. A *disposition* is a tendency for something to happen given certain conditions. For example, we say that "if the lever is disturbed, the mousetrap will snap closed." The key is the *"if . . . then"* (or "hypothetical") form of the statement. Ryle explains this in the following way:

> There are at least two quite different senses in which an occurrence is said to be 'explained'; and there are correspondingly at least two quite different senses in which we ask 'why' it occurred and two quite different senses in which we say that it happened 'because' so and so was the case. The first sense is the causal sense. To ask why the glass broke is to ask what caused it to break, and we explain, in this sense, the fracture of the glass when we report that a stone hit it. The 'because' clause in the explanation reports an event, namely the event which stood to the fracture of the glass as cause to effect.
>
> But very frequently we look for and get explanations of occurrences in another sense of 'explanation'. We ask why the glass shivered when struck by the stone and we get the answer that it was because the glass was brittle. Now 'brittle' is a dispositional adjective; that is to say, to describe the glass as brittle is to assert a general hypothetical proposition about the glass. So when we say that the glass broke when struck because it was brittle, the 'because' clause does not report a happening or a cause; it states a law-like proposition. People commonly say of explanations of this second kind that they give the 'reason' for the glass breaking when struck.
>
> How does the law-like general hypothetical proposition work? It says, roughly, that the glass, *if* sharply struck or twisted, etc. *would* not dissolve or stretch or evaporate but fly into fragments. The matter of fact that the glass did at a particular moment fly into fragments, when struck by a particular stone, is explained, in this sense of 'explain', when the first happening, namely the impact of the stone, satisfies the protasis of the general hypothetical proposition, and when the second happening, namely the fragmentation of the glass, satisfies its apodosis.

He then applies this concept of disposition to his analysis of "mind." (This occupies him for most of his book.) The main idea is this: everything "mental" is really a disposition to behave in certain ways. Consider, for example, his brief analysis of acting from vanity:

[9]Ryle, *The Concept of Mind.*

> ... The statement 'he boasted from vanity' ought, on one view, to be construed as saying that 'he boasted and the cause of his boasting was the occurrence in him of a particular feeling or impulse of vanity'. On the other view, it is to be construed as saying 'he boasted on meeting the stranger and his doing so satisfies the law-like proposition that whenever he finds a chance of securing the admiration and envy of others, he does whatever he thinks will produce this admiration and envy'.

And then the general argument:

> ... To say that a person knows something, or aspires to be something, is not to say that he is at a particular moment in process of doing or undergoing anything, but that he is able to do certain things, when the need arises, or that he is prone to do and feel certain things in situations of certain sorts.
>
> . . . . .
>
> Abandonment of the two-worlds legend involves the abandonment of the idea that there is a locked door and a still to be discovered key. Those human actions and reactions, those spoken and unspoken utterances, those tones of voice, facial expressions and gestures, which have always been the data of all the other students of men, have, after all, been the right and the only manifestations to study. They and they alone have merited, but fortunately not received, the grandiose title 'mental phenomena'.[10]

Ryle's (and Wittgenstein's) logical behaviorism differs from the radical behaviorism of the psychologists in that it is not a theory about behavior and its causes so much as it is a theory about the language of mind, about the meaning of "mentalistic" terms such as "wants," "believes," "hurts," "loves," "feels," and "thinks." Ryle's basic thesis, stripped of his polemic against "the ghost in the machine," is that applying a mental term—attributing a mental property to a person—is logically equivalent to saying that the person will act in a certain way. The advantage of this is that it eliminates all mysterious things mental by translating the mental terminology into statements about behavior, not "inner events." Instead of thinking of love as "a feeling deep inside," for example, the logical behaviorist would say, unromantically perhaps, that "John loves Mary" means that John will be with Mary every chance he gets, he will buy her flowers if flowers are available, he will take her to the movies if she utters the stimulating words, "Let's go to the movies!" As you can see from this example, the number of acts and possible acts involved in the translation of a mentalistic term can be indefinitely large, since, in various circumstances and with various opportunities, a person in love might do almost anything. (The case is not so complicated, usually, with such mental predicates as "is thirsty" and "has an itch.") But however complicated the translation from mental language to behavioral disposition, the problem of dualism does not arise. The causal interaction between mind and body has been reformulated as the causal connection between a physical state—a dis-

---

[10]*The Concept of Mind.*

position to behave in certain ways—and the actual consequent behavior. Saying "he will marry her because he loves her" is therefore no more metaphysically problematic than saying "the glass will break because it is brittle."

There is a problem with all forms of behaviorism—both radical and logical. However tempting such a theory might be when we are studying other people at a distance, it seems utterly absurd when we try to think behavioristically while talking to a friend or listening to someone talk to us. And behaviorism becomes pure nonsense in one's own case, when we are trying to understand and talk about our own mental states. My pain is not the same as my behavior, and no matter how easy it may be for you to infer from my behavior that I am in pain, that is certainly not how *I* know that I am in pain, and it is not what I mean by my report, "I am in pain." Indeed, when I tell you "I am in pain," I am not predicting my behavior. I am telling you what I *feel*, quite apart from anything I might *do*. Whatever the logic of mental language, that undeniable feeling seems to remind us that behaviorism, however therapeutic in psychology and however powerful as an antidote to Cartesianism, cannot be the whole story. Watson's behaviorism helped correct an absurd amount of mentalistic theorizing about the behavior of animals ("the rat is trying to figure out how to get the door open"). So too, Ryle's behaviorism is a vital challenge to the too-easy supposition that our "minds" are ghostly containers filled with equally ghostly entities and processes. But as an alternative account of the mind, behaviorism inevitably bangs up against that ultimate mark of the mental, Descartes's "I think." There is no way you can think consistently that you never think or think that your thinking is nothing but your tendency to behave. As one of Watson's early critics commented, "What behaviorism shows is that psychologists do not always think very well, not that they don't think at all."

The rejection of dualism need not be a rejection of the mental side of the duality, although that is the obvious preference of most scientists. We have seen at least one philosopher, however, who escapes the problems of Cartesian dualism by rejecting the physical side of the problem. That is Bishop Berkeley, who quite clearly, in attacking Locke and defending his own "subjective idealism," provides a radical solution to the mind-body problem as well. His theory is that there are only minds and their ideas, no physical bodies. Therefore, there is no problem of interaction. He too (like Leibniz), however, needs God to hold his system together. But idealism has not been as rare an answer to the mind-body problem as you might think, although we see little of it nowadays. The religious idealists of the past century, in America as well as in England and Europe, were so powerful that they virtually ruled philosophy for a number of decades.[11]

---

[11]In Eastern thought too, idealism has often been an attractive thesis, but not for theoretical reasons. The following is from *The Teaching of Buddha*:

> Everything originates within the mind. Just as a magician cleverly makes whatever he wishes to appear, so this world of delusion originates within the mind. People look upon it and observe its appearing and disappearing and they believe it to be real and call it life and death. That is, everything is mind-made and has no significance apart from mind. As people come to understand this fact, they are able to remove all delusions and there is an end of all mental disturbance forever.

THE IDENTITY THEORY

The most powerful and most plausible rejection of dualism, however, consists neither of denying consciousness nor of denying physical bodies. To deny dualism by denying mind or body strikes us as a bit simple-minded; there is a better way. Why not say that there are not two things at all, as there appear to be, but only one. In other words, mind and body, or more accurately, mental events and certain bodily events (presumably brain events) are identical. This theory, accordingly, is called the **identity theory,** and it has been one of the hottest controversies in American philosophy. You can see that it was anticipated, in a sense, by Spinoza and Russell with their dual aspect theory. But the identity theory, unlike the others, tries to tie itself as closely as possible with current scientific research, and although it is not a scientific theory itself, it will allow no such mysterious "something" such as we found in Spinoza and Russell. Accordingly, it is usually considered a form of materialism (although it does not deny the existence — only the ontological independence — of mental events).

The identity theory says that there are mental events, but they are identical to — the same thing as — certain physical events, that is, processes in the brain. Unlike behaviorism (radical or logical), the identity theory does not deny that mentalistic terms refer to something. The identity theory rather denies dualism by insisting that what mentalistic terms such as "wants," "believes," and "loves" refer to is not only some further unspecifiable mental state; it is also a neurological process that scientists, someday, will be able to specify precisely. Dualism is eliminated because there are no longer two things to interact; there is just a single event, a mental–neurological event, which can be described in either of two ways, in either of two quite different languages. One can (truthfully) say, "I have a headache" or, if one knows an extensive amount of neurology, one could just as well say, "such and such (the details are not for a philosophy book) is going on in my brain."

The following essay is one of the classic statements of the identity theory by Australian philosopher J. J. C. Smart:

"Sensations and Brain Processes," by J. J. C. Smart

It seems to me that science is increasingly giving us a viewpoint whereby organisms are able to be seen as physico-chemical mechanisms: it seems that even the behavior of man himself will one day be explicable in mechanistic terms. There does seem to be, so far as science is concerned, nothing in the world but increasingly complex arrangements of physical constituents. All except for one place: in consciousness. That is, for a full description of what is going on in a man you would have to mention not only the physical processes in his tissue, glands, nervous system, and so forth, but also his states of consciousness: his visual, auditory, and tactual sensations, his aches and pains. That these should be *correlated* with brain processes does not help, for to say that they are *correlated* is to say that they are something "over and above." You cannot correlate something with itself. You correlate footprints with burglars, but not Bill Sikes the burglar with Bill Sikes the burglar. So sensations, states of consciousness, do seem to be the one sort of thing left outside the physicalist picture, and for various reasons I just cannot believe that this can be so. That everything should be explicable in terms of physics (together of course with descriptions of the ways in which the parts are put together — roughly, biology is to physics as radio-engineering is to electro-magnetism) except the occurrence of sensations seems to me to be frankly unbelievable. Such sensations would be "nomological danglers," to use Feigl's expression. It is not often realized how odd would be the laws whereby these nomological danglers would dangle. It is sometimes asked, "Why can't there be psycho-physical laws which are of a novel sort, just as the laws of electricity and magnetism were novelties from the standpoint of Newtonian mechanics?" Certainly we are pretty sure in the future to come across new ultimate laws of a novel type, but I expect them to relate simple constituents: for example, whatever ultimate particles are then in vogue. I cannot believe that ultimate laws of nature could relate simple constituents to configurations consisting of perhaps billions of neurons (and goodness knows how many billion billions of ultimate particles) all put together for all the world as though their main purpose in life was to be a negative feedback mechanism of a complicated sort. Such ultimate laws would be like nothing so far known in science. They have a queer "smell" to them. I am just unable to believe in the nomological danglers themselves, or in the laws whereby they would dangle. If any philosophical arguments seemed to compel us to believe in such things, I would suspect a catch in the argument. In any case it is the object of this paper to show that there are no philosophical arguments which compel us to be dualists.

· · · · ·

Why should not sensations just be brain processes of a certain sort? There are, of course, well-known (as well as lesser-known) philosophical objections to the view that reports of sensations are reports of brain-processes, but I shall try to argue that these arguments are by no means as cogent as is commonly thought to be the case.

Let me first try to state more accurately the thesis that sensations are brain processes. It is not the thesis that, for example, "after-image" or "ache" means the same as "brain process of sort *X*" (where "*X*" is replaced by a description of a certain sort of brain process). It is that, in so far as "after-image" or "ache" is a report of a process, it is a report of a process that *happens to be* a brain process. It follows that the thesis does not claim that sensation statements can be *translated* into statements about brain processes. Nor does it claim that the logic of a sensation statement is the same as that of a brain-process statement. All it claims is that in so far as a sensation statement is a report of something, that something is in fact a brain process. Sensations are nothing over and above brain processes. Nations are nothing "over and above" citizens, but this does not prevent the logic of nation statements being very different from the logic of citizen statements, nor does it insure the translatability of nation statements into citizen statements. (I do not, however, wish to assert that the relation of sensation statements to brain-process statements is very like that of nation statements to citizen statements. Nations do not just *happen to be* nothing over and above citizens, for example. I bring in the "nations" example merely to make a negative point: that the fact that the logic of A-statements is different from that of B-statements does not insure that A's are anything over and above B's.)

Remarks on identity. When I say that a sensation is a brain process or that lightning is an electric discharge, I am using "is" in the sense of strict identity. (Just as in the — in this case necessary — proposition "7 is identical with the smallest prime number greater than 5.") When I say that a sensation is a brain process or that lightning is an electric discharge I do not mean just that the sensation is somehow spatially or temporally continuous with the brain process or that the lightning is just spatially or temporally continuous with the discharge. When on the other hand I say that the successful general is the same person as the small boy who stole the apples I mean only that the successful general I see before me is a time slice of the same four-dimensional object of which the small boy stealing apples is an earlier time slice. However, the four-dimensional object which has the general-I-see-before-me for its late time slice is identical in the strict sense with the four-dimensional object which has the small-boy-stealing-apples for an early time slice. I distinguish these two senses of "is identical with" because I wish to make it clear that the brain-process doctrine asserts identity in the *strict* sense.

. . . . .

In short, the reply to Objection 1 is that there can be contingent statements of the form "A is identical with B," and a person may well know that something is an A without knowing that it is a B. An illiterate peasant might well be able to talk about his sensations without knowing about his brain processes, just as he can talk about lightning though he knows nothing of electricity.

Objection 2. It is only a contingent fact (if it is a fact) that when we have a certain kind of sensation there is a certain kind of process in our brain. Indeed it is possible, though perhaps in the highest degree unlikely, that our present physiological theories will be as out of date as the ancient theory connecting mental processes with goings on in the heart. It follows that when we report a sensation we are not reporting a brain-process.

Reply. The objection certainly proves that when we say "I have an after-image" we cannot *mean* something of the form "I have such and such a brain-process." But this does not show that what we report (having an after-image) is not *in fact* a brain process. "I see lightning" does not *mean* "I see an electric discharge." Indeed, it is logically possible (though highly unlikely) that the electrical discharge account of lightning might one day be given up. . . .

Objection 3. Even if Objections 1 and 2 do not prove that sensations are something over and above brain-processes, they do prove that the qualities of sensations are something over and above the qualities of brain-processes. That is, it may be possible to get out of asserting the existence of irreducibly psychic processes, but not out of asserting the existence of irreducibly psychic *properties.* For suppose we identify the Morning Star with the Evening Star. Then there must be some properties which logically imply that of being the Morning Star, and quite distinct properties which entail that of being the Evening Star. Again, there must be some properties (for example, that of being a yellow flash) which are logically distinct from those in the physicalist story. . . .

Now how do I get over the objection that sensation can be identified with a brain process only if it has some phenomenal property, not possessed by brain processes, whereby one-half of the identification may be, so to speak, pinned down?

Reply. My suggestion is as follows. When a person says, "I see a yellowish-orange after-image," he is saying something like this: *"There is something going on which is like what is going on when* I have my eyes open, am awake, and there is an orange illuminated in good light in front of me, that is, when I really see an orange." (And there is no reason why a person should not say the same thing when he is having a veridical sense-datum, so long as we construe "like" in the last sentence in such a sense that something can be like itself.) Notice that the italicized words, namely "there is something going on which is like what is going on when," are all quasi-logical or topic-neutral words. This explains why the ancient Greek peasant's reports about his sensations can be neutral between dualistic metaphysics or my materialistic metaphysics. It explains how sensations can be brain-processes and yet how those who report them need know nothing about brain-processes. For he reports them only very abstractly as "something going on which is like what is going on when . . ." Similarly, a person may say "someone is in the room," thus reporting truly that the doctor is in the room, even though he has never heard of doctors. (There are not two people in the room: "someone" *and* the doctor.) This account of sensation statements also explains the singular elusiveness of "raw feels" — why no one seems to be able to pin any properties on them. Raw feels, in my view, are colorless for the very same reason that *something* is colorless. This does not mean that sensations do not have properties, for if they are brain-processes they certainly have properties. It only means that in speaking of them as being like or unlike one another we need not know or mention these properties.

This, then, is how I would reply to Objection 3. The strength of my reply depends on the possibility of our being able to report that one thing is like another without being able to state the respect in which it is like. I am not sure whether this is so or not, and that is why I regard Objection 3 as the strongest with which I have to deal.

.   .   .   .   .

Objection 5. It would make sense to say of a molecular movement in the brain that it is swift or slow, straight or circular, but it makes no sense to say this of the experience of seeing something yellow.

Reply. So far we have not given sense to talk of experiences as swift or slow, straight or circular. But I am not claiming that "experience" and "brain-process" mean the same or even that they have the same logic. "Somebody" and "the doctor" do not have the same logic, but this does not lead us to suppose that talking about somebody telephoning is talking about someone over and above, say, the doctor. The ordinary man when he reports an experience is reporting that something is going on, but he leaves it open as to what sort of thing is going on, whether in a material solid medium, or perhaps in some sort of gaseous medium, or even perhaps in some sort of nonspatial medium (if this makes sense). All that I am saying is that "experience" and "brain-process" may in fact refer to the same thing, and if so we may easily adopt a convention (which is not a change in our present rules for the use of experience words but an addition to them) whereby it would make sense to talk of an experience in terms appropriate to physical processes.

Objection 6. Sensations are private, brain processes are *public.* If I sincerely say, "I see a yellowish-orange after-image" and I am not making a verbal mistake, then I cannot be wrong. But I can be wrong about a brain-process. The scientist looking into my brain might be having an illusion. Moreover, it makes sense to say that two or more people are observing the same brain-process but not that two or more people are reporting the same inner experience.

Reply. This shows that the language of introspective reports has a different logic from the language of material processes. It is obvious that until the brain-process theory is much improved and widely accepted there will be no *criteria* for saying "Smith has an experience of such-and-such a sort" *except* Smith's introspective reports. So we have adopted a rule of language that (normally) what Smith says goes.

Objection 7. I can imagine myself turned to stone and yet having images, aches, pains, and so on.

Reply. I can imagine that the electrical theory of lightning is false, that lightning is some sort of purely optical phenomenon. I can imagine that lightning is not an electrical discharge. I can imagine that the Evening Star is not the Morning Star. But it is. All the objection shows is that "experience" and "brain-process" do not have the same meaning. It does not show that an experience is not in fact a brain process.

.   .   .   .   .

U. T. Place seems to hold that the [brain-process thesis] is a straight-out scientific hypothesis. If so, he is partly right and partly wrong. If the issue is between (say) a brain-process thesis and a heart thesis, or a liver thesis, or a kidney thesis, then the issue is a purely empirical one, and the verdict is overwhelmingly in favor of the brain. The right sorts of things don't go on in the heart, liver, or kidney, nor do these organs possess the right sort of complexity of structure. On the other hand, if the issue is between a brain-or-heart-or-liver-or kidney thesis (that is, some form of materialism) on the one hand and epiphenomenalism on the other hand, then the issue is not an empirical one. For there is no conceivable experiment which could decide between materialism and epiphenomenalism. If it be agreed that there are no cogent philosophical arguments which force us into accepting dualism, and if the brain process theory and dualism are equally consistent with the facts, then the principles of parsimony and simplicity seem to me to decide overwhelmingly in favor of the brain-process theory.[12]

[12]From J. J. C. Smart, "Sensations and Brain Processes," *Philosophical Review*, LXVIII (1959), pp. 141–56.

As compatible as the identity theory may seem with contemporary science and as plausible as it may seem as a way of rejecting dualism without rejecting the obvious facts about feelings and thinking, the identity theory too runs up against its share of paradoxes. The idea that one thing (a brain event = a mental event) can be referred to and described in two different languages sounds plausible and impressive. But, in this case, the two languages are so very different that there is very good reason to suppose that the thing(s) they refer to is/are very different as well. To pursue this line of criticism, here is a re-evaluation of the identity theory by the American philosopher Jerome Shaffer.

Against the Identity Theory, by Jerome Shaffer

The last version of materialism we shall consider, and currently the most seriously discussed, is known as the identity theory. It is the theory that thoughts, feelings, wishes, and the rest of so-called mental phenomena are identical with, one and the same thing as, states and processes of the *body* (and, perhaps, more specifically, states and processes of the nervous system, or even of the brain alone). Thus the having of a thought is identical with having such and such bodily cells in such and such states. . . .

The sense of "identity" relevant here is that in which we say, for example, that the morning star is "identical" with the evening star. It is not that the expression "morning star" means the same as the expression "evening star"; on the contrary, these expressions mean something different. But the object referred to by the two expressions is one and the same; there is just one heavenly body, namely, Venus, which when seen in the morning is called the morning star and when seen in the evening is called the evening star. The morning star is identical with the evening star; they are one and the same object.[13]

Of course, the identity of the mental with the physical is not exactly of this sort, since it is held to be simultaneous identity rather than the identity of a thing at one time with the same thing at a later time. To take a closer example, one can say that lightning is a particularly massive electrical discharge from one cloud to another or to the earth. Not that the word "lightning" *means* "a particularly massive electrical discharge . . . "; when Benjamin Franklin discovered that lightning was electrical, he did not make a discovery about the meaning of words. Nor when it was discovered that water was H_2O was a discovery made about the meanings of words; yet water is identical with H_2O.

In a similar fashion, the identity theorist can hold that thoughts, feelings, wishes, and the like are identical with physical states. Not "identical" in the sense that mentalistic terms are synonymous in meaning with physicalistic terms but "identical" in the sense that the actual events picked out by mentalistic terms are one and the same events as those picked out by physicalistic terms.

---

[13]Both refer to the planet Venus, one as seen in the morning, the other at night. But it took many years for this identity to be discovered.

It is important to note that the identity theory does not have a chance of being true unless a particular sort of correspondence obtains between mental events and physical events, namely, that whenever a mental event occurs, a physical event of a particular sort (or at least one of a number of particular sorts) occurs, and vice versa. If it turned out to be the case that when a particular mental event occurred it seemed a matter of chance what physical events occurred or even whether any physical event at all occurred, or vice versa, then the identity theory would not be true. So far as our state of knowledge at the present time is concerned, it is still too early to say what the empirical facts are, although it must be said that many scientists do believe that there exists the kind of correspondences needed by identity theorists. But even if these correspondences turn out to exist, that does not mean that the identity theory will be true. For identity theorists do not hold merely that mental and physical events are correlated in a particular way but that they are one and the same events, i.e., not like lightning and thunder (which are correlated in lawful ways but not identical) but like lightning and electrical discharges (which always go together because they are one and the same).

What are the advantages of the identity theory? As a form of materialism, it does not have to cope with a world which has in it both mental phenomena and physical phenomena, and it does not have to ponder how they might be related. There exist only the physical phenomena, although there do exist two different ways of talking about such phenomena: physicalistic terminology and, in at least some situations, mentalistic terminology. We have here a dualism of language, but not a dualism of entities, events, or properties.

But do we have merely a dualism of languages and no other sort of dualism? In the case of Venus, we do indeed have only one object, but the expression "morning star" picks out one phase of that object's history, where it is in the mornings, and the expression "evening star" picks out another phase of that object's history, where it is in the evenings. If that object did not have these two distinct aspects, it would not have been a *discovery* that the morning star and the evening star were indeed one and the same body, and, further, there would be no point to the different ways of referring to it.

Now it would be admitted by identity theorists that physicalistic and mentalistic terms do not refer to different phases in the history of one and the same object. What sort of identity is intended? Let us turn to an allegedly closer analogy, that of the identity of lightning and a particular sort of electrical phenomenon. Yet here again we have two distinguishable aspects, the appearance to the naked eye on the one hand and the physical composition on the other. And this is also not the kind of identity which is plausible for mental and physical events. The appearance *to the naked eye* of a neurological event is utterly different from the experience of having a thought or a pain.

It is sometimes suggested that the physical aspect results from looking at a particular event "from the outside," whereas the mental results from looking at the same event "from the inside." When the brain surgeon observes my brain he is looking at it from the outside, whereas when I experience a mental event I am "looking" at my brain "from the inside."

Such an account gives us only a misleading analogy, rather than an accurate characterization of the relationship between the mental and the physical. The analogy suggests the difference between a man who knows his own house from the inside, in that he is free to move about within, seeing objects from different perspectives, touching them, etc., but can never get outside to see how it looks from there, and a man who cannot get inside and therefore knows only the outside appearance of the house, and perhaps what he can glimpse through the windows. But what does this have to do with the brain? Am I free to roam about inside my brain, observing what the brain surgeon may never see? Is not the "inner" aspect of my brain far more accessible to the brain surgeon than to me? He has the X rays, probes, electrodes, scalpels, and scissors for getting at the inside of my brain. If it is replied that this is only an analogy, not to be taken literally, then the question still remains how the mental and the physical are related.

Usually identity theorists at this point flee to even vaguer accounts of the relationship. They talk of different "levels of analysis," or of different "perspectives," or of different "conceptual schemes," or of different "language games." The point of such suggestions is that the difference between the mental and the physical is not a basic, fundamental, or intrinsic one, but rather a difference which is merely relative to different human purposes or standpoints. The difference is supposed to exist not in the thing itself but in the eye of the beholder.

But these are only hints. They do not tell us in precise and literal terms how the mental and the physical differ and are related. They only try to assure us that the difference does not matter to the real nature of things. But until we are given a theory to consider, we cannot accept the identity theorists' assurance that some theory will do only he does not know what it is.

One of the leading identity theorists, J. J. C. Smart, holds that mentalistic discourse is simply a vaguer, more indefinite way of talking about what could be talked about more precisely by using physiological terms. If I report a red afterimage, I mean (roughly) that something is going on which is like what goes on when I really see a red patch. I do not actually *mean* that a particular sort of brain process is occurring, but when I say something is going on I refer (very vaguely, to be sure) to just that brain process. Thus the thing referred to in my report of an afterimage is a brain process. Hence there is no need to bring in any nonphysical features. Thus even the taint of dualism is avoided.

Does this ingenious attempt to evade dualistic implications stand up under philosophical scrutiny? I am inclined to think it will not. Let us return to the man reporting the red afterimage. He was aware of the occurrence of something or other, of some feature or other. Now it seems to me obvious that he was not necessarily aware of the state of his brain at that time (I doubt that most of us are ever aware of the state of our brain) nor, in general, necessarily aware of any physical features of his body at that time. He might, of course, have been incidentally aware of some physical feature but not insofar as he was aware of the red afterimage as such. Yet he was definitely aware of something, or else how could he have made that report? So he must have been aware of some nonphysical feature. That is the only way of explaining how he was aware of anything at all.

Of course, the thing that our reporter of the afterimage was aware of might well have had further features which he was *not* aware of, particularly, in this connection, physical features. I may be aware of certain features of an object without being aware of others. So it is not ruled out that the event our reporter is aware of might be an event with predominantly physical features — he just does not notice those. But he must be aware of some of its features, or else it would not be proper to say he was aware of *that* event. And if he is not aware of any physical features, he must be aware of something else. And that shows that we cannot get rid of those nonphysical features in the way that Smart suggests. . . .

Even if the identity theorist could clarify the sense of "identity" to be used in his theory, he would still face two other problems. These concern coexistence in time and space. Coexistence in time and space are conditions that must be met if there is to be identity. That is to say, for two apparently different things to turn out to be one and the same, they must exist at the same time and in the same location. If we could show that Mr. A existed at a time when Mr. B did not, or that Mr. A existed in a place where Mr. B did not, then this would show that Mr. A and Mr. B were different men. It is by virtue of these facts about identity that an alibi can exonerate a suspect: if Mr. A was not in Chicago at the time, then he could not be one and the same with the man who stole the diamonds in Chicago.

So if mental events are to be identical with physical events, then they must fulfill the conditions of coexistence in time and space. The question is, Do they?

So far as coexistence in time is concerned, very little is known. The most relevant work consists in direct stimulation of an exposed part of the brain during surgery. Since only a local anesthetic is necessary in many such cases the patient may well be fully conscious. Then, as the surgeon stimulates different parts of his brain, the patient may report the occurrence of mental events — memories, thoughts, sensations. Do the physical events in the brain and the mental events occur at precisely the same time? It is impossible to say. All that would be required is a very small time gap to prove that the physical events were not identical with the mental events. But it is very difficult to see how the existence of so small a time gap could be established. And even if it were, what would it prove? Only that the mental event was not identical with just that physical event; it would not prove it was nonidentical with any physical event. So it could well be that coexistence in time is present or is not. I do not think that we shall get much decisive imformation from empirical work of the sort here described. The identity theorist, then, does not have to fear refutation from this quarter, at least not for a long time.

How about coexistence in space? Do mental events occur in the same place the corresponding physical events occur? This is also a very difficult question to answer, for two reasons. First our present ignorance of neurophysiology, especially concerning the brain and how it functions, allows us to say very little about the location of the relevant physical events. This much does seem likely: they are located in the brain. Much more than that we do not at present know, although as the time passes, we should learn much more. The second reason for our difficulty in telling if there is coexistence in space has to do with the location of mental events. Where do thoughts, feelings, and wishes occur? Do they occur in the brain? Suppose you suddenly have the thought that it is almost suppertime; where does that occur? The most sensible answer would be that it occurs wherever you are when you have that thought. If you are in the library when you have that thought, then the thought occurs in the library. But it would be utterly unnatural to ask where inside your body the thought occurred; in your foot, or your liver, or your heart, or your head? It is not that any one of these places is more likely than another. They are all wrong. Not because thoughts occur somewhere *else* within your body than your foot, liver, heart, or head — but because it *makes no sense at all* to locate the occurrence of a thought at some place within your body. We would not understand someone who pointed to a place in his body and claimed that it was *there* that his entertaining of a thought was located. Certainly, if one *looked* at that place, one would not *see* anything resembling a thought. If it were replied to this that pains can be located in the body without being seen there, then it should be pointed out that one *feels* the pain there but one hardly feels a thought in the body.

The fact that it makes no sense at all to speak of mental events as occurring at some point within the body has the result that the identity theory cannot be true. This is because the corresponding physical events do occur at some point within the body, and if those physical events are identical with mental events, then those mental events must occur at the same point within the body. But those mental events do not occur at any point within the body, because any statement to the effect that they occurred here, or there, would be senseless. Hence the mental events cannot meet the condition of coexistence in space, and therefore cannot be identical with physical events.

Our inability to give the location within the body of mental events is different from our inability to give the location of the corresponding physical events within the body. In the latter case, it is that we do not know enough about the body, particularly the brain. Some day, presumably, we will know enough to pin down pretty exactly the location of the relevant physical events. But in the case of mental events it is not simply that at present we are ignorant but that someday we may well know. What would it be like to discover the location of a thought in the brain? What kind of information would we need to be able to say that the thought occurred exactly *here*? If by X rays or some other means we were able to see every event which occurred in the brain, we would never get a glimpse of a thought. If, to resort to fantasy, we could so enlarge a brain or so shrink ourselves that we could wander freely through the brain, we would still never observe a thought. All we could ever observe in the brain would be the *physical* events which occur in it. If mental events had location in the brain, there should be some means of detecting them there. But of course there is none. The very idea of it is senseless.

Some identity theorists believe this objection can be met. One approach is to reply that this objection begs the question: if the identity theory is true, and mental events are identical with brain events, then, paradoxical as it may sound, mental events do indeed have location, and are located precisely where the physical events are located. Another approach is to reply that the relevant physical events should be construed as events which happen to the body as a whole, and therefore occur where the body as a whole is located; then it is not so paradoxical to give location to the mental events, for they would be located where the body is located but would not be located in any particular part of the body.[14]

Shaffer disagrees with the identity theory, but both his presentation and his criticism of it are central to the ongoing debate today. In defending the identity theory, it is most important to stress that the identity of brain processes and thoughts is an empirical identity, that is, an identity that must be discovered through experiment and experience. It is not a logical identity, as if the two terms "brain process" and "thought" are synonymous. The latter suggestion is obviously false, and modern defenders of the identity theory are always emphasizing that it is only future neurophysiological research that will prove them right. Shaffer's criticism, however, is based on a principle that must be distinguished from the all-too-easy attack on the logical identity suggestion. The principle is that if two things are identical, then they must have all the same properties. But, Shaffer argues, no amount of research could possibly show that brain processes and thought have the same properties. Most importantly, brain processes take place in the brain and can be traced like any other physical processes; thoughts, on the other hand, have no spatial location, and there is nothing that research can "discover" that will show that they do. Of course, research can and has shown that certain thoughts are correlated with certain brain processes, but correlation is not yet identity, and it is only identity that will fulfill the demands of the mind-body problem, according to the defenders of the identity theory.

CHANGING OUR MINDS:
ALTERNATIVE CONCEPTIONS

It is worth reminding ourselves that these problems are relatively new. The separation of mind and body — or at least soul and body — is even older than Christian theology, but it was not considered a serious problem until Descartes. More importantly, there was no such separation in ancient times. One modern philosopher has pointed out that the Greeks didn't even have a way of characterizing "experience" in our sense. And when Aristotle wrote about "the soul," he meant nothing other than "the form of the body":

[14]Jerome Shaffer, *The Philosophy of Mind* (Englewood Cliffs, N.J.: Prentice-Hall, 1968).

from *de Anima,*
by Aristotle

One can no more ask if the body and the soul are one than if the wax and the impression it receives are one, or speaking generally the matter of each thing and the form of which it is the matter; for admitting that the terms unity and existence are used in many senses, the paramount sense is that of actuality. We have, then, given a general definition of what the soul is: it is substance expressed as form. It is this which makes a body what it . is. . . . [15]

This is not behaviorism. Aristotle is not denying the existence of anything that we normally believe in. Yet it is clearly not a dualism of the Cartesian variety, and this raises the following question: Are there ways of conceiving of ourselves without falling into the Cartesian trap of talking about minds and bodies?

We can only suggest a few possibilities here. The first, perhaps, was advanced by Ludwig Wittgenstein in his *Philosophical Investigations.* Although he is usually considered to be an unconfessed behaviorist, a more recent and perhaps more plausible interpretation is that Wittgenstein wanted to deny the very idea that human beings are a curious combination of two very different substances or kinds of entities or events. Rather, there are just people, not minds plus bodies. This Wittgensteinian view has been defended, for example, by P. F. Strawson in his essay "Persons":

"Persons,"
by P. F. Strawson

Let us think of some of the ways in which we ordinarily talk of ourselves, of some of the things which we ordinarily ascribe to ourselves. They are of many kinds. We ascribe to ourselves *actions and intentions* (I am doing, did, shall do this); *sensations* (I am warm, in pain); *thoughts and feelings* (I think, wonder, want this, am angry, disappointed, contented); *perceptions and memories* (I see this, hear the other, remember that). We ascribe to ourselves, in two senses, position: *location* (I am on the sofa) and *attitude* (I am lying down). And of course we ascribe to ourselves not only temporary conditions, states, and situations, like most of these, but also enduring characteristics, including such physical characteristics as height, coloring, shape, and weight. That is to say, among the things we ascribe to ourselves are things of a kind that we also ascribe to material bodies to which we would not dream of ascribing others of the things that we ascribe to ourselves. Now there seems nothing needing explanation in the fact that the particular height, coloring, and physical position which we ascribe to ourselves, should be ascribed to *something or other;* for that which one calls one's body is, at least, a body, a material thing. It can be picked out from others, identified by ordinary physical criteria and described in ordinary physical terms. But it can seem, and has seemed, to need explanation that

[15]Aristotle, *de Anima,* trans. W. S. Hett (Cambridge, Mass.: Harvard University Press, 1936).

one's states of consciousness, one's thoughts and sensations, are ascribed *to the very same thing* as that to which these physical characteristics, this physical situation, is ascribed. Why are one's states of consciousness ascribed to the very same thing as certain corporeal characteristics, a certain physical situation, etc.? And once this question is raised, another question follows it, viz.: Why are one's states of consciousness ascribed to (said to be of, or to belong to) anything at all? It is not to be supposed that the answers to these questions will be independent of one another.

. . . I have in mind a very simple but, in this question, a very central, thought: viz., that it is a necessary condition of one's ascribing states of consciousness, experiences, to oneself, in the way one does, that one should also ascribe them (or be prepared to ascribe them) to others who are not oneself. This means not less than it says. It means, for example, that the ascribing phrases should be used in just the same sense when the subject is another, as when the subject is oneself. Of course the thought that this is so gives no trouble to the non-philosopher: the thought, for example, that "in pain" means the same whether one says "I am in pain" or "He is in pain." The dictionaries do not give two sets of meanings for every expression which describes a state of consciousness: a first-person meaning, and a second- and third-person meaning. But to the philosopher this thought has given trouble; indeed it has. How could the sense be the same when the method of verification was so different in the two cases — or, rather, when there *was* a method of verification in the one case (the case of others) and not, properly speaking, in the other case (the case of oneself)? Or, again, how can it be right to talk of *ascribing* in the case of oneself? For surely there can be a question of ascribing only if there is or could be a question of identifying that to which the ascription is made? And though there may be a question of identifying the one who is in pain when that one is another, how can there be such a question when that one is oneself? But this last query answers itself as soon as we remember that we speak primarily to others, for the information of others. In one sense, indeed, there is no question of my having to *tell who it is* who is in pain, when I am. In another sense I may have to *tell who it is*, i.e., to let others know who it is.

What I have just said explains, perhaps, how one may properly be said to ascribe states of consciousness to oneself, given that one ascribes them to others. But how is it that one can ascribe them to others? Well, one thing is certain: that *if* the things one ascribes states of consciousness to, in ascribing them to others, are thought of as a set of Cartesian egos to which *only* private experiences can, in correct logical grammar, be ascribed, *then* this question is unanswerable and this problem insoluble. If, in identifying the things to which states of consciousness are to be ascribed, private experiences are to be all one has to go on, then, just for the very same reason as that for which there is, from one's own point of view, no question of telling that a private experience is one's own, there is also no question of telling that a private experience is another's. All private experiences, all states of consciousness, will be mine, i.e., no one's. To put it briefly: one can ascribe states of consciousness to oneself only if one can ascribe them to others; one can ascribe them to others only if one can identify other subjects of experience; and one cannot identify others if one can identify them *only* as subjects of experience, possessors of states of consciousness.

It might be objected that this way with Cartesianism is too short. After all, there is no difficulty about distinguishing bodies from one another, no difficulty about identifying bodies. And does not this give us an indirect way of identifying subjects of experience, while preserving the Cartesian mode? Can we not identify such a subject as, for example, "the subject that stands to that body in the same special relation as I stand to this one"; or, in other words, "the subject of those experiences which stand in the same unique causal relation to body N as *my* experiences stand to body M"? But this suggestion is useless. It requires me to have noted that *my* experiences stand in a special relation to body M, when it is just the right to speak of *my* experiences at all that is in question. (It requires me to have noted that *my* experiences stand in a special relation to body M; but it requires me to have noted this as a condition of being able to identify other subjects of experience, i.e., as a condition of having the idea of myself as a subject of experience, i.e., as a condition of thinking of any experience as *mine*.) So long as we persist in talking, in the mode of this explanation, of experiences on the one hand, and bodies on the other, the most I may be allowed to have noted is that experiences, *all* experiences, stand in a special relation to body M, that body M is unique in just this way, that is what makes body M unique among bodies. (This "most" is, perhaps, too much — because of the presence of the word "experiences".) The proffered explanation runs: "Another subject of experience is distinguished and identified as the subject of those experiences which stand in the same unique causal relationship to body N as *my* experiences stand to body M." And the objection is: "But what is the word 'my' doing in this explanation? (It could not get on without it.)"

What we have to acknowledge, in order to begin to free ourselves from these difficulties, is the *primitiveness* of the concept of a person. What I mean by the concept of a person is the concept of a type of entity such that *both* predicates ascribing states of consciousness *and* predicates ascribing corporeal characteristics, a physical situation, etc. are equally applicable to a single individual of that single type. And what I mean by saying that this concept is primitive can be put in a number of ways. One way is to return to those two questions I asked earlier: viz., (1) why are states of consciousness ascribed to anything at all? and (2) why are they ascribed to the very same thing as certain corporeal characteristics, a certain physical situation, etc.? I remarked at the beginning that it was not to be supposed that the answers to these questions were independent of each other. And now I shall say that they are connected in this way: that a necessary condition of states of consciousness being ascribed at all is that they should be ascribed to the *very same things* as certain corporeal characteristics, a certain physical situation, etc. That is to say, states of consciousness could not be ascribed at all, *unless* they were ascribed to persons, in the sense I have claimed for this word. . . .

So, then, the word "I" never refers to this, the pure subject. But this does not mean, as the no-ownership theorist must think and as Wittgenstein, at least at one period, seemed to think, that "I" in some cases does not refer at all. It refers, because I am a person among others. And the predicates which would, *per impossibile*, belong to the pure subject if it could be referred to, belong properly to the person to which "I" does refer.

The concept of a person is logically prior to that of an individual consciousness. The concept of a person is not to be analyzed as that of an animated body or of an embodied anima. This is not to say that the concept of a pure individual consciousness might not have a logically secondary existence, if one thinks, or finds, it desirable. We speak of a dead person — a body — and in the same secondary way we might at least think of a disembodied person, retaining the logical benefit of individuality from having been a person.[16]

In this selection, Strawson makes at least two radical departures from the traditional Cartesian dualism between mind and body. To begin with, he attacks the idea that each of us is first of all a mind who "has" a body. Each of us is first of all a person, and the concept of "having a body" is no less essential than the concept of "having a mind." In other words, Strawson rejects outright Descartes's claim that he is essentially "a thinking thing," which might in fact have no body at all. We are essentially, according to Strawson, "thinking things" only if by that we mean "thinking persons." Descartes worried about how the two parts of a person can come together; Strawson says that they should never have been separated in the first place. This is one of the most famous cases in which a seemingly obvious philosophical distinction gets us into impossible trouble later on.

Second, Strawson adapts an argument from Wittgenstein that completely turns topsy-turvy Descartes's main thesis. Descartes assumed that we knew for certain our own mental states and then by inference applied the same words to the mental states of other people. What Strawson now argues, following Wittgenstein, is that we can apply such "mental" words to our own thoughts, feelings, and experiences only if we can apply them at the same time to other people. In other words, there can be no self-knowledge without knowledge of others as well.

A very different kind of answer comes to us from Husserl's phenomenology. Although Husserl was not particularly concerned with the mind-body problem as such, he was obviously very interested in the nature of consciousness, since it is consciousness that provides the subject matter of his entire life's work. What Husserl argued began with a violent attack on the spatial metaphors we use in talking about consciousness. At the beginning of the chapter, we mentioned these, suggesting that they were "just metaphors," symptoms of a problem but not a problem themselves. Well, Husserl shows that they are a problem, that philosophers have not used them merely as metaphors, and that it is because of their taking these metaphors literally that our problems about consciousness arise in the first place.

What Husserl attacks is the very idea of consciousness as a mysterious con-

---

[16]P. F. Strawson, "Persons," in *Minnesota Studies in the Philosophy of Science*, Vol. 2 (Minneapolis, Minn.: University of Minnesota Press, 1958).

tainer, "in" which one finds ideas, thoughts, feelings, desires, etc. The same objection holds of such metaphors as "the stream of consciousness," with emotions, thoughts, and feelings floating by like so much flotsam and jetsam. Consciousness must rather be viewed in two parts (though Husserl insists these must not be thought of as a separate "dualism"): There are acts of consciousness, and there are the objects of those acts. Simply stated, a phenomenologist would analyze my seeing a tree into (1) my act of seeing, and (2) the tree as seen. So far, this looks innocent enough. But its consequences are not so innocent. First, just in passing, notice what this does to Berkeley's idealism. Berkeley's whole argument rested on his thesis that all we can experience are ideas. But this is a confusion, Husserl insists, of our act of experiencing with the objects experienced. The object experienced (the tree) is not merely my idea. Accordingly, Husserl concludes that Berkeley's idealism is "absurd." And in general, Husserl's phenomenological theory insists that philosophers have been neglectful of this crucial distinction. Many attributes of the act of experiencing do not hold of the object; for example, the object, unlike the act, is not "private." One and only one person, namely, myself, can perform my act of seeing. But any number of people can see the object of my seeing, the tree. Moreover, there can be no such thing, Husserl argues, as a conscious act without an object. You can see how this might provide a powerful argument against many traditional forms of skepticism.

Our concern here is Husserl's conception of consciousness, which he calls **intentionality**. (Accordingly, the act is often called the "intentional act," and the object is called the "intentional object.") To say that consciousness is intentional means (among other things, which are irrelevant to this chapter), that our conscious acts are always directed towards objects and that we should not, therefore, talk about conscious acts as self-contained "contents" that are mysteriously coordinated with the movements of our bodies. Rather, we can simply say that among our various acts as persons are intentional conscious acts as well as physical actions. We can look at a tree and we can kick a tree. But there is no problem of "coordination" or interaction.

This theory was never actually developed by Husserl himself, but it was worked out in great detail by one of his "existential" followers in France, Maurice Merleau-Ponty (a close friend and student of Sartre). Coming from a very different starting point, Merleau-Ponty arrives at a position that is surprisingly close to Wittgenstein. It must not be called "behaviorist," but like Wittgenstein, Merleau-Ponty does reject the traditional way of dividing up mind and body and thereby suggests a very different conception of persons in which such problematic distinctions are not allowed to arise.

Merleau-Ponty attacks dualism from the side that has so far seemed least controversial — the idea that the human body is just another "bit of matter." He introduces the notion of a "dialectic" between mind and body, by which he means that there is no ultimate distinction between them. From one point of view, he argues, it is possible to see the body as "the cause of the structure of consciousness," for example, as a physiologist interested in the workings of the brain and the sense organs. From another point of view, it is possible to see the body as a mere "object of knowledge," for example, when a medical student dissects a body in his anatomy class. But it is a mistake, Merleau-Ponty argues, to confuse either of these viewpoints with the "correct" view of the body, either as a cause of consciousness or as something wholly distinct from it. It is only the *living* body that can count as *my* body, except in a very special and not everyday sense, namely, the sense in which I can talk about what will happen to my body after I die. "The body is not a self-enclosed mechanism" he argues, nor does it make sense to treat "the soul" or consciousness as a distinct entity with some mysterious relationship with the body. "There is not a duality of substances," he writes, but only "the dialectic of living being in its biological milieu." Merleau-Ponty sometimes says that consciousness is nothing but "the meaning of one's body," all of which is to say, in extremely difficult prose, that mind and body are nothing other than a single entity, and the distinctions we make between them are always special cases. "I live my body," he says; there is no enigma of "my body" to be explained.[17]

In his difficult "dialectical" language, Merleau-Ponty defends a thesis that is strikingly similar to that defended by Wittgenstein and Strawson: One cannot treat a person as an uneasy conglomerate of mental parts and body parts but must begin with the whole person. But where Wittgenstein and Strawson proceed by attacking the mental side of Cartesian dualism, Merleau-Ponty attacks anyone who would treat the human body as "just another body." The body itself is not only alive but, in an important sense, conscious. This does not mean, as in Descartes, that it is connected with a consciousness. It is itself aware, as we often notice when we talk of "bodily awareness" or "feeling our way." The difference between the body of a living person and a corpse is not just a difference in physiology, nor is it the difference between an "inhabited" body and an "uninhabited" body. My body and myself are essentially one, and to try to separate them, as Descartes had done, is to make the relationship between "me and my body" into an unnecessary mystery.

A view that is strikingly similar to the phenomenological theory was defended in this country by William James. But instead of giving consciousness the attention it receives in Husserl, he argues that there is no such thing as consciousness as an entity, only different functions of experience:

from "Does Consciousness Exist?"
by William James

'Thoughts' and 'things' are names for two sorts of objects, which common sense will always find contrasted and will always practically oppose to each other. Philosophy, reflecting on the contrast, has varied in the past in her explanations of it, and may be expected to vary in the future. At first, 'spirit and matter,' 'soul and body,' stood for a pair of equipollent substances quite on a par in weight and interest. But one day Kant undermined the soul and

---

[17]Maurice Merleau-Ponty, *The Structure of Behavior*, trans. Alden L. Fisher (Boston, Mass.: Beacon Press, 1963).

brought in the transcendental ego, and ever since then the bipolar relation has been very much off its balance. The transcendental ego seems nowadays in rationalist quarters to stand for everything, in empiricist quarters for almost nothing. In the hands of . . . writers . . . the spiritual principle attenuates itself to a thoroughly ghostly condition, being only a name for the fact that the 'content' of experience *is known*. It loses personal form and activity — these passing over to the content — and becomes a bare [consciousness], of which in its own right absolutely nothing can be said.

I believe that 'consciousness,' when once it has evaporated to this estate . . . is on the point of disappearing altogether. It is the name of a nonentity, and has no right to a place among first principles. Those who still cling to it are clinging to a mere echo, the faint rumor left behind by the disappearing 'soul' upon the air of philosophy. During the past year, I have read a number of articles whose authors seemed just on the point of abandoning the notion of consciousness, and substituting for it that of an absolute experience not due to two factors. But they were not quite radical enough, not quite daring enough in their negations. For twenty years past I have mistrusted 'consciousness' as an entity; for seven or eight years past I have suggested its non-existence to my students, and tried to give them its pragmatic-equivalent in realities of experience. It seems to me that the hour is ripe for it to be openly and universally discarded.

To deny plumply that 'consciousness' exists seems so absurd on the face of it — for undeniably 'thoughts' do exist — that I fear some readers will follow me no farther. Let me then immediately explain that I mean only to deny that the word stands for an entity, but to insist most emphatically that it does stand for a function. There is, I mean, no aboriginal stuff or quality of being, contrasted with that of which material objects are made, out of which our thoughts of them are made; but there is a function in experience which thoughts perform, and for the performance of which this quality of being is invoked. That function is *knowing*. 'Consciousness' is supposed necessary to explain the fact that things not only are, but get reported, are known. Whoever blots out the notion of consciousness from his list of first principles must still provide in some way for that function's being carried on.

.   .   .   .   .

My thesis is that if we start with the supposition that there is only one primal stuff or material in the world, a stuff of which everything is composed, and if we call that stuff 'pure experience,' then knowing can easily be explained as a particular sort of relation towards one another into which portions of pure experience may enter. The relation itself is a part of pure experience; one of its 'terms' becomes the subject or bearer of the knowledge, the knower, the other becomes the object known. This will need much explanation before it can be understood. The best way to get it understood is to contrast it with the alternative view; and for that we may take the recentest alternative, that in which the evaporation of the definite soul-substance has proceeded as far as it can go without being yet complete. If neo-Kantism has expelled earlier forms of dualism, we shall have expelled all forms if we are able to expel neo-Kantism in its turn.

For the thinkers I call neo-Kantian, the word consciousness today does no more than signalize the fact that experience is indefeasibly dualistic in structure. It means that not subject, not object, but object-plus-subject is the minimum that can actually be. The subject-object distinction meanwhile is entirely different from that between mind and matter, from that between body and soul. Souls were detachable, had separate destinies; things could happen to them. To consciousness as such nothing can happen, for, timeless itself, it is only a witness of happenings in time, in which it plays no part. It is, in a word, but the logical correlative of 'content' in an Experience of which the peculiarity is that *fact comes to light* in it, that *awareness* of *content* takes place. Consciousness as such is entirely impersonal — 'self' and its activities belong to the content. To say that I am self-conscious, or conscious of putting forth volition, means only that certain contents, for which 'self' and 'effort of will' are the names, are not without witness as they occur.

Thus, for these belated drinkers at the Kantian spring, we should have to admit consciousness as an 'epistemological' necessity, even if we had no direct evidence of its being there.

But in addition to this, we are supposed by almost every one to have an immediate consciousness of consciousness itself. When the world of outer fact ceases to be materially present, and we merely recall it in memory, or fancy it, the consciousness is believed to stand out and to be felt as a kind of impalpable inner flowing, which, once known in this sort of experience, may equally be detected in presentations of the outer world. "The moment we try to fix our attention upon consciousness and to see *what*, distinctly, it is," says a recent writer, "it seems to vanish. It seems as if we had before us a mere emptiness. When we try to introspect the sensation of blue, all we can see is the blue; the other element is as if it were diaphanous. Yet it *can* be distinguished, if we look attentively enough, and know that there is something to look for." "Consciousness," says another philosopher, "is inexplicable and hardly describable, yet all conscious experiences have this in common that what we call their content has this peculiar reference to a centre for which 'self' is the name, in virtue of which reference alone the content is subjectively given, or appears. . . . While in this way consciousness, or reference to a self, is the only thing which distinguishes a conscious content from any sort of being that might be there with no one conscious of it, yet this only ground of the distinction defies all closer explanations. The existence of consciousness, although it is the fundamental fact of psychology, can indeed be laid down as certain, can be brought out by analysis, but can neither be defined nor deduced from anything but itself."

. . . . . .

Now my contention is exactly the reverse of this. *Experience, I believe, has no such inner duplicity; and the separation of it into consciousness and content comes, not by way of subtraction, but by way of addition* — the addition, to a given concrete piece of it, of other sets of experiences, in connection with which severally its use or function may be of two different kinds. The paint will also serve here as an illustration. In a pot in a paintshop, along with other paints, it serves in its entirety as so much saleable matter. Spread on a canvas, with other paints around it, it represents, on the contrary, a feature in a picture and performs a spiritual function. Just so, I maintain, does a given undivided portion of experience, taken in one context of associates, play the part of a knower, of a state of mind, of 'consciousness'; while in a different context the same undivided bit of experience plays the part of a thing known, of an objective 'content.' In a word, in one group it figures as a thought, in another group as a thing. And, since it can figure in both groups simultaneously we have every right to speak of it as subjective and objective both at once. The dualism connoted by such double-barrelled terms as 'experience,' 'phenomenon,' 'datum'— terms which, in philosophy at any rate, tend more and more to replace the single-barrelled terms of 'thought' and 'thing'—that dualism, I say, is still preserved in this account, but reinterpreted, so that, instead of being mysterious and elusive, it becomes verifiable and concrete. It is an affair of relations, it falls outside, not inside, the single experience considered, and can always be particularized and defined.

The entering wedge for this more concrete way of understanding the dualism was fashioned by Locke when he made the word 'idea' stand indifferently for thing and thought, and by Berkeley when he said that what common sense means by realities is exactly what the philosopher means by ideas. Neither Locke nor Berkeley thought his truth out into perfect clearness, but it seems to me that the conception I am defending does little more than consistently carry out the 'pragmatic' method which they were the first to use.

If the reader will take his own experiences, he will see what I mean. Let him begin with a perceptual experience, the 'presentation,' so called, of a physical object, his actual field of vision, the room he sits in, with the book he is reading as its centre; and let him for the present treat this complex object in the common-sense way as being 'really' what it seems to be, namely, a collection of physical things cut out from an environing world of other physical things with which these physical things have actual or potential relations. Now at the same time it is just *those self-same things* which his mind, as we say, perceives; and the whole philosophy of perception from Democritus's time downwards has been just one long wrangle over the paradox that what is evidently one reality should be in two places at once, both in outer space and in a person's mind. 'Representative' theories of perception avoid the logical paradox, but on the other hand they violate the reader's sense of life, which knows no intervening mental image but seems to see the room and the book immediately just as they physically exist.

The puzzle of how the one identical room can be in two places is at bottom just the puzzle of how one identical point can be on two lines. It can, if it be situated at their intersection; and similarly, if the 'pure experience' of the room were a place of intersection of two processes, which connected it with different groups of associates respectively, it could be counted twice over, as belonging to either group, and spoken of loosely as existing in two places, although it would remain all the time a numerically single thing.

Well, the experience is a member of diverse processes that can be followed away from it along entirely different lines. The one self-identical thing has so many relations to the rest of experience that you can take it in disparate systems of association, and treat it as belonging with opposite contexts. In one of these contexts it is your 'field of consciousness'; in another it is 'the room in which you sit,' and it enters both contexts in its wholeness, giving no pretext for being said to attach itself to consciousness by one of its parts or aspects, and to outer reality by another. What are the two processes, now, into which the room-experience simultaneously enters in this way?

One of them is the reader's personal biography, the other is the history of the house of which the room is part. The presentation, the experience, the *that* in short (for until we have decided *what* it is it must be a mere *that*) is the last term of a train of sensations, emotions, decisions, movements, classifications, expectations, etc., ending in the present, and the first term of a series of similar 'inner' operations extending into the future, on the reader's part. On the other hand, the very same *that* is the *terminus ad quem* of a lot of previous physical operations, carpentering, papering, furnishing, warming, etc., and the *terminus a quo* of a lot of future ones, in which it will be concerned when undergoing the destiny of a physical room. The physical and the mental operations form curiously incompatible groups. As a room, the experience has occupied that spot and had that environment for thirty years. As your field of consciousness it may never have existed until now. As a room, attention will go on to discover endless new details in it. As your mental state merely, few new ones will emerge under attention's eye. As a room, it will take an earthquake, or a gang of men, and in any case a certain amount of time, to destroy it. As your subjective state, the closing of your eyes, or any instantaneous play of your fancy will suffice. In the real world, fire will consume it. In your mind, you can let fire play over it without effect. As an outer object, you must pay so much a month to inhabit it. As an inner content, you may occupy it for any length of time rent-free. If, in short, you follow it in the mental direction, taking it along with events of personal biography solely, all sorts of things are true of it which are false, and false of it which are true if you treat it as a real thing experienced, follow it in the physical direction, and relate it to associates in the outer world.

.   .   .   .   .

First of all, this will be asked: "If experience has not 'conscious' existence, if it be not partly made of 'consciousness,' of what then is it made? Matter we know, and thought we know, and conscious content we know, but neutral and simple 'pure experience' is something we know not at all. Say *what* it consists of — for it must consist of something — or be willing to give it up!"

To this challenge the reply is easy. Although for fluency's sake I myself spoke early in this article of a stuff of pure experience, I have now to say that there is no *general* stuff of which experience at large is made. There are as many stuffs as there are 'natures' in the things experienced. If you ask what any one bit of pure experience is made of, the answer is always the same: "It is made of *that*, of just what appears, of space, of intensity, of flatness, brownness, heaviness, or what not. . . . " Experience is only a collective name for all these sensible natures, and save for time and space (and, if you like, for 'being') there appears no universal element of which all things are made.

But a last cry of *non possumus* will probably go up from many readers. "All very pretty as a piece of ingenuity," they will say, "but our consciousness itself intuitively contradicts you. We, for our part, *know* that we are conscious. We *feel* our thought, flowing as a life within us, in absolute contrast with the objects which it so unremittingly escorts. We can not be faithless to this immediate intuition. The dualism is a fundamental *datum*: Let no man join what God has put asunder."

My reply to this is my last word, and I greatly grieve that to many it will sound materialistic. I can not help that, however, for I, too, have my intuitions and I must obey them. Let the case be what it may in others, I am as confident as I am of anything that, in myself, the stream of thinking (which I recognize emphatically as a phenomenon) is only a careless name for what, when scrutinized, reveals itself to consist chiefly of the stream of my breathing. The 'I think' which Kant said must be able to accompany all my objects, is the 'I breathe' which actually does accompany them. There are other internal facts besides breathing (intracephalic muscular adjustments, etc., of which I have said a word in my larger Psychology), and these increase the assets of 'consciousness,' so far as the latter is subject to immediate perception; but breath, which was ever the original of 'spirit,' breath moving outwards, between the glottis and the nostrils, is, I am persuaded, the essence out of which philosophers have constructed the entity known to them as consciousness. *That entity is fictitious, while thoughts in the concrete are fully real. But thoughts in the concrete are made of the same stuff as things are.*

I wish I might believe myself to have made that plausible in this article. In another article I shall try to make the general notion of a world composed of pure experiences still more clear.[18]

Here again, but from another perspective, the traditional Cartesian dualism is rejected. James, like Wittgenstein and Strawson, attacks the idea of separate "mental" events or "consciousness" and insists that "there is no such thing." But in saying that, he is not denying that we are conscious or that we have feeling and experiences. He is rather saying that we have to think of these as "functions" of the overall person, not as independent and possibly separable entities.

FUNCTIONALISM: THE MIND AND THE COMPUTER

Ever since Descartes (and probably before), philosophers troubled by mind-body interaction have tended to focus on the obvious difference between the ontology of mind and the ontology of the brain. Minds are "non-extended," Descartes said. Minds are "non-physical," at least in the obvious sense. We might talk about "big minds" and "little minds" but no one thinks that therefore minds actually have

---

[18]William James, "Does Consciousness Exist?" in *Journal of Philosophy, Psychology and Scientific Methods*, Vol. 1, No. 18, September 1, 1904.

a physical size. But what has long been taken for granted is the physical basis of minds — the brain and the central nervous system. It is the brain that makes minds possible.

On the one hand, this was a rather remarkable discovery in the history of biology. It is by no means obvious, looking at that cauliflower-like mound inside the skull, that in that small space is packed billions of tiny neural networks that control our every experience, our every action, including the inner actions of our bodies of which we may not even be aware (control of metabolism and blood flow, for example). But, on the other hand, is it so obvious that minds could *only* be the product of brains? Could mental processes be based on physical processes that are not brain processes? Could, for example, mental processes be based upon a network of electronic signals in a properly designed complex of transistors and circuit boards? In other words, could mental processes be the product of a computer? Could the brain be nothing but an organic computer? Could computers — the kind that we make out of metal and minerals — have minds?

The computer revolution has not gone unnoticed in debates about the mind-body problem, and it is no coincidence that the past decade or so of computer breakthroughs has produced a revolution in the way some philosophers think about mind and body as well. The philosophical position is called **functionalism,** and its basic insight is that minds are produced not so much by particular kinds of materials (for example, brains) but rather by the *relations* between parts. In another few decades, it may in fact be possible, according to the most optimistic functionalists, to build a human mind out of computer parts. But whether or not computer scientists achieve such a (frightening) miracle, less optimistic functionalists hold that the mind is, in effect, a *function* of the patterns of neurological activity in the brain.

In computer technology (now at least in part included in our everyday language), there is a crucial distinction between "hardware" and "software." Hardware is the actual computer with its circuits. In the case of human minds, the hardware would be the brain and its neurological circuits. Software is the program that gives the computer specific instructions. (Sometimes, specific instructions can be "hard-wired," as in the case of instinct, but these are not the exciting cases that inspire most functionalists and computer scientists.) The view of the functionalists is that the mind is nothing other than an elaborate program of sorts, which is the product of a spectacularly complicated pattern embodied in the physical workings of the brain. To desribe this model in more detail, here is MIT philosopher-psychologist Jerry Fodor explaining the advantages of the functionalist philosophy.

from "The Mind-Body Problem," by Jerry A. Fodor

Traditional philosophies of mind can be divided into two broad categories: dualist theories and materialist theories. In the dualist approach the mind is a nonphysical substance. In materialist theories the mental is not distinct from the physical; indeed, all mental states, properties, processes and operations are in principle identical with physical states, properties, processes and operations. Some materialists, known as behaviorists, maintain that all talk of mental causes can be eliminated from the language of psychology in favor of talk of environmental stimuli and behavioral responses. Other materialists, the identity theorists, contend that there are mental causes and that they are identical with neurophysiological events in the brain.

In the past 15 years a philosophy of mind called functionalism that is neither dualist nor materialist has emerged from philosophical reflection on developments in artificial intelligence, computational theory, linguistics, cybernetics and psychology. All these fields, which are collectively known as the cognitive sciences, have in common a certain level of abstraction and a concern with systems that process information. Functionalism, which seeks to provide a philosophical account of this level of abstraction, recognizes the possibility that systems as diverse as human beings, calculating machines and disembodied spirits could all have mental states. In the functionalist view the psychology of a system depends not on the stuff it is made of (living cells, metal or spiritual energy) but on how the stuff is put together. Functionalism is a difficult concept, and one way of coming to grips with it is to review the deficiencies of the dualist and materialist philosophies of mind it aims to displace.

The chief drawback of dualism is its failure to account adequately for mental causation. If the mind is nonphysical, it has no position in physical space. How, then, can a mental cause give rise to a behavioral effect that has a position in space? To put it another way, how can the nonphysical give rise to the physical without violating the laws of the conservation of mass, of energy and of momentum?

The dualist might respond that the problem of how an immaterial substance can cause physical events is not much obscurer than the problem of how one physical event can cause another. Yet there is an important difference: there are many clear cases of physical causation but not one clear case of nonphysical causation. Physical interaction is something philosophers, like all other people, have to live with. Nonphysical interaction, however, may be no more than an artifact of the immaterialist construal of the mental. Most philosophers now agree that no argument has successfully demonstrated why mind-body causation should not be regarded as a species of physical causation.

Dualism is also incompatible with the practices of working psychologists. The psychologist frequently applies the experimental methods of the physical sciences to the study of the mind. If mental processes were different in kind from physical processes, there would be no reason to expect these methods to work in the realm of the mental. In order to justify their experimental methods many psychologists urgently sought an alternative to dualism.

. . . . .

The intuition underlying functionalism is that what determines the psychological type to which a mental particular belongs is the causal role of the particular in the mental life of the organism. Functional individuation is differentiation with respect to causal role. A headache, for example, is identified with the type of mental state that among other things causes a disposition for taking aspirin in people who believe aspirin relieves a headache, causes a desire to rid oneself of the pain one is feeling, often causes someone who speaks English to say such things as "I have a headache" and is brought on by overwork, eyestrain and tension. This list is presumably not complete. More will be known about the nature of a headache as psychological and physiological research discovers more about its causal role.

Functionalism construes the concept of causal role in such a way that a mental state can be defined by its causal relations to other mental states. In this respect functionalism is completely different from logical behaviorism. Another major difference is that functionalism is not a reductionist thesis. It does not foresee, even in principle, the elimination of mentalistic concepts from the explanatory apparatus of psychological theories.

The difference between functionalism and logical behaviorism is brought out by the fact that functionalism is fully compatible with token physicalism. The functionalist would not be disturbed if brain events turn out to be the only things with the functional properties that define mental states. Indeed, most functionalists fully expect it will turn out that way.

Since functionalism recognizes that mental particulars may be physical, it is compatible with the idea that mental causation is a species of physical causation. In other words, functionalism tolerates the materialist solution to the mind-body problem provided by the central-state identity theory. It is possible for the functionalist to assert both that mental properties are typically defined in terms of their relations and that interactions of mind and body are typically causal in however robust a notion of causality is required by psychological explanations. The logical behaviorist can endorse only the first assertion and the type physicalist only the second. As a result functionalism seems to capture the best features of the materialist alternatives to dualism. It is no wonder that functionalism has become increasingly popular.

As the simplest example of functionalist explanation, Fodor describes two Coke machines. One simply dispenses a can of Coke when one puts in a dime; the other is also capable of taking nickels, and so requires at least two internal states (depending on whether a dime or a nickel is inserted) in addition to dispensing the Coke. The first machine satisfies the behaviorist model of stimulus (insertion of a dime) and response (the dispensing of the Coke). The second requires a primitive functionalist explanation.

Machines provide good examples of two concepts that are central to functionalism: the concept that mental states are interdefined and the concept that they can be realized by many systems. The illustration [in the magazine] contrasts a behavioristic Coke machine with a mentalistic one.

Both machines dispense a Coke for 10 cents. (The price has not been affected by inflation.) The states of the machines are defined by reference to their causal roles, but only the machine on the left would satisfy the behaviorist. Its single state (*SO*) is completely specified in terms of stimuli and responses. *SO* is the state a machine is in if, and only if, given a dime as the input, it dispenses a Coke as the output.

The machine on the right in the illustration has interdefined states (*S1* and *S2*), which are characteristic of functionalism. *S1* is the state a machine is in if, and only if, (1) given a nickel, it dispenses nothing and proceeds to *S2*, and (2) given a dime, it dispenses a Coke and stays in *S1*. *S2* is the state a machine is in if, and only if, (1) given a nickel, it dispenses a Coke and proceeds to *S1*, and (2) given a dime, it dispenses a Coke and a nickel and proceeds to *S1*. What *S1* and *S2* jointly amount to is the machine's dispensing a Coke if it is given a dime, dispensing a Coke and a nickel if it is given a dime and a nickel and waiting to be given a second nickel if it has been given a first one.

Since *S1* and *S2* are each defined by hypothetical statements, they can be viewed as dispositions. Nevertheless, they are not behavioral dispositions because the consequences an input has for a machine in *S1* or *S2* are not specified solely in terms of the output of the machine. Rather, the consequences also involve the machine's internal states.

Nothing about the way I have described the behavioristic and mentalistic Coke machines puts constraints on what they could be made of. Any system whose states bore the proper relations to inputs, outputs and other states could be one of these machines. No doubt it is reasonable to expect such a system to be constructed out of such things as wheels, levers and diodes (token physicalism for Coke machines). Similarly, it is reasonable to expect that our minds may prove to be neurophysiological (token physicalism for human beings).

Nevertheless, the software description of a Coke machine does not logically require wheels, levers and diodes for its concrete realization. By the same token, the software description of the mind does not logically require neurons. As far as functionalism is concerned a Coke machine with states *S1* and *S2* could be made of ectoplasm, if there is such stuff and if its states have the right causal properties. Functionalism allows for the possibility of disembodied Coke machines in exactly the same way and to the same extent that it allows for the possibility of disembodied minds.

To say that *S1* and *S2* are interdefined and realizable by different kinds of hardware is not, of course, to say that a Coke machine has a mind. Although interdefinition and functional specification are typical features of mental states, they are clearly not sufficient for mentality. What more is required is a question to which I shall return below.

Some philosophers are suspicious of functionalism because it seems too easy. Since functionalism licenses the individuation of states by reference to their causal role, it appears to allow a trivial explanation of any observed event *E*, that is, it appears to postulate an *E*-causer. For example, what makes the valves in a machine open? Why, the operation of a valve opener. And what is a valve opener? Why, anything that has the functionally defined property of causing valves to open.

In psychology this kind of question-begging often takes the form of theories that in effect postulate homunculi with the selfsame intellectual capacities the theorist set out to explain. Such is the case when visual perception is explained by simply postulating psychological mechanisms that process visual information. The behaviorist has often charged the mentalist, sometimes justifiably, of mongering this kind of question-begging pseudo explanation. The charge will have to be met if functionally defined mental states are to have a serious role in psychological theories.

The burden of the accusation is not untruth but triviality. There can be no doubt that it is a valve opener that opens valves, and it is likely that visual perception is mediated by the processing of visual information. The charge is that such putative functional explanations are mere platitudes. The functionalist can meet this objection by allowing functionally defined theoretical constructs only where mechanisms exist that can carry out the function and only where he has some notion of what such mechanisms might be like. One way of imposing this requirement is to identify the mental processes that psychology postulates with the operations of the restricted class of possible computers called Turing machines.

A Turing machine can be informally characterized as a mechanism with a finite number of program states. The inputs and outputs of the machine are written on a tape that is divided into squares each of which includes a symbol from a finite alphabet. The machine scans the tape one square at a time. It can erase the symbol on a scanned square and print a new one in its place. The machine can execute only the elementary mechanical operations of scanning, erasing, printing, moving the tape and changing state.

The program states of the Turing machine are defined solely in terms of the input symbols on the tape, the output symbols on the tape, the elementary operations and the other states of the program. Each program state is therefore functionally defined by the part it plays in the overall operation of the machine. Since the functional role of a state depends on the relation of the state to other states as well as to inputs and outputs, the relational character of the mental is captured by the Turing-machine version of functionalism. Since the definition of a program state never refers to the physical structure of the system running the program, the Turing-machine version of functionalism also captures the idea that the character of a mental state is independent of its physical realization. A human being, a roomful of people, a computer and a disembodied spirit would all be a Turing machine if they operated according to a Turing-machine program.

The proposal is to restrict the functional definition of psychological states to those that can be expressed in terms of the program states of Turing machines. If this restriction can be enforced, it provides a guarantee that psychological theories will be compatible with the demands of mechanisms. . . .

An obvious objection to functionalism as a theory of the mind is that the functionalist definition is not limited to mental states and processes. Catalysts, Coke machines, valve openers, pencil sharpeners, mousetraps and ministers of finance are all in one way or another concepts that are functionally defined, but none is a mental concept such as pain, belief and desire. What, then, characterizes the mental? And can it be captured in a functionalist framework?

The traditional view in the philosophy of mind has it that mental states are distinguished by their having what are called either qualitative content or intentional content. I shall discuss qualitative content first.

It is not easy to say what qualitative content is; indeed, according to some theories, it is not even possible to say what it is because it can be known not by description but only by direct experience. I shall nonetheless attempt to describe it. Try to imagine looking at a blank wall through a red filter. Now change the filter to a green one and leave everything else exactly the way it was. Something about the character of your experience changes when the filter does, and it is this kind of thing that philosophers call qualitative content. I am not entirely comfortable about introducing qualitative content in this way, but it is a subject with which many philosophers are not comfortable.

The reason qualitative content is a problem for functionalism is straightforward. Functionalism is committed to defining mental states in terms of their causes and effects. It seems, however, as if two mental states could have all the same causal relations and yet could differ in their qualitative content. Let me illustrate this with the classic puzzle of the inverted spectrum.

It seems possible to imagine two observers who are alike in all relevant psychological respects except that experiences having the qualitative content of red for one observer would have the qualitative content of green for the other. Nothing about their behavior need reveal the difference because both of them see ripe tomatoes and flaming sunsets as being similar in color and both of them call that color "red." Moreover, the causal connection between their (qualitatively distinct) experiences and their other mental states could also be identical. Perhaps they both think of Little Red Riding Hood when they see ripe tomatoes, feel depressed when they see the color green and so on. It seems as if anything that could be packed into the notion of the causal role of their experiences could be shared by them, and yet the qualitative content of the experiences could be as different as you like. If this is possible, then the functionalist account does not work for mental states that have qualitative content. If one person is having a green experience while another person is having a red one, then surely they must be in different mental states.

The example of the inverted spectrum is more than a verbal puzzle. Having qualitative content is supposed to be a chief factor in what makes a mental state conscious. Many psychologists who are inclined to accept the functionalist framework are nonetheless worried about the failure of functionalism to reveal much about the nature of consciousness. Functionalists have made a few ingenious attempts to talk themselves and their colleagues out of this worry, but they have not, in my view, done so with much success. (For example, perhaps one is wrong in thinking one can imagine what an inverted spectrum would be like.) As matters stand, the problem of qualitative content poses a serious threat to the assertion that functionalism can provide a general theory of the mental.

Functionalism has fared much better with the intentional content of mental states. Indeed, it is here that the major achievements of recent cognitive science are found. To say that a mental state has intentional content is to say that it has certain semantic properties. For example, for Enrico to believe Galileo was Italian apparently involves a three-way relation between Enrico, a belief and a proposition that is the content of the belief (namely the proposition that Galileo was Italian). In particular it is an essential property of Enrico's belief that it is about Galileo (and not about, say, Newton) and that it is true if, and only if, Galileo was indeed Italian. Philosophers are divided on how these considerations fit together, but it is widely agreed that beliefs involve semantic properties such as expressing a proposition, being true or false and being about one thing rather than another.

It is important to understand the semantic properties of beliefs because theories in the cognitive sciences are largely about the beliefs organisms have. Theories of learning and perception, for example, are chiefly accounts of how the host of beliefs an organism has are determined by the character of its experiences and its genetic endowment. The functionalist account of mental states does not by itself provide the required insights. Mousetraps are functionally defined, yet mousetraps do not express propositions and they are not true or false.

There is at least one kind of thing other than a mental state that has intentional content: a symbol. Like thoughts, symbols seem to be about things. If someone says "Galileo was Italian," his utterance, like Enrico's belief, expresses a proposition about Galileo that is true or false depending on Galileo's homeland. This parallel between the symbolic and the mental underlies the traditional quest for a unified treatment of language and mind. Cognitive science is now trying to provide such a treatment.

The basic concept is simple but striking. Assume that there are such things as mental symbols (mental representations) and that mental symbols have semantic properties. On this view having a belief involves being related to a mental symbol, and the belief inherits its semantic properties from the mental symbol that figures in the relation. Mental processes (thinking, perceiving, learning and so on) involve causal interactions among relational states such as having a belief. The semantic properties of the words and sentences we utter are in turn inherited from the semantic properties of the mental states that language expresses.

Associating the semantic properties of mental states with those of mental symbols is fully compatible with the computer metaphor, because it is natural to think of the computer as a mechanism that manipulates symbols. A computation is a causal chain of computer states and the links in the chain are operations on semantically interpreted formulas in a machine code. To think of a system (such as the nervous system) as a computer is to raise questions about the nature of the code in which it computes and the semantic properties of the symbols in the code. In fact, the analogy between minds and computers actually implies the postulation of mental symbols. There is no computation without representation.

. . . . .

The current idea is that the semantic properties of a mental representation are determined by aspects of its functional role. In other words, a sufficient condition for having semantic properties can be specified in causal terms. This is the connection between functionalism and the representational theory of the mind. Modern cognitive psychology rests largely on the hope that these two doctrines can be made to support each other.

No philosopher is now prepared to say exactly how the functional role of a mental representation determines its semantic properties. Nevertheless, the functionalist recognizes three types of causal relation among psychological states involving mental representations, and they might serve to fix the semantic properties of mental representations. The three types are causal relations among mental states and stimuli, mental states and responses and some mental states and other ones.

Consider the belief that John is tall. Presumably the following facts, which correspond respectively to the three types of causal relation, are relevant to determining the semantic properties of the mental representation involved in the belief. First, the belief is a normal effect of certain stimulations, such as seeing John in circumstances that reveal his height. Second, the belief is the normal cause of certain behavioral effects, such as uttering "John is tall." Third, the belief is a normal cause of certain other beliefs and a normal effect of certain other beliefs. For example, anyone who believes John is tall is very likely also to believe someone is tall. Having the first belief is normally causally sufficient for having the second belief. And anyone who believes everyone in the room is tall and also believes John is in the room will very likely believe John is tall. The third belief is a normal effect of the first two. In short, the functionalist maintains that the proposition expressed by a given mental representation depends on the causal properties of the mental states in which that mental representation figures.

The concept that the semantic properties of mental representations are determined by aspects of their functional role is at the center of current work in the cognitive sciences. Nevertheless, the concept may not be true. Many philosophers who are unsympathetic to the cognitive turn in modern psychology doubt its truth, and many psychologists would probably reject it in the bald and unelaborated way that I have sketched it. Yet even in its skeletal form, there is this much to be said in its favor: It legitimizes the notion of mental representation, which has become increasingly important to theorizing in every branch of the cognitive sciences. Recent advances in formulating and testing hypotheses about the character of mental representations in fields ranging from phonetics to computer vision suggest that the concept of mental representation is fundamental to empirical theories of the mind.

The behaviorist has rejected the appeal to mental representation because it runs counter to his view of the explanatory mechanisms that can figure in psychological theories. Nevertheless, the science of mental representation is now flourishing. The history of science reveals that when a successful theory comes into conflict with a methodological scruple, it is generally the scruple that gives way. Accordingly the functionalist has relaxed the behaviorist constraints on psychological explanations. There is probably no better way to decide what is methodologically permissible in science than by investigating what successful science requires.[19]

SUMMARY AND CONCLUSION

Since Descartes's discussion of mind and body as two separate and different substances, philosophers have struggled with a number of theories to explain how mind and body worked together to constitute a complete human being. Certain properties of mind — its lack of "extension" and seeming "privileged access," and the "incorrigibility" of mental claims — made the connection between mind and body extremely problematic. Therefore, philosophers suggested that mental events and bodily events are different aspects of some other event (dual aspect theory), or that they occur in parallel, like the sound and visual tracks on a film (parallelism or pre-established harmony), or that bodily events cause mental events but not the other way around (epiphenomenalism), or that mental events and bodily events are in fact identical (identity theory). Many philosophers and psychologists embraced behaviorism, arguing that "mental event" is in fact only shorthand for a complex description of patterns of behavior. More recently, many philosophers have come to reject the distinction between mind and body altogether, insisting on the primacy and indivisibility of the concept of a person. Other philosophers have come to embrace functionalism, which holds that the brain is in fact an extremely sophisticated computer, causally but not logically dependent on the brain.

GLOSSARY

behaviorism: in psychology, the radical methodological thesis that insists that only what is publicly observable can be used as subject matter or as evidence in scientific research regarding human beings. In particular, all talk of "minds" and "mental events," "desires," "purposes," "ideas," "perceptions," and "experiences" is to be given up in favor of terms that refer only to the experimental situation or the behavior of the creature (or person) in question (for example, "stimulus," "response," "reinforcements"). In philosophy and metaphysics, behaviorism is the logical thesis that there are no "covert" or "private" mental events, only patterns of behavior and psychological ways of talking about behavior as "intelligent," "deceitful," "calculating," or "inattentive." All of these must be understood not in terms of some process

[19]Jerry A. Fodor, "The Mind-Body Problem," *Scientific American*, Jan., 1981.

("intelligence," "deceitful thinking," "calculating," or "lack of attending") going on "in the mind" but rather as ways of interpreting, predicting, and otherwise describing and evaluating behavior.

causal interactionism: the theory that mind and body causally interact; that mental events (for example, an "act of will") can cause a bodily consequence (for example, raising one's arm), and that a bodily change (for example, a puncture of the skin) can cause a mental consequent (for example, a pain). The theory sounds plausible enough on first hearing, but there are extremely serious objections that have been raised against it.

dual aspect theory: the theory (for example, in Spinoza) that mind and body are simply different aspects (or "attributes") of one and the same substance, thus avoiding the problem of interaction between substances.

dualism: in general, the distinction between mind and body as separate substances, or very different kinds of states and events with radically different properties.

epiphenomenalism: the thesis that mental events are epiphenomena, that is, side effects of various physical processes in the brain and nervous system but of little importance themselves. The model is a one-way causal model: Body states cause changes in the mind, but mental states have no effect in themselves on the body.

functionalism: the view that the mind is the product of a pattern in the brain, as in a computer, rather than a product of the matter of the brain as such.

identity theory: the thesis that the mind and brain are ontologically one and the same, or, more accurately, that mental states and events are in fact certain brain and nervous system processes. The theory is usually presented as a form of materialism, but it is important to emphasize that, unlike many materialistic theories, it does not deny the existence of mental events. It denies only that they have independent existence. Mental events are nothing other than certain bodily events.

immediate: for certain and without need for argument.

incorrigibility: impossible to correct; cannot be mistaken. It has long been argued that our claims about our own mental states are incorrigible — we cannot be mistaken about them.

inference-ticket: Ryle's term for referring to the proper function of a mental state: talk, as a description of a pattern of behavior and, therefore, as an "inference-ticket" that allows us to infer what a person will do in the future. (To say "George wants an olive" is to give us an inference-ticket regarding his future behavior around olives.)

intentionality: in phenomenology, the thesis that every conscious act has an object. (The act is therefore called the "intentional act" and the object the "intentional object.") The importance of this concept is that it undercuts the metaphor of mental "contents" (as in a theater, an image explicitly used by Hume, for example). The concept was used by Husserl's teacher, Franz Brentano, who borrowed it from some medieval philosophers, before Husserl used it and made it famous.

parallelism: the thesis that mental events and bodily events parallel each other and occur in perfect coordination but do not interact.

pre-established harmony: Leibniz's view that the coordination between our ideas and the physical events of the world and our bodies was set up by God in perfect order.

privacy: the seeming inaccessibility of mental states and events to anyone other than the person who "has" them.

private language argument: Wittgenstein's argument that even if there were such "private objects" as mental states and events, it would be impossible for us to talk about them and impossible for us to identify them, even in our own case.

privileged access: the technical term used by philosophers to refer to the curious fact that a person usually (if not always) can immediately know, simply by paying attention, what is going on in his own mind, while other people can find out what is going on — if they can at all — only by watching the person's behavior, listening to what he or she says, or asking (and hoping they get a truthful answer). It is important to distinguish privileged access from incorrigibility. The first means that a person knows directly what is "in his mind" without having to observe his behavior; the second means that he knows for certain and beyond the possibility of error.

unconscious: Freud's famous way of referring to the fact that there are ideas, desires, memories, and experiences in our minds to which we do not have privileged access, which we may be wrong about (and, therefore, about which our claims are not incorrigible), and which may be more evident to other people than to oneself. He also distinguishes a *preconscious* ("the antechamber of consciousness"). Preconscious ideas can be made conscious simply by being attended to. (For example, you do know what the capital of California is, but you weren't conscious of it before I mentioned it; it was preconscious.) Truly unconscious ideas, however, cannot be made conscious, even when one tries to do so.

9

Freedom

"Two plus two equals four"—as if freedom means that!

Fyodor Dostoevsky

"The murderer had been raised in a slum. His father abandoned him when he was seven months old; he was beaten by his older siblings and constantly abused by his mother. He never had the chance to attend school; he never could get or hold a job. By the time he robbed the store, he was near starvation, addicted to hard drugs, without friends, and without help of any kind. His sister said, 'I've known since he was a child that he would do this some day.' His mother complained, 'I don't understand!' The prosecutor called it a 'cold-blooded, premeditated act.' The defense accused the whole of society, claiming that it had, through its neglect as well as its negative conditioning, made this man an inevitable killer." We know the rest of the arguments, what we don't know is their resolution. Should a man be held responsible for an act for which he has been conditioned the whole of his life? Or must we not hold out that, no matter what the circumstances, he could have resisted, he could have decided not to commit the crime, and therefore he must be held responsible.

Of all the abstract problems of philosophy, the problem of freedom has the most obvious practical consequences. If we believe a person is free to choose his or her actions and destiny, we tend to load the person with moral responsibility, praise or blame; if we believe a person is simply a victim of the fates, a cog in a mechanical universe, or a pawn in the abstract hands of society, then our attitude towards his or her actions can be no different than our attitudes towards the movement of glaciers and the growth of flowers. "It happens that way," that's all.

Are we cogs in the universe? Are we pawns of the fates? People have often thought so. Most of the ancient Greeks believed that our destinies were already decided for us; no matter what our actions, the outcome was settled. Oedipus knew long before his tragedy that he would kill his father and marry his mother. He left his home town, trying to avoid the couple who raised him and whom he believed were his parents, changed his identity, took all precautions, and nevertheless did just what the fates ordered anyway. There have been powerful movements in Christianity that have taught that God has predetermined or knows in advance every action we will perform, as well as our ultimate chances for salvation. And today most people believe that a person's actions and character are the causal result of his genes and his upbringing, and perhaps also the result of unconscious fears and desires that he or she may never recognize. Then too, astrology and other theories of external determination have always been popular. (For instance, "*Virgo:* It's going to be a bad day: don't get out of bed and don't talk to anyone.") And we can see why they would be. The more our actions are the results of other forces and not our own doing, the less we need feel responsible for them, and the less we need worry about deciding what to do. It is already decided, and not by us.

Consider, for example, the following news article that appeared around the nation in April 1980:[1]

> The way lawyer John Badger saw it, he was giving the judge a chance to "follow the flow into the brotherhood of man" by entertaining the notion that his client's life of crime was ordained by the stars.
>
> But Circuit Judge Ruben Costa, who said he was "inclined to believe there is a certain verity" to astrology, threw out the proposed defense at a pretrial hearing Monday for 23-year-old John Matthew Gopel, who is charged with rape, robbery and assault.
>
> Badger had planned to argue Gopel was insane by virtue of his astrological destiny.
>
> Badger said his client, born at 8:14 p.m. on Aug. 8, 1956, was literally "a born loser."
>
> "There is a force in the life of this young man that forced him to go on transmission fluid, sniff gasoline, cocaine, anything he could get his hands on," he said.
>
> Badger said he intended to present testimony from astrologers, scientists and mental health experts, as well as a bartender who would describe the effects of the full moon on human behavior.
>
> The list of defense evidence included the song, "When You Wish Upon A Star," Spiderman comic books and the plays "King Lear" and "Hamlet."

DETERMINISM

The problem of freedom occurs on different levels of generality, from the most abstract thesis that the universe as a whole is a single great machine or "substance" (as in Newton or Spinoza) to very localized theories about the psychology

---

[1] All names in this article have been invented to protect the individuals involved.

of the human personality. At all levels, however, the problem has usually been identified with a single claim, determinism. We were briefly introduced to determinism in Chapter 2: Spinoza defended it in his metaphysical system; Newton gave it a convincing scientific interpretation with his physical theories. In a phrase, **determinism** can be characterized by a principle already familiar to us from Chapter 3, the "principle of universal causation." "Every event has its cause(s)." That is determinism. It is the thesis that everything that happens in the universe is determined according to the laws of nature. The problem is that human actions, whatever else they might be, are also events in the universe. Accordingly, by the simplest of syllogisms, they are also determined:

Every event has its cause(s).

Human actions are events.

Therefore, every human action has its cause(s).

But if an action is caused, can it also be free? How can we hold someone responsible for doing something if he or she had no choice in the matter and couldn't have done anything else? It is as if we were to start praising people (or blaming them) for obeying the law of gravity. What else could they possibly do?

It is important to separate determinism as we have defined it from traditional conceptions of fatalism and predestination. The Greek tragedies depend upon **fatalism,** the view that whatever a person's actions and whatever the circumstances, the end is inevitable. But this is not determinism, for determinism requires certain actions and circumstances as antecedent conditions of the determined outcome. According to fatalism, whatever happens, the end is inevitable. According to determinism, an event will necessarily happen if its antecedent conditions are fulfilled. Thus the Oedipus tragedy is fatalistic because whatever Oedipus decided to do, he is fated to kill his father (whether he knows that he is doing it or not) and marry his mother (whether or not he knows that it is his mother). Determinism, on the other hand, need not say that any event is inevitable; it insists only that *if* certain conditions exist, *then* a certain kind of event will take place (for example, if a pot of water is heated sufficiently, then it will boil; or if a person is forced to choose between losing his life and killing an insect, then he will take the life of the insect). This "if . . . then" structure is essential to determinism. (There need be no such "ifs" or "thens" to fatalism.)

We similarly distinguish between determinism and predestination. **Predestination** has been the view of many Christian theologians, according to whom our every action (and every event in the universe) is known, if not also caused in advance, by God. Predestination, like fatalism, does not depend upon any particular antecedent conditions, unless we want to say that God is an antecedent condition. Accordingly, we might distinguish determinism and predestination by spelling out our determinist premise further: "every event has its natural cause." The theory of predestination might hold that every event has its cause, God; but it does not hold, as determinism does, that every event has its natural cause.

Determinism, therefore, is the theory that every event in the universe, including every human action, has its natural causes; given certain antecedent conditions, then an event will take place necessarily, according to the laws of nature.

But we must fill out the determinist's premise by at least one more step. It is not enough to say, "every event has its natural cause(s)," since this would leave open the possibility that although every event requires certain antecedent conditions in order to take place, the event might still be a matter of chance, at least to some extent, or a matter of human choice. In other words, it might be that the antecedent conditions limit the possibilities, but do not fully determine them. We must say, therefore, that "every event has its sufficient natural cause(s)." **Sufficient** means capable of bringing the event about by itself. Then there is no room for chance and no room for choice. And this view, which we shall call "hard" determinism ("hard" as in "hardheaded" as well as a "hard" conclusion to accept), clearly leaves no room for human freedom. Without choice, there can be no freedom, and without freedom, there is no reason to hold a person responsible for his action, no matter how virtuous or how vicious it might be. According to the hard determinist thesis, we can barely be said to be "acting" at all, for our "actions" are nothing but the result of antecedent conditions and laws of nature that leave no room for our "doing something" at all.

ARE WE COGS IN THE UNIVERSE?
"HARD DETERMINISM"

The hard determinist premise received its greatest impetus from Newton's physics and his picture of the universe as "matter in motion," determined according to the laws of motion and gravitation that he so elegantly formulated. But his followers applied these laws not only to the movements of the planets and the stars or to the ball rolling down an inclined plane. According to them, we too are "matter in motion," physical bodies that are subject to all of the laws of nature. What we "do" is just as determined by these laws as any other event in nature.

This "hardheaded" determinism has maintained a powerful hold on philosophers ever since Isaac Newton published his theories in the seventeenth century. The philosopher Pierre Simon La Place had such confidence in the Newtonian system that he claimed that if he knew the location and motion of every object in the universe, he could predict the location and motion of every object in the universe at any time in the future. (He could also *retrodict*, or look back to, every past state of the universe.) This means that if he had a proper map of the universe, including the material parts of our own bodies, he could predict everything that would ever happen, and of course, everything that we would ever do. If this is so, what possible sense could we make of our vain claims to have choices of actions, to decide what to do, or to hold ourselves and others responsible for what we have done?

La Place's confidence in the hard determinist thesis was common among the immediate successors and enthusiasts of Newton. For example, one of the philosophers of the French Enlightenment, Baron Paul Henri d'Holbach, defended the hard determinist viewpoint so uncompromisingly that he shocked even his colleagues as well as the many traditionalists.

from *System of Nature,*
by Paul Henri d'Holbach

In whatever manner man is considered, he is connected to universal nature, and submitted to the necessary and immutable laws that she imposes on all beings she contains, according to their peculiar essences or to the respective properties with which, without consulting them, she endows each particular species. Man's life is a line that nature commands him to describe upon the surface of the earth, without his ever being able to swerve from it, even for an instant. He is born without his own consent; his organization does in nowise depend upon himself; his ideas come to him involuntarily; his habits are in the power of those who cause him to contract them; he is unceasingly modified by causes, whether visible or concealed, over which he has no control, which necessarily regulate his mode of existence, give the hue to his way of thinking, and determine his manner of acting. He is good or bad, happy or miserable, wise or foolish, reasonable or irrational, without his will being for anything in these various states. Nevertheless, in spite of the shackles by which he is bound, it is pretended he is a free agent, or that independent of the causes by which he is moved, he determines his own will, and regulates his own condition.

However slender the foundation of his opinion, of which everything ought to point out to him the error, it is current at this day and passes for an incontestable truth with a great number of people, otherwise extremely enlightened; it is the basis of religion, which supposing relations between man and the unknown being she has placed above nature, has been incapable of imagining how man could merit reward or deserve punishment from this being, if he was not a free agent. Society has been believed interested in his system; because an idea has gone abroad, that if all the actions of man were to be contemplated as necessary, the right of punishing those who injure their associates would no longer exist. At length human vanity accommodated itself to a hypothesis which, unquestionably, appears to distinguish man from all other physical beings, by assigning to him the special privilege of a total independence of all other causes, but of which a very little reflection would have shown him the impossibility.

The will, as we have elsewhere said, is a modification of the brain, by which it is disposed to action, or prepared to give play to the organs. This will is necessarily determined by the qualities, good or bad, agreeable or painful, of the object or the motive that acts upon his sense, or of which the idea remains with him, and is resuscitated by his memory. In consequence, he acts necessarily, his action is the result of the impulse he receives either from the motive, from the object, or from the idea which has modified his brain, or disposed his will. When he does not act according to this impulse, it is because there comes some new cause, some new motive, some new idea, which modified his brain in a different manner, gives him a new impulse, determines his will in another way, by which the action of the former impulse is suspended: thus, the sight of an agreeable object, or its idea, determines his will to set him in action to procure it; but if a new object or a new idea more powerfully attracts him, it gives a new direction to his will, annihilates the effect of the former, and prevents the action by which it was to be procured. This is the mode in which reflection, experience, reason, necessarily arrests or suspends the action of man's will: without this he would of necessity have followed the anterior impulse which carried him towards a then desirable object. In all this he always acts according to necessary laws from which he has no means of emancipating himself.

. . . . .

In short, the actions of man are never free; they are always the necessary consequence of his temperament, of the received ideas, and of the notions, either true or false, which he has formed to himself of happiness; of his opinions, strengthened by example, by education, and by daily experience. So many crimes are witnessed on the earth only because every thing conspires to render man vicious and criminal; the religion he has adopted, his government, his education, the examples set before him, irresistibly drive him on to evil: under these circumstances, morality preaches virtue to him in vain. In those societies where vice is esteemed, where crime is crowned, where venality is constantly recompensed, where the most dreadful disorders are punished only in those who are too weak to enjoy the privilege of committing them with impunity, the practice of virtue is considered nothing more than a painful sacrifice of happiness. Such societies chastise, in the lower orders, those excesses which they respect in the higher ranks; and frequently have the injustice to condemn those in the penalty of death, whom public prejudices, maintained by constant example, have rendered criminal.

Man, then, is not a free agent in any one instant of his life; he is necessarily guided in each step by those advantages, whether real or fictitious, that he attaches to the objects by which his passions are roused: these passions themselves are necessary in a being who unceasingly tends towards his own happiness; their energy is necessary, since that depends on his temperament; his temperament is necessary, because it depends on the physical elements which enter into his composition; the modification of this temperament is necessary, as it is the infallible and inevitable consequence of the impulse he receives from the incessant action of moral and physical beings.[2]

IS DETERMINISM TRUE? DETERMINISM VERSUS INDETERMINISM

Why should we accept the determinist's premise? Without it, determinism cannot get to first base. Well, we have already seen the arguments traditionally advanced in earlier chapters, even by philosophers who are not themselves "hard determinists": The most general argument is that only by assuming from the outset that every event has its (sufficient natural) cause(s) can we ever understand anything. Otherwise, we should have auto mechanics always giving us back our

[2]Baron Paul Henri d'Holbach, *System of Nature* (London: Kearsley, 1797).

cars (and our bills) with the unhelpful statement that "there's no cause for our troubles." We could expect the same from doctors whenever a diagnosis gave them the least bit of trouble, and we would use it ourselves every time a problem began to get difficult. A much stronger argument is made by Kant, who says that the basic rule of determinism, the principle of universal causation, is one of the rules by which we must interpret every experience. But even Hume, who denies that this principle can be justified either through reason or through experience, insists that it is a "natural habit" or custom that is indispensable to us and that we could not give up even if we wanted to. The consensus, then, has been that the principle itself is inescapable. Even Leibniz, who rejected the idea of causation altogether, insisted on his "Principle of Sufficient Reason," which came to the same end, that is, "every event has its sufficient reason."

The agreement of so many philosophers indicates the strength of the hard determinist position. Without the assumption that "every event has its sufficient natural cause(s)," human knowledge would seem to be without one of its most vital presuppositions. Not only scientific research but even our most ordinary, everyday beliefs would be forced to an intolerable skeptical standstill. Our every experience would be unintelligible, and our universe would appear to be nothing but a disconnected stream of incoherent happenings, from which nothing could be predicted and nothing understood. So the answer to the question, "Why should we accept the determinist's premise?" seems to be, "We cannot give it up; how could we possibly do without it?" For no matter how it is rephrased or philosophically altered (for example, by Leibniz, who eliminates the concept of "cause" from it), the assumption that every event in the universe, including our own actions, can be explained and understood, if only one knows enough about it and its antecedent conditions, is a presupposition of all human thinking that we cannot imagine doing without.

But even if the hard determinist's premise seems undeniable, it is not yet clear how we are to understand that premise. The older determinists of the Newtonian period (La Place, d'Holbach) understood the idea of a cause as a literal push or compulsion, as if one were given a shove down the stairs. On this model, our actions are no different, except in complexity, from the "actions" of billiard balls on a felt-covered table, the motion of each wholly determining the motion of the next. The exact movements of every ball, of course, are not always evident. In the opening break, for example, even the most expert player cannot predict with accuracy where each ball will go. But we can be sure that each one is absolutely determined by the movements of the other balls that make contact with it, just as with the simple predictable case of a single ball hitting another straight on.

If we view human beings as nothing more than physical bodies — bones, muscles, nerve cells, and the like — then this mechanical billiard ball model might make some sense. But there is a much weaker interpretation of the hard determinist premise that does not require us to so radically reduce people to mere bodies. Instead of talking about actual physical pushes and compulsions, we can interpret the determinist premise in the following way: To say that every event has its cause(s) is to say that if certain antecedent conditions are satisfied, then we can predict that such-and-such will occur. On the stronger mechanistic determinist interpretation, causes are actual pushes and, on such an interpretation, the notion of freedom is clearly impossible. But on the weaker interpretation, of determinism as predictability, there may yet be room for us to talk about freedom of action. For example, we may be able to predict our friend's decision, but that does not seem to mean that he was forced to make it. We may be able to predict his action, but only because, knowing him, we know what he will probably do. On the second interpretation, perhaps we can have determinism and freedom.

Many philosophers would defend determinism only as predictability on the basis of probability. We might easily be wrong. To say that every event is determined, on this view, means only that it is predictable if we know enough about antecedent conditions. But it has been objected, against the determinist, that the fact of such predictability is not sufficient to defend determinism in anything like the "hard" sense. It is one thing to say that all events, including human actions, are actually caused or compelled by physical forces. It is something quite different to say that all events, including human actions, are predictable. They might be predictable, for example, only on the basis of certain statistical probabilities. "Most people in this circumstance would do that." "The odds are for it," in other words. Or, in the case of human actions, the predictability might still be due to human choices; we can predict each other's actions because we know how we would probably choose in the same circumstances. But there is no need here to talk about "causes" or compulsions. Nor, it has been argued, should we even talk any longer about "determinism," if this is all that we mean by it.

In contrast, the antideterminist thesis, called **indeterminism,** rejects both versions of determinism. Indeterminism claims that not every event has its sufficient natural cause(s). This theory at least appears to leave room for free will, for as soon as we allow that there are some events that are uncaused, human actions might be among them. And thus it would seem that we can be held properly responsible for our actions. But is the indeterminist thesis plausible?

The indeterminist argument has recently received a boost from physics, the very science that gave rise to the determinist threat in the first place. It was Newtonian physics that gave determinism its strongest claims. And you remember La Place boasting that if he knew the location and motion of every particle in the universe, he could predict every future state of the universe at any time. But it has been shown in recent physics that such knowledge is impossible. One of the most important discoveries of modern physics is the **Heisenberg Uncertainty Principle** (named after its discoverer, Werner Heisenberg), which says that we cannot know both the location and the momentum of a subatomic particle. In coming to know the one, we make it impossible for us to know the other at the same time. From this principle, the British physicist-philosopher Sir Arthur Eddington advanced the indeterminist argument that determinism is false on physical grounds. Not every event in the universe is predictable. And furthermore, many scientists now agree, on the basis of such considerations, that the concept of "cause" does not apply to certain subatomic particles either. Therefore, the determinist premise that "every event in the universe has its sufficient natural cause" is false. Some events, namely those involving some subatomic particles, are not caused, not predictable, and therefore not determined, on any interpretation. But if not all events are determined, then perhaps human actions are not determined but free. And if they are predictable, it is not because they are caused.

The object of indeterminism is to deny the determinist position in order to make room for human freedom. But there are, unfortunately, two serious objections to this indeterminist argument. First, even if we suppose that the conclusions of modern physical ("quantum") theory are correct (a matter still in dispute among physicists), it is clear that determinism is of importance to us primarily as a theory of macroscopic bodies (that is, visible size — people, trees, cars) not subatomic particles. And no one has ever concluded that quantum theory and modern physics actually refute Newton's theories. Rather, it supplements them, puts them in their place, and qualifies them in ways that would have been unthinkable in the eighteenth century. But as for the determinism of the gravitation of the planets or the rolling of a ball down an inclined plane, the spectacular discoveries of modern particle physics don't affect them in the least. And with regard to the physical determinism of our own bodies, the case remains as before. It might be true that it is impossible to predict what a subatomic particle in our bodies might do. But it does not follow that it is impossible to predict what our bodies will do. Falling out of a plane, we still fall at exactly the same speed as a sack of potatoes. And that is all the determinist needs to continue his attack on our concept of freedom. Second, even if there should be such indeterminism, indeterminism is not the same as freedom. Suppose there should be a "gap" in the causal determinism of our decisions by the various neurological processes of our brains; that would mean, at most, that what we do is not determined at all — or is determined only randomly. Suppose all of a sudden your legs started moving and you found yourself kicking a fire hydrant; surely this is not what we mean by a "free action." Freedom means, at least, that we are free to choose what we shall do and that our decisions are effective. Indeterminism robs us of our freedom, therefore, just as much as determinism. And the argument against determinism, in any case, is not yet sufficiently persuasive to allow the indeterminist his conclusions.

THE ROLE OF CONSCIOUSNESS

Hard determinism is true of us as physical bodies. But, you might insist, we are not just physical bodies, we are also conscious. We can make decisions. We have a will of our own. (The somewhat antique notion of "will" often enters into these controversies, and so the problem of freedom is often called "the free will problem." But we shall not use this terminology here.)

Whatever we are besides physical bodies, our physical bodies are still subject to all of the laws of Newtonian physics. You can see the problem. If our bodies are just cogs in the universe, what does it matter whether we are conscious or not? If you fall out of an airplane, you fall and accelerate at exactly the same rate as a sack of potatoes. The fact that you, unlike the potatoes, are aware of your falling, scared out of your mind, and wishing or praying like crazy that some miracle will save you makes not a bit of difference. But perhaps this is so with all of our actions as well? Our bodies are composed of bits of matter, various molecules undergoing chemical interactions and acted upon by the various laws of physics. No one can deny that they are subject to all the laws of physical nature. But once all the parts are determined in their various movements and activities, what is left for consciousness to do?

There are two possible replies to this problem, but both seem to support the hard determinist position and leave us without the freedom we are trying to find room for. Suppose one insists that consciousness, unlike our physical bodies, is not part of the scheme of determinism? Consciousness, unlike our bodies, is free, free to make decisions, free to choose what to do. But if our bodies are determined in their movements, then what can consciousness do even if it is "free"? Whatever consciousness decides, it cannot have any possible effect on the movements of our bodies, in other words, it cannot affect our actions. Our "decisions," then, would be mere vanities, like fancy switches on a machine that in fact don't do anything at all. Consciousness, on this view, is nothing but a sideshow, for whatever it "decides," what we will do and what will happen are already determined by other antecedent conditions that have nothing to do with the "decision." In crude form, this was Spinoza's ethical position, and also that of some of the early Stoic philosophers. Everything is determined by the laws of nature; it is absurd to fight against nature, and you couldn't if you tried anyway. All that can be done is to accept the necessity of whatever happens and recognize our consciousness and our apparent freedom as a luxurious vanity. Every human action has its sufficient natural causes apart from consciousness. And so consciousness can make no difference whatsoever.

Most hard determinists, however, would probably not agree with the idea that any event, even a nonphysical event such as an act of consciousness, could be "outside" the determinism of nature. Most hard determinists would argue that our thoughts and feelings, even our decisions, are caused by the states of our brains and nervous systems. Our "decisions" are nothing but the conscious effects of complex causal antecedents, most of which we still don't understand, but definitely part of the deterministic scheme of things. How consciousness enters this deterministic scheme is open to all of the questions that we asked in the last chapter — whether, for example, there can be causal connections between consciousness and our bodies, whether consciousness is merely an "epiphenomenon" of our brain states or identical to them, or whether we should no longer speak of "consciousness" at all. But, however those disputes are resolved, the hard determinist will insist that consciousness cannot be an exception to determinism.

a secondary phenomenon accompanying another and caused by it.

If consciousness is part of the deterministic scheme of things, could we not say that what happens in consciousness, particularly our decisions, thereby cause movements of our bodies, and therefore control our actions? This attractive compromise, however, faces an overwhelming problem. If one accepts the determinist's premise, then our decisions cannot cause our actions unless it is also true that our decisions, as part of the deterministic scheme, are caused in turn. Our decisions, therefore, are also determined, and no matter that it might seem as if we have a choice of actions, what we decide is already determined by those antecedent conditions that determine our decision.

Suppose, for example, you are deciding whether or not to go to the movies. Whether or not you go depends upon your decision. But your decision, in turn, depends upon its causal antecedents. Now suppose that we knew enough about your upbringing and tastes, your character and the workings of your brain such that we could see that your decision — let's say to go to the movies — is nothing more than the result of all of these conditions. What sense would it make, then, to say that you decided to go? Of course, it is true that you went through all of the motions of "making a decision." But the outcome of that decision, even if it was the causal result of the decision, was nevertheless nothing more than the result of conditions that preceded and had nothing to do with the decision. It is as if I gave you a choice of two alternatives, only one of which was possible anyway. That is hardly a choice. And so, if a decision enters into our actions, it must be a decision whose outcome is already determined in advance. The hard determinist thus wins in either case. If consciousness is not part of the deterministic scheme, it can have no possible effects on our actions. If it is part of the deterministic scheme of things, then it cannot be free. In either case, hard determinism is undeniable and freedom turns out to be an illusion.

"SOFT DETERMINISM"

The philosophers of the Newtonian tradition, those "hard" determinists who believe that determinism precludes the possibility of freedom of choice and action, have always had a powerful and simple argument on their side. But because of the urgency of our demand that we hold ourselves and each other responsible for our actions, most philosophers have not accepted "hard" determinism, even though they have accepted the determinist argument. Accordingly, many philosophers have espoused what has been called **soft determinism.** (The name comes from William James, who was not one of them.) Soft determinists, unlike the uncompromising hard determinists, believe that human freedom and determinism are compatible positions. On the one hand, they accept the determinist's argument, but, on the other, they refuse to give up the all-important demand for human freedom and responsibility. (Accordingly, they are often called *compatibilists*, and their position, **compatibilism.**)

existing together in harmony

The key to the "soft determinist" position is that an action or a decision, though fully determined, is free if it "flows from the agent's character." John Stuart Mill, for example, defends such a position in the following way:

on "Causation" and "Necessity," by John Stuart Mill

the relation a cause between it effect and its

The question, whether the law of causality applies in the same strict sense to human actions as to other phenomena, is the celebrated controversy concerning the freedom of the will; which, from at least as far back as the time of Pelagius, has divided both the philosophical and the religious world. The affirmative opinion is commonly called the doctrine of Necessity, as asserting human volitions and actions to be necessary and inevitable. The negative maintains that the will is not determined, like other phenomena, by antecedents, but determines itself; that our volitions are not, properly speaking, the effects of causes, or at least have no causes which they uniformly and implicitly obey.

I have already made it sufficiently apparent that the former of these opinions is that which I consider the true one; but the misleading terms in which it is often expressed, and the indistinct manner in which it is usually apprehended, have both obstructed its reception, and perverted its influence when received. The metaphysical theory of free-will, as held by philosophers (for the practical feeling of it, common in a greater or less degree to all mankind, is in no way inconsistent with the contrary theory), was invented because the supposed alternative of admitting human actions to be *necessary* was deemed inconsistent with every one's instinctive consciousness, as well as humiliating to the pride and even degrading to the moral nature of man. Nor do I deny that the doctrine, as sometimes held, is open to these imputations; for the misapprehension in which I shall be able to show that they originate, unfortunately is not confined to the opponents of the doctrine, but is participated in by many, perhaps we might say by most, of its supporters.

accusation

Correctly conceived, the doctrine called Philosophical Necessity is simply this: that, given the motives which are present to an individual's mind, and given likewise the character and disposition of the individual, the manner in which he will act might be unerringly inferred; that if we knew the person thoroughly, and knew all the inducements which are acting upon him, we could foretell his conduct with as much certainty as we can predict any physical event. This proposition I take to be a mere interpretation of universal experience, a statement in words of what every one is internally convinced of. No one who believed that he knew thoroughly the circumstances of any case, and the characters of the different persons concerned, would hesitate to foretell how all of them would act. Whatever degree of doubt he may in fact feel, arises from the uncertainty whether he really knows the circumstances, or the character of some one or other of the persons, with the degree of accuracy required; but by no means from thinking that if he did know these things, there could be any uncertainty what the conduct would be. Nor does this full assurance conflict in the smallest degree with what is called our feeling of freedom. We do not feel ourselves the less free, because those to whom we are intimately known are well assured how we shall will to act in a particular case. We often, on the contrary, regard the doubt what our conduct will be, as a mark of ignorance of our character, and sometimes even resent it as an imputation. The religious metaphysicians who have asserted the freedom of the will, have always maintained it to be consistent with divine foreknowledge of our actions: and if with divine, then with any other foreknowledge. We may be free, and yet another may have reason to be perfectly certain what use we shall make of our freedom. It is not, therefore, the doctrine that our volitions and actions are invariable consequents of our antecedent states of mind, that is either contradicted by our consciousness, or felt to be degrading.

But the doctrine of causation, when considered as obtaining between our volitions and their antecedents, is almost universally conceived as involving more than this. Many do not believe, and very few practically feel, that there is nothing in causation but invariable, certain, and unconditional sequence. There are few to whom mere constancy of succession appears a sufficiently stringent bond of union for so peculiar a relation as that of cause and effect. Even if the reason repudiates, the imagination retains, the feeling of some more intimate connection, of some peculiar tie, or mysterious constraint exercised by the antecedent over the consequent. Now this it is which, considered as applying to the human will, conflicts with our consciousness, and revolts our feelings. We are certain that, in the case of our volitions, there is not this mysterious constraint. We know that we are not compelled, as by a magical spell, to obey any particular motive. We feel, that if we wished to prove that we have the power of resisting the motive, we could do so (that wish being, it needs scarcely be observed, a *new antecedent*); and it would be humiliating to our pride, and (what is of more importance) paralyzing to our desire of excellence, if we thought otherwise. But neither is any such mysterious compulsion now supposed, by the best philosophical authorities, to be exercised by any other cause over its effect. Those who think that causes draw their effects after them by a mystical tie, are right in believing that the relation between volitions and their antecedents is of another nature. But they should go farther, and admit that this is also true of all other effects and their antecedents. If such a tie is considered to be involved in the word Necessity, the doctrine is not true of human actions; but neither is it then true of inanimate objects. It would be more correct to say that matter is not bound by necessity, than that mind is so.

· · · · ·

I am inclined to think that this error is almost wholly an effect of the associations with a word, and that it would be prevented, by forbearing to employ, for the expression of the simple fact of causation, so extremely inappropriate a term as Necessity. That word, in its other acceptations, involves much more than mere uniformity of sequence: it implies irresistibleness. Applied to the will, it only means that the given cause will be followed by the effect, subject to all possibilities of counter-action by other causes; but in common use it stands for the operation of those causes exclusively which are supposed too powerful to be counter-acted at all. When we say that all human actions take place of necessity, we only mean that they will certainly happen if nothing prevents; when we say that dying of want, to those who can not get food, is a necessity, we mean that it will certainly happen whatever may be done to prevent it. The application of the same term to the agencies on which human actions depend, as is used to express those agencies of nature which are really uncontrollable, can not fail, when habitual, to create a feeling of uncontrollableness in the former also. This, however, is a mere illusion. There are physical sequences which we call necessary, as death for want of food or air; there are others which, though as much cases of causation as the former, are not said to be necessary, as death from poison, which an antidote, or the use of the stomach-pump, will sometimes avert. It is apt to be forgotten by people's feelings, even if remembered by their understandings, that human actions are in this last predicament: they are never (except in some cases of mania) ruled by any one motive with such absolute sway that there is no room for the influence of any other. The causes, therefore, on which action depends, are never uncontrollable; and any given effect is only necessary provided that the causes tending to produce it are not controlled. That whatever happens, could not have happened otherwise, unless something had taken place which was capable of preventing it, no one surely needs hesitate to admit. But to call this by the name Necessity is to use the term in a sense so different from its primitive and familiar meaning, from that which it bears in the common occasions of life, as to amount almost to a play upon words. The associations derived from the ordinary sense of the term will adhere to it in spite of all we can do; and though the doctrine of Necessity, as stated by most who hold it, is very remote from fatalism, it is probable that most necessitarians are fatalists, more or less, in their feelings.

A fatalist believes, or half believes (for nobody is a consistent fatalist), not only that whatever is about to happen will be the infallible result of the causes which produce it (which is the true necessitarian doctrine), but moreover that there is no use in struggling against it; that it will happen, however we may strive to prevent it. Now, a necessitarian, believing that our actions follow from our characters, and that our characters follow from our organization, our education, and our circumstances, is apt to be, with more or less of consciousness on his part, a fatalist as to his own actions, and to believe that his nature is such, or that his education and circumstances have so moulded his character, that nothing can now prevent him from feeling and acting in a particular way, or at least that no effort of his own can hinder it. In the words of the sect which in our own day has most perseveringly inculcated and most perversely misunderstood this great doctrine, his character is formed *for* him, and not *by* him; therefore his wishing that it had been formed differently is of no use; he has no power to alter it. But this is a grand error. He has, to a certain extent, a power to alter his character. Its being, in the ultimate resort, formed for him, is not inconsistent with its being, in part, formed *by* him as one of the intermediate agents. His character is formed by his circumstances (including among these his particular organization); but his own desire to mould it in a particular way, is one of those circumstances, and by no means one of the least influential. We can not, indeed, directly will to be different from what we are. But neither did those who are supposed to have formed our characters directly will that we should be what we are. Their will had no direct power except over their own actions. They made us what they did make us, by willing, not the end, but the requisite means; and we, when our habits are not too inveterate, can, by similarly willing the requisite means, make ourselves different. If they could place us under the influence of certain circumstances, we, in like manner, can place ourselves under the influence of other circumstances. We are exactly as capable of making our own character, *if we will*, as others are of making it for us.

Yes (answers the Owenite),[3] but these words, "if we will," surrender the whole point: since the will to alter our own character is given us, not by any efforts of ours, but by circumstances which we can not help, it comes to us either from external causes, or not at all. Most true: if the Owenite stops here, he is in a position from which nothing can expel him. Our character is formed by us as well as for us; but the wish which induces us to attempt to form it is formed for us; and how? Not, in general, by our organization, nor wholly by our education, but by our experience; experience of the painful consequences of the character we previously had; or by some strong feeling of admiration or aspiration, accidentally aroused. But to think that we have no power of altering our character, and to think that we shall not use our power unless we desire to use it, are very different things, and have a very different effect on the mind. A person who does not wish to alter his character, can not be the person who is supposed to feel discouraged or paralyzed by thinking himself unable to do it. The depressing effect of the fatalist doctrine can only be felt where there *is* a wish to do what that doctrine represents as impossible. It is of no consequence what we think forms our character, when we have no desire of our own about forming it; but it is of great consequence that we should not be prevented from forming such a desire by thinking the attainment impracticable, and that if we have the desire, we should know that the work is not so irrevocably done as to be incapable of being altered.

And indeed, if we examine closely, we shall find that this feeling, of our being able to modify our own character *if we wish*, is itself the feeling of moral freedom which we are conscious of. A person feels morally free who feels that his habits or his temptations are not his masters, but he theirs; who, even in yielding to them, knows that he could resist; that were he desirous of altogether throwing them off, there would not be required for that purpose a stronger desire than he knows himself to be capable of feeling. It is of course necessary, to render our consciousness of freedom complete, that we should have succeeded in making our character all we have hitherto attempted to make it; for if we have wished and not attained, we have, to that extent, not power over our own character; we are not free. Or at least, we must feel that our wish, if not strong enough to alter our character, is strong enough to conquer our character when the two are brought into conflict in any particular case of conduct. And hence it is said with truth, that none but a person of confirmed virtue is completely free.

[3]From Robert Owen (1771–1858), a political reformer.

The application of so improper a term as Necessity to the doctrine of cause and effect in the matter of human character, seems to me one of the most signal instances in philosophy of the abuse of terms, and its practical consequences one of the most striking examples of the power of language over our associations. The subject will never be generally understood until that objectionable term is dropped. The free-will doctrine, by keeping in view precisely that portion of the truth which the word Necessity puts out of sight, namely the power of the mind to co-operate in the formation of its own character, has given to its adherents a practical feeling much nearer to the truth than has generally (I believe) existed in the minds of necessitarians. The latter may have had a stronger sense of the importance of what human beings can do to shape the characters of one another; but the free-will doctrine has, I believe, fostered in its supporters a much stronger spirit of self culture.[4]

In this selection, Mill slides between the harsh alternatives of "hard determinism" and indeterminism. He begins by accepting determinism and the idea that all human actions are "necessary and inevitable," given their causes. But he then goes on to say that these causes are themselves within human control, that we can alter the causes of events and even, by taking certain steps, alter our own characters. But this is not in the least to deny determinism; nor does it deny that we are in control and have "free will" in an important sense. Human actions, following from their various causes (including "character" or personality), are as predictable as any other events. But predictability is not incompatible with freedom, for freedom means, according to Mill, nothing other than acting in accordance with one's own character, desires, and wishes. Since these are the causes of our actions, that means that Mill can defend both determinism and freedom at the same time.

David Hume is also a "soft determinist," and he too argues that the reconciliation of "liberty and necessity" is to be found in the fact that a person's actions "flow from one's character or disposition." In defending soft determinism, Hume argues that we cannot mean by a free action one that is uncaused, a matter of chance, for this flies in the face of our common assumption that every event must have a cause. Such a view of freedom is also incoherent: The free-will advocate wants to ensure that we can hold people responsible for their actions; but if people's actions were merely a matter of chance, over which they have no control, we surely would not hold them responsible. On the contrary, actions that we praise or blame are precisely those determined by the person's character.

Although Hume defends a soft determinist position, there is a sense in which Hume is not a determinist at all. Recall from Chapter 3 that Hume thinks that causality is a fiction and our penchant for seeking out causes merely a habit. Thus he can argue that just as we are never rationally justified in claiming that a particular event has a cause, so we are never fully justified in claiming that human actions have causes.

[4]John Stuart Mill, *A System of Logic*, 8th ed. (New York: Harper & Row, 1874).

on Causation and Character,
by David Hume

But to proceed in this reconciling project with regard to the question of liberty and necessity; the most contentious question of metaphysics, the most contentious science; it will not require many words to prove, that all mankind have ever agreed in the doctrine of liberty as well as in that of necessity, and that the whole dispute, in this respect also, has been hitherto merely verbal. For what is meant by liberty, when applied to voluntary actions? We cannot surely mean that actions have so little connexion with motives, inclinations, and circumstances, that one does not follow with a certain degree of uniformity from the other, and that one affords no inference by which we can conclude the existence of the other. For these are plain and acknowledged matters of fact. By liberty, then, we can only mean *a power of acting or not acting according to the determinations of the will;* that is, if we choose to remain at rest, we may; if we choose to move, we also may. Now this hypothetical liberty is universally allowed to belong to everyone who is not a prisoner and in chains. Here then is no subject of dispute.

Whatever definition we may give of liberty, we should be careful to observe two requisite circumstances: *first,* that it be consistent with plain matter of fact; *secondly,* that it be consistent with itself. If we observe these circumstances and render our definition intelligible, I am persuaded that all mankind will be found of one opinion with regard to it.

It is universally allowed that nothing exists without a cause of its existence, and that chance, when strictly examined, is a mere negative word and means not any real power which has anywhere a being in nature. But it is pretended that some causes are necessary, some not necessary. Here then is the advantage of definitions. Let anyone *define* a cause without comprehending, as part of the definition, a *necessary connexion* with its effect, and let him show distinctly the origin of the idea expressed by the definition, and I shall readily give up the whole controversy. But if the foregoing explication of the matter be received, this must be absolutely impracticable. Had not objects a regular conjunction with each other, we should never have entertained any notion of cause and effect; and this regular conjunction produces that inference of the understanding which is the only connexion that we can have any comprehension of. Whoever attempts a definition of cause exclusive of these circumstances will be obliged either to employ unintelligible terms or such as are synonymous to the term which he endeavours to define. And if the definition above mentioned be admitted, liberty, when opposed to necessity, not to constraint, is the same thing with chance, which is universally allowed to have no existence. . . .

All laws being founded on rewards and punishments, it is supposed as a fundamental principle, that these motives have a regular and uniform influence on the mind, and both produce the good and prevent the evil actions. We may give to this influence what name we please; but, as it is usually conjoined with the action, it must be esteemed a *cause,* and be looked upon as an instance of that necessity, which we would here establish.

The only proper object of hatred or vengeance is a person or creature, endowed with thought and consciousness; and when any criminal or injurious actions excite that passion, it is only by their relation to the person, or connexion with him. Actions are, by their very nature, temporary and perishing; and where they proceed not from some *cause* in the character and disposition of the person who performed them, they can neither redound to his honour, if good; nor infamy, if evil. The actions themselves may be blameable; they may be contrary to all the rules of morality and religion: But the person is not answerable for them; and as they proceeded from nothing in him that is durable and constant, and leave nothing of that nature behind them, it is impossible he can, upon their account, become the object of punishment or vengeance. According to the principle, therefore, which denies necessity, and consequently causes, a man is as pure and untainted, after having committed the most horrid crime, as at the first moment of his birth, nor is his character anywise concerned in his actions, since they are not derived from it, and the wickedness of the one can never be used as a proof of the depravity of the other.

Men are not blamed for such actions as they perform ignorantly and casually, whatever may be the consequences. Why? but because the principles of these actions are only momentary, and terminate in them alone. Men are less blamed for such actions as they perform hastily and unpremeditatedly than for such as proceed from deliberation. For what reason? but because a hasty temper, though a constant cause or principle in the mind, operates only by intervals, and infects not the whole character. Again, repentance wipes off every crime, if attended with a reformation of life and manners. How is this to be accounted for? but by asserting that actions render a person criminal merely as they are proofs of criminal principles in the mind; and when, by an alteration of these principles, they cease to be just proofs, they likewise cease to be criminal. But, except upon the doctrine of necessity, they never were just proofs, and consequently never were criminal.

It will be equally easy to prove, and from the same arguments, that *liberty*, according to that definition above mentioned, in which all men agree, is also essential to morality, and that no human actions, where it is wanting, are susceptible of any moral qualities, or can be the objects either of approbation or dislike. For as actions are objects of our moral sentiment, so far only as they are indications of the internal character, passions, and affections; it is impossible that they can give rise either to praise or blame, where they proceed not from these principles, but are derived altogether from external violence.[5]

In other words, Hume too suggests that not only is freedom of choice and action possible within the framework of determinism, but determinism is even necessary if we are to make sense out of the notion of freedom of choice and responsibility. His language is convoluted, but his point is plain: We can make sense of the notion of voluntary action only because there is a uniform ("neces-

[5]David Hume, *An Enquiry Concerning Human Understanding*, 2nd ed., ed. L. A. Selby-Bigge (Oxford: Oxford University Press, 1902).

sary") connection between our motives, inclinations, circumstances, and characters and what we do. But "soft determinism" raises the same old questions yet
once again. Can we be said to be responsible even for those acts that are caused
by our character? Can we choose our character, as Mill suggests? Could we have
done other than what we did? even if we had wanted to? In other words, is soft
determinism really so "soft" after all?

COMPULSION

The basis of compatibilism or "soft determinism" is that we somehow carve a
space within determinism for those actions that we insist on calling "free" and
for which we hold ourselves and other people responsible. But this means that
"free actions" must also be actions that are determined by antecedent conditions
and causes. Free as well as unfree acts (like falling down the stairs) are caused
according to the determinist argument. The distinction, therefore, as we saw in
both Mill and Hume, depends upon whether the determining factors are within
the agent or "outside" of him. In the latter case, we say that the act was not free
but *compelled* or "done under compulsion." This distinction is not a new one.
Aristotle, for example, many centuries ago defined a voluntary action as one that
was (1) not done under compulsion, and (2) not done from ignorance.

on Voluntary Action,
by Aristotle

... It is only voluntary feelings and actions for which praise and blame
are given; those that are involuntary are condoned, and sometimes even
pitied. Hence it seems to be necessary for the student of ethics to define the
difference between the Voluntary and the Involuntary; and this will also
be of service to the legislator in assigning rewards and punishments.

It is then generally held that actions are involuntary when done (a)
under compulsion or (b) through ignorance; and that (a) an act is compulsory when its origin is from without, being of such a nature that the agent,
or person compelled, contributes nothing to it: for example, when a ship's
captain is carried somewhere by stress of weather, or by people who have
him in their power. But there is some doubt about actions done through
fear of a worse alternative, or for some noble object — as for instance if a
tyrant having a man's parents and children in his power commands him to
do something base, when if he complies their lives will be spared but if he
refuses they will be put to death. It is open to question whether such actions
are voluntary or involuntary. A somewhat similar case is when cargo is
jettisoned in a storm; apart from circumstances, no one voluntarily throws
away his property, but to save his own life and that of his shipmates any
sane man would do so. Acts of this kind, then, are 'mixed' or composite;
but they approximate rather to the voluntary class. For at the actual time
when they are done they are chosen or willed; and the end or motive of an

act varies with the occasion, so that the terms 'voluntary' and 'involuntary' should be used with reference to the time of action; now the actual deed in the cases in question is done voluntarily, for the origin of the movement of the parts of the body instrumental to the act lies in the agent; and when the origin of an action is in oneself, it is in one's own power to do it or not. Such acts therefore are voluntary, though perhaps involuntary apart from circumstances — for no one would choose to do any such action in and for itself.

. . . . .

What kind of actions then are to be called 'compulsory'? Used without qualification, perhaps this term applies to any case where the cause of the action lies in things outside the agent, and when the agent contributes nothing. But when actions instrinsically involuntary are yet in given circumstances deliberately chosen in preference to a given alternative, and when their origin lies in the agent, these actions are to be pronounced intrinsically involuntary but voluntary in the circumstances, and in preference to the alternative. They approximate however rather to the voluntary class, since conduct consists of particular things done, and the particular things done in the cases in question are voluntary. But it is not easy to lay down rules for deciding which of two alternatives is to be chosen, for particular cases differ widely.

To apply the term 'compulsory' to acts done for the sake of pleasure or for noble objects, on the plea that these exercise constraint on us from without, is to make every action compulsory. For (1) pleasure and nobility between them supply the motives of all actions whatsoever. Also (2) to act under compulsion and involuntarily is painful, but actions aiming at something pleasant or noble are pleasant. And (3) it is absurd to blame external things, instead of blaming ourselves for falling an easy prey to their attractions; or to take the credit of our noble deeds to ourselves, while putting the blame for our disgraceful ones upon the temptations of pleasure. It appears therefore that an act is compulsory when its origin is from outside, the person compelled contributing nothing to it.[6]

What is compulsion? According to Aristotle, an act is compulsory "when its origin is without" such that the person who acts "contributes nothing to it." Thus a person who is literally pushed into doing something is compelled rather than free. But what are we to say of certain other cases (which Aristotle did not know about)? For example, what of the person who is neurotic, who acts compulsively or "irrationally" because of mental illness? In ancient times, it might have been said that such a person was "possessed," as if something "external" (a demon or an evil spirit) had "taken over" and compelled certain actions. But today we are fully aware that such "compulsions" are clearly within the person and not "external" at all. In fact, it is clear that the neurotic always contributes to the neurosis as well as suffers from it, and thus, according to Aristotle's criterion, such acts are not really compelled at all. Or, to take a much more difficult kind of case, what

[6]Aristotle, *Nicomachean Ethics*, Bk. III, trans. H. Rackham (Cambridge, Mass.: Harvard University Press, 1934).

are we to say of those celebrated "brainwashing" cases (as with Patty Hearst or during the Korean War) in which a person seemingly performs an action voluntarily, but only after he or she has been "conditioned" in a dramatic and sometimes brutal way. Sometimes even the person's "character" itself is changed. Should we hold a person responsible for such actions? (This question was the main point in dispute in the Patty Hearst case, for example.) Similarly, should we hold a person responsible for actions performed under great stress or as the result of a violent emotion (rage or infatuation, for example)? Should we hold a person responsible for actions performed under the influence of drugs or alcohol (assuming that we might well hold them responsible for taking the drugs or drinking in the first place)? You can see that the distinction between "free" actions and acts that are "compelled" is not nearly as clear as it first seemed. We can easily distinguish between a person who breaks into a store and a person who is pushed through the front window. But in many cases where freedom is most in question, in cases of neurosis and brainwashing, and even in cases of great passion and chemical "influences," the distinction between what is "external" to the person and what is within his or her character is not clear at all.

There are more serious problems with the notion of "compulsion," however. Even if we admit that there are some problematic examples of actions that are not clearly either "free" or "compelled" (neurosis and brainwashing, great passion and drugs), we would want to insist that at least some actions are clearly free and not compelled. For example, I write a check to the American Cancer Society just because I believe that it is an important organization and want to make a contribution. No one has solicited me, no one has encouraged me to do it, and no one need know that I do it. Can even this act, so seemingly performed "of my own free will," be counted as a "free action"? The "soft determinist" would say that this action is "free" because it flows from my generous character. But what sense does it make to say that this kind of determinism, determinism by a person's character, makes an act any more free than an act that is determined by anything else? *because it is determined by character which, in this argument is formed by us—we had a hand in it.*

Even in our "freest" acts, it can be argued that the desires and decisions, in short, our "personality" is wholly determined by forces that are outside of us and beyond our control. Consider the following argument, for example, by Professor John Hospers, who uses Freud and psychoanalysis as the basis for his claim that all of our acts are compelled and not free, insofar as all of our acts are brought about by a set of psychological determinants over which we have no control.

from "What Means This Freedom?" by John Hospers

[Are we] in the final analysis, *responsible for any of our actions at all.* The issue may be put this way: How can anyone be responsible for his actions, since they grow out of his character, which is shaped and molded and made what it is by influences—some hereditary, but most of them stemming from early parental environment—that were not of his own making or choosing? This question, I believe, still troubles many people who would agree to all the distinctions we have just made but still have the feeling that "this isn't all." They have the uneasy suspicion that there is a more ultimate sense, a "deeper" sense, in which we are *not* responsible for our actions, since we are not responsible for the character out of which those actions spring. . . .

Let us take as an example a criminal who, let us say, strangled several persons and is himself now condemned to die in the electric chair. Jury and public alike hold him fully responsible (at least they utter the words "he is responsible"), for the murders were planned down to the minutest detail, and the defendant tells the jury exactly how he planned them. But now we find out how it all came about; we learn of parents who rejected him from babyhood, of the childhood spent in one foster home after another, where it was always plain to him that he was not wanted; of the constantly frustrated early desire for affection, the hard shell of nonchalance and bitterness that he assumed to cover the painful and humiliating fact of being unwanted, and his subsequent attempts to heal these wounds to his shattered ego through defensive aggression. . . . The poor victim is not conscious of the inner forces that exact from him this ghastly toll; he battles, he schemes, he revels in pseudo-aggression, he is miserable, but he does not know what works within him to produce these catastrophic acts of crime. His aggressive actions are the wriggling of a worm on a fisherman's hook. And if this is so, it seems difficult to say any longer, "He is responsible." Rather, we shall put him behind bars for the protection of society, but we shall no longer flatter our feeling of moral superiority by calling him personally responsible for what he did.

Let us suppose it were established that a man commits murder only if, sometime during the previous week, he has eaten a certain combination of foods—say, tuna fish salad at a meal also including peas, mushroom soup, and blueberry pie. What if we were to track down the factors common to all murders committed in this country during the last twenty years and found this factor present in all of them, and only in them? The example is of course empirically absurd; but may it not be that there is *some* combination of factors that regularly leads to homicide, factors such as are described in general terms in the above quotation? (Indeed the situation in the quotation is less fortunate than in our hypothetical example, for it is easy to avoid certain foods once we have been warned about them, but the situation of the infant is thrust on him; something has already happened to him once and for all, before he knows it has happened.) When such specific factors are discovered, won't they make it clear that it is foolish and pointless, as well as immoral, to hold human beings responsible for crimes? Or, if one prefers biological to psychological factors, suppose a neurologist is called in to testify at a murder trial and produces X-ray pictures of the brain of the criminal; anyone can see, he argues, that the *cella turcica* was already calcified at the age of nineteen; it should be a flexible bone, growing, enabling the gland to grow. All the defendant's disorders might have resulted from this early calcification. Now, this particular explanation may be empirically false; but who can say that no such factors, far more complex, to be sure, exist?

When we know such things as these, we no longer feel so much tempted to say that the criminal is responsible for his crime; and we tend also (do we not?) to excuse him—not legally (we still confine him to prison) but morally; we no longer call him a monster or hold him personally responsible for what he did. Moreover, we do this in general, not merely in the case of crime: "You must excuse Grandmother for being irritable; she's really quite ill and is suffering some pain all the time." Or: "The dog always bites children after she's had a litter of pups; you can't blame her for it: she's not feeling well, and besides she naturally wants to defend them." Or: "She's nervous and jumpy, but do excuse her: she has a severe glandular disturbance." . . .

But one may still object that so far we have talked only about neurotic behavior. Isn't nonneurotic or normal or not unconsciously motivated (or whatever you want to call it) behavior still within the area of responsibility? There are reasons for answering "No" even here, for the normal person no more than neurotic one has caused his own character, which makes him what he is. Granted that neurotics are not responsible for their behavior (that part of it which we call neurotic) because it stems from undigested infantile conflicts that they had no part in bringing about, and that are external to them just as surely as if their behavior had been forced on them by a malevolent deity (which is indeed one theory on the subject); but the so-called normal person is equally the product of causes in which his volition took no part. And if, unlike the neurotic's, his behavior is changeable by rational considerations, and if he has the will power to overcome the effects of an unfortunate early environment, this again is no credit to him; he is just lucky. If energy is available to him in a form in which it can be mobilized for constructive purposes, this is no credit to him, for this too is part of his psychic legacy. Those of us who can discipline ourselves and develop habits of concentration of purpose tend to blame those who cannot, and call them lazy and weak-willed; but what we fail to see is that they literally *cannot* do what we expect; if their psyches were structured like ours, they could, but as they are burdened with a tyrannical super-ego (to use psychoanalytic jargon for the moment), and a weak defenseless ego whose energies are constantly consumed in fighting endless charges of the superego, they simply cannot do it, and it is irrational to expect it of them. We cannot with justification blame them for their inability, any more than we can congratulate ourselves for our ability. This lesson is hard to learn, for we constantly and naïvely assume that other people are constructed as we ourselves are.

. . . . . .

The position, then, is this: if we *can* overcome the effects of early environment, the ability to do so is itself a product of the early environment. We did not give ourselves this ability; and if we lack it we cannot be blamed for not having it. Sometimes, to be sure, moral exhortation brings out an ability that is there but not being used, and in this lies its *occasional* utility; but very often its use is pointless, because the ability is not there. The only thing that can overcome a desire, as Spinoza said, is a stronger contrary desire; and many times there simply is no wherewithal for producing a stronger contrary desire. Those of us who do have the wherewithal are lucky.[7]

[7]John Hospers, "What Means This Freedom?" in *Determinism and Freedom in the Age of Modern Science*, ed. Sidney Hook (New York: New York University Press, 1958).

What emerges from the foregoing arguments is not an attractive conclusion. No matter how we try to wriggle free of total determinism, it seems as if we keep finding ourselves enmeshed back in "hard" determinism. We tried to clear a small space within determinism for those acts we want to call "free," but we found such a space hard to find. We suggested that perhaps an act is free if one of its causes is a decision, but then we saw that if this were so, then the decision itself must be caused in turn and thus is not really a decision at all. We suggested that an action is free if it "flows from a person's character"; but then we saw that it can be argued that an act that "flows from a person's character" is no more within his or her control and no more his or her responsibility than any other act. We might want to say that a person's act is free if, in this case, he or she could have done otherwise, but what does this mean, given the previous arguments, except that the act would have been different if the circumstances had been different or if the person had been, in effect, another person? For example, it is true that you could have changed the course of World War II—but *if what?* If you had been born Winston Churchill, perhaps. But that is a nonsensical "if." Does it make any more sense, however, to say that "you could have been a professional football player?" If what? If circumstances had been different? If you had been born with a different body, raised in a different environment? But isn't this to say, for each of these "ifs," that you would be (slightly but significantly) a different person than you are? It looks as if we are trapped by the tautology that each of us is whoever he or she is. It is true of the geranium that if it had been planted in better soil, it would be larger; and if the ball had been dropped from a greater height it would have landed harder; and if you were raised differently, placed in different circumstances, then you might have acted other than you did. But does this have anything to do with "freedom"? Are your actions any more free than the growth of the plant or the falling of the ball? Of course, there is a difference: You think that you've made some decision. But why should what you think change the way things are determined? You might pretend to be flying after you've fallen out of the plane. But you're still falling, and what seems to be the case doesn't matter at all. Soft determinism doesn't seem to make determinism (or the fall from the plane) any "softer" after all.

A CHAMPION OF DETERMINISM

Not everyone views determinism with horror. The eminent American psychologist B. F. Skinner, for example, applauds the determinist's argument as a means of controlling human behavior and changing it for the better. In his best seller, *Beyond Freedom and Dignity*, Skinner argues that we have made a fetish of freedom and that we should replace this with an acceptance of determinism. Behavioral scientists can and should be given the power to "engineer" human behavior in accordance with an agreed-upon set of ideals (social harmony, individual happiness, and productivity). In an essay of a few decades ago, Skinner argued:

Beyond Freedom,
by B. F. Skinner

Perhaps the most crucial part of our democratic philosophy to be reconsidered is our attitude toward freedom — or its reciprocal, the control of human behavior. We do not oppose all forms of control because it is "human nature" to do so. The reaction is not characteristic of all men under all conditions of life. It is an attitude which has been carefully engineered, in large part by what we call the "literature" of democracy. With respect to some methods of control (for example, the threat of force), very little engineering is needed, for the techniques or their immediate consequences are objectionable. Society has suppressed these methods by branding them "wrong," "illegal," or "sinful." But to encourage these attitudes toward objectionable forms of control, it has been necessary to disguise the real nature of certain indispensable techniques, the commonest examples of which are education, moral discourse, and persuasion. The actual procedures appear harmless enough. They consist of supplying information, presenting opportunities for action, pointing out logical relationships, appealing to reason or "enlightened understanding," and so on. Through a masterful piece of misrepresentation, the illusion is fostered that these procedures do not involve the control of behavior; at most, they are simply ways of "getting someone to change his mind." But analysis not only reveals the presence of well-defined behavioral processes, it demonstrates a kind of control no less inexorable, though in some ways more acceptable, than the bully's threat of force.

Let us suppose that someone in whom we are interested is acting unwisely — he is careless in the way he deals with his friends, he drives too fast, or he holds his golf club the wrong way. We could probably help him by issuing a series of commands: don't nag, don't drive over sixty, don't hold your club that way. Much less objectionable would be "an appeal to reason." We could show him how people are affected by his treatment of them, how accident rates rise sharply at higher speeds, how a particular grip on the club alters the way the ball is struck and corrects a slice. In doing so we resort to verbal mediating devices which emphasize and support certain "contingencies of reinforcement" — that is, certain relations between behavior and its consequences — which strengthen the behavior we wish to set up. The same consequences would possibly set up the behavior without our help, and they eventually take control no matter which form of help we give. The appeal to reason has certain advantages over the authoritative command. A threat of punishment, no matter how subtle, generates emotional reactions and tendencies to escape or revolt. Perhaps the controllee merely "feels resentment" at being made to act in a given way, but even that is to be avoided. When we "appeal to reason," he "feels freer to do as he pleases." The fact is that we have exerted *less* control than in using a threat; since other conditions may contribute to the result, the effect may be delayed or, possibly in a given instance, lacking. But if we have worked a change in his behavior at all, it is because we have altered relevant environmental conditions, and the processes we have set in motion are just as real and just as inexorable, if not as comprehensive, as in the most authoritative coercion.

"Arranging an opportunity for action" is another example of disguised control. The power of the negative form has already been exposed in the analysis of censorship. Restriction of opportunity is recognized as far from harmless. As Ralph Barton Perry said in an article which appeared in the Spring, 1953, *Pacific Spectator*, "Whoever determines what alternatives shall be made known to man controls what that man shall choose *from*. He is deprived of freedom in proportion as he is denied access to *any* ideas, or is confined to any range of ideas short of totality of relevant possibilities." But there is a positive side as well. When we present a relevant state of affairs, we increase the likelihood that a given form of behavior will be emitted. To the extent that the probability of action has changed, we have made a definite contribution. The teacher of history controls a student's behavior (or, if the reader prefers, "deprives him of freedom") just as much in *presenting* historical facts as in suppressing them. Other conditions will no doubt affect the student, but the contribution made to his behavior by the presentation of material is fixed and, within its range, irresistible.

The methods of education, moral discourse, and persuasion are acceptable not because they recognize the freedom of the individual or his right to dissent, but because they make only *partial* contributions to the control of his behavior. The freedom they recognize is freedom from a more coercive form of control. The dissent which they tolerate is the possible effect of other determiners of action. Since these sanctioned methods are frequently ineffective, we have been able to convince ourselves that they do not represent control at all. When they show too much strength to permit disguise, we give them other names and suppress them as energetically as we suppress the use of force. Education grown too powerful is rejected as propaganda or "brain-washing," while really effective persuasion is decried as "undue influence," "demagoguery," "seduction," and so on.

If we are not to rely solely upon accident for the innovations which give rise to cultural evolution, we must accept the fact that some kind of control of human behavior is inevitable. We cannot use good sense in human affairs unless someone engages in the design and construction of environmental conditions which affect the behavior of men. Environmental changes have always been the condition for the improvement of cultural patterns, and we can hardly use the more effective methods of science without making changes on a grander scale. We are all controlled by the world in which we live, and part of that world has been and will be constructed by men. The question is this: Are we to be controlled by accident, by tyrants, or by ourselves in effective cultural design?

The danger of the misuse of power is possibly greater than ever. It is not allayed by disguising the facts. We cannot make wise decisions if we continue to pretend that human behavior is not controlled, or if we refuse to engage in control when valuable results might be forthcoming. Such measures weaken only ourselves, leaving the strength of science to others. The first step in a defense against tyranny is the fullest possible exposure of controlling techniques. A second step has already been taken successfully in restricting the use of physical force. Slowly, and as yet imperfectly, we have worked out an ethical and governmental design in which the strong man is not allowed to use the power deriving from his strength to control his fellow men. He is restrained by a superior force created for that purpose — the ethical pressure of the group, or more explicit religious and governmental measures. We tend to distrust superior forces, as we currently hesitate to relinquish sovereignty in order to set up an international police force. But it is only through such countercontrol that we have achieved what we call peace — a condition in which men are not permitted to control each other through force. In other words, control itself must be controlled.

Science has turned up dangerous processes and materials before. To use the facts and techniques of a science of man to the fullest extent without making some monstrous mistake will be difficult and obviously perilous. It is no time for self-deception, emotional indulgence, or the assumption of attitudes which are no longer useful. Man is facing a difficult test. He must keep his head now, or he must start again — a long way back.[8]

In his novel *Walden II*, Skinner gives us a prototype for his deterministic utopia:

"I think Mrs. Nash's puzzlement," said Frazier, as we left the building, "is proof enough that our children are seldom envious or jealous. Mrs. Nash was twelve years old when Walden Two was founded. It was a little late to undo her early training, but I think we were successful. She's a good example of the Walden Two product. She could probably recall the experience of jealousy, but it's not part of her present life."

"Surely that's going too far!" said Castle. "You can't be so godlike as all that! You must be assailed by emotions just as much as the rest of us!"

"We can discuss the question of godlikeness later, if you wish," replied Frazier. "As to emotions — we aren't free of them all, nor should we like to be. But the meaner and more annoying — the emotions which breed unhappiness — are almost unknown here, like unhappiness itself. We don't need them any longer in our struggle for existence, and it's easier on our circulatory system, and certainly pleasanter, to dispense with them."

"If you've discovered how to do that, you are indeed a genius," said Castle. He seemed almost stunned as Frazier nodded assent. "We all know that emotions are useless and bad for our peace of mind and our blood pressure," he went on. "But how arrange things otherwise?"

"We arrange them otherwise here," said Frazier. He was showing a mildness of manner which I was coming to recognize as a sign of confidence.

"But emotions are — fun!" said Barbara. "Life wouldn't be worth living without them."

"Some of them, yes," said Frazier. "The productive and strengthening emotions — joy and love. But sorrow and hate — and the high-voltage excitements of anger, fear, and rage — are out of proportion with the needs of modern life, and they're wasteful and dangerous. Mr. Castle mentioned jealousy — a minor form of anger, I think we may call it. Naturally we avoid it. It has served its purpose in the evolution of man; we've no further use for it. If we allowed it to persist, it would only sap the life out of us. In a cooperative society there's no jealousy because there's no need for jealousy."

[8]B. F. Skinner, "Freedom and the Control of Men," in *The American Scholar*, 1955–56.

"How do you make sure that jealousy isn't needed in Walden Two?" I said.

"In Walden Two problems can't be solved by attacking others," said Frazier with marked finality.

"That's not the same as eliminating jealousy, though," I said.

"Of course it's not. But when a particular emotion is no longer a useful part of a behavioral repertoire, we proceed to eliminate it."

"Yes, but how?"

"It's simply a matter of behavioral engineering," said Frazier.

"Behavioral engineering?"

"Each of us," Frazier began, "is engaged in a pitched battle with the rest of mankind."

"A curious premise for a Utopia," said Castle. "Even a pessimist like myself takes a more hopeful view than that."

"You do, you do," said Frazier. "But let's be realistic. Each of us has interests which conflict with the interests of everybody else. That's our original sin, and it can't be helped. Now, 'everybody else' we call 'society.' It's a powerful opponent, and it always wins. Oh, here and there an individual prevails for a while and gets what he wants. Sometimes he storms the culture of a society and changes it slightly to his own advantage. But society wins in the long run, for it has the advantage of numbers and of age. Many prevail against one, and men against a baby. Society attacks early, when the individual is helpless. It enslaves him almost before he has tasted freedom. The 'ologies' will tell you how it's done. Theology calls it building a conscience or developing a spirit of selflessness. Psychology calls it the growth of the super-ego.

"Considering how long society has been at it, you'd expect a better job. But the campaigns have been badly planned and the victory has never been secure. The behavior of the individual has been shaped according to revelations of 'good conduct,' never as the result of experimental study. But why not experiment? The questions are simple enough. What's the best behavior for the individual so far as the group is concerned? And how can the individual be induced to behave in that way? Why not explore these questions in a scientific spirit?

"We could do just that in Walden Two. We had already worked out a code of conduct — subject, of course, to experimental modification. The code would keep things running smoothly if everybody lived up to it. Our job was to see that everybody did. Now, you can't get people to follow a useful code by making them into so many jacks-in-the-box. You can't foresee all future circumstances, and you can't specify adequate future conduct. You don't know what will be required. Instead you have to set up certain behavioral processes which will lead the individual to design his own 'good' conduct when the time comes. We call that sort of thing 'self-control.' But don't be misled, the control always rests in the last analysis in the hands of society. . . ."[9]

[9] B. F. Skinner, *Walden II* (New York: Macmillan, 1965).

Not every visionary has looked upon determinism with delight. More often determinism has appeared in novels as a nightmare, as the philosophical basis of societies more oppressive and authoritarian than any we have ever seen. The most famous examples are George Orwell's *1984* and Aldous Huxley's *Brave New World*. In both novels, the techniques of psychology and drugs are used to manipulate the inhabitants of entire societies and force them to conform to a single set of behavioral standards, concerning which they have no choice whatsoever. In a more recent novel, *Clockwork Orange*, Anthony Burgess presents a nightmarish fantasy in which a young hoodlum named Alex is "reconditioned" to be good through a series of experiments in which his viewing of violent movies is accompanied by a drug that makes him violently ill. It works, but the prison chaplain summarizes the philosophical difficulties this raises:

from *A Clockwork Orange,* by Anthony Burgess

[The Prison Chaplain tells him:] 'Very hard ethical questions are involved,' he went on. 'You are to be made into a good boy, 6655321. Never again will you have the desire to commit acts of violence or to offend in any way whatsoever against the State's Peace. I hope you take all that in. I hope you are absolutely clear in your own mind about that.' I said:

'Oh, it will be nice to be good, sir.' But I had a real horrorshow smeck at that inside, brothers. He said:

'It may not be nice to be good, little 6655321. It may be horrible to be good. And when I say that to you I realize how self-contradictory that sounds. I know I shall have many sleepless nights about this. What does God want? Does God want goodness or the choice of goodness? Is a man who chooses the bad perhaps in some way better than a man who has the good imposed upon him? Deep and hard questions, little 6655321. But all I want to say to you now is this: if at any time in the future you look back to these times and remember me, the lowest and humblest of all God's servitors, do not, I pray, think evil of me in your heart, thinking me in any way involved in what is now about to happen to you. And now, talking of praying, I realize sadly that there will be little point in praying for you. You are passing now to a region where you will be beyond the reach of the power of prayer. A terrible terrible thing to consider. And yet, in a sense, in choosing to be deprived of the ability to make an ethical choice, you have in a sense really chosen the good. So I shall like to think. So, God help us all, 6655321, I shall like to think.' And he began to cry.[10]

Thus Skinner's optimistic vision of a world in which bad behavior can be controlled has to be balanced with an all-important presupposition of our moral behavior: we have free choice and responsibility. We might all agree that it would be a better world if everyone acted in a moral way, if there were no more violence

---

[10]Anthony Burgess, *A Clockwork Orange* (New York: Norton, 1962).

learned through experience?

and crime. But that has to be balanced against the view we have that it is moral responsibility that makes us human, and to guarantee our goodness through determinism at the same time undermines, therefore, our sense of humanity.

DEMANDING TO BE FREE: LIBERTARIANISM

The demand for freedom and responsibility is not going to be satisfied by these different variations of determinism, no matter how "soft" they pretend to be. What we need is a breach in determinism, a conception of our actions, or at least our decisions, as truly free and not determined in any of the ways discussed previously.

The classic statement of this claim to freedom and responsibility is to be found in the philosophy of Immanuel Kant. (I am sure that you now appreciate how truly monumental Kant's philosophy has been. We shall see more of him in the next chapter as well.) We have already seen that Kant gave an unqualified endorsement of determinism, arguing that the principle (of universal causation) upon which it is based is nothing less than a necessary rule of all human experience. And this includes human actions:

> Actions of men are determined in conformity with the order of Nature, by their empirical character and other causes; if we could exhaust all the appearances, there would not be found a single human action which would not be predicted with certainty.[11]

This is surely a statement of the hardest of "hard" determinism. But Kant also appreciated, as much as any philosopher ever has, the importance of unqualified freedom for human responsibility. (He called freedom, as he had called God, a "postulate" [or presupposition] of practical reason.) But how could he defend both universal determinism and human freedom? Determinism is true of every possible event and object of human knowledge, Kant says, but it does not follow that it is also applicable to human acts of will or decisions to act. Action is a wholly different matter than knowledge. The metaphysics with which Kant defends this view is far too complicated to even summarize here. But the basic principle is simple enough: Kant says that we adopt two different standpoints towards the world, one theoretical, one practical. Insofar as we want to know something, we adopt the standpoint of science and determinism. And within that standpoint, every event, including human actions, is determined, brought about by sufficient natural causes (including the states of our brains and various psychological factors). But when we are ready to do something, we switch to the practical standpoint. And the main point is this: Insofar as we are acting or deciding to act, we

[11]Immanuel Kant, *The Critique of Pure Reason*, trans. Norman Kemp Smith (New York: St. Martin's Press, 1933).

must consider our own acts of will and decisions as the sufficient causes of our actions, and we cannot continue the causal chain backwards to consider whether those acts of will are themselves caused. When we act, in other words, we cannot think of ourselves except as acting freely.

Suppose that you are about to make a decision: You are finally going to give up smoking. A friend offers you a cigarette on the second day. Yes or no? Do you smoke it? Now it might very well be that, given your personality, your weakness for past habits, and any number of other psychological factors, you are clearly determined to accept and thus break your resolution. Your friend, who knows you quite well, may even know this. But you can't think of yourself in this deterministic way, for insofar as you have to make a decision, you can't simply "find out" what you will do. In other words, you can't simply predict your own behavior, no matter how much you know about the various causes and factors that allow your friend to predict your behavior. If you were to predict, "I'm going to start smoking again anyway," you would not be simply predicting; you would be, in that very act, breaking your resolution, that is, deciding to break it. So, when your own acts and decisions are concerned, you have to act as if you were totally free. This in a way denies determinism. It says, as you are the one that has to make the decision, determinism isn't relevant. (Kant says, "and to have to think yourself free is to *be* free.")

Other philosophers, however, have taken a much stronger stance on this need to see oneself as free. Kant defends both determinism and freedom. Many philosophers who follow him do not. They take the practical side of his argument and defend it against determinism.

Advocates of human freedom have always rejected the determinist's premise just because it seems to close off the possibility of human freedom and responsibility. A widely read argument for this position has been formulated by the Scottish philosopher C. A. Campbell. The position he defends is called "Libertarianism" (not to be confused with the political philosophy of the same name).

from *In Defense of Free Will*, by C. A. Campbell

The present state of philosophical opinion on free will is, for certain definitely assignable reasons, profoundly unsatisfactory. In my judgement, a thoroughly perverse attitude to the whole problem has been created by the almost universal acquiescence in the view that free will in what is often called the "vulgar" sense is too obviously nonsensical a notion to deserve serious discussion. Free will in a more "refined" sense — which is apt to mean free will purged of all elements that may cause embarrassment to a Deterministic psychology or a Deterministic metaphysics — is, it is understood, a conception which may be defended by the philosopher without loss of caste. But in its "vulgar" sense, as maintained, for example, by the plain man, who clings to a belief in genuinely open possibilities, it is (we are told) a wild and even obnoxious delusion, long ago discredited for sober thinkers.

Now, as it happens, I myself firmly believe that free will, in something extremely like the "vulgar" sense, is a fact. And I am anxious to-day to do what I can, within the limits of a single lecture, to justify that belief. I propose therefore to develop a statement of the Libertarian's position which will try to make clear why he finds himself obliged to hold what he does hold.

Let us begin by noting that the problem of free will gets its urgency for the ordinary educated man by reason of its close connection with the conception of moral responsibility. When we regard a man as morally responsible for an act, we regard him as a legitimate object of moral praise or blame in respect of it. But it seems plain that a man cannot be a legitimate object of moral praise or blame for an act unless in willing the act he is in some important sense a "free" agent. Evidently free will in some sense, therefore, is a precondition of moral responsibility. Without doubt it is the realisation that any threat to freedom is thus a threat to moral responsibility — with all that that implies — combined with the knowledge that there are a variety of considerations, philosophic, scientific, and theological, tending to place freedom in jeopardy, that gives to the problem of free will its perennial and universal appeal. And it is therefore in close connection with the question of the conditions of moral responsibility that any discussion of the problem must proceed, if it is not to be academic in the worst sense of the term.

We raise the question at once, therefore, what are the conditions, in respect of freedom, which must attach to an act in order to make it a morally responsible act? It seems to me that the fundamental conditions are two. I shall state them with all possible brevity, for we have a long road to travel.

The first condition is the universally recognised one that the act must be *self*-caused, *self*-determined. But it is important to accept this condition in its full rigour. The agent must be not merely *a* cause but the *sole* cause of that for which he is deemed morally responsible. If entities other than the self have also a causal influence upon an act, then that act is not one for which we can say without qualification that the *self* is morally responsible. If in respect of it we hold the self responsible at all, it can only be for some feature of the act — assuming the possibility of disengaging such a feature — of which the self *is* the sole cause. I do not see how this conclusion can be evaded. But it has awkward implications which have led not a few people to abandon the notion of individual moral responsibility altogether.

The first condition, however, is quite clearly not sufficient. It is possible to conceive an act of which the agent is the sole cause, but which is at the same time an act *necessitated* by the agent's nature.

. . . In the case of such an act, where the agent could not do otherwise than he did, we must all agree, I think, that it would be inept to say that he *ought* to have done otherwise and is thus morally blameworthy, or *ought not* to have done otherwise and is thus morally praiseworthy. It is perfectly true that we do sometimes hold a person morally responsible for an act, even when we believe that he, being what he now is, virtually could not do otherwise. But underlying that judgement is always the assumption that the person has *come* to be what he now is in virtue of past acts of will in which he *was* confronted by real alternatives, by genuinely open possibilities: and, strictly speaking, it is in respect of these *past* acts of his that we praise or blame the agent *now*. For ultimate analysis, the agent's power of alternative action would seem to be an inexpugnable condition of his liability to moral praise or blame, i.e. of his moral responsibility.[12]

A person's act is free, according to Campbell, if (1) it is self-determined, and (2) if the person could have done otherwise. If these two conditions are to hold, Campbell then argues, both the hard determinist and the soft determinist must be wrong. The only way for these two conditions to hold is if determinism does not apply to human actions, that is, if we determine our own actions without being determined in turn. His argument then turns on the fact that such acts seem free to us as agents:

> Let us proceed, then, by following up this clue. Let us ask, why do human beings so obstinately persist in believing that there is an indissoluble core of purely *self*-originated activity which even heredity and environment are powerless to affect? There can be little doubt, I think, of the answer in general terms. They do so, at bottom, because they feel certain of the existence of such activity from their immediate practical experience of themselves. Nor can there be in the end much doubt, I think, in what function of the self that activity is to be located. There seems to me to be one, and only one, function of the self with respect to which the agent can even pretend to have an assurance of that absolute self-origination which is here at issue. But to render precise the nature of that function is obviously of quite paramount importance: and we can do so, I think, only by way of a somewhat thorough analysis—which I now propose to attempt—of the experiential situation in which it occurs, viz. the situation of "moral temptation."
>
> It is characteristic of that situation that in it I am aware of an end *A* which I believe to be morally right, and also of an end *B*, incompatible with *A*, towards which, in virtue of that system of conative dispositions which constitutes my "character" as so far formed, I entertain a strong desire. There may be, and perhaps must be, desiring elements in my nature which are directed to *A* also. But what gives to the situation its specific character as one of moral temptation is that the urge of our desiring nature towards the right end, *A*, is felt to be *relatively* weak. We are sure that if our desiring nature is permitted to issue directly in action, it is end *B* that we shall choose. That is what is meant by saying, as William James does, that end *B* is "in the line of least resistance" relatively to our conative dispositions. The expression is, of course, a metaphorical one, but it serves to describe, graphically enough, a situation of which we all have frequent experience, viz. where we recognise a specific end as that towards which the "set" of our desiring nature most strongly inclines us, and which we shall indubitably choose if no inhibiting factor intervenes.

---

[12]C. A. Campbell, *In Defence of Free Will, An Inaugural Lecture* (Glasgow: Jackson, Son and Co., 1938). All subsequent quotations from Campbell are from this edition.

power or act of striving with or without conceivable goal.

In resisting moral temptation, in other words, we have the undeniable experience of resisting desires that may be very much part of our "character," and when we succeed in resisting them, we may even act "out of character." Here is Campbell's reply to the "soft determinist," who calls an act "free" only when it is "in character." To the contrary, he argues, an act is most free precisely when it is not "in character":

> . . . if my analysis is correct, in the function of moral decision in situations of moral temptation, we have an act of the self which at least *appears to the agent* to satisfy both of the conditions of freedom which we laid down at the beginning. The vital question now is, is this "appearance" true or false? Is the act of decision really what it appears to the agent to be, determined solely by the self, and capable of alternative forms of expression? If it is, then we have here a free act which serves as an adequate basis for moral responsibility. We shall be entitled to regard the agent as morally praiseworthy or morally blameworthy according as he decides to put forth effort or let his desiring nature have its way. We shall be entitled, in short, to judge the agent as he most certainly judges himself in the situation of moral temptation. If, on the other hand, there is good reason to believe that the agent is the victim of illusion in supposing his act of decision to bear this character, then in my opinion the whole conception of moral responsibility must be jettisoned altogether. For it seems to me certain that there is no other function of the self that even looks as though it satisfied the required conditions of the free act.
>
> . . . . .
>
> Libertarianism holds that the act of moral decision is the *self's* act, and yet insists at the same time that it is not influenced by any of those determinate features in the self's nature which go to constitute its "character." But, it is asked, do not these two propositions contradict one another? Surely a *self-determination* which is determination by something other than the self's *character* is a contradiction in terms? What meaning is there in the conception of a "self" in abstraction from its "character"? If you really wish to maintain, it is urged, that the act of decision is not determined by the self's character, you ought to admit frankly that it is not determined by the *self* at all. But in that case, of course, you will not be advocating a freedom which lends any kind of support to moral responsibility; indeed very much the reverse.
>
> Now this criticism, and all of its kind, seem to me to be the product of a simple, but extraordinarily pervasive, error: the error of confining one's self to the categories of the external observer in dealing with the actions of human agents. Let me explain.
>
> It is perfectly true that the stand-point of the external observer, which we are obliged to adopt in dealing with physical processes, does not furnish us with even a glimmering of a notion of what can be meant by an entity which acts causally and yet not through any of the determinate features of its character. So far as we confine ourselves to external observation, I agree that this notion must seem to us pure nonsense. But then we are *not* obliged

to confine ourselves to external observation in dealing with the human agent. Here, though here alone, we have the inestimable advantage of being able to apprehend operations from the *inside*, from the stand-point of *living experience*. But if we do adopt this internal stand-point — surely a proper standpoint, and one which we should be only too glad to adopt if we could in the case of other entities — the situation is entirely changed. We find that we not merely can, but constantly do, attach meaning to a causation which is the self's causation but is yet not exercised by the self's character. We have seen as much already in our analysis of the situation of moral temptation. When confronted by such a situation, we saw, we are certain that it lies with our *self* to decide whether we shall let our character as so far formed dictate our action or whether we shall by effort oppose its dictates and rise to duty. We are certain, in other words, that the act is *not* determined by our *character*, while we remain equally certain that the act *is* determined by our *self*.

EXISTENTIALISM — *individuals responsibility for making himself what he is*

Kant's suggestion has been taken up in a very different way in European philosophy, particularly by the existentialists. Like Kant, they accept (or at least do not bother to reject) determinism in science. But they insist that even if determinism is true, one must always view *him or herself as agent* as necessarily free. When you have to decide what to do, all the knowledge of the possible factors determining your decision are not sufficient to cause you to decide. For you cannot predict your own decision without at the same time making it.

Jean-Paul Sartre, the leading existentialist today, has defended the Kantian claim for human freedom as far as it can possibly be defended. In his mammoth book *Being and Nothingness*, Sartre argued that we are, always, absolutely free. This means, as Kant had insisted, that insofar as we act (and Sartre says that we are always acting) our decisions and our actions cannot be viewed as having any causes whatsoever. We must make decisions, and no amount of information and no number of causal circumstances can ever replace our need to make them. We can, of course, refuse to make decisions, acting as if they were made for us, as if circumstances already determined them, as if the fates had already established the outcome. But even in these cases, we are making decisions, "choosing not to choose," in a classic Sartrian phrase. We are "condemned to be free," he says, in a phrase that has since become famous. Again, desires may enter into consideration, but only as "consideration." We can always act against a desire, any desire, no matter how strong, if only we are sufficiently decided that we shall do so. A starving man may yet refuse food if, for example, he is taking part in a hunger strike for a political cause to which he is dedicated. A mother may refuse to save her own life if it would be at the expense of her children. A student may miss his favorite television show if he has resolved to study for tomorrow's test. Whether trivial or grandiose, our every act is a decision, and our every decision is free. And even if we fail to live up to them or find that we "cannot" make them, we are responsible nevertheless. There is no escape from freedom or responsibility.

"Absolute Freedom," by Jean-Paul Sartre

Although the considerations which are about to follow are of interest primarily to the ethicist, it may nevertheless be worthwhile after these descriptions and arguments to return to the freedom of the for-itself and try to understand what the fact of this freedom represents for human destiny.

The essential consequence of our earlier remarks is that man being condemned to be free carries the weight of the whole world on his shoulders; he is responsible for the world and for himself as a way of being. We are taking the word "responsibility" in its ordinary sense as "consciousness (of) being the incontestable author of an event or of an object." In this sense the responsibility of the for-itself is overwhelming since he is the one by whom it happens that *there is* a world; since he is also the one who makes himself be, then whatever may be the situation in which he finds himself, the for-itself must wholly assume this situation with its peculiar coefficient of adversity, even though it be insupportable. He must assume the situation with the proud consciousness of being the author of it, for the very worst disadvantages or the worst threats which can endanger my person have meaning only in and through my project; and it is on the ground of the engagement which I am that they appear. It is therefore senseless to think of complaining since nothing foreign has decided what we feel, what we live, or what we are.

Furthermore this absolute responsibility is not resignation; it is simply the logical requirement of the consequences of our freedom. What happens to me happens through me, and I can neither affect myself with it nor revolt against it nor resign myself to it. Moreover everything which happens to me is *mine*. By this we must understand first of all that I am always equal to what happens to me *qua* man, for what happens to a man through other men and through himself can be only human. The most terrible situations of war, the worst tortures do not create a non-human state of things; there is no non-human situation. It is only through fear, flight, and recourse to magical types of conduct that I shall decide on the non-human, but this decision is human, and I shall carry the entire responsibility for it. But in addition the situation is *mine* because it is the image of my free choice of myself, and everything which it presents to me is *mine* in that this represents me and symbolizes me. Is it not I who decide the coefficient of adversity in things and even their unpredictability by deciding myself?

Thus there are no *accidents* in life; a community event which suddenly bursts forth and involves me in it does not come from the outside. If I am mobilized in a war, this war is *my* war; it is in my image and I deserve it. I deserve it first because I could always get out of it by suicide or by desertion; these ultimate possibles are those which must always be present for us when there is a question of envisaging a situation. For lack of getting out of it, I have *chosen* it. This can be due to inertia, to cowardice in the face of public opinion, or because I prefer certain other values to the value of the refusal to join in the war (the good opinion of my relatives, the honor of my family, *etc.*). Any way you look at it, it is a matter of a choice. This choice will be repeated later on again and again without a break until the end of the war. Therefore we must agree with the statement by J. Romains, "In war there are no innocent victims." If therefore I have preferred war to death or to dishonor, everything takes place as if I bore the entire responsibility for this war. Of course others have declared it, and one might be tempted perhaps to consider me as a simple accomplice. But this notion of complicity has only a juridical sense, and it does not hold here. For it depended on me that for me and by me this war should not exist, and I have decided that it does exist. There was no compulsion here, for the compulsion could have got no hold on a freedom. I did not have any excuse; . . . the peculiar character of human-reality is that it is without excuse. Therefore it remains for me only to lay claim to this war.

But in addition the war is *mine* because by the sole fact that it arises in a situation which I cause to be and that I can discover it there only by engaging myself for or against it, I can no longer distinguish at present the choice which I make of myself from the choice which I make of the war. To live this war is to choose myself through it and to choose it through my choice of myself. There can be no question of considering it as "four years of vacation" or as a "reprieve," as a "recess," the essential part of my responsibilities being elsewhere in my married, family, or professional life. In this war which I have chosen I choose myself from day to day, and I make it mine by making myself. If it is going to be four empty years, then it is I who bear the responsibility for this.

Finally, . . . each person is an absolute choice of self from the standpoint of a world of knowledges and of techniques which this choice both assumes and illumines; each person is an absolute upsurge at an absolute date and is perfectly unthinkable at another date. It is therefore a waste of time to ask what I should have been if this war had not broken out, for I have chosen myself as one of the possible meanings of the epoch which imperceptibly led to war. I am not distinct from this same epoch; I could not be transported to another epoch without contradiction. Thus *I am* this war which restricts and limits and makes comprehensible the period which preceded it. In this sense we may define more precisely the responsibility of the for-itself if to the earlier quoted statement, "There are no innocent victims," we add the words, "We have the war we deserve." Thus, totally free, undistinguishable from the period for which I have chosen to be the meaning, as profoundly responsible for the war as if I had myself declared it, unable to live without integrating it in *my* situation, engaging myself in it wholly and stamping it with my seal, I must be without remorse or regrets as I am without excuse; for from the instant of my upsurge into being, I carry the weight of the world by myself alone without anything or any person being able to lighten it.

Yet this responsibility is of a very particular type. Someone will say, "I did not ask to be born." This is a naïve way of throwing greater emphasis on our facticity. I am responsible for everything, in fact, except for my very responsibility, for I am not the foundation of my being. Therefore everything takes place as if I were compelled to be responsible. I am *abandoned* in the world, not in the sense that I might remain abandoned and passive in a hostile universe like a board floating on the water, but rather in the sense that I find myself suddenly alone and without help, engaged in a world for which I bear the whole responsibility without being able, whatever I do, to tear myself away from this responsibility for an instant. For I am responsible for my very desire of fleeing responsibilities. To make myself passive in the world, to refuse to act upon things and upon Others is still to choose myself, and suicide is one mode among others of being-in-the-world. Yet I find an absolute responsibility for the fact that my facticity (here the fact of my birth) is directly inapprehensible and even inconceivable, for this fact of my birth never appears as a brute fact but always across a projective reconstruction of my for-itself. I am ashamed of being born or I am astonished at it or I rejoice over it, or in attempting to get rid of my life I affirm that I live and I assume this life as bad. Thus in a certain sense I *choose* being born. This choice itself is integrally affected with facticity since I am not able not to choose, but this facticity in turn will appear only in so far as I surpass it toward my ends. Thus facticity is everywhere but inapprehensible; I never encounter anything except my responsibility. That is why I can not ask, "*Why* was I born?" or curse the day of my birth or declare that I did not ask to be born, for these various attitudes toward my birth — *i.e.*, toward the *fact* that I realize a presence in the world — are absolutely nothing else but ways of assuming this birth in full responsibility and of making it *mine*. Here again I encounter only myself and my projects so that finally my abandonment — *i.e.*, my facticity — consists simply in the fact that I am condemned to be wholly responsible for myself. I am the being which *is* in such a way that in its being its being is in question. And this "is" of my being *is* as present and inapprehensible.

Under these conditions since every event in the world can be revealed to me only as an *opportunity* (an opportunity made use of, lacked, neglected, *etc.*), or better yet since everything which happens to us can be considered as a *chance* (*i.e.*, can appear to us only as a way of realizing this being which is in question in our being) and since others as transcendences-transcended are themselves only *opportunities* and *chances*, the responsibility of the for-itself extends to the entire world as a peopled-world. It is precisely thus that the for-itself apprehends itself in anguish; that is, as a being which is neither the foundation of its own being nor of the Other's being nor of the in-itselfs which form the world, but a being which is compelled to decide the meaning of being — within it and everywhere outside of it. The one who realizes in anguish his condition as *being* thrown into a responsibility which extends to his very abandonment has no longer either remorse or regret or excuse; he is no longer anything but a freedom which perfectly reveals itself and whose being resides in this very revelation. But as we pointed out . . . , most of the time we flee anguish in bad faith.[13]

Sartre's position is the culmination of a full century of existentialist thought, beginning with Søren Kierkegaard in the 1840s. Kierkegaard too argued that one

[13]Jean-Paul Sartre, *Being and Nothingness*, trans. Hazel E. Barnes (New York: Philosophical Library, 1956).

is responsible for whatever one is and that self-conscious choice and commitment were the factors that made a person most human. Sartre's very strong sense of responsibility goes even so far as to ascribe an act of choice to those situations in which we seem clearly to be only victims, for example, in war. "There are no accidents in a life," he argues. It is always my choice as to how I shall act in and deal with a situation. One can always complain, "I didn't ask to be born," Sartre says, but this is only one of many ways we have of trying to avoid responsibility. Given the fact that we have been born, raised in certain conditions, and so forth, it is now entirely up to us as to what we shall make of all this. Instead of looking at the events of the world as problems and intrusions, Sartre ultimately says, we should learn to look at everything as an opportunity. Here is the optimistic note to his very strong defense of human freedom.

FREEDOM AND PERVERSITY

What all of these arguments demand is the following: In one's own case, in making your decision, there can be no appeal to determinism even if determinism is true. Whatever might be theoretically determined, in practice, you must choose. And since freedom is the key to our self-esteem and our pride in ourselves, some people will demand it at any cost.

The most brilliant, if bizarre, example of this existentialist demand is formulated by the strange character in Dostoevsky's short novel *Notes from the Underground*. The argument is simple. Any prediction can be thwarted as long as you know about it. If they say, "you'll do *x*"; do *y*. Now, suppose that determinism is true. In particular, suppose that psychological determinism is true and that its basic law is this: "people always act to their own advantage." Now, what does this have to do with the predictability of a person's actions? Absolutely nothing, if you are sufficiently determined not to be predictable. Accordingly, the character in this novel is, more than anything else, spiteful. His main concern is not being predictable, in proving his freedom even if it means making himself miserable. Now you might say that his spite itself is the determinant of his behavior, and of course it is. But the very point of the argument is that causes and explanations of any kind are simply beside the point. Let the underground man know what you expect him to do, and he'll do precisely the opposite. And if you predict he'll act spiteful, he'll be as agreeable as can be — just out of spite!

"The Most Advantageous Advantage," by Dostoevsky

I am a sick man . . . I am a spiteful man. I am an unpleasant man. I think my liver is diseased. However, I don't know beans about my disease, and I am not sure what is bothering me. I don't treat it and never have, though I respect medicine and doctors. Besides, I am extremely superstitious, let's say sufficiently so to respect medicine. (I am educated enough not to be superstitious, but I am.) No, I refuse to treat it out of spite. You probably will not understand that. Well, but *I* understand it. Of course, I can't explain to you just whom I am annoying in this case by my spite. I am perfectly well aware that I cannot "get even" with the doctors by not consulting them. I know better than anyone that I thereby injure only myself and no one else. But still, if I don't treat it, it is out of spite. My liver is bad, well then — let it get even worse!

. . . . .

. . . But these are all golden dreams. Oh, tell me, who first declared, who first proclaimed, that man only does nasty things because he does not know his own real interests: and that if he were enlightened, if his eyes were opened to his real normal interests, man would at once cease to do nasty things, would at once become good and noble because, being enlightened and understanding his real advantage, he would see his own advantage in the good and nothing else, and we all know that not a single man knowingly acts to his own disadvantage. Consequently, so to say, he would begin doing good through necessity. Oh, the babe! Oh, the pure, innocent child! Why, in the first place, when in all these thousands of years has there ever been a time when man has acted only for his own advantage? What is to be done with the millions of facts that bear witness that men, *knowingly*, that is, fully understanding their real advantages, have left them in the background and have rushed headlong on another path, to risk, to chance, compelled to this course by nobody and by nothing, but, as it were, precisely because they did not want the beaten track, and stubbornly, wilfully, went off on another difficult, absurd way seeking it almost in the darkness. After all, it means that this stubbornness and wilfulness were more pleasant to them than any advantage. Advantage! What is advantage? And will you take it upon yourself to define with perfect accuracy in exactly what the advantage of man consists of? And what if it so happens that a man's advantage *sometimes* not only may, but even must, consist exactly in his desiring under certain conditions what is harmful to himself and not what is advantageous. And if so, if there can be such a condition then the whole principle becomes worthless. What do you think — are there such cases? You laugh; laugh away, gentlemen, so long as you answer me: have man's advantages been calculated with perfect certainty? Are there not some which not only have been included but cannot possibly be included under any classification? After all, you, gentlemen, so far as I know, have taken your whole register of human advantages from the average of statistical figures and scientific-economic formulas. After all, your advantages are prosperity, wealth, freedom, peace — and so on, and so on. So that a man who, for instance, would openly and knowingly oppose that whole list would, to your thinking, and indeed to mine too, of course, be an obscurantist or an absolute madman, would he not? But, after all, here is something amazing: why does it happen that all these statisticians, sages and lovers of humanity, when they calculate human advantages invariably leave one out? They don't even take it into their calculation in the form in which it should be taken, and the whole reckoning depends upon that. There would be no great harm to take it, this advantage, and to add it to the list. But the trouble is, that this strange advantage does not fall under any classification and does not figure in any list. For instance, I have a friend. Bah, gentlemen! But after all he is your friend, too; and indeed there is no one, no one, to whom he is not a friend! When he prepares for any undertaking this gentleman immediately explains to you, pompously and clearly, exactly how he must act in accordance with the laws of reason and truth. What is more, he will talk to you with excitement and passion of the real normal interests of man; with irony he will reproach the short-sighted fools who do not understand their own advantage, for the true significance of virtue; and, within a quarter of an hour, without any sudden outside provocation, but precisely through that something internal which is stronger than all his advantages, he will go off on quite a different tack—that is, act directly opposite to what he has just been saying himself, in opposition to the laws of reason, in opposition to his own advantage—in fact, in opposition to everything. I warn you that my friend is a compound personality, and therefore it is somehow difficult to blame him as an individual. The fact is, gentlemen, it seems that something that is dearer to almost every man than his greatest advantages must really exist, or (not to be illogical) there is one most advantageous advantage (the very one omitted of which we spoke just now) which is more important and more advantageous than all other advantages, for which, if necessary, a man is ready to act in opposition to all laws, that is, in opposition to reason, honor, peace, prosperity—in short, in opposition to all those wonderful and useful things if only he can attain that fundamental, most advantageous advantage which is dearer to him than all.

And what is that "advantageous advantage?" Nothing other than:

One's own free unfettered choice, one's own fancy, however wild it may be, one's own fancy worked up at times to frenzy. That is the "most advantageous advantage," which is always overlooked.[14]

Freedom, in other words, is itself what we most demand, whatever the cost, whatever the difficulties, and whatever the arguments against it. Whatever else may be true, we will refuse to see ourselves as anything but free. For it is freedom that makes us human.

SUMMARY AND CONCLUSION

To say that a person's act is free is to be able to ascribe responsibility. The defense of freedom therefore becomes extremely important to us. Our confidence in the universality of scientific explanations, however, seems to imply the thesis of determinism, which holds that every event has its sufficient natural cause. Human actions, as events, thus seem to be determined and thus not free. In this

[14]Fyodor Dostoevsky, *Notes from the Underground,* in *Notes from the Underground and The Grand Inquisitor,* trans. Ralph Matlaw (New York: E. P. Dutton, 1960).

chapter, we have attempted to explore the various ways in which philosophers have attempted to reconcile these two vital beliefs — that at least some human acts are free and that science can ultimately (at least in principle) explain everything.

There have been philosophers who have defended determinism ("hard determinism") to the exclusion of freedom. There have been philosophers who have defended freedom to the exclusion of determinism ("libertarians" and "indeterminists"). Most philosophers, however, have tried to defend both theses (and so are often called "compatibilists"). They have argued that determinism does not preclude freedom if an act flows from a person's decision or character ("soft determinists"), or that even if determinism is true, we cannot help but think of ourselves as free (Kant and the existentialists).

GLOSSARY

antecedent conditions: those circumstances, states of affairs, or events that regularly precede and can be said to cause an event. The antecedent conditions of boiling water, for example, are the application of heat to water under normal atmospheric pressure, etc. A determinist would say that the antecedent conditions of a human action would be the state of his or her nervous system, a developed character (with personality traits), certain desires and beliefs, and the circumstances (or "stimulus") in which the action takes place.

cause: that which brings something about. On the hard determinist interpretation, a cause is an antecedent condition that, together with other antecedent conditions, is sufficient to make the occurrence of some event necessary, according to the laws of nature. On a weaker interpretation, a cause may simply be an event (or condition) that regularly precedes another event, and thus can be used to predict when the latter will occur. (For example, if we say "a cause of forest fires is lightning," we mean "whenever lightning strikes a sufficiently dry forest, fire will occur.") (The concept of a "cause" is also discussed in Chapters 2, 3, and 4.)

compatibilism: the thesis that both determinism (on some interpretations) and free action can be true. Determinism does not rule out free action and the possibility of free action does not require that determinism be false. They are compatible positions.

compulsion: "being forced to do something." One acts from compulsion (or is compelled to act) when he or she could not have done otherwise. Some philosophers distinguish between *external* compulsions (for example, being pushed) and *internal* compulsions (for example, a neurotic obsession).

determinism: the thesis that every event has its sufficient natural cause(s), that every event is caused by its antecedent conditions, or that every event is predictable on the basis of such conditions.

fatalism: the thesis that certain events (or perhaps all events) are going to happen inevitably, regardless of what efforts we take to prevent them.

free will: among philosophers, a somewhat antiquated expression (as in "he did it of his own free will") that means that a person is capable of making decisions that are not determined by antecedent conditions. Of course there may ·be antecedent considerations, such as what a person wants, what a person believes, but free will means that such considerations never determine a person's decision. At most they "enter into the decision."

freedom: the idea that a human decision or action is a person's own responsibility and that praise and blame may be appropriately ascribed. The most extreme interpretation of "freedom" is the absence of any causes or determinations. Thus an indeterminist would say that an event was free if it had no causes; a libertarian would say that a human act was free if it was only self-caused, but not determined by anything else (including a person's character). Certain determinists, however ("soft determinists"), would say that an act is free if only it is "in character" and based upon a person's desires and personality. Most generally, we say that a person's act was free whether or not it was the result of a conscious decision and whether or not certain causes may have been involved, if we would say that he or she could have done otherwise.

Heisenberg Uncertainty Principle: an important principle of recent physics that demonstrates that we cannot know both the position and the momentum of certain subatomic particles, for in our attempts to know one, we make it impossible to know the other. This principle has been used to attack the very idea of "determinism" in its classical formulations, for determinism requires just the "certainty" of possible prediction that the Heisenberg Principle rejects.

indeterminism: the thesis that at least some events in the universe are not determined, are not caused by antecedent conditions, and may not be predictable.

predestination: the thesis (usually in a theological context) that every event is destined to happen (as in fatalism) whatever efforts we make to prevent it. The usual version is that God knows and perhaps causes all things to happen, and therefore everything must happen precisely as He knows (and possibly causes) it to happen.

prediction: to say that some event will happen before it happens. Determinism normally includes the thesis that if we know enough about the antecedent conditions of an event, we can always predict that it will occur. But prediction does not require determinism. One might predict the outcome of some state of affairs on the basis of statistical probabilities without knowing any antecedent conditions and perhaps even without assuming that there are any such conditions (in quantum physics, for example). And it is also possible that a person might predict the future on the basis of lucky guesses or E.S.P., again without necessarily accepting determinism.

responsibility: answerable or accountable for some act or event presumed to be within a person's control.

retrodiction: to say, on the basis of certain present evidence, what must have happened in the past. For example, the astronomer who looks at the present course of a comet can retrodict certain facts about its history. For the determinist, retrodiction is as important to his thesis as prediction.

soft determinism: a thesis that accepts determinism but claims that certain kinds of causes, namely, a person's character, still allow us to call his or her actions "free." The soft determinist is therefore a compatibilist, for he believes in both freedom and determinism.

sufficient cause: capable of bringing something about by itself (for example, four healthy people are sufficient to push a Volkswagen up a hill).

10

Ethics

"From now on I'm thinking only of me."
Major Danby replied indulgently with a superior smile,
"But Yossarian, suppose everyone felt that way?"
"Then I'd certainly be a ——— fool to feel any
other way, wouldn't I?"

Joseph Heller, *Catch 22*

What should we do? And what should we not do? What acts should we praise? What acts should we condemn and blame? These are questions of **ethics,** the concern for which made Socrates willing to give up his life. The core of ethics is **morality.** Morality is a set of fundamental rules that guide our actions; for example, they may forbid us to kill each other, encourage us to help each other, tell us not to lie, command us to keep our promises.

Most of the moral rules we accept and follow are ones that we have learned and uncritically adopted from parents, friends, teachers, and our own society. At times, though, others may challenge our moral rules, demanding that we defend them. Why should we help each other? Why shouldn't we ever cheat? What reasons can we give to defend one sexual ethic rather than another? New social and technological developments may also force us to reevaluate our morality. Pressure from minorities and women for equal rights has forced many to reconsider the justice of discrimination on the basis of race or sex. And the development of sophisticated life-sustaining devices has forced both physicians and philosophers to question whether it is always a moral duty to preserve life (and refrain from killing).

Whenever we try to defend or criticize a moral belief we enter the realm of ethics. Ethics is not concerned with specific moral rules but with the foundation of morality and with providing very general principles that will both help us evaluate the validity of a moral rule and choose between different moralities (different sets of moral rules). For example, some ethical theorists called **utilitarians** hold that any good moral rule should promote the greatest happiness for the greatest number. Other theorists, for example, Aristotle and Kant, have argued that a good moral rule helps us act in the most rational way possible.

Ethics is also concerned with deciding whether we should take into account others' or our own interests and desires when deciding what we ought to do. For some ethicists, morality is tied to self-interest at least in an abstract way, and they argue that morality is the best way of satisfying everyone's interests. Other philosophers retain the rigid distinction between morality and self-interest and insist that obedience to morality is good for its own sake, or equivalent to being rational, or simply required in order to make us human. Finally some authors have argued that morality is only one among many sets of principles, which we may but need not choose to obey.

In this chapter, we will begin by raising some of the perennial problems of ethics, including the nature of morality and the problem of moral relativism. Then, we will address the familiar claim that the basis of all human behavior—moral behavior included—is selfishness, or **egoism.** Finally we will examine several different ethical theories, different ways of conceiving of morals and (or) justifying moral beliefs:

—The ethics of Aristotle, who based his view of morality on the concept of "virtue" and his idea that man is by nature a social and rational animal. Aristotle argues that being virtuous—controlling our feelings and acting rationally—enables us to become fully human. In this discussion, we have the opportunity to examine a moral system that is significantly different from our own, but still sufficiently similar for us to understand it.

—The view that morality is essentially a matter of feeling; David Hume and Jean-Jacques Rousseau are its representatives.

—The monumental ethical theory of Immanuel Kant, who insisted that morality is strictly a matter of practical reason, divorced from our personal interests and desires and based solely on universal principles or laws. Thus, according to Kant, we cannot justify the morality of our actions by appealing to the good consequences our actions have for others or ourselves.

—The ethical theories of the utilitarians, who argued (in contrast to Kant) that moral rules were merely rules of thumb for achieving the greatest good for the greatest number of people, and who thereby tried to reconcile the interests of each individual with the interests of everyone else.

—The radical theories of Nietzsche and the existentialists, who insist that, in an important sense, we choose our moralities and that this choice cannot be justified in any of the ways argued by other modern philosophers. For Nietzsche, at least, this view also included a retrospective appreciation of the morality of the ancient Greeks, and he argued that we should inject some of their conceptions into our own.

—The "metaethical" theories of G. E. Moore and A. J. Ayer, and the implications of these for practical ethics.

MORALITY

Morality gives us the rules by which we live with other people. It sets limits to our desires and our actions. It tells us what is permitted and what is not. It gives us guiding principles for making decisions. It tells us what we ought and what we ought not to do. But what is this "morality" that sounds so impersonal and "above" us? It is important to begin with an appreciation for the metaphor, which so well characterizes moral rules. Nietzsche describes it this way: "A tablet of virtues hangs over every people."

This "tablet of virtues" is morality. The prototype of morality, in this view, is those ancient codes, carved in stone, with commands that are eternal and absolute. We know best the two tablets inscribed by God, in front of Moses, which we call the Ten Commandments. And they are indeed *commandments*. "Thou shalt" and "Thou shalt not" is all they say. And this is the essence of morality. It consists of commands. These commands do not appeal to individual pleasures or desires. They do not make different demands on different individuals or societies. Quite to the contrary, they are absolute rules that tell us what we must or must not do, no matter who we are, no matter what we want, and regardless of whether or not our interests will be served by the command. "Thou shalt not kill" means that even if you want to, even if you have the power to, and even if you can escape all punishment, you are absolutely forbidden to kill.

The image of morality as coming "from above" is appropriate. First, because moral laws are often said, and not only in our society, to come from God. Second, because we learn these laws from our parents, who literally "stand over us" and indoctrinate us with them through their shouts, commands, examples, threats, and gestures. Finally and most importantly, morality itself is "above" any given individual or individuals, whether it is canonized in the laws of society or not. Morality is not just another aid in getting us what we want; it is entirely concerned with right and wrong. And these considerations are "above" tampering by any individual, no matter how powerful, as if they have a life of their own.

This characteristic of morality as independent of individual desires and ambitions has led many people to characterize morality simply in terms of some absolute and independent agency. Most often, this absolute and independent agency is God. Saint Augustine, for example, talks about morality in this way.

> . . . Unless you turn to Him and repay the existence that He gave you, you won't be "nothing"; you will be wretched. All things owe to God, first of all, what they are insofar as they are natures. Then, those who have received a will owe to Him whatever better thing they can will to be, and whatever they ought to be. No man is ever blamed for what he has not been given, but he is justly blamed if he has not done what he should have done; and if he has received free will and sufficient power, he stands under obligation. When a man does not do what he ought, God the Creator is not at fault. It is to His glory that a man suffers justly; and by blaming a man

for not doing what he should have done, you are praising what he ought to do. You are praised for seeing what you ought to do, even though you see this only through God, who is immutable Truth.[1]

And St. Thomas Aquinas: " . . . It is apparent that things prescribed by divine law are right, not only because they are put forth by law, but also because they are in accord with nature." Or "Therefore by divine law precepts had to be given, so that each man would give his neighbor his due and would abstain from doing injuries to him."[2] And in the Bible: "When thou shalt harken — to the voice of the Lord thy God, to keep all his commandments, which I command thee this day, to do that which is right in the Eyes of the Lord thy God."[3]

But whether or not one believes in God, it is clear that something further is needed to help us define morality. Even assuming that there is a God, we need a way of determining what His moral commands must be. One might say that He has given these commands to various individuals, but the fact is that different people seem to have very different ideas about the morality that God has given them. Some, for example, would say that it explicitly rules out abortion and infanticide. Others would argue that God does not rule these out but makes it clear that they are, like other forms of killing (a "holy war," for example), justifiable only in certain circumstances. And in view of such disagreements, we cannot simply appeal to God but must, for reasons that we can formulate and defend, define our morality for ourselves. There is the further question, which has often been debated, whether we should follow God's laws just because they are His or rather, whether God is good because His laws are good. If the latter, then we have to decide what is good in order to know that God is good. If the former, then one has to decide whether or not to believe in God precisely on the basis of whether we can accept those laws. Either way, we have to decide for ourselves what laws of morality we are willing to accept.

Similar considerations hold true for that familiar appeal to conscience in determining what we ought or ought not do. Even if one believes that conscience is God-given, the same problems emerge again. Should we follow our consciences just because "conscience tells us to"? Or do we follow our conscience just because we know that what our conscience commands is good. How does one decide whether a nagging thought is or is not the prompting of God? Probably on the basis of whether what it demands is good or not. (Thus one readily attributes to conscience the nagging reminder that one shouldn't have cheated an unsuspecting child, but one does not attribute to conscience the nagging thought that one could have gotten away with shoplifting if only one had had the daring to do it.) If one believes that conscience is simply the internalization of the moral teachings of one's parents and society, then the question takes an extra dimension: Should

[1]St. Augustine, *On Freedom* (New York: Bobbs-Merrill, 1956).
[2]St. Thomas Aquinas, *Summa Contra Gentiles*, Bk. III (New York: Doubleday, 1955).
[3]Deuteronomy, 13:18.

Is conscience somewhat we have been taught? (inherent)

we accept or reject what we have been taught? Since our consciences often disagree, we must still decide whose conscience and which rules of conscience one ought to obey. Identifying morality with the promptings of one's conscience is both plausible and valuable, but philosophically it only moves the question one step back: how do we know what is, and what is not, the prompting of conscience? And is it always right to follow one's conscience? But these two questions are in fact just another way of asking, what is moral? What should I do?

Morality is not just obedience — whether obedience to the king, the Pope, the law or one's conscience. Morality is doing what is *right*, whether or not it is commanded by any person or law and whether or not one "feels" it in one's conscience. One way of putting this — defended later on by Immanuel Kant — is to say that morality involves **autonomy,** that is, the ability to think for oneself and decide, for oneself, what is right and what is wrong, whom to obey and whom to ignore, what to do and what not to do. The danger is that this conception of morality as autonomy seems to leave us without a place to learn morality in the first place. How do we learn to judge right and wrong but from our parents, our friends, our teachers, and our society and its models? But if we try to tie morality too closely to our upbringing and our society, then it looks as if there is no room for autonomy, no way in which we could disagree with our family or society, no way to criticize the way in which we have been raised. Furthermore, tying morality to particular societies raises an additional question, and that is whether morality (or morali*ties*) might not be **relative** to particular societies and cultures.

IS MORALITY RELATIVE?

Moralities, like lifestyles, vary from culture to culture and even from person to person. But while there is nothing surprising about the fact that lifestyles vary, there is a problem in the variation of moralities. Morality, by its very nature, is supposed to be a set of universal principles, principles that do not distinguish between cultures or peoples or lifestyles. If it is morally reprehensible to kill for fun, then it is morally reprehensible in every society, in every culture, for every lifestyle, and for every person, no matter who he or she is. And this will be true even if the society or person in question does not agree with that moral principle. Aristotle, for example, discusses at length what he calls "the wicked man," who does evil because he believes in immoral principles and therefore acts without regret, unlike the person who acts badly from momentary weakness, force of circumstances, desperation, or misinformation. But on what grounds can one society or person claim that another society's or person's principles are immoral? How could European Christians, for example, be justified in criticizing the sexual morality of Polynesians in the South Pacific? The Polynesians were a separate society, with their own mores and principles that worked quite well for them, possibly even better in certain ways than the European customs worked in

Europe. Yet European missionaries felt no hesitation whatever in condemning their sexual practices as "immoral." And similarly but more seriously, what gives us the right to criticize a culture across the world that still believes in genocide as a legitimate consequence of war or in torture as a way of keeping civil order? We surely feel that we have the right to speak up in such cases, but then we too are asserting the universality of our morality, extending it even to people who might explicitly reject our principles. How can we do this? What justifies such an extension?

The problem of relativism has become extremely controversial since the nineteenth century, when anthropologists began telling us. of exotic societies with moralities so different from ours. In a sense, relativism has always been a threat to established morality, for even the Greeks came into contact with societies that were much different from theirs. (Thus their tendency to immediately label anything non-Greek "barbarian," so that they didn't have to consider the possibility of relativism.) Kant was the most vigorous opponent of relativism, for his conception of morality was such that if a human being was to count as rational at all, he or she had to agree to at least the basic principles of a universal morality. There were people and societies that did not, but that, according to Kant, only proved that they were less than rational (and therefore less than human as well). Today we tend to be more liberal in our acceptance of different styles of life, but few people would deny that at least some moral principles hold for every society. The principle that unnecessary cruelty is wrong, for example, would be such a principle, although people might well disagree about what was "cruel" and what was "unnecessary."

Philosophers generally distinguish two theses. First, there is the factual claim that different societies have different moralities. This is called **cultural relativism.** The difficult question is whether these different moralities are only different superficially or whether they are fundamentally different. For example, Eskimos of certain tribes kill their elders by leaving them to freeze on the ice; we consider that grossly immoral (we send most of our elders to frigid "old-age homes" instead). But the question of cultural relativity is whether this difference is merely the reflection of different interpretations of some basic moral principle (such as, don't kill anyone unless it is absolutely necessary for the survival of the rest) or whether it really is a wholly different morality. This is among the most controversial anthropological questions of our time. But philosophers are interested in a somewhat different question: Assuming that two moralities really are fundamentally different, is it possible that each is as correct as the other? The philosopher who says "yes" is an **ethical relativist.** And it is ethical relativism that will occupy us here.

In the following selection, the English-American philosopher Walter Stace presents the ethical relativist position and its traditional opponent, **ethical absolutism,** the view that there is only one correct morality. Stace's own answer to the problem is more of an absolutist solution; later in the same work he says that "happiness" is a universal and absolute value, and therefore cross-cultural evaluations are possible.

on Ethical Relativism,
by Walter Stace

There is an opinion widely current nowadays in philosophical circles which passes under the name of "ethical relativity." Exactly what this phrase means or implies is certainly far from clear. But unquestionably it stands as a label for the opinions of a group of ethical philosophers whose position is roughly on the extreme left wing among the moral theorizers of the day. And perhaps one may best understand it by placing it in contrast with the opposite kind of extreme view against which, undoubtedly, it has arisen as a protest. For among moral philosophers one may clearly distinguish a left and a right wing. Those of the left wing are the ethical relativists. They are the revolutionaries, the clever young men, the up to date. Those of the right wing we may call the ethical absolutists. They are the conservatives and the old-fashioned.

According to the absolutists there is but one eternally true and valid moral code. This moral code applies with rigid impartiality to all men. What is a duty for me must likewise be a duty for you. And this will be true whether you are an Englishman, a Chinaman, or a Hottentot. If cannibalism is an abomination in England or America, it is an abomination in central Africa, notwithstanding that the African may think otherwise. The fact that he sees nothing wrong in his cannibal practices does not make them for him morally right. They are as much contrary to morality for him as they are for us. The only difference is that he is an ignorant savage who does not know this. There is not one law for one man or race of men, another for another. There is not one moral standard for Europeans, another for Indians, another for Chinese. There is but one law, one standard, one morality, for all men. And this standard, this law, is absolute and unvarying.

Moreover, as the one moral law extends its dominion over all the corners of the earth, so too it is not limited in its application by any considerations of time or period. That which is right now was right in the centuries of Greece and Rome, nay, in the very ages of the cave man. That which is evil now was evil then. If slavery is morally wicked today, it was morally wicked among the ancient Athenians, notwithstanding that their greatest men accepted it as a necessary condition of human society. Their opinion did not make slavery a moral good for them. It only showed that they were, in spite of their otherwise noble conceptions, ignorant of what is truly right and good in this matter.

The ethical absolutist recognizes as a fact that moral customs and moral ideas differ from country to country and from age to age. This indeed seems manifest and not to be disputed. We think slavery morally wrong, the Greeks thought it morally unobjectionable. The inhabitants of New Guinea certainly have very different moral ideas from ours. But the fact that the Greeks or the inhabitants of New Guinea think something right does not make it right, even for them. Nor does the fact that we think the same things wrong make them wrong. They are *in themselves* either right or wrong. What we have to do is to discover which they are. What anyone thinks makes no difference. It is here just as it is in matters of physical science. We believe the earth to be a globe. Our ancestors may have thought it flat. This does not show that it *was* flat, and is *now* a globe. What it shows is that men having in other ages been ignorant about the shape of the earth have now learned the truth. So if the Greeks thought slavery morally legitimate, this does not indicate that it was for them and in that age morally legitimate, but rather that they were ignorant of the truth of the matter.

．　．　．　．　．

Now ethical absolutism was, in its central ideas, the product of Christian theology. The connection is not difficult to detect. For morality has been conceived, during the Christian dispensation, as issuing from the will of God. That indeed was its single and all-sufficient source. There would be no point, for the naïve believer in the faith, in the philosopher's questions regarding the foundations of morality and the basis of moral obligation. Even to ask such questions is a mark of incipient religious scepticism. For the true believer the author of the moral law is God. What pleases God, what God commands — that is the definition of right. What displeases God, what he forbids — that is the definition of wrong. Now there is, for the Christian monotheist, only one God ruling over the entire universe. And this God is rational, self-consistent. He does not act upon whims. Consequently his will and his commands must be the same everywhere. They will be unvarying for all peoples and in all ages. If the heathen have other moral ideas than ours — inferior ideas — that can only be because they live in ignorance of the true God. If they knew God and his commands, their ethical precepts would be the same as ours.

．　．　．　．　．

This explains why ethical absolutism, until very recently, was not only believed by philosophers but *taken for granted without any argument*. The ideas of philosophers, like the ideas of everyone else, are largely moulded by the civilizations in which they live. Their philosophies are largely attempts to state in abstract terms and in self-consistent language the stock of ideas which they have breathed in from the atmosphere of their social environment. This accounts for the large number of so-called "unrecognized presuppositions" with which systems of philosophy always abound. These presuppositions are simply the ideas which the authors of the systems have breathed in with the intellectual atmospheres by which they happen to be surrounded — which they have taken over therefore as a matter of course, without argument, without criticism, without even a suspicion that they might be false. . . .

We can now turn to the consideration of ethical relativity which is the proper subject of this chapter. The revolt of the relativists against absolutism is, I believe, part and parcel of the general revolutionary tendency of our times. In particular it is a result of the decay of belief in the dogmas of orthodox religion. Belief in absolutism was supported, as we have seen, by belief in Christian monotheism. And now that, in an age of widespread religious scepticism, that support is withdrawn, absolutism tends to collapse. Revolutionary movements are as a rule, at any rate in their first onset, purely negative. They attack and destroy. And ethical relativity is, in its essence, a purely negative creed. It is simply a denial of ethical absolutism. That is why the best way of explaining it is to begin by explaining ethical absolutism. If we understand that what the latter asserts the former denies, then we understand ethical relativity.

Any ethical position which denies that there is a single moral standard which is equally applicable to all men at all times may fairly be called a species of ethical relativity. There is not, the relativist asserts, merely one moral law, one code, one standard. There are many moral laws, codes, standards. What morality ordains in one place or age may be quite different from what morality ordains in another place or age. The moral code of Chinamen is quite different from that of Europeans, that of African savages quite different from both. Any morality, therefore, is relative to the age, the place, and the circumstances in which it is found. It is in no sense absolute.

This does not mean merely—as one might at first sight be inclined to suppose—that the very same kind of action which is *thought* right in one country and period may be *thought* wrong in another. This would be a mere platitude, the truth of which everyone would have to admit. Even the absolutist would admit this—would even wish to emphasize it—since he is well aware that different peoples have different sets of moral ideas, and his whole point is that some of these sets of ideas are false. What the relativist means to assert is, not this platitude, but that the very same kind of action which *is* right in one country and period may *be* wrong in another. And this, far from being a platitude, is a very startling assertion.

It is very important to grasp thoroughly the difference between the two ideas. For there is reason to think that many minds tend to find ethical relativity attractive because they fail to keep them clearly apart. It is so very obvious that moral ideas differ from country to country and from age to age. And it is so very easy, if you are mentally lazy, to suppose that to say this means the same as to say that no universal moral standard exists,—or in other words that it implies ethical relativity. We fail to see that the word "standard" is used in two different senses. It is perfectly true that, in one sense, there are many variable moral standards. We speak of judging a man by the standard of his time. And this implies that different times have different standards. And this, of course, is quite true. But when the word "standard" is used in this sense it means simply the set of moral ideas current during the period in question. It means what people *think* right, whether as a matter of fact it *is* right or not. On the other hand when the absolutist asserts that there exists a single universal moral "standard," he is not using the word in this sense at all. He means by "standard" what *is* right as distinct from what people merely think right. His point is that although what people think right varies in different countries and periods, yet what actually is right is everywhere and always the same. And it follows that when the ethical relativist disputes the position of the absolutist and denies that any universal moral standard exists he too means by "standard" what actually is right. But it is exceedingly easy, if we are not careful, to slip loosely from using the word in the first sense to using it in the second sense; and to suppose that the variability of moral beliefs is the same thing as the variability of what really is moral. And unless we keep the two senses of the word "standard" distinct, we are likely to think the creed of ethical relativity much more plausible than it actually is.

The genuine relativist, then, does not merely mean that Chinamen may think right what Frenchmen think wrong. He means that what *is* wrong for the Frenchman may *be* right for the Chinaman. And if one enquires how, in those circumstances, one is to know what actually is right in China or in France, the answer comes quite glibly. What is right in China is the same as what people think right in China; and what is right in France is the same as what people think right in France. So that, if you want to know what is moral in any particular country or age all you have to do is to ascertain what are the moral ideas current in that age or country. Those ideas are, *for that age or country*, right. Thus what is morally right is identified with what is thought to be morally right, and the distinction which we made above between these two is simply denied. To put the same thing in another way, it is denied that there can be or ought to be any distinction between the two senses of the word "standard." There is only one kind of standard of right and wrong, namely, the moral ideas current in any particular age or country.[4]

EGOISM AND ALTRUISM

Most moral rules are ones that enjoin us to take into account the interests, feelings, or welfare of other people. The commands not to lie, not to kill, and not to steal, as well as the commands to keep our promises, treat others fairly, and be generous are all commands that concern our relations to other persons. (There can, of course, be moral rules that require us to take into account our own interests; for example, the prohibition of suicide or, as Kant thought, the obligation to develop our talents.)

One of the important assumptions of any morality, then, is that it is possible for us to act in the interests of other people. In addition, morality assumes that it is possible for us to do so *because* we are concerned about others' welfare or because we recognize that we ought to be. Someone who refrains from cheating, for example, simply because he or she is afraid of being caught acts purely self-interestedly; and we would not think this person is morally praiseworthy. Again, a person who visits a dying relative in the hospital because he or she wants to ensure a substantial inheritance is not acting morally. Only if actions are motivated by a concern for others' interests do we call them truly moral actions.

There is an important theory, though, that denies that we can be motivated simply by a concern for others. This is psychological egoism. **Psychological egoism** is the thesis that everyone, in fact, acts for his or her own advantage, and the only reason why people act respectfully or kindly toward each other is that that too, for one reason or another, is to their advantage. It might be fear of punishment that makes them act "correctly." Some have "ulterior motives"; that

[4]Walter Stace, *The Concept of Morals* (New York: Macmillan, 1937).

is, they expect other things later on, perhaps a favor in return or reward in heaven after they die, or they are trying to avoid guilt or want a feeling of self-satisfaction. In popular language, the egoist position is often called **selfishness.**

One should be careful, though, to distinguish psychological egoism from ethical egoism. Psychological egoism asserts that our psychology is such that we cannot help but act in our own interests. In contrast, **ethical egoism** claims that even though we can act in others' interests because we are concerned for others, we *ought* always to act in our own interest. One of the most widely read contemporary ethical egoists is Ayn Rand, who has written of "the virtue of selfishness." It is psychological, not ethical, egoism that challenges the very possibility of any morality.

One of Socrates' opponents in *The Republic* states the psychological egoist's view with brutal clarity:

from *The Republic,* by Plato

They say that to do wrong is naturally good, to be wronged is bad, but the suffering of injury so far exceeds in badness the good of inflicting it that when men have done wrong to each other and suffered it, and have had a taste of both, those who are unable to avoid the latter and practise the former decide that it is profitable to come to an agreement with each other neither to inflict injury nor to suffer it. As a result they begin to make laws and convenants, and the law's command they call lawful and just. This, they say, is the origin and essence of justice; it stands between the best and the worst, the best being to do wrong without paying the penalty and the worst to be wronged without the power of revenge. The just then is a mean between two extremes; it is welcomed and honoured because of men's lack of the power to do wrong. The man who has that power, the real man, would not make a compact with anyone not to inflict injury or suffer it. For him that would be madness. This then, Socrates, is, according to their argument, the nature and origin of justice.

Even those who practise justice do so against their will because they lack the power to do wrong. This we could realize very clearly if we imagined ourselves granting to both the just and the unjust the freedom to do whatever they liked. We could then follow both of them and observe where their desires led them, and we would catch the just man redhanded travelling the same road as the unjust. The reason is the desire for undue gain which every organism by nature pursues as a good, but the law forcibly sidetracks him to honour equality. The freedom I just mentioned would most easily occur if these men had the power which they say the ancestor of the Lydian Gyges possessed. The story is that he was a shepherd in the service of the ruler of Lydia. There was a violent rainstorm and an earthquake which broke open the ground and created a chasm at the place where he was tending sheep. Seeing this and marvelling, he went down into it. He saw, besides many other wonders of which we are told, a hollow bronze horse. There were window-like openings in it; he climbed through them and caught sight of a corpse which seemed of more than human stature, wearing nothing but a ring of gold on its finger. This ring the shepherd put on and came out. He arrived at the usual monthly meeting which reported to the king on the state of the flocks, wearing the ring. As he was sitting among the others he happened to twist the hoop of the ring towards himself, to the inside of his hand, and as he did this he became invisible to those sitting near him and they went on talking as if he had gone. He marvelled at this and, fingering the ring, he turned the hoop outward again and became visible. Perceiving this he tested whether the ring had this power and so it happened: if he turned the hoop inwards he became invisible, but was visible when he turned it outwards. When he realized this, he at once arranged to become one of the messengers to the king. He went, committed adultery with the king's wife, attacked the king with her help, killed him, and took over the kingdom.

Now if there were two such rings, one worn by the just man, the other by the unjust, no one, as these people think, would be so incorruptible that he would stay on the path of justice or bring himself to keep away from other people's property and not touch it, when he could with impunity take whatever he wanted from the market, go into houses and have sexual relations with anyone he wanted, kill anyone, free all those he wished from prison, and do the other things which would make him like a god among men. His actions would be in no way different from those of the other and they would both follow the same path. This, some would say, is a great proof that no one is just willingly but under compulsion, so that justice is not one's private good, since wherever either thought he could do wrong with impunity he would do so. Every man believes that injustice is much more profitable to himself than justice, and any exponent of this argument will say that he is right. The man who did not wish to do wrong with that opportunity, and did not touch other people's property, would be thought by those who knew it to be very foolish and miserable. They would praise him in public, thus deceiving one another, for fear of being wronged. So much for my second topic.[5]

Both egoist positions are contrasted with what is usually called **altruism,** that is, acting for the sake of other people's interests. There are degrees of altruism. One may be altruistic because one acts morally, because he or she recognizes an obligation to other people. Or one may be altruistic in actually taking another person's interests as important or even more important than one's own interests, such as one often finds between lovers or brothers and sisters. Altruism can also be divided into two distinct theses, although these are not so often distinguished. There is *psychological altruism,* which says that people "naturally" act for each other's sakes. (We shall see this thesis defended by several important philosophers in later sections.) It has rarely been argued, however, that people are compelled to act altruistically. Thus psychological egoism is usually defended for all cases; psychological altruism, in contrast, is only defended for some cases. *Ethical altruism,* on the other hand, says that people ought to act with each other's interests

[5]Plato, *The Republic*, Bk. II, trans. G. M. A. Grube (Indianapolis, Ind.: Hackett, 1974).

in mind. This is, of course, a basic statement of morality, best summarized in the so-called **Golden Rule:** "Do unto others as you would have them do unto you." (We shall see a modern version of this ancient teaching in the philosophy of Immanuel Kant.)

The most familiar and most difficult question is about psychological egoism: Is it true that people only act for their own self-interest? A famous story about Abraham Lincoln is an apt illustration of the thesis. As he was arguing the psychological egoist position with a friend, his coach was passing a mud slide where a mother pig was squealing as her piglets were drowning. Lincoln stopped the coach, saved the piglets, then moved on. His friend asked him whether that wasn't a clear case of altruism. Lincoln replied: "Why that was the very essence of selfishness. I should have had no peace of mind all day had I gone on and left that suffering old sow worrying over those piglets. I did it to get peace of mind, don't you see?"[6]

There are many actions that are based upon self-interest and are "selfish" without any question. The question is, are there any actions that are not based on self-interest? Lincoln's response is an excellent example because it would seem as if his action is not for selfish reasons at all. Yet, according to him, there was a selfish reason behind his actions: his own sense of satisfaction and "peace of mind." Could this be true of all our actions?

The arguments that are still considered to be the most powerful and definitive against psychological egoism were formulated as sermons by an English bishop, Joseph Butler. Bishop Butler argued that such reasoning as Lincoln's turned on a number of fallacies. Butler begins by accepting the distinction between "private good and a person's own preservation and happiness" and "respect to society and the promotion of public good and the happiness of society." But then he insists that these are not, as the egoists argue, always in conflict and fighting against each other. To the contrary, they are almost always in perfect harmony.

Against Egoism,
by Joseph Butler

From this review and comparison of the nature of man as respecting self and as respecting society, it will plainly appear that there are as real and the same kind of indications in human nature that we were made for society and to do good to our fellow creatures, as that we were intended to take care of our own life and health and private good; and that the same objections lie against one of these assertions as against the other.

First, there is a natural principle of *benevolence* in man, which is in some degree to *society* what *self-love* is to the *individual*. And if there be in mankind any disposition to friendship; if there be any such thing as compassion, for compassion is momentary love; if there be any such thing as the paternal or filial affections; if there be any affection in human nature the object and end of which is the good of another — this is itself benevolence or the love of another. Be it ever so short, be it in ever so low a degree,

[6]Quoted in F. Sharp, *Ethics* (New York: Appleton-Century-Crofts, 1928).

or ever so unhappily confined, it proves the assertion and points out what we were designed for, as really as though it were in a higher degree and more extensive. I must however remind you that though benevolence and self-love are different, though the former tends most directly to public good, and the latter to private, yet they are so perfectly coincident that the greatest satisfactions to ourselves depend upon our having benevolence in a due degree, and that self-love is one chief security of our right behavior toward society. It may be added that their mutual coinciding, so that we can scarce promote one without the other, is equally a proof that we were made for both.

．　．　．　．　．　．

Secondly, this will further appear, from observing that the *several passions and affections*, which are distinct both from benevolence and self-love, do in general contribute and lead us to *public* good as really as to *private*. It might be thought too minute and particular, and would carry us too great a length, to distinguish between and compare together the several passions or appetites distinct from benevolence, whose primary use and intention is the security and good of society; and the passions distinct from self-love, whose primary intention and design is the security and good of the individual. It is enough to the present argument that desire of esteem from others, contempt and esteem of them, love of society as distinct from affection to the good of it, indignation against successful vice—that these are public affections or passions, have an immediate respect to others, naturally lead us to regulate our behavior in such a manner as will be of service to our fellow creatures. If any or all of these may be considered likewise as private affections, as tending to private good, this does not hinder them from being public affections, too, or destroy the good influence of them upon society, and their tendency to public good. It may be added that as persons without any conviction from reason of the desirableness of life would yet of course preserve it merely from the appetite of hunger, so by acting merely from regard (suppose) to reputation, without any consideration of the good of others, men often contribute to public good. In both these instances they are plainly instruments in the hands of another, in the hands of Providence, to carry on ends, the preservation of the individual and good of society, which they themselves have not in their view or intention. The sum is, men have various appetites, passions, and particular affections, quite distinct both from self-love and from benevolence—all of these have a tendency to promote both public and private good, and may be considered as respecting others and ourselves equally and in common; but some of them seem most immediately to respect others, or tend to public good, others of them most immediately to respect self, or tend to private good; as the former are not benevolence, so the latter are not self-love; neither sort are instances of our love either to ourselves or others, but only instances of our Maker's care and love both of the individual and the species, and proofs that He intended we should be instruments of good to each other, as well as that we should be so to ourselves.

Thirdly, there is a principle of reflection in men by which they distinguish between, approve and disapprove, their own actions. We are plainly constituted such sort of creatures as to reflect upon our own nature. The mind can take a view of what passes within itself, its propensions, aversions, passions, affections, as respecting such objects and in such degrees, and of the several actions consequent thereupon. In this survey it approves of one, disapproves of another, and toward a third is affected in neither of these ways, but is quite indifferent. This principle in man by which he approves or disapproves his heart, temper, and actions, is conscience. . . . That this faculty tends to restrain men from doing mischief to each other, and leads them to do good, is too manifest to need being insisted upon. Thus a parent has the affection of love to his children; this leads him to take care of, to educate, to make due provision for them; the natural affection leads to this, but the reflection that it is his proper business, what belongs to him, that it is right and commendable so to do—this added to the affection becomes a much more settled principle and carries him on through more labor and difficulties for the sake of his children than he would undergo from that affection alone, if he thought it, and the course of action it led to, either indifferent or criminal. This indeed is impossible, to do that which is good and not to approve of it; for which reason they are frequently not considered as distinct, though they really are, for men often approve of the actions of others which they will not imitate, and likewise do that which they approve not. It cannot possibly be denied that there is this principle of reflection or conscience in human nature. Suppose a man to relieve an innocent person in great distress, suppose the same man afterwards, in the fury of anger, to do the greatest mischief to a person who had given no just cause of offense; to aggravate the injury, add the circumstances of former friendship and obligation from the injured person, let the man who is supposed to have done these two different actions coolly reflect upon them afterwards, without regard to their consequences to himself; to assert that any common man would be affected in the same way toward these different actions, that he would make no distinction between them, but approve or disapprove them equally, is too glaring a falsity to need being confuted. There is therefore this principle of reflection or conscience in mankind. . . .

If it be said that there are persons in the world who are in great measure without the natural affections toward their fellow creatures, there are likewise instances of persons without the common natural affections to themselves; but the nature of man is not to be judged of by either of these, but by what appears in the common world, in the bulk of mankind.[7]

In short, Butler argues that merely acting on one's own desires does not make an action selfish, for all actions are, in some sense, based on our desires, but at least some of those desires are desires to serve someone else's interests. Thus the "object" of desire is what makes an act selfish or unselfish, not merely the fact that one's own desire is acted upon. Nor can simply acting with some benefit to oneself make an action selfish, for even if we agreed that an act gives us some benefit (for example, peace of mind), it may still be the case that most of the benefit is for someone else. Even if peace of mind typically follows virtuous

[7]Bishop Joseph Butler, *Five Sermons* (New York: Bobbs-Merrill, 1950).

actions, that does not show that our motivation is selfish. The satisfaction that accompanies good acts is itself not the motivation of the act. Here is the answer to Lincoln. His act was, despite his philosophical claims, an altruistic one; his satisfaction was not the motive of the act but only its consequence.

MORALITY AS VIRTUE: ARISTOTLE

Aristotle's *Ethics* (properly called the *Nicomachean Ethics*) is the best systematic guide to ancient Greek moral and ethical thinking. The significant feature of Greek ethics is its stress on being virtuous as opposed to merely following moral rules. Aristotle's concept of virtue is based on a very special conception of man as a rational being. Virtue, accordingly, is rational activity, activity in accordance with a rational principle. Having defined virtue in this way, Aristotle can then defend, for example, courage as a virtue by showing that the courageous man is more rational than the coward.

Aristotle arrives at his conception of man as an essentially rational being by asking what "the natural good for man" is. This, he argues, will be discovered by finding what all men desire "for its own sake" and not "for the sake of anything else."

from *The Nicomachean Ethics,* by Aristotle

Every art and every kind of inquiry, and likewise every act and purpose, seems to aim at some good; and so it has been well said that the good is that at which everything aims. But a difference is observable among these aims or ends. What is aimed at is sometimes the exercise of a faculty, sometimes a certain result beyond that exercise. And where there is an end beyond that act, there the result is better than the exercise of the faculty. Now since there are many kinds of actions and many arts and sciences, it follows that there are many ends also; *e.g.* health is the end of medicine, ships of ship-building, victory of the art of war, and wealth of economy. But when several of these are subordinated to some one art or science, — as the making of bridles and other trappings to the art of horsemanship, and this in turn, along with all else that the soldier does, to the art of war, and so on, — then the end of the master art is always more desired than the end of the subordinate arts, since these are pursued for its sake. And this is equally true whether the end in view be the mere exercise of a faculty or something beyond that, as in the above instances.

If then in what we do there be some end which we wish for on its own account, choosing all the others as means to this, but not every end without exception as a means to something else (for so we should go on *ad infinitum,* and desire would be left void and objectless), — this evidently will be the good or the best of all things.[8]

We see here the same logical strategy that Aristotle used in Chapter 1: the idea that every act is for the sake of something else (we want to earn a dollar to buy ourselves some food, and we want that to satisfy our hunger). But since there can be no "infinite regress," there must be some ultimate end. Aristotle examines two popular conceptions of this ultimate end that is the natural good for man: pleasure and success. He rejects both because neither pleasure nor success is desired for its own sake. Rather, happiness is what all men desire for its own sake and is the natural good for man.

> . . . It seems that men not unreasonably take their notions of the good or happiness from the lives actually led, and that the masses who are the least refined suppose it to be pleasure, which is the reason why they aim at nothing higher than the life of enjoyment. For the most conspicuous kinds of life are three: this life of enjoyment, the life of the statesman, and, thirdly, the contemplative life. The mass of men show themselves utterly slavish in their preference for the life of brute beasts, but their views receive consideration because many of those in high places have the tastes of Sardanapalus. Men of refinement with a practical turn prefer honour; for I suppose we may say that honour is the aim of the statesman's life. But this seems too superficial to be the good we are seeking: for it appears to depend upon those who give rather than upon those who receive it; while we have a presentiment that the good is something that is peculiarly a man's own and can scarce be taken away from him. Moreover, these men seem to pursue honour in order that they may be assured of their own excellence, — at least, they wish to be honoured by men of sense, and by those who know them, and on the ground of their virtue or excellence. It is plain, then, that in their view, at any rate, virtue or excellence is better than honour; and perhaps we should take this to be the end of the statesman's life, rather than honour. But virtue or excellence also appears too incomplete to be what we want; for it seems that a man might have virtue and yet be asleep or be inactive all his life, and, moreover, might meet with the greatest disasters and misfortunes; and no one would maintain that such a man is happy, except for argument's sake. But we will not dwell on these matters now, for they are sufficiently discussed in the popular treatises. The third kind of life is the life of contemplation: we will treat of it further on. As for the money-making life, it is something quite contrary to nature; and wealth evidently is not the good of which we are in search, for it is merely useful as a means to something else. So we might rather take pleasure and virtue or excellence to be ends than wealth; for they are chosen on their own account. But it seems that not even they are the end, though much breath has been wasted in attempts to show that they are.

[8]Aristotle, *The Nicomachean Ethics*, translated by F. H. Peters, 8th edition (1901). All subsequent quotations from Aristotle are from this edition.

... Let us return once more to the question, what this good can be of which we are in search. It seems to be different in different kinds of action and in different arts, — one thing in medicine and another in war, and so on. What then is the good in each of these cases? Surely that for the sake of which all else is done. And that in medicine is health, in war is victory, in building is a house, — a different thing in each different case, but always, in whatever we do and in whatever we choose, the end. For it is always for the sake of the end that all else is done. If then there be one end of all that man does, this end will be the realizable good, — or these ends, if there be more than one.

By this generalization our argument is brought to the same point as before. This point we must try to explain more clearly. We see that there are many ends. But some of these are chosen only as means, as wealth, flutes, and the whole class of instruments. And so it is plain that not all ends are final. But the best of all things must, we conceive, be something final. If then there be only one final end, this will be what we are seeking, — or if there be more than one, then the most final of them. Now that which is pursued as an end in itself is more final than that which is pursued as means to something else, and that which is never chosen as means than that which is chosen both as an end in itself and as means, and that is strictly final which is always chosen as an end in itself and never as means.

Happiness seems more than anything else to answer to this description: for we always choose it for itself, and never for the sake of something else; while honour and pleasure and reason, and all virtue or excellence, we choose partly indeed for themselves (for, apart from any result, we should choose each of them), but partly also for the sake of happiness, supposing that they will help to make us happy. But no one chooses happiness for the sake of these things, or as a means to anything else at all. We seem to be led to the same conclusion when we start from the notion of self-sufficiency. The final good is thought to be self-sufficing [or all-sufficing]. In applying this term we do not regard a man as an individual leading a solitary life, but we also take account of parents, children, wife, and, in short, friends and fellow-citizens generally, since man is naturally a social being. Some limit must indeed be set to this; for if you go on to parents and descendants and friends of friends, you will never come to a stop. But this we will consider further on: for the present we will take self-sufficing to mean what by itself makes life desirable and in want of nothing. And happiness is believed to answer to this description. And further, happiness is believed to be the most desirable thing in the world, and that not merely as one among other good things: if it were merely one among other good things [so that other things could be added to it], it is plain that the addition of the least of other goods must make it more desirable; for the addition becomes a surplus of good, and of two goods the greater is always more desirable. Thus it seems that happiness is something final and self-sufficing, and is the end of all that man does.

We need some idea what happiness is, and Aristotle here gives us his idea: Happiness is living according to rationality ("a rational principle").

But perhaps the reader thinks that though no one will dispute the statement that happiness is the best thing in the world, yet a still more precise definition of it is needed. This will best be gained, I think, by asking, What is the function of man? For as the goodness and the excellence of a piper or a sculptor, or the practiser of any art, and generally of those who have any function or business to do, lies in that function, so man's good would seem to lie in his function, if he has one. But can we suppose that, while a carpenter and a cobbler has a function and a business of his own, man has no business and no function assigned him by nature? Nay, surely as his several members, eye and hand and foot, plainly have each his own function, so we must suppose that man also has some function over and above all these.

What then is it? Life evidently he has in common even with the plants, but we want that which is peculiar to him. We must exclude, therefore, the life of mere nutrition and growth. Next to this comes the life of sense; but this too he plainly shares with horses and cattle and all kinds of animals. There remains then the life whereby he acts — the life of his rational nature, with its two sides or divisions, one rational as obeying reason, the other rational as having and exercising reason. But as this expression is ambiguous, we must be understood to mean thereby the life that consists in the exercise [not the mere possession] of the faculties; for this seems to be more properly entitled to the name.

The function of man, then, is exercise of his vital faculties [or soul] on one side in obedience to reason, and on the other side with reason. But what is called the function of a man of any profession and the function of a man who is good in that profession are, generically the same, *e.g.* of a harper and of a good harper; and this holds in all cases without exception, only that in the case of the latter his superior excellence at his work is added; for we say a harper's function is to harp, and a good harper's to harp well. Man's function then being, as we say, a kind of life — that is to say, exercise of his faculties and action of various kinds with reason — the good man's function is to do this well and beautifully [or nobly]. But the function of anything is done well when it is done in accordance with the proper excellence of that thing. If this be so the result is that the good of man is exercise of his faculties in accordance with excellence or virtue, or, if there be more than one, in accordance with the best and most complete virtue. But there must also be a full term of years for this exercise; for one swallow or one fine day does not make a spring, nor does one day or any small space of time make a blessed or happy man.

It is important to notice the structure of Aristotle's argument here, for we shall see it emerge often in philosophy as well as in our own thought. The argument is an argument on the basis of what is "natural" to man. The good for man is that which is "natural" to him, and that means, according to Aristotle, what is special or unique to him as well. Thus mere "nutrition and growth," that is, eating and keeping physically healthy, cannot in themselves be happiness (although it is necessary for happiness) because even plants, Aristotle says, have this "goal." Nor can happiness lie in simple experience, even exciting experiences, since even a cow has this as the "end" of its life. What is unique to man, Aristotle concludes, is his rationality, his ability to act on rational principles. But action according to rational principles is, as we shall see, precisely what Aristotle thinks virtue is. Thus happiness turns out to be an "activity of the soul in accordance with perfect virtue." (This is the key phrase of his work.) This "perfect virtue" is also called "excellence," and thus Aristotle's ethics is often called an ethics of self-realization, the goal of which is to make each individual as perfect as possible in all ways:

> Indeed, in addition to what we have said, a man is not good at all unless he takes pleasure in noble deeds. No one would call a man just who did not take pleasure in doing justice, nor generous who took no pleasure in acts of generosity, and so on. If this be so, the manifestations of excellence will be pleasant in themselves. But they are also both good and noble, and that in the highest degree — at least, if the good man's judgment about them is right, for this is his judgment. Happiness, then, is at once the best and noblest and pleasantest thing in the world. . . .

So far, however, it sounds as if virtue and happiness are strictly individual matters. But this is not the case. Aristotle's well-known belief that man is a social animal is as important as these other principles. Thus, the principles of reason and rationality that enter into his *Ethics* will have the interests of society as well as the individual built into them. (Aristotle even says that there is no real distinction between ethics and politics and that the proper end of ethics is politics.) Virtue, accordingly, is also a social conception, and most of the virtues Aristotle discusses, for example, justice and courage, have much to do with one's role in society. Happiness in general, therefore, has its social dimensions. For example, Aristotle argues that both respect and honor are ingredients in the good life. For Aristotle, the happy person, the virtuous person, is mainly a good citizen. It is necessary to add, however, that the only people who could qualify for Aristotle's good life were Greek citizens, which meant that women, children, slaves, and anyone who did not have the good fortune to be born Greek did not even have a chance at being happy, in Aristotle's sense.[9]

Not only does happiness have a social dimension and not only are the virtues socially defined, but the good life, according to Aristotle, must be taught to us by society. Accordingly, Aristotle talks a great deal about the need for "good education," and he goes so far as to say that if a person has not been brought up "properly," then no amount of philosophy will be able to make him either virtuous or happy. He also says that young people, because they are "inexperienced in the actions of life" and are "so ruled by their passions," should not try to learn moral

---

[9]Even in an introductory course, it is necessary to say something about Aristotle's special notion of *happiness*. It is not at all like our conception of "feeling happy." Aristotle's term *(eudaimonia)* means more like "living well," and it includes such matters as one's status in society and virtuous acts as well as good feelings. No matter how good you feel about yourself — even if you are in a state of ecstasy all of the time — you would not be happy in Aristotle's sense unless you had these other advantages and acted virtuously as well.

philosophy, which depends upon maturity and rationality. On this point, however, we will ignore Aristotle's warnings. For we have seen that growing older
and more "mature" is certainly no guarantee of wisdom, and the passions of
youth are sometimes more virtuous than the "rationality" of established
maturity.

We have already seen Aristotle's beginning: Every act has its goal (or "good"),
and ultimately there is a goal (or "chief good") towards which all human acts
aim, and that is generally called happiness **(eudaimonia).** But, Aristotle adds,
this is not much help, for people give very different accounts of what they take
to be the ingredients in happiness. Some say that it is pleasure, others say it is
wealth or honor. We have seen Aristotle's arguments against these views (p. 478)
and his conclusion that happiness must be "activity in accordance with rational
principle." And that means, virtuous activity. The key to Aristotle's ethics, then,
lies in his concept of virtue.

Aristotle distinguishes two kinds of virtues, the practical or moral virtues
(courage, generosity, and so on) and the intellectual virtues (skill at mathematics
and philosophy). Although Aristotle thinks the highest virtue is the intellectual
virtue of philosophic contemplation, most of his discussion of virtue centers on
the moral virtues. We will now take a closer look at how moral virtues are
acquired, what Aristotle means by a moral virtue, and what the moral virtues are.

> Excellence, then, being of these two kinds, intellectual and moral, intel-
> lectual excellence owes its birth and growth mainly to instruction, and so
> requires time and experience, while moral excellence is the result of habit
> or custom and has accordingly in our language received a name formed by
> a slight change from the word for custom. From this it is plain that none of
> the moral excellences or virtues is implanted in us by nature; for that which
> is by nature cannot be altered by training. For instance, a stone naturally
> tends to fall downwards, and you could not train it to rise upwards, though
> you tried to do so by throwing it up ten thousand times, nor could you train
> fire to move downwards, nor accustom anything which naturally behaves
> in one way to behave in any other way. The virtues, then, come neither
> by nature nor against nature, but nature gives the capacity for acquiring
> them, and this is developed by training.
>
> Again, where we do things by nature we get the power first, and put this
> power forth in act afterwards: as we plainly see in the case of the senses; for
> it is not by constantly seeing and hearing that we acquire those faculties,
> but, on the contrary, we had the power first and then used it, instead of
> acquiring the power by the use. But the virtues we acquire by doing the
> acts, as is the case with the arts too. We learn an art by doing that which
> we wish to do when we have learned it; we become builders by building,
> and harpers by harping. And so by doing just acts we become just, and by
> doing acts of temperance and courage we become temperate and coura-
> geous. . . .
>
> Again, both the moral virtues and the corresponding vices result from
> and are formed by the same acts; and this is the case with the arts also. It
> is by harping that good harpers and bad harpers alike are produced: and so
> with builders and the rest; by building well they will become good builders,

and bad builders by building badly. Indeed, if it were not so, they would not want anybody to teach them, but would all be born either good or bad at their trades. And it is just the same with the virtues also. It is by our conduct in our intercourse with other men that we become just or unjust, and by acting in circumstances of danger, and training ourselves to feel fear or confidence, that we become courageous or cowardly. So, too, with our animal appetites and the passion of anger; for by behaving in this way or in that on the occasions with which these passions are concerned, some become temperate and gentle, and others profligate and ill-tempered. In a word, acts of any kind produce habits or characters of the same kind. Hence we ought to make sure that our acts be of a certain kind; for the resulting character varies as they vary. It makes no small difference, therefore, whether a man be trained from his youth up in this way or in that, but a great difference, or rather all the difference.

Aristotle's point here is not just that the virtues are acquired by practice, he is also arguing that virtue is a state of character. The virtuous person wants to do virtuous acts and he does them "naturally." We sometimes think that we are moral just because we believe in moral principles. But believing isn't enough, virtuous action is required. But not even virtuous action by itself is enough to make us virtuous. We sometimes think a person is virtuous because he "forces himself" to do what he is supposed to. Not according to Aristotle. The virtuous person is one who does what he is supposed to do because he wants to, because it is built into his very character. It is even essential, according to Aristotle, that the virtuous man enjoys being virtuous:

> And, further, the life of these men is in itself pleasant. For pleasure is an affection of the soul, and each man takes pleasure in that which he is said to love, — he who loves horses in horses, he who loves sight-seeing in sight-seeing, and in the same way he who loves justice in acts of justice, and generally the lover of excellence or virtue in virtuous acts or the manifestation of excellence. And while with most men there is a perpetual conflict between the several things in which they find pleasure, since these are not naturally pleasant, those who love what is noble take pleasure in that which is naturally pleasant. For the manifestations of excellence are naturally pleasant, so that they are both pleasant to them and pleasant in themselves. Their life, then, does not need pleasure to be added to it as an appendage, but contains pleasure in itself.

Here Aristotle gives us perhaps his most famous doctrine, the idea that virtues are "means between the extremes." This is often misinterpreted, however, to read, "everything in moderation." In a way, what Aristotle teaches is very different from this; he tells us that we can't do too much of a good thing, that is, if it is a virtue. One can't be too courageous (as opposed to being rash or cowardly), or too just. What he intends by "the means between the extremes" is this:

> By the absolute mean, or mean relatively to the thing itself, I understand that which is equidistant from both extremes, and this is one and the same

for all. By the mean relatively to us I understand that which is neither too much nor too little for us; and this is not one and the same for all. For instance, if ten be too large and two too small, six is the mean relatively to the thing itself; for it exceeds one extreme by the same amount by which it is exceeded by the other extreme: and this is the mean in arithmetical proportion. But the mean relatively to us cannot be found in this way. If ten pounds of food is too much for a given man to eat, and two pounds too little, it does not follow that the trainer will order him six pounds: for that also may perhaps be too much for the man in question, or too little; too little for Milo, too much for the beginner. The same holds true in running and wrestling. And so we may say generally that a master in any art avoids what is too much and what is too little, and seeks for the mean and chooses it — not the absolute but the relative mean.

If, then, every art or science perfects its work in this way, looking to the mean and bringing its work up to this standard (so that people are wont to say of a good work that nothing could be taken from it or added to it, implying that excellence is destroyed by excess or deficiency, but secured by observing the mean; and good artists, as we say, do in fact keep their eyes fixed on this in all that they do), and if virtue, like nature, is more exact and better than any art, it follows that virtue also must aim at the mean — virtue of course meaning moral virtue or excellence; for it has to do with passions and actions, and it is these that admit of excess and deficiency and the mean. For instance, it is possible to feel fear, confidence, desire, anger, pity, and generally to be affected pleasantly and painfully, either too much or too little, in either case wrongly; but to be thus affected at the right times, and on the right occasions, and towards the right persons, and with the right object, and in the right fashion, is the mean course and the best course, and these are characteristics of virtue. And in the same way our outward acts also admit of excess and deficiency, and the mean or due amount. Virtue, then, has to deal with feelings or passions and with outward acts, in which excess is wrong and deficiency also is blamed, but the mean amount is praised and is right — both of which are characteristics of virtue. Virtue, then, is a kind of moderation inasmuch as it aims at the mean.

Again, there are many ways of going wrong (for evil is infinite in nature, to use a Pythagorean figure, while good is finite), but only one way of going right; so that the one is easy and the other hard — easy to miss the mark and hard to hit. On this account also, then, excess and deficiency are characteristic of vice, hitting the mean is characteristic of virtue.

Virtue, then, is a habit or trained faculty of choice, the characteristic of which lies in moderation or observance of the mean relatively to the persons concerned, as determined by reason, *i.e.* by the reason by which the prudent man would determine it. And it is a moderation, firstly, inasmuch as it comes in the middle or mean between two vices, one on the side of excess, the other on the side of defect; and, secondly, inasmuch as, while these vices fall short of or exceed the due measure in feeling and in action, it finds and chooses the mean, middling, or moderate amount. Regarded in its essence, therefore, or according to the definition of its nature, virtue is a moderation or middle state, but viewed in its relation to what is best and right it is the extreme of perfection.

But it is not all actions nor all passions that admit of moderation; there are some whose very names imply badness, as malevolence, shamelessness, envy, and, among acts, adultery, theft, murder. These and all other like things are blamed as being bad in themselves, and not merely in their excess or deficiency. It is impossible therefore to go right in them; they are always wrong: rightness and wrongness in such things (*e.g.* in adultery) does not depend upon whether it is the right person and occasion and manner, but the mere doing of any one of them is wrong. It would be equally absurd to look for moderation or excess or deficiency in unjust cowardly or profligate conduct; for then there would be moderation in excess or deficiency, and excess in excess, and deficiency in deficiency. The fact is that just as there can be no excess or deficiency in temperance or courage because the mean or moderate amount is, in a sense, an extreme, so in these kinds of conduct also there can be no moderation or excess or deficiency, but the acts are wrong however they be done. For, to put it generally, there cannot be moderation in excess or deficiency, nor excess or deficiency in moderation.

We see that Aristotle defines "moral virtue" as a mean both in feeling and action. Thus courage is a virtue because the courageous man feels neither too little nor too much fear. His fear is appropriate to the dangerousness of his situation. Because the courageous person feels the right amount of fear, he acts in the right way, neither plunging rashly into danger nor fleeing from it in terror. Now, finally, Aristotle gives us his examples of virtue:

Moderation in the feelings of fear and confidence is courage: of those that exceed, he that exceeds in fearlessness has no name (as often happens), but he that exceeds in confidence is foolhardy, while he that exceeds in fear, but is deficient in confidence, is cowardly. Moderation in respect of certain pleasures and also (though to a less extent) certain pains is temperance, while excess is profligacy. But defectiveness in the matter of these pleasures is hardly ever found, and so this sort of people also have as yet received no name: let us put them down as "void of sensibility." In the matter of giving and taking money, moderation is liberality, excess and deficiency are prodigality and illiberality. But both vices exceed and fall short in giving and taking in contrary ways: the prodigal exceeds in spending, but falls short in taking; while the illiberal man exceeds in taking, but falls short in spending. . . . But, besides these, there are other dispositions in the matter of money: there is a moderation which is called magnificence (for the magnificent is not the same as the liberal man: the former deals with large sums, the latter with small), and an excess which is called bad taste or vulgarity, and a deficiency which is called meanness. . . . With respect to honour and disgrace, there is a moderation which is pride, an excess which may be called vanity, and a deficiency which is humility.

But just as we said that liberality is related to magnificence, differing only in that it deals with small sums, so here there is a virtue related to high-mindedness, and differing only in that it is concerned with small instead of great honours. A man may have a due desire for honour, and also more or less than a due desire: he that carries this desire to excess is called ambitious, he that has not enough of it is called unambitious, but he that has the due amount has no name. . . . In the matter of anger also we find excess and deficiency and moderation. The characters themselves hardly have recognized names, but as the moderate man is here called gentle, we will call his character gentleness; of those who go into extremes, we may take the term wrathful for him who exceeds, with wrathfulness for the vice, and wrathless for him who is deficient, with wrathlessness for his character. . . .

In the matter of truth, then, let us call him who observes the mean a true [or truthful] person, and observance of the mean truth [or truthfulness]: pretence, when it exaggerates, may be called boasting, and the person a boaster; when it understates, let the names be irony and ironical. With regard to pleasantness in amusement, he who observes the mean may be called witty, and his character wittiness; excess may be called buffoonery, and the man a buffoon; while boorish may stand for the person who is deficient, and boorishness for his character. With regard to pleasantness in the other affairs of life, he who makes himself properly pleasant may be called friendly, and his moderation friendliness; he that exceeds may be called obsequious if he have no ulterior motive, but a flatterer if he has an eye to his own advantage; he that is deficient in this respect, and always makes himself disagreeable, may be called a quarrelsome or peevish fellow.

Moreover, in mere emotions and in our conduct with regard to them, there are ways of observing the mean; for instance, shame is not a virtue, but yet the modest man is praised. For in these matters also we speak of this man as observing the mean, of that man as going beyond it (as the shame-faced man whom the least thing makes shy), while he who is deficient in the feeling, or lacks it altogether, is called shameless; but the term modest is applied to him who observes the mean. Righteous indignation, again, hits the mean between envy and malevolence. These have to do with feelings of pleasure and pain at what happens to our neighbours. A man is called righteously indignant when he feels pain at the sight of undeserved prosperity, but your envious man goes beyond him and is pained by the sight of any one in prosperity, while the malevolent man is so far from being pained that he actually exults in the misfortunes of his neighbours.

It is worth making a short list of Aristotle's moral virtues. Many of them are our own virtues also, but some of them are far more appropriate to an aristocratic, warrior society than they are to our own. In order to illustrate Aristotle's idea that virtues are the means between the extremes, I have included "the extremes" in parentheses for contrast:

Courage, particularly courage in battle (extremes: cowardice, rashness). What motivates courage, Aristotle tells us, is a sense of honor, not fear of punishment nor desire for reward, nor merely a sense of duty. The courageous man is afraid, he adds, because without fear there would be no courage. The man who feels no fear in the face of danger is rather rash.
Temperance, particularly concerning bodily pleasures, such as sex, food, and drinking (extremes: self-indulgence or piggishness, insensitivity). Notice that Aristotle does not say, along with many modern moralists, that

pleasures are either "bad" or unimportant; in fact, he attacks the man who does not enjoy sex, food, and drinking as much as he attacks the man who overindulges himself. He says that such people "are not even human."

Liberality, we would say, charity (extremes: prodigality or waste, meanness or stinginess). It is worth noting that Aristotle ridicules the man who gives more than he can afford to charity as much as he chastizes the man who will not give at all.

Magnificence, in other words, how extravagantly you live (extremes: vulgarity, miserliness). Aristotle says that one ought to live "like an artist" and spend lavishly. (There is little of the ascetic in Aristotle.)

Pride (extremes: humility, vanity). It is worth noting that pride is one of the seven deadly sins in Christian morality while humility is a virtue. In Aristotle's ethics, this is reversed.

Good temper (extremes: irascibility or bad tempered, too easygoing). It is important to get angry, according to Aristotle, about the right things, but not too much (which "makes a person impossible to live with").

Friendliness (extremes: obsequious, churlish). Friendship, for Aristotle, is one of the most important ingredients in the good life, and being friendly, therefore, is an extremely important virtue. But Aristotle does not say that we should be friendly to everyone; the person who is indiscriminately friendly to everyone is not worth being a friend at all.

Truthfulness (extremes: lying, boasting). Especially telling the truth about oneself.

Wittiness (extremes: buffoonery, boorishness). We think of wittiness as a personal asset, but rarely as a virtue. Aristotle thinks that people who are incapable of telling a joke or who tell bad jokes are actually inferior. Fun is an important ingredient in Greek virtuousness.

Shame, Aristotle calls this a "quasi-virtue" (extremes: shamelessness, ————). We all make mistakes and it is a sign of virtue, according to Aristotle, that the good man feels shame when he does them. Shamelessness is a sign of wickedness. Aristotle does not even talk of the other extreme, which he did not consider a problem. (We certainly would. We call it excessive guilt.)

Justice, the cardinal virtue of the Greeks. The need for lawful and fair (which does not mean equal) treatment of other men. (The sense in which justice is a mean between extremes is too complex to discuss here. Aristotle spends a full chapter explaining it.)

Finally, Aristotle gives us his view of the good life for man; it is the life of activity in accordance with virtue, but it is also, ideally, a life of intellectual activity, or what he calls "the life of contemplation." In other words, the happiest person is the philosopher:

We said that happiness is not a habit or trained faculty. If it were, it would be within the reach of a man who slept all his days and lived the life of a vegetable, or of a man who met with the greatest misfortunes. As we cannot accept this conclusion, we must place happiness in some exercise of faculty, as we said before. But as the exercises of faculty are sometimes necessary (*i.e.* desirable for the sake of something else), sometimes desirable in themselves, it is evident that happiness must be placed among those that are desirable in themselves, and not among those that are desirable for the sake of something else: for happiness lacks nothing; it is sufficient in itself.

Now, the exercise of faculty is desirable in itself when nothing is expected from it beyond itself. Of this nature are held to be (1) the manifestations of excellence; for to do what is noble and excellent must be counted desirable for itself: and (2) those amusements which please us; for they are not chosen for the sake of anything else,—indeed, men are more apt to be injured than to be benefited by them, through neglect of their health and fortunes. Now, most of those whom men call happy have recourse to pastimes of this sort. And on this account those who show a ready wit in such pastimes find favour with tyrants; for they make themselves pleasant in that which the tyrant wants, and what he wants is pastime. These amusements, then, are generally thought to be elements of happiness, because princes employ their leisure in them. But such persons, we may venture to say, are no criterion. For princely rank does not imply the possession of virtue or of reason, which are the sources of all excellent exercise of faculty. And if these men, never having tasted pure and refined pleasure, have recourse to the pleasures of the body, we should not on that account think these more desirable; for children also fancy that the things which they value are better than anything else. It is only natural, then, that as children differ from men in their estimate of what is valuable, so bad men should differ from good.

As we have often said, therefore, that is truly valuable and pleasant which is so to the perfect man. Now, the exercise of those trained faculties which are proper to him is what each man finds most desirable; what the perfect man finds most desirable, therefore, is the exercise of virtue. Happiness, therefore, does not consist in amusement; and indeed it is absurd to suppose that the end is amusement, and that we toil and moil all our life long for the sake of amusing ourselves. We may say that we choose everything for the sake of something else, excepting only happiness; for it is the end. But to be serious and to labour for the sake of amusement seems silly and utterly childish; while to amuse ourselves in order that we may be serious, as Anacharsis says, seems to be right; for amusement is a sort of recreation, and we need recreation because we are unable to work continuously. Recreation, then, cannot be the end; for it is taken as a means to the exercise of our faculties.

Again, the happy life is thought to be that which exhibits virtue; and such a life must be serious and cannot consist in amusement. Again, it is held that things of serious importance are better than laughable and amusing things, and that the better the organ or the man, the more important is the function; but we have already said that the function or exercise of that which is better is higher and more conducive to happiness. Again, the enjoyment of bodily pleasures is within the reach of anybody, of a slave no less than the best of men; but no one supposes that a slave can participate in happiness, seeing that he cannot participate in the proper life of man. For indeed happiness does not consist in pastimes of this sort, but in the exercise of virtue, as we have already said.

7. But if happiness be the exercise of virtue, it is reasonable to suppose that it will be the exercise of the highest virtue; and that will be the virtue or excellence of the best part of us. Now, that part or faculty — call it reason or what you will — which seems naturally to rule and take the lead, and to apprehend things noble and divine — whether it be itself divine, or only the divinest part of us — is the faculty the exercise of which, in its proper excellence, will be perfect happiness. . . . this consists in speculation or theorizing.

This conclusion would seem to agree both with what we have said above, and with known truths. This exercise of faculty must be the highest possible; for the reason is the highest of our faculties and of all knowable things those that reason deals with are the highest. Again, it is the most continuous; for speculation can be carried on more continuously than any kind of action whatsoever. We think too that pleasure ought to be one of the ingredients of happiness; but of all virtuous exercises it is allowed that the pleasantest is the exercise of wisdom. At least philosophy is thought to have pleasures that are admirable in purity and steadfastness; and it is reasonable to suppose that the time passes more pleasantly with those who possess, than with those who are seeking knowledge. Again, what is called self-sufficiency will be most of all found in the speculative life. The necessaries of life, indeed, are needed by the wise man as well as by the just man and the rest; but, when these have been provided in due quantity, the just man further needs persons towards whom, and along with whom, he may act justly; and so does the temperate and the courageous man and the rest; while the wise man is able to speculate even by himself, and the wiser he is the more is he able to do this. He could speculate better, we may confess, if he had others to help him, but nevertheless he is more self-sufficient than anybody else. Again, it would seem that this life alone is desired solely for its own sake; for it yields no result beyond the contemplation, but from the practical activities we get something more or less besides action.

. . . it follows that the exercise of reason will be the complete happiness of man, *i.e.* when a complete term of days is added; for nothing incomplete can be admitted into our idea of happiness. But a life which realized this idea would be something more than human; for it would not be the expression of man's nature, but of some divine element in that nature — the exercise of which is as far superior to the exercise of the other kind of virtue, as this divine element is superior to our compound human nature. If then reason be divine as compared with man, the life which consists in the exercise of reason will also be divine in comparison with human life. Nevertheless, instead of listening to those who advise us as men and mortals not to lift our thoughts above what is human and mortal, we ought rather, as far as possible, to put off our mortality and make every effort to live in the exercise of the highest of our faculties; for though it be but a small part of us, yet in power and value it far surpasses all the rest. And indeed this part would even seem to constitute our true self, since it is the sovereign and the better part. It would be strange, then, if a man were to prefer the life of something else to the life of his true self. Again, we may apply here what we said above — for every being that is best and pleasantest which is naturally proper to it. Since, then, it is the reason that in the truest sense is the man, the life that consists in the exercise of the reason is the best and pleasantest for man — and therefore the happiest.

But it must not be thought that Aristotle's ideal philosopher does nothing but contemplate. He may also enjoy pleasure, wealth, honor, success, and power. As a man among men, he is also virtuous and chooses to act virtuously like all good men. But in addition, he has an understanding and an appreciation of reason that makes him "dearest to the Gods and presumably the happiest among men." This is surely a flattering portrait of the place of the philosopher! But if we ignore this final self-congratulation, we can see in Aristotle a powerful conception of morality, with its emphasis on virtue, excellence, and a kind of heroism (whether intellectual or moral) that is in some ways very different from our own conception of morality and the good life.

MORALITY AND SENTIMENT: HUME AND ROUSSEAU

Morality for Aristotle depended upon rules embedded and learned in a particular society, an elite society of the privileged males of the Greek aristocracy. Modern conceptions of morality, on the other hand, are usually thought to be universal, that is, not restricted to a particular society or a particular elite. It applies to women, men, poor people, rich people, adults, and children, even if they are only a few years old. At the same time, however, most modern conceptions of morality minimize Aristotle's emphasis on society and upbringing, preferring to place morals on some individual basis. In Kant's moral philosophy, we shall see that the key to morality is *individual autonomy*, the idea that every person can find for himself or herself, just through the use of reason, what acts are moral and what acts are not. Before Kant, the ruling conception of morality was based upon a conception of personal feelings of a special moral kind, a "natural desire" to help one's fellow man. (As in Aristotle, this philosophy insisted that morality had to be viewed as a part of nature.)

It should be clear how this conception of morality has a distinct advantage in reconciling personal interests and moral principles. Since strong moral feelings are a kind of personal interest, one can satisfy his personal feelings and the demands of morality at the same time. (Again, this lies at the heart of Bishop Butler's arguments.) There are, of course, other personal feelings — jealousy, greed, and envy — that act against these moral feelings. But at least some of our feelings are satisfied by moral action. And according to these philosophers, such moral feelings can be found in virtually all of us.

The two most famous philosophers to argue this position are David Hume, whom you already know quite well from earlier chapters, and the French philosopher Jean-Jacques Rousseau, whose political philosophy we shall study in the final chapter. The key to both of their philosophies is the notion of **sentiment** ("feeling") and the notion of **sympathy** ("fellow feeling" or feeling pity for other people and taking their interests into account as well as our own). Hume says

> The hypothesis which we embrace is plain. It maintains that morality is determined by sentiment. It defines virtue to be *whatever mental action or quality gives to a spectator the pleasing sentiment of approbation;* and vice the contrary.[10]

The central concern in Hume's moral philosophy distinguishes those who defend morality as a function of reason from those who say that it is rather a matter of sentiment and passion. Elsewhere Hume gives us his very strong opinion, that "reason is, and ought to be, the slave of the passions." Here is his argument:

on "Reason as Slave of the Passions," by David Hume

There has been a controversy started of late, much better worth examination, concerning the general foundation of *morals;* whether they be derived from *reason* or from *sentiment;* whether we attain the knowledge of them by a chain of argument and induction or by an immediate feeling and finer internal sense; whether, like all sound judgment of truth and falsehood, they should be the same to every rational, intelligent being, or whether, like the perception of beauty and deformity, they be founded entirely on the particular fabric and constitution of the human species.

The ancient philosophers, though they often affirm that virtue is nothing but conformity to reason, yet, in general, seem to consider morals as deriving their existence from taste and sentiment. On the other hand, our modern inquirers, though they also talk much of the beauty of virtue and deformity of vice, yet have commonly endeavored to account for these distinctions by metaphysical reasonings and by deductions from the most abstract principles of the understanding. Such confusion reigned in these subjects that an opposition of the greatest consequence could prevail between one system and another, and even in the parts of almost each individual system, and yet nobody, till very lately, was ever sensible of it.

. . . . . .

It must be acknowledged that both sides of the question are susceptible of specious arguments. Moral distinctions, it may be said, are discernible by pure *reason;* else, whence the many disputes that reign in common life, as well as in philosophy with regard to this subject, the long chain of proofs often produced on both sides, the examples cited, the authorities appealed to, the analogies employed, the fallacies detected, the inferences drawn, and

---

[10]David Hume, *Inquiry Concerning the Principles of Morals* (La Salle, Ill.: Open Court, 1912).

the several conclusions adjusted to their proper principles? Truth is disputable, not taste: what exists in the nature of things is the standard of our judgment; what each man feels within himself is the standard of sentiment. Propositions in geometry may be proved, systems in physics may be controverted, but the harmony of verse, the tenderness of passion, the brilliancy of wit must give immediate pleasure. No man reasons concerning another's beauty, but frequently concerning the justice or injustice of his actions. In every criminal trial, the first object of the prisoner is to disprove the facts alleged and deny the actions imputed to him; the second, to prove that, even if these actions were real, they might be justified as innocent and lawful. It is confessedly by deductions of the understanding that the first point is ascertained; how can we suppose a different faculty of the mind is employed in fixing the other?

On the other hand, those who would resolve all moral determinations into *sentiments* may endeavor to show that it is impossible for reason ever to draw conclusions of this nature. To virtue, say they, it belongs to be *amiable* and vice *odious*. This forms their very nature or essence. But can reason or argumentation distribute these different epithets to any subjects and pronounce beforehand that this must produce love and that hatred? Or what other reason can we ever assign for these affections but the original fabric and formation of the human mind, which is naturally adapted to receive them?

The end of all moral speculations is to teach us our duty, and, by proper representations of the deformity of vice and beauty of virtue, beget correspondent habits and engage us to avoid the one and embrace the other. But is this ever to be expected from inferences and conclusions of the understanding, which of themselves have no hold of the affections or set in motion the active powers of men? They discover truths. But where the truths which they discover are indifferent and beget no desire or aversion, they can have no influence on conduct and behavior. What is honorable, what is fair, what is becoming, what is noble, what is generous takes possession of the heart and animates us to embrace and maintain it. What is intelligible, what is evident, what is probable, what is true procures only the cool assent of the understanding and, gratifying a speculative curiosity, puts an end to our researches.

. . . . .

Extinguish all the warm feelings and prepossessions in favor of virtue, and all disgust or aversion to vice; render men totally indifferent toward these distinctions, and morality is no longer a practical study nor has any tendency to regulate our lives and actions.

These arguments on each side (and many more might be produced) are so plausible that I am apt to suspect they may, the one as well as the other, be solid and satisfactory and that *reason* and *sentiment* concur in almost all moral determinations and conclusions. The final sentence, it is probable, which pronounces characters and actions amiable or odious, praiseworthy or blamable; that which stamps on them the mark of honor or infamy, approbation or censure; that which renders morality an active principle and constitutes virtue our happiness, and vice our misery — it is probable, I say, that this final sentence depends on some internal sense or feeling which nature has made universal in the whole species.

It is worth noting here that Hume's moral philosophy, like his philosophy of knowledge, is strictly empiricist:

> ... Men are now cured of their passion for hypotheses and systems in natural philosophy and will hearken to no arguments but those which are derived from experience. It is full time they should attempt a like reformation in all moral disquisitions and reject every system of ethics, however subtle or ingenious, which is not founded on fact and observation.

Reason, Hume argues, may be of use in deciding how we can get what we want, but it is incapable of ever telling us what we ultimately want. Notice the familiar argument against an infinite regress; notice also Hume's sharp distinction between reason (which is concerned with knowledge, truth, and falsehood) and taste or sentiment (that judges values, which ultimately depend upon pleasure and pain):

> ... It appears evident that the ultimate ends of human actions can never, in any case, be accounted for by *reason*, but recommend themselves entirely to the sentiments and affections of mankind without any dependence on the intellectual faculties. Ask a man *why he uses exercise*; he will answer, *because he desires to keep his health*. If you then inquire *why he desires health*, he will readily reply, *because sickness is painful*. If you push your inquiries further and desire a reason *why he hates pain*, it is impossible he can ever give any. This is an ultimate end and is never referred to any other object.
> Perhaps to your second question, *why he desires health*, he may also reply that *it is necessary for the exercise of his calling*. If you ask *why he is anxious on that head*, he will answer, *because he desires to get money*. If you demand, *why? It is the instrument of pleasure*, says he. And beyond this, it is an absurdity to ask for a reason. It is impossible there can be a progress *in infinitum* and that one thing can always be a reason why another is desired. Something must be desirable on its own account and because of its immediate accord or agreement with human sentiment and affection.
> Now, as virtue is an end and is desirable on its own account, without fee or reward, merely for the immediate satisfaction which it conveys, it is requisite that there should be some sentiment which it touches — some internal taste or feeling, or whatever you please to call it, which distinguishes moral good and evil and which embraces the one and rejects the other.
> Thus, the distinct boundaries and offices of *reason* and of *taste* are easily ascertained. The former conveys the knowledge of truth and falsehood; the latter gives the sentiment of beauty and deformity, vice and virtue. The one discovers objects as they really stand in nature, without addition or diminution; the other has a productive faculty; and gliding or straining all natural objects with the colors borrowed from internal sentiment, raises, in a manner, a new creation. Reason, being cool and disengaged, is no motive to action and directs only the impulse received from appetite or inclination by showing us the means of attaining happiness or avoiding misery. Taste, as it gives pleasure or pain, and thereby constitutes happiness or misery,

becomes a motive to action and is the first spring or impulse to desire and volition. From circumstances and relations, known or supposed, the former leads us to the discovery of the concealed and unknown. After all circumstances and relations are laid before us, the latter makes us feel from the whole a new sentiment of blame or approbation.[11]

Elsewhere Hume argues a razor-sharp distinction between facts and values. He argues with characteristic conciseness that "it is impossible to derive an 'ought' from an 'is,'" that is, any notions of value or what we *ought to do* cannot be derived from any statements of fact. One can know, as a matter of fact, that pushing this button will kill a thousand innocent children, but from that fact alone, it does not follow that I ought not push the button. What I ought to do — or ought not to do — depends on something that is not a matter of fact or reason at all, my moral feelings or sentiments. Without these sentiments, no action is either moral or immoral, praiseworthy or blameworthy, or of any value whatever. Accordingly, in one of his most shocking statements Hume says that it would not be irrational for him to prefer the death of half the world to the pricking of his little finger. This is not to say that he would prefer this, but there is *nothing in reason* to forbid it. Values are a matter of sentiment, not of reason.

A similar theory of sentiment is defended by Jean-Jacques Rousseau. Although he is often characterized as the first great "Romantic," it is worth noting that Rousseau is not nearly so antagonistic to reason as his reputation suggests. Sentiment, by his theory, is tied to a kind of "natural reason." And the key to his theory, therefore, is the concept of conscience, a powerful kind of moral feeling that has its own kind of divine reason. As in Hume, it is only detached reason that offers us no guidance. Notice that he too reconciles "self-love" and "moral goodness" as ultimately having the same goals:

from *Emile,*
by Jean-Jacques Rousseau

Let us lay it down as an incontrovertible rule that the first impulses of nature are always right; there is no original sin in the human heart, the how and why of the entrance of every vice can be traced. The only natural passion is self-love or selfishness taken in a wider sense. This selfishness is good in itself and in relation to ourselves; and as the child has no necessary relations to other people he is naturally indifferent to them; his self-love only becomes good or bad by the use made of it and the relations established by its means. Until the time is ripe for the appearance of reason, that guide of selfishness, the main thing is that the child shall do nothing because you are watching him or listening to him; in a word, nothing because of other people, but only what nature asks of him; then he will never do wrong.

I do not mean to say that he will never do any mischief, never hurt himself, never break a costly ornament if you leave it within his reach. He might do much damage without doing wrong, since wrong-doing depends

[11]Hume, *Inquiry Concerning the Principles of Morals.*

on the harmful intention which will never be his. If once he meant to do harm, his whole education would be ruined; he would be almost hopelessly bad. . . .

The morality of our actions consists entirely in the judgments we ourselves form with regard to them. If good is good, it must be good in the depth of our heart as well as in our actions; and the first reward of justice is the consciousness that we are acting justly. If moral goodness is in accordance with our nature, man can only be healthy in mind and body when he is good. If it is not so, and if man is by nature evil, he cannot cease to be evil without corrupting his nature, and goodness in him is a crime against nature. If he is made to do harm to his fellow-creatures, as the wolf is made to devour his prey, a humane man would be as depraved a creature as a pitiful wolf; and virtue alone would cause remorse.

My young friend, let us look within, let us set aside all personal prejudices and see whither our inclinations lead us. Do we take more pleasure in the sight of the sufferings of others or their joys? Is it pleasanter to do a kind action or an unkind action, and which leaves the more delightful memory behind it? Why do you enjoy the theatre? Do you delight in the crimes you behold? Do you weep over the punishment which overtakes the criminal? They say we are indifferent to everything but self-interest; yet we find our consolation in our sufferings in the charms of friendship and humanity, and even in our pleasures we should be too lonely and miserable if we had no one to share them with us. If there is no such thing as morality in man's heart, what is the source of his rapturous admiration of noble deeds, his passionate devotion to great men? What connection is there between self-interest and this enthusiasm for virtue?

· · · · ·

Take from our hearts this love of what is noble and you rob us of the joy of life. The mean-spirited man in whom these delicious feelings have been stifled among vile passions, who by thinking of no one but himself comes at last to love no one but himself, this man feels no raptures, his cold heart no longer throbs with joy, and his eyes no longer fill with the sweet tears of sympathy, he delights in nothing; the wretch has neither life nor feeling, he is already dead.

There are many bad men in this world, but there are few of these dead souls, alive only to self-interest, and insensible to all that is right and good. We only delight in injustice so long as it is to our own advantage; in every other case we wish the innocent to be protected. If we see some act of violence or injustice in town or country, our hearts are at once stirred to their depths by an instinctive anger and wrath, which bids us go to the help of the oppressed; but we are restrained by a stronger duty, and the law deprives us of our right to protect the innocent. On the other hand, if some deed of mercy or generosity meets our eye, what reverence and love does it inspire! Do we not say to ourselves, "I should like to have done that myself"? What does it matter to us that two thousand years ago a man was just or unjust? and yet we take the same interest in ancient history as if it happened yesterday. What are the crimes of Cataline to me? I shall not be his victim. Why then have I the same horror of his crimes as if he were living now? We do not hate the wicked merely because of the harm they do to our-

selves, but because they are wicked. Not only do we wish to be happy ourselves, we wish others to be happy too, and if this happiness does not interfere with our own happiness, it increases it. In conclusion, whether we will
or not, we pity the unfortunate; when we see their suffering we suffer too.
Even the most depraved are not wholly without this instinct, and it often
leads them to self-contradiction. The highwayman who robs the traveller,
clothes the nakedness of the poor; the fiercest murderer supports a fainting
man.

Men speak of the voice of remorse, the secret punishment of hidden
crimes, by which such are often brought to light. Alas! who does not know
its unwelcome voice? We speak from experience, and we would gladly stifle
this imperious feeling which causes us such agony. Let us obey the call of
nature; we shall see that her yoke is easy and that when we give heed to
her voice we find a joy in the answer of a good conscience. The wicked
fears and flees from her; he delights to escape from himself; his anxious
eyes look around him for some object of diversion; without bitter satire and
rude mockery he would always be sorrowful; the scornful laugh is his one
pleasure. Not so the just man, who finds his peace within himself; there is
joy not malice in his laughter, a joy which springs from his own heart; he
is as cheerful alone as in company, his satisfaction does not depend on those
who approach him; it includes them.

. . . . . .

It is no part of my scheme to enter at present into metaphysical discussions which neither you nor I can understand, discussions which really lead
nowhere. I have told you already that I do not wish to philosophise with
you, but to help you to consult your own heart. If all the philosophers in
the world should prove that I am wrong, and you feel that I am right, that
is all I ask.

For this purpose it is enough to lead you to distinguish between our
acquired ideas and our natural feelings; for feeling precedes knowledge; and
since we do not learn to seek what is good for us and avoid what is bad for
us, but get this desire from nature, in the same way the love of good and
the hatred of evil are as natural to us as our self-love. The decrees of conscience are not judgments but feelings. Although all our ideas come from
without, the feelings by which they are weighed are within us, and it is by
these feelings alone that we perceive fitness or unfitness of things in relation
to ourselves, which leads us to seek or shun these things.

To exist is to feel; our feeling is undoubtedly earlier than our intelligence, and we had feelings before we had ideas. Whatever may be the cause
of our being, it has provided for our preservation by giving us feelings suited
to our nature; and no one can deny that these at least are innate. These
feelings, so far as the individual is concerned, are self-love, fear, pain, the
dread of death, the desire for comfort. Again, if, as it is impossible to doubt,
man is by nature sociable, or at least fitted to become sociable, he can only
be so by means of other innate feelings, relative to his kind; for if only
physical well-being were considered, men would certainly be scattered
rather than brought together. But the motive power of conscience is derived
from the moral system formed through this twofold relation to himself and
to his fellow-men. To know good is not to love it; this knowledge is not

innate in man; but as soon as his reason leads him to perceive it, his conscience impels him to love it; it is this feeling which is innate.

So I do not think, my young friend, that it is impossible to explain the immediate force of conscience as a result of our own nature, independent of reason itself. And even should it be impossible, it is unnecessary; for those who deny this principle, admitted and received by everybody else in the world, do not prove that there is no such thing; they are content to affirm, and when we affirm its existence we have quite as good grounds as they, while we have moreover the witness within us, the voice of conscience, which speaks on its own behalf. If the first beams of judgment dazzle us and confuse the objects we behold, let us wait till our feeble sight grows clear and strong, and in the light of reason we shall soon. behold these very objects as nature has already showed them to us. Or rather let us be simpler and less pretentious; let us be content with the first feelings we experience in ourselves, since science always brings us back to these, unless it has led us astray.

Conscience! Conscience! Divine instinct, immortal voice from heaven; sure guide for a creature ignorant and finite indeed; yet intelligent and free; infallible judge of good and evil, making man like to God! In thee consists the excellence of man's nature and the morality of his actions; apart from thee, I find nothing in myself to raise me above the beasts—nothing but the sad privilege of wandering from one error to another, by the help of an unbridled understanding and a reason which knows no principle.[12]

But, as we pointed out before, there is a problem with this notion of conscience and with all appeals of morality to personal feeling. What if different people disagree? Whose conscience, or whose feelings should we accept? And even if we find ourselves in agreement, how do we know that our consciences or feelings are right? It is with these questions in mind that we turn to the moral philosophy of Kant.

MORALITY AND REASON: KANT

Aristotle, Hume, and Rousseau all give feeling an important place in their conceptions of morality. For Aristotle, the virtuous man wants to act virtuously and enjoys doing so. For Hume and Rousseau, sentiment defines morality. On all such accounts, our concept of *duty*—what we ought to do—is derivative, at least in part, from such feelings and from our upbringing. But what if feelings disagree? What if people are brought up to value different things? What are we to say of a person who is brought up by criminals to value what is wicked and to enjoy cruelty? And what are we to say, most importantly of all, in those familiar cases in which a person's feelings all draw him or her towards personal interests but duty calls in the opposite direction? This is the problem that Kant considered, and

[12]Jean-Jacques Rousseau, *Emile*, trans. Barbara Foxley (New York: E. P. Dutton, 1968).

because of it, he rejected all attempts to base morality on feelings of any kind. Morality, he argued, must be based solely on reason and reason alone. Its central concept is the concept of **duty,** and so morality is a matter of **deontology** (from the Greek word *dein,* or "duty").

Hume had restricted the notion of reason to concern with knowledge, truth, and falsity; Kant replies that reason also has a practical side, one that is capable of telling us what to do as well as how to do it. Rousseau had said that morality must be universal, common to all men, even in a presocietal "state of nature"; Kant (who very much admired Rousseau) agrees but says that the nature of this universality cannot lie in people's feelings, which may vary from person to person and society to society, but only in reason, which by its very nature must be universal. And Aristotle had insisted that morality must be taught within society and that morals were very much a matter of public opinion and practices; but unlike most modern philosophers, Kant insisted on the independence of morality from society. What is most important, he argues, is that morality be autonomous, a function of individual reason, such that every rational person is capable of finding out what is right and what is wrong for himself or herself. But where Hume and Rousseau had looked for morality in individual feeling, Kant again insists that it must be found through an examination of reason, nothing else. This is the key to Kant's moral philosophy: Morality consists solely of rational principles.

Since morality is based on reason, according to Kant, it does not depend on particular societies or particular circumstances; it does not depend on individual feelings or desires (Kant summarizes all such personal feelings, desires, ambitions, impulses, and emotions as **inclinations**). The purpose of moral philosophy, therefore, is to examine our ability to reason practically and to determine from this examination the fundamental principles that lie at the basis of every morality, for every person, and in every society. In direct contrast to Aristotle, Kant begins by saying that what is ultimately good is none of those benefits and virtues that make up Greek happiness, but rather what he calls a good will. And a good will, in turn, is the will that exercises pure practical reason.

from *Fundamental Principles of the Metaphysics of Morals,* by Immanuel Kant

Nothing can possibly be conceived in the world, or even out of it, which can be called good without qualification, except a *good will.* Intelligence, wit, judgment, and other *talents* of the mind, however they may be named, or courage, resolution, perseverance, as qualities of temperament, are undoubtedly good and desirable in many respects; but these gifts of nature may also become extremely bad and mischievous if the will which is to make use of them, and which, therefore, constitutes what is called *character,* is not good. It is the same with the *gifts of fortune.* Power, riches, honor, even health, and the general well-being and contentment with one's condition which is called *happiness,* inspire pride, and often presumption, if there is not a good will to correct the influence of these on the mind, and with this also to rectify the whole principle of acting, and adapt it to its end. The sight of a being who is not adorned with a single feature of a pure and good will, enjoying unbroken prosperity, can never give pleasure to an impartial rational spectator. Thus a good will appears to constitute the indispensable condition even of being worthy of happiness.[13]

The argument behind this opening move is this: It makes no sense to blame or praise a person for his or her character or abilities or the consequences of his or her actions. There are many factors that contribute to a person's control. Whether or not a person is wealthy, intelligent, courageous, witty, and so on (Aristotle's virtues) is often due to his or her upbringing and heredity rather than any personal choice. But what we *will*, that is, what we try to do, is wholly within our control. Therefore it is the only thing that is ultimately worth moral consideration. Notice that Kant is concerned with questions of morality and not questions of the good life in general. What makes us happy is not particularly his concern. He is only concerned with what makes a person morally worthy of being happy.

> A good will is good not because of what it performs or effects, not by its aptness for the attainment of some proposed end, but simply by virtue of the volition — that is, it is good in itself, and considered by itself is to be esteemed much higher than all that can be brought about by it in favor of any inclination, nay, even of the sum-total of all inclinations. Even if it should happen that, owing to special disfavor of fortune, or the niggardly provision of a stepmotherly nature, this will should wholly lack power to accomplish its purpose, if with its greatest efforts it should yet achieve nothing, and there should remain only the good will (not, to be sure, a mere wish, but the summoning of all means in our power), then, like a jewel, it would still shine by its own light, as a thing which has its whole value in itself. Its usefulness or fruitlessness can neither add to nor take away anything from this value. It would be, as it were, only the setting to enable us to handle it the more conveniently in common commerce, or to attract to it the attention of those who are not yet connoisseurs, but not to recommend it to true connoisseurs, or to determine its value.
>
> There is, however, something so strange in this idea of the absolute value of the mere will, in which no account is taken of its utility, that notwithstanding the thorough assent of even common reason to the idea, yet a suspicion must arise that it may perhaps really be the product of mere high-flown fancy, and that we may have misunderstood the purpose of nature in assigning reason as the governor of our will. Therefore we will examine this idea from this point of view.

Kant's argument here is surprisingly similar to Aristotle's argument in his *Ethics*. You remember that Aristotle argues that the good for man must be found in

---

[13]Immanuel Kant, *Fundamental Principles of the Metaphysics of Morals*, trans. T. K. Abbot (New York: Longmans, Green, 1898). All subsequent quotations from Kant are from this edition.

man's nature, in that which is unique to him. The assumption is that since man is singularly endowed with reason, then reason must have a special significance in human life. Kant's argument also begins with the observation that man, unlike other creatures, is capable of reasoning. But why should he have such a capacity? Not in order to make him happy, Kant argues, because any number of instincts would have served that end more effectively. (Remember that Kant is presupposing God as Creator here, so he believes, like Leibniz, that everything exists for some sufficient reason.)

> ... our existence has a different and far nobler end, for which and not for happiness, reason is properly intended, and which must, therefore, be regarded as the supreme condition to which the private ends of man must, for the most part, be postponed.

This "far nobler end" and "supreme condition" is what Kant calls *duty*. "The notion of duty," he tells us, "includes that of a good will," but a good will that subjects itself to rational principles. Those rational principles are moral laws, and it is action in accordance with such laws that alone makes a man good.

It is important, however, to make a distinction, which Aristotle makes too: It is one thing to do what duty requires for some personal interest, and it is something else to do one's duty just because it is one's duty. For example, a grocer might refuse to cheat his customers (which is his duty) because it would be bad for business; then he is not acting for the sake of duty, but for personal interests. But he may refuse to cheat his customers just because he knows that he ought not to. This does count as doing his duty and thereby makes him morally worthy.

> I omit here all actions which are already recognized as inconsistent with duty, although they may be useful for this or that purpose, for with these the question whether they are done *from duty* cannot arise at all, since they even conflict with it. I also set aside those actions which really conform to duty, but to which men have **no** direct *inclination*, performing them because they are impelled thereto by some other inclination. For in this case we can readily distinguish whether the action which agrees with duty is done *from duty* or from a selfish view. It is much harder to make this distinction when the action accords with duty, and the subject has besides a *direct* inclination to it. For example, it is always a matter of duty that a dealer should not overcharge an inexperienced purchaser; and wherever there is much commerce the prudent tradesman does not overcharge, but keeps a fixed price for everyone, so that a child buys of him as well as any other. Men are thus *honestly* served; but this is not enough to make us believe that the tradesman has so acted from duty and from principles of honesty; his own advantage required it; it is out of the question in this case to suppose that he might besides have a direct inclination in favor of the buyers, so that, as it were, from love he should give no advantage to one over another. Accordingly the action was done neither from duty nor from direct inclination, but merely with a selfish view.
>
> On the other hand, it is a duty to maintain one's life; and, in addition,

everyone has also a direct inclination to do so. But on this account the often anxious care which most men take for it has no intrinsic worth, and their maxim has no moral import. They preserve their life *as duty requires*, no doubt, but not *because duty requires*. On the other hand, if adversity and hopeless sorrow have completely taken away the relish for life, if the unfortunate one, strong in mind, indignant at his fate rather than desponding or dejected, wishes for death, and yet preserves his life without loving it—not from inclination or fear, but from duty—then his maxim has a moral worth.

To be beneficent when we can is a duty; and besides this, there are many minds so sympathetically constituted that, without any other motive of vanity or self-interest, they find a pleasure in spreading joy around them, and can take delight in the satisfaction of others so far as it is their own work. But I maintain that in such a case an action of this kind, however proper, however amiable it may be, has nevertheless no true moral worth, but is on a level with other inclinations, for example, the inclination to honor; which, if it is happily directed to that which is in fact of public utility and accordant with duty, and consequently honorable, deserves praise and encouragement, but not esteem. For the maxim lacks the moral import, namely, that such actions be done *from duty*, not from inclination. Put the case that the mind of that philanthropist was clouded by sorrow of his own extinguishing all sympathy with the lot of others, and that while he still has the power to benefit others in distress, he is not touched by their trouble because he is absorbed with his own; and now suppose that he tears himself out of this dead insensibility and performs the action without any inclination to it, but simply from duty, then first has his action its genuine moral worth. Further still, if nature has put little sympathy in the heart of this or that man, if he, supposed to be an upright man, is by temperament cold and indifferent to the sufferings of others, perhaps because in respect of his own he is provided with the special gift of patience and fortitude, and supposes, or even requires, that others should have the same—and such a man would certainly not be the meanest product of nature—but if nature had not specially framed him for a philanthropist, would he not still find in himself a source from whence to give himself a far higher worth than that of a good-natured temperament could be? Unquestionably. It is just in this that the moral worth of the character is brought out which is incomparably the highest of all, namely, that he is beneficent, not from inclination, but from duty.

In a curious two short paragraphs, Kant tells us that we have a duty to make ourselves happy, not because we want to be happy (wants are never duties) but because it is necessary for us to do our other duties. Then, with reference to the Bible, Kant makes a famous (or infamous) distinction between two kinds of love, practical love, which is commanded as a duty, and pathological love, in other words, what we would call the *emotion* of love.

To secure one's own happiness is a duty, at least indirectly; for discontent with one's condition, under a pressure of many anxieties and amidst unsatisfied wants, might easily become a great *temptation to transgression of duty*. But here again, without looking to duty, all men have already the strongest and most intimate inclination to happiness, because it is just in this idea that all inclinations are combined in one total. But the precept of happiness is often of such a sort that it greatly interferes with some inclinations, and yet a man cannot form any definite and certain conception of the sum of satisfaction of all of them which is called happiness. It is not then to be wondered at that a single inclination, definite both as to what it promises and as to the time within which it can be gratified, is often able to overcome such a fluctuating idea, and that a gouty patient, for instance, can choose to enjoy what he likes, and to suffer what he may, since, according to his calculation, on this occasion at least, he has [only] not sacrificed the enjoyment of the present moment to a possibly mistaken expectation of a happiness which is supposed to be found in health. But even in this case, if the general desire for happiness did not influence his will, and supposing that in his particular case health was not a necessary element in this calculation, there yet remains in this, as in all other cases, this law — namely, that he should promote his happiness not from inclination but from duty, and by this would his conduct first acquire true moral worth.

It is in this manner, undoubtedly, that we are to understand those passages of Scripture also in which we are commanded to love our neighbor, even our enemy. For love, as an affection, cannot be commanded, but beneficence for duty's sake may, even though we are not impelled to it by any inclination — nay, are even repelled by a natural and unconquerable aversion. This is *practical* love, and not *pathological* — a love which is seated in the will, and not in the propensions of sense — in principles of action and not of tender sympathy; and it is this love alone which can be commanded.

Having thus defended his primary proposition that what is ultimately good is a good will acting in accordance with practical reason, in other words, from duty, Kant moves on to two corollary propositions:

The second proposition is: That an action done from duty derives its moral worth, *not from the purpose* which is to be attained by it, but from the maxim by which it is determined, and therefore does not depend on the realization of the object of the action, but merely on the *principle of volition* by which the action has taken place, without regard to any object of desire. It is clear from what precedes that the purposes which we may have in view in our actions, or their effects regarded as ends and springs of the will cannot give to actions any unconditional or moral worth. In what, then, can their worth lie if it is not to consist in the will and in reference to its expected effect? It cannot lie anywhere but in the *principle of the will* without regard to the ends which can be attained by the action. For the will stands between its *a priori* principle, which is formal, and its *a posteriori* spring which is material, as between two roads, and as it must be determined by something, it follows that it must be determined by the formal principle of volition when an action is done from duty, in which case every material principle has been withdrawn from it.

The third proposition, which is a consequence of the two preceding, I would express thus: *Duty is the necessity of acting from respect for the law.* I may have *inclination* for an object as the effect of my proposed action, but I cannot have *respect* for it just for this reason that it is an effect and not an energy of will. Similarly, I cannot have respect for inclination, whether my own or another's; I can at most, if my own, approve it; if another's, sometimes even love it, that is, look on it as favorable to my own interest. It is only what is connected with my will as a principle, by no means as an effect — what does not subserve my inclination, but overpowers it, or at least in case of choice excludes it from its calculation — in other words, simply the law of itself, which can be an object of respect, and hence a command. Now an action done from duty must wholly exclude the influence of inclination, and with it every object of the will, so that nothing remains which can determine the will except objectively the *law*, and subjectively *pure respect* for this practical law, and consequently the maxim that I should follow this law even to the thwarting of all my inclinations.

Thus the moral worth of an action does not lie in the effect expected from it, nor in any principle of action which requires to borrow its motive from this expected effect. For all these effects — agreeableness of one's condition, and even the promotion of the happiness of others — could have been also brought about by other causes, so that for this there would have been no need of the will of a rational being; whereas it is in this alone that the supreme and unconditional good can be found. The pre-eminent good which we call moral can therefore consist in nothing else than *the conception of law* in itself, *which certainly is only possible in a rational being,* in so far as this conception, and not the expected effect, determines the will. This is a good which is already present in the person who acts accordingly, and we have not to wait for it to appear first in the result.

But what sort of law can that be the conception of which must determine the will, even without paying any regard to the effect expected from it, in order that this will may be called good absolutely and without qualification? As I have deprived the will of every impulse which could arise to it from obedience to any law, there remains nothing but the universal conformity of its actions to law in general, which alone is to serve the will as a principle. . . .

This conception of "universal conformity to law" is Kant's central notion of duty. He defines it, as we shall see, as a generalized version of the Golden Rule: "Do unto others as you would have them do unto you." The point is, decide what you ought to do by asking yourself the question, "What if everyone were to do that?" The rule, as he states it, is

> . . . I am never to act otherwise than so *that I could also will that my maxim should become a universal law.* Here, now, it is the simple conformity to law in general, without assuming any particular law applicable to certain actions, that serves the will as its principle, and must so serve it if duty is not to be a vain delusion and a chimerical notion. The common reason of men in its practical judgments perfectly coincides with this, and

always has in view the principle here suggested. Let the question be, for example: May I when in distress make a promise with the intention not to keep it? I readily distinguish here between the two significations which the question may have: whether it is prudent or whether it is right to make a false promise? The former may undoubtedly often be the case. I see clearly indeed that it is not enough to extricate myself from a present difficulty by means of this subterfuge, but it must be well considered whether there may not hereafter spring from this lie much greater inconvenience than that from which I now free myself, and as, with all my supposed *cunning*, the consequences cannot be so easily foreseen but that credit once lost may be much more injurious to me than any mischief which I seek to avoid at present, it should be considered whether it would not be more *prudent* to act herein according to a universal maxim, and to make it a habit to promise nothing except with the intention of keeping it. But it is soon clear to me that such a maxim will still only be based on the fear of consequences. Now it is a wholly different thing to be truthful from duty, and to be so from apprehension of injurious consequences. In the first case, the very notion of the action implies a law for me; in the second case, I must first look about elsewhere to see what results may be combined with it which would affect myself. For to deviate from the principle of duty is beyond all doubt wicked; but to be unfaithful to my maxim of prudence may often be very advantageous to me, although to abide by it is certainly safer. The shortest way, however, and an unerring one, to discover the answer to this question whether a lying promise is consistent with duty, is to ask myself, Should I be content that my maxim (to extricate myself from difficulty by a false promise) should hold good as a universal law, for myself as well as for others; and should I be able to say to myself, "Every one may make a deceitful promise when he finds himself in a difficulty from which he cannot otherwise extricate himself?" Then I presently become aware that, while I can will the lie, I can by no means will that lying should be a universal law. For with such a law there would be no promises at all, since it would be in vain to allege my intention in regard to my future actions to those who would not believe this allegation, or if they over-hastily did so, would pay me back in my own coin. Hence my maxim, as soon as it should be made a universal law, would necessarily destroy itself.

The impressive name Kant gives to this general formulation of his notion of duty is **The Categorical Imperative.** An imperative, however, is just what we called a command in our preliminary discussion of morality. It is of the form "do this!" or "don't do this!" The word that distinguishes moral commands in general is the word **ought,** and this tells us something about the term *categorical.* Some imperatives tell us to "do this!" but only in order to get or do something else. Kant calls these "hypothetical imperatives." For example, "go to law school" (if you want to be a lawyer) or "don't eat very hot curry" (unless you don't mind risking an ulcer). But imperatives with a moral *ought* in them are not tied to any such "if" or "in order to" conditions. They are simply "do this" or "don't do this," whatever the circumstances, whatever you would like or enjoy personally. For example, "don't lie" (no matter what). This is what Kant means by "categorical."

Now all *imperatives* command either *hypothetically* or *categorically*. The former represent the practical necessity of a possible action as means to something else that is willed (or at least which one might possibly will). The categorical imperative would be that which represented an action as necessary of itself without reference to another end, that is, as objectively necessary.

Since every practical law represents a possible action as good, and on this account, for a subject who is practically determinable by reason as necessary, all imperatives are formulae determining an action which is necessary according to the principle of a will good in some respects. If now the action is good only as a means *to something else*, then the imperative is *hypothetical*; if it is conceived as good *in itself* and consequently as being necessarily the principle of a will which of itself conforms to reason, then it is *categorical*.

With hypothetical imperatives, what is commanded depends upon particular circumstances. With moral or categorical imperatives, there are universal laws that tell us what to do in every circumstance. (A **maxim,** according to Kant, is a "subjective principle of action," or what we would call an *intention*. It is distinguished from an "objective principle," that is, a universal law of reason.)

There is therefore but one categorical imperative, namely, this: *Act only on that maxim whereby thou canst at the same time will that it should become a universal law.*

Now if all imperatives of duty can be deduced from this one imperative as from their principle, then, although it should remain undecided whether what is called duty is not merely a vain notion, yet at least we shall be able to show what we understand by it and what this notion means.

Since the universality of the law according to which effects are produced constitutes what is properly called *nature* in the most general sense (as to form) — that is, the existence of things so far as it is determined by general laws — the imperative of duty may be expressed thus: *Act as if the maxim of thy action were to become by thy will a universal law of nature.*

We will now enumerate a few duties, adopting the usual division of them into duties to ourselves and to others, and into perfect and imperfect duties.

1. A man reduced to despair by a series of misfortunes feels wearied of life, but is still so far in possession of his reason that he can ask himself whether it would not be contrary to his duty to himself to take his own life. Now he inquires whether the maxim of his action could become a universal law of nature. His maxim is: From self-love I adopt it as a principle to shorten my life when its longer duration is likely to bring more evil than satisfaction. It is asked then simply whether this principle founded on self-love can become a universal law of nature. Now we see at once that a sys-

tem of nature of which it should be a law to destroy life by means of the very feeling whose special nature it is to impel to the improvement of life would contradict itself, and therefore could not exist as a system of nature; hence that maxim cannot possibly exist as a universal law of nature, and consequently would be wholly inconsistent with the supreme principle of all duty.

2. Another finds himself forced by necessity to borrow money. He knows that he will not be able to repay it, but sees also that nothing will be lent to him unless he promises stoutly to repay it in a definite time. He desires to make this promise, but he has still so much conscience as to ask himself: Is it not unlawful and inconsistent with duty to get out of a difficulty in this way? Suppose, however, that he resolves to do so, then the maxim of his action would be expressed thus: When I think myself in want of money, I will borrow money and promise to repay it, although I know that I never can do so. Now this principle of self-love or of one's own advantage may perhaps be consistent with my whole future welfare; but the question now is, Is it right? I change then the suggestion of self-love into a universal law, and state the question thus: How would it be if my maxim were a universal law? Then I see at once that it could never hold as a universal law of nature, but would necessarily contradict itself. For supposing it to be a universal law that everyone when he thinks himself in a difficulty should be able to promise whatever he pleases, with the purpose of not keeping his promise, the promise itself would become impossible, as well as the end that one might have in view in it, since no one would consider that anything was promised to him, but would ridicule all such statements as vain pretenses.

3. A third finds in himself a talent which with the help of some culture might make him a useful man in many respects. But he finds himself in comfortable circumstances and prefers to indulge in pleasure rather than to take pains in enlarging and improving his happy natural capacities. He asks, however, whether his maxim of neglect of his natural gifts, besides agreeing with his inclination to indulgence, agrees also with what is called duty. He sees then that a system of nature could indeed subsist with such a universal law, although men (like the South Sea islanders) should let their talents rest and resolve to devote their lives merely to idleness, amusement, and prop-agation of their species — in a word, to enjoyment; but he cannot possibly *will* that this should be a universal law of nature, or be implanted in us as such by a natural instinct. For, as a rational being, he necessarily wills that his faculties be developed, since they serve him, and have been given him, for all sorts of possible purposes.

4. A fourth, who is in prosperity, while he sees that others have to con-tend with great wretchedness and that he could help them, thinks: What concern is it of mine? Let everyone be as happy as Heaven pleases, or as he can make himself; I will take nothing from him nor even envy him, only I do not wish to contribute anything to his welfare or to his assistance in distress! Now no doubt, if such a mode of thinking were a universal law, the human race might very well subsist, and doubtless even better than in a state in which everyone talks of sympathy and good-will, or even takes care occasionally to put it into practice, but, on the other side, also cheats when he can, betrays the rights of men, or otherwise violates them. But

although it is possible that a universal law of nature might exist in accordance with that maxim, it is impossible to *will* that such a principle should have the universal validity of a law of nature. For a will which resolved this would contradict itself, inasmuch as many cases might occur in which one would have need of the love and sympathy of others, and in which, by such a law of nature, sprung from his own will, he would deprive himself of all hope of the aid he desires.

These are a few of the many actual duties, or at least what we regard as such, which obviously fall into two classes on the one principle that we have laid down. We must be *able to will* that a maxim of our action should be a universal law. This is the canon of the moral appreciation of the action generally. Some actions are of such a character that their maxim cannot without contradiction be even *conceived* as a universal law of nature, far from it being possible that we should *will* that it *should* be so. In others, this intrinsic impossibility is not found, but still it is impossible to *will* that their maxim should be raised to the universality of a law of nature, since such a will would contradict itself. It is easily seen that the former violate strict or rigorous (inflexible) duty; the latter only laxer (meritorious) duty. Thus it has been completely shown by these examples how all duties depend as regards the nature of the obligation (not the object of the action) on the same principle.

Another way of describing the categorical imperative, using a term from Kant that we've already encountered, is to say that it is an *a priori* principle, in this case, independent of any particular circumstances. Moral principles are necessary for the same reason that certain principles of knowledge are necessary, according to Kant, that is, because they are essential to human nature. It is important, therefore, for Kant to insist that moral principles, as *a priori* principles of reason, hold for every human being, in fact, even more generally, for every rational creature. (There is an extremely important point hidden in this phrase; traditionally, morality has always been defended on the basis of God's will, that is, we ought to be moral because God gave us the moral laws. According to Kant, however, God does not give the laws but as a rational creature He is bound to them just as we are. Thus, in answer to the question, "Are the laws of morality good because God is good or is God good because he obeys the laws of morality?" Kant would accept the latter.)

Kant's discussion of the categorical imperative is made confusing because after he has told us that "there is but one categorical imperative," he then goes on to give us others. He calls these "alternative formulations of the categorical imperative," but their effect on most readers is to confuse them unnecessarily. In actuality, for Kant there are a great many categorical imperatives. The first one Kant gave us is merely the most general. More specific examples are "don't lie!" and "keep your promises!" Another general categorical imperative is "never use people!" There is, however, a sense in which "using people" may be perfectly innocent. For example, I "use" you in order to play tennis, since I could not play alone. In such a case, you derive as much benefit from my "using you" as I do, and we could say that you are "using me" as well. But there are cases in which we are tempted to "use" people for our own benefit without any regard to their interests. This is what Kant forbids.

Now I say: man and generally any rational being *exists* as an end in himself, *not merely as a means* to be arbitrarily used by this or that will, but in all his actions, whether they concern himself or other rational beings, must be always regarded at the same time as an end. All objects of the inclinations have only a conditional worth; for if the inclinations and the wants founded on them did not exist, then their object would be without value. But the inclinations themselves, being sources of want, are so far from having an absolute worth for which they should be desired that, on the contrary, it must be the universal wish of every rational being to be wholly free from them. Thus the worth of any object which is *to be acquired* by our action is always conditional. Beings whose existence depends not on our will but on nature's, have nevertheless, if they are not rational beings, only a relative value as means, and are therefore called *things*; rational beings, on the contrary, are called *persons*, because their very nature points them out as ends in themselves, that is, as something which must not be used merely as means, and so far therefore restricts freedom of action (and is an object of respect). These, therefore, are not merely subjective ends whose existence has a worth *for us* as an effect of our action, but *objective ends*, that is, things whose existence is an end in itself—an end, moreover, for which no other can be substituted, which they should subserve *merely* as means, for otherwise nothing whatever would possess *absolute worth*; but if all worth were conditioned and therefore contingent, then there would be no supreme practical principle of reason whatever.

If then there is a supreme practical principle or, in respect of the human will, a categorical imperative, it must be one which, being drawn from the conception of that which is necessarily an end for everyone because it is *an end in itself*, constitutes an *objective* principle of will, and can therefore serve as a universal practical law. The foundation of this principle is: *rational nature exists as an end in itself*. Man necessarily conceives his own existence as being so; so far then this is a *subjective* principle of human actions. But every other rational being regards its existence similarly, just on the same rational principle that holds for me; so that it is at the same time an objective principle from which as a supreme practical law all laws of the will must be capable of being deduced. Accordingly the practical imperative will be as follows: *So act as to treat humanity, whether in thine own person or in that of any other, in every case as an end withal, never as means only.* We will now inquire whether this can be practically carried out.

To abide by the previous examples:

First, under the head of necessary duty to oneself: He who contemplates suicide should ask himself whether his action can be consistent with the idea of humanity *as an end in itself*. If he destroys himself in order to escape from painful circumstances, he uses a person merely as *a mean* to maintain a tolerable condition up to the end of life. But a man is not a thing, that is to say, something which can be used merely as means, but must in all his actions be always considered as an end in himself. I cannot, therefore, dispose in any way of a man in my own person so as to mutilate him, to damage or kill him. (It belongs to ethics proper to define this principle more precisely, so as to avoid all misunderstanding, for example, as to the amputation of the limbs in order to preserve myself; as to exposing my life to danger with a view to preserve it, etc. This question is therefore omitted here.)

Secondly, as regards necessary duties, or those of strict obligation, towards others: He who is thinking of making a lying promise to others will see at once that he would be using another man *merely as a mean*, without the latter containing at the same time the end in himself. For he whom I propose by such a promise to use for my own purposes cannot possibly assent to my mode of acting towards him, and therefore cannot himself contain the end of this action. This violation of the principle of humanity in other men is more obvious if we take in examples of attacks on the freedom and property of others. For then it is clear that he who transgresses the rights of men intends to use the person of others merely as means, without considering that as rational beings they ought always to be esteemed also as ends, that is, as beings who must be capable of containing in themselves the end of the very same action.

Thirdly, as regards contingent (meritorious) duties to oneself: It is not enough that the action does not violate humanity in our own person as an end in itself, it must also *harmonize with it*. Now there are in humanity capacities of greater perfection which belong to the end that nature has in view in regard to humanity in ourselves as the subject; to neglect these might perhaps be consistent with the *maintenance* of humanity as an end in itself, but not with the *advancement* of this end.

Fourthly, as regards meritorious duties towards others: The natural end which all men have is their own happiness. Now humanity might indeed subsist although no one should contribute anything to the happiness of others, provided he did not intentionally withdraw anything from it; but after all, this would only harmonize negatively, not positively, with *humanity as an end in itself*, if everyone does not also endeavor, as far as in him lies, to forward the ends of others. For the ends of any subject which is an end in himself ought as far as possible to be *my* ends also, if that conception is to have its *full* effect with me.

This principle that humanity and generally every rational nature is *an end in itself* (which is the supreme limiting condition of every man's freedom of action), is not borrowed from experience, *first*, because it is universal, applying as it does to all rational beings whatever, and experience is not capable of determining anything about them; *secondly*, because it does not present humanity as an end to men (subjectively), that is, as an object which men do of themselves actually adopt as an end; but as an objective end which must as a law constitute the supreme limiting condition of all our subjective ends, let them be what we will; it must therefore spring from pure reason.

In Kant's own terms, every human will is a will capable of acting according to universal laws of morality, not based upon any personal inclinations or interests but obeying rational principles that are categorical. Using this as a definition of morality, Kant then looks back at his predecessors:

> Looking back now on all previous attempts to discover the principle of morality, we need not wonder why they all failed. It was seen that man was bound to laws by duty, but it was not observed that the laws to which he is subject are *only those of his own giving,* though at the same time they are *universal,* and that he is only bound to act in conformity with his own will—a will, however, which is designed by nature to give universal laws. For when one has conceived man only as subject to a law (no matter what), then this law required some interest, either by way of attraction or constraint, since it did not originate as a law from *his own will,* but this will was according to a law obliged by *something else* to act in a certain manner. Now by this necessary consequence all the labor spent in finding a supreme principle of *duty* was irrevocably lost. For men never elicited duty, but only a necessity of acting from a certain interest.

Any morality worthy of the name, in other words, must be a product of a person's own autonomous reason yet universal at the same time, as a product of rational will and independent of personal feeling or interest. All previous philosophy, however, has insisted upon appealing to such personal feelings and interests and thus ended up with principles that were in every case hypothetical and not, according to Kant, categorical or moral. Thus morality for Aristotle depended upon a person's being a male Greek citizen. For Kant, morality and duty are completely set apart from such personal circumstances and concerns. Morality and duty have no qualifications, and, ultimately, they need have nothing to do with the good life or with happiness. In a perfect world, perhaps, doing our duty might also bring us happiness. But this is not such a world, Kant observes, and so happiness and morality are two separate concerns, with the second always to be considered the most important. (It is at this point, however, that Kant introduces his "Postulates of Practical Reason," and God in particular, in order to give us some assurance that, at least in the [very] long run, doing our duty will bring us some reward.)

Kant's conception of morality is so strict that it is hard for most people to accept. What is most difficult to accept is the idea that morality and duty have nothing to do with our personal desires, ambitions, and feelings, which Kant called our inclinations. We can agree that at least sometimes our duties and our inclinations are in conflict. But many philosophers have felt that Kant went much too far the other way in separating them entirely. Furthermore, Kant's emphasis on the categorical imperative systematically rules out all reference to particular situations and circumstances. In response to Kant, one may ask: Isn't the right thing to do often determined only within the particular context or situation? (A very recent moral philosophy called "situation ethics" has renewed this ancient demand.) Don't we have to know the particular problems and persons involved? What is right in one situation might very well be wrong in another, just because of different personalities, for example. Some people may be extremely hurt if we tell them the "truth" about themselves. On the other hand, a little "white" lie will make them feel much better. Other people are offended at any lie, however, and prefer even hurtful truths to the "ignorant bliss" of not knowing. Must not all moral rules be tempered to the particular situation?

The Kantian response to this objection would be that there are many ways to avoid hurting people other than telling lies. One can say, "no comment." One can cough conveniently, or drop the platter in one's hand. The fact that certain deceptions are institutionalized in our society (such as "regrets" for a dinner party) does not mean that a Kantian should defend them. The question, then, becomes how one formulates an accurate description of the options in such cases. Is it ever simply the case that one has a choice — hurt someone or tell a lie?

In a more general way, it has been objected that Kant's unqualified concept of morality is much too general to help us decide what to do in any particular situation. As an example, take the categorical imperative "don't steal!" Although the imperative itself, as a categorical one, must be unqualified, in order to apply it at all, we have to understand the kinds of circumstances to which it applies. Can't we have a right to steal in certain circumstances? Or, to put the same point differently, aren't there some circumstances in which "stealing" isn't really stealing at all? But what then of the situation in which a starving man steals a loaf of bread from an extremely wealthy baker. Surely he is stealing, but wouldn't we say that under the circumstances he is justified in doing so? The Kantian reply here is to distinguish between the question whether that person is *wrong* in stealing and the question of whether (or how) he should be punished. In this case, we can presume, Kant would insist that the man did wrong, but nevertheless agree that he should not be punished.

How do we decide "under which circumstances" a moral law is to be applied? Kant's formulation of the categorical imperative only tells us that we must act in such a way that anyone in similar circumstances should act the same way. What defines these "similar" circumstances? Suppose I were to say that "anyone in these circumstances, namely, being five-foot-seven and born in Detroit in 1942, having blond hair and blue eyes, and being a graduate of C. High School, may steal." Anyone in the same circumstances can steal, but, of course, I have defined the circumstances in such a way that it is extremely unlikely that anyone but myself will ever qualify. How can we avoid such trickery? Not by any considerations within the categorical imperative itself, for by its very nature it is incapable of telling us under what circumstances a moral law applies. Another way of making the same objection is to complain that there is no way of deciding how detailed the imperative must be. For example, should we simply say, "don't steal!" or rather "don't steal unless you're starving and the other person is not!" or else, "don't steal unless you're blond and blue-eyed!" and so on? Kant's reply, to prevent such abuses, is to quite clearly leave out all mention of particular circumstances in the formulation of principles. Nevertheless, we have to decide in what circumstances to apply what principles, and here the question comes up once again: how narrowly must we define the circumstances? Which circumstances are relevant to the formulation of a categorical imperative? Surely it won't do to say that *none* are relevant; at least we must know enough to know whether or not this act is an instance of stealing.

There have been other objections to Kant's severe philosophy. For example, if moral principles are categorical, then what do we do when two different moral principles conflict? The rule that tells us "don't lie!" is categorical; so is the rule that tells us "keep your promises!" Suppose that I promise not to tell anyone where you will be this weekend. Then some people wishing to kill you force me to tell. I have to say something. Either I break the promise or I lie. Kant gives us no adequate way of choosing between the promise and the lie. He has ruled out any appeal to the consequences of our actions. In Kant's argument, even if your enemies are trying to kill you, it is not morally relevant. And, most importantly, Kant has ruled out any appeal to what will make people happy, not only the person who must either lie or break a promise but everyone else who is involved as well. Kant would reply, presumably, that such cases of apparent conflict are due to a misrepresentation of the case. For example, one could respond to the intruders by playing dumb, or refusing to say anything, or trying to make them go away with force. The question of moral conflict thus becomes critical for Kant's moral philosophy. If moral principles conflict, we need a way of choosing between them. If they do not conflict, then we need a way of accounting for apparent conflicts and resolving them. But it is not clear that the Kantian theory gives us either a satisfactory criterion for getting out of moral quandaries or for explaining away some of the very painful moral conflicts in which we occasionally find ourselves.

UTILITARIANISM

In response to the harsh Kantian view of morality, with its neglect of happiness and the good life, a number of British philosophers, chiefly Jeremy Bentham, James Mill, and his son John Stuart Mill, developed a conception of morality that is called **utilitarianism.** It was an attempt to bring back personal inclinations and interests into moral considerations. Utilitarians wished to reconsider the consequences as well as the "will" of an action and to consider the particular circumstances of an action in an attempt to determine what is morally right. Most importantly, it was an attempt to return morality to the search for the personally satisfying life, which Kant had neglected.

The basis of utilitarianism is a form of **hedonism,** the conception of the good life that says the ultimate good is pleasure and that in the final analysis we want and ought to want this pleasure. But where traditional hedonism is concerned only with one's personal pleasure, utilitarianism is concerned with pleasure in general; that is, with one's own pleasure, the pleasure of other people involved, and even the pleasure of other people who are not directly involved. In many utilitarian writings, the notions of pleasure and happiness are used interchangeably. From our earlier discussion (and especially our discussion of Aristotle), we know that we must be cautious of any such exchange. There are many short-lived pleasures that do not make us happy; and happiness is much more than mere pleasure. But this is a major concern for the utilitarians; their whole theory revolves around a single aim, to make the most people as happy as possible, sometimes sacrificing short-term pleasures for enduring ones. Their central principle is often summarized as "the greatest good for the greatest number."

Jeremy Bentham was motivated to formulate his utilitarian theories not so much by the strict moralism of Kant's philosophy as by the absurd complexity of the British legal system. Just as Kant sought a single principle that would simplify all morality, Bentham looked for a single principle that would simplify the law. Bentham began with the fact that people seek pleasure and avoid pain and developed the "principle of utility" on just this basis:

from *The Principles of Morals and Legislation,* by Jeremy Bentham

I. Nature has placed mankind under the governance of two sovereign masters, *pain* and *pleasure*. It is for them alone to point out what we ought to do, as well as to determine what we shall do. On the one hand the standard of right and wrong, on the other the chain of causes and effects, are fastened to their throne. They govern us in all we do, in all we say, in all we think; every effort we can make to throw off our subjection, will serve but to demonstrate and confirm it. In words a man may pretend to abjure their empire: but in reality he will remain subject to it all the while. The *principle of utility* recognizes the subjection, and assumes it for the foundation of that system, the object of which is to rear the fabric of felicity by the hands of reason and of law. Systems which attempt to question it, deal in sounds instead of sense, in caprice instead of reason, the darkness instead of light.

But enough of metaphor and declamation: it is not by such means that moral science is to be improved.

II. The principle of utility is the foundation of the present work; it will be proper therefore at the outset to give an explicit and determinate account of what is meant by it. By the principle of utility is meant that principle which approves or disapproves of every action whatsoever, according to the tendency which it appears to have to augment or diminish the happiness of the party whose interest is in question; or, what is the same thing in other words, to promote or to oppose that happiness. I say of every action whatsoever; and therefore not only of every action of a private individual, but of every measure of government.

III. By utility is meant that property in any object, whereby it tends to produce benefit, advantage, pleasure, good, or happiness, (all this in the present case comes to the same thing) or (what comes again to the same thing) to prevent the happening of mischief, pain, evil, or unhappiness to the party whose interest is considered: if that party be the community in general, then the happiness of the community: if a particular individual, then the happiness of that individual.

IV. The interest of the community is one of the most general expressions that can occur in the phraseology of morals: no wonder that the meaning of it is often lost. When it has a meaning, it is this. The community is a fictitious *body*, composed of the individual persons who are considered as constituting as it were its *members*. The interest of the community then is, what? — the sum of the interests of the several members who compose it.

V. It is in vain to talk of the interest of the community, without understanding what is the interest of the individual. A thing is said to promote the interest, or to be *for* the interest, of an individual, when it tends to add to the sum total of his pleasures: or, what comes to the same thing, to diminish the sum total of his pains.

VI. An action then may be said to be conformable to the principle of utility, or, for shortness' sake, to utility, (meaning with respect to the community at large) when the tendency it has to augment the happiness of the community is greater than any it has to diminish it.

VII. A measure of government (which is but a particular kind of action, performed by a particular person or persons) may be said to be conformable to or dictated by the principle of utility, when in like manner the tendency which it has to augment the happiness of the community is greater than any which it has to diminish it.[14]

Morality, according to Bentham's principle of utility, means nothing other than action that tends to increase the amount of pleasure rather than diminish it.

X. Of an action that is conformable to the principle of utility, one may always say either that it is one that ought to be done, or at least that it is not one that ought not to be done. One may say also, that it is right it should be done; at least that it is not wrong it should be done: that it is a right action; at least that it is not a wrong action. When thus interpreted, the words *ought*, and *right* and *wrong*, and others of that stamp, have a meaning: when otherwise, they have none.

How does one defend this principle of utility? One cannot. To try to prove the principle is "as impossible as it is needless." People quite "naturally," whether they admit to it or not, act on the basis of it. This is not to say that they always act on it, but that is only because, according to Bentham, people do not always know what is best for them. That is the reason for formulating the principle in philosophy.

The heart of Bentham's theory is the formulation of a procedure for deciding, in every possible case, the value of alternative courses of action. The procedure simply involves the determination of alternative amounts of pleasures and pain, according to what has appropriately been called **the happiness calculus.**

---

[14]Jeremy Bentham, *An Introduction to the Principles of Morals and Legislation* (New York: Hafner, 1948). All subsequent quotations from Bentham are from this edition.

I. Pleasures then, and the avoidance of pains, are the *ends* which the legislator has in view: it behoves him therefore to understand their *value*. Pleasures and pains are the *instruments* he has to work with: it behoves him therefore to understand their force, which is again, in other words, their value.

II. To a person considered *by himself*, the value of a pleasure or pain considered *by itself*, will be greater or less, according to the four following circumstances.

1. Its *intensity*.   3. Its *certainty* or *uncertainty*.
2. Its *duration*.   4. Its *propinquity* or *remoteness*.

III. These are the circumstances which are to be considered in estimating a pleasure or a pain considered each of them by itself. But when the value of any pleasure or pain is considered for the purpose of estimating the tendency of any *act* by which it is produced, there are two other circumstances to be taken into the account; these are,

5. Its *fecundity*, or the chance it has of being followed by sensations of the *same* kind: that is, pleasures, if it be a pleasure: pains, if it be a pain.

6. Its *purity*, or the chance it has of *not* being followed by sensations of the *opposite* kind: that is, pains, if it be a pleasure: pleasures, if it be a pain.

. . . . .

Then the test itself:

V. To take an exact account then of the general tendency of any act by which the interests of a community are affected, proceed as follows. Begin with any one person of those whose interests seem most immediately to be affected by it: and take an account,

1. Of the value of each distinguishable *pleasure* which appears to be produced by it in the *first* instance.

2. Of the value of each *pain* which appears to be produced by it in the *first* instance.

3. Of the value of each pleasure which appears to be produced by it *after* the first. This constitutes the *fecundity* of the first *pleasure* and the *impurity* of the first *pain*.

4. Of the value of each *pain* which appears to be produced by it after the first. This constitutes the *fecundity* of the first *pain*, and the *impurity* of the first pleasure.

5. Sum up all the values of all the *pleasures* on the one side, and those of all the pains on the other. The balance, if it be on the side of pleasure, will give the *good* tendency of the act upon the whole, with respect to the interests of that *individual* person; if on the side of pain, the *bad* tendency of it upon the whole.

6. Take an account of the *number* of persons whose interests appear to be concerned; and repeat the above process with respect to each. *Sum up* the numbers expressive of the degrees of *good* tendency, which the act has, with respect to each individual, in regard to whom the tendency of it is *good* upon the whole: do this again with respect to each individual, in regard to whom the tendency of it is *bad* upon the whole. Take the balance;

which, if on the side of *pleasure,* will give the general *good tendency* of the act, with respect to the total number of community of individuals concerned; if on the side of pain the general *evil tendency,* with respect to the same community.

Let us take an example. Bentham himself discusses the problem of lust (Prop. XXX), which he says is always bad. Why? "Because if the effects of the motive are not bad, then we do not call it lust." Lust, in other words, is sexual desire that is so excessive that it brings about more pain than pleasure. Suppose you are sexually attracted to another person. How do you decide (assuming that there is already mutual agreement) whether to follow through or not? First, you estimate the amount of pleasure each person will gain. An important question is whether the pleasure of only these two people should be estimated or the pleasure of others besides. If it is a question of adultery, then the interests of at least a third person should be considered. But assuming that no such direct complications are involved, even the indirect interests of the rest of society must be considered. (If you and your potential lover are sufficiently young, should the happiness of your parents enter into your decision?) Then, after you have considered its initial pleasure, estimate the initial pain. (In this case, we may presume it will be slight.) Then ask about the longer term pleasures and pains for each person involved. If a sexual relationship will leave you feeling happy about yourself and the other person, then the subsequent pleasure will be considerable. If either person will feel regrets, or degraded, or embarrassed, or if sex will spoil a good friendship, or if a sexual relationship will set up expectations that one or both of you is unwilling to fulfill, then the amount of subsequent pain may be overwhelming. Then add up the pleasures and pains for each person, match the total amount of pleasure against the total pain, and if the balance is positive, go ahead. If the balance is negative, don't do it. Suppose, for example, you each expect a great deal of initial pleasure, and one of you expects nothing but good feelings afterwards while the other expects only mild regrets. No one else need even know, and so the balance, clearly, is very positive. But suppose neither of you expects to enjoy it all that much, and the subsequent hassles will be a prolonged and troublesome bother, then, very likely the balance will be negative. We don't often make this kind of decision in this way, we simply do what we want to do at the time. And this is precisely what Bentham says we shouldn't do. He argues that it is because we so often act on the basis of impulses without rational calculations that we end up unhappy. In other words, the fact that we are usually irrational is not an argument against Bentham's principles. Their purpose is precisely to make us rational, to help us get what we really want.

There are problems with Bentham's theory. All that is considered, according to his "happiness calculus," is solely the amount of pleasure and pain. But some of you, in response to our preceding example, might well say, "it doesn't matter how much pleasure and how little pain two people will gain if they get into a sexual relationship. Under certain circumstances (if it is adultery, or simply if they are not married) such behavior is wrong! Mere happiness is not enough!" And here we see the beginning of a swing back towards Kant. To see why such a move is necessary, let us examine the following objection to Bentham. Suppose a great many people would get a great deal of pleasure out of seeing some innocent person tortured and slaughtered like a beast. Of course the victim would suffer a great deal of pain, but by increasing the size of the crowd we could eventually obtain an amount of pleasure on the part of everyone else that more than balanced the suffering of the victim. Bentham's calculus has no way of rejecting such a gruesome outcome. A less horrible example is this: If a person gets great pleasure from some activity and no pain, there are no other considerations that apply to him or her (assuming that his or her actions do not affect others). Are we then to say that a life of sloth and self-indulgence, if it satisfies everyone and gives them a lot of pleasure and no pain, is to be preferred to any other life of any kind? Does Bentham give us any reason to try for anything "better" than being happy pigs? This was the problem that bothered Bentham's godson, John Stuart Mill.

Mill's version of utilitarianism added an important qualification to Bentham's purely quantitative calculus. He said that it is not only the quantity of pleasure that counts, but the quality as well. Needless to say, this makes the calculations much more complicated. In fact, it makes them impossible, for there cannot be precise calculation of quality, even though there can be precise calculations of quantity. Mill's now famous example is the following: If a pig can live a completely satisfied life, while a morally concerned and thoughtful individual like Socrates cannot ever be so satisfied, is the life of the pig therefore preferable? Mill's answer is this:

> It is better to be a human being dissatisfied than a pig satisfied; better to be Socrates dissatisfied than a fool satisfied.

On what grounds can he say this? Aren't the pig and the fool happier?

> If the fool, or the pig, are of a different opinion, it is because they only know their own side of the question. The other party [Socrates] knows both sides.[15]

There are problems that emerge from this theory. How are we to evaluate different "qualities" of pleasure, even if we have tried them all? But first let us look at Mill's revision of utilitarianism, as summarized in his popular pamphlet, appropriately called *Utilitarianism*. (It was Mill, not Bentham, who invented this term.) It begins with a general consideration of morality, and of Kant's moral philosophy in particular.

from *Utilitarianism*, by J. S. Mill

Our moral faculty, according to all those of its interpreters who are entitled to the name of thinkers, supplies us only with the general principles of moral judgments; it is a branch of our reason, not of our sensitive faculty;

[15]John Stuart Mill, *Utilitarianism* (New York: Bobbs-Merrill, 1957).

and must be looked to for the abstract doctrines of morality, not for perception of it in the concrete. The intuitive, no less than what may be termed the inductive, school of ethics insists on the necessity of general laws. They both agree that the morality of an individual action is not a question of direct perception, but of the application of a law to an individual case. They recognize also, to a great extent, the same moral laws but differ as to their evidence and the source from which they derive their authority. According to the one opinion, the principles of morals are evident *a priori*, requiring nothing to command assent except that the meaning of the terms be understood. According to the other doctrine, right and wrong, as well as truth and falsehood, are questions of observation and experience. But both hold equally that morality must be deduced from principles; and the intuitive school affirm as strongly as the inductive that there is a science of morals. Yet they seldom attempt to make out a list of the *a priori* principles which are to serve as the premises of the science; still more rarely do they make any effort to reduce those various principles to one first principle, or common ground of obligation. They either assume the ordinary precepts of morals as of *a priori* authority, or they lay down as the common groundwork of those maxims, some generality much less obviously authoritative than the maxims themselves, and which has never succeeded in gaining popular acceptance. Yet to support their pretensions there ought either to be some one fundamental principle or law at the root of all morality, or, if there be several, there should be a determinate order of precedence among them; and the one principle, or the rule for deciding between the various principles when they conflict, ought to be self-evident.

To inquire how far the bad effects of this deficiency have been mitigated in practice, or to what extent the moral beliefs of mankind have been vitiated or made uncertain by the absence of any distinct recognition of an ultimate standard, would imply a complete survey and criticism of past and present ethical doctrine. It would, however, be easy to show that whatever steadiness or consistency these moral beliefs have attained has been mainly due to the tacit influence of a standard not recognized. Although the non-existence of an acknowledged first principle has made ethics not so much a guide as a consecration of men's actual sentiments, still, as men's sentiments, both in favor and of aversion, are greatly influenced by what they suppose to be the effect of things upon their happiness, the principle of utility, or, as Bentham latterly called it, the greatest happiness principle, has had a large share in forming the moral doctrines even of those who most scornfully reject its authority. Nor is there any school of thought which refuses to admit that the influence of actions on happiness is a most material and even predominant consideration in many of the details, of morals, however unwilling to acknowledge it as the fundamental principle of morality and the source of moral obligation. I might go much further and say that to all those *a priori* moralists who deem it necessary to argue at all, utilitarian arguments are indispensable. It is not my present purpose to criticize these thinkers; but I cannot help referring, for illustration, to a systematic treatise by one of the most illustrious of them, the *Metaphysics of Ethics* by Kant. This remarkable man, whose system of thought will long remain one of the landmarks in the history of philosophical speculation, does, in the treatise in question, lay down a universal first principle as the origin and ground of moral obligation; it is this: "So act that the rule on which thou actest would admit of being adopted as a law by all rational beings." But when he begins to deduce from this precept any of the actual duties of morality, he fails, almost grotesquely, to show that there would be any contradiction, and logical (not to say physical) impossibility, in the adoption by all rational beings of the most outrageously immoral rules of conduct. All he knows is that the *consequences* of their universal adoption would be such as no one would choose to incur.

Then Mill gets down to the business of redefining utilitarianism. Like Bentham, he insists that the principle of utility cannot be proven as such, for it is the ultimate end in terms of which everything else is justified. But there is, Mill tells us, a "larger sense of the word 'proof'":

On the present occasion, I shall, without further discussion of the other theories, attempt to contribute something towards the understanding and appreciation of the "utilitarian" or "happiness" theory, and towards such proof as it is susceptible of. It is evident that this cannot be proof in the ordinary and popular meaning of the term. Questions of ultimate ends are not amenable to direct proof. Whatever can be proved to be good must be so by being shown to be a means to something admitted to be good without proof. The medical art is proved to be good by its conducing to health; but how is it possible to prove that health is good? The art of music is good, for the reason, among others, that it produces pleasure; but what proof is it possible to give that pleasure is good? If, then, it is asserted that there is a comprehensive formula, including all things which are in themselves good, and that whatever else is good is not so as an end but as a means, the formula may be accepted or rejected, but is not a subject of what is commonly understood by proof. We are not, however, to infer that its acceptance or rejection must depend on blind impulse, or arbitrary choice. There is a larger meaning of the word "proof," in which this question is as amenable to it as any other of the disputed questions of philosophy. The subject is within the cognizance of the rational faculty; and neither does that faculty deal with it solely in the way of intuition. Considerations may be presented capable of determining the intellect either to give or withhold its assent to the doctrine; and this is equivalent to proof.

WHAT UTILITARIANISM IS

A passing remark is all that needs be given to the ignorant blunder of supposing that those who stand up for utility as the test of right and wrong use the term in that restricted and merely colloquial sense in which utility is opposed to pleasure. An apology is due to the philosophical opponents of utilitarianism, for even the momentary appearance of confounding them with anyone capable of so absurd a misconception; which is the more extraordinary, inasmuch as the contrary accusation, of referring everything to pleasure, and that, too, in its grossest form, is another of the common charges against utilitarianism: and, as has been pointedly remarked by an able writer, the same sort of persons, and often the very same persons, denounce the theory "as impracticably dry when the word 'utility' precedes the word 'pleasure,' and as too practicably voluptuous when the word 'pleasure' precedes the word 'utility'." Those who know anything about the matter are aware that every writer, from Epicurus to Bentham, who maintained the theory of utility, meant by it, not something to be contradistinguished from pleasure, but pleasure itself, together with exemption from pain; and instead of opposing the useful to the agreeable or the ornamental, have always declared that the useful means these, among other things. Yet the common herd, including the herd of writers, not only in newspapers and periodicals, but in books of weight and pretension, are perpetually falling into this shallow mistake. Having caught up the word "utilitarian," while knowing nothing whatever about it but its sound, they habitually express by it the rejection or the neglect of pleasure in some of its forms: of beauty, of ornament, or of amusement. Nor is the term thus ignorantly misapplied solely in disparagement, but occasionally in compliment, as though it implied superiority to frivolity and the mere pleasures of the moment. And this perverted use is the only one in which the word is popularly known, and the one from which the new generation are acquiring their sole notion of its meaning. Those who introduced the word, but who had for many years discontinued it as a distinctive appellation, may well feel themselves called upon to resume it if by doing so they can hope to contribute anything towards rescuing it from this utter degradation.

The creed which accepts as the foundation of morals "utility" or the "greatest happiness principle" holds that actions are right in proportion as they tend to promote happiness, wrong as they tend to produce the reverse of happiness. By happiness is intended pleasure, and the absence of pain; by unhappiness, pain, and the privation of pleasure. To give a clear view of the moral standard set up by the theory, much more requires to be said; in particular, what things it includes in the ideas of pain and pleasure; and to what extent this is left an open question. But these supplementary explanations do not affect the theory of life on which this theory of morality is grounded—namely, that pleasure and freedom from pain are the only things desirable as ends, and that all desirable things (which are as numerous in the utilitarian as in any other scheme) are desirable either for the pleasure inherent in themselves, or as means to the promotion of pleasure and the prevention of pain.

Now such a theory of life excites in many minds, and among them in some of the most estimable in feeling and purpose, inveterate dislike. To suppose that life has (as they express it) no higher end than pleasure—no better and nobler object of desire and pursuit—they designate as utterly mean and groveling; as a doctrine worthy only of swine, to whom the followers of Epicurus were, at a very early period, contemptuously likened; and modern holders of the doctrine are occasionally made the subject of equally polite comparisons by its German, French, and English assailants.

When thus attacked, the Epicureans have always answered that it is not they, but their accusers, who represent human nature in a degrading light, since the accusation supposes human beings to be capable of no pleasures except those of which swine are capable. If this supposition were true, the charge could not be gainsaid, but would then be no longer an imputation; for if the sources of pleasure were precisely the same to human beings and to swine, the rule of life which is good enough for the one would be good enough for the other. The comparison of the Epicurean life to that of beasts is felt as degrading, precisely because a beast's pleasures do not satisfy a human being's conceptions of happiness. Human beings have faculties more elevated than the animal appetites and, when once made conscious of them, do not regard anything as happiness which does not include their gratification. I do not, indeed, consider the Epicureans to have been by any means faultless in drawing out their scheme of consequences from the utilitarian principle. To do this in any sufficient manner, many Stoic, as well as Christian, elements require to be included. But there is no known Epicurean theory of life which does not assign to the pleasures of the intellect, of the feelings and imagination, and of the moral sentiments, a much higher value of pleasures than to those of mere sensation. It must be admitted, however, that utilitarian writers in general have placed the superiority of mental over bodily pleasures chiefly in the greater permanency, safety, uncostliness, etc., of the former — that is, in their circumstantial advantages rather than in their intrinsic nature. And on all these points utilitarians have fully proved their case; but they might have taken the other and, as it may be called, higher ground with entire consistency. It is quite compatible with the principle of utility to recognize the fact that some kinds of pleasure are more desirable and more valuable than others. It would be absurd that, while, in estimating all other things, quality is considered as well as quantity, the estimation of pleasures should be supposed to depend on quantity alone.

If I am asked what I mean by difference of quality in pleasures, or what makes one pleasure more valuable than another, merely as a pleasure, except its being greater in amount, there is but one possible answer. Of two pleasures, if there be one to which all or almost all who have experience of both give a decided preference, irrespective of a feeling of moral obligation to prefer it, that is the more desirable pleasure. If one of the two is, by those who are competently acquainted with both, placed so far above the other that they prefer it, even though knowing it to be attended with a greater amount of discontent, and would not resign it for any quantity of the other pleasure which their nature is capable of, we are justified in ascribing to the preferred enjoyment a superiority in quality so far outweighing quantity as to render it, in comparison, of small account.

Now it is an unquestionable fact that those who are equally acquainted with and equally capable of appreciating and enjoying both, do give a most marked preference to the manner of existence which employs their higher faculties. Few human creatures would consent to be changed into any of the lower animals for a promise of the fullest allowance of a beast's pleasures; no intelligent human being would consent to be a fool, no instructed person would be an ignoramus, no person of feeling and conscience would be selfish and base, even though they should be persuaded that the fool, the dunce, or the rascal is better satisfied with his lot than they are with theirs. They would not resign what they possess more than he for the most complete satisfaction of all the desires which they have in common with him. If they ever fancy they would, it is only in cases of unhappiness so extreme that to escape from it they would exchange their lot for almost any other, however undesirable in their own eyes. A being of higher faculties requires more to make him happy, is capable probably of more acute suffering, and certainly accessible to it at more points, than one of an inferior type; but in spite of these liabilities, he can never really wish to sink into what he feels to be a lower grade of existence. We may give what explanation we please of this unwillingness; we may attribute it to pride, a name which is given indiscriminately to some of the most and to some of the least estimable feelings of which mankind are capable: we may refer it to the love of liberty and personal independence, an appeal to which was with the Stoics one of the most effective means for the inculcation of it; to the love of power or to the love of excitement, both of which do really enter into and contribute to it; but its most appropriate appellation is a sense of dignity, which all human beings possess in one form or other, and in some, though by no means in exact, proportion to their higher faculties, and which is so essential a part of the happiness of those in whom it is strong that nothing which conflicts with it could be otherwise than momentarily an object of desire to them. Whoever supposes that this preference takes place at a sacrifice of happiness — that the superior being, in anything like equal circumstances, is not happier than the inferior — confounds the two very different ideas of happiness and content. It is indisputable that the being whose capacities of enjoyment are low has the greatest chance of having them fully satisfied; and a highly endowed being will always feel that any happiness which he can look for, as the world is constituted, is imperfect. But he can learn to bear its imperfections, if they are at all bearable; and they will not make him envy the being who is indeed unconscious of the imperfections, but only because he feels not at all the good which those imperfections qualify. It is better to be a human being dissatisfied than a pig satisfied; better to be Socrates dissatisfied than a fool satisfied. And if the fool, or the pig, are of a different opinion, it is because they only know their own side of the question. The other party to the comparison knows both sides.

It may be objected that many who are capable of the higher pleasures occasionally, under the influence of temptation, postpone them to the lower. But this is quite compatible with a full appreciation of the intrinsic superiority of the higher. Men often, from infirmity of character, make their election for the nearer good, though they know it to be the less valuable; and this no less when the choice is between two bodily pleasures than when it is between bodily and mental. They pursue sensual indulgences to the injury of health, though perfectly aware that health is the greater good. It may be further objected that many who begin with youthful enthusiasm for everything noble, as they advance in years, sink into indolence and selfishness. But I do not believe that those who undergo this very common change voluntarily choose the lower description of pleasures in preference to the higher. I believe that, before they devote themselves exclusively to the one, they have already become incapable of the other. Capacity for the nobler feelings is in most natures a very tender plant, easily killed, not only by hostile influences, but by mere want of sustenance; and in the majority of young persons it speedily dies away if the occupations to which their position in life has devoted them, and the society into which it has thrown them, are not favorable to keeping that higher capacity in exercise. Men lose their high aspirations as they lose their intellectual tastes, because they have not time or opportunity for indulging them; and they addict themselves to inferior pleasures, not because they deliberately prefer them, but because they are either the only ones to which they have access, or the only ones which they are any longer capable of enjoying. It may be questioned whether any one who has remained equally susceptible to both classes of pleasures, ever knowingly and calmly preferred the lower, though many, in all ages, have broken down in an ineffectual attempt to combine both.

I have dwelt on this point, as being a necessary part of a perfectly just conception of utility or happiness considered as the directive rule of human conduct. But it is by no means an indispensable condition to the acceptance of the utilitarian standard; for that standard is not the agent's own greatest happiness, but the greatest amount of happiness altogether; and if it may possibly be doubted whether a noble character is always the happier for its nobleness, there can be no doubt that it makes other people happier, and that the world in general is immensely a gainer by it. Utilitarianism, therefore, could only attain its end by the general cultivation of nobleness of character, even if each individual were only benefited by the nobleness of others, and his own, so far as happiness is concerned, were a sheer deduction from the benefit. But the bare enunciation of such an absurdity as this last renders refutation superfluous.

According to the greatest happiness principle, as above explained, the ultimate end, with reference to and for the sake of which all other things are desirable — whether we are considering our own good or that of other people — is an existence exempt as far as possible from pain, and as rich as possible in enjoyments, both in point of quantity and quality; the test of quality and the rule for measuring it against quantity being the preference felt by those who, in their opportunities of experience, to which must be added their habits of self-consciousness and self-observation, are best furnished with the means of comparison. This, being, according to the utilitarian opinion, the end of human action, is necessarily also the standard of morality, which may accordingly be defined "the rules and precepts for human conduct," by the observance of which an existence such as has been described might be, to the greatest extent possible, secured to all mankind; and not to them only, but, so far as the nature of things admits, to the whole sentient creation.[16]

THE CREATION OF MORALITY:
NIETZSCHE AND EXISTENTIALISM

The single term "morality" must not mislead us. We have been discussing not simply different theories of morality (ethics) but different conceptions of morality, and that means different moralities, even if they should have many principles

---

[16]Mill, *Utilitarianism*.

in common. The problem of relativism, in other words, is not confined to the comparison of exotically different cultures. It faces us in a far more urgent form in our own conceptions of morality. We might agree that killing without extreme provocation is wrong. But why do we believe that it is wrong? One person claims that it is wrong because the Ten Commandments (and therefore God) forbid it. Another says it is wrong because it is a mark of insensitivity and therefore a flaw in character. Another says it is wrong because it violates peoples' rights, while still another says it is wrong because it increases the amount of pain in the world without equally adding to happiness. They all agree that killing is wrong, but the different reasons point to different circumstances in which each would kill. The first, if God commanded him or her to. The second, if the killing could be seen as a sign of strength and heroism. The third, if he or she found a way to take away people's right to live or found another right that was overriding. The fourth, as a utilitarian, would only have to find a circumstance in which the death of one person was more than balanced by the increased welfare of the others (as in a criminal execution).

From the three great moral philosophies we have studied, four such conceptions emerge. They all agree on many principles, but the reasons differ widely, and some of the principles do also. But most dramatic is the difference between Aristotle's ancient Greek morality and Kant's modern morality of duty. Kant's morality may be taken as a fair representation of the modern Judeo-Christian morality in its strictest form: the emphasis on moral principle and laws, the emphasis on reason and individual autonomy, the emphasis on good intentions ("a good will") and doing one's duty. There are small differences that we have already pointed out: the Greek emphasis on pride as a virtue in contrast to the Christian condemnation of pride as a "deadly sin" (or at least a personality flaw) and its emphasis on humility. One of Aristotle's first virtues was courage in battle, while most modern moralities consider that as a special case, not as a matter of being an everyday "good person" at all. This difference might well be attributed to the different political climates of the two societies. But that is not enough. As we shall see, the differences are much deeper than that.

There are crucial differences between ancient and modern moral perspectives; the most striking is the difference in the scope of their applicability. In Aristotle's moral philosophy, only a small elite is thought to be capable of true happiness *(eudaimonia)* through virtuous action and contemplation. Other people (women, slaves, noncitizens) may live comfortably enough and do their duties and chores efficiently, but they cannot be called "happy." The elite, however, are characterized by their excellence, by their individual achievements, including wealth, power, honor, intelligence, wit, and all of those rewards that come with an aristocratic upbringing, the best of education and a life that is guaranteed in basic comforts from birth. In Kant's conception of morality, by contrast, all people who are rational (that is, everyone except morons and very young children) are to be judged by the same moral standards, the standards of duty. There are no elites. And since the judgments of moral worth are made solely on the basis of good intentions, no "external" advantages are relevant to a person's goodness or badness. In fact, it is possible that a perfectly "good" person would, with only the best intentions, cause chaos and unhappiness around him wherever he goes. And the harder he tries to make amends, the more he fouls them up. Dostoevsky wrote one of his greatest novels, *The Idiot*, about just this — a perfectly good man, with all the right intentions, causes suffering and even death every time he tries to do good. Yet the point is, he is, by this modern conception, still the perfectly good man. Aristotle would find this laughable. How could we call a man virtuous just because of his intentions? How can a perfect failure be an example of ideal goodness?

In Aristotle's morality, the only people who operate on the basis of duty are those who are incapable of being truly good and truly happy. Duty is a morality for women and servants. For the elite, it is rather a question of personal excellence — in battle, in games, in business, in love, in debate, and in all things, especially philosophy. And where Kant's morality mostly consists (like the Ten Commandments) of "thou shalt not . . ." Aristotle's morality appropriately consists of personal desires and ambitions, not commands to achieve, and certainly not negative commands. The key element of Kant's philosophy, duty, is treated minimally in Aristotle, where the emphasis is on personal growth and achievement. But, on the other side, the image of the well-rounded, successful man, excellent in all things and the envy of his fellow men, plays only a secondary role in Kant's philosophy (for example, in his *Doctrine of Virtue*, the second part of the *Metaphysics of Morals*). For him, what is important is the person who does what he or she is supposed to do. For Aristotle, the ideal is to strive for personal excellence, and doing what a person is supposed to do is simply taken for granted along the way.

Now notice that both moralities have many of the same results. Aristotle's morality will praise many and condemn most of the same acts as Kant's morality: Killing needlessly and stealing are wrong; telling the truth and keeping promises are right. But their conceptions of morality, and consequently, their conceptions of people are distinctively different. And as we appreciate the nature of this difference, we will be in a position to understand one of the most dramatic moral revolutions of modern times, initiated by Friedrich Nietzsche. Nietzsche called himself an **immoralist,** and he attacked morality as viciously as he attacked Christianity. But though he has often been interpreted as saying that we should give up morality and feel free to kill, steal, and commit crimes of all kinds, his moral philosophy does not in fact say that at all. What he did was to attack modern morality, as summarized by Kant and Christianity, and urge us to return to ancient Greek morality as summarized by Aristotle. He also attacked utilitarianism, which he considered "vulgar." Like a great many philosophers of the nineteenth century (particularly German philosophers: Fichte, Hegel, Marx), Nietzsche saw in the ancient Greeks a sense of personal harmony and a sense of excellence that had been lost in the modern world. Nietzsche, like Aristotle, saw the concept of duty as fit for servants and slaves, but such a morality was wholly inadequate to motivate us to personal excellence and achievement. And Nietzsche, like Aristotle, was an unabashed elitist. Only a few people were capable of this "higher" morality. For the rest, the "slave morality" of duty would have to suffice. But for those few, nothing was more important than to give up the "thou shalt not . . ."'s of Morality (with a capital *m*) and seek out one's own virtues and abilities. This does not mean that such a person need ever violate the laws of morality although it must be said that Nietzsche's belligerent style and often war-like terminology certainly suggests that his master morality will include a good amount of cruelty and immorality. But it is clear that Nietzsche does not consider obedience to laws as the most important thing in life. Nor does this mean that Nietzsche is (as he is often thought to be) an **ethical egoist.** To say that a person should develop his or her own virtues and become excellent in as many ways as possible is not at all to say that one must act only in one's own interests. As in Aristotle, the excellence of the individual is part of and contributes to the excellence of society as a whole.

Nietzsche takes his central project as a philosopher to be what he calls "the creation of values." In this he is rightly listed as one of the existentialist philosophers, or at least as one of their most important predecessors. The phrase is perhaps misleading, however. What Nietzsche is doing is not inventing new values so much as reasserting very old ones. Furthermore, Nietzsche, like Aristotle, takes ethics to be based solely upon human nature, and so it is not a question of "creating values" so much as finding them in oneself. But where such a philosophy for Aristotle was in agreement with most of the thinking of his times, Nietzsche's thought was a radical disruption of the usual Kantian style of thinking of the modern period and so takes on the tone of violent destructiveness rather than — as in Aristotle — the self-satisfied tones of a gentleman. And since Nietzsche, unlike Aristotle, did not believe that every human "nature" was the same, he taught that different individuals would most assuredly find and follow different values, different conceptions of excellence and thus have different moralities. For this reason, students who read Nietzsche looking for concrete moral advice, a set of principles to act on, are always disappointed. His central teaching is rather "follow yourself, don't follow me." Consequently, he can't — and won't — try to tell you how to live. But he does tell you to live and to give up the servile views that we have held of ourselves for many centuries.

Nietzsche's moral philosophy is largely critical, and most of his efforts have gone into the rejection of Kant's conception of morality in order to make room for individual self-achieving as found in Aristotle. His argument, however, is not a refutation in the usual sense. Instead, he undermines morality by showing that the motivation behind it is decrepit and weak. The central categories of Nietzsche's philosophy are strength and weakness, and he considers the Greek tradition of personal excellence a source of strength, the modern conception of morality a façade for weakness. Accordingly, he calls the first a "master morality," the second, a "slave morality" or, with reference to modern mass movements, a "herd morality." The excerpts that follow, therefore, are illustrative of Nietzsche's general attack on morality. But never forget that his purpose is not merely destructive but, in his eyes, creative, and the point is to get us to look to ourselves for values and to excel each in our own ways (the phrase "will to power" refers to just this effort to excel as individuals).

on "Master and Slave Morality," by Friedrich Nietzsche

What does your conscience say? "You should become him who you are."

Herd-Instinct. — Wherever we meet with a morality we find a valuation and order of rank of the human impulses and activities. These valuations and orders of rank are always the expression of the needs of a community or herd: that which is in the first place to *its* advantage — and in the second place and third place — is also the authoritative standard for the worth of every individual. By morality the individual is taught to become a function of the herd, and to ascribe to himself value only as a function. As the conditions for the maintenance of one community have been very different from those of another community, there have been very different moralities; and in respect to the future essential transformations of herds and communities, states and societies, one can prophesy that there will still be very divergent moralities. Morality is the herd-instinct in the individual.[17]

Apart from the value of such assertions as "there is a categorical imperative in us," one can always ask: What does such an assertion indicate about him who makes it? There are systems of morals which are meant to justify their author in the eyes of other people; other systems of morals are meant to tranquillise him, and make him self-satisfied; with other systems he wants to crucify and humble himself; with others he wishes to take revenge; with others to conceal himself; with others to glorify himself and gain superiority and distinction; — this system of morals helps its author to forget, that system makes him, or something of him, forgotten; many a moralist would like to exercise power and creative arbitrariness over mankind; many another, perhaps, Kant especially, gives us to understand by his morals that "what is estimable in me, is that I know how to obey — and with you it *shall* not be otherwise than with me!" In short, systems of morals are only a *sign-language of the emotions.* . . .

In a tour through the many finer and courser moralities which have hitherto prevailed or still prevail on the earth, I found certain traits recurring regularly together, and connected with one another, until finally two primary types revealed themselves to me, and a radical distinction was brought to light. There is *master-morality* and *slave-morality*; — I would at once add, however, that in all higher and mixed civilisations, there are also attempts at the reconciliation of the two moralities; but one finds still oftener the confusion and mutual misunderstanding of them, indeed, sometimes their close juxtaposition — even in the same man, within one soul. The distinctions of moral values have either originated in a ruling caste, pleasantly conscious of being different from the ruled — or among the ruled class, the slaves and dependents of all sorts. In the first case, (when it is the rulers who determine the conception "good," it is the exalted, proud disposition which is regarded as the distinguishing feature, and that which

---

[17]Friedrich Nietzsche, *The Joyful Wisdom*, trans. Thomas Common, in *The Complete Works of Friedrich Nietzsche*, Oscar Levy, General Editor (1909–11)

determines the order of rank. The noble type of man separates from himself the beings in whom the opposite of this exalted, proud disposition displays itself: he despises them. Let it at once be noted that in this first kind of morality the antithesis "good" and "bad" means practically the same as "noble" and "despicable"; — the antithesis "good" and "*evil*" is of a different origin. The cowardly, the timid, the insignificant, and those thinking merely of narrow utility are despised; moreover, also, the distrustful, with their constrained glances, the self-abasing, the dog-like kind of men who let themselves be abused, the mendicant flatterers, and above all the liars: — it is a fundamental belief of all aristocrats that the common people are untruthful. "We truthful ones" — the nobility in ancient Greece called themselves. It is obvious that everywhere the designations of moral value were at first applied to *men*, and were only derivatively and at a later period appled to *actions*; it is a gross mistake, therefore, when historians of morals start questions like, "Why have sympathetic actions been praised?" (The noble type of man regards *himself* as a determiner of values; he does not require to be approved of; he passes the judgment: "What is injurious to me is injurious in itself"; he knows that it is he himself only who confers honour on things; he is a *creator of values*. He honours whatever he recognises in himself: such morality is self-glorification. In the foreground there is the feeling of plenitude, of power, which seeks to overflow, the happiness of high tension, the consciousness of a wealth which would fain give and bestow: — the noble man also helps the unfortunate, but not — or scarcely — out of pity, but rather from an impulse generated by the super-abundance of power. The noble man honours in himself the powerful one, him also who has power over himself, who knows how to speak and how to keep silence, who takes pleasure in subjecting himself to severity and hardness, and has reverence for all that is severe and hard. "Wotan placed a hard heart in my breast," says an old Scandinavian Saga: it is thus rightly expressed from the soul of a proud Viking. Such a type of man is even proud of *not* being made for sympathy; the hero of the Saga therefore adds warningly; "He who has not a hard heart when young, will never have one." The noble and brave who think thus are the furthest removed from the morality which sees precisely in sympathy, or in acting for the good of others, or in *désintéressement*, the characteristic of the moral; faith in oneself, pride in oneself, a radical enmity and irony towards "selflessness," belong as definitely to noble morality, as do a careless scorn and precaution in presence of sympathy and the "warm heart." — It is the powerful who *know* how to honour, it is their art, their domain for invention. The profound reverence for age and for tradition — all law rests on this double reverence, — the belief and prejudice in favour of ancestors and unfavourable to newcomers, is typical in the morality of the powerful; and if, reversely, men of "modern ideas" believe almost instinctively in "progress" and the "future," and are more and more lacking in respect for old age, the ignoble origin of these "ideas" has complacently betrayed itself thereby. A morality of the ruling class, however, is more especially foreign and irritating to present-day taste in the sternness of its principle that one has duties only to one's equals; that one may act towards beings of a lower rank, towards all that is foreign, just as seems good to one, or "as the heart desires," and in any case "beyond good and evil": it is here that sympathy and similar sentiments can have a place. The ability and obligation to exercise prolonged gratitude and prolonged revenge — both only within the circle of equals, — artfulness in retaliation, *raffinement* of the idea in friendship, a certain necessity to have enemies (as outlets for the emotions of envy, quarrelsomeness, arrogance — in fact, in order to be a good *friend*): all these are typical characteristics of the noble morality, which, as has been pointed out, is not the morality of "modern ideas," and is therefore at present difficult to realise, and also to unearth and disclose. — It is otherwise with the second type of morality, *slave-morality*. Supposing that the abused, the oppressed, the suffering, the unemancipated, the weary, and those uncertain of themselves, should moralise, what will be the common element in their moral estimates? Probably a pessimistic suspicion with regard to the entire situation of man will find expression, perhaps a condemnation of man, together with his situation. The slave has an unfavourable eye for the virtues of the powerful; he has a scepticism and distrust, a *refinement* of distrust of everything "good" that is there honoured — he would fain persuade himself that the very happiness there is not genuine. On the other hand, *those* qualities which serve to alleviate the existence of sufferers are brought into prominence and flooded with light; it is here that sympathy, the kind, helping hand, the warm heart, patience, diligence, humility, and friendliness attain to honour for here these are the most useful qualities, and almost the only means of supporting the burden of existence. Slave-morality is essentially the morality of utility. Here is the seat of the origin of the famous antithesis "good" and "evil": — power and dangerousness are assumed to reside in the evil, a certain dreadfulness, subtlety, and strength, which do not admit of being despised. According to slave-morality, therefore, the "evil" man arouses fear; according to master-morality, it is precisely the "good" man who arouses fear and seeks to arouse it, while the bad man is regarded as the despicable being. The contrast attains its maximum when, in accordance with the logical consequences of slave-morality, a shade of depreciation — it may be slight and well-intentioned — at last attaches itself to the "good" man of this morality; because, according to the servile mode of thought, the good man must in any case be the *safe* man: he is good-natured, easily deceived, perhaps a little stupid, *un bonhomme*. Everywhere that slave-morality gains the ascendency, language shows a tendency to approximate the significations of the words "good" and "stupid." — At last fundamental difference: the desire for *freedom*, the instinct for happiness and the refinements of the feeling of liberty belong as necessarily to slave-morals and morality, as artifice and enthusiasm in reverence and devotion are the regular symptoms of an aristocratic mode of thinking and estimating. — Hence we can understand without further detail why love *as a passion*— it is our European specialty — must absolutely be of noble origin. . . .

And on the philosopher:

... The philosophical workers, after the excellent pattern of Kant and Hegel, have to fix and formalise some great existing body of valuations — that is to say, former *determinations of value*, creations of value, which have become prevalent, and are for a time called "truths" — whether in the domain of the *logical*, the *political* (moral), or the *artistic*. It is for these investigators to make whatever has happened and been esteemed hitherto, conspicuous, conceivable, intelligible, and manageable, to shorten everything long, even "time" itself, and to *subjugate* the entire past: an immense and wonderful task, in the carrying out of which all refined pride, all tenacious will, can surely find satisfaction. *The real philosophers, however, are commanders and law-givers;* they say: "Thus *shall* it be!" They determine first the Whither and the Why of mankind, and thereby set aside the previous labour of all philosophical workers, and all subjugators of the past — they grasp at the future with a creative hand, and whatever is and was, becomes for them thereby a means, an instrument, and a hammer. Their "knowing" is *creating,* their creating is a law-giving, their will to truth is — *Will to Power.* — Are there at present such philosophers? Have there ever been such philosophers? *Must* there not be such philosophers some day? . . .[18]

Nietzsche is often viewed as the most extreme of the antimoralists, those who attack the traditional duty-bound Kantian-Christian conception of morality. In fact, he is but one among many philosophers who have rejected that morality in exchange for a more personal and individual set of principles. And given his emphasis on human "nature," we can say that even Nietzsche is much more traditional than is usually supposed (though it is the Aristotelian, not the Kantian tradition). In the past few decades, however, morality has become far more personalized than even Nietzsche suggested. In Anglo-American philosophy, largely in the wake of logical positivism, ethics has been reduced to a matter of emotions, prescriptions, and attitudes rather than principles and rational laws. (Ironically, Nietzsche has always been in extreme disfavor among such philosophers while Kant has been considered with extreme favor.)

The attack on the absolute moral principles of reason, which are the same for everyone, has been one of the most vigorous philosophical movements of the twentieth century, so much so that many philosophers, religious leaders, and moralists have become alarmed at the destruction of uniform moral codes and have attempted to reassert the old moral laws in new ways. The problem is one of relativism. Is there a single moral code? Or are there possibly as many moralities as there are people? There are intermediary suggestions, such as relativizing morals to particular groups or societies, but the question is still the same: "Is there ultimately any way of defending one moral code against any other?"

The most extreme relativist position of all has emerged from Nietzsche's existentialist successors, particularly Jean-Paul Sartre. In Sartre's philosophy, not only the idea of a uniform morality but the idea of a human nature upon which this morality might be based is completely rejected. Not because different people might have different "natures," as in Nietzsche, but because for Sartre our values

---

[18]Friedrich Nietzsche, *Beyond Good and Evil,* trans. Helen Zimmern, in *The Complete Works of Friedrich Nietzsche,* Oscar Levy, General Editor (1909–11) (New York: Russell & Russell, 1964).

are quite literally a question of creation, of personal commitment. In answer to any question about morality, the only ultimate answer is "because I choose to accept these values." But what is most fascinating about Sartre's conception of morality as choice is that he does not therefore abandon general principles as Nietzsche does. Quite the contrary, he adopts an almost Kantian stance about the need to choose principles for all mankind, not just oneself. The difference is that Sartre, unlike Kant, makes no claims about the singular correctness of these principles. All he can say is "this is what I choose mankind to be." Thus Sartre's moral philosophy is a curious mixture of the most radical relativism and the most traditional moralizing.

from "Existentialism," by Sartre

Man is nothing else but that which he makes of himself. That is the first principle of existentialism. And this is what people call its "subjectivity," using the word as a reproach against us. But what do we mean to say by this, but that man is of a greater dignity than a stone or a table? For we mean to say that man primarily exists — that man is, before all else, something which propels itself towards a future and is aware that it is doing so. Man is, indeed, a project which possesses a subjective life, instead of being a kind of moss, or a fungus or a cauliflower. Before that projection of the self nothing exists; not even in the heaven of intelligence: man will only attain existence when he is what he purposes to be. Not, however, what he may wish to be. For what we usually understand by wishing or willing is a conscious decision taken — much more often than not — after we have made ourselves what we are. I may wish to join a party, to write a book or to marry — but in such a case what is usually called my will is probably a manifestation of a prior and more spontaneous decision. If, however, it is true that existence is prior to essence, man is responsible for what he is. Thus, the first effect of existentialism is that it puts every man in possession of himself as he is, and places the entire responsibility for his existence squarely upon his own shoulders. And, when we say that man is responsible for himself, we do not mean that he is responsible only for his own individuality, but that he is responsible for all men. The word "subjectivism" is to be understood in two senses, and our adversaries play upon only one of them. Subjectivism means, on the one hand, the freedom of the individual subject and, on the other, that man cannot pass beyond human subjectivity. It is the latter which is the deeper meaning of existentialism. When we say that man chooses himself, we do mean that every one of us must choose himself; but by that we also mean that in choosing for himself he chooses for all men. For in effect, of all the actions a man may take in order to create himself as he wills to be, there is not one which is not creative, at the same time, of an image of man such as he believes he ought to be. To choose between this or that is at the same time to affirm the value of that which is chosen; for we are unable ever to choose the worse. What we choose is always the better; and nothing can be better for us unless it is better for all. If, moreover, existence precedes essence and we will to exist at the same time as we fashion our image, that image is valid for all and for the entire epoch in which we find ourselves. Our responsibility is thus much greater than we had supposed, for it concerns mankind as a whole. If I am a worker, for instance, I may choose to join a Christian rather than a Communist trade union. And if, by that membership, I choose to signify that resignation is, after all, the attitude that best becomes a man, that man's kingdom is not upon this earth, I do not commit myself alone to that view. Resignation is my will for everyone, and my action is, in consequence, a commitment on behalf of all mankind. Or if, to take a more personal case, I decide to marry and to have children, even though this decision proceeds simply from my situation, from my passion or my desire, I am thereby committing not only myself, but humanity as a whole, to the practice of monogamy. I am thus responsible for myself and for all men, and I am creating a certain image of man as I would have him to be. In fashioning myself I fashion man.

. . . . .

. . . Who can prove that I am the proper person to impose, by my own choice, my conception of man upon mankind? I shall never find any proof whatever; there will be no sign to convince me of it.

. . . . .

If I regard a certain course of action as good, it is only I who choose to say that it is good and not bad. . . . nevertheless I also am obliged at every instant to perform actions which are examples. Everything happens to every man as though the whole human race had its eyes fixed upon what he is doing and regulated its conduct accordingly.

. . . . .

As an example by which you may the better understand this state of abandonment, I will refer to the case of a pupil of mine, who sought me out in the following circumstances. His father was quarrelling with his mother and was also inclined to be a "collaborator"; his elder brother had been killed in the German offensive of 1940 and this young man, with a sentiment somewhat primitive but generous, burned to avenge him. His mother was living alone with him, deeply afflicted by the semi-treason of his father and by the death of her eldest son, and her one consolation was in this young man. But he, at this moment, had the choice between going to England to join the Free French Forces or of staying near his mother and helping her to live. He fully realized that this woman lived only for him and that his disappearance — or perhaps his death — would plunge her into despair. He also realized that, concretely and in fact, every action he performed on his mother's behalf would be sure of effect in the sense of aiding her to live, whereas anything he did in order to go and fight would be an ambiguous action which might vanish like water into sand and serve no purpose. For instance, to set out for England he would have to wait indefinitely in a Spanish camp on the way through Spain; or, on arriving in England or in Algiers he might be put into an office to fill up forms. Consequently, he found himself confronted by two very different modes of action; the one concrete, immediate, but directed towards only one individual; and the other an action addressed to an end infinitely greater, a national collectivity, but for that very reason ambiguous—and it might be frustrated on the way. At the same time, he was hesitating between two kinds of morality; on the one side the morality of sympathy, of personal devotion and, on the other side, a morality of wider scope but of more debatable validity. He had to choose between those two. What could help him to choose? Could the Christian doctrine? No. Christian doctrine says: Act with charity, love your neighbour, deny yourself for others, choose the way which is hardest, and so forth. But which is the harder road? To whom does one owe the more brotherly love, the patriot or the mother? Which is the more useful aim, the general one of fighting in and for the whole community, or the precise aim of helping one particular person to live? Who can give an answer to that *à priori?* No one. Nor is it given in any ethical scripture. The Kantian ethic says, Never regard another as a means, but always as an end. Very well; if I remain with my mother, I shall be regarding her as the end and not as a means: but by the same token I am in danger of treating as means those who are fighting on my behalf; and the converse is also true, that if I go to the aid of the combatants I shall be treating them as the end at the risk of treating my mother as a means.

If values are uncertain, if they are still too abstract to determine the particular, concrete case under consideration, nothing remains but to trust in our instincts. That is what this young man tried to do; and when I saw him he said, "In the end, it is feeling that counts; the direction in which it is really pushing me is the one I ought to choose. If I feel that I love my mother enough to sacrifice everything else for her—my will to be avenged, all my longings for action and adventure—then I stay with her. If, on the contrary, I feel that my love for her is not enough, I go." But how does one estimate the strength of a feeling? The value of his feeling for his mother was determined precisely by the fact that he was standing by her. I may say that I love a certain friend enough to sacrifice such or such a sum of money for him, but I cannot prove that unless I have done it. I may say, "I love my mother enough to remain with her," if actually I have remained with her. I can only estimate the strength of this affection if I have performed an action by which it is defined and ratified. But if I then appeal to this affection to justify my action, I find myself drawn into a vicious circle. . . .

In other words, feeling is formed by the deeds that one does; therefore I cannot consult it as a guide to action. And that is to say that I can neither seek within myself for an authentic impulse to action, nor can I expect, from some ethic, formulae that will enable me to act. You may say that the youth did, at least, go to a professor to ask for advice. But if you seek counsel—from a priest, for example—you have selected that priest; and at bottom you already knew, more or less, what he would advise. In other words, to choose an adviser is nevertheless to commit oneself by that choice. If you are a Christian, you will say, Consult a priest; but there are collaborationists, priests who are resisters and priests who wait for the tide to turn: which will you choose? Had this young man chosen a priest of the resistance, or one of the collaboration, he would have decided beforehand the kind of advice he was to receive. Similarly, in coming to me, he knew what advice I should give him, and I had but one reply to make. You are free, therefore choose — that is to say, invent. No rule of general morality can show you what you ought to do.

To say that it does not matter what you choose is not correct. In one sense choice is possible, but what is not possible is not to choose. I can always choose, but I must know that if I do not choose, that is still a choice. This although it may appear merely formal, is of great importance as a limit to fantasy and caprice. For, when I confront a real situation — for example, that I am a sexual being, able to have relations with a being of the other sex and able to have children — I am obliged to choose my attitude to it, and in every respect I bear the responsibility of the choice which, in committing myself, also commits the whole of humanity. . . . Man finds himself in an organized situation in which he is himself involved: his choice involves mankind in its entirety, and he cannot avoid choosing. Either he must remain single, or he must marry without having children, or he must marry and have children. In any case, and whichever he may choose, it is impossible for him, in respect of this situation, not to take complete responsibility. Doubtless he chooses without reference to any pre-established values, but it is unjust to tax him with caprice. Rather let us say that the moral choice is comparable to the construction of a work of art.

· · · · ·

No one can tell what the painting of tomorrow will be like; one cannot judge a painting until it is done. What has that to do with morality? We are in the same creative situation. We never speak of a work of art as irresponsible; when we are discussing a canvas by Picasso, we understand very well that the composition became what it is at the time when he was painting it, and that his works are part and parcel of his entire life.

It is the same upon the plane of morality. There is this in common between art and morality, that in both we have to do with creation and invention. We cannot decide *à priori* what it is that should be done. I think it was made sufficiently clear to you in the case of that student who came to see me, that to whatever ethical system he might appeal, the Kantian or any other, he could find no sort of guidance whatever; he was obliged to invent the law for himself. Certainly we cannot say that this man, in choosing to remain with his mother — that is, in taking sentiment, personal devotion and concrete charity as his moral foundations — would be making an irresponsible choice, nor could we do so if he preferred the sacrifice of going away to England. Man makes himself; he is not found ready-made; he makes himself by the choice of his morality, and he cannot but choose a morality, such is the pressure of circumstances upon him.[19]

Sartre says that "man makes himself." He believes this to be true both individually and collectively. It is through my actions that I commit myself to values, not through principles I accept *a priori* or rules that are imposed upon me by God or society. If you accept the voice of some authority, you have chosen to accept that authority rather than some other. If you appeal for advice or help, you have

[19]Jean-Paul Sartre, *Existentialism As a Humanism*, trans. Philip Mairet (New York: Philosophical Library, 1949).

chosen to seek that kind of advice rather than some other kind. If you refuse to choose between alternatives, then you are responsible for neglecting both or all the alternatives, for "copping-out." In any case, you must do something, even if what you do is "doing nothing" (that is, not taking one of the important alternatives before you).

Here is Sartre's reply to his predecessors. We are no longer in the position of Aristotle, in which morality appears to us as a given, as "natural," and without alternatives of the most irresolvable kind. We can no longer trust our "sentiments," as Hume did, for we now find ourselves torn with conflicting sentiments of every kind. We can no longer accept the *a priori* moralizing of Kant, for we now see that the circumstances in which we must act are never so simple that they will allow for a simple "categorical" imperative. And even "the greatest good for the greatest number" no longer provides a guide for our actions, for we no longer pretend that we can calculate the consequences of our actions with any such accuracy. And besides, who is to say what "the greatest good" or, for that matter, "the greatest number" is today? Against all of this, Sartre argues that there is simply our choice of actions and values, together with their consequences, whatever they are. There is no justification for these, and no "right" or "wrong." But this does not mean that we need not choose or that it is all "arbitrary." To the contrary, the upshot of Sartre's thesis is precisely that we are always choosing and that morality is nothing other than our commitments, at least for the present, to those values we choose to follow through our actions.

ETHICS UNNATURALIZED: METAETHICS AND ITS CONSEQUENCES

Each of the theories we have examined, from Aristotle to the existentialists and the pragmatists, is an attempt to say what is good and right, as opposed to what is bad and wrong. In some cases, this moral advice is specific and straightforward, as in Aristotle's list of the virtues. In other cases, it is not specific at all, as in Hume and Rousseau's celebration of sympathy, Nietzsche's enthusiasm about strength and creativity, and Jean-Paul Sartre's exhortation of responsibility. Both Kant and Mill present us with a conception of morality in which abstract principles are to be used to figure out specific actions. All of these theories, in other words, are *normative* theories of ethics. They present us with *norms* or standards and ideals of good (and bad) behavior. They tell us, specifically or abstractly, what we are to do.

But in addition to this central normative concern, there is also a second level of analysis in each of the above theories. It is the more abstract analysis of what the key terms of ethics *mean*—words such as "good" and "ought" and "right" for example. And with this analysis of the meaning of ethical terms, each philosopher also makes a statement about the nature of the justification of ethical statements. Aristotle justifies such statements by reference to the *telos* of being human; Kant justifies them by appeal to reason; Mill to the principle of utility and, ultimately, individual well-being. One might formulate each author's views by way of a definition of "good," such as: for Mill, "good" means conducive to the general happiness, or, for Nietzsche, "good" means expressing the strength of the strongest, or, for Kant, "good" means in accordance with the principles of practical reason. Such analyses of the meaning and justification of ethical terms, as opposed to the actual presentation of a normative ethics telling us what to do, is called **metaethics.** Metaethical theories do not tell us what to do but rather tell us about the nature of ethics and ethical statements. What are they? How are they to be justified? Can they be ultimately justified?

What is common to all of the theories we have examined so far is that, in addition to being normative theories, they have also assumed a position which metaethicists call **naturalism.** Ethical naturalism is the view that ethical statements are based on facts — facts about human nature, facts about what makes us happy, facts about human feelings such as sympathy, facts about human faculties such as practical reason. Sometimes, the naturalism in an ethical theory is quite straightforward, as in John Stuart Mill's equation of goodness and pleasure, and as in Aristotle's appeal of all ethical questions to human nature or *telos.* Sometimes, the naturalism is paradoxical; for example, Hume explicitly denies that ethics is based on facts in his sharp separation of "is" and "ought," but then he goes ahead and develops an ethical system in which morals are firmly (if not rationally) based on natural human sentiments, in particular our sympathy or "fellow-feeling." Sometimes, the ethical naturalism of an author can be convoluted indeed; Kant's ethics seems clearly to distinguish between questions of fact and nature (such as, "what makes us happy?" and "what feelings are natural?") and questions of morals, which are always questions of reason and will. But on what ground does he make such a distinction? On the basis of the *fact* that we have a faculty of reason. Nevertheless, it is clear that Kant, even more than Hume, adamantly insists on a distinction between the facts of nature and the nature of morality, between any concern for the empirically verifiable state of affairs in which an action is performed and the rational, normative considerations which govern the goodness of that action. Indeed, despite the rationality of Kant's ethics, he insists that moral principles are not matters of *knowledge.* Thus he anticipates the position of a great many metaethicists in this century — **non-naturalism** and **non-cognitivism.** The non-naturalist believes that ethical statements are not based on empirically verifiable facts. The non-cognitivist further believes that the truth of ethical statements cannot be known at all; indeed, ethical statements are neither true nor false.

Non-naturalism can be traced as far back as Plato, to Socrates' view that the Form of the Good is something distinct from all factual questions about happiness, pleasure, and power. In modern times, the father of non-naturalism is David Hume, who argued the unbreachable logical gap between "is" and "ought." In this century, the patriarch of non-naturalism is the Cambridge philosopher G. E. Moore, who pursued Hume's distinction with a tough-minded argument and the name of a new kind of logical fallacy — the **naturalistic fallacy.** The argument is what Moore called "the open question argument." It picks up with Hume's distinction and asks, "well, you've told me that Phaedo is housebroken, obedient, playful with children and threatening to strangers, but — the question is still open — is Phaedo a *good* dog?" In other words, no matter how many facts are accumulated in an ethical matter, it is still always an "open question" whether the thing or act in question is good or not. The fallacy — the naturalistic fallacy — is ignoring just this logical gap and arguing, wrongly, that a thing or an action is good *because* such and such facts are true of it.

The following selection is from G. E. Moore's classic *Principia Ethica,* which was published in 1903.

from *Principia Ethica,* by G. E. Moore

... What, then, is good? How is good to be defined? Now, it may be thought that this is a verbal question. A definition does indeed often mean the expressing of one word's meaning in other words. But this is not the sort of definition I am asking for. ... My business is solely with that object or idea, which I hold, rightly or wrongly, that the word is generally used to stand for. What I want to discover is the nature of that object or idea, and about this I am extremely anxious to arrive at an agreement.

But, if we understand the question in this sense, my answer to it may seem a very disappointing one. If I am asked 'What is good?' my answer is that good is good, and that is the end of the matter. Or if I am asked 'How is good to be defined?' my answer is that it cannot be defined, and that is all I have to say about it. But disappointing as these answers may appear, they are of the very last importance. To readers who are familiar with philosophic terminology, I can express their importance by saying that they amount to this: That propositions about the good are all of them synthetic and never analytic; and that is plainly no trivial matter. And the same thing may be expressed more popularly, by saying that, if I am right, then nobody can foist upon us such an axiom as that 'Pleasure is the only good' or that 'The good is the desired' on the pretence that this is 'the very meaning of the word.'

Let us, then, consider this position. My point is that 'good' is a simple notion, just as 'yellow' is a simple notion; that, just as you cannot, by any manner of means, explain to any one who does not already know it, what yellow is, so you cannot explain what good is. Definitions of the kind that I was asking for, definitions which describe the real nature of the object or notion denoted by a word, and which do not merely tell us what the word is used to mean, are only possible when the object or notion in question is something complex. You can give a definition of a horse, because a horse has many different properties and qualities, all of which you can enumerate. But when you have enumerated them all, when you have reduced a horse to his simplest terms, then you can no longer define those terms. They are simply something which you think of or perceive, and to any one who cannot think of or perceive them, you can never, by any definition, make their nature known. It may perhaps be objected to this that we are able to describe to others, objects which they have never seen or thought of. We can, for instance, make a man understand what a chimaera is, although he has never heard of one or seen one. You can tell him that it is an animal with a lioness's head and body, with a goat's head growing from the middle of its back, and with a snake in place of a tail. But here the object which you are describing is a complex object; it is entirely composed of parts, with which we are all perfectly familiar — a snake, a goat, a lioness; and we know, too, the manner in which those parts are to be put together, because we know what is meant by the middle of a lioness's back, and where her tail is wont to grow. And so it is with all objects, not previously known, which we are able to define: they are all complex; all composed of parts, which may themselves, in the first instance, be capable of similar definition, but which must in the end be reducible to simplest parts, which can no longer be defined. But yellow and good, we say, are not complex: they are notions of that simple kind, out of which definitions are composed and with which the power of further defining ceases.

. . . . .

'Good,' then, if we mean by it that quality which we assert to belong to a thing, when we say that the thing is good, is incapable of any definition, in the most important sense of that word. The most important sense of 'definition' is that in which a definition states what are the parts which invariably compose a certain whole; and in this sense 'good' has no definition because it is simple and has no parts. It is one of those innumerable objects of thought which are themselves incapable of definition, because they are the ultimate terms by reference to which whatever *is* capable of definition must be defined. That there must be an indefinite number of such terms is obvious, on reflection; since we cannot define anything except by an analysis, which, when carried as far as it will go, refers us to something, which is simply different from anything else, and which by that ultimate difference explains the peculiarity of the whole which we are defining: for every whole contains some parts which are common to other wholes also. There is, therefore, no intrinsic difficulty in the contention that 'good' denotes a simple and indefinable quality. . . . Ethics aims at discovering what are those other properties belonging to all things which are good. But far too many philosophers have thought that when they named those other properties they were actually defining good; that these properties, in fact, were simply not 'other,' but absolutely and entirely the same with goodness. This view I propose to call the 'naturalistic fallacy' and of it I shall now endeavour to dispose.

Let us consider what it is such philosophers say. And first it is to be noticed that they do not agree among themselves. They not only say that they are right as to what good is, but they endeavour to prove that other people who say that it is something else, are wrong. One, for instance, will affirm that good is pleasure, another, perhaps, that good is that which is desired; and each of these will argue eagerly to prove that the other is wrong. But how is that possible? One of them says that good is nothing but the object of desire, and at the same time tries to prove that it is not pleasure.

But from his first assertion, that good just means the object of desire, one of two things must follow as regards his proof:

(1) He may be trying to prove that the object of desire is not pleasure. But, if this be all, where is his Ethics? The position he is maintaining is merely a psychological one. Desire is something which occurs in our minds, and pleasure is something else which so occurs; and our would-be ethical philosopher is merely holding that the latter is not the object of the former. But what has that to do with the question in dispute? His opponent held the ethical proposition that pleasure was the good, and although he should prove a million times over the psychological proposition that pleasure is not the object of desire, he is no nearer proving his opponent to be wrong. The position is like this. One man says a triangle is a circle: another replies 'A triangle is a straight line, and I will prove to you that I am right: for' (this is the only argument) 'a straight line is not a circle.' 'That is quite true,' the other may reply, 'but nevertheless a triangle is a circle, and you have said nothing whatever to prove the contrary. What is proved is that one of us is wrong, for we agree that a triangle cannot be both a straight line and a circle: but which is wrong, there can be no earthly means of proving, since you define triangle as straight line and I define it as circle.' — Well, that is one alternative which any naturalistic Ethics has to face; if good is *defined* as something else, it is then impossible either to prove that any other definition is wrong or even to deny such definition.

(2) The other alternative will scarcely be more welcome. It is that the discussion is after all a verbal one. When A says 'Good means pleasant' and B says 'Good means desired,' they may merely wish to assert that most people have used the word for what is pleasant and for what is desired respectively. And this is quite an interesting subject for discussion: only it is not a whit more an ethical discussion than the last was. Nor do I think that any exponent of naturalistic Ethics would be willing to allow that this was all he meant. They are all so anxious to persuade us that what they call the good is what we really ought to do. 'Do, pray, act so, because the word "good" is generally used to denote actions of this nature': such, on this view, would be the substance of their teaching. And in so far as they tell us how we ought to act, their teaching is truly ethical, as they mean it to be. But how perfectly absurd is the reason they would give for it! 'You are to do this, because most people use a certain word to denote conduct such as this.' 'You are to say the thing which is not, because most people call it lying.' That is an argument just as good! — My dear sirs, what we want to know from you as ethical teachers, is not how people use a word; it is not even, what kind of actions they approve, which the use of this word 'good' may certainly imply: what we want to know is simply what *is* good. We may indeed agree that what most people do think good, is actually so; we shall at all events be glad to know their opinions: but when we say their opinions about what *is* good, we do mean what we say; we do not care whether they call that thing which they mean 'horse' or 'table' or 'chair,' 'gut' or 'bon' or 'α'γαθός'; we want to know what it is that they so call. When they say 'Pleasure is good,' we cannot believe that they merely mean 'Pleasure is pleasure' and nothing more than that. . . .

My objections to Naturalism are then, in the first place, that it offers no reason at all, far less any valid reason, for any ethical principle whatever; and in this it already fails to satisfy the requirements of Ethics, as a scientific study. But in the second place I contend that, though it gives a reason for no ethical principle, it is a *cause* of the acceptance of false principles—it deludes the mind into accepting ethical principles, which are false; and in this it is contrary to every aim of Ethics. It is easy to see that if we start with a definition of right conduct as conduct conducive to general happiness; then, knowing that right conduct is universally conduct conducive to the good, we very easily arrive at the result that the good is general happiness. If, on the other hand, we once recognize that we must start our Ethics without a definition, we shall be much more apt to look about us, before we adopt any ethical principle whatever; and the more we look about us, the less likely are we to adopt a false one. . . .

Our first conclusion as to the subject-matter of Ethics is, then, that there is a simple, indefinable, unanalysable object of thought by reference to which it must be defined. By what name we call this unique object is a matter of indifference, so long as we clearly recognise what it is and that it does differ from other objects. The words which are commonly taken as the signs of ethical judgments all do refer to it; and they are expressions of ethical judgments solely because they do so refer.[20]

Moore rejects naturalism, but he still insists that ethical statements refer to something—namely, an indefinable non-natural property of goodness. Accordingly, although one cannot prove that something is good through an argument based on the facts, one can still "see that it is so," and that is a justification of sorts. But other philosophers, following Moore, reject even this kind of justification, insisting that there is *no* property referred to by ethical statements and therefore no grounds for knowing whether such a statement is true or false. These are the *non-cognitivists*, who maintain the Humean-Kantian distinction between "is" and "ought" with such fervor that ethics threatens to disappear as a rational discipline. Indeed, some of the leading non-cognitivists—who call themselves **emotivists**—have argued that there can be no justification of ethical statements. At most, we can encourage and persuade one another to accept certain ethical positions, but the positions themselves are merely matters of emotion or attitude, not questions of belief that can be rationally challenged or rationally justified.

The following statement of emotivism is by A. J. Ayer, from *Language, Truth and Logic*.

on "Emotivism"
by A. J. Ayer

. . . It is our business to give an account of "judgements of value" which is both satisfactory in itself and consistent with our general empiricist principles. We shall set ourselves to show that in so far as statements of value

[20]G. E. Moore, *Principia Ethica* (Cambridge: Cambridge Univ. Press, First Edition 1903).

are significant, they are ordinary "scientific" statements; and that in so far as they are not scientific, they are not in the literal sense significant, but are simply expressions of emotion which can be neither true nor false. . . .

The ordinary system of ethics, as elaborated in the works of ethical philosophers, is very far from being a homogeneous whole. Not only is it apt to contain pieces of metaphysics, and analyses of non-ethical concepts: its actual ethical contents are themselves of very different kinds. We may divide them, indeed, into four main classes. There are, first of all, propositions which express definitions of ethical terms, or judgements about the legitimacy or possibility of certain definitions. Secondly, there are propositions describing the phenomena of moral experience, and their causes. Thirdly, there are exhortations to moral virtue. And, lastly, there are actual ethical judgements. It is unfortunately the case that the distinction between these four classes, plain as it is, is commonly ignored by ethical philosophers; with the result that it is often very difficult to tell from their works what it is that they are seeking to discover or prove.

In fact, it is easy to see that only the first of our four classes, namely that which comprises the propositions relating to the definitions of ethical terms, can be said to constitute ethical philosophy. The propositions which describe the phenomena of moral experience, and their causes, must be assigned to the science of psychology, or sociology. The exhortations to moral virtue are not propositions at all, but ejaculations or commands which are designed to provoke the reader to action of a certain sort. Accordingly, they do not belong to any branch of philosophy or science. As for the expressions of ethical judgements, we have not yet determined how they should be classified. But inasmuch as they are certainly neither definitions nor comments upon definitions, nor quotations, we may say decisively that they do not belong to ethical philosophy. A strictly philosophical treatise on ethics should therefore make no ethical pronouncements. But it should, by giving an analysis of ethical terms, show what is the category to which all such pronouncements belong. And this is what we are now about to do.

A question which is often discussed by ethical philosophers is whether it is possible to find definitions which would reduce all ethical terms to one or two fundamental terms. But this question, though it undeniably belongs to ethical philosophy, is not relevant to our present enquiry. We are not now concerned to discover which term, within the sphere of ethical terms, is to be taken as fundamental; whether, for example, "good" can be defined in terms of "right" or "right" in terms of "good," or both in terms of "value." What we are interested in is the possibility of reducing the whole sphere of ethical terms to non-ethical terms. We are enquiring whether statements of ethical value can be translated into statements of empirical fact.

That they can be so translated is the contention of those ethical philosophers who are commonly called subjectivists, and of those who are known as utilitarians. For the utilitarian defines the rightness of actions, and the goodness of ends, in terms of the pleasure, or happiness, or satisfaction, to which they give rise; the subjectivist, in terms of the feelings of approval which a certain person, or group of people, has towards them. Each of these types of definition makes moral judgements into a sub-class of psychological or sociological judgements; and for this reason they are very attractive to us. For, if either was correct, it would follow that ethical assertions were not generically different from the factual assertions which are ordinarily contrasted with them; and the account which we have already given of empirical hypotheses would apply to them also.

Nevertheless we shall not adopt either a subjectivist or a utilitarian analysis of ethical terms. We reject the subjectivist view that to call an action right, or a thing good, is to say that it is generally approved of, because it is not self-contradictory to assert that some actions which are generally approved of are not right, or that some things which are generally approved of are not good. And we reject the alternative subjectivist view that a man who asserts that a certain action is right, or that a certain thing is good, is saying that he himself approves of it, on the ground that a man who confessed that he sometimes approved of what was bad or wrong would not be contradicting himself. And a similar argument is fatal to utilitarianism. We cannot agree that to call an action right is to say that of all the actions possible in the circumstances it would cause, or be likely to cause, the greatest happiness, or the greatest balance of pleasure over pain, or the greatest balance of satisfied over unsatisfied desire, because we find that it is not self-contradictory to say that it is sometimes wrong to perform the action which would actually or probably cause the greatest happiness, or the greatest balance of pleasure over pain, or of satisfied over unsatisfied desire. And since it is not self-contradictory to say that some pleasant things are not good, or that some bad things are desired, it cannot be the case that the sentence "x is good" is equivalent to "x is pleasant," or "x is desired." And to every other variant of utilitarianism with which I am acquainted the same objection can be made. And therefore we should, I think, conclude that the validity of ethical judgements is not determined by the felicific tendencies of actions, any more than by the nature of people's feelings; but that it must be regarded as "absolute" or "intrinsic," and not empirically calculable. . . .

In admitting that normative ethical concepts are irreducible to empirical concepts, we seem to be leaving the way clear for the "absolutist" view of ethics — that is, the view that statements of value are not controlled by observation, ordinary empirical propositions are, but only by a mysterious "intellectual intuition." A feature of this theory, which is seldom recognized by its advocates, is that it makes statements of value unverifiable. For it is notorious that what seems intuitively certain to one person may seem doubtful, or even false, to another. So that unless it is possible to provide some criterion by which one may decide between conflicting intuitions, a mere appeal to intuition is worthless as a test of a proposition's validity. But in the case of moral judgements, no such criterion can be given. Some moralists claim to settle the matter by saying that they "know" that their own moral judgements are correct. But such an assertion is of purely psychological interest, and has not the slightest tendency to prove the validity of any moral judgement. For dissentient moralists may equally well "know" that their ethical views are correct. And, as far as subjective certainty goes, there will be nothing to choose between them. When such differences of opinion arise in connection with an ordinary empirical proposition, one may attempt to resolve them by referring to, or actually carrying out, some relevant empirical test. But with regard to ethical statements, there is, on the "absolutist" or "intuitionist" theory, no relevant empirical test. We are therefore justified in saying that on this theory ethical statements are held to be unverifiable. . . .

Considering the use which we have made of the principle that a synthetic proposition is significant only if it is empirically verifiable, it is clear that the acceptance of an "absolutist" theory of ethics would undermine the whole of our main argument. And as we have already rejected the "naturalistic" theories which are commonly supposed to provide the only alternative to "absolutism" in ethics, we seem to have reached a difficult position. We shall meet the difficulty by showing that the correct treatment of ethical statements is afforded by a third theory, which is wholly compatible with our radical empiricism.

We begin by admitting that the fundamental ethical concepts are unanalysable, inasmuch as there is no criterion by which one can test the validity of the judgements in which they occur. So far we are in agreement with the absolutists. But, unlike the absolutists, we are able to give an explanation of this fact about ethical concepts. We say that the reason why they are unanalysable is that they are mere pseudo-concepts. The presence of an ethical symbol in a proposition adds nothing to its factual content. Thus if I say to someone, "You acted wrongly in stealing that money," I am not stating anything more than if I had simply said, "You stole that money." In adding that this action is wrong I am not making any further statement about it. I am simply evincing my moral disapproval of it. It is as if I had said, "You stole that money," in a peculiar tone of horror, or written it with the addition of some special exclamation marks. The tone, or the exclamation marks, adds nothing to the literal meaning of the sentence. It merely serves to show that the expression of it is attended by certain feelings in the speaker.

If now I generalise my previous statement and say, "Stealing money is wrong," I produce a sentence which has no factual meaning — that is, expresses no proposition which can be either true or false. It is as if I had written "Stealing money!!" — where the shape and thickness of the exclamation marks show, by a suitable convention, that a special sort of moral disapproval is the feeling which is being expressed. It is clear that there is nothing said here which can be true or false. Another man may disagree with me about the wrongness of stealing, in the sense that he may not have the same feelings about stealing as I have, and he may quarrel with me on account of my moral sentiments. But he cannot, strictly speaking, contradict me. For in saying that a certain type of action is right or wrong, I am not making any factual statement, not even a statement about my own state of mind. I am merely expressing certain moral sentiments. And the man who is ostensibly contradicting me is merely expressing his moral sentiments. So that there is plainly no sense in asking which of us is in the right. For neither of us is asserting a genuine proposition.

What we have just been saying about the symbol "wrong" applies to all normative ethical symbols. Sometimes they occur in sentences which record ordinary empirical facts besides expressing ethical feeling about those facts: sometimes they occur in sentences which simply express ethical feeling about a certain type of action, or situation, without making any statement of fact. But in every case in which one would commonly be said to be making an ethical judgement, the function of the relevant ethical word is purely "emotive." It is used to express feeling about certain objects, but not to make any assertion about them.[21]

The problems with emotivism are rather obvious, but their exploration quickly takes us deep into the nature of ethics. What happens, in the emotivist theory, to questions of justification, for surely we do justify our actions and appeal to principles? Why should a statement be unjustifiable just because it is based on emotion, for are not emotions — at least sometimes — justifiable? (One can have a right to be jealous, and one can be angry without reason.) And does emotivism mean that any ethical opinion is as warranted as any other, if only it is the sincere expression of a felt attitude or emotion? (But then, why should sincerity be important either?) Today, almost every ethicist agrees that emotivism is an inadequate and extreme theory. But if one accepts the distinction between "is" and "ought" in any of its versions and consequently accepts Moore's "open question argument," what alternatives to emotivism are there? In fact, as you can imagine, ethicists have suggested a great many more plausible metaethical theories, but these must be the substance of another course.

The rise of emotivism in ethics does suggest, however, that something has gone very wrong, not only in metaethical theory, but in the realm of normative ethics as well. Could it be, for example, that the rise of emotivism reflects a society in which — unlike the society of Aristotle or even Kant — no one knows with any confidence what is to be done, what is good or right, whether some values are really better than others? This is the argument of moral philosopher Alasdair MacIntyre, who combines normative ethics, metaethics and sociology to arrive at a diagnosis of what has gone wrong in contemporary ethical theory. (What he ultimately advocates is a return to the ethics of Aristotle.)

from *After Virtue,*
by Alasdair MacIntyre

Imagine that the natural sciences were to suffer the effects of a catastrophe. A series of environmental disasters are blamed by the general public on the scientists. Widespread riots occur, laboratories are burnt down, physicists are lynched, books and instruments are destroyed. Finally a Know-Nothing political movement takes power and successfully abolishes science teaching in schools and universities, imprisoning and executing the remaining scientists. Later still there is a reaction against this destructive movement and enlightened people seek to revive science, although they have largely forgotten what it was. But all that they possess are fragments: a knowledge of experiments detached from any knowledge of the theoretical context which gave them significance; parts of theories unrelated either to the other bits and pieces of theory which they possess or to experiment;

[21]A. J. Ayer, *Language, Truth and Logic* (New York: Dover, 1936).

instruments whose use has been forgotten; half-chapters from books, single pages from articles, not always fully legible because torn and charred. None the less all these fragments are reembodied in a set of practices which go under the revived names of physics, chemistry and biology. Adults argue with each other about the respective merits of relativity theory, evolutionary theory and phlogiston theory, although they possess only a very partial knowledge of each. Children learn by heart the surviving portions of the periodic table and recite as incantations some of the theorems of Euclid. Nobody, or almost nobody, realises that what they are doing is not natural science in any proper sense at all. For everything that they do and say conforms to certain canons of consistency and coherence and those contexts which would be needed to make sense of what they are doing have been lost, perhaps irretrievably.

In such a culture men would use expressions such as 'neutrino', 'mass', 'specific gravity', 'atomic weight' in systematic and often interrelated ways which would resemble in lesser or greater degrees the ways in which such expressions had been used in earlier times before scientific knowledge had been so largely lost. But many of the beliefs presupposed by the use of these expressions would have been lost and there would appear to be an element of arbitrariness and even of choice in their application which would appear very surprising to us. What would appear to be rival and competing premises for which no further argument could be given would abound. Subjectivist theories of science would appear and would be criticised by those who held that the notion of truth embodied in what they took to be science was incompatible with subjectivism.

· · · · ·

What is the point of constructing this imaginary world inhabited by fictitious pseudo-scientists and real, genuine philosophy? The hypothesis which I wish to advance is that in the actual world which we inhabit the language of morality is in the same state of grave disorder as the language of natural science in the imaginary world which I described. What we possess, if this view is true, are the fragments of a conceptual scheme, parts which now lack those contexts from which their significance derived. We possess indeed simulacra of morality, we continue to use many of the key expressions. But we have — very largely, if not entirely — lost our comprehension, both theoretical and practical, of morality.

· · · · ·

[ON EMOTIVISM AND MORAL DECLINE]

It is, I take it, no accident that the acutest of the modern founders of emotivism . . . were pupils of Moore; it is not implausible to suppose that they did in fact confuse moral utterance at Cambridge (and in other places with a similar inheritance) after 1903 with moral utterance as such, and that they therefore presented what was in essentials a correct account of the former as though it were an account of the latter. Moore's followers had behaved as if their disagreements over what is good were being settled by an appeal to an objective and impersonal criterion; but in fact the stronger and psychologically more adroit will was prevailing. It is unsurprising that emotivists sharply distinguished between factual, including perceptual, disagreement and what Stevenson called 'disagreement in attitude'. But if the claims of emotivism, understood as claims about the use of moral utterance at Cambridge after 1903 and its heirs and successors in London and elsewhere rather than about the meaning of moral expressions at all times and places, seem remarkably cogent, it turns out to be for reasons which at first sight seem to undermine emotivism's universal claims and with them emotivism's apparent threat to my original thesis.

What makes emotivism convincing as a thesis about a certain kind of moral utterance at Cambridge after 1903 are certain features specific to that historical episode. Those whose evaluative utterances embodied Moore's interpretations of those utterances could not have been doing what they took themselves to be doing because of the falsity of Moore's thesis. But nothing whatsoever seems to follow about moral utterance in general. Emotivism on this account turns out to be an empirical thesis, or rather a preliminary sketch of an empirical thesis, presumably to be filled out later by psychological and sociological and historical observations, about those who continue to use moral and other evaluative expressions, as if they were governed by objective and impersonal criteria, when all grasp of any such criterion has been lost. We should therefore expect emotivist types of theory to arise in a specific local circumstance as a response to types of theory and practice which share certain key features of Moore's intuitionism. Emotivism thus understood turns out to be, as a cogent theory of use rather than a false theory of meaning, connected with one specific stage in moral development or decline, a stage which our own culture entered early in the present century.

· · · · ·

The scheme of moral decline which these remarks presuppose would, as I suggested earlier, be one which required the discrimination of three distinct stages; a first at which evaluative and more especially moral theory and practice embody genuine objective and impersonal standards which provide rational justification for particular policies, actions and judgments and which themselves in turn are susceptible of rational justification; a second stage at which there are unsuccessful attempts to maintain the objectivity and impersonality of moral judgments, but during which the project of providing rational justifications both by means of and for the standards continuously breaks down; and a third stage at which theories of an emotivist kind secure wide implicit acceptance because of a general implicit recognition in practice, though not in explicit theory, that claims to objectivity and impersonality cannot be made good. . . . What I have suggested to be the case by and large about our own culture — that in moral argument the apparent assertion of principles functions as a mask for expressions of personal preference — is what emotivism takes to be universally the case.

· · · · ·

[THE SOCIAL CONTEXT OF EMOTIVISM]

A moral philosophy — and emotivism is no exception — characteristically presupposes a sociology. For every moral philosophy offers explicitly or implicitly at least a partial conceptual analysis of the relationship of an agent to his or her reasons, motives, intentions and actions, and in so doing generally presupposes some claim that these concepts are embodied or at least can be in the real social world. Even Kant, who sometimes seems to restrict moral agency to the inner realm of the noumenal, implies otherwise in his writings on law, history and politics. Thus it would generally be a decisive refutation of a moral philosophy to show that moral agency on its own account of the matter could never be socially embodied; and it also follows that we have not yet fully understood the claims of any moral philosophy until we have spelled out what its social embodiment would be. Some moral philosophers in the past, perhaps most, have understood this spelling out as itself one part of the task of moral philosophy. So, it scarcely needs to be said, Plato and Aristotle, so indeed also Hume and Adam Smith; but at least since Moore the dominant narrow conception of moral philosophy has ensured that the moral philosophers could ignore this task; as notably do the philosophical proponents of emotivism. We therefore must perform it for them.

What is the key to the social content of emotivism? It is the fact that emotivism entails the obliteration of any genuine distinction between manipulative and non-manipulative social relations. Consider the contrast between, for example, Kantian ethics and emotivism on this point. For Kant ... the difference between a human relationship uninformed by morality and one so informed is precisely the difference between one in which each person treats the other primarily as a means to his or her ends and one in which each treats the other as an end. To treat someone else as an end is to offer them what I take to be good reasons for acting in one way rather than another, but to leave it to them to evaluate those reasons. It is to be unwilling to influence another except by reasons which that other he or she judges to be good. It is to appeal to impersonal criteria of the validity of which each rational agent must be his or her own judge. By contrast, to treat someone else as a means is to seek to make him or her an instrument of my purposes by adducing whatever influences or considerations will in fact be effective in this or that occasion. The generalisations of the sociology and psychology of persuasion are what I shall need to guide me, not the standards of a normative rationality.

If emotivism is true, this distinction is illusory. For evaluative utterance can in the end have no point or use but the expression of my own feelings or attitudes and the transformation of the feelings and attitudes of others. I cannot genuinely appeal to impersonal criteria, for there are no impersonal criteria. I may think that I so appeal and others may think that I so appeal, but these thoughts will always be mistakes. The sole reality of distinctively moral discourse is the attempt of one will to align the attitudes, feelings, preferences and choices of another with its own. Others are always means, never ends.

What then would the social world *look* like, if seen with emotivist eyes? And what would the social world *be* like, if the truth of emotivism came to be widely presupposed? The general form of the answer to these questions is now clear, but the social detail depends in part on the nature of particular social contexts; it will make a difference in what milieu and in the service of what particular and specific interests the distinction between manipulative and non-manipulative social relationships has been obliterated. William Gass has suggested that it was a principal concern of Henry James to examine the consequences of the obliteration of this distinction in the lives of a particular kind of rich European in *The Portrait of a Lady* . . . that the novel turns out to be an investigation, in Gass's words, 'of what it means to be a consumer of persons, and of what it means to be a person consumed.' The metaphor of consumption acquires its appropriateness from the milieu; James is concerned with rich aesthetes whose interest is to fend off the kind of boredom that is so characteristic of modern leisure by contriving behaviour in others that will be responsive to their wishes, that will feed their stated appetites. Those wishes may or may not be benevolent, but the distinction between characters who entertain themselves by willing the good of others and those who pursue the fulfilment of their desires without a concern for any good but their own . . . is not as important to James as the distinction between a whole milieu in which the manipulative mode of moral instrumentalism has triumphed and one, such as the New England of *The Europeans*, of which this was not true . . . The unifying preoccupation of that tradition is the condition of those who see in the social world nothing but a meeting place for individual wills each with its own set of attitudes and preferences and who understand that world solely as an arena for the achievement of their own satisfaction, who interpret reality as a series of opportunities for their enjoyment and for whom the last enemy is boredom.

Another social context is that provided by the life of organisations, of those bureaucratic structures which, whether in the form of private corporations or of government agencies, define the working tasks of so many of our contemporaries. One sharp contrast with the lives of the aesthetic rich secures immediate attention. The rich aesthete with a plethora of means searches restlessly for ends on which he may employ them; but the organisation is characteristically engaged in a competitive struggle for scarce resources to put to the service of its predetermined ends. It is therefore a central responsibility of managers to direct and redirect their organisations' available resources, both human and non-human, as effectively as possible toward those ends. Every bureaucratic organisation embodies some explicit or implicit definition of costs and benefits from which the criteria of effectiveness are derived. Bureaucratic rationality is the rationality of matching means to ends economically and efficiently.

·   ·   ·   ·   ·

[CONCLUSION]

It is always dangerous to draw too precise parallels between one historical period and another; and among the most misleading of such parallels are those which have been drawn between our own age in Europe and North America and the epoch in which the Roman empire declined into the Dark Ages. None the less certain parallels there are. A crucial turning point in that earlier history occurred when men and women of good will turned aside from the task of shoring up the Roman *imperium* and ceased to iden-

tify the continuation of civility and moral community with the maintenance of that *imperium*. What they set themselves to achieve instead —
often not recognising fully what they were doing — was the construction of
new forms of community within which the moral life could be sustained
so that both morality and civility might survive the coming ages of barbarism and darkness. If my account of our moral condition is correct, we
ought also to conclude that for some time now we too have reached that
turning point. What matters at this stage is the construction of local forms
of community within which civility and the intellectual and moral life can
be sustained through the new dark ages which are already upon us. And if
the tradition of the virtues was able to survive the horrors of the last dark
ages, we are not entirely without grounds for hope. This time however the
barbarians are not waiting beyond the frontiers; they have already been governing us for quite some time. . . .[22]

SUMMARY AND CONCLUSION

In this chapter, we have reviewed a half dozen or so theories of morality. (1)
Aristotle takes the key to morality to be the concept of "virtue," which he argues
to be activity in accordance with rational principles. He bases this argument on
a concept of what is "natural" for man, but his discussion is clearly limited to a
small class of Greek male citizens, whom he views as the ideal specimens of
humanity. (2) Hume and Rousseau both argue that morality must be based on
certain kinds of feelings or "sentiments." "Reason is and ought to be the slave of
the passions," Hume argues, and Rousseau similarly argues that man is "naturally" good. (3) Kant insists that morality is strictly a matter of rational principle
divorced from all personal interests and desires ("inclinations"). This includes a
rejection of Hume and Rousseau, who base morality on feelings (which are inclinations in Kant's sense). This also includes a rejection of Aristotle. Although both
philosophers use the notion of a "rational principle," Kant intends his notion to
apply to every human being, and therefore every person has the same duties and
obligations. (4) The utilitarians, Bentham and Mill, reject Kant's divorce between
morality and personal interest and argue that morality is our guide to the satisfaction of the greatest number of interests of the greatest number of people. (5)
Nietzsche rejects both Kant and the utilitarians, preferring a return to the elitism
and "virtue" orientation of Aristotle's morality. He argues that we create our values and live with them according to our personal needs. Following him, the existentialists, particularly Jean-Paul Sartre, argue that all values are chosen by us;
there is no "true" morality, only those values to which we have voluntarily committed ourselves. (6) American pragmatism rejects the sharp boundaries between
"is" and "ought," and (7) shifting to the "metaethical" level of analysis, contem-

[22]Alasdair MacIntyre, *After Virtue* (Notre Dame, Ind.: Univ. of Notre Dame Press, 1981).

porary English and American ethicists have suggested that the whole idea of justification by reference to happiness or reason may be mistaken, with some disturbing consequences.

GLOSSARY

a priori: in moral philosophy, independent of particular circumstances. In Kant's philosophy, moral laws are said to be *a priori* in this sense.

altruism: the thesis that one ought to act for the sake of the interests of others.

autonomy: independence. Moral autonomy is the ability of every rational person to reach his or her own moral conclusions about what is right and what is wrong. (This does not mean that they will therefore come to different conclusions.)

categorical imperative: in Kant's philosophy, a moral law, a command that is unqualified and not dependent on any conditions or qualifications. In particular, that rule that tells us to act in such a way that we would want everyone else to act the same way.

commitment: to form a binding obligation voluntarily. In Sartre's moral philosophy, a commitment is a freely chosen adoption of a moral principle or project, which one thereby vows to defend and practice, even in the absence of any other reasons for doing so. And since, according to Sartre, there are never conclusive reasons for adopting any particular moral position, one must always defend his or her position through commitment and nothing else.

conscience: a sense or feeling about what is right and wrong, usually without argument. (It is like intuition in matters of knowledge.) In Christian moral theory, it is a moral sense instilled in us by God. In Freudian psychology, it is the internalization of the moral lessons given us as children by our parents and teachers.

contemplation (the life of): according to Aristotle (and other philosophers), the happiest life, the life of thought and philosophy.

cultural relativism: the descriptive anthropological thesis that different societies have different moralities. It is important to stress that these moralities must be fundamentally different, not only different in details. Some societies consider an act as stealing while others do not, but a society that does not have a conception of private property might be fundamentally different from one that does.

deontology: ethics based on duty (Gk: *dein*). Kant's ethic is deontological in that it stresses obedience to principle rather than attention to consequences (including happiness).

duty: what one is morally bound to do.

egoism: the thesis that people act for their own interests. *Psychological egoism* is merely the thesis that they in fact act in their own interests; *ethical egoism* is the thesis that people ought to act in their own interests.

emotivism: the view that ethical statements are simply an expression of feeling or attitude and therefore not justifiable or knowable as true or false.

ethics: a system of general moral principles and a conception of morality and its foundation. Or, the study of moral principles.

ethical absolutism: the thesis that there is one and only one correct morality.

ethical egoism: the thesis that people ought to act in their own interests.

ethical absolutism [handwritten annotation in top margin]

ethical relativism: the thesis that different moralities should be considered equally correct even if they directly contradict each other. A morality is "correct," by this thesis, merely if it is correct according to the particular society that accepts it.

eudaimonia: Aristotle's word for "happiness," or, more literally, "living well."

existentialism: the modern movement in philosophy that puts great emphasis on individual choice and the voluntary acceptance of all values.

Golden Rule: "Do unto others as you would have them do unto you."

happiness: the achievement of the good life. In Aristotle, the name we all agree to give to the good life, whatever it is. Happiness, in this sense, must not be confused with pleasure, which is but one (among many) concerns and conceptions of the good life.

happiness calculus (also *felicity calculus*): Bentham's technique for quantifying and adding up pleasures and pains as a way of deciding what to do.

hedonism: the conception of the good life that takes pleasure to be the ultimate good. Hedonism is the premise of most forms of utilitarianism. It is often the premise — though sometimes a consequence — of ethical egoism. (These two are not the same: hedonism refers to the *end*; egoism refers to *whose* ends.)

hypothetical imperative: in Kant, a command that is conditional, depending upon particular aims or inclinations. For example, "if you want to be a doctor, then go to medical school." According to Kant, all other philosophers (Aristotle, Hume, Rousseau) took morality to be a hypothetical imperative. He does not.

immoralist: a person who rejects the ultimate claims of morality. An immoralist need not actually break the rules of morality; he does not consider them absolute rules and claims that other considerations (even personal considerations) may override them.

imperative: a command.

inclination: Kant's term for all personal considerations: desires, feelings, emotions, attitudes, moods, etc.

law: an objective rule that is binding on individuals whether they personally accept it or not. Contrasted with *maxim*.

master morality: in Nietzsche, a morality that takes personal self-realization as primary, so-called because it was the morality of the "masters" in the slave states of the ancient world (including Greece).

maxim: in Kant, a personal rule or intention. Contrasted with *law*.

mean (between the extremes): in Aristotle, the middle course, not too much, not too little. Courage, for example, is a mean because a person with courage is neither too timid to fight nor so lacking in fear that he or she is rash or reckless in the face of danger.

metaethics: the study of ethical language and the nature of justification of ethical statements.

morality: in general, the rules for right action and prohibitions against wrong acts. Sometimes morality is that single set of absolute rules and prohibitions that are valid for all men at all times and all societies. More loosely, a morality can be any set of ultimate principles, and there might be any number of moralities in different societies.

naturalism: the view that ethical statements are ultimately based on facts (about human nature, happiness, reason, feeling).

naturalistic fallacy: according to Moore, inferring an "ought" statement from factual premises.

non-cognitivism: the view that ethical statements are neither true nor false and so cannot be *known* to be true or false.

non-naturalism: the view that ethical statements are not ultimately based on facts.

obligation: bound by duty. For example, "you have an obligation to keep your promises."

ought: the verb most often used to express moral duty or obligation. Sometimes "should" is used, but this is ambiguously between "ought" and merely "preferable." Sometimes "must" or "have to" is used, but this is ambiguously between "ought to" and "forced to." In Hume's ethics (and in many others as well) "ought" is contrasted with "is" as the hallmark of value (esp. moral) judgment.

principle of utility: in Bentham, the principle that one ought to do what gives the greatest pleasure to the greatest number of people.

psychological egoism: the thesis that people always act for their own self-interest, even when it seems as if they are acting for other people's benefit (for example, in giving to charity, the egoist would say, the person is simply making himself or herself feel self-righteous).

rationality: acting in the best possible way; according to reason. Sometimes, rationality means simply doing what is best under the circumstances, without insisting that there is only one rational way of acting. In other words, rationality is considered relative to particular interests and circumstances. In Kant's philosophy, however, rationality refers to that faculty that allows us to act in the correct way, without reference to particular interests and circumstances.

relativism: the thesis that morals are relative to particular societies, particular interests, particular circumstances, or particular individuals. (See *cultural relativism, ethical relativism.*)

selfishness: acting in one's own interest to the exclusion of other's interests. The word has a nasty connotation and so should be separated from the more neutral claims of the psychological egoist. To say that a person is acting selfishly is to condemn him or her and say that the action is blameworthy. It is possible to act for one's own interests, however, and not be selfish, for one may also act for the benefit of others. A selfish act is to the exclusion of other people's interests; an act may be both in one's own interests and in the interests of others, however.

sentiment: feeling, emotion; particularly moral feelings (as in Hume, Rousseau).

slave morality: in Nietzsche's moral philosophy, a morality that takes duties and obligations as primary, so-called because it was the morality of the slaves who were not allowed to aspire any higher than mere efficiency and personal comfort.

sympathy: fellow feeling; felt concern for other people's welfare. In the ethics of Hume and Rousseau, the necessary and universal sentiment without which morals—and society—would be impossible.

utilitarianism: the moral philosophy that says that we should act in such ways as to make the greatest number of people as happy as possible.

virtue: moral excellence. In Aristotle's philosophy, a state of character according to which we enjoy doing what is right. In Kant, willing what is right (whether or not we enjoy it, in fact, especially if we don't enjoy it).

will: the power of mind that allows us to choose our own actions, or, at least, what we shall try to do. In Kant, a good will is the only thing that is good "without qualification," in other words, acting for the right reasons and good intentions.

will to power: in Nietzsche's philosophy, the thesis that every act is ultimately aimed at superiority, sometimes over other people, but, more importantly, superiority according to one's own standards. In other words, it is what Aristotle meant by excellence. (Nietzsche has often been interpreted, however, to mean political power.)

11

Politics

Man is by nature an animal designed for living in states.

Aristotle

"Man is a social animal," wrote Aristotle. Therefore, he is a political animal as well. We live with other people, not just our friends and families but thousands and millions of others, most of whom we will never meet and many of whom we come across in only the most casual way — passing them as we cross the street or buying a ticket at the movie theater. Yet we have to be concerned about them, and they about us, for there is a sense in which we are all clearly dependent upon each other. For example, we depend on them not to attack us without reason or steal our possessions. Of course, our confidence varies from person to person and from city to city. But it is clear that, in general, we have duties towards people we never know, for example, the duty not to contaminate their water or air supplies, or place their lives in danger. And they have similar duties to us. We also claim certain rights for ourselves: for example, the right not to be attacked as we walk down the street, the right to speak our mind about politically controversial issues without being thrown in jail, the right to believe in this religion or that religion or no religion without having our jobs, our homes, or our freedom taken from us.

Political and social philosophy is the study of people in societies with particular attention the abstract claims they have on each other in the form of "rights," "duties,"and "privileges," and their demands for "justice," "equality," and "freedom." (It is important to distinguish this sense of *political* freedom from the causal or metaphysical freedom that we discussed in Chapter 9. These can be and are almost always discussed independently of each other.) At least ideally, politics is continuous with morality. Our political duties and obligations, for example, are often the same as our moral duties and obligations. Our claims to certain "moral rights" are often claims to political rights as well, and political rights — particularly those very general and absolute rights which we call human rights (for example, the right not to be tortured or degraded, the right not to be exploited by powerful institutions or persons) — are typically defended on the basis of moral principles. The virtues of government are ideally the virtues of individuals: Government should be just, temperate, courageous, honest, humane, considerate, and reasonable. Plato and Aristotle, for example, portrayed their visions of the ideal state in precisely these terms. (Both Plato and Aristotle, unlike most modern philosophers, actually had the opportunity to set up such governments; both failed, but for reasons that were hardly their fault.) This is not to say that all politics or all politicians are moral; we know much better than that. But it is to say that our politics are constrained and determined by our sense of morality. Morality is concerned more with relations between particular people while politics is concerned more with large and impersonal groups. But the difference is one of degree. In ancient Greece, Plato and Aristotle lived in relatively small "city-states" (each called a *polis*), with fewer citizens than even most American towns. It was much easier for them to treat morality and politics together. But even today, we still speak hopefully of "the human family" and "international brother-sisterhood," which is to reassert our belief that politics — even international hot-and-cold war politics — ought to be based on interpersonal moral principles.

The key to a successful society is cooperation. With few exceptions, it is in everyone's interest that society work smoothly, without vast bureaucratic confusion, without corruption, without general chaos, without exploitation of the weaker members of society, and without forcing anyone to feel that he or she is justified in stealing, cheating, murdering, or "getting even" with society as a whole. But the smooth working of society as a whole, even though it generally benefits everyone, is not the only concern. Societies of ants and bees work more "smoothly" than any human society, but they are not to be envied or imitated. Even if it is agreed that the smooth working of society is generally in everyone's interest, what we may call the public interest, individual interests deserve and sometimes demand recognition even in opposition to this broader public interest. A person who is critical of the government may very well disrupt the smooth operations of that government. He or she may even, at least for a short time, interfere with the public interest. But most of us would agree that such a person has a right to speak his or her mind and that he or she has a right to be heard as well. Or, to take a very different example, scientists or artists might feel the need to act in ways that are very unpopular or antisocial in order to do their work with the intensity they require. Despite the fact that they might annoy us, we would say that they have a right to live that way. Or, to take still a different example, people who have sexual preferences and desires that are not approved of by most people around them — perhaps they just enjoy an occasional obscene movie — can claim to have rights as well, so long as they don't force their preferences on other people or otherwise interfere with other people's lives. But you can see that with this last set of examples we have entered an area of continuing controversy. Do people have rights to enjoy things that are disapproved of by the rest of society? Should governments dictate morals (for example, by passing laws against the things that most people or at least some powerful people consider "immoral")? And the very existence of such controversies shows very clearly how different we are from ants and bees. In their societies, species preservation and instinct dictate all; in our societies, there must always be a balance between the public interest on the one hand and individual rights and interests on the other. Ideally, these will agree as much as possible. In fact, they often do not agree. And political and social philosophy makes this disagreement its primary concern.

If people do not cooperate, the success of society requires that some authority have the power to bring individual interests into line with the public interest. This authority is generally called the state. The state passes laws and enforces them; its purpose is to protect the public interest. But is it only this? We would probably say "no." Its purpose is also to protect individual rights, for example, against powerful corporations and against strongly mobilized pressure groups that try to interfere with individual lives. In general, we might say that the function of the state is to protect justice. But there has been disagreement ever since ancient times about what that means and how much the primary emphasis should be placed on the public interest and how much on individual rights and interests.

Our concept of the state and the extent of its power and **authority** depends very much on our conception of human nature and of people's willingness to cooperate without being forced to do so. At one extreme there are those who place such strong emphasis on the smooth workings of society that they are willing to sacrifice most individual rights and interests; they are generally called *authoritarians*, and their confidence in willing individual cooperation is very slight compared to their confidence in a strong authoritarian state. ("But he did make the trains run on time" is often said of the fascist Italian dictator Benito Mussolini.) At the other extreme there are people with so much confidence in individual cooperation and so little confidence in the state that they argue that the state should be eliminated altogether. They are called **anarchists.** Between these extremes are those positions that are more moderate, for example, there are people who have some confidence both in individual cooperation and in the possibility of a reasonably just state but don't have complete confidence in either. Democrats and Republicans, for example, both believe in a government that is at least partially run by the people themselves but with sufficient power to enforce its laws over individual interests whenever necessary. All these people believe in varying solutions to the same central problem: the problem of a balance between the public interest and the need for cooperation on the one hand and individual rights and interests on the other — in other words, the problem of **justice.**

THE PROBLEM OF JUSTICE

When we think of justice, we first tend to think of criminal cases and problems of punishment. Justice, in this sense, is catching the criminal and "making him pay for his crime." The oldest sense of the word "justice," therefore, is what philosophers call **retributive justice,** or simply, "getting even." Retribution for a crime is making the criminal suffer or pay an amount appropriate to the severity of the crime. In ancient traditions, the key phrase was "an eye for an eye, a tooth for a tooth." If a criminal caused a person to be blind, he was in turn blinded. We now view this as brutal and less than civilized. But is it so clear that we have in fact given up this retributive sense of justice? Do we punish our criminals (that is, demand retribution), or do we sincerely attempt to reform them? Or is the purpose of prison simply to keep them off the street? Should we ever punish people for crimes, or should we simply protect ourselves against their doing the same thing again? If a man commits an atrocious murder, is it enough that we guarantee that he won't do another one? Or does he deserve punishment even if we know that he won't do it again?

But retributive justice and the problems of punishment are really only a small piece of a much larger concern. Justice is not just "getting even" for crimes and offenses. It concerns the running of society as a whole in day-to-day civil matters as well as the more dramatic criminal concerns. Given the relative scarcity of wealth and goods, how should they be distributed? Should everyone receive exactly the same amount? Should the person who works hard at an unpleasant job receive no more than the person who refuses to work at all and prefers to watch T.V. all day and just amuse himself or herself? Should the person who uses his wealth to the benefit of others receive no more than the person who "throws away" his or her money on gambling, drinking, and debauchery? If a class of people have been historically deprived of their adequate share because of the color of their skin, their religious beliefs, or their sex or age, should they now be given more than their share in compensation, or is this too an injustice against other people?

It is not only wealth and goods that are at issue here, however. Distribution of privileges and power are equally important. Who will vote? Will everyone's vote count exactly the same? Should the opinions of an illiterate who does not even know the name of his political leaders have as much say in the government as the political scientist or economist who has studied these matters for years? Should everyone be allowed to drive? Or to drink? Should everyone receive exactly the same treatment before the law? Or are there concerns that would indicate that some people (for example, congressmen or foreign diplomats) should receive special privileges? Enjoyment of society's cultural gifts is also at issue. Should everyone receive the same education? What if that turns out to be "impractical" (since job training is much more efficient than "liberal arts")? But doesn't that mean that some — the workers and career persons who are trained to do a job — are deprived of the training that is necessary to enjoy great books, music, poetry, philosophy, intellectual debate, proficiency in foreign languages, which give considerable enjoyment to those who have been taught to appreciate them?

There are also questions of status. Should there be social classes? What if it could be proved that such divisions make a society run more smoothly? How minimal should distinctions in status be? And this in turn leads to the more general question, shouldn't all members of society be able to expect equal treatment and respect not only by the law but in every conceivable social situation? All of these are the concerns of justice. But what is just? Who decides? And how?

Theories of justice, in one sense, are as old as human society. The ancient codes of the Hebrews, the Persians, and the Babylonians were theories of justice in the sense that they tried, in their various ways, to develop rules to cover fair dealing and distribution of goods, the punishment of criminals, and the settling of disputes. A fully developed theory of justice, however, should go beyond this and try to analyze the nature of justice itself. The first great theories of justice to try to do this were those of Plato and Aristotle. In the *Republic*, Plato argued that justice in the state is precisely the same as justice in the individual, that is, a harmony between the various parts for the good of the whole. In other words, cooperation among all for the sake of a successful society is the key to justice. But this means that the interests of the individual take a clearly secondary role to the interests of society. In ancient Greece, this may have been only rarely true for the wealthy and powerful, but for the majority of people — especially the slaves — this secondary role was the norm. Because their docile submission was seen as necessary to the overall success of society, their individual interests and rights were extremely minimal. They expected to be rewarded and satisfied only insofar as their efforts benefited their betters, and then they expected their betters to reap far more reward from their labor than they themselves. In Plato's universe, everyone has his or her "place," and justice means that they act and are treated accordingly:

from *The Republic*,
by Plato

I think that justice is the very thing, or some form of the thing which, when we were beginning to found our city, we said had to be established throughout. We stated, and often repeated, if you remember, that everyone must pursue one occupation of those in the city, that for which his nature best fitted him.

Yes, we kept saying that.

Further, we have heard many people say, and have often said ourselves, that justice is to perform one's own task and not to meddle with that of others.

We have said that.

This then, my friend, I said, when it happens, is in some way justice, to do one's own job. And do you know what I take to be a proof of this?

No, tell me.

I think what is left over of those things we have been investigating, after moderation and courage and wisdom have been found, was that which made it possible for those three qualities to appear in the city and to continue as long as it was present. We also said that what remained after we found the other three was justice.

It had to be.

And surely, I said, if we had to decide which of the four will make the city good by its presence, it would be hard to judge whether it is a common belief among the rulers and the ruled, or the preservation among the soldiers of a law-inspired belief as to the nature of what is, and what is not, to be feared, or the knowledge and guardianship of the rulers, or whether it is, above all, the presence of this fourth in child and woman, slave and free, artisan, ruler and subject, namely that each man, a unity in himself, performed his own task and was not meddling with that of others.

How could this not be hard to judge?

It seems then that the capacity for each in the city to perform his own task rivals wisdom, moderation, and courage as a source of excellence for the city.

It certainly does.

You would then describe justice as a rival to them for excellence in the city?

Most certainly.

Look at it this way and see whether you agree: you will order your rulers to act as judges in the courts of the city?

Surely.

And will their exclusive aim in delivering judgement not be that no citizen should have what belongs to another or be deprived of what is his own?

That would be their aim.

That being just?

Yes.

In some way then possession of one's own and the performance of one's own task could be agreed to be justice.

That is so.

Consider then whether you agree with me in this: if a carpenter attempts to do the work of a cobbler, or a cobbler that of a carpenter, and they exchange their tools and the esteem that goes with the job, or the same man tries to do both, and all the other exchanges are made, do you think that this does any great harm to the city?

No.

But I think that when one who is by nature a worker or some other kind of moneymaker is puffed up by wealth, or by the mob, or by his own strength, or some other such thing, and attempts to enter the warrior class, or one of the soldiers tries to enter the group of counsellors and guardians, though he is unworthy of it, and these exchange their tools and the public esteem, or when the same man tries to perform all these jobs together, then I think you will agree that these exchanges and this meddling bring the city to ruin.

They certainly do.

The meddling and exchange between the three established orders does very great harm to the city and would most correctly be called wickedness.

Very definitely.

And you would call the greatest wickedness worked against one's own city injustice?

Of course.

That then is injustice. And let us repeat that the doing of one's own job by the moneymaking, auxiliary, and guardian groups, when each group is performing its own task in the city, is the opposite, it is justice and makes the city just.

I agree with you that this is so.[1]

Plato's rigid hierarchy of social classes and insistence on the inequality of people offends our sense of universal equality, but it is important to see that equality (or, more properly, **egalitarianism,** the view that all men and women are equal just by virtue of their being human) is a position that must be argued and is not a "natural" state of affairs or a belief that has always been accepted by everyone. The same is true of Aristotle's theory of justice. In his *Politics*, he gives an unabashed defense of slavery, not only on the grounds that slaves are efficient and good for society as a whole, but because those who are slaves are "naturally" meant to be slaves and would be unhappy and unable to cope if they were granted freedom and made citizens. (This is not just an ancient argument, however. I am sure you have heard similar arguments about other groups of people in your own lifetimes.) For Aristotle as for Plato, different people have different roles, and to treat unequals equally is as unjust, according to them, as it is to treat equals unequally. They would consider the view that morons and children and foreigners deserve the same respect and treatment as citizens ridiculous. So too would they find the contemporary argument that we should treat men and women as equals. But despite these opinions, Plato and Aristotle laid the foundations of much of our own conceptions of justice. The idea that equals must be treated as equals is the foundation of our sense of justice just as much as theirs. The difference is that we are taught to believe that everybody is an equal. Similarly, the theory of what is called **distributive justice,** the fair distribution of wealth and goods among the members of society, is a current international as well as national concern that owes much to Aristotle's original formulations. The idea that individuals are due certain rewards for their labor is also Aristotle's idea. But despite his aristocratic opinions and his harsh elitism, Aristotle saw quite clearly that the members of society who depended most upon an adequate theory of justice were the poorer and less powerful members. It was for them that the just society was most vital (since the powerful and wealthy had a much better chance of taking care of themselves). And it was Aristotle who made the vital distinction, with which we began this section, between that restricted concern for justice that rights certain wrongs (in crimes, in bad business deals, and in public misfortunes) and the general concern of justice for a well-balanced and reasonable society. What follows are brief excerpts from Aristotle's analysis of the virtue of justice in his *Nicomachean Ethics:*

> Let us take as a starting-point, then, the various meanings of "an unjust man." Both the lawless man and the greedy and unfair man are thought to be unjust, so that evidently both the law-abiding and the fair man will be

[1]Plato, *The Republic*, Bk. VI, trans. G. M. A. Grube (Indianapolis, Ind.: Hackett, 1974).

just. The just, then, is the lawful and the fair, the unjust the unlawful and the unfair.

Since the lawless man was seen to be unjust and the law-abiding man just, evidently all lawful acts are in a sense just acts; for the acts laid down by the legislative art are lawful, and each of these, we say, is just. Now the laws in their enactments on all subjects aim at the common advantage either of all or of the best or of those who hold power, or something of the sort; so that in one sense we call those acts just that tend to produce and preserve happiness and its components for the political society. And the law bids us do both the acts of a brave man (*e.g.* not to desert our post nor take to flight nor throw away our arms), and those of a temperate man (*e.g.* not to commit adultery nor to gratify one's lust), and those of a good-tempered man (*e.g.* not to strike another nor to speak evil), and similarly with regard to the other virtues and forms of wickedness, commanding some acts and forbidding others; and the rightly-framed law does this rightly, and the hastily conceived one less well.

This form of justice, then, is complete virtue, but not absolutely, but in relation to our neighbour. And therefore justice is often thought to be the greatest of virtues, and "neither evening nor morning star" is so wonderful; and proverbially "in justice is every virtue comprehended." And it is complete virtue in its fullest sense, because it is the actual exercise of complete virtue. It is complete because he who possesses it can exercise his virtue not only in himself but towards his neighbour also; for many men can exercise virtue in their own affairs, but not in their relations to their neighbour.

· · · · ·

But at all events what we are investigating is the justice which is a *part* of virtue; for there is a justice of this kind, as we maintain. Similarly it is with injustice in the particular sense that we are concerned.

That there is such a thing is indicated by the fact that while the man who exhibits in action the other forms of wickedness acts wrongly indeed, but not graspingly (*e.g.* the man who throws away his shield through cowardice or speaks harshly through bad temper or fails to help a friend with money through meanness), when a man acts graspingly he often exhibits none of these vices — no, nor all together, but certainly wickedness of some kind (for we blame him) and injustice. There is, then, another kind of injustice which is a part of injustice in the wide sense, and a use of the word "unjust" which answers to a part of what is unjust in the wide sense of "contrary to the law." Again, if one man commits adultery for the sake of gain and makes money by it, while another does so at the bidding of appetite though he loses money and is penalized for it, the latter would be held to be self-indulgent rather than grasping, but the former is unjust, but not self-indulgent; evidently, therefore, he is unjust by reason of his making gain by his act. Again, all other unjust acts are ascribed invariably to some particular kind of wickedness, for example adultery to self-indulgence, the desertion of a comrade in battle to cowardice, physical violence to anger; but if a man makes gain, his action is ascribed to no form of wickedness but injustice. Evidently, therefore, there is apart from injustice in the wide sense another, "particular," injustice which shares the name and nature of the first, because its definition falls within the same genus; for the significance of both consists in a relation to one's neighbour, but the one is concerned with honour or money or safety — or that which includes all these, if we had a single name for it — and its motive is the pleasure that arises from gain; while the other is concerned with all the objects with which the good man is concerned.

It is clear, then, that there is more than one kind of justice, and that there is one which is distinct from virtue entire; we must try to grasp its genus and differentia.

. . . . .

Of particular justice and that which is just in the corresponding sense, (A) one kind is that which is manifested in distributions of honour or money or the other things that fall to be divided among those who have a share in the constitution (for in these it is possible for one man to have a share either unequal or equal to that of another), and (B) one is that which plays a rectifying part in transactions between man and man. Of this there are two divisions; of transactions (1) some are voluntary and (2) others involuntary — voluntary such transactions as sale, purchase, loan for consumption, pledging, loan for use, depositing, letting (they are called voluntary because the origin of these transactions is voluntary), while of the involuntary (a) some are clandestine, such as theft, adultery, poisoning, procuring, enticement of slaves, assassination, false witness, and (b) others are violent, such as assault, imprisonment, murder, robbery with violence, mutilation, abuse, insult.

. . . . .

(A) We have shown that both the unjust man and the unjust act are unfair or unequal; now it is clear that there is also an intermediate between the two unequals involved in either case. And this is the equal; for in any kind of action in which there is a more and a less there is also what is equal. If, then, the unjust is unequal, the just is equal, as all men suppose it to be, even apart from argument. And since the equal is intermediate, the just will be an intermediate. Now equality implies at least two things. The just, then, must be both intermediate and equal and relative (*i.e.* for certain persons). And *qua* intermediate it must be between certain things (which are respectively greater and less); *qua* equal, it involves *two* things; *qua* just, it is for certain people. The just, therefore, involves at least four terms; for the persons for whom it is in fact just are two, and the things in which it is manifested, the objects distributed, are two. And the same equality will exist between the persons and between the things concerned; for as the latter — the things concerned — are related, so are the former; if they are not equal, they will not have what is equal, but this is the origin of quarrels and complaints — when either equals have and are awarded unequal shares, or unequals equal shares. Further, this is plain from the fact that awards should be "according to merit;" for all men agree that what is just in distribution must be according to merit in some sense, though they do not all specify the same sort of merit, but democrats identify it with the status of freeman, supporters of oligarchy with wealth (or with noble birth), and supporters of aristocracy with excellence.

This, then, is what the just is — the proportional; the unjust is what violates the proportion. Hence one term becomes too great, the other too small, as indeed happens in practice, for the man who acts unjustly has too much, and the man who is unjustly treated too little, of what is good. In the case

of evil the reverse is true; for the lesser evil is reckoned a good in comparison with the greater evil, since the lesser evil is rather to be chosen than
the greater, and what is worthy of choice is good, and what is worthier of
choice a greater good.

This, then, is one species of the just.

(B) The remaining one is the rectificatory, which arises in connexion with
transactions both voluntary and involuntary. This form of the just has a
different specific character from the former. For the justice which distrib-
utes common possessions is always in accordance with the kind of proportion mentioned above (for in the case also in which the distribution is made
from the common funds of a partnership it will be according to the same
ratio which the funds put into the business by the partners bear to one
another); and the injustice opposed to this kind of justice is that which violates the proportion. But the justice in transactions between man and man
is a sort of equality indeed, and the injustice a sort of inequality; not according to that kind of proportion, however, but according to arithmetical proportion. For it makes no difference whether a good man has defrauded a bad
man or a bad man a good one, nor whether it is a good or a bad man that
has committed adultery; the law looks only to the distinctive character of
the injury, and treats the parties as equal, if one is in the wrong and the
other is being wronged, and if one inflicted injury and the other has
received it. Therefore, this kind of injustice being an inequality, the judge
tries to equalize it; for in the case also in which one has received and the
other has inflicted a wound, or one has slain and the other been slain, the
suffering and the action have been unequally distributed; but the judge tries
to equalize things by means of the penalty, taking away from the gain of
the assailant. For the term "gain" is applied generally to such cases, even if
it be not a term appropriate to certain cases, for example to the person who
inflicts a wound—and "loss" to the sufferer; at all events when the suffering has been estimated, the one is called loss and the other gain. Therefore
the equal is intermediate between the greater and the less, but the gain and
the loss are respectively greater and less in contrary ways; more of the good
and less of the evil are gain, and the contrary is loss; intermediate between
them is, as we saw, the equal, which we say is just; therefore corrective
justice will be the intermediate between loss and gain. This is why, when
people dispute, they take refuge in the judge; and to go to the judge is to go
to justice; for the nature of the judge is to be a sort of animate justice; and
they seek the judge as an intermediate; and in some states they call judges
mediators, on the assumption that if they get what is intermediate they will
get what is just. The just, then, is an intermediate, since the judge is so. The
judge restores equality. . . .[2]

In contrast to the Greeks, the premise of most modern theories of justice has
been the equality of everyone with everyone else. No one is "better" than anyone
else, whatever his or her talents, achievements, wealth, family, or intelligence.
This view rules out slavery on principle, whatever the benefits to society as a
whole and whatever the alleged benefits to the slaves. Slavery is inequality and

[2]Aristotle, *Nicomachean Ethics*, trans. W. D. Ross (Oxford: Oxford University Press, 1925).

is thus to be condemned. But this egalitarian principle has its problems too. It is obvious that, as a matter of fact, all people are not equally endowed with intelligence or talent, good looks or abilities. Is it therefore to the good of all that everyone should be treated equally? One person is a doctor, capable of saving many lives; another is a chronic profligate and drunkard. If they were to commit exactly the same crime, would it be to the public interest to give them equal jail terms? Obviously not. But would it be just to give them different terms? It doesn't appear so. One problem that recent theorists have tried to answer is connected with cases in which the public interest seems at odds with the demands for equal treatment. A similar problem gives rise to one of the "paradoxes of democracy," which we mentioned before. Does it make sense to treat the opinions of an ignorant person whose only knowledge of current events comes from fifteen minutes (at best) of television news a day in the same way that we treat the opinions of a skilled political veteran? But the ballots we vote on make no such distinction. And it is obvious that our society, despite its egalitarian principles, treats people who are cleverer at business or power-brokering much better than everyone else. Is this an example of systematic injustice? Or are there cases, even for us, in which inequality can still be justified as justice?

The theory of justice has been one of the central concerns of British philosophy for several centuries. Thomas Hobbes developed a theory that began with equality as a "natural fact" and took justice to be that which "assured peace and security to all" enforced by the government. Several years later, John Locke and then David Hume argued a similar theory of justice; again, equality was the premise, and mutual agreement the basis of government authority. For both philosophers, the ultimate criterion of justice was utility, the public interest, and therefore the satisfaction of the interests of at least most citizens. This would have been rejected by Plato and Aristotle. The most explicit statement of this modern position could be expected to be found in the most explicit "utility" theorist of all, John Stuart Mill. The selection that follows is from his pamphlet *Utilitarianism.*

from *Utilitarianism,*
by J. S. Mill

In the case of this, as of our other moral sentiments, there is no necessary connexion between the question of its origin and that of its binding force. That a feeling is bestowed on us by nature does not necessarily legitimate all its promptings. The feeling of justice might be a peculiar instinct, and might yet require, like our other instincts, to be controlled and enlightened by a higher reason. If we have intellectual instincts leading us to judge in a particular way, as well as animal instincts that prompt us to act in a particular way, there is no necessity that the former should be more infallible in their sphere than the latter in theirs; it may as well happen that wrong judgments are occasionally suggested by those, as wrong actions by these.

. . . . .

In the first place, it is mostly considered unjust to deprive anyone of his personal liberty, his property, or any other thing which belongs to him by law. Here, therefore, is one instance of the application of the terms "just" and "unjust" in a perfectly definite sense, namely, that it is just to respect, unjust to violate, the *legal rights* of anyone. But this judgment admits of several exceptions, arising from the other forms in which the notions of justice and injustice present themselves. For example, the person who suffers the deprivation may (as the phrase is) have forfeited the rights which he is so deprived of—a case to which we shall return presently. But also—

Secondly, the legal rights of which he is deprived may be rights which *ought* not to have belonged to him; in other words, the law which confers on him these rights may be a bad law. When it is so or when (which is the same thing for our purpose) it is supposed to be so, opinions will differ as to the justice or injustice of infringing it. Some maintain that no law, however bad, ought to be disobeyed by an individual citizen; that his opposition to it, if shown at all, should only be shown in endeavoring to get it altered by competent authority. This opinion (which condemns many of the most illustrious benefactors of mankind, and would often protect pernicious institutions against the only weapons which, in the state of things existing at the time, have any chance of succeeding against them) is defended by those who hold it on grounds of expediency, principally on that of the importance to the common interest of mankind, of maintaining inviolate the sentiment of submission to law. Other persons, again, hold the directly contrary opinion that any law, judged to be bad, may blamelessly be disobeyed, even though it be not judged to be unjust but only inexpedient, while others would confine the license of disobedience to the case of unjust laws; but, again, some say that all laws which are inexpedient are unjust, since every law imposes some restriction on the natural liberty of mankind, which restriction is an injustice unless legitimated by tending to their good. Among these diversities of opinion it seems to be universally admitted that there may be unjust laws, and that law, consequently, is not the ultimate criterion of justice, but may give to one person a benefit, or impose on another an evil, which justice condemns. When, however, a law is thought to be unjust, it seems always to be regarded as being so in the same way in which a breach of law is unjust, namely, by infringing somebody's right, which, as it cannot in this case be a legal right, receives a different appellation and is called a moral right. We may say, therefore, that a second case of injustice consists in taking or withholding from any person that to which he has a *moral right*.

Thirdly, it is universally considered just that each person should obtain that (whether good or evil) which he *deserves*, and unjust that he should obtain a good or be made to undergo an evil which he does not deserve. This is, perhaps, the clearest and most emphatic form in which the idea of justice is conceived by the general mind. As it involves the notion of desert, the question arises what constitutes desert? Speaking in a general way, a person is understood to deserve good if he does right, evil if he does wrong; and in a more particular sense, to deserve good from those to whom he does or has done good, and evil from those to whom he does or has done evil. The precept of returning good for evil has never been regarded as a case of the fulfillment of justice, but as one in which the claims of justice are waived, in obedience to other considerations.

Fourthly, it is confessedly unjust to *break faith* with anyone: to violate an engagement, either express or implied, or disappoint expectations raised by our own conduct, at least if we have raised those expectations knowingly and voluntarily. Like the other obligations of justice already spoken of, this one is not regarded as absolute, but as capable of being overruled by a stronger obligation of justice on the other side, or by such conduct on the part of the person concerned as is deemed to absolve us from our obligation to him and to constitute a *forfeiture* of the benefit which he has been led to expect.

Fifthly, it is, by universal admission, inconsistent with justice to be *partial*—to show favor or preference to one person over another in matters to which favor and preference do not properly apply. Impartiality, however, does not seem to be regarded as a duty in itself, but rather as instrumental to some other duty; for it is admitted that favor and preference are not always censurable, and, indeed, the cases in which they are condemned are rather the exception than the rule. A person would be more likely to be blamed than applauded for giving his family or friends no superiority in good offices over strangers when he could do so without violating any other duty; and no one thinks it unjust to seek one person in preference to another as a friend, connection, or companion. Impartiality where rights are concerned is of course obligatory, but this is involved in the more general obligation of giving to everyone his right. A tribunal, for example, must be impartial because it is bound to award, without regard to any other consideration, a disputed object to the one of two parties who has the right to it. There are other cases in which impartiality means being solely influenced by desert, as with those who, in the capacity of judges, preceptors, or parents, administer reward and punishment as such. There are cases, again, in which it means being solely influenced by consideration for the public interest, as in making a selection among candidates for a government employment. Impartiality, in short, as an obligation of justice, may be said to mean being exclusively influenced by the considerations which it is supposed ought to influence the particular case in hand, and resisting solicitation of any motives which prompt to conduct different from what those considerations would dictate.

Nearly allied to the idea of impartiality is that of *equality*, which often enters as a component part both into the conception of justice and into the practice of it, and, in the eyes of many persons, constitutes its essence. But in this, still more than in any other case, the notion of justice varies in different persons, and always conforms in its variations to their notion of utility. Each person maintains that equality is the dictate of justice, except where he thinks that expediency requires inequality. The justice of giving equal protection to the rights of all is maintained by those who support the most outrageous inequality in the rights themselves. Even in slave countries it is theoretically admitted that the rights of the slave, such as they are, ought to be as sacred as those of the master, and that a tribunal which fails to enforce them with equal strictness is wanting in justice; while, at the same time, institutions which leave to the slave scarcely any rights to enforce are not deemed unjust because they are not deemed inexpedient. Those who think that utility requires distinctions of rank do not consider it unjust that riches and social privileges should be unequally dispensed;

but those who think this inequality inexpedient think it unjust also. Whoever thinks that government is necessary sees no injustice in as much inequality as is constituted by giving to the magistrate powers not granted to other people. Even among those who hold leveling doctrines, there are differences of opinion about expediency. Some communists consider it unjust that the produce of the labor of the community should be shared on any other principle than that of exact equality; others think it just that those should receive most whose wants are greatest; while others hold that those who work harder, or who produce more, or whose services are more valuable to the community, may justly claim a larger quota in the division of the produce. And the sense of natural justice may be plausibly appealed to in behalf of every one of these opinions.

Mill then goes on to define a **right:**

When we call anything a person's right, we mean that he has a valid claim on society to protect him in the possession of it, either by the force of law or by that of education and opinion. If he has what we consider a sufficient claim, on whatever account, to have something guaranteed to him by society, we say that he has a right to it.

To have a right, then, is, I conceive, to have something which society ought to defend me in the possession of. If the objector goes on to ask why it ought, I can give him no other reason than general utility. If that expression does not seem to convey a sufficient feeling of the strength of the obligation, nor to account for the peculiar energy of the feeling, it is because there goes to the composition of the sentiment, not a rational only but also an animal element — the thirst for retaliation; and this thirst derives its intensity, as well as its moral justification, from the extraordinarily important and impressive kind of utility which is concerned. The interest involved is that of security, to everyone's feelings the most vital of all interests. All other earthly benefits are needed by one person, not needed by another; and many of them can, if necessary, be cheerfully foregone or replaced by something else; but security no human being can possibly do without; on it we depend for all our immunity from evil and for the whole value of all and every good, beyond the passing moment, since nothing but the gratification of the instant could be of any worth to us if we could be deprived of everything the next instant by whoever was momentarily stronger than ourselves. Now this most indispensable of all necessaries, after physical nutriment, cannot be had unless the machinery for providing it is kept unintermittedly in active play. Our notion, therefore, of the claim we have on our fellow creatures to join in making safe for us the very groundwork of our existence gathers feelings around it so much more intense than those concerned in any of the more common cases of utility that the difference in degree (as is often the case in psychology) becomes a real difference in kind. The claim assumes that character of absoluteness, that apparent infinity and incommensurability with all other considerations which constitute the distinction between the feeling of right and wrong and that of ordinary expediency and inexpediency. The feelings concerned are so powerful, and we count so positively on finding a responsive feeling in others (all being alike interested) that *ought* and *should* grow into *must*, and recognized indispensability becomes a moral necessity, analogous to physical, and often not inferior to it in binding force.[3]

Mill's utilitarian theory of justice is a logical extension of his ethical theories: What is good and desirable is what is best for the greatest number of people. But although it might at first seem as if the greatest happiness of the greatest number leaves no room for such abstract concerns as "justice," Mill argues that, to the contrary, it is only utility that can give that abstract sense of justice some concrete basis in human life.

The problem with the utilitarian theory of justice is identical to the problem we saw with the utilitarian theory of morals. Could there not be a case in which the public interest and general utility would be served only at the clearly unjust expense of a single unfortunate individual? Suppose we lived in a society that ran extremely well, such that we had few if any complaints about our government and the way it was run, when a single muckraking journalist started turning the peace upside down with his insistence that something was very wrong in the government. We might easily suppose that, at least in the short run, the public confusion and trauma would be much more harmful to the public interest than the slight correction that would result from public exposure. Should the government forcefully silence the journalist? We would say "no." He has a right to his inquiries and a right to speak his mind. Or suppose that the most efficient way to solve a series of on-going crimes was to torture a recently captured suspect and hold him without evidence? Here again public interest and justice are at odds. Or more generally, should the government have the authority to throw people in jail just because it has reason (even good reason) to believe that they will create a public disturbance or commit certain crimes? Public interest says "yes"; justice says "no."

A partial answer to this utilitarian dilemma was clearly stated by Hume and then later by Mill. They distinguished between the utility of a single act and the utility of a system, so that an unjust act is to be challenged not as an isolated occurrence but as an example of a general set of rules and practices.

on "Justice and Utility," by David Hume

To make this more evident, consider, that though the rules of justice are established merely by interest, their connection with interest is somewhat singular, and is different from what may be observed on other occasions. A single act of justice is frequently contrary to *public interest;* and were it to stand alone, without being followed by other acts, may, in itself, be very prejudicial to society. When a man of merit, of a beneficent disposition, restores a great fortune to a miser, or a seditious bigot, he has acted justly and laudably, but the public is a real sufferer. Nor is every single act of

---

[3]John Stuart Mill, *Utilitarianism* (New York: Bobbs-Merrill, 1957).

justice, considered apart, more conducive to private interest, than to public; and it is easily conceived how a man may impoverish himself by a single instance of integrity, and have reason to wish that with regard to that single act, the laws of justice were for a moment suspended in the universe. But however single acts of justice may be contrary, either to public or private interest, it is certain, that the whole plan or scheme is highly conducive, or indeed absolutely requisite, both to the support of society, and the well-being of every individual.[4]

What Hume makes clear is that the utility of an act by itself cannot give us an adequate concept of justice. We need a theory of general practices as well (a theory that, still within the confines of utilitarianism, is sometimes called *rule utilitarianism*, as opposed to *act utilitarianism*). But even this qualification allows for the possibility of a practice that is unjust but which nonetheless systematically increases general utility. It is for this reason that a concern for individual rights must always come back into the picture, not just in the sense of simple utility argued by Mill and Hume, but in a more forceful way that may even go against public utility. The most powerful contemporary theory of justice attempts to do just this by placing the emphasis on the advantages of a practice to the least advantaged members of society. The American philosopher John Rawls has argued such a theory of justice. The following selection is taken from one of his early essays, "Justice as Fairness."

from "Justice as Fairness," by John Rawls

It might seem at first sight that the concepts of justice and fairness are the same, and that there is no reason to distinguish them, or to say that one is more fundamental than the other. I think that this impression is mistaken. In this paper I wish to show that the fundamental idea in the concept of justice is fairness; and I wish to offer an analysis of the concept of justice from this point of view. To bring out the force of this claim, and the analysis based upon it, I shall then argue that it is this aspect of justice for which utilitarianism, in its classical form, is unable to account, but which is expressed, even if misleadingly, by the idea of the social contract.

. . . . .

Throughout I consider justice only as a virtue of social institutions, or what I shall call practices.[5] The principles of justice are regarded as formulating restrictions as to how practices may define positions and offices, and

---

[4]David Hume, *Inquiry Concerning the Principles of Morals* (La Salle, Ill: Open Court, 1912.)

[5]I use the word "practice" throughout as a sort of technical term meaning any form of activity specified by a system of rules which defines offices, roles, moves, penalties, defences, and so on, and which gives the activity its structure. As examples one may think of games and rituals, trials and parliaments, markets and systems or property. I have attempted a partial analysis of the notion of a practice in a paper, "Two Concepts of Rules," *Philosophical Review*, LXIV (1955), pp. 3–32 [Rawls'note].

assign thereto powers and liabilities, rights and duties. Justice as a virtue of particular actions or of persons I do not take up at all. It is important to distinguish these various subjects of justice, since the meaning of the concept varies according to whether it is applied to practices, particular actions, or persons. These meanings are, indeed, connected, but they are not identical. I shall confine my discussion to the sense of justice as applied to practices, since this sense is the basic one. Once it is understood, the other senses should go quite easily.

The conception of justice which I want to develop may be stated in the form of two principles as follows: first, each person participating in a practice, or affected by it, has an equal right to the most extensive liberty compatible with a like liberty for all; and second, inequalities are arbitrary unless it is reasonable to expect that they will work out for everyone's advantage, and provided the positions and offices to which they attach, or from which they may be gained, are open to all. These principles express justice as a complex of three ideas: liberty, equality, and reward for services contributing to the common good.

The term "person" is to be construed variously depending on the circumstances. On some occasions it will mean human individuals, but in others it may refer to nations, provinces, business firms, churches, teams, and so on. The principles of justice apply in all these instances, although there is a certain logical priority to the case of human individuals. As I shall use the term "person," it will be ambiguous in the manner indicated.

The first principle holds, of course, only if other things are equal: that is, while there must always be a justification for departing from the initial position of equal liberty (which is defined by the pattern of rights and duties, powers and liabilities, established by a practice), and the burden of proof is placed on him who would depart from it, nevertheless, there can be, and often there is, a justification for doing so. Now, that similar particular cases, as defined by a practice, should be treated similarly as they arise, is part of the very concept of a practice; it is involved in the notion of an activity in accordance with rules. The first principle expresses an analogous conception, but as applied to the structure of practices themselves. It holds, for example, that there is a presumption against the distinctions and classifications made by legal systems and other practices to the extent that they infringe on the original and equal liberty of the persons participating in them. The second principle defines how this presumption may be rebutted.

It might be argued at this point that justice requires only an equal liberty. If, however, a greater liberty were possible for all without loss or conflict, then it would be irrational to settle on a lesser liberty. There is no reason for circumscribing rights unless their exercise would be incompatible, or would render the practice defining them less effective. Therefore no serious distortion of the concept of justice is likely to follow from including within it the concept of the greatest equal liberty.

The second principle defines what sorts of inequalities are permissible; it specifies how the presumption laid down by the first principle may he put aside. Now by inequalities it is best to understand not *any* differences between offices and positions, but differences in the benefits and burdens attached to them either directly or indirectly, such as prestige and wealth, or liability to taxation and compulsory services. Players in a game do not protest against there being different positions, such as batter, pitcher, catcher, and the like, nor to there being various privileges and powers as specified by the rules; nor do the citizens of a country object to there being the different offices of government such as president, senator, governor, judge, and so on, each with their special rights and duties. It is not differences in the resulting distribution established by a practice, or made possible by it, of the things men strive to attain or avoid. Thus they may complain about the pattern of honors and rewards set up by a practice (*e.g.* the privileges and salaries of government officials) or they may object to the distribution of power and wealth which results from the various ways in which men avail themselves of the opportunities allowed by it (*e.g.* the concentration of wealth which may develop in a free price system allowing large entrepreneurial or speculative gains).

It should be noted that the second principle holds that an inequality is allowed only if there is reason to believe that the practice with the inequality, or resulting in it, will work for the advantage of *every* party engaging in it. Here it is important to stress that *every* party must gain from the inequality. Since the principle applies to practices, it implies that the representative man in every office or position defined by a practice, when he views it as a going concern, must find it reasonable to prefer his condition and prospects with the inequality to what they would be under the practice without it. The principle excludes, therefore, the justification of inequalities on the grounds that the disadvantages of those in one position are outweighed by the greater advantages of those in another position. This rather simple restriction is the main modification I wish to make in the utilitarian principle as usually understood. When coupled with the notion of a practice, it is a restriction of consequence, and one which some utilitarians, for example Hume and Mill, have used in their discussions of justice without realizing apparently its significance, or at least without calling attention to it. Why it is a significant modification of principle, changing one's conception of justice entirely, the whole of my argument will show.

Further, it is also necessary that the various offices to which special benefits or burdens attach are open to all. It may be, for example, to the common advantage, as just defined, to attach special benefits to certain offices. Perhaps by doing so the requisite talent can be attracted to them and encouraged to give its best efforts. But any offices having special benefits must be won in a fair competition in which contestants are judged on their merits. If some offices were not open, those excluded would normally be justified in feeling unjustly treated, even if they benefited from the greater efforts of those who were allowed to compete for them. Now if one can assume that offices are open, it is necessary only to consider the design of practices themselves and how they jointly, as a system, work together. It will be a mistake to focus attention on the varying relative positions of particular persons, who may be known to us by their proper names, and to require that each such change, as a once for all transaction viewed in isolation, must be in itself just. It is the system of practices which is to be judged, and judged from a general point of view: unless one is prepared to criticize it from the standpoint of a representative man holding some particular office, one has no complaint against it.[6]

Rawls, like Hume in particular, ties the concept of "justice" to the concept of "equality." The main theme of his work is an attempt to develop this connection and to state precisely the kind of "equality" that is most important for justice. Against the conservative suggestion that people are equal in legal rights and "opportunities" alone, without any right to material goods and social services, he argues that a just society will consider the welfare of the worst-off members of society as an obligation. Here he differs with Mill and the utilitarians, who would say that such help is a matter of utility; for Rawls, it is more like a Kantian duty. Moreover, Rawls clearly distinguishes himself from socialists as well, who would argue that all property should be shared; he says only that it is obligatory to help out the worst-off members of society, but nowhere does he suggest that all people therefore ought to have equal wealth and property. Justice, in other words, does not equate fair distribution with equal distribution. Equality becomes a far more complex notion, therefore, than simple egalitarianism often takes it to be.

THE LEGITIMACY OF THE STATE

If people will not cooperate willingly and act for the public interest, then they may be forced to do so. The authority with the power to define the public interest and to enforce its definition is what philosophers call the **state**.[7] But it must not be thought that the state or its instrument — the government — is merely a book-keeping and organizational institution. Ideally, in a well-functioning society in which most people act in the public interest, it may be not much more than this, and then as minimally as necessary. But since people do not always act in the public interest, the role of the state is necessarily that of *legislator*, making laws and rules that tell people how to act (and how not to act), and that of *enforcer*, applying enough force through threat of punishment to make sure that people obey those laws and rules. Then too it is the state that may have to step in when the rights of an individual are threatened, and pass laws to protect those rights and punish those who violate them. Ideally, the function of the state is to keep the balance between the public interest and individual rights, in other words, to preserve justice. Some theorists would add that the function of the state is to make life for its citizens such that the public interest and individual rights and interests almost always coincide. Others would hope that the state would serve this function so well that it would no longer be needed, except perhaps as a bureau of

[6]John Rawls, "Justice as Fairness," in *The Philosophical Review*, LXVII (April 1958).
[7]This is a general term for any highest authority in a society; it includes federal government as well as "states" in a more restricted sense, for example, Alabama and Massachusetts. Thus the sovereign cities of the ancient Greeks were called "city-states."

records and an occasional enforcer of contracts. Some people think that the state is an end in itself, a matter of pride and a rallying point for its citizens, something like a football team in a small town. Still others would say that the only proper state is virtually no state at all.

We have been talking about the state as the center of power and authority, and many people would simply define "politics" in terms of "power." But "power" alone is not enough to characterize the state; we must add that it is legitimate power. **Legitimacy** means that this power must be justified. A person or organization might have tremendous power and rule a society with an iron hand. But rulers might be gangsters who rule by force alone. Or they might be invaders from another country who rule without popular consent. Or they might be citizens who, because of powerful positions in the government or the army, acquire this power in illegal or unacceptable ways. The idea of the state, therefore, is not simply that it is the center of power; it is the center of legitimate power or, in other words, *authority*. When philosophers and political scientists use the term "authority," they almost always mean "legitimate authority." And sometimes, when they say that "the state has the power to do such and such," they mean "that the state has the legitimate power to do such and such." Legitimate authority (or simply, authority) has the legal power to make laws. Crude military or political power is only the ability to force people to do what one wants; it is not therefore legitimate. A central question of political philosophy, accordingly, is "what makes a state's power legitimate?" In other words, "what gives a state its authority?"

It is necessary to distinguish three different levels on which the question of legitimacy and authority must be raised. First, there is the question of the legitimacy of the state itself. On what authority did the English, for example, rule over the American colonies and consider them a part of the British Empire? Conversely, what authority did the American colonists claim when they declared themselves independent of England and set themselves up as a separate state? Much recent history involves the creation, re-creation, and realignment of various states. If we look at maps of Europe for the past fifty years, for example, we will see that states go into and out of existence, sometimes several times. The question of the legitimacy of the state itself, therefore, is one of the main causes of the wars and political battles of our times (and earlier times as well). Second, there is the question of the legitimacy of a certain form of government. In some Asian and Latin American countries, for example, there are frequent changes between military dictatorships and republics or democracies. In the recent history of Spain, as another example, there have been changes from a monarchy to a republic to a dictatorship back to a monarchy trying to establish democratic processes. The geographical boundaries of the state in all these instances remain the same, the population also remains pretty much the same (making allowances for casualties and refugees), but the form of government changes radically. It is possible that the same people or party, however, will remain in power even though the form of government changes. (For example, the president of a democracy may become the dictator in a dictatorship.) This brings us to our third level of legitimacy: Particular governments must be shown to be legitimate within the framework of the form of government in a state. It is the form of government that confers legitimacy: For example, a democracy confers legitimacy through elections, a monarchy confers legitimacy on a new king or queen through birth. In our own state, the form of government has remained constant for the past two hundred years, but the particular governments have changed quite frequently, from one party to the other, and sometimes new parties are created and succeed in getting elected. A particular government (whether Republican or Democratic, for example) is made legitimate by the election laws created by our form of government. Usually these laws make it clear which particular government (that is, which party) is the legitimate government at a particular time. In a close election, however, this may be in hot dispute, and it is in such instances that the distinction between the form of government and particular governments is thrown into sharp contrast.

Five Theories of Legitimacy

The legitimacy of a particular government, a form of government, or a state means that its power is justified. But what justifies this power? We might say that what justifies a particular government, form of government, or state is the willingness of its citizens to obey its laws, the recognition of it by other governments and states whom it in turn recognizes, and in general the widespread belief in its legitimacy by virtue of which the people or party in power are accepted as such. But this extremely loose definition encounters many problems, particularly in dictatorships where people are forced to accept governments, in powerful military states that can force recognition from other states, and powerful governments that are able to force their citizens to obey them, whether the citizens really want to or not. Moreover, the crucial belief in a government, form of government, or state may be based on many different kinds of justifications. It is necessary, therefore, to mention at least five different kinds of justifications for this belief, each of which might be called a theory of legitimacy.

DIVINE RIGHT TO RULE THEORY   Since ancient times it has been argued that kings, queens, pharoahs, princes, and emperors have been given their authority directly by God or gods. Until modern times this was a difficult theory to refute and a dangerous one to argue against. But even in ancient times, for example, in Greece, it was maintained that this divine right had to be supported by justice and a modicum of wisdom and, at least to a small extent, the acceptance of the people ruled. But since the people who were ruled were more often than not forced to accept the authority of the divinely appointed ruler, this last qualification was mostly nominal. Kings sometimes enjoyed the support of the people, but it is debatable whether they actually needed it.

MIGHT MAKES RIGHT THEORY   This theory holds that power itself makes a government legitimate. In a sense, therefore, this theory rejects the very idea of legitimacy, since according to it any government or state that has power has legitimate power and therefore the distinction between legitimate and illegitimate power disappears. For obvious reasons, this theory is usually favored more by those who are already in power than by those who are not in power. But it is rare that a government or state that has power will publicly state the might makes right theory. Usually it will invoke one of the other theories in its defense.

UTILITARIAN THEORY   Just as utilitarianism in moral theory defends that action that will promote the greatest good for the greatest number, utilitarianism in political theory defends the government or state that will promote the greatest good for the greatest number of its citizens. Jeremy Bentham's classic treatise, for example, is called *An Introduction to the Principles of Morals and Legislation.* And Mill's pamphlet, *Utilitarianism,* is partly devoted to the political problem of justice. According to the utilitarian theory, a government is legitimate so long as it provides the most services and best protection for its citizens in general. Or to characterize this theory slightly differently, the utilitarian theory says that a government is justified insofar as it furthers the public interest. (Thus it might also be called "public interest theory.")

JUSTICE THEORY   One possible problem with the utilitarian theory, as we have seen in other contexts in this chapter, is that it may promote the best interests of most of the people at the expense of a small minority. Neither the divine right nor might makes right theories include any mention of justice at all, and so it is important that the demand that governments and states be just be made independently of these others. Plato and Aristotle, for example, used a justice theory to defend their conceptions of the state. But the fact that Plato's and Aristotle's conception of the state was so different from ours (and so unjust in some respects) points to an important qualification of this kind of theory. What the theory amounts to depends wholly on the concept of justice one defends. If justice means equality, then the legitimate state will maximize equality; if justice means "everyone in his or her proper place" (as in Plato and Aristotle), then the state will be legitimate if the various parts of the state are "in harmony" and working together smoothly.

CONSENT OF THE GOVERNED THEORY   This theory is the one that most people accept today. It is assumed, however, that the consent of the governed will also ensure the public interest and justice for everyone as well. Consent of the governed theory is based on the idea that the people who are ruled should have some say in how they are ruled and perhaps even have a choice in who rules them. These two ideas are not equivalent, although they usually go together in our society. People might have a say in government policies without being able to choose the government, as in most monarchies, for example. Even Plato accepted this theory to some degree. In *The Republic,* he argues (through Socrates), "in our state, if anywhere, the governors and the governed will share the same conviction on the question who ought to rule. Don't you think so?"[8]

The most powerful modern versions of the consent of the governed theory are summed up in the phrase, "social contract." According to the theory of the social contract, governments and states are legitimate only because the citizens agree to be ruled by them.

The Social Contract

The single most influential defense of the legitimacy of the state in modern times has been called the "social contract theory." The **social contract** is an agreement among people to share certain interests and make certain compromises for the good of them all. It is, in other words, a "consent of the governed theory." In one form or another, it existed even in ancient times. For example, reread Socrates' argument in the *Crito* (pp. 4–8) where he says that by staying in Athens he had implicitly agreed to abide by its laws, even when those laws unfairly condemned him to death. But what is most important in understanding the nature of this social contract is that, as in Socrates' argument, there need not have been any actual, physical contract or even oral agreement in order to talk about it. We are bound by social contract, in other words, even if we never signed or saw such a contract. Moreover, it may not be the case that there was ever such a contract, even in past history. It happens, however, that Americans are among the few people in the world whose state was actually formed explicitly by such a contract, namely, our *Constitution.* But the actual existence of such a piece of paper is not necessary to a discussion about a social contract. Simply to live in a society, according to these philosophers, is to have agreed, at least implicitly, to such an agreement. (Thus, living in a society you are expected to obey its laws; "ignorance is no excuse," and you cannot get out of an arrest by saying "I don't really live here," much less "I don't recognize your right to arrest me.")

Two very different pictures of the original social contract are presented to us by the English philosopher Thomas Hobbes and the French philosopher Jean-Jacques Rousseau. Both begin by considering man in "the state of nature," without laws and without society, before men and women came together to accept the social contract. Hobbes based his conception of the social contract, however, on an extremely unfavorable conception of human nature. He attacked the idealistic political philosophies of Plato and Aristotle for being unrealistic and assuming wrongly that people were naturally capable of virtue and wisdom. Like Machiavelli, whom he followed with praise, he considered himself to be a "realist." As with most realists, this meant seeing the nasty side of things. So, according to his theory of human nature, natural man was a selfish beast, fighting for his own interests against everyone else. Human life was a "war of all against all" and

[8]Plato, *The Republic,* trans. Francis M. Cornford (Oxford: Oxford University Press, 1941).

a person's life, consequently, was "nasty, brutish and short." He dismissed reason and appealed to human passions, particularly the passion for self-preservation. The social contract, therefore, was mainly an agreement of equally selfish and self-seeking persons not to commit mutual murder.

from *Leviathan,* by Thomas Hobbes

OF THE NATURAL CONDITION OF MANKIND AS CONCERNING THEIR FELICITY, AND MISERY

Men by nature equal. Nature hath made men so equal, in the faculties of the body, and mind; as that though there be found one man sometimes manifestly stronger in body, or of quicker mind than another; yet when all is reckoned together, the difference between man, and man, is not so considerable, as that one man can thereupon claim to himself any benefit, to which another may not pretend, as well as he. For as to the strength of body, the weakest has strength enough to kill the strongest, either by secret machination, or by confederacy with others, that are in the same danger with himself.

. . . . .

For such is the nature of men, that howsoever they may acknowledge many others to be more witty, or more eloquent, or more learned; yet they will hardly believe there be many so wise as themselves; for they see their own wit at hand, and other men's at a distance. But this proveth rather that men are in that point equal, than unequal. For there is not ordinarily a greater sign of the equal distribution of any thing, than that every man is contented with his share.

From equality proceeds diffidence. From this equality of ability, ariseth equality of hope in the attaining of our ends. And therefore if any two men desire the same thing, which nevertheless they cannot both enjoy, they become enemies; and in the way to their end, which is principally their own conservation, and sometimes their delectation only, endeavour to destroy, or subdue one another. And from hence it comes to pass, that where an invader hath no more to fear, than another man's single power; if one plant, sow, build, or possess a convenient seat, others may probably be expected to come prepared with forces united, to dispossess, and deprive him, not only of the fruit of his labour, but also of his life, or liberty. And the invader again is in the like danger of another.

From diffidence war. And from this diffidence of one another, there is no way for any man to secure himself, so reasonable, as anticipation; that is, by force, or wiles, to master the persons of all men he can, so long, till he see no other power great enough to endanger him: and this is no more than his own conservation requireth, and is generally allowed. Also because there be some, that taking pleasure in contemplating their own power in the acts of conquest, which they pursue farther than their security requires; if others, that otherwise would be glad to be at ease within modest bounds, should not by invasion increase their power, they would not be able, long time, by standing only on their defence, to subsist. And by consequence, such augmentation of dominion over men being necessary to a man's conservation, it ought to be allowed him.

Again, men have no pleasure, but on the contrary a great deal of grief, in keeping company, where there is no power able to over-awe them all. For every man looketh that his companion should value him, at the same rate he sets upon himself: and upon all signs of contempt, or undervaluing, naturally endeavors, as far as he dares, (which amongst them that have no common power to keep them in quiet, is far enough to make them destroy each other), to extort a greater value from his contemners, by damage; and from others, by the example.

So that in the nature of man, we find three principal causes of quarrel. First, competition; secondly, diffidence; thirdly, glory.

The first, maketh men invade for gain; the second, for safety; and the third, for reputation. The first use violence, to make themselves masters of other men's persons, wives, children, and cattle; the second, to defend them; the third, for trifles, as a word, a smile, a different opinion, and any other sign of undervalue, either direct in their persons, or by reflection in their kindred, their friends, their nation, their profession, or their name.

Out of civil states, there is always war of every one against every one. Hereby it is manifest, that during the time men live without a common power to keep them all in awe, they are in that condition which is called war; and such a war, as is of every man, against every man. For war, consisteth not in battle only, or the act of fighting; but in a tract of time, wherein the will to contend by battle is sufficiently known. . . .

The incommodities of such a war. Whatsoever therefore is consequent to a time of war, where every man is enemy to every man; the same is consequent to the time, wherein men live without other security, than what their own strength, and their own invention shall furnish them withal. In such condition, there is no place for industry; because the fruit thereof is uncertain: and consequently no culture of the earth; no navigation, nor use of the commodities that may be imported by sea; no commodious building; no instruments of moving, and removing, such things as require much force; no knowledge of the face of the earth; no account of time; no arts; no letters; no society; and which is worst of all, continual fear, and danger of violent death; and the life of man, solitary, poor, nasty, brutish, and short.

It may seem strange to some man, that has not well weighed these things; that nature should thus dissociate, and render men apt to invade, and destroy one another: and he may therefore, not trusting to this inference, made from the passions, desire perhaps to have the same confirmed by experience. Let him therefore consider with himself, when taking a journey, he arms himself, and seeks to go well accompanied; when going to sleep, he locks his doors; when even in his house he locks his chests; and this when he knows there be laws, and public officers, armed, to revenge all injuries shall be done him; what opinion he has of his fellow-subjects, when he rides armed; of his fellow citizens, when he locks his doors; and of his children, and servants, when he locks his chests. Does he not there as much accuse mankind by his actions, as I do by my words? But neither of us accuse man's nature in it. The desires, and other passions of man, are in themselves no sin. No more are the actions, that proceed from those passions, till they know a law that forbids them: which till laws be made they cannot know: nor can any law be made, till they have agreed upon the person that shall make it.

It may peradventure be thought, there was never such a time, nor condition of war as this; and I believe it was never generally so, over all the world: but there are many places, where they live so now. For the savage people in many places of America, except the government of small families, the concord whereof dependeth on natural lust, have no government at all; and live at this day in that brutish manner, as I said before. Howsoever, it may be perceived what manner of life there would be, where there were no common power to fear, by the manner of life, which men that have formerly lived under a peaceful government, use to degenerate into, in a civil war.

OF THE FIRST AND SECOND NATURAL LAWS, AND OF CONTRACTS

Right of nature what. The right of nature, which writers commonly call *jus naturale*, is the liberty each man hath, to use his own power, as he will himself, for the preservation of his own nature; that is to say, of his own life; and consequently, of doing any thing, which in his own judgment, and reason, he shall conceive to be the aptest means thereunto.

Liberty what. By liberty, is understood, according to the proper signification of the word, the absence of external impediments: which impediments, may oft take away part of a man's power to do what he would; but cannot hinder him from using the power left him, according as his judgment, and reason shall dictate to him.

A law of nature what. A law of nature, *lex naturalis*, is a precept or general rule, found out by reason, by which a man is forbidden to do that, which is destructive of his life, or taketh away the means of preserving the same; and to omit that, by which he thinketh it may be best preserved.

Difference of right and law. For though they that speak of this subject, use to confound *jus*, and *lex*, *right* and *law*: yet they ought to be distinguished; because right, consisteth in liberty to do, or to forbear: whereas law, determineth, and bindeth to one of them: so that law, and right, differ as much, as obligation, and liberty; which in one and the same matter are inconsistent.

Naturally every man has right to every thing. And because the condition of man, as hath been declared in the precedent chapter, is a condition of war of every one against every one; in which case every one is governed by his own reason; and there is nothing he can make use of, that may not be a help unto him, in preserving his life against his enemies; it followeth, that in such a condition, every man has a right to every thing; even to one another's body. And therefore, as long as this natural right of every man to every thing endureth, there can be no security to any man, how strong or wise soever he be, of living out the time, which nature ordinarily alloweth men to live.

The fundamental law of nature. And consequently it is a precept, or general rule of reason, *that every man, ought to endeavour peace, as far as he has hope of obtaining it; and when he cannot obtain it, that he may seek, and use, all helps, and advantages of war.*

. . . . .

The second law of nature. From this fundamental law of nature, by which men are commanded to endeavour peace, is derived this second law; *that a man be willing, when others are so too, as far-forth, as for peace, and defence of himself he shall think it necessary, to lay down this right to all things; and be contented with so much liberty against other men, as he would allow other men against himself.* For as long as every man holdeth this right, of doing any thing he liketh; so long are all men in the condition of war. But if other men will not lay down their right, as well as he; then there is no reason for any one, to divest himself of his: for that were to expose himself to prey, which no man is bound to, rather than to dispose himself to peace. This is that law of the Gospel; *whatsoever you require that others should do to you, that do ye to them.*

. . . . .

What it is to lay down a right. To *lay down* a man's *right* to any thing, is to *divest* himself of the *liberty*, of hindering another of the benefit of his own right to the same. For he that renounceth, or passeth away his right, giveth not to any other man a right which he had not before; because there is nothing to which every man had not right by nature: but only standeth out of his way, that he may enjoy his own original right, without hindrance from him; not without hindrance from another. So that the effect which redoundeth to one man, by another man's defect of right, is but so much diminution of impediments to the use of his own right original.

. . . . .

Not all rights are alienable. Whensoever a man transferreth his right, or renounceth it; it is either in consideration of some right reciprocally transferred to himself; or for some other good he hopeth for thereby. For it is a voluntary act: and of the voluntary acts of every man, the object is some *good to himself*. And therefore there be some rights, which no man can be understood by any words, or other signs, to have abandoned, or transferred. As first a man cannot lay down the right of resisting them, that assault him by force, to take away his life; because he cannot be understood to aim thereby, at any good to himself. The same may be said of wounds, and chains, and imprisonment; both because there is no benefit consequent to such patience; as there is to the patience of suffering another to be wounded, or imprisoned: as also because a man cannot tell, when he seeth men proceed against him by violence, whether they intend his death or not. And lastly the motive, and end for which this renouncing, and transferring of right is introduced, is nothing else but the security of a man's person, in his life, and in the means of so preserving life, as not to be weary of it. And therefore if a man by words, or other signs, seem to despoil himself of the end, for which those signs were intended; he is not to be understood as if he meant it, or that it was his will; but that he was ignorant of how such words and actions were to be interpreted.

Contract what. The mutual transferring of right, is that which men call CONTRACT.

· · · · ·

Covenants of mutual trust, when invalid. If a covenant be made, wherein neither of the parties perform presently, but trust one another; in the condition of mere nature, which is a condition of war of every man against every man, upon any reasonable suspicion, it is void: but if there be a common power set over them both, with right and force sufficient to compel performance, it is not void. For he that performeth first, has no assurance the other will perform after; because the bonds of words are too weak to bridle men's ambition, avarice, anger, and other passions, without the fear of some coercive power; which in the condition of mere nature, where all men are equal, and judges of the justness of their own fears, cannot possibly be supposed. And therefore he which performeth first, does but betray himself to his enemy; contrary to the right, he can never abandon, of defending his life, and means of living.

But in a civil estate, where there is a power set up to constrain those that would otherwise violate their faith, that fear is no more reasonable; and for that cause, he which by the covenant is to perform first, is obliged so to do.

The cause of fear, which maketh such a covenant invalid, must be always something arising after the covenant made; as some new fact, or other sign of the will not to perform: else it cannot make the covenant void. For that which could not hinder a man from promising, ought not to be admitted as a hindrance of performing.

Right to the end, containeth right to the means. He that transferreth any right, transferreth the means of enjoying it, as far as lieth in his power. As he that selleth land, is understood to transfer the herbage, and whatsoever grows upon it: nor can he that sells a mill turn away the stream that drives it. And they that give to a man the right of government in sovereignty, are understood to give him the right of levying money to maintain soldiers; and of appointing magistrates for the administration of justice.[9]

Hobbes begins his argument with the perhaps surprising observation that people are basically equal in nature. He is not talking here about legal equality or equal rights (for there are no laws and no legal rights) but rather equality in abilities, talents, and power. This seems strange because the problem of equality usually pays attention to the great differences between people. Instead Hobbes points out our similarities. In particular, he points out that almost everyone is strong and smart enough to kill or inflict grievous injury on others. Even a puny moron can, with a knife or a handgun, kill the strongest and smartest person on earth. Accordingly, the basis of the social contract (or "covenant") according to Hobbes is our mutual protection. Everyone agrees not to kill other people and in return is guaranteed that he or she won't be killed. Although it is a cynical view of human nature, it also continues to be one of the most powerful arguments for strong governments. (Hobbes himself was a conservative monarchist.)

[9]Thomas Hobbes, *Leviathan* (New York: Hafner, 1926).

Rousseau, quite to the contrary, had an extremely optimistic view of human nature, as we saw in the preceding chapter. He believed that people were "naturally good," and it was only the corruptions of society that made them selfish and destructive. Rousseau does not take the social contract, therefore, to be simply a doctrine of protection between mutually brutish individuals. The function of the state is rather to allow people to develop the "natural goodness" that they had in the absence of any state at all. This is not to say (although Rousseau is often interpreted this way) that he was nostalgic and wanted to "go back to the state of nature." That is impossible. (It is not even clear that Rousseau believed that there ever was a "state of nature" as such; his example, like Hobbes's example, is a way of giving a picture of "human nature," whether or not it is historically accurate.) We are already in society, that is a given fact. So Rousseau's aim is to develop a conception of the state that will allow us to live as morally as possible. This is important, for Rousseau, unlike most social contract theorists, is not at all a utilitarian; it is not happiness that is most important but goodness. (Hobbes, by way of contrast, took utility, pleasure and well-being, in addition to self-preservation, to be the purpose of the social contract.)

Rousseau's ambition, therefore, is not to "get us back to nature" but rather to revise our conception of the state. His "revision," however, is one of the most radical documents in modern history and has rightly been said to be one of the causes of both the American and French revolutions. The main thesis is one that Rousseau inherits from Locke: The state has legitimate power only so long as it serves the people it governs. The revolutionary corollary is that when a state ceases to serve its citizens, the citizens have a right to overthrow that government. This was a radical claim, again reminiscent of Locke. Even Rousseau was not comfortable with it. (Locke had made his statement *after* the English Revolution.) He called revolution "the most horrible alternative," to be avoided wherever possible. But subsequent French history took his theories quite literally and demonstrated too the "horror" that may follow too radical and abrupt a change in the authority that citizens accept as legitimate.

In earlier works, Rousseau had argued his famous thesis that "natural man" is "naturally good" and that contemporary society has corrupted him (and her). He went on to say that it was competition and the artificiality of our lust for private property that was responsible for this corruption, and he even included marriage and romantic love as forms of this "lust for private property." In the state of nature, he suggests, people mated when they felt like it, with whomever they felt like, and duels fought between jealous rivals were unheard of. Rousseau does not suggest that we return to that prehistoric custom, but he does use it as a wedge to pry open even the most sacred of our modern civil institutions. All of these, he argues, must be reexamined, and the tool for that reexamination is the social contract.

The key to his most famous book, appropriately called *The Social Contract*, is that man must regain his freedom within society. This does not mean, however, that a person can do whatever he or she would like to do. Quite the contrary, to be a citizen, according to Rousseau, is to want and do what is good for the society as well. To be free is precisely to want to do what is good for the society as well. And in one of the most problematic statements of the social contract, Rousseau says that a person who does not so act for the good of the society may have to "be forced to be free." Here is the basis for a strange paradox. On the one hand, Rousseau has properly been regarded as the father of the most liberal and revolutionary political theories of our time. (Marx, for example, claims a great debt to Rousseau.) His political philosophy stresses individual freedom and rights above all, even above the state itself. But there is another side to Rousseau that emerges in this paradoxical phrase; his stress on the state as an entity in itself ("the sovereign," presumably the king, but essentially any government) and the subservience of the individual to the state has also caused him to be labeled an authoritarian and the forerunner of totalitarian and fascist governments.

This paradox is not easily resolved, but we can at least explain how it comes about. Rousseau believes that the state is subject to and receives its legitimacy from the people it governs. But that does not mean that individual people need have any real power in determining the form or functions of government. Rousseau is not a democrat. What he says instead is that the state is subject to what he calls the general will, which is not simply a collection of individuals but something more. For example, we talk about "the spirit of the revolution" or "the discontent of the working class," but this spirit or discontent is not simply the product of each individual person. A poll of workers or revolutionaries would not show it either way. The revolution may have spirit even though some participants do not; indeed, they may even dislike the whole idea. And here is the source of the paradox: Legitimacy is given to the state by the general will, not by every individual person. And the person who does not agree with the general will, therefore, may very well find himself or herself forced into compliance with the state. (As Rousseau says, "forced to be free.") How much force, however, is a matter that Rousseau is not very clear about, nor have his many followers agreed on that crucial point either. On one extreme, Rousseau's authoritarian followers have insisted that all dissent from the general will must be stifled; on the other extreme, Rousseau's most libertarian and anarchist followers have insisted that the rights of the individual to be free from government intervention and to live according to his or her own "natural goodness" outweigh any claims that the state may have. What follows are a few selections from *The Social Contract*, beginning with one of Rousseau's best-known slogans.

from *The Social Contract*, by Rousseau

Man is born free; and everywhere he is in chains. One thinks himself the master of others, and still remains a greater slave than they. How did this change come about? I do not know. What can make it legitimate? That question I think I can answer.

If I took into account only force, and the effects derived from it, I should say: 'As long as a people is compelled to obey, and obeys, it does well; as soon as it can shake off the yoke, and shakes it off, it does still better; for, regaining its liberty by the same right as took it away, either it is justified in resuming it, or there was no justification for those who took it away.' But the social order is a sacred right which is the basis of all other rights. Nevertheless, this right does not come from nature, and must therefore be founded on conventions. Before coming to that, I have to prove what I have just asserted.

THE FIRST SOCIETIES

The most ancient of all societies, and the only one that is natural, is the family: and even so the children remain attached to the father only so long as they need him for their preservation. As soon as this need ceases, the natural bond is dissolved. The children, released from the obedience they owed to the father, and the father, released from the care he owed his children, return equally to independence. If they remain united, they continue so no longer naturally, but voluntarily; and the family itself is then maintained only by convention.

This common liberty results from the nature of man. His first law is to provide for his own preservation, his first cares are those which he owes to himself; and, as soon as he reaches years of discretion, he is the sole judge of the proper means of preserving himself, and consequently becomes his own master.

The family then may be called the first model of political societies; the ruler corresponds to the father, and the people to the children; and all, being born free and equal, alienate their liberty only for their own advantage. The whole difference is that, in the family, the love of the father for his children repays him for the care he takes of them, while, in the State, the pleasure of commanding takes the place of the love which the chief cannot have for the peoples under him.

. . . . .

THE SOCIAL COMPACT

I suppose men to have reached the point at which the obstacles in the way of their preservation in the state of nature show their power of resistance to be greater than the resources at the disposal of each individual for his maintenance in that state. That primitive condition can then subsist no longer; and the human race would perish unless it changed its manner of existence.

But, as men cannot engender new forces, but only unite and direct existing ones, they have no other means of preserving themselves than the formation, by aggregation, of a sum of forces great enough to overcome the resistance. These they have to bring into play by means of a single motive power, and cause to act in concert.

This sum of forces can arise only where several persons come together: but, as the force and liberty of each man are the chief instruments of his self-preservation, how can he pledge them without harming his own interests, and neglecting the care he owes to himself? This difficulty, in its bearing on my present subject, may be stated in the following terms:

'The problem is to find a form of association which will defend and protect with the whole common force the person and goods of each associate, and in which each, while uniting himself with all, may still obey himself alone, and remain as free as before.' This is the fundamental problem of which the *Social Contract* provides the solution.

The clauses of this contract are so determined by the nature of the act that the slightest modification would make them vain and ineffective; so that, although they have perhaps never been formally set forth, they are everywhere the same and everywhere tacitly admitted and recognized, until, on the violation of the social compact, each regains his original rights and resumes his natural liberty, while losing the conventional liberty in favour of which he renounced it.

These clauses, properly understood, may be reduced to one — the total alienation of each associate, together with all his rights, to the whole community; for, in the first place, as each gives himself absolutely, the conditions are the same for all; and, this being so, no one has any interest in making them burdensome to others.

Moreover, the alienation being without reserve, the union is as perfect as it can be, and no associate has anything more to demand: for, if the individuals retained certain rights, as there would be no common superior to decide between them and the public, each, being on one point his own judge, would ask to be so on all; the state of nature would thus continue, and the association would necessarily become inoperative or tyrannical.

Finally, each man, in giving himself to all, gives himself to nobody; and as there is no associate over which he does not acquire the same right as he yields others over himself, he gains an equivalent for everything he loses, and an increase of force for the preservation of what he has.

If then we discard from the social compact what is not of its essence, we shall find that it reduces itself to the following terms:

'Each of us puts his person and all his power in common under the supreme direction of the general will, and, in our corporate capacity, we receive each member as an indivisible part of the whole.'

At once, in place of the individual personality of each contracting party, this act of association creates a moral and collective body, composed of as many members as the assembly contains voters, and receiving from this act its unity, its common identity, its life, and its will. This public person, so formed by the union of all other persons, formerly took the name of *city*, and now takes that of *Republic* or *body politic*; it is called by its members *State* when passive, *Sovereign* when active, and *Power* when compared with others like itself. Those who are associated in it take collectively the name of *people*, and severally are called *citizens*, as sharing in the sovereign power, and *subjects*, as being under the laws of the State. But these terms are often confused and taken one for another: it is enough to know how to distinguish them when they are being used with precision.

THE SOVEREIGN

This formula shows us that the act of association comprises a mutual undertaking between the public and the individuals, and that each individual, in making a contract, as we may say, with himself, is bound in a double capacity; as a member of the Sovereign he is bound to the individuals, and as a member of the State to the Sovereign. But the maxim of civil right, that no one is bound by undertakings made to himself, does not apply in this case; for there is a great difference between incurring an obligation to yourself and incurring one to a whole of which you form a part.

Attention must further be called to the fact that public deliberation, while competent to bind all the subjects to the Sovereign, because of the two different capacities in which each of them may be regarded, cannot, for the opposite reason, bind the Sovereign to itself; and that it is consequently against the nature of the body politic for the Sovereign to impose on itself a law which it cannot infringe. Being able to regard itself in only one capacity, it is in the position of an individual who makes a contract with himself; and this makes it clear that there neither is nor can be any kind of fundamental law binding on the body of the people — not even the social contract itself. This does not mean that the body politic cannot enter into undertakings with others, provided the contract is not infringed by them; for in relation to what is external to it, it becomes a simple being, an individual.

But the body politic or the Sovereign, drawing its being wholly from the sanctity of the contract, can never bind itself, even to an outsider, to do anything derogatory to the original act, for instance, to alienate any part of itself, or to submit to another Sovereign. Violation of the act by which it exists would be self-annihilation; and that which is itself nothing can create nothing.

As soon as this multitude is so united in one body, it is impossible to offend against one of the members without attacking the body, and still more to offend against the body without the members resenting it. Duty and interest therefore equally oblige the two contracting parties to give each other help; and the same men should seek to combine, in their double capacity, all the advantages dependent upon that capacity.

Again, the Sovereign, being formed wholly of the individuals who compose it, neither has nor can have any interest contrary to theirs; and consequently the sovereign power need give no guarantee to its subjects, because it is impossible for the body to wish to hurt all its members. We shall also see later on that it cannot hurt any in particular. The Sovereign, merely by virtue of what it is, is always what it should be.

This, however, is not the case with the relation of the subjects to the Sovereign, which, despite the common interest, would have no security that they would fulfil their undertakings, unless it found means to assure itself of their fidelity.

In fact, each individual, as a man, may have a particular will contrary or dissimilar to the general will which he has as a citizen. His particular interest may speak to him quite differently from the common interest: his absolute and naturally independent existence may make him look upon what he owes to the common cause as a gratuitous contribution, the loss of which will do less harm to others than the payment of it is burdensome to himself; and, regarding the moral person which constitutes the State as a *persona ficta*, because not a man, he may wish to enjoy the rights of citizenship without being ready to fulfil the duties of a subject. The continuance of such an injustice could not but prove the undoing of the body politic.

In order then that the social compact may not be an empty formula, it tacitly includes the undertaking, which alone can give force to the rest, that whoever refuses to obey the general will shall be compelled to do so by the whole body. This means nothing less than that he will be forced to be free; for this is the condition which, by giving each citizen to his country, secures him against all personal dependence. In this lies the key to the working of the political machine; this alone legitimizes civil undertakings, which, without it, would be absurd, tyrannical, and liable to the most frightful abuses.

THE CIVIL STATE

The passage from the state of nature to the civil state produces a very remarkable change in man, by substituting justice for instinct in his conduct, and giving his actions the morality they had formerly lacked. Then only, when the voice of duty takes the place of physical impulses and right of appetite, does man, who so far had considered only himself, find that he is forced to act on different principles, and to consult his reason before listening to his inclinations. Although, in this state, he deprives himself of some advantages which he got from nature, he gains in return others so great, his faculties are so stimulated and developed, his ideas so extended, his feelings so ennobled, and his whole soul so uplifted, that, did not the abuses of this new condition often degrade him below that which he left, he would be bound to bless continually the happy moment which took him from it for ever, and, instead of a stupid and unimaginative animal, made him an intelligent being and a man.

Let us draw up the whole account in terms easily commensurable. What man loses by the social contract is his natural liberty and an unlimited right to everything he tries to get and succeeds in getting; what he gains is civil liberty and the proprietorship of all he possesses. If we are to avoid mistake in weighing one against the other, we must clearly distinguish natural liberty, which is bounded only by the strength of the individual, from civil liberty, which is limited by the general will; and possession, which is merely the effect of force or the right of the first occupier, from property, which can be founded only on a positive title.

We might, over and above all this, add, to what man acquires in the civil state, moral liberty, which alone makes him truly master of himself; for the mere impulse of appetite is slavery, while obedience to a law which we prescribe to ourselves is liberty.[10]

Although Rousseau shares with Hobbes a belief in the social contract theory, the differences between them could not be more striking. Where Hobbes begins with a brutal view of human nature forced into agreement by fear of mutual violence, Rousseau begins by saying that "man is born free." For Rousseau, the social contract is not an instrument of mutual protection but a means of improving people and bringing out what is best in them. His central theme is not antag-

---

[10]Jean-Jacques Rousseau, *The Social Contract and Discourses,* trans. G. D. H. Cole (New York: Everyman's Library Edition, E. P. Dutton, 1947).

onism but humanity's "natural goodness." With unmistakable clarity, Rousseau rejects all might makes right theories and insists that legitimacy must always be a matter of the consent of the governed. "The general will" is not a general compromise but the creation of a new power, the power of the people, which for Rousseau is the ultimate voice of authority.

The most famous example of social contract theory at work is in our own *Declaration of Independence*. In that document, social contract theory combined with a theory of "natural" ("inalienable") rights provided an epoch-making announcement of the right of a people to overthrow an established government:

from "The Declaration of Independence," by Jefferson *et al.*

We hold these Truths to be self-evident, that all Men are created equal, that they are endowed by their Creator with certain unalienable Rights, that among these are Life, Liberty, and the pursuit of Happiness — That to secure these rights, Governments are instituted among Men, deriving their just Powers from the Consent of the Governed, that whenever any Form of Government becomes destructive of these Ends, it is the Right of the People to alter or to abolish it, and to institute new Government, laying its Foundation on such Principles, and organizing its Powers in such Form, as to them shall seem most likely to effect their Safety and Happiness. Prudence, indeed, will indicate that Governments long established should not be changed for light and transient causes; and accordingly all Experience hath shewn, that Mankind are more disposed to suffer, while Evils are sufferable, than to right themselves by abolishing the Forms to which they are accustomed. But when a long Train of Abuses and Usurpations, pursuing invariably the same Object, evinces a Design to reduce them under absolute Despotism, it is their Right, it is their Duty, to throw off such Government, and to provide new Guards for their future Security.

INDIVIDUAL RIGHTS AND FREEDOM

If our concern were only the smooth workings of society, almost any government would do — the stronger the better, the more authoritarian the more efficient. But efficiency is only one of several concerns and probably not the most important. You might argue that the public interest could be served by such a government, but it is clear that justice and individual rights could not. The importance of the social contract theory (and consent of the governed theories in general) is precisely its clear emphasis on justice and rights, even when these go against the general public interest. However, the social contract theory by itself is not entirely clear about the status of individual rights. Those rights concerning freedom are of particular concern here. How much personal freedom does the social contract guarantee us? Thus any discussion of justice and the state must include some special concern for the status of basic freedoms and "unalienable rights" (that is, rights that no one and no government may take away), such as freedom to speak one's political opinions without harassment, freedom to worship (or not worship) without being penalized or punished, freedom to defend oneself against attack ("the right to bear arms" is a controversial case), and the freedom to pursue one's own interests (where these do not interfere with the rights of others). In addition, we can add the right not to be imprisoned without reason, or accused without a fair trial, or punished unduly for a crime committed. Our best-known list of such freedoms and rights is the American "Bill of Rights," appended to the main body of the Constitution as a kind of contractual guarantee of personal rights.

But even if the importance of such rights is indisputable, the precise formulation and extent of those rights are highly debatable. We speak of "unalienable rights," but should such rights be left unrestricted, for example, even in wartime? It is clear, to mention the most common example, that freedom of speech does not extend so far as the right to falsely yell "fire" in a crowded theater. Freedom of speech, therefore, like other rights, is limited by considerations of public welfare and utility. But how limited? Is mere annoyance to the government sufficient? or general boredom among the populace? Similarly, we can go back to the difficult examples we raised in earlier sections. Are the rights against imprisonment and harsh punishment always valid against overwhelming public interest? For example, are they valid in the case of a criminal who has committed crimes repeatedly? Or, to take a difficult example, is "free enterprise" an "unalienable" right in our society? Or is free enterprise rather a theory (and a debatable one) that suggests that public interest and justice will best be served by open competition and a free market? But that theory evolved before modern monopolies developed and before it was obvious that "free" markets could be manipulated so as not to be either free or in the public interest at all. Is that "freedom" still a right? Or should it also be tempered by other concerns?

One of the most important basic rights is the presumed right to own private property. John Locke, writing just after the English ("Glorious") Revolution of 1688, listed three basic rights that would become the main ingredients of both the American Declaration of Independence and a still-prominent political philosophy called liberalism. Foremost among them were "life, liberty, and the right to own private property." (The original draft of the American Declaration included just these three, but Jefferson replaced the last with the less commital "pursuit of happiness.") For Locke, private property is the bulwark of freedom and the basis of other human rights. One's own body is private property in the most basic sense; no one else has the authority to violate or use it without permission. Most contemporary societies recognize this right to one's own body as fundamental. But then Locke adds that the right to own property that one has helped cultivate with his or her body ("hath mixed his labour with it") is also basic to freedom and human dignity. The Protestant work ethic emerges very powerfully in this view, in which work and rights are treated together, the first being our way of earning the second:

from *The Second Treatise* *on Government,* by John Locke

Though the earth and all inferior creatures be common to all men, yet every man has a *property* in his own *person*. This nobody has any right to but himself. The *labour* of his body and the *work* of his hands, we may say, are properly his. Whatsoever, then, he removes out of the state that nature hath provided and left it in, he hath mixed his labour with it, and joined to it something that is his own, and thereby makes it his property. It being by him removed from the common state nature placed it in, it hath by this labour something annexed to it that excludes the common right of other men. For this labour being the unquestionable property of the labourer, no man but he can have a right to what that is once joined to, at least where there is enough, and as good left in common for others.

He that is nourished by the acorns he picked up under an oak, or the apples he gathered from the trees in the wood, has certainly appropriated them to himself. Nobody can deny but the nourishment is his. I ask, then, when did they begin to be his? when he digested? or when he ate? or when he boiled? or when he brought them home? or when he picked them up? And 'tis plain, if the first gathering made them not his, nothing else could. That labour put a distinction between them and common. That added something to them more than Nature, the common mother of all, had done, and so they became his private right. And will any one say he had no right to those acorns or apples he thus appropriated because he had not the consent of all mankind to make them his? Was it a robbery thus to assume to himself what belonged to all in common? If such a consent as that was necessary, man had starved, notwithstanding the plenty God had given him. We see in commons, which remain so by compact, that 'tis the taking any part of what is common, and removing it out of the state Nature leaves it in, which begins the property, without which the common is of no use. And the taking of this or that part does not depend on the express consent of all the commoners. Thus, the grass my horse has bit, the turfs my servant has cut, and the ore I have digged in any place, where I have a right to them in common with others, become my property without the assignation or consent of any body. The labour that was mine, removing them out of that common state they were in, hath fixed my property in them.

And thus, I think, it is very easy to conceive, without any difficulty, how labour could at first begin a title of property in the common things of nature, and how the spending it upon our uses bounded it; so that there could then be no reason of quarrelling about title, nor any doubt about the largeness of possession it gave. Right and conveniency went together. For as a man had a right to all he could employ his labour upon, so he had no temptation to labour for more than he could make use of. This left no room for controversy about the title, nor for encroachment on the right of others. What portion a man carved to himself was easily seen; and it was useless as well as dishonest to carve himself too much, or take more than he needed.[11]

---

[11]John Locke, *The Second Treatise on Government* (New York: Hafner, 1956).

It is important to point out that discussions of rights should never be set apart from discussions of political duties and obligations. As the several versions of the social contract make clear, these are always part of one and the same agreement — certain rights in return for certain obligations. To discuss freedom of speech, for example, without also discussing the obligation to be well informed and logically coherent, is to provide a dangerously one-sided view of the problem. One way of developing this idea of an exchange of rights and obligations has been to distinguish two different senses of "freedom": a *negative* freedom from interference and a *positive* freedom to realize one's own potential and find one's place in society. Freedom from interference may be necessary for a person to enjoy life and contribute to the welfare of those around him or her, but a person also needs positive goods — health and education, for example. Thus freedom takes on a double meaning, freedom *from* interference but freedom *to* participate in society too. And since positive freedom also includes a person's being able to take on responsibilities, some philosophers have pointed out a paradox in the idea of being "free to perform obligations."

The idea that one is "free to perform obligations" may sound odd to us because we are so used to talking exclusively about freedom from constraints and the demands made by authority. But one of the themes that has recurred since the ancient Greeks is that all rights and "freedoms from" must be coupled with duties and obligations and the freedom to perform them. In Rousseau, for example, the citizen's obligations to the state are just as important as the state's obligations to its citizens. Many philosophers are concerned that simple freedom from constraint leaves people without direction or morality and can easily degenerate into chaos and anarchy. Thus these philosophers stress the necessity of laws and guidelines as an essential part of freedom. This is why they call it "positive" freedom, since it necessarily includes "positive" goods (health and education) as well as a set of roles, duties, obligations, and constraints. This notion can be abused easily, however, for "positive freedom" can be made compatible with the most authoritarian state. (The Italian and German fascists, for example, often used the term "freedom" in this "positive" sense.) But despite possible abuses, it is important to see that there is more to freedom than simple freedom from interference. Whenever someone demands freedom, it is important to ask not only "from what?" but also "for what?"

It is also worth distinguishing several different kinds of rights. We can distinguish between "negative" and "positive" rights as well as freedoms; one has a right not to be interfered with, and one has rights *to* certain goods that society can provide. We have mostly been discussing negative rights (the right to be left alone, the right not to be arrested without good reason). But there are positive rights that are equally important, although they are often more controversial in this society, for example, the right to a minimal income regardless of the work one performs, the right to adequate health care regardless of one's ability to pay for it. Many rights are clearly localized to a particular state or a particular community, as, for example, the right of university regents to free football game tickets and lunches at taxpayers' expense. These rights exist by convention only, and cannot be generalized from one community to another. Then, more generally, there are **civil** rights, rights that are guaranteed in a particular state. One example can be the right to equal treatment despite differences in skin color or sex or religion, as required by various state and federal laws. These are clearly much more important than the conventional rights, and they have a clearly moral basis. For that reason, even though they are defined by reference to a particular state and society, they are often generalized to other societies as well. Insofar as they are generalized in this way, they become *moral* rights or **human rights,** extendable to all people, in any society, regardless of the laws and customs of the society in which they live. Some apparent human rights have been hotly debated: for example, whether the American government has the moral authority to interfere with the infringements of certain human rights of citizens in the Soviet Union. If the right in question is harsh punishment for a seemingly minor crime, it might be argued that their system of punishment is simply more severe than ours, and we should not apply our values to their people. If the right in question is the ability of citizens to speak out against the government without threat of imprisonment or worse, a strong argument has been made that the American government does indeed have that moral authority (whether or not it wishes to risk the consequences is another matter). But if the right in question is one of those basic human rights against torture or debasement or pointless murder, then it can be argued that everyone has a moral obligation to defend such rights. Human rights are those that transcend all social and national boundaries; they demand that people deserve certain treatment just because they are human, regardless of all else.

A right is a kind of demand, the demand that one is owed something by society and the state, usually a certain sort of consideration or treatment. But most of the rights we have been discussing are in fact rights to freedom or to liberty, that is, the right to be left alone and not interfered with. It is a belief in individual freedom that forms the basis of the liberal political philosophy, which is defined most of all by a commitment to the right of each individual to be free to do whatever he or she wishes as long as it doesn't interfere with similar rights of others. The classic statement of this position is another pamphlet by John Stuart Mill, *On Liberty* (1859). In it, he defends the rights of individuals and minorities against the tyranny of democratic majorities, for Mill sees that liberty can be as endangered in a democracy as it can be in an authoritarian state. Mill goes on to offer a "very simple principle," that individual liberty is to be considered inviolable except when other people are threatened with harm.

from *On Liberty,* by J. S. Mill

The object of this Essay is to assert one very simple principle, as entitled to govern absolutely the dealings of society with the individual in the way of compulsion and control, whether the means used be physical force in the form of legal penalties, or the moral coercion of public opinion. That principle is, that the sole end for which mankind are warranted, individually

or collectively, in interfering with the liberty of action of any of their number, is self-protection. That the only purpose for which power can be rightfully exercised over any member of a civilised community, against his will,
is to prevent harm to others. His own good, either physical or moral, is not
a sufficient warrant. He cannot rightfully be compelled to do or forbear
because it will be better for him to do so, because it will make him happier,
because, in the opinions of others, to do so would be wise, or even right.
These are good reasons for remonstrating with him, or reasoning with him,
or persuading him, or entreating him, but not for compelling him, or visiting him with any evil in case he do otherwise. To justify that, the conduct
from which it is desired to deter him must be calculated to produce evil to
some one else. The only part of the conduct of any one, for which he is
amenable to society, is that which concerns others. In the part which
merely concerns himself, his independence is, of right, absolute. Over himself, over his own body and mind, the individual is sovereign.

It is, perhaps, hardly necessary to say that this doctrine is meant to apply
only to human beings in the maturity of their faculties. We are not speaking of children, or of young persons below the age which the law may fix
as that of manhood or womanhood. Those who are still in a state to require
being taken care of by others, must be protected against their own actions
as well as against external injury. For the same reason, we may leave out of
consideration those backward states of society in which the race itself may
be considered as in its nonage. The early difficulties in the way of spontaneous progress are so great, that there is seldom any choice of means for
overcoming them; and a ruler full of the spirit of improvement is warranted
in the use of any expedients that will attain an end, perhaps otherwise unat-
tainable. Despotism is a legitimate mode of government in dealing with
barbarians, provided the end be their improvement,[12] and the means justified by actually affecting that end. Liberty, as a principle, has no application
to any state of things anterior to the time when mankind have become
capable of being improved by free and equal discussion.

It is proper to state that I forego any advantage which could be derived
to my argument from the idea of abstract right, as a thing independent of
utility. I regard utility as the ultimate appeal on all ethical questions; but it
must be utility in the largest sense, grounded on the permanent interests of
a man as a progressive being. Those interests, I contend, authorise the subjection of individual spontaneity to external control, only in respect to those
actions of each, which concern the interest of other people. If any one does
an act hurtful to others, there is a *prima facie* case for punishing him, by
law, or, where legal penalties are not safely applicable, by general disappro-
bation. There are also many positive acts for the benefit of others, which
he may rightfully be compelled to perform; such as to give evidence in a
court of justice; to bear his fair share in the common defence, or in any
other joint work necessary to the interest of the society of which he enjoys
the protection; and to perform certain acts of individual beneficence, such

---

[12]Notice the political implications for this qualification, however, in "underdeveloped" countries
and colonies. The principle of *paternalism* — that one ought to take care of those who cannot take
care of themselves — is easily abused, and therefore always dangerous.

as saving a fellow creature's life, or interposing to protect the defenceless against ill-usage, things which whenever it is obviously a man's duty to do, he may rightfully be made responsible to society for not doing. A person may cause evil to others not only by his actions but by his inaction, and in either case he is justly accountable to them for the injury. The latter case, it is true, requires a much more cautious exercise of compulsion than the former. To make any one answerable for doing evil to others is the rule; to make him answerable for not preventing evil is, comparatively speaking, the exception. Yet there are many cases clear enough and grave enough to justify that exception. In all things which regard the external relations of the individual, he is *de jure* amenable to those whose interests are concerned, and, if need be, to society as their protector. There are often good reasons for not holding him to the responsibility; but these reasons must arise from the special expediencies of the case: either because it is a kind of case in which he is on the whole likely to act better, when left to his own discretion, than when controlled in any way in which society have it in their power to control him; or because the attempt to exercise control would produce other evils, greater than those which it would prevent. When such reasons as these preclude the enforcement of responsibility, the conscience of the agent himself should step into the vacant judgment seat, and protect those interests of others which have no external protection; judging himself all the more rigidly, because the case does not admit of his being made accountable to the judgment of his fellow creatures.

But there is a sphere of action in which society, as distinguished from the individual, has, if any, only an indirect interest; comprehending all that portion of a person's life and conduct which affects only himself, or if it also affects others, only with their free, voluntary, and undeceived consent and participation. When I say only himself, I mean directly, and in the first instance; for whatever affects himself, may affect others through himself; and the objection which may be grounded on this contingency, will receive consideration in the sequel. This, then, is the appropriate region of human liberty. It comprises, first, the inward domain of consciousness; demanding liberty of conscience in the most comprehensive sense; liberty of thought and feeling; absolute freedom of opinion and sentiment on all subjects, practical or speculative, scientific, moral, or theological. The liberty of expressing and publishing opinions may seem to fall under a different principle, since it belongs to that part of the conduct of an individual which concerns other people; but, being almost of as much importance as the liberty of thought itself, and resting in great part on the same reasons, is practically inseparable from it. Secondly, the principle requires liberty of tastes and pursuits; of framing the plan of our life to suit our own character; of doing as we like, subject to such consequences as may follow: without impediment from our fellow creatures, so long as what we do does not harm them, even though they should think our conduct foolish, perverse, or wrong. Thirdly, from this liberty of each individual, follows the liberty, within the same limits, of combination among individuals; freedom to unite, for any purpose not involving harm to others: the persons combining being supposed to be of full age, and not forced or deceived.

No society in which these liberties are not, on the whole, respected, is free, whatever may be its form of government; and none is completely free in which they do not exist absolute and unqualified. The only freedom which deserves the name, is that of pursuing our own good in our own way, so long as we do not attempt to deprive others of theirs, or impede their efforts to obtain it. Each is the proper guardian of his own health, whether bodily, or mental and spiritual. Mankind are greater gainers by suffering each other to live as seems good to themselves, than by compelling each to live as seems good to the rest.[13]

Mill's main concern in this essay is the extent to which government and public interest have authority over individuals and individual actions. If an action harms other people or presents a public menace, then government does have the authority to prevent it or punish a person for doing it. But if an action is not harmful to others, the government has no such authority. In the question of freedom of speech, for example, this means that governments have no authority to censor some comment or publication unless it clearly harms other people, not merely annoys or personally offends them. Mill is particularly concerned with protecting individuals against "the tyranny of the majority." The public interest is authoritative to "a limit," but that limit does not include interfering with personal affairs or opinions.

A DIFFERENT SENSE OF FREEDOM: MARX

From a liberal perspective, this English emphasis on rights and liberty seems indisputable. But what happens when the "natural right" to private property is abused, when people take more than they can use personally and use their excess possession merely as a means to manipulate other people? And it is all well and good to defend such rights as freedom of speech and religion, but what if many people in the society find themselves far more concerned just with the exigencies of existence — putting food on the table, surviving a dangerous job, and not having enough protection under the law to prevent them from being grossly exploited and underpaid for unrewarding and painful labor? There is an obvious sense in which people in such conditions are not at all "free," even if they are guaranteed freedom of speech and religion. Freedom from government persecution is not necessarily freedom from economic exploitation. And it is the latter freedom that concerns Karl Marx and his frequent coauthor Friedrich Engels.

It is worth mentioning that Locke wrote his two treatises on government before the industrial revolution; Marx wrote when that revolution was at its peak, transforming cities like Manchester, England, into virtual slave-farms of underpaid, overworked laborers. With this in mind, the freedoms of speech and religion protected by well-to-do and comfortable liberals seemed not nearly so important

[13]John Stuart Mill, *On Liberty* (London: Longmans, 1859).

as the basic freedom to a decent life. So Marx turned from political liberties to economic necessities and turned his attention from the supposed right to private property to the abuse of private property.

Although Marx insists on "the abolition of private property" as the central theme of communism, he still retains the idea that a man or woman has the right to the products of his or her own labor. What he rejects is the ownership of property that one has not personally produced and that serves only as a means for getting richer at the expense of other people, who are thereby forced to work without enjoying the products of their labor. This is what Marx means by his very important notion of **alienation.** A person is alienated if he or she is no longer working for himself or herself but only for the benefit of another person. Even though a person might get paid for this labor, that does not make it less alienated. Factory workers may be well paid, but they are alienated insofar as their work is meaningless to them, and the profits of their work do not go to them but to someone else. Thus, despite their obvious differences, Marx and Locke agree to this extent: A person has a right to something "if he has mixed his labour with it." Both philosophers agree on the importance of human productivity and creativity to the good life, and the person's right to his or her own creation is therefore essential to any adequate society.

Marx was a *historical materialist*, which means that he placed new emphasis on the economic modes of production of goods and saw history and politics (and all other human enterprises) as conditioned by economic relations. Accordingly, the key to human freedom and the lack of freedom was also economic. In the following passage from his early writings (of 1844), Marx summarizes his notion of alienation as the unnatural separation of a person from the object he or she creates, resulting in separation ("alienation") from other people and ultimately from oneself. Quite the contrary of the "natural" identity the worker should feel with what he or she has made, the object produced is "set against him [or her] as an alien and hostile force." Instead of pride or enjoyment, the worker feels only resentment against those who have made the labor meaningless, and the pay received for this only makes it clearer how personally irrelevant it is.

from "Alienated Labor," by Karl Marx

We shall begin from a *contemporary* economic fact. The worker becomes poorer the more wealth he produces and the more his production increases in power and extent. The worker becomes an ever cheaper commodity the more goods he creates. The *devaluation* of the human world increases in direct relation with the *increase in value* of the world of things. Labor does not only create goods; it also produces itself and the worker as a *commodity,* and indeed in the same proportion as it produces goods.

This fact simply implies that the object produced by labor, its product, now stands opposed to it as an *alien being,* as a *power independent* of the producer. The product of labor is labor which has been embodied in an object and turned into a physical thing; this product is an *objectification* of labor. The performance of work is at the same time its objectification. The performance of work appears in the sphere of political economy as a *vitiation* of the worker, objectification as a *loss* and as *servitude to the object,* and appropriation as *alienation.*

So much does the performance of work appear as vitiation that the worker is vitiated to the point of starvation. So much does objectification appear as loss of the object that the worker is deprived of the most essential things not only of life but also of work. Labor itself becomes an object which he can acquire only by the greatest effort and with unpredictable interruptions. So much does the appropriation of the object appear as alienation that the more objects the worker produces the fewer he can possess and the more he falls under the domination of his product, of capital.

All these consequences follow from the fact that the worker is related to the *product of his labor* as to an *alien* object. For it is clear on this presupposition that the more the worker expends himself in work the more powerful becomes the world of objects which he creates in face of himself, the poorer he becomes in his inner life, and the less he belongs to himself. The life which he has given to the object sets itself against him as an alien and hostile force.[14]

Marx introduces the new concept of freedom from alienation, which requires a return to the "natural" state in which people and their labor are one. (In this notion of return to the natural state, Marx is heavily influenced by Rousseau.) It is important to emphasize that nowhere does Marx suggest or desire that people should someday be free of work. According to him, work makes us human. Instead he argues that we should make ourselves free of alienated work. This does not mean that he denies other freedoms — freedom of speech, for example — but he does argue that such freedoms are meaningless in the face of the cruel economic necessities that rule most people's lives. Men and women, desperate for a job and forced to undertake meaningless tasks for forty hours a week, need more than just the freedom to speak out. They require freedom from the economic exploitation that keeps them in such desperate circumstances. They must have, in general, freedom from material need. Marx makes a great deal of what he considers humanity's crucial difference from the animals: their ability to work and produce, thereby freeing themselves from the needs of nature.

Marx is a very modern theorist. He no longer argues on the basis of endless human requirements for food and shelter but sees that in the modern world the means of producing enough food and shelter for everyone are already at hand. What is needed is simply a more equitable form of distribution. This means no private property except for those products a person makes directly. There can be factories but no "owners," as opposed to the laborers. There might be "corporations" but only if they are nothing more than a coalition of the workers, who share in the benefits of their own work.

But this Marxist vision, in which there are no owners except the workers and

[14]Karl Marx, *Early Writings,* trans. T. Bottomore (New York: McGraw-Hill, 1964).

in which everyone is a worker and no one is alienated from his or her work, is not going to come about without enormous upheaval. Marx's "classless society" requires a thoroughgoing revolution — not so much a political revolution as an economic one. This is the key to Marx's concept of freedom. It proposes freedom from want and freedom from economic exploitation, not political freedom in terms of rights and the freedom from government interference that we have mainly discussed so far. The revolution he envisions, in which the various economic classes of society will continue to war against each other until all such classes disappear, may therefore be called a battle for freedom just as much as the traditional liberal battles for freedom of speech and self-government. It is a revolution that he sees as inevitable, which has been in the making since ancient times, and in which the theme "workers of the world unite; you have nothing to lose but your chains" will become the rallying cry around which the human world will experience its greatest upheaval ever.

The excerpt that follows, the *Communist Manifesto* of 1848, is the most popular statement of Marx's theory. Marx wrote it with his friend and long-time collaborator, Friedrich Engels. In it, they explain human history in terms of historical materialism, define the two social classes they see at war with each other, the *bourgeoisie* or ownership class and the *proletariat* or working class, and suggest the course that history now has to take. They are not just predicting and theorizing, however, but are also advocating the revolution they describe in no uncertain terms.

from the *Communist Manifesto*, by Marx and Engels

BOURGEOIS AND PROLETARIANS

The history of all hitherto existing society is the history of class struggles.

Freeman and slave, patrician and plebeian, lord and serf, guild-master and journeyman, in a word, oppressor and oppressed, stood in constant opposition to one another, carried on an uninterrupted, now hidden, now open fight, a fight that each time ended, either in a revolutionary re-constitution of society at large, or in the common ruin of the contending classes.

In the earlier epochs of history, we find almost everywhere a complicated arrangement of society into various orders, a manifold gradation of social rank. In ancient Rome we have patricians, knights, plebeians, slaves; in the middle ages, feudal lords, vassals, guild-masters, journeymen, apprentices, serfs; in almost all of these classes, again, subordinate gradations.

The modern bourgeois society that has sprouted from the ruins of feudal society, has not done away with class antagonisms. It has but established new classes, new conditions of oppression, new forms of struggle in place of the old ones.

Our epoch, the epoch of the bourgeoisie, possesses, however, this distinctive feature; it has simplified the class antagonisms. Society as a whole is more and more splitting up into two great hostile camps, into two great classes directly facing each other: Bourgeoisie and Proletariat.

THE RISE OF THE BOURGEOISIE

From the serfs of the middle ages sprang the chartered burghers of the earliest towns. From these burgesses the first elements of the bourgeoisie were developed.

The discovery of America, the rounding of the Cape, opened up fresh ground for the rising bourgeoisie. The East-Indian and Chinese markets, the colonization of America, trade with the colonies, the increase in the means of exchange and in commodities generally, gave to commerce, to navigation, to industry, an impulse never before known, and thereby, to the revolutionary element in the tottering feudal society, a rapid development.

The feudal system of industry, under which industrial production was monopolized by closed guilds, now no longer sufficed for the growing wants of the new markets. The manufacturing system took its place. The guild-masters were pushed on one side by the manufacturing middle-class; division of labor between the different corporate guilds vanished in the face of division of labor in each single workshop.

Meantime the markets kept ever growing, the demand, ever rising. Even manufacture no longer sufficed. Thereupon, steam and machinery revolutionized industrial production. The place of manufacture was taken by the giant, Modern Industry, the place of the industrial middle-class, by industrial millionaires, the leaders of whole industrial armies, the modern bourgeois.

Modern industry has established the world-market, for which the discovery of America paved the way. This market has given an immense development to commerce, to navigation, to communication by land. This development has, in its turn, reacted on the extension of industry; and in proportion as industry, commerce, navigation, railways extended, in the same proportion the bourgeoisie developed, increased its capital, and pushed into the background every class handed down from the Middle Ages.

We see, therefore, how the modern bourgeoisie is itself the product of a long course of development, of a series of revolutions in the modes of production and of exchange.

Each step in the development of the bourgeoisie was accompanied by a corresponding political advance of that class. An oppressed class under the sway of the feudal nobility, an armed and self-governing association in the mediaeval commune, here independent urban republic (as in Italy and Germany), there taxable "third estate" of the monarchy (as in France), afterwards, in the period of manufacture proper, serving either the semifeudal or the absolute monarchy as a counterpoise against the nobility, and, in fact, cornerstone of the great monarchies in general, the bourgeoisie has at last, since the establishment of Modern Industry and of the world-market, conquered for itself, in the modern representative State, exclusive political sway. *The executive of the modern State is but a committee for managing the common affairs of the whole bourgeoisie.*

REVOLUTIONARY ROLE OF THE BOURGEOISIE

The bourgeoisie, historically, has played a most revolutionary part.

The bourgeoisie, wherever it has got the upper hand, has put an end to all feudal, patriarchal, idyllic relations. It has pitilessly torn asunder the motley feudal ties that bound man to his "natural superiors," and has left remaining no other nexus between man and man than naked self-interest, callous "cash payment." It has drowned the most heavenly ecstasies of religious fervor, of chivalrous enthusiasm, of philistine sentimentalism, in the icy water of egotistical calculation. It has resolved personal worth into exchange value, and in place of the numberless indefeasible chartered freedoms, has set up that single, unconscionable freedom — Free Trade. In one word, for exploitation, veiled by religious and political illusions, it has substituted naked, shameless, direct, brutal exploitation.

The bourgeoisie has stripped of its halo every occupation hitherto honored and looked up to with reverent awe. It has converted the physician, the lawyer, the priest, the poet, the man of science, into its paid wage-laborers.

The bourgeoisie has torn away from the family its sentimental veil, and has reduced the family relation to a mere money relation.

The bourgeoisie has disclosed how it came to pass that the brutal display of vigor in the Middle Ages, which Reactionists so much admire, found its fitting complement in the most slothful indolence. It has been the first to show what man's activity can bring about. It has accomplished wonders far surpassing Egyptian pyramids, Roman aqueducts, and Gothic cathedrals; it has conducted expeditions that put in the shade all former Exoduses of nations and crusades.

The bourgeoisie cannot exist without constantly revolutionizing the instruments of production, and thereby the relations of production, and with them the whole relations of society. Conservation of the old modes of production in unaltered form, was, on the contrary, the first condition of existence for all earlier industrial classes. Constant revolutionizing of production, uninterrupted disturbance of all social conditions, everlasting uncertainty and agitation distinguish the bourgeois epoch from all earlier ones. All fixed, fast-frozen relations, with their train of ancient and venerable prejudices and opinions, are swept away, all new-formed ones become antiquated before they can ossify. All that is solid melts into air, all that is holy is profaned, and man is at last compelled to face, with sober senses, his real conditions of life, and his relations with his kind.

The need of a constantly expanding market for its products chases the bourgeoisie over the whole surface of the globe. It must nestle everywhere, settle everywhere, establish connections everywhere.

The bourgeoisie has through its exploitation of the world-market given a cosmopolitan character to production and consumption in every country. To the great chagrin of Reactionists, it has drawn from under the feet of industry the national ground on which it stood. All old-established national industries have been destroyed or are daily being destroyed. They are dislodged by new industries, whose introduction becomes a life and death question for all civilized nations, by industries that no longer work up indigenous raw material, but raw material drawn from the remotest zones; industries whose products are consumed, not only at home, but in every quarter of the globe. In place of the old wants, satisfied by the productions of the country, we find new wants, requiring for their satisfaction the products of distant lands and climes. In place of the old local and national seclusion and self-sufficiency, we have intercourse in every direction, universal interdependence of nations. And as in material, so also in intellectual production. The intellectual creations of individual nations become common property. National one-sidedness and narrow-mindedness become more and more impossible, and from the numerous national and local literatures there arises a world-literature.

The bourgeoisie, by the rapid improvement of all instruments of production, by the immensely facilitated means of communication, draws all, even the most barbarian, nations into civilization. The cheap prices of its commodities are the heavy artillery with which it batters down all Chinese walls, with which it forces the barbarians' intensely obstinate hatred of foreigners to capitulate. It compels all nations, on pain of extinction, to adopt the bourgeois mode of production; it compels them to introduce what it calls civilization into their midst, i.e., to become bourgeois themselves. In a word, it creates a world after its own image.

The bourgeoisie has subjected the country to the rule of the towns. It has created enormous cities, has greatly increased the urban population as compared with the rural, and has thus rescued a considerable part of the population from the idiocy of rural life. Just as it has made the country dependent on the towns, so it has made barbarian and semi-barbarian countries dependent on the civilized ones, nations of peasants on nations of bourgeois, the East on the West.

The bourgeoisie keeps more and more doing away with the scattered state of the population, of the means of production, and of property. It has agglomerated population, centralized means of production, and has concentrated property in a few hands. The necessary consequence of this was political centralization. Independent, or but loosely connected provinces, with separate interests, laws, governments and systems of taxation, became lumped together in one nation, with one government, one code of laws, one national class-interest, one frontier and one customs-tariff.

The bourgeoisie, during its rule of scarce one hundred years, has created more massive and more colossal productive forces than have all preceding generations together. Subjection of Nature's forces to man, machinery, application of chemistry to industry and agriculture, steam-navigation, railways, electric telegraphs, clearing of whole continents for cultivation, canalization of rivers, whole populations conjured out of the ground—what earlier century had even a presentiment that such productive forces slumbered in the lap of social labor?

THE REVOLT OF PRODUCTIVE FORCES
AGAINST PROPERTY RELATIONS

We see then: the means of production and of exchange on whose foundation the bourgeoisie built itself up, were generated in feudal society. At a certain stage in the development of these means of production and of exchange, the conditions under which feudal society produced and exchanged, the feudal organization of agriculture and manufacturing industry, in one word, the feudal relations of property became no longer compatible with the already developed productive forces; they became so many fetters. They had to burst asunder; they were burst asunder.

Into their places stepped free competition, accompanied by a social and political constitution adapted to it, and by the economical and political sway of the bourgeois class.

A similar movement is going on before our own eyes. *Modern bourgeois society* with its relations of production, of exchange and of property, a society that has conjured up such gigantic means of production and of exchange, *is like the sorcerer, who is no longer able to control the powers of the nether world whom he has called up by his spells.* For many a decade past the history of industry and commerce is but the history of the revolt of modern productive forces against modern conditions of production, against the property relations that are the conditions for the existence of the bourgeoisie and of its rule. It is enough to mention the commercial crises that by their periodical return put on its trial, each time more threateningly, the existence of the entire bourgeois society. In these crises a great part not only of the existing products, but also of the previously created productive forces, are periodically destroyed. In these crises there breaks out an epidemic that, in all earlier epochs, would have seemed an absurdity — the epidemic of over-production. Society suddenly finds itself put back into a state of momentary barbarism; it appears as if a famine, a universal war of devastation had cut off the supply of every means of subsistence; industry and commerce seem to be destroyed; and why? Because there is too much civilization, too much means of subsistence, too much industry, too much commerce. The productive forces at the disposal of society no longer tend to further the development of the conditions of bourgeois property; on the contrary, they have become too powerful for these conditions, by which they are fettered, and so soon as they overcome these fetters, they bring disorder into the whole of bourgeois society, endanger the existence of bourgeois property. The conditions of bourgeois society are too narrow to comprise the wealth created by them. And how does the bourgeoisie get over these crises? On the one hand by enforced destruction of a mass of productive forces; on the other, by the conquest of new markets, and by the more thorough exploitation of the old ones. That is to say, by paving the way for more extensive and more destructive crises, and by diminishing the means whereby crises are prevented. The weapons with which the bourgeoisie felled feudalism to the ground are now turned against the bourgeoisie itself.

But not only has the bourgeoisie forged the weapons that bring death to itself; it has also called into existence the men who are to wield those weapons — the modern working-class — the proletarians.

THE STRUGGLE AND VICTORY OF THE PROLETARIAT

The proletariat goes through various stages of development. With its birth begins its struggle with the bourgeoisie. At first the contest is carried on by individual laborers, then by the workpeople of a factory, then by the operatives of one trade, in one locality, against the individual bourgeois who directly exploits them. They direct their attacks not against the bourgeois conditions of production, but against the instruments of production themselves; they destroy imported wares that compete with their labor, they smash to pieces machinery, they set factories ablaze, they seek to restore by force the vanished status of the workman of the Middle Ages.

At this stage the laborers still form an incoherent mass scattered over the whole country, and broken up by their mutual competition. If anywhere they unite to form more compact bodies, this is not yet the consequence of their own active union, but of the union of the bourgeoisie, which class, in order to attain its own political ends, is compelled to set the whole proletariat in motion, and is moreover, yet, for a time, able to do so. At this stage, therefore, the proletarians do not fight their enemies, but the enemies of their enemies, the remnants of absolute monarchy, the landowners, the non-industrial bourgeois, the petty bourgeoisie. Thus the whole historical movement is concentrated in the hands of the bourgeoisie; every victory so obtained is a victory for the bourgeoisie.

But with the development of industry the proletariat not only increases in number, it becomes concentrated in greater masses, its strength grows, and it feels that strength more. The various interests and conditions of life within the ranks of the proletariat are more and more equalized, in proportion as machinery obliterates all distinctions of labor, and nearly everywhere reduces wages to the same low level. The growing competition among the bourgeois, and the resulting commercial crises, make the wages of the workers ever more fluctuating. The unceasing improvement of machinery, ever more rapidly developing, makes their livelihood more and more precarious; the collisions between individual workmen and individual bourgeois take more and more the character of collisions between two classes. Thereupon the workers begin to form combinations (Trades' Unions) against the bourgeois; they club together in order to keep up the rate of wages; they found permanent associations in order to make provision beforehand for these occasional revolts. Here and there the contest breaks out into riots.

Now and then the workers are victorious, but only for a time. The real fruit of their battle lies, not in the immediate result, but in the ever-expanding union of the workers. This union is helped on by the improved means of communication that are created by modern industry, and that place the workers of different localities in contact with one another. It was just this contact that was needed to centralize the numerous local struggles, all of the same character, into one national struggle between classes. But every class struggle is a political struggle. And that union, to attain which the burghers of the Middle Ages, with their miserable highways, required centuries, the modern proletarians, thanks to railways, achieve in a few years.

This organization of the proletarians into a class, and consequently into a political party, is continually being upset again by the competition between the workers themselves. But it ever rises up again, stronger, firmer, mightier. It compels legislative recognition of particular interest of the workers, by taking advantage of the divisions among the bourgeoisie itself. Thus the ten-hour bill in England was carried.

Altogether collisions between the classes of the old society further, in many ways, the course of development of the proletariat. The bourgeoisie finds itself involved in a constant battle. At first with the aristocracy; later on, with those portions of the bourgeoisie itself, whose interests have become antagonistic to the progress of industry; at all times, with the bourgeoisie of foreign countries. In all these battles it sees itself compelled to appeal to the proletariat, to ask for its help, and thus, to drag it into the political arena. The bourgeoisie itself, therefore, supplies the proletariat with its own elements of political and general education, in other words, it furnishes the proletariat with weapons for fighting the bourgeoisie.

Further, as we have already seen, entire sections of the ruling classes are, by the advance of industry, precipitated into the proletariat, or are at least threatened in their conditions of existence. These also supply the proletariat with fresh elements of enlightenment and progress.

Finally, in times when the class-struggle nears the decisive hour, the process of dissolution going on within the ruling class, in fact, within the whole range of old society, assumes such a violent, glaring character, that a small section of the ruling class cuts itself adrift, and joins the revolutionary class, the class that holds the future in its hands. Just as, therefore, at an earlier period, a section of the nobility went over to the bourgeoisie, so now a portion of the bourgeoisie goes over to the proletariat, and in particular, a portion of the bourgeois ideologists, who have raised themselves to the level of comprehending theoretically the historical movements as a whole.

PROPERTY AND FREEDOM

All property relations in the past have continually been subject to historical change consequent upon the change in historical conditions.

The French Revolution, for example, abolished feudal property in favor of bourgeois property.

The distinguishing feature of Communism is not the abolition of property generally, but the abolition of bourgeois property. But modern bourgeois private property is the final and most complete expression of the system of producing and appropriating products, that is based on class antagonism, on the exploitation of the many by the few.

In this sense, the theory of the Communists may be summed up in the single sentence: Abolition of private property. . . .

You are horrified at our intending to do away with private property. But in your existing society, private property is already done away with for nine-tenths of the population; its existence for the few is solely due to its nonexistence in the hands of those nine-tenths. You reproach us, therefore, with intending to do away with a form of property, the necessary condition for whose existence is the nonexistence of any property for the immense majority of society.

In a word, you reproach us with intending to do away with your property. Precisely so; that is just what we intend.

From the moment when labor can no longer be converted into capital, money, or rent, into a social power capable of being monopolized, *i.e.*, from the moment when individual property can no longer be transformed into bourgeois property, into capital, from that moment, you say, individuality vanishes.

You must, therefore, confess that by "individual" you mean no other person than the bourgeois, than the middle-class owner of property. This person must, indeed, be swept out of the way, and made impossible.

Communism deprives no man of the power to appropriate the products of society; all that it does is to deprive him of the power to subjugate the labor of others by means of such appropriation. . . .

And then Marx's final optimism:

When, in the course of development, class distinctions have disappeared, and all production has been concentrated in the hands of a vast association of the whole nation, the public power will lose its political character. Political power, properly so called, is merely the organized power of one class for oppressing another. If the proletariat during its contest with the bourgeoisie is compelled, by the force of circumstances, to organize itself as a class; if, by means of a revolution, it makes itself the ruling class, and, as such sweeps away by force the old conditions of production, then it will, along with these conditions, have swept away the conditions for the existence of class antagonisms, and of classes generally, and will thereby have abolished its own supremacy as a class.

In place of the old bourgeois society, with its classes and class antagonisms, we shall have an association, in which the free development of each is the condition for the free development of all.[15]

THE ABSOLUTE STATE: FASCISM

We think of "fascism" as a nasty word. People of very different political persuasions accuse their opponents of "fascism" if they consider their policies oppressive. But this is a new meaning of the word. "Fascism" once was the proud name of a political theory, the theory of the absolute state. In the 1920s, Benito Mussolini swept into power in Italy with enormous popularity, a popularity he retained until his disastrous alliance with Adolf Hitler (also a fascist) in the Second World War. For Mussolini, and for most of his followers, "fascism" had an almost religious significance: the state was raised to an almost divine status. The state was like a god, the source of laws and duties not unlike those discussed in the Bible. The individual existed only to serve and identify with the state. According to fascism, if some people were brutally repressed, it was only for the good of the general will and the state. (Rousseau's notion of "the general will"

---

[15]Karl Marx and Friedrich Engels, *Communist Manifesto*, trans. Samuel Moore (Chicago: Regnery, 1969).

often enters into fascist theory.) If fascism had to use force to protect the govern-ment, that force, so it was argued, was ultimately for the good of its people. And if fascism so often meant war, what better way to bring the citizens together into a virtual family? This identification of the state with the family plays a central part in the almost religious language of fascism. What follows is an extract from one of Mussolini's most often-quoted speeches:

on "Fascism," by Mussolini

Fascism is a religious conception in which man is seen in his immanent relationship with a superior law and with an objective Will that transcends the particular individual and raises him to conscious membership of a spir-itual society. Whoever has seen in the religious politics of the Fascist regime nothing but mere opportunism has not understood that Fascism besides being a system of government is also, and above all, a system of thought.

Fascism is a historical conception, in which man is what he is only in so far as he works with the spiritual process in which he finds himself, in the family or social group, in the nation and in the history in which all nations collaborate. From this follows the great value of tradition, in mem-ories, in language, in customs, in the standards of social life. Outside history man is nothing. Consequently, Fascism is opposed to all the individualistic abstractions of a materialistic nature like those of the eighteenth century; and it is opposed to all Jacobin utopias and innovations. It does not consider that "happiness" is possible upon earth, as it appeared to be in the desire of the economic literature of the eighteenth century, and hence it rejects all teleological theories according to which mankind would reach a definitive stabilized condition at a certain period in history. This implies putting one-self outside history and life, which is a continual change and coming to be. Politically, Fascism wishes to be a realistic doctrine; practically, it aspires to solve only the problems which arise historically of themselves and that of themselves find or suggest their own solution. To act among men, as to act in the natural world, it is necessary to enter into the process of reality and to master the already operating forces.

Against individualism, the Fascist conception is for the State; and it is for the individual in so far as he coincides with the State, which is the con-science and universal will of man in his historical existence. It is opposed to classical Liberalism, which arose from the necessity of reacting against absolutism, and which brought its historical purpose to an end when the State was transformed into the conscience and will of the people. Liberalism denied the State in the interests of the particular individual; Fascism reaf-firms the State as the true reality of the individual. And if liberty is to be the attribute of the real man, and not of that abstract puppet envisaged by individualistic Liberalism, Fascism is for liberty. And for the only liberty which can be a real thing, the liberty of the State and of the individual within the State. Therefore, for the Fascist, everything is in the State, and nothing human or spiritual exists, much less has value, outside the State.

In this sense Fascism is totalitarian, and the Fascist State, the synthesis and unity of all values, interprets, develops and gives strength to the whole life of the people.

.   .   .   .   .

This higher personality is truly the nation in so far as it is the State. It is not the nation that generates the State, as according to the old naturalistic concept which served as the basis of the political theories of the national States of the nineteenth century. Rather the nation is created by the State, which gives to the people, conscious of its own moral unity, a will and therefore an effective existence. The right of a nation to independence derives not from a literary and ideal consciousness of its own being, still less from a more or less unconscious and inert acceptance of a *de facto* situation, but from an active consciousness, from a political will in action and ready to demonstrate its own rights: that is to say, from a state already coming into being. The State, in fact, as the universal ethical will, is the creator of right.[16]

In the other political theories we have discussed, the state and its interests are always balanced against the interests of the public and the individual citizen. This is the main point of most social contract theories, of consent of the governed theories, of utilitarian and justice theories, and the main goal of Marx's theory as well (although Marx is more concerned with economic power than just political power). In fascism, by contrast, the balance tips towards the interests of the state. This is not to say that the purpose of fascism is not also to serve the public interest and the individual citizen, but in terms of priorities, the state comes first. In social contract theories (including democratic theories), a state that does not serve the public interest can be legitimately overthrown; in fascist theory, the state has absolute legitimacy whether or not it succeeds in satisfying its citizens, and this is part of its religious significance.

In view of the fascist doctrine of the absolute state, it is in the interest of the state, but not its obligation, to have its citizens support it as enthusiastically as possible. This means that the fascist state will try to get the approval of its people perhaps just as fervently as a democratic state but primarily in order to enhance its own power. About four hundred years before the advent of modern fascism, one of Mussolini's countrymen, Niccolo Machiavelli, wrote a short treatise designed to instruct the leaders of absolute states on the art of keeping their power, including the art of winning and keeping public support. In *The Prince* (1513), Machiavelli writes a "how to" book for rulers, telling them the best ways of winning wars, tricking their enemies, and, in general, keeping power. (Machiavelli himself was not a fascist; he also wrote the *Discourses*, which deals in part with how to establish a republic. But *The Prince* has always served as the classic book for fascist theories.) The following is a representative excerpt from *The*

---

[16]Benito Mussolini, "The Doctrine of Fascism," trans. I. S. Munro (Rome: Encyclopedie Italiano, 1934).

Prince. Notice that its concern throughout is "how to stay in power," not how to be just or fair or even good. Justice or compassion are but means of keeping power, and that is the key to modern fascism as well.

from *The Prince,* by Machiavelli

OF CRUELTY AND CLEMENCY, AND WHETHER IT IS BETTER TO BE LOVED THAN FEARED

Coming down now to the other aforementioned qualities, I say that every prince ought to desire the reputation of being merciful, and not cruel; at the same time, he should be careful not to misuse that mercy. Cesare Borgia was reputed cruel, yet by his cruelty he reunited the Romagna to his states, and restored that province to order, peace, and loyalty; and if we carefully examine his course, we shall find it to have been really much more merciful than the course of the people of Florence, who, to escape the reputation of cruelty, allowed Pistoia to be destroyed. A prince, therefore, should not mind the ill repute of cruelty, when he can thereby keep his subjects united and loyal; for a few displays of severity will really be more merciful than to allow, by an excess of clemency, disorders to occur, which are apt to result in rapine and murder; for these injure a whole community, while the executions ordered by the prince fall only upon a few individuals. And, above all others, the new prince will find it almost impossible to avoid the reputation of cruelty because new states are generally exposed to many dangers. It was on this account that Virgil made Dido to excuse the severity of her government, because it was still new, saying, —

'My cruel fate,
And doubts attending an unsettled state,
Force me to guard my coasts from foreign foes.'[17]

A prince, however, should be slow to believe and to act; nor should he be too easily alarmed by his own fears, and should proceed moderately and with prudence and humanity, so that an excess of confidence may not make him incautious, nor too much mistrust make him intolerant. This, then, gives rise to the question "whether it be better to be beloved than feared, or to be feared than beloved." It will naturally be answered that it would be desirable to be both the one and the other; but as it is difficult to be both at the same time, it is much more safe to be feared than to be loved, when you have to choose between the two. For it may be said of men in general that they are ungrateful and fickle, dissemblers, avoiders of danger, and greedy of gain. So long as you shower benefits upon them, they are all yours; they offer you their blood, their substance, their lives, and their children, provided the necessity for it is far off; but when it is near at hand, then they revolt. And the prince who relies upon their words, without having otherwise provided for his security, is ruined; for friendships that are won by

---

[17]Translated from Latin by John Dryden.

rewards, and not by greatness and nobility of soul, although deserved, yet are not real, and cannot be depended upon in time of adversity.

Besides, men have less hesitation in offending one who makes himself beloved than one who makes himself feared; for love holds by a bond of obligation which, as mankind is bad, is broken on every occasion whenever it is for the interest of the obliged party to break it. But fear holds by the apprehension of punishment, which never leaves men. A prince, however, should make himself feared in such a manner that, if he has not won the affections of his people, he shall at least not incur their hatred; for the being feared, and not hated, can go very well together, if the prince abstains from taking the substance of his subjects, and leaves them their women. And if you should be obliged to inflict capital punishment upon any one, then be sure to do so only when there is manifest cause and proper justification for it; and, above all things, abstain from taking people's property, for men will sooner forget the death of their fathers than the loss of their patrimony. Besides, there will never be any lack of reasons for taking people's property; and a prince who once begins to live by rapine will ever find excuses for seizing other people's property. On the other hand, reasons for taking life are not so easily found, and are more readily exhausted. But when a prince is at the head of his army, with a multitude of soldiers under his command, then it is above all things necessary for him to disregard the reputation of cruelty; for without such severity an army cannot be kept together, nor disposed for any successful feat of arms.

Among the many admirable qualities of Hannibal, it is related of him that, having an immense army composed of a very great variety of races of men, which he led to war in foreign countries, no quarrels ever occurred among them, nor were there ever any dissensions between them and their chief, either in his good or in his adverse fortunes; which can only be accounted for by his extreme cruelty. This, together with his boundless courage, made him ever venerated and terrible in the eyes of his soldiers; and without that extreme severity all his other virtues would not have sufficed to produce that result.

Inconsiderate writers have, on the one hand, admired his great deeds, and, on the other, condemned the principal cause of the same. And the proof that his other virtues would not have sufficed him may be seen from the case of Scipio, who was one of the most remarkable men, not only of his own time, but in all history. His armies revolted in Spain solely in consequence of his extreme clemency, which allowed his soldiers more license than comports with proper military discipline. This fact was censured in the Roman Senate by Fabius Maximus, who called Scipio the corrupter of the Roman soldiers. The tribe of the Locrians having been wantonly destroyed by one of the lieutenants of Scipio, he neither punished him for that nor for his insolence, — simply because of his own easy nature; so that, when somebody wished to excuse Scipio in the Senate, he said, "that there were many men who knew better how to avoid errors themselves than to punish them in others." This easy nature of Scipio's would in time have dimmed his fame and glory if he had persevered in it under the Empire; but living as he did under the government of the Senate, this dangerous quality of his was not only covered up, but actually redounded to his honor.

To come back now to the question whether it be better to be beloved than feared, I conclude that, as men love of their own free will, but are inspired with fear by the will of the prince, a wise prince should always rely upon himself, and not upon the will of others; but, above all, should he always strive to avoid being hated, as I have already said above.[18]

THE ALTERNATIVE TO GOVERNMENT: ANARCHISM

We have all known and heard about bad governments. Sometimes it is a single corrupt politician that is bad, other times it is the political system itself. But those political (or perhaps "antipolitical") philosophers who call themselves "anarchists" would say that it is the very nature of government that is "bad," insofar as every government has and exercises unjustified power over its citizens. No one and no institution, including governments, have the right to interfere with our lives, according to the anarchist. Of course we must agree not to kill each other (as the social contract insists), but we don't need a government in order to enforce such agreements. Proper upbringing and mutual respect alone will be sufficient. Sometimes anarchists are also tied to theories of revolution insofar as they believe that it is economic inequality and desperation that force most people to commit crimes and destroy social harmony. But in a society where people had no unsatisfied needs, they argue, there would be no need for violence or robbery either. It is essential to anarchism to have an optimistic Rousseauian view of human nature as "naturally good." It is impossible to accept a Hobbesian "mutual-murder" view and still have faith in people's ability to live together without governments. Anarchists often suggest breaking mass societies into smaller units, such as communes and local communities in which mutual personal relationships make the need for impersonal government unnecessary. In such communities, there may be those who are in charge of certain tasks, but this is a matter of efficiency and administration, not a matter of power. There may be rules but not laws, for the very idea of enforcement of laws presupposes a government in power and is antithetical to the anarchist ideal.

"Anarchism" has often been used as a nasty word pointing to total chaos. Politicians in power often refer to the alternative to their rule as "anarchy and chaos," as if anarchy must always be sheer confusion. Although the word originally meant simply "without a leader," it perhaps has taken on the meaning of chaos because of those anarchists in history who have attacked their governments in a wild and destructive fashion. The word now conjurs up images of "bomb-throwing anarchists" and widespread rape and murder. But this is not essential to anarchism as a political theory. (Sometimes the word "anarchism" is used to refer to the theory; "anarchy" is used to point to political confusion and chaos.) Many anarchists would argue that it is only because governments treat us like children

[18]Niccolo Machiavelli, *The Prince*, trans. Christian E. Detmold (New York: Airmont, 1965).

that we can no longer conceive what it would be like without them. But if we are to take the notion of individual freedom and rights seriously, according to the anarchist, then we will have to conclude that the only good government is no government, for any government is by its very existence a threat to individual freedom and an infringement of individual rights.

The anarchist position is here represented by Benjamin R. Tucker, an American who believed in the social contract theory but argued that the only logical conclusion to a social contract would be no state at all:

"For Anarchism,"
by Benjamin R. Tucker

Presumably the honor which you have done me in inviting me to address you to-day upon "The Relation of the State to the Individual" is due principally to the fact that circumstances have combined to make me somewhat conspicuous as an exponent of the theory of Modern Anarchism, — a theory which is coming to be more and more regarded as one of the few that are tenable as a basis of political and social life. In its name, then, I shall speak to you in discussing this question, which either underlies or closely touches almost every practical problem that confronts this generation. The future of the tariff, of taxation, of finance, of property, of woman, of marriage, of the family, of the suffrage, of education, of invention, of literature, of science, of the arts, of personal habits, of private character, of ethics, of religion, will be determined by the conclusion at which mankind shall arrive as to whether and how far the individual owes allegiance to the State.

Anarchism, in dealing with this subject, has found it necessary, first of all, to define its terms. Popular conceptions of the terminology of politics are incompatible with the rigorous exactness required in scientific investigation. . . . Take the term "State," for instance, with which we are especially concerned to-day. It is a word that is on every lip. But how many of those who use it have any idea of what they mean by it? And, of the few who have, how various are their conceptions! We designate by the term "State" institutions that embody absolutism in its extreme form and institutions that temper it with more or less liberality. We apply the word alike to institutions that do nothing but aggress and to institutions that, besides aggressing, to some extent protect and defend. But which is the State's essential function, aggression or defence, few seem to know or care. . . . Brought face to face with these diverse views, the Anarchists, whose mission in the world is the abolition of aggression and all the evils that result therefrom, perceived that, to be understood, they must attach some definite and avowed significance to the terms which they are obliged to employ, and especially to the words "State" and "government." Seeking, then, the elements common to all the institutions to which the name "State" has been applied, they have found them two in number: first, aggression; second, the assumption of sole authority over a given area and all within it, exercised generally for the double purpose of more complete oppression of its subjects and extension of its boundaries. That this second element is common to all States, I think, will not be denied, — at least, I am not aware that any State has ever tolerated a rival State within its borders; and it seems plain that any State which should do so would thereby cease to be a State and to be considered as such by any. The exercise of authority over the same area by two States is a contradiction. That the first element, aggression, has been and is common to all States will probably be less generally admitted. Nevertheless, I shall not attempt to reenforce here the conclusion of Spencer, which is gaining wider acceptance daily, — that the State had its origin in aggression, and has continued as an aggressive institution from its birth. Defence was an afterthought, prompted by necessity; and its introduction as a State function, though effected doubtless with a view to the strengthening of the State, was really and in principle the initiation of the State's destruction. Its growth in importance is but an evidence of the tendency of progress toward the abolition of the State. Taking this view of the matter, the Anarchists contend that defence is not an essential of the State, but that aggression is. Now what is aggression? Aggression is simply another name for government. Aggression, invasion, government, are interconvertible terms. The essence of government is control, or the attempt to control. He who attempts to control another is a governor, an aggressor, an invader; and the nature of such invasion is not changed, whether it is made by one man upon another man, after the manner of the ordinary criminal, or by one man upon all other men, after the manner of an absolute monarch, or by all other men upon one man, after the manner of a modern democracy. On the other hand, he who resists another's attempt to control is not an aggressor, an invader, a governor, but simply a defender, a protector; and the nature of such resistance is not changed whether it be offered by one man to another man, as when one repels a criminal's onslaught, or by one man to all other men, as when one declines to obey an oppressive law, or by all other men to one man, as when a subject people rises against a despot, or as when the members of a community voluntarily unite to restrain a criminal. This distinction between invasion and resistance, between government and defence, is vital. Without it there can be no valid philosophy of politics. Upon this distinction and the other considerations just outlined, the Anarchists frame the desired definitions. This, then, is the Anarchistic definition of government: the subjection of the non-invasive individual to an external will. And this is the Anarchistic definition of the State: the embodiment of the principle of invasion in an individual, or a band of individuals, assuming to act as representatives or masters of the entire people within a given area. As to the meaning of the remaining term in the subject under discussion, the word "individual," I think there is little difficulty. Putting aside the subtleties in which certain metaphysicians have indulged, one may use this word without danger of being misunderstood. Whether the definitions thus arrived at prove generally acceptable or not is a matter of minor consequence. I submit that they are reached scientifically, and serve the purpose of a clear conveyance of thought. The Anarchists, having by their adoption taken due care to be explicit, are entitled to have their ideas judged in the light of these definitions.

Now comes the question proper: What relations should exist between the State and the individual? The general method of determining these is to apply some theory of ethics involving a basis of moral obligation. In this method the Anarchists have no confidence. The idea of moral obligation, of inherent rights and duties, they totally discard. They look upon all obligations, not as moral, but as social, and even then not really as obligations except as these have been consciously and voluntarily assumed. If a man makes an agreement with men, the latter may combine to hold him to his agreement; but, in the absence of such agreement, no man, so far as the Anarchists are aware, has made any agreement with God or with any other power of any order whatsoever. The Anarchists are not only utilitarians, but egoists in the farthest and fullest sense. So far as inherent right is concerned, might is its only measure. . . .

If this, then, were a question of right, it would be, according to the Anarchists, purely a question of strength. But, fortunately, it is not a question of right: it is a question of expediency, of knowledge, of science, — the science of living together, the science of society. The history of humanity has been largely one long and gradual discovery of the fact that the individual is the gainer by society exactly in proportion as society is free, and of the law that the condition of a permanent and harmonious society is the greatest amount of individual liberty compatible with equality of liberty. The average man of each new generation has said to himself more clearly and consciously than his predecessor: "My neighbor is not my enemy, but my friend, and I am his, if we would but mutually recognize the fact. We help each other to a better, fuller, happier living; and this service might be greatly increased if we would cease to restrict, hamper, and oppress each other. Why can we not agree to let each live his own life, neither of us transgressing the limit that separates our individualities?" It is by this reasoning that mankind is approaching the real social contract, which is not, as Rousseau thought, the origin of society, but rather the outcome of a long social experience, the fruit of its follies and disasters. It is obvious that this contract, this social law, developed to its perfection, excludes all aggression, all violation of equality of liberty, all invasion of every kind. Considering this contract in connection with the Anarchistic definition of the State as the embodiment of the principle of invasion, we see that the State is antagonistic to society; and, society being essential to individual life and development, the conclusion leaps to the eyes that the relation of the State to the individual and of the individual to the State must be one of hostility, enduring till the State shall perish.

"But," it will be asked of the Anarchists at this point in the argument, "what shall be done with those individuals who undoubtedly will persist in violating the social law of invading their neighbors?" The Anarchists answer that the abolition of the State will leave in existence a defensive association, resting no longer on a compulsory but on a voluntary basis, which will restrain invaders by any means that may prove necessary. "But that is what we have now," is the rejoinder. "You really want, then, only a change of name?" Not so fast, please. Can it be soberly pretended for a moment that the State, even as it exists here in America, is purely a defensive institution? Surely not, save by those who see of the State only its most palpable manifestation, — the policeman on the street-corner. And one would not have to watch him very closely to see the error of this claim. Why, the very first act of the State, the compulsory assessment and collection of taxes, is itself an aggression, a violation of equal liberty, and, as such, vitiates every subsequent act, even those acts which would be purely defensive if paid for out of a treasury filled by voluntary contributions. How is it possible to sanction, under the law of equal liberty, the confiscation of a man's earnings to pay for protection which he has not sought and does not desire? And if this is an outrage, what name shall we give to such confiscation when the victim is given, instead of bread, a stone, instead of protection, oppression? To force a man to pay for the violation of his own liberty is indeed an addition of insult to injury. But that is exàctly what the State is doing. Read the "Congressional Record"; follow the proceedings of the State legislatures; examine our statute-books; test each act separately by the law of equal liberty, — you will find that a good nine-tenths of existing legislation serves, not to enforce that fundamental social law, but either to prescribe the individual's personal habits, or, worse still, to create and sustain commercial, industrial, financial, and proprietary monopolies which deprive labor of a large part of the reward that it would receive in a perfectly free market. "To be governed," says Proudhon, "is to be watched, inspected, spied, directed, law-ridden, regulated, penned up, indoctrinated, preached at, checked, appraised, sized, censured, commanded, by beings who have neither title nor knowledge nor virtue. To be governed is to have every operation, every transaction, every movement noted, registered, counted, rated, stamped, measured, numbered, assessed, licensed, refused, authorized, indorsed, admonished, prevented, reformed, redressed, corrected. To be governed is, under pretext of public utility and in the name of the general interest, to be laid under contribution, drilled, fleeced, exploited, monopolized, extorted from, exhausted, hoaxed, robbed; then, upon the slightest resistance, at the first word of complaint, to be repressed, fined, vilified, annoyed, hunted down, pulled about, beaten, disarmed, bound, imprisoned, shot, mitrailleused, judged, condemned, banished, sacrificed, sold, betrayed, and, to crown all, ridiculed, derided, outraged, dishonored." And I am sure I do not need to point out to you the existing laws that correspond to and justify nearly every count in Proudhon's long indictment. How thoughtless, then, to assert that the existing political order is of a purely defensive character instead of the aggressive State which the Anarchists aim to abolish![19]

SUMMARY AND CONCLUSION

In some areas of philosophy, the question arises, "What does this have to do with everyday life?" In political philosophy, as in moral philosophy, the connection between philosophy and "everyday life" is obvious. It is no coincidence that the major revolutions of the eighteenth and nineteenth centuries came soon after a flurry of philosophical radicalism. And we know that much of the world is divided and ruled according to rival political philosophies at the present time.

What is always at issue is the concept of justice. The idea that people are equal

[19]Benjamin R. Tucker, *Instead of a Book* (New York: Benjamin R. Tucker, 1893).

and should be treated equally, the idea that people have natural or human rights that no one and no government can take away from them, and the idea that people should equally share the material goods of society have all been the subject of constant debate — and sometimes wars and revolutions — for most of modern times. Then too, the nature of the state itself has been part of that debate as well as the stage on which the debate has been carried out. How much should the state serve the people and how much the people serve the state? What constitutes a good state? And when, if ever, do people have the right to overthrow the state, or a particular government, or a particular law? There is no way we can even begin to give adequate answers to these complex questions in the context of a general introduction to philosophy; but neither is there any way in which we can avoid asking them in the world as it is today.

GLOSSARY

alienation: in Marx, the unnatural separation of a person from the products he or she makes, from other people, or from oneself.

anarchism: the view that no government has the legitimate authority to coerce people and that the public interest and individual rights can only be served without a state of any kind.

authority: that which controls; usually, that which has the right to control. (For example, the government has the authority to tax your income.)

civil rights: those rights that are determined by a particular state and its laws; constitutional rights, for example, are civil rights in this sense, guaranteed by the law of the land.

democracy: that form of government in which policies or at least the makers of policy are chosen by popular mandate.

distributive justice: the ideal of everyone receiving his or her fair share. For example, concerns over ownership of land, just wages, and fair prices are all matters of distributive justice.

egalitarianism: the view that all people are equal in rights and respect.

equality: in political philosophy, the nondiscriminatory treatment of every person, regardless of sex, race, religion, physical or mental abilities, wealth, social status, etc.

fascism: the view that the best government is the strongest, and that the government has the right — and perhaps the duty — to control the lives of every citizen for the sake of the most efficient society.

freedom: see liberty

government: the instrument of authority; that body that rules, passes and enforces laws, etc.

human rights: those rights that are considered to be universal, "unalienable," and common to every person regardless of where or when he or she lives. For example, freedom from torture and degradation would be a human right.

justice: in the general sense, the virtues of an ideal society. In the more particular sense, the balance of public interest and individual rights, the fair sharing of the available goods of society, the proper punishment of criminals, and the fair restitution of victims of crime and misfortune within society.

legitimacy: the right to have authority; sanctioned power (for example, through the grace of god, or by means of legal succession, or by appeal to justice, or to the general consent of the people governed).

liberty: (political freedom) the ability to act without restraint or threat of punishment. For example, the ability to travel between states without a passport, the ability to speak one's opinions without prosecution, the ability to work for or choose one's own profession or career. This ability, however, is not mere physical or mental ability; one might have the liberty to travel or to try to become a doctor without having the means to do so. It is also important to distinguish this political sense of liberty or freedom from the metaphysical or causal sense discussed in Chapter 9: Whether our acts are really free in that sense must be distinguished from the question whether we are constrained or free to act in this political sense. The first refers to the causes of human behavior; the second refers only to the existence of legislation and political forces constraining our behavior.

retributive justice: "getting even," "an eye for an eye. . . ."

rights: demands that a member of society is entitled to make upon his society. Everyone, for example, has a right to police protection. Some people, by virtue of their position, have special rights; for example, congressmen have the right to send mail to their constituents without paying postage.

social contract: an agreement, tacit or explicit that all members of society shall abide by the laws of the state in order to maximize the public interest and ensure cooperation among themselves. It is important that such a contract need never have actually been signed in history; what is important is that every member of a society, by choosing to remain in that society, implicitly makes such an agreement.

society: a group of people with common historical and cultural ties; usually, but not always, members of the same state and ruled by the same government.

sovereign: independent. A sovereign state is one that is subject to the laws of no other state. A sovereign is a person (for example, a king) who is not subject or answerable to the commands of anyone else. A people are sovereign when their wishes are ultimate in the same way and not subject to commands by anyone else or any government. (To say that a people is sovereign is not to say that the will of any individual or group is sovereign within it.)

state: the center of authority in a society, for example, the largest political unit in a society. Usually a state is a nation, for example, America, West Germany, etc. Usually, but not always, coextensive with a society, and usually, but not always, distinguished by a single form of government and a single government (for example, the American federal government).

unalienable rights: those rights that no one and no government can take away, for example, the right of a person to protect his or her own life. In other words, *human rights*.

BRIEF BIOGRAPHIES

Anaximander (611–547? B.C.): Pre-Socratic philosopher who taught that reality is ultimately composed of an indeterminate something that we can never know directly through experience.

Anaximenes (6th century B.C.): Pre-Socratic philosopher who taught that the basic element of reality was air and that all things in the universe are different forms of air.

Anselm, Saint (1033–1109): Archbishop of Canterbury and author of the ontological argument for God's existence. He was one of the main defenders of the intellect and "understanding" against the then current anti-intellectualism of the church. He is best known for his *Monologion* and *Proslogion*, in which the ontological argument is developed.

Aquinas, Saint Thomas (1225–74): Architect of the most comprehensive theological structure of the Roman Catholic Church, the *Summa Theologica*, which has long been recognized as the "official" statement of orthodox Christian beliefs by many theologians. Aquinas borrowed many of his arguments from Aristotle, as can be seen in his "five ways" of demonstrating the existence of God.

Aristippus (435?–356? B.C.): One of the Cynics and a student of Socrates, who taught that the good life consists solely of immediate pleasures.

Aristotle (384–322 B.C.): One of the greatest Western philosophers. Aristotle was born in northern Greece (Stagira). His father was the physician to Philip, king of Macedonia, and he himself was to become the tutor to Philip's son, Alexander the Great. For eighteen years Aristotle was a student in Plato's academy in Athens, where he learned and parted from Plato's views. After Plato's death, he turned to the study of biology, and many of his theories ruled Western science until the Renaissance. He was with Alexander until 335 B.C., when he returned to Athens to set up his own school, the Lyceum. After Alexander's death, the anti-Macedonian sentiment in Athens forced Aristotle to flee (commenting that the Athenians would not sin twice against philosophy). In addition to his biological studies, Aristotle virtually created the sciences of logic and linguistics, developed extravagant theories in physics and astronomy, and made significant contributions to metaphysics, ethics, politics, and aesthetics. His *Metaphysics* is still a basic text on the subject, and *Nicomachean Ethics* codified ancient Greek morality. This latter work stresses individual virtue and excellence for a small elite of Greek citizens. The best life of all, according to Aristotle, is the life of contemplation, that is, the life of a philosopher, for it is the most self-contained and the "closest to the gods." But such contemplation must be together with the pleasures of life, honor, wealth, and virtuous action.

Augustine, Saint (354–430): The main figure in the development of medieval Christian thought from its roots in classical Greece and Rome. Augustine was born in North Africa and lived during the "decline" of the Roman Empire. After exploring various pagan beliefs, he was converted to Christianity and became Bishop of Hippo in North Africa. He is best known for his theological treatise *The City of God* and for his very personal *Confessions*.

Austin, John Langshaw (1911–60): Oxford "ordinary-language" philosopher who had enormous influence on the development of "therapeutic" philosophy through attention to the details and nuances of everyday speech.

Ayer, Alfred J. (b. 1910): Oxford philosopher who became the major British defender of the powerful philosophical movement called logical positivism (logical empiricism). His *Language, Truth and Logic* (1936) was England's (and soon America's) first introduction to the very important work that had been developed in Austria by Rudolf Carnap, Hans Reichenbach, Moritz Schlick, C. G. Hempel, and Otto Neurath (the "Vienna Circle"). The main thesis of *Language, Truth and Logic,* and of logical positivism in general, is, in an updated version of Hume, that all knowledge can only be divided into matters of empirical fact and matters of language and logic and that all other claims are "meaningless," including the concepts of metaphysics, religion, ethics, and aesthetics.

Bayle, Pierre (1647–1706): Enlightenment philosopher and teacher. His *Historical and Critical Dictionary* (1697) influenced Voltaire and much of the Enlightenment.

Bentham, Jeremy (1748–1832): A leader in the legal reform movement in England and the founding father of that ethical position called utilitarianism. His *principle of utility*, which says that one should act to produce the greatest good for the greatest number of people, was the central theme of utilitarianism and slowly worked its way into the confusion of rules and statutes that constituted the English legal system of his day. His best-known work is his *Introduction to the Principles of Morals and Legislation* (1789).

Berkeley, Bishop George (1685–1753): Wrote virtually all the works that made him famous before he turned twenty-eight. He was born, raised, and educated in Ireland, and as a student he immersed himself in the writings of the important philosophers of the time, particularly Locke, Newton, and some of the French metaphysicians. In later life, Berkeley became an educational missionary, visiting America and Bermuda, and then a bishop, eventually moving to Oxford. Unlike Locke and Hume, whose interests spread across the whole of philosophy, science, and human affairs, Berkeley restricted himself to a single problem — perception — and his entire philosophy is aptly summarized in his famous phrase "to be is to be perceived" *(esse est percipi)*. His arguments for this position are most thoroughly outlined in his *Treatise Concerning the Principles of Human Knowledge* (1710).

Blanshard, Brand (b. 1892): Contemporary idealist and main American defender of the coherence theory of truth, still working at Yale University.

Bradley, Francis Herbert (1846–1924): The best-known and perhaps the most brilliant of the "British idealists" working at the turn of this century. He is best known for his work *Appearance and Reality* (1893), in which he argues a very strong version of the coherence theory of truth.

Butler, Bishop Joseph (1692–1752): Powerful English clergyman who formulated what are still recognized as the standard arguments against psychological egoism in his *Fifteen Sermons* (1726).

Cynics (4th century B.C.): Group of post-Socratic philosophers who taught that the good life was a life of complete autonomy. Therefore they minimized the social values of success, wealth, and honor and focused their attention on what makes a person wholly self-sufficient. For Diogenes, this consisted of the simplest life possible, based upon simple pleasures and simple virtues. For Aristippus, this consisted of a life of immediate pleasure.

Davidson, Donald (b. 1917): Contemporary American philosopher who has become one of the leading philosophers of language in the world. One of his continuing efforts is to generalize Alfred Tarski's semantic theory of truth as a general theory of truth for natural languages.

Democritus (5th century B.C.): Pre-Socratic philosopher who taught that reality is divisible into small "atoms," which combine to make up all things but which themselves are eternal and indivisible.

Descartes, René (1596–1650): French philosopher who is usually considered the "father of modern philosophy." He was raised in the French aristocracy and educated at the excellent Jesuit College of La Flèche. He became skilled in the classics, law, and medicine; however, he decided that they fell far short of proper knowledge, and so he turned to modern science and mathematics. His first book was a defense of Copernicus, which he prudently did not publish. He discovered, while still a young man, the connections between algebra and geometry (which we now call "analytic geometry") and used this discovery as a model for the rest of his career. Basing the principles of philosophy and theology on a similar mathematical basis, he was able to develop a method in philosophy that could be carried through according to individual reason and no longer depended upon appeal to authorities whose insights and methods were questionable. In *Discourse on Method* (1637), he set out these basic principles, which he had already used in *Meditations on First Philosophy* (not published until 1641), to reexamine the foundations of philosophy. He sought a basic premise from which, as in a geometrical proof, he could deduce all those principles that could be known with certainty.

Diogenes (412?–323? B.C.): Cynic philosopher who lived an extremely simple life. Offered anything he wanted by Alexander the Great, he replied, "Get out of my light."

Epicurus (342?–270 B.C.): Greek philosopher who argued that the good life was pleasure but not just the immediate pleasure talked about by Aristippus. Some pleasures last longer than others; some have a lower price than others. Accordingly, he taught self-control and avoidance of violent pleasures, which often caused more pain than ultimate pleasure. Ultimately what was most pleasurable, according to Epicurus, was a life of peace and quiet. Today we use the word "Epicurean" to describe someone who often indulges in pleasures, particularly sophisticated pleasures (gourmet food, for example).

Fichte, Johann Gottlieb (1762–1814): German philosopher, student of Immanuel Kant, who turned Kant's "transcendental" philosophy into a practically oriented and relativistic "ethical idealism." He taught that "the kind of philosophy a man chooses depends upon the kind of man he is." One of the first German nationalists.

Fodor, Jerry (b. 1935): Professor of Psychology, Linguistics, and Philosophy at MIT. One of the leading voices in the current discussion of "functionalism" in minds and computers.

Frege, Gottlob (1848–1925): Brilliant logician whose work on the foundations of arithmetic inspired Bertrand Russell and Alfred North Whitehead and turned the current of logical thinking from the Mill-like empiricism that was then reigning (in Germany as well as England) to a hardheaded mathematical discipline. He is often said to have been the pioneer and innovator of modern mathematical logic. Most important, perhaps, is his *Foundations of Arithmetic* (1884).

Gadamer, Hans-Georg (b. 1900): Leading German promoter of hermeneutics.

Goodman, Nelson (b. 1906): Contemporary American pragmatist who, together with W. V. O. Quine, has made pragmatism once again a dominant force in philosophy.

Hegel, Georg Wilhelm Friedrich (1770–1831): German philosopher who, during the age of Napoleon, wrote his *Phenomenology of Spirit* (1807), which was the single most powerful influence in European philosophy — after Kant's works — for the next hundred years. He argued that there were many different views of the world, that none of them should be thought to be wholly correct or incorrect in exclusion of the others, but that these various views could still be compared and evaluated according to a "dialectic," in which some views are shown to be more developed, more inclusive, and more adequate than others.

Heidegger, Martin (1889–1976): German phenomenologist and student of Edmund Husserl, whose rebellion against his teacher began the "existential" movement in phenomenology. His best-known work is *Being and Time* (1927). Although focusing on metaphysics and phenomenology, this work is also one of the first existentialist studies of "human nature."

Hempel, Carl Gustav (b. 1905): Contemporary American philosopher of science and mathematics, member of the "Vienna Circle," and one of the continuing most powerful voices of the empiricist tradition. A good collection of his essays is *Aspects of Scientific Explanation* (1965).

Heraclitus (5th century B.C.): Pre-Socratic philosopher who taught that the basic element of reality was fire and that all things are in constant flux but yet are unified by an underlying logic or *logos*.

Hobbes, Thomas (1588–1679): The author of *Leviathan* (1651) and one of England's first great modern philosophers. He is generally credited with the formulation of the theory of the "social contract" for the establishment of governments and society, and he was one of the first philosophers to base his theory of government on a conception of man prior to his "civilization," in what he called "the state of nature." This was, according to Hobbes, "selfish, nasty, brutish and short." Therefore people were motivated to become part of society for their mutual protection. Hobbes also defended a materialist conception of the universe. Even the human mind, he argued, was nothing more than "matter in motion."

d'Holbach, Baron Paul Henri (1723–89): French philosopher and one of the leaders of the Enlightenment. An ardent materialist and atheist, he represented the most radical fringe of the brilliant free-thinkers of prerevolutionary France.

Hospers, John (b. 1918): Professor of philosophy at the University of Southern California, articulate follower of Ayn Rand, and one-time Libertarian candidate for President of the United States.

Hume, David (1711–76): Often admired as the outstanding genius of British philosophy. Born in Scotland (Edinburgh), where he spent much of his life, he often traveled to London and Paris. After a vacation in France, he wrote the *Treatise of Human Nature* (1739). He achieved notoriety as well as literary fame in his lifetime, was involved in scandals and proscribed by the Church. He was refused professorships at the leading universities for his "heresies." Yet he was, by all accounts, an utterly delightful man who never lost his sense of humor. He was "the life of the party" in

London, Edinburgh, and Paris, and he has long set the standard of the ideal thinker for British philosophers. Hume's *Inquiry Concerning the Principles of Morals* (1751) created as much of a stir in the intellectual world as his *Inquiry Concerning Human Understanding* (1748). Like the latter book, the book on morality was a rewriting of his youthful *Treatise*, which never received the attention it deserved. Hume's thesis in moral philosophy was as skeptical and shocking as his thesis in epistemology: There is no knowledge of right and wrong and no rational defense of moral principles. These are based upon sentiment or feeling and, as such, cannot be defended by argument.

Husserl, Edmund (1859–1938): German-Czech philosopher and mathematician who was the founder of phenomenology, a modern form of rationalist intuitionism. With Gottlob Frege, he fought against the empiricist view of necessary truth defended by John Stuart Mill and developed an alternative view in which matters of necessity were not matters of ordinary experience but rather of a special kind of intuition. His best-known works are *Ideas* (Vol. 1) (1913) and *Cartesian Meditations* (1931).

James, William (1842–1910): Perhaps the greatest American philosopher (and psychologist) to this day. He developed the particularly American philosophy of pragmatism from the brilliant but obscure formulations of his colleague at Harvard, Charles Sanders Peirce, into a popular and still very powerful intellectual force. James was born in New York City and graduated from Harvard with a medical degree, but he decided to teach (at Harvard) rather than to practice medicine. His best-known work in philosophy, besides his work called *Pragmatism: A New Name for Some Old Ways of Thinking* (1907), is *The Varieties of Religious Experience* (1902). He also established himself as one of the fathers of modern psychology with his *Principles of Psychology* (1890).

Kant, Immanuel (1724–1804): German philosopher, probably the greatest philosopher since Plato and Aristotle, who lived his entire life in a small town in East Prussia (Königsburg). He was a professor at the university there for over thirty years; he never married, and his neighbors said that his habits were so regular that they could set their watches by him. (A later German poet said, "It is hard to write about Kant's life, for he had no life.") Yet, from a safe distance, he was one of the most persistent defenders of the French Revolution and, in philosophy, created no less a revolution himself. His philosophical system, embodied in three huge volumes called *Critique of Pure Reason* (1781), *Critique of Practical Reason* (1788), and *Critique of Judgment* (1790), changed the thinking of philosophers as much as the revolution changed France. His central thesis was the defense of what he called "synthetic *a priori*" judgments (and their moral and religious equivalents) by showing their necessity for all human experience. In this way, he escaped from Hume's skepticism and avoided the dead-end intuitionism of his rationalist predecessors.

Kierkegaard, Søren (1813–1855): Danish philosopher and theologian who is generally recognized as the father of existentialism and the founder of many varieties of contemporary religious irrationalism. Kierkegaard dedicated himself to religious writing after a short and not altogether successful attempt at the wild life and a brief engagement, which he broke off in order to devote himself to his work. The basic tenet of Kierkegaard's philosophy was the need for each individual to choose his own way of life. Christianity, as one of the possible choices, could not be considered anything other than just such a choice, a passionate choice, which had nothing to do with doctrines, churches, social groups, and ceremonies.

Leibniz, Gottfried Wilhelm von (1646–1716): Leibniz has been called "the last of the universal geniuses." He was one of the inventors of the calculus, the father of modern formal linguistics, the inventor of a primitive computer, a military strategist (who may have influenced Napoleon), a physicist who in his own time was thought to be the rival of Newton, and most of all a great philosopher. He grew up in Leipzig but traveled considerably (to Paris and Amsterdam and all over Germany). He spoke personally with most of the great philosophers of his time and debated with them constantly. His metaphysics is a curious combination of traditional theology and a radical alternative to the physical theories of Newton, to whose philosophy he had once been attracted but which he had given up as "absurd." His short *Monadology* (1714) is a summary of his mature metaphysical theories.

Locke, John (1632–1704): Spent his early life in the English countryside, including many years at Oxford where he taught philosophy and the classics until he earned a medical degree and turned to medicine. Much of Locke's mature life, however, was spent in politics, and he joined a more or less revolutionary group that was fighting for the overthrow of the government. He was forced to flee England in 1683, and he lived in Holland until the Glorious Revolution of 1688. For his part in the struggle, he received a government position, although he spent most of his time writing his two *Treatises on Government* (1689) to justify the revolution and its political principles and defending his *Essay Concerning Human Understanding* (1690), which he had written while in exile. He is generally credited not only as the founder of British empiricism but as the father of modern political liberalism as well.

Logical positivism (roughly from 1929 until the Nazis proscribed it in 1938): A powerful school of philosophy that originated in Vienna with a group of scientists and philosophers of anti-Nazi, liberal, antimetaphysical, and scientific persuasion—the "Vienna Circle." Against the horrendous mythologies and superstitions propagandized by the Nazis, using the old metaphysics as a tool, these philosophers used the clarity of science to dispel nonsense and to defend common sense. Accordingly, the group was broken by the Nazis, and most of its members, except for Moritz Schlick, who was shot by an insane student, left for America, England, and Holland. The main thrust of logical positivism is its total rejection of metaphysics in favor of a strong emphasis on science and verifiability through experience. The method of the logical positivists, accordingly, is strongly empiricist (they actually called themselves "logical empiricists") and has much in common with the method of Hume, according to which all knowledge is to be defended either as a matter of empirical fact to be verified (that is, confirmed) through experience or as a matter of logic and language to be demonstrated through analysis. Arithmetic and geometry, for the logical positivists, consist of analytic truths.

Marx, Karl (1818–83): German philosopher and social theorist who formulated the philosophical basis for one of the most powerful political ideologies of this century. He received a doctorate in philosophy but could not teach in Germany because of his radical views. He spent most of his life abroad, in Paris, Brussels, and London, developing his theories and writing for various journals and newspapers (including the *New York Herald Tribune*). His attacks on established beliefs and advocacy of revolution were constant throughout his life and forced him into exile. As a young man he wrote a devastating critique of G. W. F. Hegel, whom he had studied and followed as a young student, and whose concept of "dialectic" he used in developing a powerful social-political philosophy of class conflict and economic determination.

Merleau-Ponty, Maurice (1908–61): French "existentialist," the most serious of the existential phenomenologists who followed Husserl in France. His most important work is generally considered the *Phenomenology of Perception* (1945). He is also well known for his political writings and his art criticism. In his early *Structure of Behavior* (1942), he argued that the human body cannot be considered merely another "fragment of matter," in other words, merely a body, but must be viewed as the center of our experience.

Michaels, Meredith (b. 1950): American philosopher, Mount Holyoke College.

Mill, John Stuart (1806–73): Son of James Mill, also a philosopher, and one of the documented geniuses of modern history. His intellectual feats by the age of ten would have been to the credit of most scholars at the age of sixty. He pushed himself so hard, however, that he suffered a nervous breakdown in 1826, at the age of twenty, and turned his attention from the "hard" sciences to poetry and political reform. He is best known for his moral and political writings, particularly *On Liberty* (1859) and *Utilitarianism* (1861). His logic and epistemology are the best to be found in the British empiricist tradition of the nineteenth century. His views on mathematics, for example, became one of those positions that every writer on the subject had either to accept or to fight forcefully.

Nietzsche, Friedrich (1844–1900): German philosopher who declared himself the arch-enemy of traditional morality and Christianity and spent much of his life writing polemics against them. His most sustained and vicious attack (partly included in the text) is in one of his last books, *Antichrist* (1888). Although generally known as an immoralist (a name he chose for himself), Nietzsche's moral philosophy is actually an attack on one conception of morality in order to replace it with another. The morality he attacked was the morality of traditional Christianity as defined by Kant. The morality he sought to defend was the ancient morality of personal excellence, as defined by Aristotle. He referred to the first as "slave morality," suggesting that it was suitable only for the weak and servile, and to the latter as "master morality," suggesting that it was the morality of the strong and independent few.

Parmenides (5th century B.C.): Pre-Socratic philosopher who taught that reality was eternal and unchanging and that therefore we could not know it as such.

Pascal, Blaise (1623–62): French scientist and philosopher with mildly mystical tendencies. He stressed confidence in the "heart" rather than in reason, and many of his best-known writings are concerned with the problems of religious faith. However, he was also one of the inventors of the computer and a famous mathematician. His best-known work is *Pensées* ("Thoughts") (1669).

Plato (427–347 B.C.): Plato was born into a family of wealth and political power. But in Athens he fell under the influence of Socrates and turned his talents to philosophy. He combined his heritage with his interests in his famous conception of the "philosopher-king," the ideal wise ruler, who certainly did not exist in Athens. He was disillusioned by Socrates' death and devoted his life to continuing his work. Plato set up the Academy for this purpose and spent the rest of his life teaching there. He first set down his reminiscences of Socrates' life and death, and, using the dialogue form, with Socrates as his mouthpiece, he extended Socrates' thought into entirely new areas, notably, metaphysics and the theory of knowledge. Plato incorporated a theory of morality into his metaphysics and politics, particularly in *The Republic*. Like all Greeks, he saw ethics as a part of politics and the good life for the individual in terms of the strength and harmony of the society. In *The Republic*, accordingly, Socrates argues against the various views of selfishness and hedonism that would interfere with such a conception. Virtue, he argues, is the harmony of the individual soul as well as the harmony of the individual within the society. It is still difficult, since we have nothing from Socrates himself, to know how much is original Plato and how much is transcribed Socrates.

Pythagoras (6th–5th century B.C.): The religious mystic who believed that numbers were the essence of all things. One of the Pre-Socratics.

Quine, Willard Van Orman (b. 1908): Contemporary American pragmatist whose early attacks on logical positivism and its basic tenets have been responsible for several of the dominant concerns of recent American philosophy. His attack on Immanuel Kant's distinction between "analytic" and "synthetic" sentences, for example, along with the more traditional distinctions between necessity and contingency, have thrown the entire philosophical enterprise into considerable turmoil. According to Quine, there are no indubitably "necessary" statements or beliefs, just those that happen, at a particular point in our knowledge and interests, to hold a relatively protected place in the overall system of our beliefs for ostensibly practical reasons. He is the author of *Word and Object* (1960) and many other works in logic and the philosophy of language.

Rawls, John (b. 1921): Author of *A Theory of Justice* (1971) and professor of philosophy at Harvard University.

Rousseau, Jean-Jacques (1712–78): Stormy Enlightenment philosopher who fought with most of his peers (including David Hume) and developed a dramatic conception of "natural morality," which he contrasted to what he saw as the fraud and hypocrisy of contemporary civilized man. He formulated a picture of man in "the state of nature," before civilization, in which his "natural goodness" was not yet "corrupted" by society. The key to this idea was his conception of moral sentiment, which was innate in all people and not learned from society. His writings were condemned, and he spent much of his life running from the police. He died in total poverty, but only a few years after his death his political ideas became the central ideology of the French Revolution.

Russell, Bertrand (1872–1970): One of the greatest philosophers of our century. As a young man, he wrote, with Alfred North Whitehead, a book called *Principia Mathematica* (1903), which set the stage for modern logic and foundations of mathematics and gave logic a central role as a philosophical tool. He wrote an enormous number of philosophical books on virtually every topic, including several notorious polemics in favor of what was branded "free love" and atheism. He was a persistent and harsh critic of religion in general and Christianity in particular, as a source of superstition and legitimized murder. Russell was a committed pacifist during World War I and wrote at least one of his most famous books while sitting in prison for his antiwar activities. Like his famous predecessor, David Hume (with whom he has much in common), Russell was too controversial for most universities, and a famous court case prevented him from teaching at the City College of New York. He won the Nobel prize in 1950.

Ryle, Gilbert (1900–1978): Oxford "ordinary-language" philosopher whose book *The Concept of Mind* (1949) set the stage for several decades of debate over his quasi-behavioristic resolution of the mind-body problem. His main thesis is that the distinction between mind and body rests on what he calls a "category mistake," that is, wrongly believing something to be one kind of thing when it is really another. In particular, it has been thought that mental events were events on a par with, but wholly different from, bodily events. Instead, Ryle argues, to talk about mind is to talk about behavioral dispositions and abilities. (To say that a person *wants* to do something is to say that he *would* do that if given the opportunity.)

Sartre, Jean-Paul (1905–1980): Contemporary French philosopher who began as a literary writer and a phenomenologist, in the style of Edmund Husserl, but who converted that austere philosophy to his own radical ends. He is generally regarded as the main proponent of the philosophy of "existentialism." Sartre's existentialism is a moral philosophy as well as a philosophy of freedom. It denies that there is any such thing as "human nature" and therefore insists that "man makes himself." That is, through our various choices and moral commitments we define what we want humanity to be. According to Sartre, we do not simply find moral principles upon which we should act, but rather we *choose* those moral principles *through our acting.* Thus Sartre's moral philosophy places most of its emphasis on action and minimizes the importance of moral deliberation and all that sort of moralizing in which we simply talk about what is good rather than actually doing it. For Sartre, it is action that is ultimately good, rather than simply a "good will" as in Kant. In his novels and plays, Sartre's characters are always torn by alternative identities, suffering just because they cannot make up their minds. In his greatest work, *Being and Nothingness* (1943), Sartre argues that everyone "is who he is not, and is not who he is," by which he means (in a paradoxical phrase) that our identity is never simply the totality of facts ("facticity") that are true of us, but we always identify ourselves with our plans and intentions for the future (our "transcendence") as well. And this means that so long as we are alive, we have no fixed "identity" at all.

Shaffer, Jerome (b. 1929): American philosopher, presently teaching at the University of Connecticut. One of the best-known critics of the now influential "identity theory" of mind and body.

Smart, J. J. C. (b. 1920): Australian philosopher at the Australian National University in Canberra. Classic defender of the mind-body "identity theory."

Socrates (470–399 B.C.): Athenian philosopher with a gift for rhetoric and debating. He had a notoriously poor marriage, had several children, and lived in poverty most of his life. Socrates began his studies in the physical sciences but soon turned to the study of human nature, morality, and politics. He became famous debating with the many "sophists" who wandered about giving practical training in argument and persuasion (the ancient equivalent of law school). Socrates found their general skepticism intolerable and urged a return to the absolute ideals of wisdom, virtue, justice, and the good life. In his philosophy, he approached these questions as matters of finding the exact definitions of these concepts in order to clarify our pursuit of them. In doing so, he developed a brilliant technique of dialogue or "dialectic" in which he would discover these definitions by constant debating, forcing his opponents or students to advance varying theories, which he in turn would knock down. In the process, the correct definition would slowly emerge. In his not always tactful search for truth, however, Socrates made many enemies, who eventually had him condemned to death, a cruel and unfair verdict he accepted with dignity.

Spinoza, Benedictus de (1632–77): Spinoza was born Baruch ben Michael, the son of Jewish refugees from the Spanish Inquisition. He was born and grew up in Amsterdam, a relative haven of toleration in a world still dangerous because of religious hatreds. He studied to be a rabbi, making himself familiar with Christian theology as well. He was always a recluse and was later ostracized by his fellow Jews for his heretical beliefs, wandering about the country making a living by grinding lenses. His best-known book is *Ethics* (1677); it is a radical reinterpretation of God as identical to the universe (pantheism) and a protracted argument concerning the uselessness of human struggle in the face of a thoroughly determined universe.

Stoics (4th century B.C., with revisions until the 1st century A.D.): An ancient movement in philosophy that taught self-control and minimized passion, with a willingness to endure whatever fate has in store. Some believers were Zeno of Citium in Greece (not the same as Zeno of the paradoxes), Seneca, and Marcus Aurelius in Rome.

Strawson, Peter Frederick (b. 1919): Contemporary Oxford philosopher whose book *Individuals* (1959) was responsible for reintroducing systematic metaphysics into current British philosophy. He called his metaphysics "descriptive," however, by which he meant to insist that it was only to be construed as an analysis and description of "our conceptual framework," not of "reality-in-itself." In the third chapter of that book, Strawson argues the thesis that the distinction between mind and body can be made only after we have recognized the primary category of "persons." Persons are not conglomerates of minds and bodies, and we can talk of minds and bodies only because we first have a way of specifying the different attributes of a person.

Swoyer, Chris (b. 1949): American philosopher, Oklahoma University.

Tarski, Alfred (b. 1902): American logician who formulated the still controversial "semantic theory of truth" in 1944.

Thales (6th century B.C.): The first known Greek philosopher, who taught that all things were ultimately composed of water.

Tillich, Paul (1886–1965): German-born philosopher who spent many of his later years teaching in the United States. He is among the best known of those modern theologians who, like the Romantics of the last century, place the emphasis on emotion and "concern" rather than on reason in religion. In Tillich's theology, God is no longer the transcendent judge of the scriptures but simply the symbol of our "ultimate concern." He is the author of *Systematic Theology* (1953–63), *The Dynamics of Faith* (1957), and *The Courage to Be* (1952).

Watson, John (1878–1958): American psychologist generally recognized as the founder of behaviorism. He attacked the notion of "consciousness" as a remnant of the age-old religious belief in the "soul" and urged that we give up such "magical" nonsense in favor of a purely scientific view, which allows us to talk sensibly only about observables, in other words, human behavior rather than the human "mind." He is the author of *Behaviorism* (1924).

Whitehead, Alfred North (1861–1947): Famous logician who, together with Bertrand Russell, established the basis of modern logic and who late in life turned to metaphysics. In place of the concept of substance, however, he argued for a concept of process, a universe in constant evolutionary change.

Wittgenstein, Ludwig (1889–1951): Austrian-born philosopher who became the single most powerful influence on twentieth-century "analytic" philosophy. He entered philosophy as an engineer, studied with Bertrand Russell, and wrote the book *Tractatus Logico-Philosophicus* (1922), which inspired logical positivism. Giving up philosophy for a number of years and changing his mind about his arguments in the *Tractatus*, he returned to philosophy at Cambridge and developed that "therapeutic" brand of philosophy that became known as "ordinary-language" philosophy. In his later works, culminating in his *Philosophical Investigations* (1953, published posthumously), Wittgenstein initiated a devastating attack on Cartesian dualism and the problems it carried with it. His so-called "private language argument," in fact culled from a series of aphorisms, argues that even if there were such "private" occurrences as mental events, we should have no way of talking about them and no way of knowing about them, even in our own case. But although he is often described as a "behaviorist," Wittgenstein is better described as one of those philosophers who was groping for an entirely new conception of a "person" or at least attempting to reject all the old ones.

Zeno of Elea (5th century B.C.): Pre-Socratic philosopher and student of Parmenides who taught that motion was unreal and developed a series of brilliant paradoxes in order to prove it.

BIBLIOGRAPHY

INTRODUCTION: PHILOSOPHY

A large number of alternative views of philosophy are available in Charles I. Bontempo and S. Jack Odell, eds., *The Owl of Minerva* (New York: McGraw-Hill, 1975). The trial, imprisonment, and death of Socrates are recounted by Plato in the dialogues *Apology*, *Crito*, and *Phaedo* in *The Last Days of Socrates*, trans. Hugh Tredennick (London: Penguin, 1954). An excellent account of Socrates' life is A. E. Taylor, *Socrates* (New York: Doubleday, Anchor, 1959). The best single book on the Enlightenment is Peter Gay, *The Enlightenment: An Interpretation* (New York: Vintage, 1966); a simpler discussion is Robert Anchor, *The Enlightenment Tradition* (New York: Harper & Row, 1967); and a philosophical anthology of the period is Isaiah Berlin, *The Age of Enlightenment* (New York: Mentor, 1955). Two standard introductions to logic are W. Salmon, *Logic* (Englewood Cliffs, N.J.: Prentice-Hall, 1963) and I. Copi, *Introduction to Logic* (New York: Macmillan, 1961). A more original approach is R. D. Bradley and N. Schwartz, *Possible Worlds* (Indianapolis, Ind.: Hackett, 1979).

CHAPTER 1—REALITY: ANCIENT VIEWS

General surveys of ancient Greek philosophy can be found in J. Burnet, *Early Greek Philosophy* (London: Black, 1958) and W. K. C. Guthrie, *The Greek Philosophers: From Thales to Aristotle* (New York: Harper & Row, 1960). The most important texts from the Pre-Socratics are in G. S. Kirk and J. E. Raven, *The Presocratic Philosophers* (Cambridge: Cambridge University Press, 1957). Plato's dialogues are collected in *Plato, Dialogues*, 4th ed., trans. Benjamin Jowett (Oxford: Oxford University Press, 1953); a helpful survey of his work is A. E. Taylor, *Plato: The Man and His Work* (New York: Dial, 1936). Aristotle's works are collected in R. McKeon, ed., *The Basic Works of Aristotle* (New York: Random House, 1941). An excellent survey of all Aristotle's works is W. D. Ross, *Aristotle* (New York: Meridian, 1959). Brief surveys of the Pre-Socratics, Socrates, Plato, and Aristotle are D. J. O'Connor, ed., *A Critical History of Western Philosophy* (New York: Free Press, 1964) and P. Edwards, ed., *The Encyclopedia of Philosophy* (New York: Macmillan, 1967). General introductions to metaphysics are Richard Taylor, *Metaphysics* (Englewood Cliffs, N.J.: Prentice-Hall, 1963) and D. F. Pears, ed., *The Nature of Metaphysics* (London: Macmillan, 1957). An exciting history of metaphysics is A. Lovejoy, *The Great Chain of Being* (Cambridge, Mass.: Harvard University Press, 1936).

CHAPTER 2—REALITY: TWO MODERN VIEWS

Benedictus de Spinoza's *Ethics* is in *The Rationalists* (New York: Doubleday, 1960); an excellent account of Spinoza's philosophy is S. Hampshire, *Spinoza* (London: Penguin, 1951). A convenient collection of Gottfried W. von Leibniz's major works is Philip Wiener, ed., *Leibniz, Selections* (New York: Charles Scribner's Sons, 1951). Two recent studies of Leibniz are Ruth Saw, *Leibniz* (London: Penguin, 1954) and Hidé Ishiguro, *Leibniz's Philosophy of Logic and Language* (Ithaca, N.Y.: Cornell University Press, 1972). An important but biased study is Bertrand Russell, *A Critical Exposition of the Philosophy of Leibniz* (London: George Allen and Unwin, 1937). To study more recent metaphysical systems, see A. Lovejoy, *The Great Chain of Being* (Cambridge, Mass.: Harvard University Press, 1936); Jacques Maritain, *A Preface to Metaphysics* (London: Sheed, 1948); Henri Bergson, *An Introduction to Metaphysics*, trans. T. E. Hulme (New York: Bobbs-Merrill, 1949); Martin Heidegger, *An Introduction to Metaphysics*, trans. Ralph Manheim (New Haven, Conn.: Yale University Press, 1959); and R. G. Collingwood, *An Essay on Metaphysics* (Oxford: Clarendon Press, 1940).

CHAPTER 3—KNOWLEDGE

Several studies of the various problems in René Descartes's epistemology are in Willis Doney, ed., *Descartes* (New York: Doubleday, Anchor, 1967). Gottfried W. von Leibniz's reply to John Locke is spelled out at length in Leibniz's *New Essays on Human Understanding*, trans. A. G. Langley (La Salle, Ill.: Open Court, 1949). Locke's *Essay Concerning Human Understanding* is published by Dover Publications (New York, 1959). Bishop Berkeley's *Treatise* is printed in full in T. E. Jessop, ed., *Berkeley: Philosophical Writings* (Austin, Texas: University of Texas Press, 1953). Of special interest is Berkeley's *Three Dialogues Between Hylas and Philonous* (La Salle, Ill.: Open Court, 1935), in which the arguments of his *Treatise* are worked out in entertaining dialogue form. David Hume's *Treatise of Human Nature* is available edited by L. A. Selby-Bigge (Oxford: Oxford University Press, 1888), but most beginners will find Hume's *Enquiry Concerning Human Understanding* (Oxford: Oxford University Press, 1902) much easier reading. Bertrand Russell, *Problems of Philosophy* (London: Oxford University Press, 1912) is an excellent introduction to the problems of epistemology and some of the problems of metaphysics. Two more modern epistemological studies are A. J. Ayer, *The Problem of Knowledge* (New York: St. Martin's Press, 1956) and Roderick Chisholm, *Theory of Knowledge* (Englewood Cliffs, N.J.: Prentice-Hall, 1956). A modern series of studies is R. J. Swartz, ed., *Perceiving, Sensing, Knowing* (New York: Doubleday, Anchor, 1965). For a comprehensive anthology on epistemology, see E. Nagel and R. Brandt, eds., *Meaning and Knowledge* (New York: Harcourt Brace Jovanovich, 1965). A modern defense of skepticism is Peter Unger, *Ignorance* (London: Oxford University Press, 1975).

CHAPTER 4—TRUTH

Discussion and criticism of the various theories of truth can be found in Alan R. White, *Truth* (New York: Doubleday, Anchor, 1970). A discussion of Alfred Tarski's theory is in W. V. O. Quine, *Philosophy of Logic* (Englewood Cliffs, N.J.: Prentice-Hall, 1970). Brand Blanshard's argument is developed in his *Nature of Thought* (New York: Macmillan, 1941). William James develops his pragmatic theory in his *Pragmatism: A New Name for Some Old Ways of Thinking* (New York: Longmans Green, 1907). Two brief but helpful introductions to Immanuel Kant's philosophy are J. Kemp, *The Philosophy of Kant* (London: Oxford University Press, 1968) and G. J. Warnock, "Kant," in *A Critical History of Western Philosophy*, ed. D. J. O'Connor (New York: Free Press, 1964). A short introduction to German Idealism is R. Solomon, *Introducing the German Idealists* (Indianapolis, Ind.: Hackett, 1981). The best basic discussion of hermeneutics is David Hoy, *The Critical Circle* (Berkeley: Univ. of California Press, 1978). A compendium of writings by Gadamer is *Philosophical Hermeneutics*, trans. Linge (Berkeley: Univ. of California Press, 1976). *Relativism* is the subject of the essays collected by M. Kraucze and J. Meiland, eds. (Notre Dame, Ind.: Univ. of Notre Dame Press, 1982). A controversial discussion of the whole problem of truth and its complications is Richard Rorty, *Philosophy and the Mirror of Nature* (Princeton: Princeton University Press, 1979).

CHAPTER 5 — NECESSITY

Two recent anthologies are Robert Sleigh, ed., *Necessary Truth* (Englewood Cliffs, N.J.: Prentice-Hall, 1972) and L. W. Sumner and John Woods, *Necessary Truth: A Book of Readings* (New York: Random House, 1970). For a comprehensive anthology on the foundations of mathematics, see P. Benacerraf and H. Putnam, eds., *Philosophy of Mathematics* (Englewood Cliffs, N.J.: Prentice-Hall, 1964). W. V. O. Quine's now-classic attack on the notion of "analytic truth" is in "Two Dogmas of Empiricism" in *From a Logical Point of View* (Cambridge, Mass.: Harvard University Press, 1953). An attempted rebuttal is by H. P. Grice and P. F. Strawson, "In Defense of a Dogma," in *Philosophical Review*, 65 (1956). Selections in the chapter are developed at length in A. J. Ayer, *Language, Truth and Logic* (New York: Dover Publications, 1946); John Stuart Mill, *A System of Logic*, 8th ed. (New York: Harper, 1874); Edmund Husserl, *Ideas*, trans. W. R. Boyce-Gibson (New York: Macmillan, 1962); Immanuel Kant, *The Critique of Pure Reason*, trans. Norman Kemp-Smith (London: St. Martin's Press, 1933). Reasonably straightforward expositions of Husserl and Kant can be found in R. Schmitt, "Phenomenology," in *The Encyclopedia of Philosophy*, ed. P. Edwards (New York: Macmillan, 1967) and S. Körner, *Kant* (London: Penguin, 1955).

CHAPTER 6 — RELIGION

Several good anthologies on the philosophy of religion are S. Cahn, ed., *Philosophy of Religion* (New York: Harper & Row, 1970); J. Hick, ed., *Faith and the Philosophers* (New York: St. Martin's Press, 1964); and N. Smart, ed., *Historical Selections in the Philosophy of Religion* (New York: Harper & Row, 1962). A general discussion of religious issues is J. Hick, *Faith and Knowledge*, 2nd ed. (Ithaca, N.Y.: Cornell University Press, 1966). A good series of studies on the problem of evil is N. Pike, ed., *God and Evil* (Englewood Cliffs, N.J.: Prentice-Hall, 1964). David Hume's *Dialogues on Natural Religion* (New York: Bobbs-Merrill, 1963) makes excellent and provocative reading. A convenient collection of Søren Kierkegaard's writings is W. H. Auden, *The Living Thoughts of Kierkegaard* (Bloomington, Ind.: Indiana University Press, 1963). Two good studies of Kierkegaard are J. Collins, *The Mind of Kierkegaard* (Chicago: Regnery, 1953) and Louis Mackey, *Kierkegaard: A Kind of Poet* (Philadelphia: University of Pennsylvania Press, 1972). The selections from Karl Marx, Friedrich Nietzsche, and Sigmund Freud are developed in Karl Marx, *Early Writings*, trans. T. Bottomore (New York: McGraw-Hill, 1963); Friedrich Nietzsche, *The Antichrist* in *The Viking Portable Nietzsche*, trans. Walter Kaufmann (New York: Viking, 1959); and Sigmund Freud, *The Future of an Illusion*, trans. W. D. Robson-Scott (New York: Doubleday, Anchor, 1953).

CHAPTER 7 — SELF-IDENTITY

A recent anthology on the question of self-identity is J. Perry, *Personal Identity* (New York: Lieber-Atherton, 1975). An extended study of this traditional problem is Sidney Shoemaker, *Self-Knowledge and Self-Identity* (Ithaca, N.Y.: Cornell University Press, 1963). Jean-Paul Sartre's existentialist view of the self is developed in his essay "Transcendence of the Ego" (New York: Noonday, 1957). Hermann Hesse's complex theory of the self is best developed in *Steppenwolf*, rev. ed., trans. Basil Creighton (New York: Holt, Rinehart and Winston, 1970), but it is most simply portrayed in *Siddhartha*, trans. H. Rosner (New York: New Directions, 1951). Further reading in Eastern conceptions of the self may begin with D. Suzuki, *Zen Buddhism*, ed. W. Barrett (New York: Doubleday, 1956) or C. Moore, ed., *The Individual in East and West* (Honolulu: East-West Center Press, 1967). A good introduction to G. W. F. Hegel's very difficult philosophy is the introduction to his lectures on the philosophy of history in his *Reason in History*, trans. R. Hartman (New York: Bobbs-Merrill, 1953).

CHAPTER 8 — MIND AND BODY

A good short survey of the "mind-body problem" is Keith Campbell, *Body and Mind* (New York: Doubleday, Anchor, 1970); a helpful introduction to the problem and the various alternatives is J. Shaffer, *The Philosophy of Mind* (Englewood Cliffs, N.J.: Prentice-Hall, 1968). A good historical discussion of the reactions against Cartesian dualism is A. Lovejoy, *The Revolt Against Dualism* (La Salle, Ill.: Open Court, 1955). Two more recent anthologies, with special attention to the "identity theory," are David Rosenthal, ed., *Materialism and the Mind-Body Problem* (Englewood Cliffs, N.J.: Prentice-Hall, 1971) and C. V. Borst, ed., *The Mind-Brain Identity Theory* (New York: St. Martin's Press, 1970). A delightful presentation of the functionalist position is the collection of essays by Dan Dennett, *Brainstorms* (Newton Center, Mass.: Bradford Books, 1979). See also J. Margolis, *The Philosophy of Psychology* (Englewood Cliffs, N.J.: Prentice-Hall, 1983).

CHAPTER 9 — FREEDOM

General anthologies are Sidney Hook, ed., *Determinism and Freedom in the Age of Modern Science* (New York: Macmillan, Collier, 1961); B. Berofsky, ed., *Free Will and Determinism* (New York: Harper & Row, 1966); and H. Morris, ed., *Freedom and Responsibility* (Stanford, Calif.: Stanford University Press, 1961). See also D. F. Pears, ed., *Freedom and the Will* (New York: St. Martin's Press, 1963).

CHAPTER 10 — ETHICS

A comprehensive but brief history of ethics is A. MacIntyre, *A Short History of Ethics* (New York: Macmillan, 1966). A general schematic discussion of the problems of ethics is W. Frankena, *Ethics* (Englewood Cliffs, N.J.: Prentice-Hall, 1963). A much more detailed survey of the problems and the recent history of ethics is Richard R. Brandt, *Ethical Theory* (Englewood Cliffs, N.J.: Prentice-Hall, 1959). Also available is a companion anthology, Richard R. Brandt, *Value and Obligation* (New York: Harcourt Brace Jovanovich, 1961). The classic arguments against egoism are in J. Butler, *Fifteen Sermons Upon Human Nature* (London: Macmillan, 1900). A more modern and technical set of arguments is in T. Nagel, *The Possibility of Altruism* (New York: Oxford University Press, 1970). Textbooks that include various discussions of ethical options are R. N. Beck and J. B. Orr, *Ethical Choice* (New York: Free Press, 1970) and John Hospers, *Human Conduct* (New York:

Harcourt Brace Jovanovich, 1962). Aristotle's *Nicomachean Ethics* is translated by W. D. Ross (Oxford: Oxford University Press, 1925). Ross also has a good summary of the arguments in his *Aristotle* (New York: Meridian, 1959). Some excellent articles on Aristotle's ethics are collected in J. Walsh and H. Shapiro, eds., *Aristotle's Ethics* (Belmont, Calif.: Wadsworth, 1967) and J. Moravscik, ed., *Aristotle* (New York: Doubleday, Anchor, 1966). David Hume's moral philosophy is most accessible in his *Enquiry Concerning the Principles of Morals* (La Salle, Ill.: Open Court, 1912). Jean Jacques Rousseau's moral theories are to be found in his second discourse "On the Origins of Inequality" in *The Social Contract* (New York: Dutton, 1950) and in *Emile* (New York: Dutton, 1970). The best summary of Immanuel Kant's moral philosophy is his own *Foundations of the Metaphysics of Morals*, available in various translations, the most helpful, because of the commentary, being *Groundwork of the Metaphysics of Morals*, trans. H. J. Paton (New York: Harper & Row, 1957). See also Immanuel Kant, *Lectures on Ethics*, trans. L. Infield (New York: Harper & Row, 1963). John Stuart Mill's utilitarianism is well summarized in his pamphlet *Utilitarianism* (New York: Dutton, 1910). A good summary of Friedrich Nietzsche's ethics is in Walter Kaufmann, *Nietzsche* (Princeton, N.J.: Princeton University Press, 1950). A good summary of existentialist ethics is M. Warnock, *Existentialist Ethics* (New York: St. Martin's Press, 1967). For a concise history of twentieth century metaethics, see M. Warnock, *Ethics Since 1900* (London: Oxford Univ. Press, 1974). MacIntyre's *After Virtue* is published by the University of Notre Dame Press (2nd ed. 1984).

CHAPTER 11 — POLITICS

Plato, *The Republic*, trans. Francis M. Cornford (Oxford: Oxford University Press, 1941) is still standard reading for the basics and some thought-provoking alternatives in political philosophy. See also Aristotle, *Politics*, in *The Basic Works of Aristotle*, ed. R. McKeon (New York: Random House, 1941). Our own national documents, the Declaration of Independence and the Constitution, are always important reading. John Stuart Mill, *On Liberty*, ed. C. Shields (New York: Bobbs-Merrill, 1956) has long been the classic defense of liberalism. Michael Oakeshott, *Rationalism in Politics* (New York: Basic Books, 1962) is an important challenge to liberal philosophy. Karl Marx's *Communist Manifesto*, trans. S. Moore (Chicago: Regnery, 1969) and his early political writings, *Early Writings*, trans. T. Bottomore (New York: McGraw-Hill, 1963) are essential reading for beginning students in political philosophy. Niccolò Machiavelli, *The Prince*, trans. C. Detmold (New York: Airmont, 1965) and Jean Jacques Rousseau, *The Social Contract* (New York: Dutton, 1950) are both important and rewarding reading. For more general discussions of the philosophy of politics, see F. Olafson, ed., *Justice and Social Policy* (Englewood Cliffs, N.J.: Prentice-Hall, 1961); G. Sabine, *A History of Political Theory*, 3rd ed. (New York: Holt, Rinehart and Winston, 1961); and P. Laslett and W. G. Runciman, eds., *Philosophy, Politics and Society* (Oxford: Blackwell, 1964).

INDEX OF GLOSSARY TERMS

absolute, 103
absolutism, 202, 550
abstract, 37
action-at-a-distance, 104
ad hominem argument, 38
agnosticism, 318
alienation, 614
altruism, 550
analytic, 233
analytic philosophy, 202
anarchism, 614
animism, 76
antecedent conditions, 460
anthropomorphic, 318
a posteriori, 233
appearance, 156
a priori, 156, 233, 550
argument, 38
argument from design, 318
assertion, 38
association of ideas, 157
assumption, 38
atheism, 318
attribute, 104
authority, 614
autonomy, 38, 550
axiom, 38

bad faith, 363
Becoming, 76
begging the question, 38
behaviorism, 416
Being, 77
best of all possible worlds, 104

calculus, 233
Cartesianism, 38
categorical imperative, 550
categories, 202
causal interactionism, 417

causal theory of perception, 157
causation, 157
cause, 77, 157, 460
cause-of-itself, 104
certainty, 38
civil rights, 614
cogito ergo sum, 157
coherence, 38
coherence theory of truth, 202
commitment, 550
compatibilism, 460
compulsion, 460
conceptual truth, 77, 233
conscience, 550
consistent, 38
constitute, 202
contemplation, 550
contingent, 234
continuity (spacio-temporal continuity),
    363
contradiction, 38
correspondence theory of truth, 202
cosmological argument, 318
cosmology, 77
counter-example, 38
criterion, 38, 363
critical, 38
cultural relativism, 550

datum, 157
declarative sentence, 38
deduction (deductive argument), 38
definition, 234
deism, 318
democracy, 614
deontology, 550
determinism, 104, 460
dialectic, 39, 202
distributive justice, 614
doubt, 39

dual aspect theory,   417
dualism,   417
duty,   550

egalitarianism,   614
egoism,   550
eidos,   234
emotivism,   550
empirical,   234
empirical ego,   363
empiricism,   157
Enlightenment,   39
epiphenomenalism,   417
epistemology,   157
equality,   614
essence,   77, 202, 234, 363
ethical absolutism,   550
ethical egoism,   550
ethical relativism,   551
ethics,   550
eudaimonia,   551
excluded middle, law of the,   234
existentialism,   363, 551
explanation,   157
extended,   104

facticity,   363
faith,   318
fallacy,   39
fascism,   614
fatalism,   460
first principles,   39
form (in Plato),   77
formal logic,   39
freedom,   461, 614
free will,   460
functionalism,   417

generalization,   39
generalization from experience,   157
God,   319
Golden Rule,   551
government,   614

happiness,   551
happiness calculus,   551
hedonism,   551
Heisenberg Uncertainty Principle,   461
hermeneutics,   203
historicism,   203
human rights,   614
Hume's Fork,   157
hypothesis,   39, 234
hypothetical imperative,   551

idea,   157; in Plato,   77
idealism,   104
Identity of Indiscernibles,   104
identity theory,   417

illusion,   319
immaterialism,   77
immediate,   417
immoralist,   551
immortality,   77
imperative,   551
implication,   39
impression,   157
inclination,   551
incoherent,   39
inconsistent,   39
incorrigibility,   417
indeterminism,   461
induction,   157
induction, principle of,   158
inductive argument,   39
ineffable,   319
inference,   39
inference-ticket,   417
infinite regress,   77
innate ideas,   77, 158
intentionality,   417
intuition,   158, 234
invalid,   40

justice,   614
justification,   158

law,   551
law of contradiction,   234
law of the excluded middle,   234
legitimacy,   614
liberty,   614
logic,   40, 235
logical truth,   235
logicism,   235

master morality,   551
materialism,   77
matter of fact,   235
maxim,   551
mean,   551
metaethics,   551
metaphysics,   78
method,   40
method of doubt,   40
modern philosophy,   40
modes,   104
monad,   104
monism,   78
morality,   551
mysticism,   319

naturalism,   551
naturalistic fallacy,   551
necessary truth,   78, 235
necessity,   235
non-cognitivism,   551
non-naturalism,   552

obligation, 552
omnipotent, 319
omniscient, 319
ontological argument, 319
ontology, 78
ought, 552

pantheism, 319
paradigm, 78
paradox, 40
parallelism, 417
participation, 78
phenomenology, 203, 235
pluralism, 78
pragmatic theory of truth, 203
pragmatism, 203
predestination, 461
predicate, 40
prediction, 461
pre-established harmony, 104, 417
premise, 40
presupposition, 40
primary qualities, 158
prime mover, 78
principle of induction, 158
Principle of Sufficient Reason, 104
principle of universal causation, 158
principle of utility, 552
privacy, 417
private language argument, 417
privileged access, 418
probable, 158
problem of evil, 319
proof, 40
property, 78
proposition, 40
psychological egoism, 552

quality, 158

rational, 203
rationalism, 158
rationality, 552
realism, 203
reason, 40, 78, 158
reasons, 40
reductio ad absurdum, 40
reflection, 40
relations of ideas, 158, 235
relativism, 203, 552
resemblance, 363
responsibility, 461
retributive justice, 614
retrodiction, 461
rhetoric, 40
rights, 614
rule of inference, 40, 235

secondary qualities, 158
self-consciousness, 364
self-contradictory, 40
self-evident, 41
self-identity, 364
selfishness, 552
semantics, 203
semantic theory of truth, 203
sensation, 158
sense-data, 159
sentiment, 552
skepticism, 41, 159
slave morality, 552
social contract, 614
society, 614
soft determinism, 461
sophists, 79
sound, 41
sovereign, 614
state, 614
subjective idealism, 159
substance, 79
sufficient cause, 461
syllogism, 40
sympathy, 552
synthetic, 235
synthetic *a priori*, 235
system, 40

tabula rasa, 159
tautology, 235
teleological argument, 319
teleology, 79
theism, 319
transcendence (in Sartre), 364
transcendent (God), 319
transcendental, 204
transcendental deduction, 204
transcendental ego, 364
trivial, 40
truth of reason, 235

unalienable rights, 614
unconscious, the, 418
unextended, 104
universal causation, principle of, 158
unsound, 40
utilitarianism, 552
utility, principle of, 552

valid, 40
vicious circle, 40
virtue, 552
void, 104

will, 552
will to power, 552

SUBJECT INDEX

Absolute, 103
Absolute space, 99–100
Absolute time, 100, 186
Absolutism, 200; ethical, 467, 550
Abstract, 37
Accidental property, 70
Action-at-a-distance (Newton), 99, 104
Act utilitarianism, 586
Ad hominem arguments, 34, 38
Agnosticism, 11, 240, 281, 302, 318
Alienation (Marx), 596, 614
Altruism, 471, 550
Ambiguity, fallacy involving, 35
Analogy, argument by, 29
Analytic judgment (Kant), 233
Analytic philosophy, 202
Analytic truths, 207–10, 211, 233
Anarchism, 555, 609–13, 614
Anaximander, 47–48
Anaximenes, 47
Animism, 50, 76, 194
Anselm, Saint, 241–43, 246
Antecedent conditions, 460
Anthropomorphism, 239, 318
Apeiron, 47
Apology (Plato), 2–4, 13
A posteriori, 219, 233; Kant's distinction between *a priori* knowledge and, 222
Appearance(s), 105–109, 134, 156
A priori, 97, 148–50, 153–54, 193, 206; in Kant, 182–83, 233, 550; synthetic, 221–225
Aquinas, Saint Thomas, 54, 71; on God's existence, 249–52, 254; on morality, 465

Argument, 10–12, 17–33, 38; by analogy, 29; by counter-examples, 27–29, 31–32; deductive, *see* Deduction; inappropriate, 37; inductive, 19, 26–29; questions with which to attack an, 30–31; by *reductio ad absurdum*, 32–33
Aristophanes, 1–2
Aristotle, 53, 68–74, 463, 477–90, 553, 559–62, 575; on contemplation, 69, 487; cosmology of, 72; essence in, 72, 251; on happiness, 478, 487; on justice, 559–63; on law of contradiction, 209; metaphysics of, 52, 53, 66–76, 163; on morality, 447–90, 549; on rationality, 483; on the soul, 83, 87, 396–97; Spinoza and, 231; on substance, 52, 69; teleological views of, 71; on voluntary actions, 437–38
Arithmetic, truths of, 112, 207, 210–30
Assertion, mere, 33, 38
Association of ideas, 157
Assumptions (of metaphysics), 74–76
Atheism, 11, 240, 312–18
Atoms, 49
Attributes (Spinoza), 82–83, 104
Augustine, Saint, 271–76, 464
Authoritarianism, 555
Authority, 555; appeals to, 15
Autonomy of the individual, 14, 15, 38, 550; morality and, 466
Axioms, 17; of Spinoza, 38, 83–84
Ayer, A. J., 212–13, 463, 540; on ethics, 463, 540–44; on God, 307–12; on mathematics and logic, 212–13, 217

Bad faith (Sartre), 345, 363
Barth, Karl, 249
Bayle, Pierre, 275, 276–79
Becoming, 55, 67, 76
Begging the question, 38, 152
Behaviorism, 377, 409, 416
Being, 49, 55, 60, 75, 77; *see also* Ontology
Being and Nothingness (Sartre), 346–47; 453–56
Being and Time (Heidegger), 190
Bentham, Jeremy, 513, 549
Berkeley, Bishop George, 109, 133–41, 156, 161
"Best of all possible worlds" (Leibniz), 104
Beyond Freedom and Dignity (Skinner), 443
Beyond Good and Evil (Nietzsche), 527–30
Bill of Rights, 588
Blanshard, Brand, 167–68
Body-mind problem, *see* Dualism
Bourgeoisie, Marx on, 596–605
British empiricism, 109
Brothers Karamazov, The (Dostoevksy), 281–84, 303–307
Buddha, 296, 351
Buddhism, 296–99; the self in, 351–52, 385n
Burgess, Anthony, 447
Butler, Bishop Joseph, 474–76

Calculus, 211, 233
Campbell, C. A., 449–53
Carroll, Lewis, 323
Cartesian dualism, *see* Dualism
Cartesianism, 38; *see also* Descartes, René
Categorical imperative (Kant), 504, 550
Category mistakes (Ryle), 381
Catholic Church, 15
Causal interactionism, 375, 417
Causal theory of perception (Locke), 127, 157
Causation (causality), 127, 157; Hume on, 145–51; *see also* Determinism; Universal causation, principle of
Cause, 71, 77, 145, 157; in Aristotle, 72; sufficient, 249–52; *see also* Determinism
Cause-of-itself (Spinoza), 82–84, 104
Certainty, 16, 38; Descartes on, 38, 110
Change, reality and, 48, 50–51

Choice: Determinism and, 428; Sartre on, 453
Chomsky, Noam, 125
Christianity (Christian theology), 15, 51, 54; God in, 237–56; mysticism and, 285; Nietzsche's attack on, 313–16
Chuang-Tzu, 105
Civil rights, 591, 614
Cleanthes, 255
Clouds (Aristophanes), 1–2
Cogito, ergo sum (Descartes), 115, 157
Coherence, 38
Coherence theory of truth, 166–68, 176–77, 202
Commandments, 464
Commitment, 531, 550
Common sense, 111, 120
Communist Manifesto (Marx and Engels), 594–605
Compatibilism (soft determinism), 429–437, 460
Compulsion, 437; Aristotle on, 437–38, 460
Computer, 407
Concept of Mind, The (Ryle), 378–84
Conceptual truth, 69, 77, 208, 233
Conclusions, unclear or shifting, 34
Confessions (St. Augustine), 270–74
Consciousness, 95, 324, 329, 369, 402, 427; determinism and, 427; Husserl on, 401; incorrigibility and, 369; James on, 401; Merleau-Ponty on, 402; Nietzsche on, 354–57; *see also* Self-consciousness
Consent of the governed theory, 574
Consistent, 38
Constitute, 179, 202
Constitution: Kant's concept of, 179–83
Contemplation, life of (Aristotle), 69, 497
Contingent truths, 234
Continuity, spacio-temporal, 263, 338
Contradiction, 38; law of, 209
Conze, Edward, 298
Correspondence theory of truth, 84, 163–65, 176, 202
Cosmological argument for God's existence, 249–52, 318
Cosmology, 52–53; Aristotle's, 77
Counter-examples, 27, 38; argument by, 38
Criterion, 16, 38, 363

Critical, 12, 13
Critique of Pure Reason (Kant), 178, 185, 222–24, 246–48
Crito (Plato), 4–8, 18
Cultural relativism, 467, 550

Darwin, Charles, 255
Datum (data), 108, 157, 227
Davidson, Donald, 176
Declaration of Independence, 14, 587
Declarative sentence, 38
Deduction (deductive argument), 19–26, 38; transcendental (Kant), 204
Definitions, 67, 234
Deism, 280, 318
Democracy, 575, 614
Democritus, 44–51
Deontology, 498, 550
Descartes, René, 15–18, 75–76, 80–81, 94, 105–21, 161, 163; basic rules of, 17; causal dualism of, *see* Dualism; epistemology of, 109–20, 156; on God, 106, 112–14, 374–75; on God's existence, 112–13, 119–20, 243–46; method of doubt of, 15–18, 109–10; on self-consciousness, 324, 337, 365–69, 378; on self-identity, 324; on substance, 80–81, 87–88
Determinism, 104, 420–27, 460; compulsion and, 437; consciousness and, 427; fatalism and predestination distinguished from, 421; hard, 422; Hume on, 435; Kant on, 448; Skinner on, 442–46; soft, 429; Spinoza on, 84, 89, 90–91
Dewey, John, 168–69
Dialectic, 39, 187; in Hegel, 202; between mind and body (Merleau-Ponty), 401–402
Dialogues on Natural Religion (Hume), 245–55
Dilthey, Wilhelm, 188, 190
Discourse on Method (Descartes), 17, 115
Disposition (Ryle), 383
Distributive justice, 559, 614
Divine right to rule theory, 573
Dostoevsky, Fyodor, 281–84, 302–307, 419, 457–59
Doubt, 302–307; method of (Descartes), 16, 17, 39, 109–20
Dual aspect theory, 376, 417

Dualism (Cartesian dualism; mind-body problem), 372, 417; behaviorism and, 374; Descartes on, 366; identity theory and, 386; Merleau-Ponty on, 401; rejection of, 377, 396; Wittgensteinian view and, 397
Duty, 498; Kant on, 500

Eddington, Sir Arthur, 426
Egalitarianism, 559, 563, 614
Egoism, 463; psychological, 471, 550
Eidetic intuition (Husserl), 226
Eidos, 54, 225–28, 234; *see also* Forms, in Plato
Einstein, Albert, 75, 99, 100, 252–53
Emotivism, 540, 545
Empirical ego, 338, 363
Empirical knowledge, 206, 234
Empiricism, 108–109, 118, 125, 155–57, 208–209; Hume's, 141–56; mathematical truths and, 211–26
Engels, Friedrich, 594, 597
Enlightenment, the, 14–15, 101, 275–76
Enquiry Concerning Human Understanding, An (Hume), 142
Epimenides the Cretan, 16
Epiphenomenalism, 377, 417
Epistemology, 105–51, 157
Equality, 559, 565, 568, 614; Hobbes on, 575; justice and, 555, 559, 561, 565; Mill on, 563; *see also* Egalitarianism
Essay Concerning Human Understanding, An (Locke), 105, 121–23, 125–33, 326–29
Essence (essential characteristics or properties), 70, 77, 202, 234, 363; in Aristotle, 70; existence as coming before (Sartre), 343; in Husserl, 226
Essential intuition (Husserl), 225
Ethical absolutism, 467, 550
Ethical altruism, 471
Ethical egoism, 472, 526, 550
Ethical relativism, 467, 551
Ethics, 462–550; *see also* Morality
Ethics (Aristotle), 447–90, 559–63
Ethics (Spinoza), 82–91, 103
Euclidean geometry, 17, 210
Eudaimonia, 482, 551
Evil, problem of, 270–84
Excluded middle, law of the, 234

Existentialism, 286, 343, 363, 453, 531; choice in, 453; freedom and, 453–57; morality and, 531–35; self-identity in, 341–49
Explanation, 157
Extended, bodies as, 104

Facticity (Sartre; Heidegger), 345, 363
Faith, 284, 318; in God's existence, 257–70; irrationality and, 284–93; leap of (Kierkegaard), 286; problem of evil and, 270
Fallacies, 19, 25–26, 33–37, 39
Fascism, 604–606, 614
Fatalism, 421, 460
Fichte, Johann Gottlieb, 185
First principles, 17, 39
Flew, Antony, 257–59, 263–64
Fodor, Jerry A., 408–16
Form, 70, 77
Formal logic, 39
Forms: of consciousness (Hegel), 186; in Plato, 54–68
Freedom, 419–61, 587, 594, 614; Dostoevsky on, 457–59; existentialism and, 453; Hume on, 435; indeterminism and, 426; Kant on, 448; libertarianism and, 448; Marx and, 594–605; *see also* Determinism; Liberty (political freedom)
Free will, 82, 419, 460; Spinoza on, 82
Frege, Gottlob, 217
Freud, Sigmund, 95, 316, 370; on religion, 316; on the unconscious, 370
Functionalism, 407–17
Fundamental Principles of the Metaphysics of Morals (Kant), 497–512
Future of an Illusion, The (Freud), 316–17

Gadamar, Hans Georg, 190–93
Galileo, 110
Generalization, 19, 39; from experience, 157; *see also* Induction
General will (Rousseau), 581
Geometry, Euclidean, 112, 207, 210–30
German Romantic philosophers, 187
God, 237–57, 265, 269, 285, 291; anthropomorphic conception of, 81, 237; Aristotle on, 72; Ayer on, 307; Berkeley on, 139–40;

Descartes on, 112–14; as experience, 285; Leibniz on, 92–94, 101–102, 113–14; problem of evil and, 113, 270–84; Spinoza on, 82, 88–90; traditional conception of, 237; transcendence of, 237–40; as ultimate concern, 290; *see also* Faith; Religion
Gödel, Kurt, 211
God's existence, 13, 240–57; cosmological argument for, 240, 249–52; Descartes on, 53, 112–14, 119–20, 257–70; Kierkegaard on, 286–90; ontological argument for, 240–49; Pascal's wager on, 269; teleological argument (argument from design) for, 252–57
Golden Rule, 474, 551; Kant's version of, 503
Gorgias, 51
Greek philosophers, Pre-Socratic, 45–53

Happiness, 479, 512, 517–23; utilitarianism and, 517
Happiness calculus (Bentham), 514, 551
Hare, R. M., 259–61
Hartshorne, Charles, 248
Hawking, Stephen, 253–54
Hedonism, 512, 551
Hegel, Georg Wilhelm Friedrich, 186, 360, 525; on the individual, 360
Heidegger, Martin, 190, 358–59
Heisenberg, Werner, 461
Heisenberg Uncertainty Principle, 426, 461
Heller, Joseph, 462
Hempel, C. G., 217–20
Heraclitus, 48, 50–52, 55, 66, 75, 90
Herd-instinct (Nietzsche), 356, 527
Hermeneutics, 189–93, 203
Hesse, Hermann, 349–50
Hinduism, 299–302
Historical materialism, 594
Historicism, 188–89
Hobbes, Thomas, 563, 575; social contract theory of, 563, 575–80
Holbach, Baron Paul Henri d', 422–24
Hospers, John, 439–41
Huguenots, 275
Human rights, 591–614
Hume, David, 109, 141–56, 163, 178–79, 231–32, 260; on causality, 145–51; on God, 255; on induction, 27,

Hume, David (continued)
145, 150–55, 161; on justice, 567–
68; Kant and, 182; on liberty and
necessity, 435–36; on morality,
491–94; on reason and sentiment,
491; on self-identity, 331–34
Hume's fork, 142, 149, 152, 157
Husserl, Edmund, 188, 221–30; on
consciousness, 229; on historicism,
188–89; on mathematical truths,
221, 225–30
Hypothesis, 19, 26, 29–31, 39, 234
Hypothetical imperatives (Kant), 505,
551

Idealism, 81; subjective, 133
Ideas, 54, 77; association of, 142, 157;
in Berkeley, 140–41; in
epistemology, 134–42; in Husserl,
226; Locke on, 125; relations of
(Hume), 142; *see also* Forms;
Innate ideas
"Ideas" (Husserl), 226–27
Ideas and Opinions (Einstein), 252–53
Identity theory, 386–96, 409, 417
Immaterial objects (immaterialism),
49, 60, 77, 81, 92
Immoralism, 525, 551
Immortality, 50, 60, 77
Imperative, 551
Implication, 39
Impression, 142, 157
Inclinations, 498, 551
Incoherent, 39
Inconsistent, 39
Incorrigibility, 369–72, 417
Indeterminism, 426, 461
Individual, the: Hegel on, 360–61;
Marx on, 362
Individual intuition (Husserl), 225
Individualism, 353, 362; Mussolini on,
605
Individual rights, 587–94
Induction (inductive reasoning;
inductive generalization), 26;
Hume on, 121, 150–55; principle
of, 158
Inductive arguments, 19, 26–29, 39
Ineffable, 319
Inference, 24, 39; rule of, 208
Inference-ticket, 382, 417
Infinite regress, 73, 77, 87
Innate ideas, 60, 77, 121

Intentionality (Husserl), 229, 401, 417
"Introduction to Phenomenology, An"
(Husserl), 228–30
Intuition, 158, 224–25, 234; essential
or eidetic (Husserl), 225–26; Locke
on, 129, 225; rationalism and, 118,
226; rules of inference and, 208–
209
Invalid, 25, 40
Islam, 293–96

James, William, 168–74, 267, 286,
402–407; on belief in God, 267–69;
on consciousness, 402–407; on
mysticism, 286; on truth, 168–69,
172–74
Jefferson, Thomas, 587
Judaism, God in, 238, 285, 293–96
Justice, 555–71, 574, 614; Aristotle's
theory of, 559–62; distributive,
559; equality and, 555, 559, 561,
565; Hume on, 567–68; Mill on,
563–67; Plato on, 557–59; Rawls
on, 568–71; retributive, 556
"Justice as Fairness" (Rawls), 568–71
Justice theory of legitimacy, 574

Kant, Immanuel, 53, 178–86, 189, 246,
336, 364, 448, 497, 500; on
arithmetic and geometry, 180, 181,
211; on duty, 497, 500; on
freedom, 448; on God's existence,
53, 246–49, 265–67; on intuition,
224–25; on knowledge, 181; on
mathematical truths, 221; Mill on
moral philosophy of, 518; on
morality, 497–512; on self-
consciousness and self-identity,
336; on the soul, 337; on space and
time, 179; on synthetic *a priori*
knowledge, 181, 221–25;
transcendental argument of, 185;
on transcendental ego, 335; on
truth, 179–85
Karma, 298–99
Kierkegaard, Søren, 286–90, 357, 456;
on the individual, 357–58
Knowledge, 59, 105–56; *a priori*, see *A
priori*; empiricist theory of, 125–
33; faith and, *see* Faith; innate,
121; Russell on, 106; *see also*
Epistemology
Knox, Ronald, 140

Laing, R. D., 353
Language, Truth and Logic (Ayer),
    212–13
La Place, Pierre Simon, 256
Leap of faith (Kierkegaard), 286
Legitimacy of the state, 571–87, 614;
    consent of the governed theory of,
    574–75; divine right to rule theory
    of, 573; justice theory of, 574;
    might makes right theory of, 574;
    social contract theory of, 575–87;
    utilitarian theory of, 574
Leibniz, Gottfried Wilhelm von, 80–
    81, 90–103, 231, 368; "best of all
    possible worlds" concept of, 92; on
    innate ideas, 123–25; on
    interaction between monads, 92,
    99, 100; Newton and, 81, 88, 91,
    225; on pre-established harmony
    between monads, 99; principle of
    the identity of indiscernibles, 93,
    101; principle of sufficient reason,
    91, 101; on space and time, 92, 99,
    102
Lewis, C. I., 301
Libertarianism, 448–53
Liberty (political freedom), 587–94,
    615; individual rights and, 587;
    Marx's view of, 594; negative
    versus positive, 590
Lichtenberg, Georg Christoph, 254
Lincoln, Abraham, 474
Locke, John, 105, 108, 120–33, 141,
    161, 581; causal theory of
    perception of, 129; epistemology
    of, 120–33; on innate ideas, 121–
    23; on primary and secondary
    qualities, 126–32; on rights, 589;
    on self-consciousness and self-
    identity, 326–30, 339; on sensation,
    125–32; on substance, 132–33
Logic, 18–37, 40, 49, 51, 235; *see also*
    Argument; Fallacies
Logical behaviorism, 378
Logicism, 235
Logos, 41, 51, 66, 75
Love, practical and pathological (Kant),
    499
Luther, Martin, 110

Machiavelli, Niccolo, 607–609
MacIntyre, Alasdair, 190–93, 544–
    49

Marx, Karl, 187, 594; on alienation,
    594–605; on freedom, 595–97; on
    religion, 312–13
Master morality (Nietzsche), 527–30,
    551
Materialism, 49, 77, 81
Mathematics, 50–51
Matters of fact (Hume), 142, 235
Maxim (Kant), 505–507, 551
Meaning: fallacy involving changing,
    34–35
Meaningful/meaningless, 307
Means between the extremes
    (Aristotle), 483, 551
Meditations on First Philosophy
    (Descartes), 109–20, 325–26, 366–
    68
Meno (Plato), 60–66
Mere assertion, 34
Merleau-Ponty, 401–402
Metaethics, 535–49, 551
Metaphysical doctrines, 52
Metaphysics, 52, 73, 78; of Aristotle,
    36, 74; assumptions of, 105, 161;
    Kant and, 183; necessary truths of,
    75–76, 207, 230–33; of Plato, 52
Metaphysics (Aristotle), 73, 163, 209
Method, 40
Method of doubt (Descartes), 17–18,
    40, 109
Michaels, Meredith, 338
Might makes right theory, 574
Mill, John Stuart, 35, 213, 218, 430,
    563, 571, 591; on freedom and
    determinism, 430–34, 571; on
    justice, 563–67; on liberty, 591–94;
    on mathematical truths, 213–18;
    on utilitarianism, 512, 517–23, 549
Mind, *see* Consciousness
Mind-body problem, 365–418
Mitchell, Basil, 261–63
Modes (Spinoza), 82–83, 104
Monadology (Leibniz), 92–98, 103
Monads (Leibniz), 92–104; *see also*
    Leibniz, Gottfried Wilhelm von
Monism, 48, 78
Moore, G. E., 463, 537–40
Morality, 462–550; altruism and, 471;
    Aristotle on 477; existentialism
    and, 531; Hume on, 491–94; Kant
    on, 265–67, 497–512; modern
    conceptions of, 535–49; Nietzsche
    on, 523–31; politics and, 553;

Morality (continued)
   psychological egoism and, 471;
   relativism in, 466–71; Rousseau
   on, 494–97; Sartre on, 531–35
Moral virtues (Aristotle), 483
Mussolini, Benito, 605–606
Mysticism, 285–86, 319
"Myth of the Cave" (Plato), 55–59, 67,
   106

Naturalism, 536, 551
Naturalistic fallacy, 537, 551
Natural law, Hobbes on, 575
Necessary truths, 205, 210–30; analytic
   truths as, 207; conceptual truths
   as, 208; mathematical truths as,
   75–76, 78, 205, 235; metaphysical
   principles as, 205, 207, 230–33
Necessity, 205–33, 235; *see also*
   Determinism; Necessary truths
Newton, Sir Isaac, 14, 81, 88, 100, 179,
   184, 219, 225; Leibniz and, 94, 99,
   225
Nicomachean Ethics (Aristotle), 447–
   90, 559–63
Nietzsche, Friedrich, 187–88, 313, 354,
   523; on Christianity, 313; on herd
   instinct, 523; on morality, 523–31;
   on self-consciousness, 354–57
Nirvana, 296–99
No Exit (Sartre), 347–48
Non-cognitivism, 536, 551
Non-naturalism, 536, 552
Notes from the Underground
   (Dostoevsky), 457–59

Obligation, 552
Omnipotent, 238, 319
Omniscient, 238, 319
On Liberty (Mill), 591–94
"On the Nature of Mathematical
   Truth" (Hempel), 218–20
Ontological argument for God's
   existence, 240–49, 319
Ontology, 52; Aristotle's, 69, 78
Orwell, George, 447
Ought, 504, 552

Pantheism, 88, 280, 319; Spinoza's, 88
Paradigm, 74, 78
Paradox, 16, 40
Parallelism, 376, 416–17

Parmenides, 51, 54–55, 105–106
Participation, Plato's concept of, 67, 78
Pascal, Blaise, 269–70
Pathological love (Kant), 502
"Paulicians" (Bayle), 276–79
Peano, Giuseppe, 217
Peirce, Charles, 168–72
Perception: causal theory of (Locke),
   127; Leibniz on, 95–98, 126; *see
   also* Sense-data
Personal identity, *see* Self-identity
"Persons" (Strawson), 397–400
Persuasion, 18
Phaedo (Plato), 8–9
Phenomenology, 203, 235; Husserl's,
   188, 221, 225–26, 228–30
Philosophical Investigations
   (Wittgenstein), 397
Philosophy, 10–13; modern approach
   to, 13–18; Nietzsche on, 9–10, 529;
   Socrates on, 13
Physics, 81; indeterminist thesis and,
   426; Newtonian, 422
Physics (Aristotle), 72
Plato, 54–68, 472, 575; forms in, 54; on
   justice, 557–59; metaphysics of,
   52–54, 60–68, 72, 74–75; "Myth of
   the Cave," 55–59, 67; two-worlds
   view of, 55
Pleasure: Aristotle on, 478, 488;
   utilitarianism and, 512
Pluralism, 49, 78
Politics, 553–615; morality and, 553;
   see also Liberty; State, the
Politics (Aristotle), 553
Popper, Karl, 28–29
Power, 526, 555
Practical love (Kant), 499
Pragmatic theory of truth, 52, 168–74,
   177, 203
Pragmatism, 168, 203
Pragmatism (James), 172–74
Predestination, 421, 461
Predicate, 21, 40, 247
Prediction, 461
Pre-established harmony (Leibniz),
   104, 417
Premises, 17, 20–21, 40
Pre-Socratics, 45–54, 74–75
Presupposition, 40, 51
Primary qualities, 126; Berkeley on,
   134; Locke on, 126–30
Prime mover, 78, 87
Prince, The (Machiavelli), 607–609

Principia Ethica (Moore), 537–40
Principia Mathematica (Russell and
  Whitehead), 217
Privacy, 417
Private language argument, 417
Private property: Marx on, 603; right
  to own, 588–600
Privileged access, 372, 418
Probable, 27, 158
Problem of evil, 270–84, 319
Problems of Philosophy, The (Russell),
  106–108
*Prolegomena to Any Future
  Metaphysics* (Kant), 182–83, 224–
  25
Proletariat, Marx on, 597–605
Proof, 40
Property, 78; *see also* Private property
Proposition, 40
Protagoras, 51, 194
Psychological altruism, 473, 552
Psychological egoism, 471, 552
Pythagoras, 49–52, 59, 60

Quantum theory, 427

Rand, Ayn, 472
Rational, 13, 162, 203
Rationalism, 81, 156, 158; continental,
  108; intuition and, 118;
  mathematical truths and, 220
Rationality, 68, 479; Aristotle on
  happiness and, 479; *see also*
  Reason
Rawls, John, 568–71
Realism, 162, 203
Reality: Kant's conception of, 185; Pre-
  Socratics' view of, 45–53; *see also*
  Metaphysics
Reason, 40, 78, 109, 158; Hume on
  morality and, 491; intuition and,
  109; Kant on morality and, 497–
  512; truth of, 265–67
Reasons, 40
Reductio ad absurdum, 40, 85–86
Reflection, 14, 17, 40
Reisman, David, 359
Relations of ideas (Hume), 142
"Relative Truth" (Swoyer), 194–
  201
Relativism, 158, 162, 186, 193–201,
  203, 235, 552; cultural, 467;
  ethical, 52, 466–71

Religion, 237–319; Flew-Hare-Mitchell
  symposium on, 257–64; Freud on,
  316; James on, 267; Marx on, 312–
  13; Nietzsche's attack on, 313–16;
  see also Atheism; Buddhism;
  Christianity; Faith; God;
  Hinduism; Judaism
Religious symbols, Tillich on, 290–93
Republic, The (Plato), 9–10, 55–59,
  472–73, 557–59
Resemblance, 363
Responsibility, 461; Sartre on, 453,
  530
Retributive justice, 556, 614
Retrodiction, 461
Rhetoric, 18, 40
Rights, 566; civil, 576; Hobbes on, 574;
  human, 594, 614; individual, 579,
  587–94; Mill on, 591–94; negative
  versus positive, 590; unalienable,
  587
Rousseau, Jean-Jacques, 494, 575; on
  morality, 494–97; on the social
  contract, 575, 581–87
Rule of inference, 40, 235
Rule utilitarianism, 568
Russell, Bertrand, 100, 106, 109, 217;
  on Hume, 141; on knowledge of
  reality, 106
Ryle, Gilbert, 378–85

Sartre, Jean-Paul, 343, 453, 531; on
  freedom, 453–57; moral
  philosophy of, 531–35; on self,
  343–45
Schelling, Friedrich, 186
Schliermacher, Friedrich, 286
Science, 12; philosophy as, 76; reality
  and, 46–50
Secondary qualities: Berkeley on, 134;
  Locke on, 126–30
Self, the, 323; in Buddhism, 349–52;
  empirical (Kant), 338; multiple or
  pluralistic, 349–53
Self-caused (Spinoza), 82–84
Self-consciousness, 324–41, 364;
  Descartes on, 325; Hume on,
  333; Kant on, 334; Locke on, 326;
  Nietzsche on, 354
Self-contradictory, 40
Self-evident, 17, 40
Self-evident axioms, *see* Axioms
Self-evident truths, mathematical truths
  as, 218

Self-identity, 323–64; Buddhism and, 351–52; Descartes on, 351–52; existentialism and, 343; Hume on, 333; Kant on, 334; Locke on, 326; Sartre on, 343; self-consciousness and, 324; society and, 353–62

Selfishness, 472, 494, 557, 575; *see also* Egoism

Semantics, 203

Semantic theory of truth, 166, 174–78, 203

Sensation, 125; Locke on, 125–33, 158

Sense-data, 108, 159

Sentiment, 490, 552; Hume on morality and, 491–94

Shaffer, Jerome, 391–96

Skepticism, 16, 41, 159; Hume's 141–56, 159

Skinner, B. F., 378, 442–46

Slave morality (Nietzsche), 527–30, 552

Slavery, 559

Smart, J. J. C., 386–91, 393

Smith, Huston, 293

Social contract, 575–78, 614; Hobbes on, 576; Rousseau on, 581–87

Social Contract, The (Rousseau), 581–87

Socrates, 1–10, 13–16, 46, 52, 55–67, 76, *et passim*

Sophists, 51

Soul, the: Aristotle on, 83, 87; Buddhist denial of, 351; Kant on, 337; Plato's doctrine of the immortality and immateriality of, 60

Sound, 21, 41

Sovereign, 584, 614

Space: absolute, 99; intuition of (Kant), 179; Leibniz on time and, 98; Newton's view of, 99

Spacio-temporal continuity, 326

Spinoza, Benedictus de, 80–91, 103, 231; axioms of, 83–84; definitions of, 82–83, 88; on determinism, 89, 102, 369; on God, 83, 88; mind-body problem and, 88, 94; pantheism of, 88; on substance, 82–91

Stace, Walter, 468–71

State, the, 563, 571, 614; fascist theory of, 604; legitimacy of, *see* Legitimacy of the state

Steppenwolf (Hesse), 349

Strawson, P. F., 397–400

Structuralism, 125

Subjective idealism, 133, 159

Substance, 52, 69, 79, 106, 109; Aristotle on, 79; Berkeley on, 133; Descartes on, 80–81; Leibniz on, 92; Locke on, 132; Spinoza on, 82–91

Sufficient cause, 422, 461

Sufficient reason, principle of, 101

Swoyer, Chris, 193–201

Syllogism, 21–22, 40–41

Sympathy, 491, 552

Synthetic *a priori* (Kant), 221–25, 235

Synthetic judgment (Kant), 235

System, 40–41

System of Logic, A (Mill), 213–18

Tabula rasa (Locke), 123, 159

Tarski, Alfred, 175–76

Tautologies, 208, 258; mathematical truths as, 235

Teleological argument for God's existence, 252–57, 319

Teleology, 71; Aristotle's, 79

Ten Commandments, 464

Thales, 45–47, 49–51, 75

Theism, 240, 310–12, 319

Tillich, Paul, 290–93

Time: absolute, 99; intuition of (Kant), 179; Leibniz on space and, 99

Toynbee, Arnold, 299

Transcendence: of God, 345, 364; in Sartre, 239, 319

Transcendent, 319

Transcendental, 204

Transcendental deduction (Kant), 204

Transcendental ego (or self), Kant's conception of, 335, 364

Transcendental phenomenology, 189

Treatise Concerning the Principles of Human Knowledge (Berkeley), 134–41

Treatise of Human Nature, A (Hume), 142–44, 146–55, 331–34

Trivial, 40–41

Truth(s), 12, 161–78; analytic, 207–10; of arithmetic and geometry, 207, 210–30; coherence theory of, 166–68, 176–77; conceptual, 67, 208; contingent, 205–206; correspondence theory of, 84, 163–65, 176; Kant on, 178; mathematical, 210; necessary, *see*

Necessary truths; pragmatic theory of, 166, 168–74, 177; semantic theory of, 174–78, 235; skepticism and paradox as obstacles to, 16
"Truth and Method" (Gadamar), 190–93
Tucker, Benjamin R., 610–13

Unalienable rights, 587, 614
Uncertainty principle (Heisenberg), 401, 426
Unconscious, the, 370–71, 418
Unextended, mind and ideas as, 90, 104
Universal causation, principle of, 141–45, 158
Universal conformity to law (Kant), 505
Unsound, 40–41
Utilitarianism, 517, 552; justice and, 563–67; legitimacy of the state and 574; morality and, 517–23; rule versus act, 568

Utilitarianism (Mill), 517–23, 563–67
Utility, principle of, 512, 552

Valid, 25, 40–41
Values; creation of (Nietzsche), 523; Hume's distinction between facts and, 491, 493
Vicious circle, 33, 40–41, 152
Virtue(s), 477; Aristotle on, 481–87, 552; as means between extremes, 483
Void, the, 100, 104
Voltaire, 101, 256, 280–81

Walden II (Skinner), 445–46
Watson, John, 378, 385
Whitehead, Alfred North, 75, 217
Whorf, Benjamin, 197
Will, 499, 552
Will to power, 530, 552
Wisdom, John, 256
Wittgenstein, Ludwig, 256, 397

Zeno, 51

COPYRIGHTS AND ACKNOWLEDGMENTS

For permission to use the selections reprinted in this book, the author is grateful to the following publishers and copyright holders:

GEORGE ALLEN & UNWIN LTD. For the excerpt from *The Nature of Thought* by Brand Blanshard. For the excerpt from *Ideas* by Edmund Husserl, translated by W. R. Boyce-Gibson. For the excerpts from *The Complete Works of Friedrich Nietzsche*, translated by Helen Zimmern. All reprinted by permission of the publisher, George Allen & Unwin Ltd.

BANTAM BOOKS, INC. For the excerpts from *The Brothers Karamazov* by Fyodor Dostoevsky, translated by Andrew R. MacAndrew. English language translation copyright © 1970 by Bantam Books, Inc. Reprinted by permission of Bantam Books, Inc.

BOSTON UNIVERSITY JOURNAL For the excerpt "On Gadamar's *Truth and Method*," from "Contexts of Interpretation," by Alasdair MacIntyre, *Boston University Journal*, vol. 24, no. 1, 1976. Reprinted by permission.

THE BOBBS-MERRILL COMPANY, INC. For the excerpts from *Prolegomena to Any Future Metaphysics* by Immanuel Kant, edited by Lewis White Beck, copyright © 1950 by The Liberal Arts Press, Inc., reprinted by permission of the publisher, The Bobbs-Merrill Company, Inc., Indianapolis.

DOVER PUBLICATIONS, INC. For the excerpts from *Language, Truth and Logic* by A. J. Ayers, 1946, Gollancz, London, 1952, Dover Publications, New York. Reprinted by permission.

W. H. FREEMAN AND COMPANY PUBLISHERS For the excerpts from "The Mind-Body Problem" by Jerry Fodor. Copyright © 1981 by Scientific American, Inc. All rights reserved.

HAIGH AND HOCHLAND LTD. For the excerpt "Husserl's Syllabus for the Paris Lectures on 'Introduction to Transcendental Phenomenology,'" *Journal of the British Society for Phenomenology* 7 (1976); reprinted in F. Elliston and M. McCormick, eds., *Husserl: Shorter Works*, University of Notre Dame Press. Reprinted by permission of Haigh and Hochland Ltd.

HARPER & ROW, PUBLISHERS, INC. For the excerpts from *The Religions of Man* by Huston Smith: pp. 64–67 ("Hinduism"), pp. 111–14 ("Buddhism"), pp. 204–208 ("Islam"). Copyright © 1958 by Huston Smith. For the excerpts abridged from pp. 11–17, 18, 22, 88–89, 116–117, 319, 320–321 in *The Concept of Mind* by Gilbert Ryle. Copyright 1949 by Gilbert Ryle (A Barnes & Noble Book). For the excerpt "Religious Symbols" (pp. 44–48) in *Dynamics of Faith* by Paul Tillich, volume 10 of *World Perspectives*, planned and edited by Ruth Nanda Anshen. Copyright © 1957 by Paul Tillich. Reprinted by permission of Harper & Row, Publishers, Inc.

HUTCHINSON PUBLISHING GROUP LTD. For the excerpts from *The Concept of Mind* by Gilbert Ryle. Reprinted by permission of the publisher, Hutchinson Publishing Group Ltd.

MACMILLAN PUBLISHING CO., INC. Reprinted with permission of Macmillan Publishing Company from *Ideas* by Edmund Husserl, translated by W. R. Boyce-Gibson (New York: Macmillan, 1931).

MEREDITH MICHAELS For the excerpt "Personal Identity" by Meredith Michaels. Reprinted by permission.

W. W. NORTON & COMPANY INC. For the excerpt reprinted from *The Future of an Illusion* by Sigmund Freud, translated from the German and edited by James Strachey, by permission of W. W. Norton & Company, Inc. Copyright © 1961 by James Strachey. For the excerpt reprinted from *New Introductory Lectures on Psychoanalysis* by Sigmund Freud, translated and edited by James Strachey, with the permission of W. W. Norton & Company, Inc. Copyright © 1964, 1965 by James Strachey.

OXFORD UNIVERSITY PRESS For the excerpt from *The Problems of Philosophy* by Bertrand Russell. Reprinted by permission of the Oxford University Press.

PENGUIN BOOKS LTD. For the excerpts from Saint Augustine, *Confessions*, trans. R. S. Pine-Coffin (Penguin Classics 1961), pp. 136–149. Copyright © R. S. Pine-Coffin, 1961. Reprinted by permission of Penguin Books Ltd.

PHILOSOPHICAL REVIEW For the excerpt from "Sensations and Brain Processes" by J. J. C. Smart, *Philosophical Review*, 68 (1959), pp. 141–56. Reprinted by permission.

PRINCETON UNIVERSITY PRESS For the excerpts from Søren Kierkegaard, *Concluding Unscientific Postscript*, trans. David F. Swenson and Walter Lowrie. Copyright 1941, © 1969 by Princeton University Press, selections pp. 189–356, reprinted by permission of Princeton University Press. For the excerpts from Søren Kierkegaard, *Philosophical Fragments*, trans. David Swenson. Copyright 1936, © 1962 by Princeton University Press. Selections pp. 49–53, reprinted by permission of Princeton University Press.

5
C 6
D 7
E 8
F 9
G 0
H 1
I 2
J 3